THE NAVAL POLICY OF AUSTRIA-HUNGARY, 1867–1918

THE NAVAL POLICY OF AUSTRIA-HUNGARY, 1867–1918 〰〰〰

Navalism, Industrial Development, and the Politics of Dualism

Lawrence Sondhaus

Purdue University Press
West Lafayette, Indiana

98   97   96   95   94   5   4   3   2   1

The paper used in this book meets the minimum requirements of American National Standard for Information Sciences—Permanence of Paper for Printed Library Materials, ANSI Z39.48-1984.

Printed in the United States of America
Design by Anita Noble

Library of Congress Cataloging-in-Publication Data
Sondhaus, Lawrence, 1958–
    The naval policy of Austria-Hungary, 1867–1918 : navalism, industrial development, and the politics of dualism / by Lawrence Sondhaus.
        p.   cm.
    Includes bibliographical references and index.
    ISBN 1-55753-034-3 (alk. paper)
        1. Austro-Hungarian Monarchy. Kriegsmarine—History—19th century. 2. Austro-Hungarian Monarchy. Kriegsmarine—History—20th century. 3. Sea-power—Austria—History—19th century. 4. Sea-power—Austria—20th century. 5. Austria—History, Naval—19th century. 6. Austria—History, Naval, 20th century.
    I. Title.
VA473.S663 1994
335'.009436—dc20   93-15906
                                                                  CIP

CONTENTS

PREFACE

Austria's connection with the sea traces back to 1382, when the free city of Trieste, fearful of its powerful Venetian neighbor, placed itself under Habsburg protection. The Austrian foothold on the Adriatic remained very small until 1797, when the demise of the Venetian Republic left the Habsburgs in possession of Venetia, Istria, and Dalmatia, along with Venice's large navy and merchant marine. Thereafter the navy endured years of neglect, then recovered slowly to emerge as a respectable force in the early 1860s, when Archduke Ferdinand Max, Emperor Francis Joseph's younger brother, oversaw the construction of Austria's first ironclad battle fleet. In the war of 1866, this force defeated its rival, the navy of the newly united kingdom of Italy, preserving the empire's outlet to the sea and extending Austrian hegemony over the Adriatic. The history of the navy from 1867 onward mirrored that of the first decades after 1797, as the fleet once again became weak and technologically backward compared to other European navies. After another slow recovery, a naval buildup begun late in the century left Austria-Hungary with a respectable battle fleet by 1914, which figured even in the Mediterranean strategic calculations of Britain, the greatest sea power. On the eve of the First World War, the navy was responsible for protecting a merchant marine that had grown to become the tenth largest in the world, and for keeping open a maritime commerce that carried over one sixth of all Austro-Hungarian imports and exports. But most important of all, the battle fleet stood guard on an Adriatic border that, even discounting the coastal frontage of the maze of Dalmatian islands, was as long as the Austro-Hungarian border with Russia.

As a sequel to my work *The Habsburg Empire and the Sea: Austrian Naval Policy, 1797–1866* (1989), the present volume seeks not just to relate the operational history of the navy from the war of 1866 through the First World War, but also to trace the growth of popular navalism in Austria-Hungary, the role of naval expansion in stimulating industrial development, and the trials and tribulations of navy commanders in dealing with the Habsburg Empire's nationality problem and the cumbersome politics of Austro-Hungarian dualism. In rejecting the narrow service history perspective in favor of an approach that gives full consideration to the forces behind naval expansion, I count among my models Arthur J. Marder's *The Anatomy of British Sea Power: A History of British Naval Policy in the Pre-Dreadnought Era, 1880–1905* (1940), Theodore Ropp's *The Development of a Modern Navy: French Naval Policy, 1871–1904* (1987), and a work that has not received the attention it deserves, B. Franklin Cooling's *Gray Steel and Blue Water Navy: The Formative Years of America's Military-Industrial Complex, 1881–1917* (1979).

The recent literature on the Austrian navy includes two works covering the years 1848–1914, Hans Hugo Sokol's *Des Kaisers Seemacht* (1980) and Lothar Höbelt's section "Die Marine" in *Die Habsburgermonarchie, 1848–1918* (1987). The former is a traditional service history, albeit not a particularly detailed one; the latter attempts to be comprehensive in scope, including a section on the budget process, but is only seventy-seven pages in length. Anthony Sokol's *The Imperial and Royal Austro-Hungarian Navy* (1968) is a richly illustrated overview of the navy's history from its earliest times through 1918. While its appearance generated an interest in the Austrian navy in the United States and, after its publication in German translation, rekindled enthusiasm for the subject in Austria as well, it is too general in scope to be of much use to scholars.

Of the handful of unpublished Austrian dissertations, the most useful are Leo Reiter's account of the navy's budget battles in the annual Austrian delegation and Erich Krenslehner's thesis on the economic repercussions of naval expansion. American dissertations on the navy include Louis Gebhard's political history of the navy from 1897 to 1914 and Milan Vego's account of naval expansion in the years 1904–1914. The former deals almost exclusively with politics and the budget, while the latter is more of a traditional service history. Both Gebhard and Vego use the fleet and the strategic problems of 1914 as their point of departure, going backward in time searching for the roots; as a consequence of this approach, neither provides adequate coverage of earlier developments. Austrian naval enthusiasts have taken a similar approach in their popular and semi-scholarly works on the navy; this tendency naturally leads to conclusions dwelling on the fact that Austria-Hungary had the smallest navy of any great power as of the First World War, rather than on how remarkable it was that the Dual Monarchy had managed to build up its sea power to the extent that it did.

Among more general works on naval affairs in the region, Paul G. Halpern's *The Mediterranean Naval Situation, 1908–1914* (1971) provides a comprehensive account of Austria-Hungary's strategic position in the Mediterranean in the years before the First World War, including the negotiations for a Triple Alliance naval convention, based on extensive archival research. Halpern's excellent *The Naval War in the Mediterranean, 1914–1918* (1987) likewise gives the Austro-Hungarian navy its fair share of attention. Hans Hugo Sokol's *Österreich-Ungarns Seekrieg, 1914–1918* (1933), in contrast to his very general history of the years 1848–1914, is a meticulously detailed two-volume study of the navy in the war years. The quarterly magazine *Marine—Gestern, Heute,* published from 1974 to 1988 by the Arbeitsgemeinschaft für österreichische Marinegeschichte, includes a number of articles that supplement or correct Sokol's overall account. The same may be said of the information provided in various memoirs published since the appearance of Sokol's work.[1] Recent specialized treatments of Austro-Hungarian submarines and naval aviation provide additional detail on the wartime experiences of these branches of the service.[2] French and Italian histories of the war in the Adriatic differ from Austrian accounts in certain details and help balance the picture.[3] I found these works indispensable when crafting my account of the years 1914 through 1918.

The libraries of the Österreichisches Staatsarchiv in Vienna and the Archivio di Stato in Trieste were invaluable to my research, and I would like to thank Hofrat Dr. Adolf Gaisbauer and Dott. Ugo Cova and their staffs for their help and consideration. Archival materials were consulted in various branches of the Österreichisches Staatsarchiv: the Haus- Hof- und Staatsarchiv, Kriegsarchiv, and Finanzarchiv. I am especially indebted to Dr. Gaisbauer for his assistance in providing me with the navy's published annual reports and other rare books from the library of the Kriegsarchiv, which was being relocated during my most recent visit to Vienna. The collection of the Nationalbibliothek in Vienna includes the protocols of the Austrian delegation of the *Reichsrat* so important to my research, along with newspapers and a number of monographs virtually unavailable elsewhere. I also used the library of the Museo Civico del Mare in Trieste and the Library of Congress in Washington, D.C. I am grateful to Christine Guyonneau and the interlibrary loan staff of Krannert Memorial Library at the University of Indianapolis for facilitating much of my secondary research. Radio Austria International provided a taped interview of Ruppert von Trapp, son of Captain Georg von Trapp. I am indebted to Erwin Sieche for information on the postwar fate of other former Austro-Hungarian naval personnel, and for providing the warship profiles, which were drawn by Mr. Sieche and Georg Pawlik. I would like to thank my colleague John Batey for drafting the diagram of the Austrian naval-industrial complex. This volume benefits from the careful handling of the staff of Purdue University Press, in particular the editing of Margaret Hunt and the design work of Anita Noble, who are now veterans of two Austrian navy book projects.

I dedicate this book to my colleagues at the University of Indianapolis, in appreciation of their friendship and moral support.

NOTES

1. These include Georg von Trapp, *Bis zum letzten Flaggenschuss: Erinnerungen eines österreichischen U-Boots-Kommandanten;* Miklós Horthy, *Memoirs;* Gottfried von Banfield, *Der Adler von Triest;* and Alfred von Koudelka, *Denn Österreich lag einst am Meer: Das Leben des Admirals Alfred von Koudelka.*

2. E.g. Wladimir Aichelburg, *Die Unterseeboote Österreich-Ungarns;* Peter Schupita, *Die k.u.k. Seeflieger.*

3. Adrien Thomazi, *La guerre navale dans l'Adriatique;* Ufficio Storico della R. Marina, *La marina italiana nella grande guerra.*

Linz
Vienna
Mariazell
Danube River
Budapest
Zeltweg
Graz
CARINTHIA
STYRIA
HUNGARY
CARNIOLA
Celje
Caporetto
Zagreb
Drava River
TYROL
Ljubljana
CROATIA
Piave River
Trieste
Julian Alps
Vukovar
VENETIA
ISTRIA
Rijeka
Sava River
Belgrade
Custoza
Venice
Buccari
Po River
Pola
Porto Ré
Ferrara
Goro
Lussin
BOSNIA
Ravenna
Premuda
Rimini
DALMATIA
Sarajevo
Novi Pazar
Pesaro
Fano
Sebenico
Senigallia
Ancona
Cape Planka
Split
Iesi
Recanati
Lissa
Klek
MONTENEGRO
Potenza River
Curzola
Ragusa
Cattaro
Lagosta
Mount Lovčen
Antivari
Scutari
Pelagosa
Dulcigno
Termoli
Adriatic Sea
Durazzo
Rome
Manfredonia
Barletta
ALBANIA
Naples
Brindisi
Valona
Taranto
Otranto
Straits of Otranto
Cape Santa
Maria di Leuca
Corfu

Messina
Ionian Sea
Augusta

Gorizia
Isonzo River
Monfalcone
Cantiere Navale Triestino
Miramar
Gulf of Trieste
Trieste
Grado
Lloyd Arsenal
San Marco shipyard
San Rocco shipyard
Muggìa

UKRAINE

Dnieper River

Bug River

Dniester River

HUNGARY

Odessa

CRIMEA

• Novorossiysk

Braila

Sebastopol •

Black Sea

Belgrade

Giurgiu

• Constanza

Danube River

Novi Pazar   Svishtov

Varna

Sinope

Trebizond

Bosporus

Constantinople •

Salonika

Gallipoli
Peninsula

Dardanelles

Volos

**Aegean
Sea**

Cephalonia

• Smyrna

Piraeus

**Dodecanese
Islands**

Cyprus

Cape
Matapan

Crete

The Mediterranean

• Alexandria

• Suez

THE ERA OF TEGETTHOFF

PROLOGUE:
THE BATTLE OF LISSA AND THE NAVY OF 1866

Rear Admiral Wilhelm von Tegetthoff had every reason to be pessimistic as he led the Austrian battle fleet out of the harbor of Pola (Pula) on the morning of 19 July 1866. The Austrian Empire was well on its way to losing a two-front war against Prussia and Italy, which would bring an end to the traditional Habsburg influence in German and Italian affairs. In an attempt to neutralize Italy and to prevent France from intervening as well, Emperor Francis Joseph and his ministers had even agreed in early June to cede Venetia to the kingdom of Italy via France as soon as the war ended. Italy went to war anyway, talking openly of seizing all of *Italia irredenta*, the "unredeemed" lands of the South Tyrol, Trieste, Istria, and Dalmatia in addition to Venetia, but these plans went awry on 24 June when the Italian army was defeated at Custoza by a vastly inferior Austrian force. Habsburg luck was not as good in the north, where the Prussian victory at Königgrätz on 3 July decided the overall course of the war. With the Prussians advancing on Vienna, Francis Joseph ordered an evacuation of Venetia to free more troops to hold the line of the Danube. The Italians occupied Venetia, regained their confidence, and turned their attention to the Adriatic, hoping for a victory at sea that would offset their army's defeat at Custoza and open the way for greater territorial gains. On 16 July, the Italian fleet left Ancona and two days later anchored off Lissa (Vis), opening fire on the Austrian forts that guarded the strategic Dalmatian island. In addition to being an excellent springboard for operations against the Dalmatian mainland, Lissa—almost exactly halfway between Venice and Corfu— was the key to controlling the Adriatic.

CHAPTER 1

The Italian fleet at Lissa consisted of twelve armored and twenty-two unarmored warships, the latter including transports with 3,000 troops. All but one of the Italian ironclads had been built in foreign shipyards (eight in France, two in the United States, one in Britain), nine had iron hulls, and eight displaced more than 4,000 tons. In contrast, the force at Tegetthoff's disposal consisted of seven armored and twenty unarmored warships. The Austrian ironclads were all armor-plated wooden ships, constructed in Trieste on a tight budget, and only the largest pair displaced over 4,000 tons.[1] Tegetthoff knew that in a full-scale fleet action against the Italians he would have to commit his unarmored vessels to battle; some were draped in chains and scrap iron before leaving Pola, an improvised protection with a value more psychological than practical. As soon as he received word that the Italians were at Lissa, he prepared to steam southward with his less than formidable fleet. To skeptics, Tegetthoff expressed an absolute confidence that the superiority of his officers and seamen would compensate for the material deficiencies of the fleet, remarking that "behind wooden walls beat hearts of iron."[2]

As the Austrian warships approached Lissa from the northwest on the morning of 20 July, the Italian ironclads steamed out in a traditional line of battle to meet them. Tegetthoff, aware that his own inferior artillery would be overmatched in a conventional duel between parallel lines of warships, went into the battle hoping for a melee in which ramming tactics could carry the day. The Austrians fell upon the Italian line in three V-shaped squadrons: the armored frigates, led by Tegetthoff aboard the flagship *Erzherzog Ferdinand Max;* seven larger wooden propeller steamers, led by Commodore Anton von Petz aboard the ship of the line *Kaiser;* and a third wave of thirteen propeller gunboats and paddle steamers. After the Austrians broke the Italian line, the battle degenerated into a chaotic close action that went on for four hours. Even though the larger wooden steamers on the Austrian side were fully engaged along with the ironclads, Tegetthoff did not lose a ship. The Italians ultimately committed only their eleven foreign-built armored warships to the battle and lost two of them: the American-built *Re d'Italia,* victim of a ramming attack by the *Ferdinand Max;* and the gun-boat *Palestro,* which sank after its powder magazine exploded. The remaining Italian ironclad and wooden ships either missed or ignored repeated signals to enter the fray. Only 38 men were killed on the Austrian side, while the Italians lost 612.[3] As the defeated fleet withdrew westward toward Ancona, Tegetthoff did not attempt to give chase. In addition to their other deficiencies, his iron-clads were much slower than their Italian counterparts and stood little chance of catching their prey.[4]

After securing the island of Lissa, the Austrians returned to their main base at Pola. Despite his inability to pursue the advantage, Tegetthoff could take pride in the outcome. In the words of a contemporary American commentator, "superior intelligence and seamanship secured victory to the Austrians."[5] The Habsburg fleet continued to patrol the northern Adriatic until 12 August, when Austria and Italy concluded an armistice, but the Italians did not venture out of Ancona. The Battle of Lissa was one of the few bright spots for the Habsburg Empire in the disastrous war of 1866. Coming after the army's defeat in the northern theater of the conflict, the navy's success prevented Italy from achieving its ambitious war aims in the Adriatic. Italy left the postwar peace conference with only Venetia, which it would have received without fighting at all, thanks to the prewar diplomacy of France.

Except for a brief period at the end of the Napoleonic Wars, Austria had ruled in Venice since the demise of the Venetian Republic in 1797. For decades the port served as headquarters of the navy command, main base of the fleet, and home of the naval academy, while the ancient Venice Arsenal handled all construction and repairing of warships. Nevertheless, by the time of its cession to the kingdom of Italy, Venice had been reduced to a minor base with little strategic significance to the Austrian navy. The Istrian harbor of Pola, site of an ancient Roman naval base, was not used regularly until the eve of the revolutions of 1848, but after the Venetian revolution of 1848–49 it became the principal anchorage of the fleet. Trieste, the leading commercial port of the Austrian Empire, became home to the naval command and also inherited the naval academy. As late as the mid-1850s, the navy built a pair of wooden propeller corvettes in the Venice Arsenal, but after 1848 the shipyards of Trieste handled most construction. Giuseppe Tonello's San Marco wharves, eventually incorporated as the Cantiere Navale Adriatico, built all seven of the ironclads that saw action at Lissa. A new arsenal at Pola, begun in 1856, provided additional facilities for the shipbuilding and repair projects once carried out at Venice.[6]

A shift away from the navy's traditional dependence upon Venetian officers and seamen accompanied the transfer of facilities away from Venice, to such an extent that the cession of Venetia in 1866 also had little impact in the area of personnel. The navy pardoned and took back many common sailors who deserted in the wake of the Venetian revolution of 1848, but throughout the 1850s and early 1860s the Venetian share of the fleet's manpower gradually declined. At Lissa, roughly half of Tegetthoff's eight thousand sailors were non-Venetian Italians from Trieste, Istria, Rijeka (Fiume), and Dalmatia, another third were Croatians, several hundred (mostly machinists and gunners) were German Austrians or Czechs, and only six hundred were Venetians. Almost all of the latter were repatriated after the war. The transition away from a Venetian-dominated officer corps had been far more abrupt; 64 percent of the navy's officers quit in the spring of 1848, and 59 percent ended up serving in the rebel Venetian navy. None were allowed to return to Habsburg service afterward.

The implementation of German as the official language of command and of study at the naval academy after 1848 naturally encouraged German officer candidates and discouraged most others. The Italian share of the officer corps, consistently more than 60 percent before 1848, fell to fewer than 15 percent in the years after the revolution. Meanwhile, the German share increased from 15 percent to more than 60 percent by 1866, thanks in part to north Germans entering the corps. Given the relative lack of interest in the navy among Hungarians, Czechs, and other inland Habsburg nationalities, an influx of foreign officers—many of them Scandinavians—was needed to cushion the transition from an Italian- to a German-dominated officer corps. A Dane, Hans Birch von Dahlerup, served as commander from 1849 to 1851, and Scandinavians dominated the corps of navy engineers throughout the 1850s. By 1866 there were few Scandinavians left, however, and the last to reach captain's rank, the Swede Erik af Klint, was killed at Lissa, where he commanded the frigate *Novara*. The cession of Venetia had little effect on the Italian minority in the officer corps; five sea officers and one cadet resigned their commissions after the war, and four Italian officers left the land-based branches of the navy. All Italian sea officers above the rank of ensign opted to remain in Habsburg service.[7]

The multinational navy of 1866 worked well enough for Tegett-hoff, to the extent that on the eve of the Lissa campaign he had far more confidence in his personnel than in the matériel of the fleet. The latter, of course, was spearheaded by the ironclad squadron. All seven of the navy's armored warships were built as broadside battery frig-ates: the 2,800-ton *Drache* and *Salamander* (launched in 1861); the 3,600-ton *Kaiser Max, Juan d'Austria,* and *Prinz Eugen* (1862); and the 5,100-ton *Erzherzog Ferdinand Max* and *Habsburg* (1865). The core of the unarmored fleet consisted of seventeen wooden propeller steam-ers: the ship of the line *Kaiser* (1858); the frigates *Radetzky* (1854), *Adria* (1856), and *Donau* (1856); the converted sailing frigates *Novara* and *Schwarzenberg* (both rebuilt in 1861–62); the corvettes *Erzherzog Friedrich* (1857) and *Dandolo* (1858); and nine gunboats. An eighteenth propeller ship, the corvette *Helgoland,* was still under construction in 1866 and would not be launched until the following year. The navy also had twelve seagoing and four auxiliary paddle steamers; a few of these ships accompanied the fleet to Lissa as scout and signal vessels, but most were designated for local defense at stations along the coast or held in reserve as transports. Still more obsolete were the sailing vessels, deleted from the active list in the late 1850s but still used as school ships or for harbor watch duties: the frigates *Venus* (1832) and *Bellona* (1842), the corvettes *Diana* (1834) and *Carolina* (1847), and eight brigs.[8] The navy entered the postwar years with no warships other than those in the Adriatic fleet. A flotilla on Lake Garda was disbanded after the cession of Venetia, and as of 1866 there were no naval vessels deployed on the Danube, even though the navy had inherited the responsibility for defending internal waterways from the army five years earlier.[9]

In addition to Tonello's San Marco shipyard, which dated from 1840, the facilities available to the navy in Trieste included Wilhelm Strudthoff's machine shop, the Stabilimento Tecnico Triestino. In 1857 Strudthoff established the San Rocco shipyard at Muggia on the outskirts of Trieste, but before 1866 all of his contracts with the navy involved the machine shop. Six of the seven ironclads built by Tonello's shipyard had Stabilimento Tecnico Triestino engines, as did the con-verted sailing frigate *Novara,* which had its machinery installed in the San Rocco yard. Of the larger vessels built in the early 1860s, the only ones not equipped with Strudthoff's engines were the armored frigate *Erzherzog Ferdinand Max* and the converted sailing frigate *Schwarzenberg*. Both were powered by machinery from the Stabilimento Tecnico Fiume in Rijeka, established in 1854 and managed by British émigré Robert Whitehead. The Trieste and Rijeka machine shops shared the engine contracts for the navy's small propeller schooners and gunboats with the Georg Sigl firm of Vienna.[10]

Austria's self-sufficiency in engines and basic warship construction unfortunately did not carry over into the area of iron and armor plate production. At a time when most of the newest British, French, and Italian ironclads featured all-iron construction, all of the Austrian ironclads built in the early 1860s had less expensive wooden frames and hulls. Most of their armor came from the Styrian ironworks of Henkel von Donnersmark, in Zeltweg, and Johann von Putzer, near Celje, but these firms could not produce heavy wrought-iron plates in a quantity and quality sufficient to fulfill their contracts. The navy supplemented these domestic sources by importing armor from the foundries of Russery, Lacombe et Compagnie and Marrel Frères, both of Rive-de-Gier on the Loire in France; these purchases remained small, however, owing to the cost and the fact that the plates had to be shipped covertly, in defiance of Napoleon III's ban on French armor exports. The situation regarding naval artillery also left much to be desired. The guns of the fleet came from the *k.k. Eisengusswerk* at Mariazell, Styria; the newest ironclads, the *Erzherzog Ferdinand Max* and *Habsburg,* were supposed to be armed with imported Krupp guns, but on the eve of the war the Prussians had blocked the transaction out of deference to their Italian allies. As of 1866, Austria had no ironworks, public or private, capable of producing modern heavy naval guns.[11]

These weaknesses notwithstanding, after the defeat of the Italian fleet at Lissa the Austrian navy at least momentarily could claim to have the fourth most powerful seagoing battle fleet in the world, inferior only to the British, French, and Russian. It was a fitting legacy to the earlier tenure of Tegetthoff's mentor, Archduke Ferdinand Max. The emperor's brother had commanded the navy from 1854 to 1864, when he became emperor of Mexico, and was responsible for the construction of the ironclad fleet, including the flagship that bore his name. Tegetthoff hoped to maintain the momentum from the archduke's accomplishments in the years after 1866 and to make the navy's wartime success pay off in peacetime. Like previous Austrian naval leaders, he would encounter stiff political resistance, led in the late 1860s by the postwar foreign minister, Count Friedrich Ferdinand von Beust. Refusing to accept the fact that Austria had lost the contest for Germany, Beust sought to build an anti-Prussian coalition among the powers of Europe. Much to the dismay of Tegetthoff and the navy, his diplomatic strategy included a policy of reconciliation, even friendship, toward Italy. The threat of a hostile Italy had provided the raison d'être for Austria's naval expansion in the early 1860s; in the immediate postwar years, and indeed until the fall of the monarchy in 1918, the fortunes of the navy would always be linked directly to the status of Austro-Italian relations.

FROM AFTERGLOW TO STATUS QUO ANTE

On the day after the Battle of Lissa, Francis Joseph promoted Tegetthoff to vice admiral. Aside from members of the imperial house, Tegetthoff, at thirty-eight, was the youngest man ever to reach such heights. The advancement was his second in two years, his promotion to rear admiral having come in 1864 after the Battle of Helgoland, in which his Austrian squadron broke the Danish blockade of Germany's North Sea ports.[12] In further acknowledgment of the navy's triumph at Lissa, Tegetthoff, Rear Admiral Petz, and Captain Max von Sterneck received the prestigious Order of Maria Theresa.[13] The rapid recognition left Tegetthoff with high hopes for himself and the fleet, but it soon became clear that any broader rewards would be slow in coming.

When the emperor declined to attend a postwar review of the fleet in Trieste harbor, the fiery Tegetthoff found it hard to conceal his bitter disappointment. By late September 1866, when the battle fleet was demobilized and Tegetthoff relieved of his squadron command, rumors abounded in Vienna that he had somehow fallen from grace. Francis Joseph's decisions regarding the navy's postwar leadership only fueled the speculation. The emperor decided to leave vacant the post of naval commander (*Marinekommandant*), last held by Ferdinand Max in 1864. His cousin Archduke Leopold, an army corps commander on the northern front during the war of 1866, returned to the ill-defined post of *Marine Truppen- und Flotteninspektor*, which Francis Joseph had created for him in July 1865 when he abolished the Austrian Ministry of Marine. Meanwhile, at the war ministry in Vienna, Vice Admiral Louis Fautz remained on duty as chief of the *Marinesektion,* a position also created in July 1865. Neither Leopold nor Fautz had done much in the year before the war to build upon Ferdinand Max's earlier achievements, and there was little reason to expect more from them in the future. Because Tegetthoff did not get along well with either of them, there appeared to be little chance that he would receive an influential peacetime position.[14]

As he went to Vienna to await further orders, Tegetthoff's fate remained a topic of speculation at court and among the informed public. In the past, most subjects of the monarchy had known little about the navy and cared even less, but the recent victory at sea—certainly not a place where one would expect Austria to prevail—captured the public's imagination and made the young admiral a celebrity. Even Francis Joseph's mother felt compelled to inquire about his future. The emperor assured her that there was no cause for alarm; Tegetthoff had been relieved of command "because the squadron has been disarmed and the few ships that remain in service would be a far too insignificant command for his high rank." In answer to the alleged disappointment of the fleet over the lack of recognition for its services, he remarked that no Austrian *Truppe* was ever "showered with honors" to the extent that the navy had been after the Battle of Lissa.[15]

Irrespective of the dubious accuracy of this claim, the emperor would have been at a loss to list any tangible ways in which the lot of the navy was being improved as a reward for its success in battle. Among his ministers, the fleet had few true friends aside from Vice Admiral Bernhard von Wüllerstorf, appointed minister for trade in 1865 after his retirement from active naval service.[16] Wüllerstorf argued for the continued growth and expansion of the navy, citing the stimulus that new ironclad warship construction would give to the "depressed domestic ironworks." He tried to persuade the wartime foreign minister, Count Alexander von Mensdorff, that "the fruits of the victory of Lissa" lay in the Levant, where Austria, because of its navy, would have a decisive edge over Italy in commercial competition.[17] The war minister, *Feldmarschalleutnant* Carl von Franck, agreed that Austrian industry needed a renewed ironclad program. He felt that the postwar cession of Venetia only increased the necessity for a strong posture in the Adriatic and observed that "under the present circumstances" the strengthening of Habsburg sea power "appears to be of decisive importance."[18] But Francis Joseph saw things differently. In late October 1866, he reorganized the cabinet, replacing Mensdorff with Beust and Franck with Major General Franz von John, a determined revanchist who was to spend most of his time planning for Beust's rematch with Prussia. Leopold and Fautz were not likely to challenge the course that John would take in the future. For the navy, the situation had returned to the status quo ante.

Rather than find a place for Tegetthoff at home, the emperor in November 1866 decided to send him abroad on an extended mission to Britain, France, and the United States, ostensibly to acquaint himself with the latest innovations in warship construction and other recent naval developments.[19] With his reassignment came a decline in morale, especially in the officer corps. Max von Sterneck, the admiral's flag captain aboard the *Erzherzog Ferdinand Max* at Lissa, complained that "with all of the successes of the navy, things remain the same as before." Bitter that Tegetthoff had been sent overseas rather than assigned an important role at home, Sterneck expressed his disgust at the "armchair" admirals who continued to run the fleet from Vienna and lamented the fate of "the sea officers, whose voices are never heard." Fautz in particular was singled out for "believ[ing] himself to be the Lord God." Attempting to dispel the gloom, Sterneck dreamed of an Austrian fleet "consisting of armored ships with broadside guns of heavy caliber and ramming capability, supported by armored rams such as the Italian *Affondatore*," the British-built twin-turreted monitor that was the pride of Italy's navy. He observed, with good reason, that "under the leadership of a Tegetthoff," such a force "would be frightful." His dream was to remain a fantasy.[20]

As for the prevailing material state of the fleet, most navy men thought it left much to be desired. Sterneck condemned the seven armored frigates as "poor ships," an observation that Tegetthoff himself had made, and envied the Italian navy for its high-quality foreign-built ironclads. But in denigrating their own warships, the heroes of Lissa were being quite unfair to Austrian industry, which had performed admirably during the prewar naval arms race. If the shipyards of the kingdom of Italy had been as efficient as those of Trieste, the Italian navy in 1866 would have had enough of an advantage in armored vessels to make an Austrian victory impossible.[21] Of course there was plenty of room for improvement. In approving the navy budget for 1867, imperial officials acknowledged the need for another ironclad, to be constructed in Trieste by Tonello's San Marco shipyard. Additional funds were provided for the remodeling of the *Salamander* and *Drache,* the oldest of the original armored frigates, and for the rearming of the entire ironclad fleet. The new 7-inch Armstrong guns, imported from Britain, were a vast improvement over the antiquated domestic batteries they had carried at Lissa. The purchase also set the precedent for a dependence on foreign producers for heavy guns that would continue until the end of the century. In 1866 future armaments magnate Emil von Skoda had just taken over his first factory in Pilsen (Plzeň), commanded a work force of only thirty-three employees, and was still a quarter century away from being competitive in the business of producing guns for warships. At 7.7 million gulden, the navy's appropriation for 1867 was slightly less than the prewar allocation for 1866. The cost of the British guns strained the budget, and by the time the new ironclad *Lissa* had been laid down and repairs begun on the other two ships, the navy had spent 10.2 million.[22]

These modest improvements hardly compensated for the psychological effects of Tegetthoff's reassignment. Without the charismatic admiral, the fleet was in danger of losing what remained of the confidence it had gained in the wars of 1864 and 1866. Ironically, a great tragedy paved the way for Tegetthoff to return to a position of prominence. He was in Paris, near the end of his inspection tour, when on 19 June 1867, Emperor Maximilian of Mexico was executed at Queretaro by troops of the republican leader Benito Juarez. After the Juarez government made known its intention to use the return of the corpse to extort a de facto Austrian recognition of the Mexican Republic, Francis Joseph recalled Tegetthoff to Vienna and made him his personal envoy to secure the recovery of the remains.[23] He hastened to Washington, D.C., to lay the diplomatic groundwork for his delicate task, then proceeded to Mexico, where he arrived in late August. Thanks to Juarez and his macabre game, Tegetthoff was to win even greater esteem in the eyes of the emperor, a development that would do more good for the navy than its performance at Lissa.[24]

THE NAVY AND AUSTRO-ITALIAN RELATIONS (1866–71)

When the defeat of 1866 necessitated the replacement of Mensdorff as Habsburg foreign minister, Francis Joseph took the controversial step of appointing an outsider, the Saxon Count Beust, to fill the post. Formerly minister of state and foreign minister of Saxony, Beust had to leave these offices when Otto von Bismarck made known his intention to incorporate Saxony into the new North German Confederation. During his first months in Vienna, Beust was preoccupied with the negotiation of the Austro-Hungarian Compromise (*Ausgleich*), which in February 1867 converted the Austrian Empire into the Dual Monarchy of Austria-Hungary. His long-term goal, however, was to rekindle the German question and revive Austria's voice in German affairs. By selecting Beust as his foreign minister, Francis Joseph demonstrated his own refusal to abandon Germany to Prussian domination.

Not wanting to lead Austria into another hopeless two-front war, Beust sought to make a stable, peaceful Austro-Italian relationship a pillar of his anti-Prussian foreign policy.[25] A favorable reaction to the initiative from Italy would open the way for Italian participation in a new alliance against Prussia, which ideally would also include France. But in order for his plans to succeed, serious obstacles would have to be overcome. Italy remained bitter over its land and sea defeats of 1866 and held out hope that the Habsburg Empire's remaining Italian-speaking communities in the Alps and on the Adriatic would someday be brought under Italian control. The French likewise would have to withdraw their garrison from Rome, where the troops of Napoleon III supported the pope's temporal authority and blocked the city's incorporation into the kingdom of Italy.

Beust's initial overtures fell on deaf ears, and his policy encountered still more difficulties in the spring of 1867, when the pro-Prussian liberal Urbano Rattazzi became Italian prime minister. It was under an earlier Rattazzi ministry, in 1862, that the Italians had made their decisive commitment to construct an ironclad battle fleet. But Rattazzi's navy minister from his previous cabinet, Count Carlo Pellion di Persano, was in no condition to take office again in 1867. After using his political connections to gain command of the Italian fleet before the war of 1866, Persano had to shoulder the blame for the disaster at Lissa and became the principal scapegoat for the entire lost war effort.[26]

Ironically, while victory had brought an unwanted return to obscurity for the navy in Austria, defeat had caused the navy to become the center of attention in Italy. But in focusing on Persano alone, the Italian government neglected to conduct a broader investigation into the causes of the defeat at Lissa, and for the navy as a whole there was no postwar reform program.[27] The only bright spot for the Italian navy was that a backlog of ironclads unavailable in 1866 finally started to enter service. The commissioning of a new armored frigate in 1867 gave Italy eleven ironclads in service and another five under construction, compared to Austria's seven completed and one just begun.[28]

In the fall of 1867, following a crisis over Giuseppe Garibaldi's abortive invasion of the Papal State, the hostile Rattazzi gave way to the conservative General Luigi Menabrea. The new prime minister responded favorably to overtures from Beust, who considered him Vienna's best hope among the circle of postwar Italian leaders. In the area of naval competition, Menabrea's Italy posed no threat to Austria's hegemony over the Adriatic. An opponent of ironclad construction during an earlier term as navy minister (1860–62), Menabrea saw to it that no new seagoing warships were ordered. The decline in Austro-Italian animosity gave Beust reason to hope that an alliance of Austria-Hungary, Italy, and France could be formed to contain Bismarck and Prussia. Coincidentally, Menabrea also made a favorable impression on Napoleon III, who took the initiative in opening alliance talks with the Italians during 1868. In the spring of 1869, two drafts of a Franco-Austro-Italian pact circulated among the three capitals, but the project failed when Italy demanded France's withdrawal from Rome as a prerequisite.[29]

Beust, too, had his share of difficulties even with the friendly regime of Menabrea, but the problems were not quite as thorny as the Roman question. In late July 1869, tensions rose after an Italian sailor from the steamer *Monzambano*, which was engaged in a joint Austro-Italian project to map the Adriatic, was killed by a local mob during his ship's visit to the Dalmatian port of Sebenico (Šibenik). The riot, which also left several other sailors and townspeople injured, had started when the Slavic populace welcomed the crew to its shore leave with a taunting song about the Battle of Lissa.[30] Dalmatian Italian irredentists publicized the incident and ultimately the Italian Chamber of Deputies called for an Austrian statement on the matter. Menabrea's ministry, by then burdened by various domestic problems, had no choice but to demand an explanation.

A subsequent Austrian investigation of the Sebenico affair failed to satisfy the Italians. In December 1869, Menabrea fell from power, to be replaced by the equally conservative but much less friendly Giovanni Lanza. The new foreign minister, Emilio Visconti Venosta, served notice that Italy would not forget Sebenico without a formal Austrian apology. Beust refused to yield on this point, but in February 1870 he reiterated that he "deplore[d] the excesses" of the mob at Sebenico and regretted the disruption the affair had brought to "la bonne harmonie" between their two countries.[31] Nevertheless, Visconti Venosta refused to forget the incident entirely, and the Sebenico affair remained an irritant in Austro-Italian relations until it finally lost its relevance amid the greater issues of the summer of 1870.[32]

A rebellion in the Bocche di Cattaro (Boka Kotorska) at the southern tip of Dalmatia placed further strains on the Austro-Italian relationship over the winter of 1869–70. The uprising occurred after local inhabitants rejected the terms of a new imperial military law, the *Wehrgesetz* of 1868. In early October 1869, when the revolt started, the Habsburg army had only three thousand men in all of Dalmatia and only nominal forces in the Cattaro region. Because poor roads made Cattaro virtually inaccessible by land, all reinforcements had to be transported by the navy. The main body of rebels was defeated by late November, but only after the fleet had ferried over ten thousand men to Dalmatia.[33] Throughout the revolt, Beust suspected Italy of supplying the rebels with arms, although Austrian consular officials found no evidence of weapons shipments crossing the Adriatic to Cattaro. The concurrent publication in Italy of a polemic urging the annexation of Albania did little to ease Beust's fears about Italian ambitions in the eastern littoral.[34]

Notwithstanding the importance of cordial Austro-Italian ties in his overall strategy, Beust by the spring of 1870 had made little progress toward a rapprochement with Italy. The Sebenico affair brought age-old anti-Austrian sentiments to the surface in Italy, while the Cattaro rebellion revived Austrian suspicions of Italy's intentions in the Adriatic. But when France and Prussia went to war in July 1870, Beust's apprehensions suddenly evaporated. The Franco-Prussian War had the potential to escalate into the general conflict he had been hoping for ever since 1866, and he was prepared to do whatever was necessary to bring the Franco-Austro-Italian alliance to fruition.

Napoleon III almost immediately offered Visconti Venosta a deal on the Roman question in return for a Franco-Italian alliance. The subsequent withdrawal of the French garrison from Rome removed a major stumbling block. Thereafter, Beust pushed the Italian foreign minister to join him in a sham "joint mediation" of the Franco-Prussian conflict that would lead both of their countries into the war on the French side. Visconti Venosta hesitated, however, hoping to gain Rome without involving Italy in the war.[35] Meanwhile, both Paris and Vienna proposed increasingly lucrative terms designed to lure the Italians into the fold.

In late July, Beust met with Count Ottaviano Vimercati, a personal adjutant of King Victor Emmanuel II, and hammered out a draft treaty that promised Italy the Italian South Tyrol (Trentino) and, east of Venetia, a border adjustment to the line of the Isonzo River; from France, Italy would gain a free hand to annex Rome, the return of part of Nice (ceded to France in 1860), and commercial concessions in Tunis. On 6 August, Visconti Venosta finally offered his own version of an Austro-Italian alliance, virtually identical to the Beust-Vimercati draft except for an addendum that the Austrian and Italian navies commence joint operations before a declaration of war.[36] Memories of Lissa were still fresh in the minds of Italian statesmen, and the foreign minister would not agree to go to war unless Italy knew in advance precisely what the Austrian navy would be doing during the conflict.

The same day that Visconti Venosta produced his terms for an alliance, the Prussians defeated the French army at Wörth, and the tide of war started to turn against Napoleon III. Italy lost interest in intervention and proposed to Britain a joint mediation of the conflict by all neutral powers. Beust promptly dropped his campaign for an Austro-Italian alliance and, in the weeks to come, acquiesced as Habsburg policy toward Italy took a very different turn. For years, Francis Joseph and Catholic Austria had been more than willing to let France act as protector of the Papal State. Even as the French garrison withdrew and Napoleon III hinted that the Roman question was negotiable, Italy had to respect the position of the French emperor as final arbiter of the pope's political fate. But with the Prussians advancing and Napoleon III's throne for the first time appearing shaky, there was little to deter a unilateral Italian annexation of Rome; indeed, the Italian Left urged immediate action, and the Lanza ministry was hard pressed to explain why it had to continue to be so cautious. Francis Joseph resolved that Austria-Hungary would fill the breach until the fortunes of war changed and France again could act as guardian of the pope's temporal authority.[37]

The coercion, starting within days of the French defeat at Wörth, included noisy defensive preparations in the Tyrol and the mobilization of Tyrolese reserve battalions, but the primary role went to the navy, which was to be used in a show of force at Italian ports. In the summer of 1870, the fleet had one of its newest ironclads, the *Habsburg*, on patrol in the Mediterranean, but out of consideration for the budget the rest of the armored warships were disarmed and docked in Pola. The Austrian naval demonstration therefore was entirely makeshift, consisting of all ships that could assemble in Italian waters. In early August, the *Habsburg* departed from its designated itinerary and proceeded to Naples with its escort, the gunboat *Kerka*. Shortly thereafter, other wooden steamers arrived as well: the corvette *Dandolo* from Gibraltar, where it was visiting en route home from a mission to South America, and the frigate *Novara* from Toulon, where it had put in while on a training cruise in the western Mediterranean. The demonstration lasted from 19 August until 3 September, with all four ships present in Naples from 27–31 August. The *Habsburg* was the first of the vessels to arrive and the last to leave, its departure coinciding with the arrival of news that the French army had been defeated at Sedan.[38]

The ensuing collapse of the French Empire doomed the cause of the pope, and Francis Joseph accepted the fact that Austria-Hungary was in no position to actually prevent Italy from annexing the Papal State. The Italian army completed the occupation on 20 September, and Lanza announced the transfer of the capital from Florence to Rome. For the remainder of Beust's tenure on the Ballhausplatz, relations between the two governments hinged on the question of whether Vienna would recognize the change in capital cities. Meanwhile, Habsburg recognition of Bismarck's new German Empire eliminated once and for all any German motivation for Austria-Hungary to seek an Italian alliance.

In a clear overreaction to the Austrian threat at sea, the Italian fleet mobilized eleven ironclads to support the army's occupation of the Papal State. Even though the Habsburg naval demonstration brought no tangible benefit, the response from the Italian side was a comforting affirmation that, four years after Lissa, Italy still respected Austrian sea power.[39] In any event, the emperor appears to have been satisfied. In October 1870, the commander of the demonstration, Captain Georg von Millosicz, was promoted to rear admiral.[40]

TEGETTHOFF AND THE ONSET OF DUALISM (1868–71)

In January 1868, Tegetthoff returned to Trieste from his special mission to Mexico. With him aboard the frigate *Novara* were the remains of Ferdinand Max, recovered from the Juarez government after months of difficult negotiations.[41] Throughout his reign in Mexico, the former navy commander had never forgotten the Habsburg fleet. He had the Mexican consul in Trieste send him periodic reports on the progress of the service, and after the Battle of Lissa he awarded his Order of Guadalupe to Tegetthoff and other officers who had distinguished themselves in the victory. Ironically, his homecoming was aboard the same ship that had taken him to the New World four years earlier.[42]

For Francis Joseph and the imperial family, the return of the archduke's body marked the end of a great ordeal. The emperor felt a deep personal gratitude toward Tegetthoff for the manner in which he had carried out his assignment. Upon his arrival in Vienna, the new war minister, *Feldzeugmeister* Baron Franz von Kuhn, informed him confidentially that Francis Joseph was going to appoint him commander.[43] At the end of February, Tegetthoff succeeded Vice Admiral Fautz as chief of the *Marinesektion* and was also appointed *Marinekommandant*. For the first time in four years, the navy had a commander, and for the first time since 1862, when Ferdinand Max turned over the naval administration to the short-lived Ministry of Marine, one man was in charge of both the fleet and the bureaucracy.[44]

Because of the political changes that had followed the war of 1866, Tegetthoff had to labor under a set of circumstances different from those faced by any previous commander. As a result of the *Ausgleich* of February 1867, the Habsburg Empire became the Dual Monarchy of Austria-Hungary, and each half of the empire was granted control over most of its own affairs. There were two cabinets, two parliaments, and only three joint or "common" ministries: for foreign affairs, war, and finance. The joint budget, including military expenditure, had to be approved by the Delegations, consisting of sixty members from each of the two parliaments. These bodies met annually, alternating their sessions between Vienna and Budapest; they did not hold a joint session unless each had failed to pass the budget on two attempts. Needless to say, the political hurdles facing the navy were greater after 1867 than before.

In late February 1868, Tegetthoff drafted a proposal to reorganize the navy. Knowing that the emperor would never agree to an independent fleet, he called for an autonomous service under the auspices of the army. Francis Joseph satisfied his wish for autonomy by making the chief of the *Marinesektion* the representative of the war minister on all naval matters, with the right to present the naval portion of the military budget before the Delegations. The war minister, however, would remain "responsible" for the navy as well as the army, and the chief of the *Marinesektion* was to have no ministerial powers or prerogatives. Tegetthoff, as *Marinekommandant,* answered directly to the emperor in matters pertaining to the battle readiness of the fleet.[45]

The arrangement would cause problems for future commanders, but Tegetthoff formed a tolerable working relationship with Kuhn. Indeed, he enjoyed relatively good relations with the leading personalities of the army. Count Friedrich Beck, chief of the emperor's military chancellery and later chief of the General Staff, considered himself a personal friend of the admiral, and Archduke Albrecht, the victor of Custoza in 1866, admired him enough to lend political support, if only occasionally. One such instance came early in 1868, when proponents of coastal fortifications sought approval for their projects before Tegetthoff had a chance to build his own case for a seagoing defense. Albrecht came down on the side of the navy, freeing the new *Marinekommandant* from what would have been a debate over the battle fleet's very existence.[46]

In March 1868, Tegetthoff formally assumed the duties of commander. Archduke Leopold resigned from his post as *Marine Truppen- und Flotteninspektor,* which Francis Joseph then abolished. Rear Admiral Friedrich von Pöck, Leopold's protégé and adjutant and an old rival of Tegetthoff, lost his influence at the top but was placated with command of the active squadron.[47] Because the Delegations had just met to approve the common budget for 1868, the new commander had to wait almost a full year before presenting his own plans for a larger armored fleet. In the meantime, he implemented reforms in virtually every area under his control.

Ever since Venetian times, the navy had maintained a separate marine infantry regiment and artillery corps alongside the "corps of sailors" (*Matrosencorps*); the marines and artillerymen were commanded by their own officers on land but were under a sea officer when serving aboard ship. As in other navies, the crew of every larger warship traditionally had included a detachment of marines to lead a boarding or landing party in battle and to keep order aboard ship at other times; in the Austrian navy, however, no marines had served on ships since 1858. Tegetthoff abolished both the marine regiment and the naval artillery corps in favor of an enlarged *Matrosencorps* that would serve as the pool of all common manpower. Most sailors not serving aboard active warships were organized into companies on land and subjected to infantry drill; others received gunnery training either on land or aboard hulks designated as artillery school ships. Detachments from the *Matrosencorps*, armed as infantrymen, performed duties normally associated with marine troops, garrisoning coastal installations not manned by the army and eventually providing guards for some Habsburg embassies and consulates outside of Europe.[48]

After the reforms, there were no naval infantry officers. Naval artillery officers were redesignated "technical officials" (*technische Beamte*) and given a separate but equal status alongside the corps of sea officers, following a precedent set in 1858–59 in the reclassification of all engineering officers as technical officials. Eventually the social status of the *Beamten* became a heated political issue, but favorable conditions of service sufficed to keep most of them content: they enjoyed a higher pay scale than the sea officers, and those marrying paid a lower *Heiratskaution*.[49] For the common manpower of the navy as well as their leaders, the basic structure introduced by Tegetthoff would remain intact until 1918.

In the administrative realm, a provisional restructuring of the *Marinesektion* in May 1868 gained definitive approval from Francis Joseph in December. Changes included the introduction of the post of *Marinekommando-Adjutant,* which Tegetthoff gave to his old friend Captain Sterneck. While the navy, as before, would have no equivalent to the army General Staff, Tegetthoff hoped the reforms would improve staff work in Vienna.[50] To facilitate the navy's access to information on the latest developments, he sent the first Habsburg naval attaché, Captain Count Alexander Kielmannsegge, to the embassy in London. Kielmannsegge assumed his post in 1869, and the British reciprocated by sending a naval attaché to Vienna.

The end of 1868 also brought the introduction of the new military law (*Wehrgesetz*) for the Austro-Hungarian armed forces, which reduced the term of active service from the traditional eight years to just three. Tegetthoff opposed the change, having often questioned whether even eight years were adequate for producing good seamen.[51] Under the law, the navy had its equivalent of the army's new option of one year of volunteer duty for young men whose social, economic, or educational background ruled out service in the ranks. In the army, most men successful in using this conscription loophole went on to become reserve officers in the Austrian *Landwehr* or Hungarian *Honvéd*. For its *Einjährig-Freiwillige*, the navy hoped to attract officers from the merchant marine to form a cadre of reserve sea officers, or those holding diplomas from technical institutes for training as reserve engineers. Eventually a two-year volunteer option offered the rank of reserve machinist noncommissioned officer (NCO) to mechanics and graduates of technical schools.

Tegetthoff also initiated reforms of the curriculum at the naval academy, which had reopened in Rijeka in the fall of 1866 after a hiatus of several years. The commander, whose personal tastes in literature ranged from Kant's philosophical works to the poetry of Lord Byron, believed firmly that the academy should provide more than just a specialized naval education. His radical proposal called for the first three years of study to follow the standard Austrian *Oberrealschule* curriculum, with courses taught by qualified civilian instructors. Navy officers would teach only the naval and technical courses, concentrated in the fourth year. The controversial plan marked a decisive turn away from a British-style program of shipboard learning and practical seamanship adopted in the early 1860s by Ferdinand Max in favor of a broad naval education on the French model. It gained acceptance only slowly and was not fully implemented until 1871.[52] Civilian faculty hired under the new program included the *Marinekommandant*'s younger brother, Dr. Albrecht von Tegetthoff, a professor of mathematics.[53]

In addition to the considerable changes on land, Tegetthoff also reevaluated the material strength of the fleet and ordered the decommissioning of a number of obsolete vessels. He reduced the sail-powered contingent to one corvette and three brigs; the remaining corvette, two frigates, and five brigs were either scrapped or designated as hulks. He also removed almost half of the paddle steamers from active duty as well as the two least seaworthy propeller frigates, *Schwarzenberg* and *Adria*. In September 1868, Tegetthoff submitted to the emperor a formal fleet plan, the first comprehensive naval program in ten years.[54] It provided for an armored battle fleet of fifteen ships, supplemented by an unarmored force of frigates, corvettes, and gunboats totaling thirty-four vessels. The expanded fleet of ironclads would be the empire's maritime muscle in times of war or international crisis, while the unarmored steam fleet, maintained at the strength of 1866, would show the flag, conduct special missions, and protect commerce in peacetime. To bring the plan to fruition, Tegetthoff called for 25.3 million gulden to be budgeted for naval construction over the next decade. The emperor sanctioned the program, but it was up to the Delegations to fund it.[55]

Many of the unarmored auxiliary ships decommissioned in the modernization campaign were vessels that Ferdinand Max had considered for sale to the Confederate States during the first years of the American Civil War.[56] By deleting them from the active list, Tegetthoff reaffirmed their expendability, along with his belief that in an emergency, the resources of the Austrian Lloyd would be more than adequate to supplement the unarmored strength of the fleet.[57] The Lloyd was the largest steamship line under Habsburg colors and, since 1851, the largest of any in the Mediterranean. Its contribution to the war effort in 1866 was not as extensive as in 1848–49 or 1859,[58] but in the postwar years, the Lloyd's value to the navy increased when it, too, pursued a program of modernization. The opening of the Lloyd Arsenal in Trieste in 1861 enabled the company to build its own ships; thereafter it started to add modern propeller vessels to its fleet and began to phase out its old paddle steamers. In 1867 and 1868, the last of the original Lloyd steamers were finally retired after thirty years of service, and the much larger liners that replaced them raised the total capacity of the fleet to unprecedented heights. Whereas the number of vessels remained roughly the same (63 in 1869, compared to 61 in 1856), the total displacement of the company's ships increased from 21,300 tons in 1856 to 58,640 in 1869. With a large and modern fleet, the Lloyd was an even greater strategic asset than before.[59]

After setting in motion his modernization program and implementing the reforms on land, in the autumn of 1868 Tegetthoff prepared his case for a larger navy budget for the following year. An appropriation of 8.4 million gulden for 1868 had included no money for new armored ships but did provide funds to convert the fleet's only ship of the line, the *Kaiser*, into an ironclad, the work to be done in the navy's own Pola Arsenal.[60] With seven ironclads in service and two more (the *Lissa* and *Kaiser*) under construction, Tegetthoff needed another six to reach his goal of fifteen. He decided to ask for three for 1869, but the council of ministers rejected his proposal on the grounds that the victory at Lissa had eliminated the immediate threat from the Italian fleet and that Beust's policy of friendship toward Italy ruled out another conflict in the Adriatic, at least for the foreseeable future. Furthermore, the army had been vanquished in 1866 and required a greater share of military spending to get back into fighting shape, while the victorious navy, in the opinion of the council, did not need rebuilding. An exasperated Tegetthoff found that the fleet was the victim of its own success.[61]

Under the constitutional arrangement of the *Ausgleich*, the head of the *Marinesektion* could submit his budget proposal to the Delegations without the sanction of the council of ministers or even the war ministry. When he faced the Delegations in Budapest in December 1868, Tegetthoff took advantage of the opportunity and kept two of the new ironclads in his budget. As he prepared for the deliberations, it did not help matters that he had such poor relations with politicians and, indeed, detested most of them. As a young officer, the events of 1848 had made him a solid German nationalist and liberal; consequently, he despised Beust's Prussophobia and, even more, the conservative, pro-clerical, pro-Slavic policies of the Austrian minister-president, Count Eduard Taaffe, and his successor, Count Alfred Potocki. At the same time, however, his personal interest in the navy budget put him at odds with the leaders of the German liberal political group in the *Reichsrat*, in particular Karl Giskra, an outspoken opponent of all increases in military spending.[62]

In the budget debate, the navy received unexpected support from Count Mensdorff, the former foreign minister, now a conservative representative from the Austrian House of Lords (*Herrenhaus*). Mensdorff highlighted the weaknesses of Austria's Italian front in the wake of the loss of Venetia in 1866 and called it "the duty of every patriot to do everything to maintain the best possible defenses on this border of the empire." In particular, he called for a fleet "in battle-ready condition," observing that anything less would be "practically worthless."[63] But Tegetthoff was his own strongest asset. The *Marinekommandant* stood before the politicians of the Delegations as the naval version of the victorious *Feldherr*, the sort of man that unfortunately was a rarity in the Habsburg Empire. Largely on the strength of his prestige, he secured authorization for the two new ironclads, although the total appropriation for 1869—8.8 million gulden—represented only a modest increase over the previous year's allotment.[64]

Out of deference to the army, the two ships were named *Erzherzog Albrecht* and *Custoza*. The contract for the former went to Tonello's Navale Adriatico, while the latter was to be built in the San Rocco yard of the Stabilimento Tecnico Triestino, a firm heretofore awarded contracts only for engines, repairs, and alterations. Tegetthoff had little time to savor the accomplishment, for in March 1869 Francis Joseph was scheduled to visit the Adriatic provinces and inspect the fleet. It would be the emperor's first direct contact with the navy in eight years, and Tegetthoff resolved to take full advantage of the opportunity. In Trieste, Francis Joseph's itinerary included tours of the Stabilimento Tecnico as well as the San Marco yard of Navale Adriatico, where the ironclad *Lissa* was nearing completion. The emperor came away favorably impressed, if not converted to the navy's cause. In the future, he would at least not actively obstruct efforts to strengthen the fleet.[65]

After the emperor's tour, the cramped political calendar for 1869 compelled Tegetthoff to start work almost immediately on his estimates for 1870. In the fall of 1869, the admiral and many of the political leaders of the empire were to accompany Francis Joseph to the opening of the Suez Canal; with the Delegations scheduled to meet in August rather than December, Tegetthoff had to have his new budget proposals ready for the council of ministers by early June. The ministers once again challenged his figures and in the category of new warships were willing to concede only an unarmored propeller frigate to replace the

Radetzky, which had exploded in an accident off Lissa in February 1869.[66] But the budget went on to the Delegations with no reductions after the emperor refused to force a compromise.

In addition to his request for more money than the ministers were willing to concede, Tegetthoff's budget for 1870 also sought to establish a principle of annual fixed expenditure, to bring his ten-year construction plan of 1868 to fruition by means of a navy law along the lines of the one Admiral Alfred von Tirpitz would be granted in Germany at the turn of the century. When the Delegations convened in Vienna, the navy budget became a topic of lively debate in which the bedfellows were strange indeed. The former admiral Wüllerstorf, now a liberal representative from the *Herrenhaus,* had to temper his support for a bigger fleet out of regard for the views of his antinavy political colleagues, while former foreign minister Count Johann von Rechberg, a conservative member from the same body, abandoned his earlier antinavy convictions and supported Tegetthoff, citing the numerical superiority of the Italian fleet and the danger it posed to the Adriatic coast.[67] In defense of the idea of annual fixed expenditure, Tegetthoff contended that his plan took into consideration the empire's "financial status" as well as its "strategic posture"; he dismissed the notion that the program would embroil Austria-Hungary "in a competition with the great sea powers." The navy received 9.8 million gulden for 1870, including money to continue work on the four ironclads under construction and for an unarmored frigate to replace the *Radetzky.* The Delegations rejected fixed expenditure, however, and budgeted no funds for additional armored ships.[68]

For better or worse, the financial battle was over for another year, and Tegetthoff finally was able to focus his attentions on the trip to Egypt. The emperor's entourage, which included foreign minister Beust, Hungarian minister-president Count Gyula Andrássy, and former finance minister (now Austrian trade minister) Ignaz von Plener, was to travel from Budapest to Constantinople by way of the Danube and Black Sea, then by sea to Greece and Palestine before arriving at the Isthmus of Suez. Austria long had appreciated the importance of the canal to the future prosperity of Trieste and the other ports of the Adriatic littoral, but little had been done to lay the groundwork for its exploitation. An Austrian naval expedition to the Far East, scheduled for 1866, had been postponed by the war, and as a result the Habsburg

Empire had not negotiated the necessary trade treaties with the Oriental governments. Plans for the mission were resurrected following the war, with Rear Admiral Petz, the commander of the wooden ships at the Battle of Lissa, placed in charge. Before sailing, Petz was granted the authority of minister plenipotentiary to Siam, China, and Japan and instructed to conclude commercial agreements with their governments. The expedition ended up being much smaller than initially planned, consisting only of the propeller frigate *Donau* and corvette *Erzherzog Friedrich,* and did not leave Trieste until October 1868, just one year before the emperor, Tegetthoff, and the rest of the Habsburg dignitaries began their journey to Egypt. The two ships would not return home until early in 1871.[69]

After arriving in the Levant in the autumn of 1869, Francis Joseph embarked on the seldom-used imperial yacht, *Greif,* while his entourage boarded two of the navy's paddle steamers. The ironclads *Erzherzog Ferdinand Max* and *Habsburg,* under Rear Admiral Pöck, escorted the flotilla on the final leg of its voyage to Port Said. On 17 November, in ceremonies opening the canal, the *Greif* fell into line behind the French imperial yacht, which, with Empress Eugénie aboard, led the procession through the waterway. Except for the two armored frigates, all of the Habsburg warships cruised on to the Red Sea, as did three steamers sent by the Austrian Lloyd. The *Greif* and its escorts returned to Trieste in December; the expedition as a whole went smoothly, marred only by Beust's frequent seasickness.[70]

The cruise home from the Suez Canal was to be the last sea voyage of Tegetthoff's career. As the new year began, the admiral was beset not only by worries over another navy budget but also by more serious concerns about his own health. A heavy smoker for many years, he had been receiving treatment for a nagging lip cancer since 1866. After doctors treated the tumor again during the summer of 1870, Tegetthoff asked the war ministry for time off to recuperate. Kuhn granted his wish and heeded a subsequent request, in late October, for an extension of the leave.[71]

The treatment and convalescence coincided with the Franco-Prussian War. Keenly interested in the conflict, Tegetthoff, like most German Austrian liberals, found the alternatives frustrating. His German nationalism made him wish for an Austro-Prussian alliance to rid Europe of the French menace once and for all, but he was enough of a realist to recognize that such a combination and result would do nothing for Austria. In his more pragmatic moments, he lamented the decision to remain neutral and speculated that, had Beust's foreign policy worked, Germany south of the Main River could have been annexed to Austria, bringing millions more Germans under Habsburg rule and strengthening the German Austrian cause against the other nationalities of the empire. While the admiral's liberalism made him a firm believer in representative institutions, in his private letters he railed against the *"Ausgleichs-komödie"* and speculated that the power-sharing arrangement with the Hungarians would not last long.[72]

In any event, the outcome of the war had been decided by the time the Delegations convened in Budapest late in the year. For Tegetthoff the months of rest seemed to help, and he appeared to be in fighting trim for the debate. The most controversial element of his budget for 1871 was a request for money to accelerate work on the ironclads already under construction. The Navale Adriatico had launched the *Lissa* in February 1869, but by the fall of 1870 its British armor still had not been delivered. The *Erzherzog Albrecht*, under construction at the Navale Adriatico since November 1869, the *Custoza*, laid down by the Stabilimento Tecnico Triestino in August 1869, and the former ship of the line *Kaiser*, out of the water in the Pola Arsenal since February 1869 for its conversion to an ironclad, were all far from ready. The latter project was plagued by cost overruns on armor and other iron fittings that had to be purchased from British suppliers; indeed, the high price of imported building materials caused the navy to exceed its budget by more than 600,000 gulden in 1870. Before turning his thoughts to new construction, Tegetthoff naturally gave his highest priority to the completion of these four warships. In his quest to finish the projects, the commander at least could be grateful that labor problems were not yet a factor. In 1869 Trieste workers formed the Società Operaia Triestina, a union with a Mazzinian ideology, but it did not attract much of a following. The Trieste shipyards would not experience a significant strike until the early 1880s.[73]

International developments during the course of 1870 naturally shaped the new round of debate over naval spending. Two of the great powers of Europe, France and Prussia, had just fought a war in which sea power played little role; a financially strapped Italy had reduced military spending; and for the fifth year in a row, the Italians had ordered no new seagoing ironclads.[74] But supporters of the navy could point to the fact that Russia had taken advantage of the Franco-Prussian War to denounce the Black Sea clauses of 1856. The revival of a Russian Black Sea fleet was certain to have repercussions for the balance of power in the eastern Mediterranean, where Austria-Hungary had considerable commercial and strategic interests.[75] In the end, Tegetthoff's prestige once again carried more weight than the best of arguments. In January 1871, when they finally voted on the navy budget, the Delegations increased the naval allocation to 11 million gulden. A substantial sum went to the construction projects, including almost 2.5 million for imported armor plate for the *Custoza* and *Erzherzog Albrecht*. A supporter of the budget, delegate Eduard Sturm of Iglau (Jihlava), observed wryly that the victory at Lissa was getting more expensive every year.[76]

The allocation ensured that the four new ironclads would be completed in a reasonable amount of time, bringing Tegetthoff to within four of his 1868 goal of fifteen armored warships for the fleet. But his emphasis on ironclads had not caused him to neglect the need for unarmored vessels to replace those he had deleted from the active list. Being less expensive, wooden-hulled warships were far less controversial with politicians. In addition to the new frigate *Radetzky*, Tegetthoff had two propeller corvettes under construction by the end of 1870, with another frigate and two corvettes to be laid down during 1871. The six vessels were built as "composite" ships, with wooden hulls covering an iron frame. They proved to be quite durable and, during the remainder of the century, carried much of the burden in showing the flag outside of European waters.[77]

Similar progress in subsequent years may well have brought to fruition the unarmored portion of Tegetthoff's fleet plan of 1868, but as fate would have it, the budget for 1871 was the last the admiral ever prepared. Over the winter of 1870–71, respiratory problems joined lip cancer on his list of health worries, and by the time spring arrived Tegetthoff considered asking for another leave of absence. Still, he attempted to keep up with his social obligations in the imperial capital. On the first Sunday in April, the *Marinekommandant*, ill with a fever, attended a dinner at the Palais Schwarzenberg; afterward he could not find a *Fiaker* for the ride home and had to walk to his quarters in the Schenkenstrasse in a driving rain. The following day found him bedridden with pneumonia, which worsened as the week progressed. He died on the morning of 7 April 1871. As his hagiographers have noted, it was a Good Friday.[78]

The funeral procession to the Matzleinsdorfer Friedhof included the entire Vienna army garrison, almost half of the navy officer corps, a detachment of five hundred sailors, dozens of dignitaries, and several thousand Viennese. Francis Joseph was conspicuously absent, having decided not to return from an Easter holiday in the Tyrol.[79] Tegetthoff's passing, at the age of forty-three, was mourned as a great national tragedy. The liberal *Neue Freie Presse*, no great supporter of naval spending, issued the most sorrowful of eulogies. Forecasting a promising political career for the admiral had he lived, the obituary speculated that Austria had lost "a hope for the future, an anchor through which the tottering, sinking ship of state—tossed about on the waves of nationality movements and confessional battles—again would have been able to take hold of solid ground." Beust, however, no doubt expressed the views of many when he remarked that fate was perhaps kind to Tegetthoff, because a man "with his reckless audacity . . . could not always have achieved victories such as that at Lissa."[80]

When Tegetthoff took command of the navy, it was assumed that he would lead it for the next generation; he was destined, however, to hold office for just over three years. His death marked the second time in seven years that fate had deprived the navy of a charismatic commander: in 1864, Ferdinand Max's departure for Mexico likewise left the fleet facing unstable times without a leader.[81] In the meantime, the war of 1866 and the *Ausgleich* of 1867 had resolved, for better or worse, the German, Italian, and Hungarian questions that had nagged Austria for decades, but in 1871 the leaders of the Dual Monarchy were on the verge of defining future priorities in the international arena, and Austria's interest in the sea was hanging in the balance. Tegetthoff, the man best equipped to battle politicians for a larger navy, was also the most respected advocate of the maritime cause in general. Proponents of a more aggressive Habsburg commercial and strategic posture overseas joined his comrades in the fleet in mourning an irreplaceable loss.

For the navy, Tegetthoff's brief time at the helm had a lasting impact. Many of his reforms in education and training survived long after his death, and his basic administrative scheme, considered the best alternative in the absence of an independent navy ministry, was to remain intact until the eve of the First World War. And in the long run, his fighting spirit, the spirit of Lissa, became a distinguishing characteristic of the navy, to a great extent immunizing it from the malaise that was to plague the Habsburg army and, indeed, the empire as a whole.

NOTES

1. For a chart comparing the strength of the Austrian and Italian fleets in 1866, see Sondhaus, *The Habsburg Empire and the Sea,* Appendix C (279–80).

2. Tegetthoff to Baroness Emma Lutteroth (wife of Prussian consul, Trieste), Fasana, n.d. [June 1866], in Maximilian Daublebsky von Sterneck zu Ehrenstein, *Admiral Max Freiherr von Sterneck: Erinnerungen aus den Jahren 1847 bis 1897,* 143.

3. The Austrians also suffered 138 wounded, while the Italians recorded 38 wounded and 19 men taken prisoner.

4. For an overview of the Lissa campaign, see Sondhaus, *The Habsburg Empire and the Sea,* 247–59. Josef Fleischer, *Geschichte der k.k. Kriegsmarine während des Krieges im Jahre 1866;* and Angelo Iachino, *La campagna navale di Lissa 1866,* are the most detailed accounts of the war in the Adriatic in 1866.

5. Green Clay (secretary of legation) to William H. Seward (U.S. secretary of state), Florence, 25 August 1866, in Howard R. Marraro, "Unpublished American Documents on the Naval Battle of Lissa," 354.

6. On the navy's initial shift away from Venice, see Sondhaus, *The Habsburg Empire and the Sea,* 150–67, 175–79. The naval academy moved from Trieste to Rijeka in 1855, then moved back to Trieste in 1858.

7. See Lawrence Sondhaus, *In the Service of the Emperor: Italians in the Austrian Armed Forces, 1814–1918,* 82–95; and idem, "Croatians in the Habsburg Navy, 1797–1918," 151–53.

8. Franz F. Bilzer, "Die Schiffe und Fahrzeuge der k.(u.)k. Kriegsmarine" will be used as the principal source of Austro-Hungarian warship data. There was no universally recognized method for computing warship tonnage until the Washington Naval Conference of 1922; in contemporary Austrian publications, tonnages listed for individual vessels at times varied from one year to the next. Thus, all displacement figures should be considered approximate. For the sake of simplicity, for ships of 1,000 tons or more the displacement will be rounded off to the nearest 100 tons; for those under 1,000 tons, the displacement will be rounded off to the nearest ten tons.

9. In 1865 the navy disbanded the small Danube flotilla it had inherited from the army in 1861. See Manfred Rauchensteiner, "Austro-Hungarian Warships on the Danube: From the Beginning of the Nineteenth Century to World War I," 157.

10. The Rijeka firm, originally known as the Fonderia Metalli, changed its name to the Stabilimento Tecnico Fiume in 1863. In the same year, the Stabilimento Tecnico Triestino sold its first shares of stock; the Rijeka firm was a joint-stock company since its founding. See Fulvio Babudieri, *Squeri e cantiere a Trieste e nella regione Giulia dal settecento agli inizi del novecento,* 21–22; Leopoldo Cupez, *Cenni sullo sviluppo dei Cantieri Riuniti dell'Adriatico, 1825–1952,* 3; Antonio Casali and Marina Cattaruzza, *Sotto i mari del mondo:*

La Whitehead, 1875-1990, 16, 21. Casali and Cattaruzza contend that Whitehead's firm also built the engines for the armored frigate *Kaiser Max* (8), but the contracts indicate that it, too, had machinery from the Stabilimento Tecnico Triestino. See STT contract, Trieste, 6 October 1861, in Vienna, Österreichisches Staatsarchiv, Kriegsarchiv, Marineakten (hereafter cited as KA, MA), T/c 5 (1862), no. 20 a-s, fols. 19–46.

11. On the navy's attempts to import French armor and Krupp guns, see Sondhaus, *The Habsburg Empire and the Sea*, 211, 213, 243, 249, and 252.

12. On the war of 1864, see Sondhaus, *The Habsburg Empire and the Sea*, 237–42.

13. A fourth navy officer, Captain Moriz Manfroni von Manfort, received the Order of Maria Theresa in 1866 for his service as commander of a gunboat flotilla on Lake Garda.

14. Ferdinand Max, determined to remove the navy from the administrative jurisdiction of the army, finally succeeded in creating the navy ministry in 1862. Shortly after his departure for Mexico in April 1864, the emperor and his council of ministers resolved to abolish the new department, although it lingered for more than a year before being disbanded in July 1865. At that time, the navy returned to the jurisdiction of the war ministry but was granted some autonomy with the creation of the *Marinesektion*. On the demise of the navy ministry and Tegetthoff's poor relations with Leopold and Fautz, see Sondhaus, *The Habsburg Empire and the Sea*, 244–46.

15. Francis Joseph to Archduchess Sophie, Schönbrunn, 17 October 1866, *Briefe Kaiser Franz Josephs I. an seine Mutter, 1838-1872*, 359.

16. Wüllerstorf entered the navy in 1833, at the age of seventeen. The highlight of his career came during the years 1857-59, when he commanded the frigate *Novara* on its celebrated circumnavigation of the globe. He held overall command of the fleet during the war of 1864, only to be upstaged by Tegetthoff. Forced to retire after the war, he used his political connections to secure the appointment as minister for trade in September 1865. The most recent biography of Wüllerstorf is Friedrich Wallisch's *Sein Schiff Hiess Novara: Bernhard von Wüllerstorf, Admiral und Minister.*

17. Wüllerstorf to Franck, Vienna, 30 July 1866, Vienna, Österreichisches Staatsarchiv, Haus- Hof- und Staatsarchiv, Administrative Registratur (hereafter cited as HHSA, AR), F44 - Marinewesen, Carton 3: Generalia 1860-70; Wüllerstorf to Mensdorff, Vienna, 25 August 1866, ibid.

18. Franck to Wüllerstorf, Vienna, 4 September 1866, HHSA, AR, F44 - Marinewesen, Carton 3: Generalia 1860-70.

19. Peter Handel-Mazzetti and Hans Hugo Sokol, *Wilhelm von Tegetthoff: Ein grosser Österreicher*, 289–303, describe Tegetthoff's travels and his personal reaction to the assignment.

20. Sterneck diary, December 1866 [excerpts], Sterneck, *Erinnerungen*, 143.

21. In the years 1860-65, the Italian government had ordered eleven armored warships from foreign shipbuilders and seven from domestic yards. All of the foreign orders were delivered before the war, but only one of the domestic ironclads was completed in time. Two armored floating batteries under construction in Italian shipyards were also not finished by 1866. See Mariano Gabriele, *La politica navale italiana dall'unita alla viglia di Lissa*, passim.

22. Ulrich Schöndorfer, "Der österreichische Kriegsschiffbau von 1848 bis 1914," 27. Budget figures from Adolf Beer, *Die Finanzen Oesterreichs*, 370. In 1866 Skoda took over management of the Waldstein firm of Pilsen, which he purchased in 1869. See Karl M. Brousek, *Die Grossindustrie Böhmens 1848-1918*, 63.

23. In Tegetthoff to Baroness Emma von Lutteroth, Vienna, 9 July 1867, the admiral notes that his mission has "a completely private character" (*Tegetthoffs Briefe an seine Freundin,* 94).

24. Arnold Blumberg, *The Diplomacy of the Mexican Empire, 1863–1867,* 287–88. The Austrian navy had maintained a steamship off Veracruz ever since Maximilian's arrival in Mexico in 1864. After the war of 1866, a second steamer was sent, and late that year, when it appeared that Maximilian would leave Mexico, "thousands of crates" of his personal property and Mexican archives were loaded aboard the two vessels (see ibid., 220).

25. For a more detailed account of this topic, see Lawrence Sondhaus, "Austria-Hungary's Italian Policy under Count Beust, 1866–1871."

26. After being tried by the Italian Senate, Persano was forced to retire in disgrace, stripped of his rank and pension. Iachino, *La campagna navale di Lissa,* 538–638, provides the most comprehensive account of the proceedings against the admiral.

27. See Brian R. Sullivan, "A Fleet in Being: The Rise and Fall of Italian Sea Power, 1861–1943," 110.

28. See Franco Bargoni, *Le prime navi di linea della marina italiana (1861–1880),* passim.

29. A French draft of March 1869 covered every contingency of various combinations of Austria-Hungary, France, and Italy engaging Prussia and Russia. In scrutinizing the terms, Beust questioned the absence of any role for the French navy against Russia in a general war. The naval issue raised by Beust in fact was not crucial for Habsburg interests because the settlement ending the Crimean War had prohibited Russia from maintaining a Black Sea fleet. Should Beust's war occur, it was assumed that the Mediterranean would remain peaceful with the Austrian navy seeing little action. ("Note répondant au contre-projet envoyé de Vienne le 18 Mars 1869," HHSA, Politisches Archiv [hereafter cited as PA], IX, Carton 177: Geheime Allianzverhandlungen, 3. Konvolut, fols. 1–12.)

30. Croatian nationalism traditionally was stronger in Sebenico than in any of the other ports of Dalmatia. In 1848 local Croatians led an unsuccessful campaign to unite the province with the kingdom of Croatia. See Grga Novak, "Narodni preporod u Dalmaciji," 78.

31. Beust to Pepoli (Italian chargé), Vienna, 3 February 1870, HHSA, AR, F 44 - Marinewesen, Carton 2: Generalia 1860-70.

32. After another five years of haggling, the Austro-Hungarian government finally agreed to pay a modest indemnity to an Italian merchant whose vessel and cargo were damaged in Sebenico harbor on the night of the riot. Count Gyula Andrássy to Count Carlo Robilant, Vienna, 13 July 1875, HHSA, AR, F 44 - Marinewesen, Carton 6: Generalia ab 1871. Correspondence over the merchant's claims fills an entire folder in this carton ("Conflikte 1869-75").

33. See Theodor Sosnosky, *Die Balkanpolitik Österreich-Ungarns seit 1866,* 1:73–90.

34. Pietro Chiari's *L'Albania* (Palermo: Tipografia de Giornale di Sicilia, 1869), forwarded to Vienna by Beust's ambassador, Baron Alois von Kübeck, as an enclosure to Kübeck to Beust, Florence, 20 November 1869, HHSA, PA, XI, Carton 75: Kgr. Italien, Berichte 1869 IX–XII, fols. 246–347.

35. Kübeck to Beust, Florence, 16 July 1870, HHSA, PA, XI, Carton 77: Kgr. Italien, Berichte 1870 VII–VIII, fols. 77–80; see also S. William Halperin, *Italy and the Vatican at War: A Study of Their Relations from the Outbreak of the Franco-Prussian War to the Death of*

Pius IX, 2. On 18 July 1870, Francis Joseph and the Austro-Hungarian council of ministers had resolved that the empire would remain neutral in the war but would improve strategic fortifications and take measures preparatory to mobilization. Beust considered neutrality to be a temporary formality, ignoring domestic German Austrian and Hungarian opposition to an alliance with France against Prussia.

36. Visconti Venosta, counterproject, [Florence], 6 August 1870, HHSA, PA, IX, Carton 177: Geheime Allianzverhandlungen, 3. Konvolut.

37. For a more detailed argument in support of this thesis, see Sondhaus, Austria-Hungary's Italian Policy under Count Beust," 49–52.

38. Kübeck to Beust, Florence, 19 August 1870, HHSA, AR, F44 - Marinewesen, Carton 2: Generalia 1860–70; and Kübeck to Beust, Florence, 5 September 1870, ibid., report the arrival and departure of the *Habsburg.* In the interim, Ambassador Alois von Kübeck kept Beust informed of the movements of each of the four warships in dispatches containing no other information. While it was common for a consular official to inform an ambassador when warships of their country visited a port, it was very unusual for an ambassador to pass on such information to a foreign minister unless the movements had considerable political significance.

39. Franco Micali Baratelli, *La marina militare italiana nella vita nazionale (1860– 1914),* 164–66, covers the Italian navy's operations during the occupation of the Papal State. Baratelli confirms Italy's concern over the Austrian naval demonstration at Naples (164). The ensuing Italian naval mobilization came in spite of the fact that the French navy was no longer a potentially hostile factor. After the defeat of the French field armies, tens of thousands of sailors were assigned to man fortifications on land against the advancing Prussians. See Theodore Ropp, *The Development of a Modern Navy: French Naval Policy, 1871–1904,* 24–25.

40. *Rangsliste der k.k. Kriegsmarine* (1874), 3.

41. On Tegetthoff's mission to Mexico see Blumberg, *Diplomacy of the Mexican Empire,* 288–90.

42. Fautz to Min. des Äussern, Vienna, 29 December 1864, HHSA, AR, F 44 - Marinewesen, Carton 3: Generalia 1860–70, gives notice of the approval of the first request for naval information by the Mexican consul in Trieste.

43. Kuhn had replaced Franz von John as war minister in January 1868. John was fired after falling out with the emperor's influential cousin, Archduke Albrecht. See Gunther E. Rothenberg, *The Army of Francis Joseph,* 79.

44. Handel-Mazzetti and Sokol, *Tegetthoff,* 317–18. The title *Marinekommandant* represented a return to the naval commander's official designation from the years before 1824. From 1824 until 1864, the title had been *Marine-Ober-Kommandant.* Before accepting the new appointment, a frustrated Tegetthoff had considered an offer from the khedive of Egypt to take command of the Egyptian navy. In Tegetthoff to Lutteroth, Pittsburgh, 8 April 1867, *Tegetthoffs Briefe,* 87, the admiral acknowledges the temptation "to try my luck in the shadow of the pyramids."

45. See Höbelt, "Die Marine," 733.

46. For the text of Albrecht's 1868 statement on the coastal fortification issue, see *Österreich-Ungarns letzter Krieg,* Ergänzungsheft 10: *Die Reichsbefestigung Österreich-Ungarns zur Zeit Conrads von Hötzendorf* (Vienna: Verlag der "Militärwissenschaftlichen Mitteilungen," 1937), 43. For Beck's views of Tegetthoff, see Edmund von Glaise-Horstenau, *Franz Josephs Weggefährte: Das Leben des Generalstabschefs Grafen Beck,* 164–65n.

47. Walter Wagner, "Die obersten Behörden der k.u.k. Kriegsmarine 1856-1918," 138-39. On the rivalry between Tegetthoff and Pöck, see Sondhaus, *The Habsburg Empire and the Sea,* 246, 248.

48. See Höbelt, "Die Marine," 734-37.

49. Ibid., 735-36. The *Heiratskaution,* which had to be handled by a bank, has no parallel among modern financial accounts or transactions. The principle behind it involved elements akin to posting bond and taking out a life insurance policy; the cash sums, once deposited, were restricted under terms not unlike those regulating current individual retirement accounts in the United States. Erwin A. Schmidl, *Jews in the Habsburg Armed Forces, 1788-1918,* 134, gives the best concise explanation of the *Heiratskaution.* See also Lawrence Sondhaus, "The Austro-Hungarian Naval Officer Corps, 1867-1918," 67-68.

50. Wagner, "Die obersten Behörden," 61-71.

51. E.g. Tegetthoff to his father, off Sulina, 9 June 1856, in *Aus Wilhelm von Tegetthoff's Nachlass,* 132, arguing that eight years are sufficient only if good use is made of the time.

52. Peter Salcher, *Geschichte der k.u.k. Marine-Akademie,* 32, 69. On Tegetthoff's literary tastes, see *Tegetthoff's Nachlass,* 82-83, 88. The naval academy at Trieste closed after the 1858-59 school year, when the higher classes were mustered out for service in the war of 1859. From 1860 to 1866, most instruction took place aboard the frigate *Venus,* docked in Trieste harbor, in emulation of the British navy's school ship *Britannia.* In contrast, the five-year French naval curriculum followed that of the French *lycée,* with specialized naval subjects reserved for late in the program. See Ropp, *The Development of a Modern Navy,* 43.

53. Dr. Tegetthoff's tenure at the academy was very brief; he died in July 1871 "after a long, hard illness" (*Jahrbuch der k.k. Kriegsmarine* [1872], 76). Handel-Mazzetti and Sokol, *Tegetthoff,* 356, confuse Albrecht with Bernhard von Tegetthoff, another younger brother of the admiral.

54. The last fleet plan, approved by Francis Joseph in July 1858, included Ferdinand Max's revisions of an earlier Navy Law of 1850. See Sondhaus, *The Habsburg Empire and the Sea,* 188.

55. Leo Reiter, "Die Entwicklung der k.u.k. Flotte und die Delegationen des Reichsrates," 16-18. Tegetthoff's unarmored fleet was to include eight large (*hochbord*) and twenty-six small (*niederbord*) vessels.

56. See Sondhaus, "Die österreichische Kriegsmarine und der amerikanische Sezessionskrieg 1861-1865," 81-84; and idem, *The Habsburg Empire and the Sea,* 224-25.

57. Tegetthoff was a bit ahead of his time in placing so much faith in converted merchantmen as unarmored auxiliary warships. Similar philosophies took hold in Britain, Russia, and France during the 1880s. See Ropp, *The Development of a Modern Navy,* 88-91, 109-10.

58. On the Lloyd's role in Austria's earlier wars, see Sondhaus, *The Habsburg Empire and the Sea,* 161, 166, 190-91, 194.

59. Figures from *Fünfundsiebzig Jahre österreichischer Lloyd,* 34, 72.

60. The navy asked for 8.5 million for 1868. The most controversial item in the budget, and the only one not funded, was an iron and metal foundry for the Pola Arsenal. See *Stenographische Protokolle der Delegation des Reichsrathes,* I. Session, 1st part (3 March 1868), 137-52, especially 145-49 (cited hereafter as *StPD* with session number, date, and pages). In the protocols, the deliberations for the 1868 budget (February-March 1868) and for the 1869 budget (November-December 1868) are both classified as the "first session."

61. Reiter, "Entwicklung," 18-19.

62. On Tegetthoff's views of the leading politicians of his time, see Handel-Mazzetti and Sokol, *Tegetthoff,* 336–39, 349. *Tegetthoffs Briefe,* 116, includes an excerpt of a letter to an unspecified friend, written in the autumn of 1870, in which the admiral refers to "the dream of our youth, a united Germany."

63. *StPD,* I/2 (1 December 1868), 297.

64. Reiter, "Entwicklung," 20. Tegetthoff had asked for just under 9.5 million; almost all of the items deleted were improvements to the base and arsenal at Pola. The budget numbers used here and below are drawn from the *Stenographische Protokolle (StPD),* rounded off to the nearest 100,000. Tables in Walter Wagner, "Die k.(u.)k. Armee: Gliederung und Aufgabenstellung," 590–91, give the actual amounts spent in each year.

65. Francis Joseph's tour of the Trieste shipyards on 19 March is described in the *Neue Freie Presse,* 20 March 1869. See also Karl Harbauer, *Der Kaiser und die Kriegsmarine,* 103–10.

66. The *Radetzky,* delivered in 1854 from the British shipyard of Money, Wigram & Sons, was the navy's first propeller frigate; it was lost when a fire of undetermined origin ignited its powder magazine. From a crew of almost four hundred men, there were only two dozen survivors. In terms of lives lost, the accident by far was the greatest the Habsburg navy ever suffered, in war or peacetime.

67. *StPD,* II (17 August 1869), 216. On Rechberg's opposition to Ferdinand Max's naval expansion during the early 1860s, see Sondhaus, *The Habsburg Navy and the Sea,* 213–18 passim. Wüllerstorf resigned from the cabinet in April 1867 rather than become the trade minister of just the Austrian half of the empire. Before the *Ausgleich,* he had argued in vain for a common Austro-Hungarian trade ministry.

68. Reiter, "Entwicklung," 25–28; Tegetthoff quoted in *StPD,* II (17 August 1869), 222. The navy's original proposal for 1870 called for more than 11.5 million gulden.

69. The two ships sailed via the Cape of Good Hope to the Far East, where they visited Bangkok, various Chinese ports, and Yokohama. The *Erzherzog Friedrich,* heavily damaged in a typhoon off Japan, returned home by the westward route, arriving in January 1871. After leaving Japan, the *Donau* continued eastward across the Pacific and circled the globe en route to Pola, which it reached in March 1871. On the way home, Petz concluded commercial treaties with Guatemala, Peru, Chile, Argentina, and Uruguay. See Heinrich Bayer von Bayersburg, *Die k.u.k. Kriegsmarine auf weiter Fahrt,* 47–49; Höbelt, "Die Marine," 756. The London office of the Anglo-Austrian Bank handled most of the foreign bills for the expedition; see Österreichisches Staatsarchiv, Finanzarchiv (hereafter cited as FA), RFM/1869, fascicle 18.21.

70. Handel-Mazzetti and Sokol, *Tegetthoff,* 325–34; and Friedrich Ferdinand von Beust, *Memoirs of Friedrich Ferdinand Count von Beust,* 2:126–58, give complete accounts of the emperor's Near Eastern tour.

71. Handel-Mazzetti and Sokol, *Tegetthoff,* 291; *Tegetthoff's Nachlass,* 84; Marinesektion to Kriegsministerium [memo], Vienna, 14 July 1870, KA, Kriegsministerium, Präsidialreihe (hereafter cited as KA, KM, Präs.) 1870/18-24/2; Tegetthoff to Kriegsministerium, Vienna, 21 October 1870, ibid., Präs. 1870/18-24/3.

72. Handel-Mazzetti and Sokol, *Tegetthoff,* 337–38. On the admiral's views of the *Ausgleich,* see Tegetthoff to Lutteroth, Vienna, 3 June 1870, *Tegetthoffs Briefe,* 115.

73. *Jahrbuch der k.k. Kriegsmarine* (1871), 74–75, 77; Schöndorfer, "Kriegsschiffbau," 28. For details on the design and construction of these postwar ironclads, see Chapter Two, part 2 below. On problems with the *Kaiser* and the budget for 1870, see Rear Admiral Julius von Wissiak to Reichsfinanzministerium, Vienna, 7 December 1869, FA, 9,308-RFM/

1869. On the formation of the Società Operaia Triestina, see Giuseppe Piemontese, *Il movimento operaio a Trieste: Dalle origini alla fine della prima guerra mondiale,* 13, 236.

74. Kübeck to Beust, Florence, 21 May 1870, HHSA, PA, XI, Carton 76: Kgr. Italien, Berichte 1870 I–VI, fols. 102–256, gives an extensive account of the heated debate over the reduction of the Italian military budget. Ironically, the relative inactivity of the French navy during 1870 did not hurt its cause after the fall of the empire. Following the collapse of the imperial army at Sedan, the performance of French navy officers and seamen in manning defensive positions on land, particularly around Paris, earned the admiration of the French public. See Ropp, *The Development of a Modern Navy,* 24–25.

75. In the first years after the opening of the Suez Canal, only the British and French ranked ahead of the Austrian merchant marine in their use of the waterway. See figures in Giuseppe Lo Giudice, *Trieste, L'Austria ed il Canale di Suez,* 180.

76. *StPD,* III (27 January 1871), 299–325. For Sturm's remarks, see 303–4.

77. Schöndorfer, "Kriegsschiffbau," 31.

78. Handel-Mazzetti and Sokol, *Tegetthoff,* 349–54.

79. Ibid., 356–57. In October 1872, Tegetthoff's body was moved to the Sankt-Leonhard-Friedhof in Graz at the request of his family. See *Tegetthoffs Briefe,* 118.

80. *Neue Freie Presse,* 8 April 1871, 2; Beust quoted in *Memoirs,* 2:150. Early in 1868, coinciding with his appointment as *Marinekommandant,* Tegetthoff had been appointed a life member of the Austrian House of Lords. While his naval duties limited his participation, his obituary noted that "in the *Herrenhaus* he voted loyally with the Left."

81. On the situation facing the navy after the departure of Ferdinand Max, see Sondhaus, *The Habsburg Empire and the Sea,* 244–46.

FROM TEGETTHOFF TO THE TRIPLE ALLIANCE

Following the death of Tegetthoff, his old adversary, Baron Friedrich von Pöck, was promoted to vice admiral and *Marinekommandant.*[1] Unpopular in his own time, Pöck has been criticized by Austrian naval historians for failing to build upon the achievements of his predecessor.[2] He had the great misfortune, though, of presiding over the navy in an era when even the principal maritime powers of Europe were not actively engaged in expanding their fleets.[3] The dozen years of Pöck's tenure were an active time for naval operations, but in the face of budget reductions the new commander could do no better than maintain the strength of the fleet at the level of the early 1870s. Nevertheless, as long as Austro-Italian relations remained uncertain, there was still some hope for future naval expansion.

"THE STRENGTH, SPIRIT, AND INSIGHT ARE LACKING": THE NAVY UNDER PÖCK (1871–78)

The political consequences of Tegetthoff's departure became evident only gradually, but to many of the officers and seamen serving under Pöck, the change in personalities at the top brought a dramatic decline in morale. Shortly after the new commander took over, Tegetthoff's friend and adjutant Max von Sterneck noted that "although the desire and the will are present to carry on the leadership of the navy in the manner of [Tegetthoff], the strength, spirit, and insight are lacking."[4]

Pöck, forty-five in the spring of 1871, was two years older than the late *Marinekommandant.* Like Tegetthoff, he was the son of a Habsburg army officer, and both men had received their education in the Italian language at the old naval academy in Venice, where Pöck graduated in

1843, two years before his rival. During the 1850s, the two young officers gravitated toward separate cliques, Tegetthoff to the circle of Archduke Ferdinand Max, Pöck toward Baron von Wüllerstorf. Pöck was second in command to Wüllerstorf on the frigate *Novara*'s celebrated circumnavigation of the globe, a duty that kept him away from the Adriatic during the war of 1859. He commanded the ship of the line *Kaiser* during the war of 1864 against Denmark, but the vessel was attached to Wüllerstorf's main fleet, which did not reach the North Sea until Tegetthoff's advance squadron had already engaged the Danes at the Battle of Helgoland.[5]

Following Wüllerstorf's retirement, Pöck became the protégé of Archduke Leopold, the new *Marine Truppen- und Flotteninspektor*, and served as his adjutant until 1868. Leopold promoted Pöck to rear admiral and restored his seniority over Tegetthoff, which he had lost with the latter's extraordinary promotion in 1864. But at the onset of the war of 1866, Tegetthoff received command of the battle fleet in the Adriatic and Pöck had to settle for the position of naval liaison officer to Archduke Albrecht at army headquarters in Venetia. According to one account, the news from Lissa brought an angry reaction from Pöck, who could not conceal his bitterness over his rival's victory.[6] After Tegetthoff took over as *Marinekommandant* and chief of the *Marinesektion*, Pöck commanded the active squadron until January 1870, when he became second in command of the navy. Fifteen months later, his position as heir apparent placed him among those last to see Tegetthoff alive.[7]

After taking over the navy, Pöck solidified his own position of authority by giving Tegetthoff's protégés assignments far removed from both Vienna and the Adriatic. The shake-up and ensuing scramble for vacant posts sickened Sterneck, who observed that the common goal of strengthening the fleet had been "pushed aside" in favor of "the interests of individuals."[8] Sterneck himself ended up, of all places, in the Arctic, as captain of an expedition to Novaya Zemlya in the Barents Sea, paving the way for a more extensive Austrian polar expedition in 1872.[9] Other casualties included Captain Hermann von Spaun, Sterneck's aide at Lissa in 1866, appointed naval attaché at the Austro-Hungarian embassy in London; and Lieutenant Rudolf Berghofer, whom Pöck declined to promote throughout his dozen years at the helm.[10] Under the new commander, a fellow former adjutant to Archduke Leopold, Captain Maximilian von Pitner, took over as head of the central chancellery of the *Marinesektion,* while the older Rear Admiral Millosicz, head of the demonstration at Naples in August 1870, served as a quiet second in command.[11]

These and other changes of personnel alienated a substantial faction within the officer corps and contributed to a general decline of morale. To make matters worse, Pöck fared no better in Vienna than on the Adriatic. In his capacity as chief of the *Marinesektion,* the new commander's temperament left him no better suited than Tegetthoff to cope with the frustrating debates in the council of ministers and the annual Delegations. But where his predecessor had been able to carry the day on the strength of his prestige as a victorious admiral, Pöck had not even been under fire since serving as an ensign on the blockade of revolutionary Venice in 1849.[12] Circumstances had kept him away from the action in 1859 and 1864, and worst of all, he had played no role in the Battle of Lissa.

Pöck's inability to command the respect of ministers and politicians was compounded by his relatively lukewarm relationship with Francis Joseph. By securing the remains of Ferdinand Max after his execution in Mexico, Tegetthoff had won the undying gratitude of the emperor and could at least count on his benevolent neutrality in any debate between the navy and politicians. But Francis Joseph owed no similar debt to Pöck, and the new commander never received the same sort of support from the throne that Tegetthoff had enjoyed. As for other members of the imperial family, there is no evidence that Pöck's service at army headquarters in Venetia in 1866 left him any closer to the powerful Archduke Albrecht. Nevertheless, in 1876, Albrecht's sixteen-year-old nephew, Charles Stephen, began to audit classes at the naval academy in Rijeka. He was commissioned as an ensign in 1879, raising hopes in naval circles of a revived interest in the fleet within the Habsburg family.[13] But it remained to be seen whether Charles Stephen would ever become as important to the navy as his great predecessor, Ferdinand Max, had been.

Notwithstanding Pöck's political weaknesses, at least initially the navy's budget appropriations did not suffer. When the Delegations met in Vienna in the summer of 1871, they granted the navy 11.1 million gulden for the following year, a slight increase from the last allocation given to Tegetthoff.[14] A more aggressive Pöck sought a higher budget for 1873, including over a million gulden to start construction on two new ironclads, tentatively named *Tegetthoff* and *Erzherzog Karl,* the latter in memory of Austria's hero of the Napoleonic wars.[15] The two new armored ships would give the navy a total of thirteen either completed or under construction, just two short of the goal of Tegetthoff's fleet plan, which the late commander had hoped to reach by 1878. But the German liberal majority in the Austrian Delegation opposed higher naval expenditure in the face of a decreased Italian threat, while a majority of Hungarians viewed all maritime issues as "Austrian" concerns and were antinavy as a matter of principle. The Austrians approved one of the new ironclads, but the Hungarian Delegation vetoed both warship proposals. The navy emerged with a reduced budget of 10.1 million gulden for 1873.[16]

Pöck persevered, however, and when the Delegations met in Vienna in early May 1873 he submitted a budget for 1874 including the projected new ironclads *Tegetthoff* and *Erzherzog Karl.* After extensive debate the Austrian Delegation once again approved funding for one of the two ships, swayed by the arguments of war minister Kuhn, Count Rechberg, and Johann von Scrinzi-Montecroce of Trieste, who emerged as the leading supporter of the fleet from among the representatives of the *Herrenhaus.* The Hungarians again decided the issue, however, by refusing to fund even one new ironclad. It was of some consolation to Pöck that his overall appropriation rose to 10.8 million gulden.[17]

Pöck's next battle with the Delegations found him hamstrung by deteriorating economic and political conditions. A mere four days after the approval of the navy budget for 1874, the Vienna stock market crash of May 1873 signaled the onset of a long depression. To make matters worse, subsequent elections for the Austrian parliament returned a solid majority (200 of 353 seats) for the antinavy German liberals. For the six-year duration of their mandate, the liberals were to provide thirty-one of the lower house's forty representatives to the Austrian Delegation, while the liberal lords of the Austrian *Herrenhaus* would control fourteen of their house's quota of twenty seats. The antinavy majority counted among its members some of the most influential liberals: Karl Giskra, an opponent of the fleet since the early 1860s; Matthias von Wickenburg, former trade and navy minister and earlier proponent of naval expansion; and Eduard Herbst, the former justice minister, a harsh critic of cost overruns in warship contracts.[18] Given the questionable financial health of the Dual Monarchy and the prevailing calm in the international arena, it would be more difficult than ever to make a successful case for more warships and a larger budget.

The exclusion of funding for new warships in the budget for 1874 had sealed the fate of Tegetthoff's fleet plan, making the goal of four more ironclads by 1878 impossible to achieve, but a persistent Pöck included the two ships in his estimates for 1875. On this third attempt, the *Tegetthoff* won both Austrian and Hungarian approval; construction on the warship finally started in 1876. The *Erzherzog Karl* did not fare as well, meeting with rejection on the floor of the Delegations in the deliberations for 1875. Pöck could hardly celebrate his hard-fought victory to fund the *Tegetthoff* because by 1875 the condition of the ironclad *Drache*, one of the navy's original pair (launched in 1862), had deteriorated to such a degree that it had to be taken out of service, making the new warship not an addition to the armored fleet but merely a replacement for another vessel. Indeed, as early as May 1874 Pöck had pointed out to the Austrian Delegation that the delays in warship construction would mean that the vessels, when finally built, would only maintain rather than increase the strength of the fleet. To emphasize this fact, the *Marinekommandant*, attempting to win approval for a sister ship for the *Tegetthoff*, referred to the *Erzherzog Karl* project as the *Ersatz Drache* in his estimates for 1876, but to no avail. He could take no solace in the size of the overall naval appropriation, either, as it fell to ten million gulden for 1875 and remained at that level for 1876.[19]

Even though Tegetthoff's timetable had to be abandoned, Pöck clung stubbornly to his predecessor's fleet plan, hoping against all odds to reach the target of fifteen armored warships. When the Delegations met in Budapest in May 1876 to approve the budget for 1877, the Austrian side deliberated over Pöck's estimates for less than an hour, the shortest navy debate thus far. His new *Drache* again failed to gain funding, and he emerged with a reduced budget of 9.4 million gulden only after the Austrian minister-president, Prince Adolf Auersperg, succeeded in brokering a compromise with the Hungarians, whose finance minister, Kálmán Széll, wanted to cut naval spending even more.[20] Ironically, the foes of the fleet did not include the most prominent Hungarian in the Dual Monarchy. Gyula Andrássy, Beust's successor as foreign minister, never intervened to oppose Pöck's efforts. Indeed, in July 1876, when Turkey offered to sell Austria-Hungary three ironclads that the sultan had ordered in Britain but could not pay for,

Andrássy promptly sent the proposition along to Pöck. Unfortunately, Pöck's finances were in no better shape than the sultan's. Even though the ironclads would have given him a total of fourteen, one short of Tegetthoff's goal, he had to inform Andrássy that the navy was "in no position" to buy them.[21]

The reduced budget and lack of progress in the area of matériel created more difficulties for the *Marinekommandant* within the service, exacerbating the problem of morale. But Pöck could claim modest successes on land in the form of better facilities in Vienna: in 1874, the *Marinesektion* moved from the Schenkenstrasse to more spacious quarters in the Doblhoffgasse, near the site where construction had just begun on the new Austrian parliament building. Meanwhile, Pola finally got an officers' club (*Marinekasino*) in 1872, thanks to the personal patronage of Francis Joseph, and a rail link to Trieste in 1876. These developments made life at Pola seem like less of an exile from civilization, but navy officers continued to grouse about the Istrian port's sleepy social life, a perennial complaint ever since the main fleet base moved away from Venice. Because the trip to Trieste, for the passenger, remained faster by steamship than by train, the railway line benefited the navy mostly by reducing the cost of transporting domestic coal to Pola.[22]

In the depressed atmosphere of the early 1870s, overseas missions provided the navy with a valuable distraction from the monotony of duty in the Adriatic and Mediterranean. Because Francis Joseph, in 1869, had approved a proposal by Tegetthoff to send each graduating class of sea cadets on an extended overseas voyage, the cruises occurred almost on an annual basis and were usually staffed by the youngest officers in the service. The first voyage of the Pöck era was entrusted to the veteran frigate *Novara*, which visited the West Indies and North America during 1871–72, waters it had not touched since transporting the body of Ferdinand Max back from Mexico in 1868. In the same years, the corvette *Fasana* traveled to Siam, China, and Japan, delivering ratified copies of the trade treaties negotiated during the Petz mission of 1868–71.[23]

In 1872–73, the corvette *Helgoland* cruised to Brazil, the West Indies, and North America, then, using the Suez Canal, circumnavigated Africa in 1873–75. The corvette *Dandolo* subsequently shouldered the burden, visiting the West Indies in 1874-75, cruising the North and South Atlantic during 1875-76, then calling at a number of North and South American ports in 1877-78. But the most extensive and eventful overseas mission of the Pöck era was the circumnavigation of the globe by the corvette *Erzherzog Friedrich* in 1874-76, only the third such voyage ever undertaken by a Habsburg ship. Its itinerary included visits to Siam, China, and Japan, and a reconnoitering of the island of Borneo to determine the feasibility of claiming territory there for an Austrian colony. This project was abandoned in the spring of 1875, when hostile local residents killed two sailors during a landing attempt on the northern coast of the island. After leaving the Orient, the ship visited San Francisco and a number of South American ports before returning home.

In ambition and adventure, the mission of the *Erzherzog Friedrich* was rivaled only by the earlier Arctic voyage of the wooden sloop *Admiral Tegetthoff*. Led by Lieutenant Carl Weyprecht and army *Jäger* Lieutenant Julius Payer, the expedition included two officers and a dozen NCOs from the navy. The Austrians were in the Arctic from August 1872 until August 1874 and drifted as far north as 82.5°N after their ship was trapped in pack ice. Ultimately Weyprecht and Payer abandoned the *Admiral Tegetthoff* and led their men by sled southward to open sea, where a Russian fishing boat rescued them. Although they failed to get within 500 miles of the North Pole, Austria's Arctic explorers discovered the northernmost extension of the Eurasian land mass—the archipelago that still bears the name Franz Josef Land— and brought home a wealth of scientific data.[24]

While the navy's smaller wooden-hulled propeller ships were showing the Austrian flag on a worldwide basis, the ironclad fleet remained in reserve at Pola, in danger of becoming obsolete. Complicating Pöck's other problems, the pace of technological change led to the development of larger warships, bigger guns, thicker armor, and stronger engines, all of which threatened to turn the balance against any naval power, large or small, lacking the resolve to keep pace. While the innovations of the late 1860s and early 1870s were not as dramatic as those of a decade earlier, when the ironclad first replaced the wooden battleship, the ever-increasing cost of naval vessels plagued Pöck just as it had his more talented predecessors.

CHAPTER 2

TACTICS, TECHNOLOGY, AND
SHIPBUILDING IN THE PÖCK ERA

At the time of Tegetthoff's death, the Habsburg navy had seven iron-clads available for service; all were wooden-hulled armored frigates, built during the years 1860–65. Even though most of the Italian warships at the Battle of Lissa were iron-hulled ironclads, in basic technology of design the first Austrian armored battle fleet had not been inferior to its Italian rival in 1866. Except for the Italian ram *Affondatore*, which carried its guns in two rotating turrets mounted on deck, all of the ironclads involved at Lissa were armored versions of the standard pre-ironclad designs, with guns mounted in a broadside arrangement below deck. Reflecting the latest tactical breakthroughs of the American Civil War, the newest of the armored frigates—including the *Erzherzog Ferdinand Max* and *Habsburg*, both completed in 1865—had more exaggerated ram bows designed to pierce enemy armor in a close action.

The success of Tegetthoff's tactics at Lissa reinforced the view that ramming rather than gunfire henceforth would carry the day in naval battles. While the Italian fleet had steamed out to meet him in a line-ahead formation, just as wooden sailing ships of the line would have assembled in Lord Nelson's time or earlier, Tegetthoff had attacked them line abreast, organizing his ships in three V-shaped waves that steamed straight into the Italian broadsides, breaking the enemy line and forcing a general melee. A French account of the campaign concluded that "the ram is today the principal arm of combat by sea," and Admiral Jurien de la Gravière went so far as to claim that in the future it would be suicidal for any captain to turn his broadside to the enemy. "We must win victories by the ram," he argued; gunfire "will not be worth the danger of a cloud of smoke . . . at the moment when the ship's safety depends upon the precision of her maneuvers."[25] Tegetthoff's line abreast became the preferred battle formation as naval tacticians abandoned the line ahead. The close action at Lissa, the ramming and attempted ramming by vessels on both sides, sent naval architects scrambling to design more flexible warships that could fire forward and aft as well as to the side.

Only two of the nineteen ironclads involved in the Lissa campaign were sunk and only one of these was lost as a result of enemy fire, attesting to the fact that, at least in 1866, armor technology was still ahead of gun design. But the introduction of bigger and more powerful guns caused the balance to swing quickly in the other direction, necessitating, in turn, even thicker armor plate to protect guns and engines from a more lethal enemy fire. The turret ship answered the problem of flexibility, but turrets were widely held to be too vulnerable to enemy fire. Critics of the design pointed to the action at Lissa, where a shot from the wooden ship of the line *Kaiser* had disabled a turret on the *Affondatore*, reducing its firing capability by half.

Nevertheless, there were proponents of turret ships in every country. They completely dominated the United States navy, whose famous *Monitor* had been the first such vessel constructed. American shipyards built a number of twin-turreted "monitors" during and after the Civil War, and even a few triple-turreted models, but it was not money well spent. While experimental cruises by American turret ships in the late 1860s demonstrated that they could function as ocean-going vessels, their low freeboard left their decks awash much of the time, and they were in danger of sinking in heavy seas. The *Monitor* itself had perished in this manner off Cape Hatteras not long after the Battle of Hampton Roads in 1862, and the *Affondatore*, returning to port after the Battle of Lissa, almost went under in a storm. But the most tragic loss of a turret ship came in September 1870, when the British *Captain*, a fully rigged twin-turreted vessel of nearly 7,000 tons, capsized in a storm off Cape Finisterre. Commissioned only five months earlier, the *Captain* sank with almost five hundred men aboard.[26] The question of seaworthiness and of vulnerability to the enemy spelled the end of the low freeboard turret ship as a design of seagoing ironclad. Austria-Hungary's only monitors were built specifically for service on the Danube. Launched in Budapest in 1871, the 310-ton *Maros* and *Leitha* were the most tangible result of Tegetthoff's postwar tour of the United States; while the admiral saw little use for monitors on the high seas, he admired the manner in which the Union had used the shallow-draft ironclads on the rivers of the American South in its successful naval war against the Confederacy. The monitors were the first significant Habsburg warships deployed on the Danube since the time of Maria Theresa.[27]

To answer the complaints against the broadside design, avoid the problems of turret ships, and accommodate the needs of heavier guns and thicker armor, the Habsburg navy built its postwar seagoing ironclads as casemate ships. The basic design of the hull was similar to the French *Gloire,* the British *Warrior,* and the Austrian and Italian armored frigates that saw action at Lissa, but instead of having two or three dozen guns mounted in side batteries for its entire length, the casemate ship had no more than a dozen heavier guns, mounted below deck in a heavily armored central battery or casemate. Owing to the arrangement of guns, some navies—most notably the British—called them "central battery ships." The lines of the hull were modified so that the guns nearest the bow could pivot, firing forward as well as to the side. Guns mounted at the rear of the casemate often were given a similar ability to fire to stern.

To compensate for their heavy plating amidships, most casemate ships had little or no armor at the bow and stern. This made the design controversial with more conservative navy men, but its advocates could point to a number of positive features: it had a high freeboard and was as seaworthy as any armored frigate; the central casemate protected the engines as well as all of the heavy guns; and the lack of armor fore and aft saved weight and made the ships faster. Aside from the embrasures in their hulls—recessed to allow the end guns to fire forward or to the rear—casemate ships had the same general appearance as standard broadside armored frigates. Like most ironclad warships built before the late 1880s, their full set of masts and yards also gave them the ability to sail.

The casemate ship marked an important step away from the broadside ironclads of the earlier 1860s; the design did not become altogether obsolete until turrets again became common in the 1880s and 1890s. Britain built eighteen casemate ships in all, more than any other naval power. The second of these, the *Hercules,* completed in November 1868, introduced the layout of main armament adopted later by Austrian designers and common to most casemate ships. The warship mounted eight 10-inch guns in its casemate and could fire two forward, two to stern, or four to either side.[28]

The first casemate ship in the Habsburg navy was the *Lissa,* begun in February 1867 from plans by chief naval engineer Josef von Romako, designer of all Austrian ironclads built during the 1860s and 1870s. It had a wooden frame and a combination wooden and iron hull, the latter material used for the unarmored portions of the ship above the waterline. Because Austria's own ironworks were unable to produce the quality of armor needed for a casemate ship, the plates were imported from the John Brown and Charles Cammell firms of Sheffield, England. This made the armor the most expensive item of all, even more so since Romako, reflecting the conservatism of Austrian designers, provided his casemate ships with thicker plating than British engineers gave theirs. Notwithstanding the navy's earlier problems in doing business with the Krupp works of Prussia, the *Lissa* was equipped with ten 9.4-inch Krupp guns, arranged like those of the British *Hercules*, only with an additional gun on each side of the casemate. Delays in the importation and installation of its armor postponed the commissioning of the *Lissa* until the summer of 1871.[29]

Although the *Lissa* was under construction throughout Tegetthoff's time as *Marinekommandant*, he had no direct influence on its design and missed seeing it enter service by a few months. The same was true of the conversion of the wooden ship of the line *Kaiser* to a casemate ship, a project inherited by Tegetthoff in 1868 but not completed until February 1874. The rebuilt *Kaiser* was a vessel of similar construction to the *Lissa*, only slightly smaller (5,800 tons, to *Lissa*'s 6,100) and with ten 9-inch British Armstrong guns instead of Krupps.[30] Tegetthoff's preferences were, however, incorporated into the two casemate ships laid down during his tenure, the *Custoza* and *Erzherzog Albrecht*. In contrast to the iron-plated wooden construction of all previous Austrian ironclads, these had iron frames and iron hulls.[31] They also had double-decked casemates, with six guns mounted above and two below.[32] The forward positioning of the lower two guns enabled the vessels to fire four toward the bow, four in a broadside, or two to stern. The overall design and, in particular, the layout of guns fit the aggressive forward ramming tactics that Tegetthoff had used at the Battle of Lissa. The *Custoza* displaced 7,100 tons, while the *Erzherzog Albrecht*—out of concern for the budget—was built somewhat smaller, at 5,900 tons. The *Custoza* was armed with 10.25-inch guns, the *Erzherzog Albrecht* with 9.4-inch guns, all ordered from Krupp. Owing to construction delays, again caused in part by the importation and installation of British armor, the ships were not ready for service until 1875.[33]

After failing to secure funding for new ironclad construction in either of his first two budgets, Pöck rather cleverly asked for money to "convert" some of the armored frigates of the 1860s into warships of the new design. Amid the furor over new construction, the "rebuilding" projects slipped through the budget process virtually unnoticed, with only the wily Eduard Herbst questioning the expenditure. The navy's allocation for 1874 included funds to begin the process, and starting at the end of 1873 the three oldest armored frigates yet to be refurbished—the *Kaiser Max, Prinz Eugen,* and *Juan d'Austria,* all launched in 1862—underwent a radical transformation into casemate ships. Called "rebuilding" for political purposes, the process in fact amounted to new construction. The old vessels were completely dismantled, their engines and armor plate removed, their wooden hulls broken up. The new iron hulls were then plated with the salvaged armor, supplemented by new imported British plates in the case of the *Prinz Eugen.* When completed, the three casemate ships had roughly the same dimensions as the original frigates. The old engines were installed in the new vessels, and each received eight 8.25-inch Krupp guns for its casemate.[34]

In service by the end of the decade, the three ships remained a part of the fleet until after the turn of the century. Nevertheless, their quality as warships was much maligned. At 3,600 tons, they were small for vessels of their type, their old engines made them rather slow, and the layout of their guns further limited their fighting ability. While the *Custoza* and *Erzherzog Albrecht,* also armed with eight guns, could fire four forward or two to the rear, the new ships could train only two guns forward and none to stern. To resentful officers, they were evidence of the navy's low standing in Vienna and Budapest.[35]

For the armored fleet, the only bright spot of Pöck's time in office was the construction of the new casemate ship *Tegetthoff,* laid down in April 1876 by the Stabilimento Tecnico Triestino. The initial project called for a first-class battleship, but the vessel that won approval after three years of bitter political warfare was built on a tight budget, which limited its displacement to no more than 8,000 tons. Within the strict guidelines, however, chief engineer Romako designed the largest, fastest, most heavily armed and armored warship the Habsburg navy had ever had: 7,550 tons, powered by engines capable of making fourteen knots, with casemate armor fourteen inches thick, protecting a battery of six 11-inch Krupp guns. The *Tegetthoff* remained the most powerful vessel in the fleet until just after the turn of the century, but by the time of its first sea trials—in October 1881—it was already a questionable match for the newest warships of other navies. The British and French fleets each had a number of casemate ships considerably larger than the *Tegetthoff,* and even the fledgling German navy could boast of two that were both larger and faster.[36]

The navy's dependence on foreign firms continued during the construction of the *Tegetthoff,* which, in addition to its German guns, had British armor plate. The *Tegetthoff* and the three smaller "rebuilt" casemate ships of the mid-1870s were also the first Habsburg warships to have hulls constructed of both iron and steel. In this regard, Austria-Hungary was not far behind the leading naval powers: French builders switched from iron to steel in 1873, the British in 1875.[37] For the Habsburg navy, much of the steel, as well as the iron, came from abroad, most of it from Britain. Along with the armor from Brown and Cammell of Sheffield, the navy imported propeller shafts from the Mersey Iron Works and steel cable from Brown & Lenox of London.[38] But domestic suppliers satisfied at least some of the navy's needs; this was always true with iron and continued to be the case after the introduction of steel. In the 1870s, the shipbuilders of Trieste and Pola used iron and steel from the Wodley firm of Klagenfurt, the Österreichisch-Alpinen-Montangesellschaft, the Prevalj works, and the Witkowitz works of Moravia, supplemented by the Royal Hungarian Staats-Eisenwerke in Budapest and the private ironworks in Krompach, Hungary.[39]

Even as the transition from iron to steel began, navies refused to abandon wood construction, especially for the unarmored cruisers employed to show the flag in distant waters. In addition to Tegetthoff's ironclad program, Pöck also inherited the six composite ships under construction as of 1871. These fully rigged unarmored steamships, their wooden hulls reinforced by iron frames, included the 3,400-ton frigates *Radetzky* and *Laudon* and four corvettes; Pöck initiated the construction of another two corvettes and two gunboats. All were completed by 1879.[40] As the vessels entered service, most of the remaining wooden propeller frigates and corvettes built during the 1850s were retired.

While introducing more ships of traditional design, the navy under Pöck also exploited one of the latest innovations in naval weaponry. The self-propelled torpedo, invented in 1864 by Austrian navy captain Johann Luppis, was produced exclusively in Rijeka at Robert Whitehead's Stabilimento Tecnico Fiume until the early 1870s, when international demand for the product compelled the inventors to authorize its production in Britain and other interested countries. Under Tegetthoff the Habsburg navy, in 1868, became the first to arm its ships with

Whitehead torpedoes; the British followed suit in 1871.[41] Pöck pursued
the experimentation with the new weapon, and even after the torpedoes
were being produced under license in other countries, the Austrians
remained in the forefront of torpedo research. Eventually a Habsburg
navy technical officer, Ludwig Obry, developed a gyroscope for torpedoes, vastly enhancing their accuracy and reliability.[42] The navy likewise led the way in developing tactics for the use of the torpedo, while
abroad, the deadly invention came to occupy a central place in the
radical new strategies of the French *Jeune Ecole*. Austria-Hungary only
attempted to limit the export of torpedo technology on one occasion, to
Russia during the Russo-Turkish War of 1877–78.[43] Ironically, the Austrians were not pioneers in designing new vessels specifically to use
torpedoes. In this area, the lead went to Thornycroft of Britain, which in
1875 built *Torpedoboot I* for Austria-Hungary.[44]

The Dual Monarchy's edge in torpedo production almost fell
victim to the economic depression that set in after the Vienna stock
market crash of 1873. In March 1874, the Stabilimento Tecnico Fiume
went bankrupt and closed, but its director, Robert Whitehead, armed
with a patent for a very marketable product, had little trouble lining up
investors for Whitehead & Company, which reopened the torpedo factory in Rijeka in January 1875.[45] The proprietors and employees of the
San Marco shipyard in Trieste were not so lucky. In 1870, after the death
of Giuseppe Tonello, the Navale Adriatico was reincorporated as a joint-
stock company. The firm continued to prosper, but only briefly; following the completion of the *Lissa* in 1871, the *Erzherzog Albrecht* was
the only warship still under construction in its San Marco yard. After
the *Albrecht* left for Pola in June 1874 to be armed and fitted out in the
navy's own arsenal, the Navale Adriatico had to lay off most of its
shipyard workers. By then the rival San Rocco yard of the Stabilimento
Tecnico Triestino already had won the "rebuilding" contracts for the
Kaiser Max and *Don Juan d'Austria;* the following year, the same firm
secured the contract for the new *Tegetthoff*. With little reason to hope for
a major navy contract in the near future, the San Marco shipyard closed
completely in 1875. The Navale Adriatico continued to operate its
Trieste machine shop for a few more years, building boilers for smaller
Habsburg navy ships.[46]

Amid the declining budgets and general malaise of the Pöck era,
the Habsburg naval leadership could take comfort in the fact that, at

least until the end of the 1870s, their fleet was still superior to its rival of 1866, the Royal Italian navy. In 1871 the Italians could boast of sixteen seagoing ironclads built or being built to Austria-Hungary's eleven, but aside from the twin-turreted ram *Affondatore,* all were designed with a broadside battery arrangement of guns. Because they laid down no new ironclads between 1863 and 1867, the Austrians had no armored frigates under construction when the navies of Europe adopted the casemate ship design; the Italians, however, had six armored frigates still on the stocks at that time, and all were destined to be obsolete as soon as they were launched. In an attempt to adjust to the new technology, three of the six were modified while under construction, but only one—the *Venezia,* completed in 1873—emerged as a true casemate ship.[47]

As the 1870s began, the political troubles of the Italian navy were even worse than those facing the Habsburg fleet. The defeat at Lissa caused some officers to give up hope of ever developing a competent battle fleet; in 1871, a special commission went so far as to reject a high seas deterrent in favor of a coastal defense system with thirty-one fortified bases to protect Italy's long, vulnerable coastline. After a bitter debate over defense expenditure during 1870, the navy budget for 1871 was slashed to a mere 26.8 million lire, its lowest allocation ever and the only year in history that the Italian navy budget actually was lower than the Austrian.[48] But the fortunes of the two fleets went in opposite directions thereafter. During the dismal year of 1871, Benedetto Brin became inspector of naval engineering. He was destined to become the driving force behind the recovery of the Italian navy.

After taking over as chief engineer, Brin designed an ironclad to be constructed entirely of iron and steel, larger, faster, and more heavily armed than any warship then afloat. Ignoring the casemate design so popular with naval architects in other countries, he revived the turret ship, but in a form barely recognizable, with four very large guns paired in two armored turrets atop a vessel with a much higher freeboard than the *Affondatore* or any other monitor of the 1860s. Unlike the casemate ship, Brin's new design eliminated all masts and yards, a break from the past that would place it among the vessels called "pre-dreadnoughts" by the navies of the early twentieth century.[49]

The ships, of course, would be expensive, but proponents of an Italian naval revival had plenty of arguments to support their construction. Italy's refusal to intervene on the side of France in the latter stages of the Franco-Prussian War poisoned relations with the new French Republic, while Visconti Venosta's rejection of Beust's diplomatic overtures left Austro-Italian relations strained as well, at a time when the Italians considered their own fleet inferior to both the French and the Austro-Hungarian navies. Supporters of the navy also pointed to the fact that the opening of the Suez Canal once again made the Mediterranean the center of world maritime trading routes. To make the most of the anticipated future prosperity, Italian commerce needed protection from a fleet respected by the rest of Europe.[50]

Brin wanted to build three ships of his new design, but the Chamber of Deputies provided funding for only two, eventually named *Duilio* and *Dandolo*, which were laid down in 1873. At 11,100 tons, the *Duilio* was a giant battleship for its time; the *Dandolo* was even larger, at 11,200 tons. Their speed and power depended upon imported British engines and 17.7-inch primary armament, the latter reflecting a decisive turn back toward faith in the gun and away from the ram.[51] The unprecedented size of the new warships would have made them expensive in any event, but their price was driven even higher by the fact that Italy could not produce even the basic materials for their construction. In addition to the guns and engines, the iron and steel for their hulls and armor also had to be imported.[52]

In 1875 the Chamber of Deputies allocated funds to start construction on two more battleships, to be laid down in 1876. At 13,900 tons, the *Italia* and *Lepanto* were much larger than the *Duilio* and *Dandolo*, or any casemate ship then afloat; the *Tegetthoff*, begun the same year, was barely more than half their size. The two new warships, like their predecessors, had four guns mounted in two turrets, but of slightly smaller caliber (17 inches).[53] After securing funding for these warships, Brin was appointed navy minister in the cabinet of Agostino Depretis in March 1876. Looking to the future, he drafted a construction program calling for sixteen battleships, ten cruisers, and forty-six smaller vessels, at a cost of 146 million lire for the first ten years. Victor Emmanuel II sanctioned the plan in November 1876, and the Chamber approved it in July 1877. To help soften the financial blow of Brin's program, the Italian navy resorted to a house-cleaning program surpassing even the one Tegetthoff had carried out in Austria-Hungary a few years earlier. As the four new warships neared completion, four of

Italy's ten surviving ironclads from the war of 1866 were decommissioned and scrapped, a fate shared by a number of obsolete unarmored propeller and paddle steamers.[54]

Although he was most famous for his battleships, Brin's plans also included unarmored vessels. Throughout the 1870s and 1880s, Italy, like Austria-Hungary, used fully rigged unarmored steamers for missions beyond European waters, including new composite ships similar to those introduced by the Habsburg navy.[55] Keeping abreast of the latest developments in smaller vessels, Brin in 1876 ordered the first Italian torpedo boat from Thornycroft of London, builders of the Austrian *Torpedoboot I* the previous year.[56]

In 1878 Depretis's fall brought the departure of Brin from the navy ministry, but not before he had secured a budget of 43.2 million lire for that fiscal year, a sum more than 60 percent greater than the figure for 1871.[57] Brin would return to head the ministry on four occasions during the next twenty years. Under his direct leadership or indirect guidance, the Italian navy continued on a course soon to make it vastly superior to its Austrian rival.

STAGNATION AND RETREAT:
THE NAVY UNDER PÖCK (1878–82)

As the *Duilio* and Brin's other projects neared completion, navy men in Austria-Hungary had little reason to hope that they would some day have similar battleships, even less so given Pöck's record of political ineffectiveness. As early as the summer of 1878, Sterneck observed that the situation actually had regressed from the conditions prevailing at the time of Tegetthoff's death: "it is no longer stagnation, it is retreat."[58]

The fleet's allocation for 1878 was 9.5 million gulden, a slight increase over the previous year, but a negative domestic political backlash from the Austro-Hungarian occupation of Bosnia subsequently left the Delegations in no mood to be generous to the armed forces. The navy budget fell to 9 million gulden for 1879 and 8.5 million for 1880. After the defeat of Auersperg and the German liberals in the *Reichsrat* elections of 1879, Count Taaffe returned to power as Austrian minister-president, and the Austrian contingent to the Delegations took on a more conservative character, but it remained to be seen if the navy would benefit from the change.[59] In the meantime, Italian naval spending continued to rise steadily, and with it the size and strength of the Italian fleet. In 1880 the budget for the Italian fleet stood at 45.1 million lire (18 million gulden), a level more than twice as great as the Habsburg total. In 1871, Pöck's first year in office, the Austrian appropriation had been greater than the Italian.[60]

The navy's relative lack of good fortune came despite Pöck's persistent efforts in the Delegations. For 1878 he resubmitted his proposal for the new *Drache,* this time with a smaller, less expensive design of just under 5,500 tons, but to no avail.[61] In November 1878, Pöck finally secured approval for the ship in the Hungarian Delegation only to have the Austrian side veto it, thus deleting it from the budget for 1879. For the first time since the war of 1866, political leaders openly questioned the need for armored warships, and indeed for any sort of seagoing strike force. In the Austrian Delegation's debate for 1879, Michael Klaić of Dalmatia remarked that Lissa had been won by Tegetthoff's bravado, not by ironclads; in the intervening years, France in 1870 and Turkey in 1877–78 had lost wars in which their expensive armored warships had played little role. Victor Wilhelm Russ of Bohemia echoed Klaić's remarks, arguing that in the event of war the Dual Monarchy's fate would be decided on land alone. Austria-Hungary, like Germany, did not need sea power.[62] In the late 1870s, Johann Michael Teuschl, representing Gorizia, joined Scrinzi-Montecroce of Trieste as an active spokesman for the navy's cause, but Pöck's political supporters found themselves in a distinct minority as the antinavy diatribes of Herbst, Russ, and others continued to draw cheers from the liberals in the Austrian Delegation. For 1880 an exasperated Pöck proposed the *Drache* for the fifth time, but only as a symbolic gesture, including no money for it in his own estimates. The budget committee of the Austrian Delegation made note of this "very unusual" move on the part of the *Marinekommandant.* The Delegation itself welcomed the absence of a proposal for a new armored warship and granted the navy's smallest appropriation in years (8.5 million gulden) in a matter of minutes, with no debate at all.[63]

While he failed in his attempts to increase the strength of the battle fleet, Pöck ultimately also had to fight to keep the ships he already had. In 1879 Peru, embroiled in the so-called Saltpeter War with Chile, approached Austria-Hungary through a London banking house with an offer to pay cash for three armored warships of less than 4,000 tons displacement. Later the same year, Spain made a cash offer for two large unarmored frigates. The new casemate ships *Kaiser Max, Don Juan d'Austria,* and *Prinz Eugen* and the composite frigates *Radetzky* and *Laudon* fit these descriptions, but the navy was not prepared to part with any of them. Pöck finally sent the foreign ministry a sharply worded letter stating that he had no ships available for sale "in any category," armored or unarmored.[64]

Given insufficient funds to maintain a potent ironclad fleet, the navy sought to develop expertise in other, less expensive means of naval warfare. While Italy continued to build battleships, Austria-Hungary reinforced its position in home waters by developing mines and especially torpedoes, weapons cursed by the Italians as the *mezzi insidiosi* of naval warfare.[65] By 1882 the Habsburg navy already had a torpedo flotilla of ten boats available to employ these "insidious means." After Thornycroft built *Torpedoboot I* in 1875, Pöck ordered five more boats from British firms and had four constructed in the Pola Arsenal, copying a British design.[66] Meanwhile, chief engineer Romako turned his attentions from casemate ships to a new type of unarmored seagoing vessel capable of firing torpedoes. His design for four new warships was a cross between the composite ship of the 1870s and the modern cruiser of the 1880s: a steel-hulled vessel with nominal rigging, but with the graceful lines of a sailing ship. The first Austro-Hungarian warships of all-steel construction, they were also built largely with domestic steel: the *Zara* (launched in 1879) and *Sebenico* (1882) at the Pola Arsenal, the *Spalato* (1879) and *Lussin* (1883) at the San Rocco yard of Stabilimento Tecnico Triestino.[67] Ranging between 850 and 1,000 tons, the four vessels were roughly the size of the future destroyers of the First World War and much larger than the first torpedo boats, all of which displaced less than 50 tons. In the evolving terminology of the day, they were just large enough to be classified as cruisers; the Habsburg navy officially called them "torpedo ships." The Italians had nothing like them, and were also slower both in buying torpedo boats from Britain and building their own at home.[68]

As the first Austro-Hungarian navy projects of all-steel construction, the torpedo ship projects touched off a crisis in the shipyards that only added to Pöck's woes. Especially at the Stabilimento Tecnico Triestino, craftsmen trained in the traditional woodworking trades protested the changes in work and wages stemming from the introduction of the new primary building material. The tension had been brewing ever since the introduction of the first ironclad battleships two decades earlier, but until the torpedo ships, at least the unarmored vessels— such as the composite ships completed during the 1870s—still used a considerable amount of wood. The resentments of workers finally boiled over in 1883 in a strike at the San Rocco wharves, which delayed the completion of the torpedo ship *Lussin*. The first strike ever to affect the construction of a navy vessel in Austria-Hungary, it was a hopeless protest by men whose skills unfortunately were tied to the technology of the past. Because the depressed economy already had caused the work force at San Rocco to shrink from over two thousand men in 1871 to fewer than three hundred by 1882, there were plenty of unemployed workers ready to take the strikers' jobs, and they had little alternative but to return to work.[69]

Even though the pioneering work in the development of the torpedo and the design of the steel-hulled torpedo cruiser came under his command, Pöck never abandoned his conviction that a strong armored fleet mattered most. He persevered in his annual campaigns for some sort of sister ship for the *Tegetthoff*, at least until 1880, despite the strength of the political opposition and the hopelessness of the cause. As the new decade began, the emperor took more of an interest in the navy, apparently concerned by Pöck's perennial lack of success with the Delegations and the resulting low budgets, which made Tegetthoff's fleet plan of 1868 a dead letter. The appearance of the Italian *Duilio* in the Adriatic shortly after its commissioning in January 1880 touched off the greatest navy scare to sweep the Habsburg littoral since the early 1860s and created a new sense of urgency in Vienna. Francis Joseph responded by appointing a committee of inquiry to study the navy's future.

The committee that convened in July 1880 consisted exclusively of representatives from the armed forces. The army's four spokesmen included the emperor's influential cousin Archduke Albrecht, the inspector-general of the army; Albrecht's brother Archduke William, the inspector-general of artillery; *Feldmarschalleutnant* Baron Franz von Vlasits, representing the war minister, *Feldzeugmeister* Count Artur Bylandt-Rheidt; and *Feldmarschalleutnant* Baron Anton von Schönfeld, the chief of the General Staff. The navy's three representatives were the *Marinekommandant*, Pöck; his leading protégé, Captain Pitner; and his principal adversary, Rear Admiral Sterneck. Archduke Albrecht served as chairman.[70]

At the beginning of the proceedings, Pöck and Pitner called for a new fleet plan that would match Brin's program of 1876, which was supposed to produce sixteen battleships and ten cruisers by 1888. Austria-Hungary, with a battle fleet of eight casemate ships and two usable armored frigates, would have to build six new armored warships to match the Italian total. Pöck estimated that the total cost of the program would be 25.6 million gulden for the seven budget years 1882–88, over and above the navy's regular annual appropriations.[71] Sterneck, somewhat more enamored with the evolving torpedo and cruiser tactics that would be cornerstones of the *Jeune Ecole* of the 1880s, wavered in his support of the *Marinekommandant's* emphasis on battleships. Pöck held firm, however; even though his plan also set goals of eight large and eight small unarmored cruisers, he proposed that money could be saved for armored warships by postponing the construction of new unarmored vessels. While he recognized the importance of such ships to show the flag in peacetime and acknowledged the theoretical merits of a *guerre de course* against an enemy's colonies and seagoing trade, Pöck insisted that cruisers "would have no purpose" in a war against Italy, "which has neither overseas possessions nor a significant merchant marine."[72]

The skepticism of the army's representatives centered around the question of funding Pöck's ambitious new program. To cut costs, the *Marinekommandant* was willing to sacrifice cruisers for the sake of building more battleships.[73] Vlasits and Archduke William ultimately agreed that a fleet of sixteen battleships was a desirable goal but rejected Pöck's contention that parity with the Italians in battleships was an absolute necessity. In the committee's final session, Albrecht stressed the same point, arguing that parity at sea with Italy was out of the question. In their recent support for Brin's program, the Italians had shown an enthusiasm for maritime greatness and a willingness to pay the price for it; this would never be the case, he contended, in the Dual Monarchy. Even if Austria-Hungary achieved the goal of parity in battleships and a future Habsburg battle fleet won another victory of the magnitude of Lissa, such a triumph would not automatically guarantee victory in a war against Italy.[74]

All things considered, Albrecht concluded that the navy should abandon all thought of catching up with Italy and instead seek only to *maintain* its current strength in battleships. A future Italian threat in the Adriatic should be met not by an offensive stance à la Tegetthoff, but with a well-developed strategy designed to defend ports and coastal waters. The goal should not be "open sea battles, but the conduct of a brilliant defensive 'little war' (*Verteidigungskrieg im Kleinen*)." The archduke closed the committee's work by praising the fleet for its past and present service but warned "against illusions [of maritime might] and against the results they would produce, if our limited resources are concentrated on the pursuit of the unattainable." His prophetic advice and admonitions were heeded in the short term but, alas, not in the years before 1914 or during the First World War. Albrecht's conclusions no doubt left Pöck feeling just as Tegetthoff had felt in the late 1860s: that the navy, ironically, was a prisoner of its own success. The Battle of Lissa had demonstrated that a smaller Austrian force with inferior equipment could defeat a larger Italian rival on the strength of its superior training and tactics. It was a lesson not forgotten by Albrecht and other army leaders.

The verdict of the committee of inquiry obliged Pöck to formulate a new fleet plan conforming to Albrecht's guideline that the number of armored warships should be maintained rather than increased. Before doing so, however, he tried once again to secure funding for an immediate construction start on a new battleship. When the council of ministers convened in September 1880, Pöck included the warship proposal in the navy estimates for 1881 and also asked for enough money to finally complete the *Tegetthoff*, which had first been funded in the budget for 1875. Francis Joseph and foreign minister Count Heinrich von Haymerle both supported the *Marinekommandant*, but Pöck's plan soon came unraveled. The Hungarian finance minister, Count Gyula Szápáry, carried the day with the argument that no new battleship should be laid down until after the *Tegetthoff* was finished. Szápáry then persuaded the ministers to cut by 50 percent the sum Pöck proposed for the *Tegetthoff* project for 1881, ensuring that the ship would not be completed until 1882 and a new battleship could not be started until 1883, at the earliest.[75] Fortunately for the navy, the ministers cut little else from Pöck's estimates, and the Delegations subsequently granted him 9.5 million gulden for 1881, more than in any year since 1876.[76]

In February 1881, Pöck presented his new fleet plan to Francis Joseph. The proposal called for the maintenance of current levels of strength in all categories: eleven armored warships, supplemented by seven large and twenty-four small unarmored vessels. For each general type of ship, the numbers represented a reduction of the goals of Tegetthoff's plan of 1868 (fifteen ironclads, eight large and twenty-six small unarmored vessels). Under a building program covering the next eight fiscal years (1882 through 1889), Pöck planned to replace the navy's four weakest ironclads: the three remaining armored frigates (*Salamander, Habsburg*, and *Erzherzog Ferdinand Max*) and the casemate ship *Kaiser*, which had begun life as a wooden ship of the line in the late 1850s. He proposed the construction of an *Ersatz Salamander* for 1882–86 and an *Ersatz Kaiser* for 1886–89, at 3.8 million gulden apiece. For the remaining pair of replacement ships, he employed the same device already used successfully in the mid-1870s, calling them "rebuilding" projects rather than new construction: the *Ferdinand Max* for 1883–86 and the *Habsburg* for 1886–89, at 2.5 million apiece. Among the smaller unarmored warships, Pöck proposed to replace three obsolete steamers with three new light cruisers at 600,000 gulden apiece, with the cost spread over the first six years of the program. Another 400,000 gulden would go toward the construction of eight new torpedo boats, with 1.5 million designated for new boilers for almost all of the remaining ships in the fleet. At 17.2 million gulden (2.15 million per year) over eight years, the program was far less expensive than the one Pöck had first proposed to Albrecht's committee inquiry the previous summer, which would have cost 3.65 million per year over a period of just seven years.[77]

In May 1881, the plan won the approval of the three common Austro-Hungarian ministers—Haymerle, war minister Bylandt-Rheidt, and finance minister József Szlávy—but they warned Pöck that the political leaders of the two halves of the Dual Monarchy were not likely to approve the necessary annual increases in the navy budget.[78] In the larger council of ministers the following September, the Hungarian finance minister, Count Szápáry, once again proved to be the navy's greatest nemesis. Szápáry touched off a long debate by proposing a ten-year timetable for the program that would reduce the annual cost to just over 1.7 million gulden. Haymerle and Bylandt-Rheidt supported Pöck, but Szlávy favored a compromise with his Hungarian countrymen. The council ultimately accepted his proposal, which retained the eight-year timetable for all but the two replacement battleships; these were now targeted for completion between 1890 and 1892.[79] Pöck argued that this revision would leave the fleet dangerously weak in the early 1890s and, in the meantime, would require the navy to spend too much money to keep obsolete ships afloat. He appealed to Francis Joseph to force a compromise more favorable to the navy, but the emperor accepted Szlávy's formula.[80]

A frustrated Pöck could be thankful that at least the Delegations posed no difficulties this time around. In November 1881, they voted the navy 9.8 million gulden for the following year, including enough money to finish the *Tegetthoff* and to start the *Ersatz Salamander*. During the course of the Austrian deliberations, delegate Teuschl of Gorizia introduced an economic argument in support of a stronger fleet, citing the need to encourage "the development of the merchant marine" and to protect Austro-Hungarian business interests in distant waters. His speech, while not entirely original, foreshadowed the rhetoric of future pronavy politicians, who would cite the needs of commerce and industry more than the traditional strategic argument of defending the coast.[81] It marked a decisive break from the navy debates of the past decade. It had become customary for supporters of the fleet to preface their remarks with a tribute to Tegetthoff's memory or the glories of Lissa, and aside from delegates speaking on behalf of the coal industry, no one had ever raised the point of the domestic businesses that would benefit from higher naval spending. Indeed, as recently as 1874, Pöck had apologized to the Austrian Delegation for the navy's use of the private shipyards in Trieste rather than its own Pola Arsenal, which alone could not handle all repairs and construction projects.[82] In contrast, future commanders would boast of the extent to which the navy patronized private industry. Ever so slowly, times were changing.

Meanwhile, on the Italian side, the *Duilio* and *Dandolo* both were in service by 1882, and in addition to the *Italia* and *Lepanto*, Italy also had three other pre-dreadnoughts under construction, the *Ruggiero di*

Lauria, Andrea Doria, and *Francesco Morosini.* Other armored vessels already serving with the fleet included the ram *Affondatore,* the casemate ship *Venezia,* and ten other ironclads laid down during the 1860s. Against Brin's wishes, political considerations dictated that the three newest ships be closer in size to the *Duilio* and *Dandolo* than to their larger, more immediate predecessors.[83] Nevertheless, the smallest of his seven pre-dreadnoughts was still over 3,500 tons heavier than the *Tegetthoff.* The strength of the Italian fleet clearly reflected Rome's commitment to sea power, while the motley collection of ships at Pola and the promise of only modest progress in the future reflected the commitment to mediocrity dictated by Albrecht and the committee of inquiry.

By the early 1880s, the relative lack of material progress under Pöck had disappointed virtually everyone involved with the service. Throughout the 1850s and 1860s, the steady growth of the fleet necessitated a constant expansion in personnel, and for officers, growth had meant rapid promotion. Whereas in 1850 the navy had only 123 active sea officers (including 30 cadets), by the end of the Tegetthoff era the number almost tripled, to 374 (including 58 cadets). The corps continued to grow during the dozen years of Pöck's administration, but for most, the rate of advancement slowed to a crawl. Some officers promoted to ensign in the spring of 1866 had to wait until 1878 to become second lieutenants, and the corps became increasingly bottom-heavy with cadets awaiting promotion to ensign. In the fall of 1883, the navy had 505 active sea officers, of whom 129 were cadets.[84]

The stagnation and absence of opportunity also made the navy an unpopular option for one-year volunteers (*Einjährig-Freiwillige*). During the 1870s, it was not uncommon for fewer than two dozen to be attracted to the navy in any given year.[85] On the positive side, the slowdown enabled the naval academy to satisfy the need for career officers without help from supplementary programs. The practice of taking on *Gymnasium* and *Oberrealschule* graduates as provisional sea cadets (*See-Aspiranten*) was discontinued after 1874 and not resumed for over a decade.[86] The resulting homogeneity of education and training for members of the corps to some degree helped offset the negative effects that slow advancement inevitably had on morale. Despite having to wait longer for their first promotion, the sea cadets commissioned under

Pöck's command suffered a lower rate of attrition in the first years after graduation than their predecessors.[87] The multinational Austro-Hungarian naval officer corps paradoxically was more cohesive than its Italian counterpart, which was bitterly divided among Venetian, Neapolitan, and Piedmontese-Genoese cliques.[88]

Tegetthoff's naval academy curriculum, finally introduced in 1871, remained in effect through the 1881–82 school year. The general education of the first three years included a heavy dose of languages: Italian, Serbo-Croatian, English, and French were all required, as was a full course in German language and literature. A revised curriculum introduced in 1882 reflected, to a large extent, political pressure from Budapest. Hungarian language instruction was made mandatory for all academy students from the Hungarian half of the monarchy; to avoid requiring non-Magyars in this category to learn an unreasonable number of languages, all students subsequently were given the option of taking either French or English.[89] Hungarians in the class enrolling under the new curriculum in the fall of 1882 included the fourteen-year-old Miklós Horthy, son of a landowner from Kenderes. Notwithstanding the new language requirements, years were to pass before it became common to hear Magyar spoken aboard ship. Horthy later recalled that after returning from an extended cruise early in his career, he "could scarcely understand a word" of his native tongue.[90]

Eventually the nationality question would make it more of a challenge for the navy to maintain cohesion in its officer corps and loyalty among the common seamen. For the moment, however, problems tended to be more emotional than political. For officers in the higher and middle ranks, life toward the end of the Pöck era was a far cry from the heady days of 1866 and from the high hopes of Tegetthoff's brief tenure as commander. Meanwhile, cadets and younger officers learning of the triumph of Lissa in the classrooms at Rijeka—the eventual commanders of the Austro-Hungarian navy in the First World War—found it difficult to become very enthusiastic about a service in which the likelihood of similar glory appeared dim indeed. And in all cases, it certainly did not help matters that the *Marinekommandant* himself had not even been with the fleet in 1866. Notwithstanding the best efforts and intentions, Pöck could never hope to command respect or generate enthusiasm as Tegetthoff had.

In the later Pöck years, as in the early and mid-1870s, overseas missions continued to be the most exciting duty regularly available to the sea officers and their men. Far from being mere excursions, these voyages, designed to defend and encourage commercial navigation in distant waters, became increasingly important. Two missions were sent overseas in 1879–80, the *Helgoland* to Australia, where it represented Austria-Hungary at the opening of the Sydney World's Fair in September 1879, and the corvette *Saida* to Brazil, South Africa, the West Indies, and New York. The staff of the latter voyage included the newly commissioned ensign Archduke Charles Stephen. The graduating academy class of the following year visited South, Central, and North American ports aboard the *Fasana,* and in 1882–83 the corvette *Erzherzog Friedrich* repeated the *Saida's* itinerary to Brazil, South Africa, the West Indies, and New York.[91] In the last two years of Pöck's time in office, Habsburg seamen returned to the Arctic for the first time since the mission of Weyprecht and Payer in 1872–74. Austria-Hungary manned the international scientific observation station on the island of Jan Mayen during the winter of 1882–83 with a contingent consisting almost exclusively of naval personnel. The transport steamer *Pola* left the group on the island in the summer of 1882 and returned a year later to take them home.[92] Under Pöck's command, the navy showed the flag in waters it had never visited before and cruised to other parts of the world far more often than in previous decades.

Throughout the 1870s and early 1880s, Habsburg merchant shipping also continued to expand, while the Adriatic ports prospered and new railway links between the littoral and the hinterland brought more of Austria-Hungary closer to the sea. Thanks to the opening of the Suez Canal, the total value of Trieste's trade reached the 200 million gulden mark in 1869 for the first time since before the war of 1859. The 300 million level was surpassed in 1882, delayed by the depression that followed the Vienna stock market crash in 1873 but also by the emergence of Rijeka as a new competitor.[93] An Italian city with Croatian suburbs, Rijeka became "Hungarian" after the *Ausgleich* of 1867, and the political leaders of Hungary aggressively promoted its development. Even though Budapest already was linked by rail to the main Vienna-Trieste line, which had been completed in 1857, the Hungarian government opened its own Budapest-Rijeka railway in 1873.[94] The new connection to the interior of Hungary subsequently caused a boom in Rijeka. Whereas in 1870 the total tonnage of merchant vessels arriving at the port amounted to just 13.5 percent of the arrivals at Trieste, in 1883 the figure stood at 48.1 percent.[95]

After 1867 the Austrian Lloyd became the Austro-Hungarian Lloyd, since the steamship line agreed to carry exports from Rijeka as well as Trieste in exchange for the Hungarian government's assumption of part of its state subsidy. But Budapest's dissatisfaction with the arrangement led, in 1882, to the decision to sponsor a separate Hungarian steamship company, the Adria Line (the Adria Magyar Tengerhajózási Tarsasag). The company prospered from the start, concentrating primarily on routes to Western European and western Mediterranean ports not already served by the Lloyd. Unlike its older competitor, which built at least some of its own vessels in the Lloyd Arsenal at Trieste, the Adria Line ordered all of its ships from British shipyards.[96] The Lloyd continued to receive Hungarian subsidies for another decade but after 1892 was supported by just Austria and reverted to its former name.

Because its primary orientation always had been toward the east, the Lloyd did not suffer greatly from competition with the Adria Line. While continuing to serve the eastern Mediterranean, the Lloyd established regular service between Trieste and Bombay in 1878, via the Suez Canal. The line was extended to Colombo (Ceylon) the following year and to Singapore and Hong Kong in 1880.[97] Thanks largely to the Lloyd, the Austro-Hungarian merchant marine initially ranked third behind only the British and French in its use of the new waterway. But while Habsburg shipping continued to expand, the merchant fleets of other powers grew at an even greater rate. By 1882 Austria-Hungary had slipped to fifth in Suez Canal use, surpassed by both Germany and Italy.[98]

In number, frequency, and variety of destinations, the navy's overseas missions during the Pöck era compared favorably with those undertaken by the Italian navy, which also assigned the same types of ships to such duties.[99] But by employing on every voyage fully rigged vessels that used their sails much more than their engines, the Austro-Hungarian navy hardly cut an imposing figure. There was a difference between showing the flag and making a show of force; while the missions no doubt were beneficial for training, diplomacy, and public relations, the exposure did not necessarily generate respect. Furthermore, this type of exercise—aboard ships that would have no usefulness in combat—did nothing to prepare officers and seamen for wartime service in the armored battle fleet. While the wooden cruisers traversed every ocean, high operating costs prevented the navy from sending any ironclads out of the Mediterranean, and even in the Adriatic and Mediterranean the active squadron often included only one armored warship. In closing the committee of inquiry, Archduke Albrecht had concluded that the navy must put its faith in the maintenance of high standards of training and the development of new tactics rather than the construction of large expensive warships. But the archduke, the army, the emperor, and the Delegations failed to recognize that these goals, too, could not be achieved without adequate funding.

THE NAVY AND
AUSTRO-HUNGARIAN FOREIGN POLICY (1871–82)

The failure of Beust's diplomacy during 1870 ultimately led to his ouster as foreign minister in the fall of 1871. By that time, Vienna and Berlin were well on their way toward a rapprochement, there were no plans for a future "anti-Prussian" coalition, and there was no longer the same pressing need for Austria-Hungary to persist in soliciting Italian friendship. Nevertheless, Beust's successor, Andrássy, soon found new reasons to remain on good terms with Italy. After 1870 a resurgent Russia appeared to be the most likely future adversary for the Habsburg Empire, and should such a conflict occur, it would be disastrous for the Austrians to have a hostile Italy at their rear. In part reacting to Russian attempts to court Italy's favor, in November 1871 Andrássy made Austria-Hungary one of the first countries to move its embassy from Florence to Rome. It was a controversial step, but Andrássy defended it as evidence of "the high price we attach to friendly relations *and close union* with Italy, which I have at heart not only to maintain but to strengthen still more."[100]

But for the remainder of the decade—indeed, until the First World War—the value that Habsburg statesmen placed upon friendship with Italy waxed and waned according to the status of Austro-Russian relations. By the fall of 1873, a year of diplomatic maneuvering had brought Austria-Hungary together with Germany and Russia in the

Three Emperors' League, and Italy ceased to be so crucial to Habsburg foreign policy. Far from making friendly overtures, war minister Kuhn explored the possibility of establishing a major military and naval base at Sebenico in response to a similar project at Taranto in the boot heel of Italy. At the same time, the temporary abeyance of the Russian threat in the eastern Balkans left Andrássy free to worry about an Italian bid for a foothold in the western Balkans.

In Vienna, the Italian decision to develop Taranto only reinforced suspicions. The Italian navy already had main bases at La Spezia and Venice to serve as defensive strongholds for wars against France and Austria-Hungary, respectively; the new works at Taranto represented a departure, an expression of what one historian has called Italy's "Balkan megalomania."[102] But the conservative Italian governments of the early 1870s had no clear Balkan goals, at least for the short term. When the Near Eastern question heated up once again during 1875, Benedetto Brin's campaign to revive the Italian navy was still in its infancy. When asked, in the Chamber of Deputies, why he was not attempting to capitalize on the chaos in the Balkans, Visconti Venosta specifically cited Italy's naval weakness as one of the restraining factors.[103] But the cautious conservatives who had dominated Italian politics for most of the years since unification lost power in 1876, and subsequent liberal cabinets would be less circumspect in the field of foreign policy, especially as the naval buildup progressed.[104]

Italy played the role of a jealous spectator throughout the Russo-Turkish War of 1877–78, the abortive Russian project for a greater Bulgaria, and the subsequent Congress of Berlin. Meanwhile, Austria-Hungary emerged with the right to administer Bosnia-Hercegovina and garrison the strategically important Sanjak of Novi Pazar, both of which would remain technically under Turkish sovereignty. The occupation of the territories began in late July 1878 and was completed within two months. Because of stiff local resistance, mostly from Muslim rebels, the operation required some 150,000 troops, 26,000 of whom were shipped to Dalmatia by the navy. Sea transport was also used to evacuate hundreds of sick and wounded soldiers to Trieste. The navy kept three armored warships in service for most of the year and in July 1878 mined the approaches to the Turkish Dalmatian enclave of Klek, but there was no action on the Adriatic. The river monitors *Maros* and *Leitha* were the only Austro-Hungarian warships directly involved in the fighting, patrolling the Sava River and covering the army's crossings from Croatia southward into Bosnia.[105]

Once the troops were in place in Bosnia and Sanjak, Austria-Hungary's sphere of influence had been extended halfway to Salonika (Thessaloniki) and a direct outlet to the Aegean Sea. With some justification, military and naval men tended to view the events of 1878 as the start of a formal or informal incorporation of the western Balkans into the empire. Tegetthoff's old friend Sterneck, languishing at a relatively unimportant post in Pola, fantasized about a bold grab for Salonika but at the same time mused over the international reaction, noting that the Italian irredentists did not even acknowledge the Austrian right to be in Pola.[106] But Habsburg aggrandizement in the Balkans faced greater obstacles than resistance from Italy. Within the Dual Monarchy those opposing the annexation of more Slavic territory included all Hungarian parties as well as the German liberals of Austria. The latter, in particular, condemned the occupation of Bosnia in the strongest terms. In the months that followed, they held up the passage of a new military law and used their power of the purse to punish both the army and navy at budget time.[107]

The navy subsequently defended Austro-Hungarian interests in the lands adjacent to the new acquisitions. After local Albanians refused to turn over the port of Dulcigno (Ulcinj) to Montenegro, as prescribed by the Treaty of Berlin, the great powers conducted a joint naval demonstration. On station from August to December 1880, the international fleet included a Habsburg contingent under Rear Admiral Alexander Eberan von Eberhorst consisting of the casemate ships *Custoza* and *Prinz Eugen,* the unarmored frigate *Laudon,* and one gunboat.[108] At the end of 1881, when an attempt to call up the local *Landwehr* sparked a rebellion in the Bocche di Cattaro, the navy played a more active role in restoring order than it had in the previous Cattaran uprising a dozen years earlier. The casemate ship *Erzherzog Albrecht* entered the bay along with the *Laudon* and several smaller vessels. By the time the revolt was crushed in March 1882, the guns of the squadron had been used to bombard rebel strongholds ashore, and a landing party from the *Laudon* led by Lieutenant Leodegar Kneissler had distinguished itself in two weeks of fighting alongside the army.[109]

As Austria-Hungary solidified its control over the hinterland of the eastern Adriatic littoral, Italy also longed for new conquests. After the Congress of Berlin, Andrássy had scoffed at suggestions that Italy should be compensated for Austrian gains by a cession of parts of *Italia irredenta,* either in the Alps or on the Adriatic. But with Russia again cast in the role of a potential enemy, Italy assumed a renewed importance in Habsburg foreign policy. When Andrássy left office in October 1879, his ambassador to Italy, Count Haymerle, became foreign minister. Haymerle hoped to redirect Italian ambitions toward goals not in conflict with Austrian interests, and Italy's leaders gave him their full cooperation.

Keenly aware that an Austro-Italian rapprochement would be disastrous for the navy, Pöck opposed Haymerle's Italian policy with all the energy he could muster. In March 1880, he warned Francis Joseph of the continuing Italian danger to the Dual Monarchy's interests at sea, pointing to Brin's battleship program, "which no doubt is directed against us."[110] Nevertheless, the breakthrough, when it came, stemmed not from a conscious desire for friendship on either side but because Italian politics were no longer completely dominated by the Piedmontese. Consequently, there was room in Rome for a worldview not fixed rigidly on the Alps and the unredeemed lands under Habsburg rule.[111] In evidence of the new orientation, the Italians pinned their hopes on acquiring land in North Africa. By the beginning of 1881, Haymerle was prepared to support their claims to Tunisia in exchange for a renunciation of all Italian ambitions in the Balkans.[112]

France's occupation of Tunisia in the spring of 1881 foiled these plans, but the resulting wave of Francophobia in Italy made the country eager for closer ties with Austria-Hungary or, to be more precise, with the Austro-German alliance that Andrássy had concluded in his last days as foreign minister. In the Italian view, the road to Berlin passed through Vienna; Italy's overtures thus included a visit by King Umberto to the Austrian capital in October 1881. Initially the campaign drew a cool response both from Bismarck and from Haymerle's successor, Count Gustav Kálnoky, neither of whom wanted war with France over Italy's ambitions in North Africa. Negotiations finally progressed, but only after the Italians dropped their claims to Tunisia. On 20 May 1882, Kálnoky's revision of an Italian draft became the treaty of the Triple Alliance, signed by the three powers in Vienna.[113]

Although the alliance ultimately became one of the longest running in the history of European diplomacy, the initial treaty had a duration of just five years. Its terms committed Germany and Italy to help one another in case either became the victim of an unprovoked attack by France. Austria-Hungary was obligated to join Italy and Germany against France if France attacked Italy, but not if France attacked Germany. Should an alliance member be attacked by two or more nonmembers, the other members were bound to intervene. If any member attacked a nonmember, the other members were committed to observe a benevolent neutrality toward their ally. They pledged to consult one another during crises and, should war break out, not to conclude peace separately. All terms were to be secret and subject to renewal in May 1887. A week after signing the treaty, the allies exchanged notes affirming their understanding that their pact was not directed against Britain.[114]

Because it was highly unlikely that France would ever attack Italy without provocation, and since Germany, too, was pledged to intervene should such an attack ever come, Kálnoky considered the alliance a fair trade for the neutralization of Italy in the event of an Austro-Russian war. He also felt that friendship with Austria-Hungary would give the Italian government a good excuse to muzzle the irredentist movement; because many irredentists were also radicals and republicans, such a development could only bode well for the future stability of the Italian monarchy.[115] For Italy, the Triple Alliance brought an end to years of diplomatic isolation. In concrete terms, it offered protection against a likely future adversary—France—without compromising Anglo-Italian relations. Indeed, the treaty gave Italy the confidence to consider itself a legitimate challenger to France in North Africa and the Mediterranean. The price, however, was a de facto concession of Austro-Hungarian hegemony over the Adriatic.[116] As Brin's naval buildup continued into the 1880s, now with France as the clear rival, the Italian navy had to accept the fact that the verdict of Lissa would not be overturned.

Though not a bad deal for Austro-Hungarian foreign policy, the Triple Alliance was nothing short of a disaster for the navy. The onset of formal Austro-Italian friendship made 1882 almost the darkest year since 1848, when the Venetian revolution had divided the fleet and threatened its very existence. There was no question this time that the navy would continue to function in some form; nevertheless, with the neutralization of the Italian threat, the need for vigilance in the Adriatic all but evaporated. As early as 1882, the navy drafted plans for the contingency of a war with Russia, but patrolling the Adriatic against a phantom threat from the east generated little more enthusiasm than the various cruises to show the flag abroad.

Even before the Triple Alliance, the Austrian and Hungarian governments had been reluctant to provide the navy with the funding necessary to keep up with the Italians or other potential rivals. But given the perennial financial weakness of the Dual Monarchy, the reservations of political leaders were quite understandable. In a time of rapid technological change, heavy investment in one type of battleship was risky for countries without the strongest of resources. The navy's modest commitment to build armored frigates in the 1860s kept Austria-Hungary from being left with a large number of them in the fleet or under construction when the technology moved on to casemate ships. A decade later, however, the Habsburg fleet was caught with eight casemate ships when Brin and the Italians led the move to more modern pre-dreadnought turret battleships. Conversely, after 1866 Italy was caught with several armored frigates still on the stocks when casemate ships were introduced. But a decade later, having invested little in casemate ships, the Italian navy had a strong argument before parliament for the necessity of Brin's program of pre-dreadnoughts. It was a high-stakes game for even the wealthiest naval powers, and at least at this point, Austria-Hungary appeared to be among the losers. But the competition was not over; it would continue—and indeed, intensify—after the turn of the century.

Even in the early 1880s, the news was not all bad. In spite of the problems with matériel, the navy's personnel remained relatively well trained, arguably better than ever. At the same time, the Pöck era embodied the formative years for a generation of talented young officers who would provide the navy's leadership during the First World War. Thanks to the overseas cruises, the Habsburg fleet had logged more sea miles under Pöck than in the rest of its history combined. And as it sought to find its niche in Austria-Hungary's new strategic constellation, the navy began to develop bold and innovative torpedo tactics that would be praised and copied by most of the larger navies of Europe in the years to come. In the twilight of the Pöck era, as the technologically antiquated battle fleet lost its relevance in the European naval balance, there were at least some reasons for optimism.

NOTES

1.   The leadership of the *Marinesektion* of the war ministry technically remained vacant until October 1872, when Pöck was officially appointed as chief; in the interim, he served as its provisional head. See Wagner, "Die obersten Behörden," 138.

2.   Handel-Mazzetti and Sokol, *Tegetthoff*, 323–24, allege that Pöck "would rather have commanded a cavalry regiment" than the fleet. Anthony Sokol, *Austro-Hungarian Navy*, 57, repeats the story that Pöck "wanted to command not a fleet, but an army corps." Other critics include Schöndorfer, "Kriegsschiffbau," 30; and Heinrich Bayer von Bayersburg, *Österreichs Admirale 1867–1918*, 140.

3.   Most notably, the fall of the Second Empire in 1870 brought an end to Anglo-French naval competition, the cornerstone of the overall drive toward steam and armor during the previous two decades. See Arthur J. Marder, *The Anatomy of British Sea Power: A History of British Naval Policy in the Pre-Dreadnought Era, 1880–1905*, 120; and Ropp, *The Development of a Modern Navy*, 26–28.

4.   Sterneck to sister, Pola, 14 June 1871, Sterneck, *Erinnerungen*, 168.

5.   See Sondhaus, *The Habsburg Empire and the Sea*, 186–87, 193, 240–41.

6.   On Pöck's earlier career and rivalry with Tegetthoff before 1866, see ibid., 246, 248. Karl Paschen, *Aus der Werdezeit zweier Marinen: Erinnerungen aus meiner Dienstzeit in der k.k. österreichischen und kaiserlich deutschen Marine*, 133, describes Pöck's reaction to the Battle of Lissa but gives no source for his account. Paschen served at Lissa as a lieutenant aboard the armored frigate *Juan d'Austria*.

7.   Officially, the second in command served as *Stellvertreter* of the commander in his capacity as chief of the war ministry's *Marinesektion*. Rear Admiral Julius von Wissiak assumed this capacity under Tegetthoff in April 1868 and held the post until his retirement at the end of 1869.

8.   Sterneck to sister, Pola, 14 June 1871, Sterneck, *Erinnerungen*, 168.

9.   Sterneck, in the open sailboat *Isbjörn*, reached a latitude of 78°N.

10.   Spaun, as a lieutenant, had been second in command of the flagship *Erzherzog Ferdinand Max* at the Battle of Lissa. He served in London from 1873 until 1879. Berghofer, promoted to the highest grade of lieutenant in 1869, remained at that rank for fifteen years. The careers of both men advanced markedly after Sterneck became *Marinekommandant* in November 1883. See Chapter Three below and Bayer von Bayersburg, *Österreichs Admirale*, 25, 168.

11.   For biographies of Millosicz (1818–90) and Pitner (1833–1911), see ibid., 128–29 and 143–44.

12.   See Jerolim Benko von Boinik, *Geschichte der k.k. Kriegsmarine während der Jahre 1848 und 1849*, 630.

13.   Salcher, *Marine-Akademie*, 73; Bayer von Bayersburg, *Österreichs Admirale*, 72. Albrecht assumed responsibility for the education of Charles Stephen and his brothers after the death, in 1874, of their father, Charles Ferdinand.

14. *StPD*, IV (14 July 1871), 192.

15. On the role of Archduke Charles in promoting the growth of the Austrian navy during the Napoleonic era, see Sondhaus, *The Habsburg Empire and the Sea*, 10–17 passim.

16. *StPD*, V (5 October 1872), 56; see also ibid., 226; Reiter, "Entwicklung," 38–40.

17. *StPD*, VI (5 May 1873), 120, 163; Reiter, "Entwicklung," 44; Krenslehner, "Die k.u.k. Kriegsmarine als wirtschaftlicher Faktor," 73.

18. Reiter, "Entwicklung," 39, 43–45. For Herbst's criticism of additional expenditure on the *Custoza* and *Erzherzog Albrecht*, see *StPD*, VI (5 May 1873), 112.

19. *StPD*, VII (15 May 1874), 47, 122; ibid., VIII (11 October 1875), 98. For Pöck's remarks regarding *Ersatzbauten*, see ibid., VII (15 May 1874), 45. See also Reiter, "Entwicklung," 45–53. According to Höbelt, the navy tried to sell the *Drache* to China in 1875, but the deal ultimately fell through ("Die Marine," 702). A supporter of Pöck's campaign for the *Ersatz Drache* attributed the rapid deterioration of the original *Drache* and its sister ship *Salamander* to their hasty construction during the Austro-Italian naval arms race of the early 1860s. See Leonhard Libert de Paradis, *Das Seewesen in Oesterreich-Ungarn: Seine Wichtigkeit, Entwicklungsfähigkeit und Literatur*, 94.

20. *StPD*, IX (22 May 1876), 22, 30, 199–201, 239–40, 242; Krenslehner, "Kriegsmarine als wirtschaftlicher Faktor," 75–76.

21. Andrássy to Marinesektion, Vienna, 4 July 1876, and Pöck to Min. des Äussern, Vienna, 11 July 1876, in HHSA, PA, XL, Carton 134: Korr. mit inneren und Militärbehörden 1876. The Turks wanted £1 million (well over ten million gulden at the prevailing exchange rate) for the ironclads; as of the summer of 1876, the sultan already had invested £800,000 in their construction and was having trouble meeting the remaining payments. The vessels, not referred to by name in the correspondence, most likely were the 5,350-ton sister ships *Messudieh* and *Memduhieh* (launched in 1875 and 1876, respectively) and the 4,200-ton *Nussratieh*, still under construction as of 1877. All were eventually delivered to the Turkish navy (*Almanach für S.M. Kriegs-Marine* [1877], 92).

22. Höbelt, "Die Marine," 725, 733n. On the completion of the railway, see Igor Karaman, "Die Industrialisierung des bürgerlichen Kroatiens und ihre wirtschaftliche Infrastruktur bis zum Ersten Weltkrieg," 254. In *StPD*, IX (22 May 1876), 21, Pöck comments on the new Pola railway and its effect on the cost of transporting coal.

23. This and the following paragraphs are based upon Bayer von Bayersburg, *Auf weitere Fahrt*, 50–70.

24. The most extensive account of the expedition is Payer's own *Die österreichisch-ungarische Nordpol-Expedition in den Jahren 1872–1874;* for briefer accounts, see Günther Hamann, "Die österreichische Kriegsmarine im Dienste der Wissenschaften," 75–77; and Sokol, *Des Kaisers Seemacht*, 133–36. The expedition was not an official undertaking of the Austro-Hungarian government, nor was the *Admiral Tegetthoff* a Habsburg naval vessel. The entire operation was funded by private benefactors; the sloop was constructed in Bremerhaven, Germany, the port of departure of the expedition.

25. Account of Lissa by Admiral Philippe-Victor Touchard, and manuscript on tactics by Admiral Jean-Pierre-Edmond Jurien de Gravière, both quoted in Ropp, *The Development of a Modern Navy*, 13.

26. G. A. Ballard, *The Black Battlefleet*, 100–113, discusses the short life of the *Captain*. The ship was built between January 1867 and January 1870.

27. Olaf Richard Wulff, *Die österreichisch-ungarische Donauflottille im Weltkrieg 1914–1918*, 11; Rauchensteiner, "Austro-Hungarian Warships on the Danube," 158.

28. Ballard, *Black Battlefleet*, 69, 230.

29. Schöndorfer, "Kriegsschiffbau," 28; *Jahrbuch der k.k. Kriegsmarine* (1871), 74. Sterneck to sister, at sea, 8 December 1869, Sterneck, *Erinnerungen,* 164, refers to the problems of the Putzer ironworks of Styria, supplier of much of the armor for Austria's older ironclads.

30. Schöndorfer, "Kriegsschiffbau," 28. Information on the construction starts, launching, and completion of vessels is often imprecise or conflicting; in most cases the dates cited are from Bilzer, "Die Schiffe und Fahrzeuge der k.(u.)k. Kriegsmarine."

31. Ernesto Gellner and Paolo Valentini claim that the *Custoza,* laid down in August 1869 at the San Rocco yard of Stabilimento Tecnico Triestino, was the first warship built outside of Britain with a double iron hull (*San Rocco: Storia di un cantiere navale,* 28). Erich Gröner indicates that the North German Confederation's armored frigate *Friedrich Karl,* completed in 1867 by the Forges et Chantiers de la Mediterranée in La Seyne (Toulon), had a double iron hull (*Die deutschen Kriegsschiffe 1815–1945,* 1:25).

32. Eight of Britain's eighteen casemate ships had double-decked casemates like the *Custoza* and *Erzherzog Albrecht;* the first was the *Audacious,* completed in September 1870. See Ballard, *Black Battlefleet,* 230, 240. On the subject of building materials, "all-iron construction" at this stage did not mean that no wood was used at all. For example, every one of the British navy's "all-iron" armored warships of the 1860s and 1870s had a layer of teak—sometimes as thick as 20 inches—sandwiched between its iron hull and armor plating.

33. Schöndorfer, "Kriegsschiffbau," 28–29; *Jahresbericht der k.k. Kriegsmarine* (1875), 17–18. Delays were worse on the *Custoza,* the first larger warship ever built by the Stabilimento Tecnico Triestino; it was laid down in August 1869 but not launched until August 1872. The more experienced Navale Adriatico built the shell of the *Erzherzog Albrecht* much faster, between November 1869 and April 1872.

34. The initial outlay for the "reconstruction" projects passed without debate; see *StPD,* VI (5 May 1873), 102–3. For Herbst's comments, see ibid., VII (15 May 1874), 40–42. Expenditure for British armor for the *Prinz Eugen* is mentioned in ibid., VII (15 May 1874), 59; and ibid., IX (22 May 1876), 25. The new *Prinz Eugen* was built at the Pola Arsenal, its sister ships at the San Rocco yard of Stabilimento Tecnico Triestino. The navy initially used the wooden hulk of the original *Prinz Eugen* as an artillery school ship in Pola; the Stabilimento Tecnico disposed of the hulks of the other two vessels. See *Jahrbuch der k.k. Kriegsmarine* (1875), 97, 116. In a slight name change, the reincarnation of the *Juan d'Austria* was christened *Don Juan d'Austria.*

35. The three vessels were considerably smaller than most other casemate ships. The British had one casemate ship of only 3,200 tons, but their other seventeen displaced 3,800 tons or more. See Ballard, *The Black Battlefleet,* 241. The *Kaiser Max,* the fastest of the trio, had a top speed of 13.43 knots. See Franz F. Bilzer, "Schiffstypenblatt S.M.S. *Kaiser Max," Marine—Gestern, Heute* 11 (1984): 64.

36. The *Tegetthoff,* launched in October 1878, registered a top speed of 14.37 knots in its trials in October 1881. See Franz F. Bilzer, "Schiffstypenblatt S.M.S. *Tegetthoff," Marine—Gestern, Heute* 13 (1986): 34–35; and Schöndorfer, "Kriegsschiffbau," 30–31. The largest casemate ships ever built were the three 9,600-ton vessels of the French *Dévastation* class (1876–79).

37. Ropp, *The Development of a Modern Navy,* 36–37.

38. *Jahrbuch der k.k. Kriegsmarine* (1872), 90, 97.

39. Alexander Dorn, *Kriegsmarine und Volkswirthschaft in Oesterreich-Ungarn,* 96; *Jahrbuch der k.k. Kriegsmarine* (1874), 168.

40. The *Radetzky* was completed in 1873, *Laudon* in 1874. The others, with years of completion, were the corvettes *Fasana* (1871), *Zrinyi* (1871), *Frundsberg* (1873), *Aurora* (1874), *Donau* (1875), and *Saida* (1879) and the gunboats *Albatros* (1874) and *Nautilus* (1874).

41. Casali and Cattaruzza, *Sotto i mari del mondo*, 6–7, 12–13. France introduced Whitehead torpedoes in its navy in 1872, followed by Germany (1873), Italy (1873), and Russia (1876).

42. Obry's gyroscope was in use by the mid-1890s; Archduke Francis Ferdinand referred to the gyroscope in a report of May 1898. Obry entered the navy in 1885 and served with the navy's technical committee in Pola until his retirement in February 1896, rising to the rank of *Konstruktionszeichner 1. Klasse*. See Gilbert von Randich, "Die Besichtigung Polas im Mai 1898 durch Erzherzog Franz Ferdinand von Österreich-Este," 91, 94.

43. Ropp, *The Development of a Modern Navy*, 112, 134, 136, and passim.

44. Schöndorfer, "Kriegsschiffbau," 32. *Torpedoboot I* displaced just 7.5 tons and, at 12 knots, was relatively slow. Most sources refer to the much larger British *Lightning*, completed by Thornycroft in 1877, as the first torpedo boat ever built.

45. Luppis, ennobled by Francis Joseph as "Ritter von Rammer" in 1869, sold his share of the torpedo enterprise to Whitehead before the bankruptcy of the Stabilimento Tecnico Fiume; he retired to Milan, where he died in 1875. See Casali and Cattaruzza, *Sotto i mari del mondo*, 12–13, 22, 25.

46. Giovanni Gerolimi, *Cantiere Riuniti dell'Adriatico: Origini e sviluppo 1857–1907–1957*, 18. *Jahresbericht der k.k. Kriegsmarine* (1878), 32; and ibid. (1880), 28, refer to contracts with the firm "Ex Navale Adriatico" for replacement boilers for four navy steamers.

47. Giorgio Giorgerini, *Almanacco storico delle navi militare italiane: La Marina e le sue navi dal 1861 al 1975*, 220–23, 706–7; Bargoni, *Le prime navi di linea*, passim. The *Palestro* (II) and *Principe Amadeo*, completed in 1874 and 1875, respectively, each had a heavily armored central battery, but their hulls had no embrasures, and none of their guns could fire forward or aft. Italy was not the only naval power to build this sort of casemate ship; some of Britain's eighteen "central battery ships" also had no heavy guns capable of firing to the bow or stern.

48. At the nominal exchange rate of 2.5 lire = 1 gulden, the Italian navy budget of 1871 was worth just over 10.7 million gulden, compared to Tegetthoff's last budget of 11 million. Italian figure from Lucio Ceva, *Le forze armate*, 103. On the fortification proposal, see Baratelli, *La marina militare italiana*, 237–38.

49. Giorgerini, *Almanacco*, 198–99. For the sake of simplicity, "barbette" will be rendered as "turret" in all subsequent discussion of naval technology. The British *Devastation*, a 9,200-ton twin-turreted ironclad (laid down in November 1869, completed in April 1873) was the first true seagoing warship to be built with no masts or yards. See Ballard, *The Black Battlefleet*, 224–27.

50. See Sullivan, "A Fleet in Being," 110.

51. Giorgerini, *Almanacco*, 198–99; Franco Bargoni, *Corazzate italiane classi Duilio - Italia - Ruggiero di Lauria (1880–1892)*, 4–5. The *Duilio*'s engines were built by Penn and Sons, the *Dandolo*'s by Maudsley and Sons, both of London. Their guns, considered experimental by the British navy, were manufactured by Armstrong. In comparison, the heaviest armaments of any British pre-dreadnought were the 16.5-inch guns of the *Benbow* (1885). See Marder, *The Anatomy of British Sea Power*, 5.

52. The cost of the two ships ultimately surpassed original estimates by 43 percent. See Baratelli, *La marina militare italiana*, 176-77.

53. Bargoni, *Corazzate italiane (1880-1892)*, 26-27. The Italian policy of sacrificing armor for the sake of speed, referred to by Sullivan, "A Fleet in Being," 111, began with the *Italia* and *Lepanto*. See Ceva, *Le forze armate*, 101.

54. Baratelli, *La marina militare italiana*, 179-80. Heinrich von Haymerle (ambassador) to Andrássy, Rome, 16 Mar. 1877, HHSA, AR, F 44 - Marinewesen, Carton 9: Varia 2/22, conveys the first detailed account of Brin's fleet plan to Vienna. The Italians tried to sell thirty-three obsolete warships (seven of the original ironclads plus twenty-six unarmored vessels); they hoped to raise six million lire from the sales, but ultimately most of the warships were sold for scrap or broken up by the navy itself. See Alois von Haymerle, "Italicae Res," 105-6.

55. The *Cristoforo Colombo*, built in 1873-76, was the first Italian composite ship and the first larger vessel constructed in the Venice Arsenal since the 1850s, when the facility was still in Austrian hands. See Giorgerini, *Almanacco*, 235. Because the Italians had so many more wooden steamers left over from the 1860s, they never built as many composite ships as the Austrians.

56. The torpedo boat *Nibbio* entered Italian service in 1881. See Giorgerini, *Almanacco*, 379.

57. Figures from Ceva, *Le forze armate*, 103.

58. Sterneck to sister, Pola, 20 August 1878, Sterneck, *Erinnerungen*, 209.

59. The elections to the Austrian House of Representatives, held in the spring of 1879, left the German liberals with one hundred seventy seats, seven short of a majority. They managed to dominate the Austrian Delegation for the ensuing debate over the 1880 budget only by piecing together a fragile coalition with splinter groups such as the Vienna Democrats and the Styrian Progressive Party. This alignment soon gave way to conservative rule under Taaffe's "Iron Ring." See Reiter, "Entwicklung," 80; Krenslehner, "Kriegsmarine als wirtschaftlicher Faktor," 76-77.

60. Italian budget figures from Ceva, *Le forze armate*, 103.

61. *StPD*, X (4 June 1878), 271-77. The smaller *Drache* would have been a "citadel ship," a variation of casemate ship pioneered by the French navy.

62. *StPD*, XI (21 November 1878), 24-39, 153.

63. *StPD*, XII (6 February 1880), 83-85, 111.

64. Count Alois Károlyi (ambassador) to Min. des Äussern, London, 31 May 1879; Károlyi to Min. des Äussern, London, 9 August 1879; Pöck to Min. des Äussern, Vienna, 14 August 1879; all in HHSA, AR, F44 - Marinewesen, Carton 8: Varia 1/16.

65. Baratelli, *La marina militare italiana*, 235.

66. Schöndorfer, "Kriegsschiffbau," 32.

67. Regarding the construction of the *Zara*, the *Jahresbericht der k.k. Kriegsmarine* (1879), 25, notes that it involved the first "large-scale" use of "domestic Bessemer steel." Romako's design followed the model of the German navy's 1,000-ton *Zieten*, built by the Thames Iron Works of London in 1875-76. See Gröner, *Die deutschen Kriegsschiffe*, 1:116-17.

68. Schöndorfer, "Kriegsschiffbau," 32. In 1882 Italy had eight torpedo boats, all built by the British firms of Thornycroft and Yarrow. See Giorgerini, *Almanacco*, 418-19.

69. On the strike of 1883, see Marina Cattaruzza, "'Organisierter Konflikt' und 'Direkte Aktion': Zwei Formen des Arbeiterkampfes am Beispiel der Werftarbeiterstreiks in

CHAPTER 2

Hamburg und Triest (1880-1914)," 347. Employment figures for Stabilimento Tecnico Triestino for 1871 cited in Babudieri, *Squeri e cantiere*, 21; for 1882 in Paolo Sema, *Il Cantiere San Rocco: Lavoro e lotta operaia, 1858-1982*, 18.

70. *Feldmarschalleutnant* Baron Daniel Salis-Soglio, future inspector-general of engineers, represented Archduke William at some of the committee's sessions. Reiter, "Entwicklung," 63.

71. Reiter, "Entwicklung," 67.

72. Quoted in ibid., 66.

73. Ibid., 64-66.

74. Albrecht's concluding remarks, here and below, are quoted from KA, KM/MS, Präs. 1880, I 4/5, 1386, in both Reiter, "Entwicklung," 68-70, and Krenslehner, "Kriegsmarine als wirtschaftlicher Faktor," 80.

75. HHSA, PA, XL, Carton 292: Gemeinsamer Ministerrat, Protokolle (hereafter cited as GMR) 272 (13 September 1880) and 273 (20 September 1880).

76. *StPD*, XIII (9 November 1880), 193-94, indicates that the navy was budgeted a sum of 9.1 million, ultimately raised to 9.5 million by a supplementary grant; see ibid., XIV (12 November 1881), 250-51.

77. Pöck *Vortrag* to Francis Joseph, Vienna, 28 February 1881, with supplementary "Denkschrift über Ersatz und Instandhaltung des Flottenmateriales während der Periode 1882-1889," HHSA, PA, I, Carton 560, Liasse V: Militaria, fols. 549-73. In ibid., fols. 572-73, Pöck anticipates the alternative of a timetable of ten rather than eight years.

78. Cabinet Protocol, Vienna, 11 May 1881, ibid., fols. 579-88.

79. HHSA, PA, XL, Carton 292: GMR 284 (19 September 1881).

80. Ibid., GMR 287 (21 September 1881).

81. *StPD*, XIV (12 November 1881), 89-90. Ironically, the speech was Teuschl's last in support of the fleet. In December 1881, he accompanied a delegation from the Trieste Chamber of Commerce to an audience with Francis Joseph; at the close of their meeting, the emperor noted that "the interests of the city of Trieste are close to my heart" but also observed that the petitioners were "in opposition to my [i.e., Taaffe's] government." Teuschl, a member of the "Club of the United Left," took the reproach much harder than his colleagues, resigning his seat in parliament in January 1882. See Gustav Kolmer, *Parlament und Verfassung in Österreich*, 3:210.

82. *StPD*, VII (15 May 1874), 46.

83. In the spring of 1880, the Italian Chamber of Deputies limited the size of new warships to 10,000 tons, a restriction the navy ultimately ignored. See Baratelli, *La marina militare italiana*, 184. The new ships (laid down in August 1881, December 1881, and January 1882) displaced just over 11,200 tons. Like the *Italia* and *Lepanto*, they carried a primary armament of four 17-inch guns, paired in two turrets. As in the past, their Italian builders imported all vital materials from Britain. See Bargoni, *Corazzate italiane (1880-1892)*, 57-58.

84. Figures on officer corps from *Militär-Schematismus des österreichischen Kaiserthums*, 1850 and 1871, and *Rangs- und Eintheilungsliste der k.k. Kriegsmarine* (1883). Numbers include all ranks from ensign (*Fähnrich*) through admiral.

85. For example, there were only twenty-two one-year volunteers serving in the navy in 1876. They included a dozen merchant seamen, five "technicians," three medical students, and two engineering students. Figures from *Jahresbericht der k.k. Kriegsmarine* (1876).

86. Starting in 1838, it had been possible for a young man to become a cadet by taking a number of specialized courses and passing examinations. Between 1848 and 1871, the navy's educational establishments graduated 293 cadets, while 399 became cadets after receiving civilian schooling. Under Pöck the academy graduated another 293 cadets, the classes of 1872 through 1883, while only 22 were commissioned from civilian schools, all in the years 1872–74. See Salcher, *Marine-Akademie,* 65–67.

87. Of the 293 navy-educated cadets entering service in the years 1848–71, 53 (18 percent) resigned from the corps before reaching the rank of ensign. Of the 293 academy cadets from 1872–83, only 22 (7.5 percent) quit before making ensign. See Salcher, *Marine-Akademie,* 66–67.

88. In an effort to remedy this problem, rival naval academies at Genoa and Naples were replaced in 1881 by a single school at La Spezia. See Baratelli, *La marina militare italiana,* 186–91.

89. The naval academy first introduced Hungarian in 1869 as an elective. See Salcher, *Marine-Akademie,* 39–40. The revised course of study also eliminated the required Roman Catholic religious instruction. Henceforth, religious education was limited to Sunday school and, for the first time, non-Catholic students (almost all of whom were from the Hungarian half of the monarchy) were given the opportunity to attend services and receive instruction in their own religion. See ibid., 38. The navy traditionally was more overwhelmingly Catholic than the Habsburg army, but as early as 1873–74, 10 percent (11 of 110) of the students at the naval academy were Protestant (*Jahrbuch der k.k. Kriegsmarine* [1875], 88).

90. Nicholas Horthy [Miklós Horthy de Nagybánya], *Memoirs,* 13, 28. Horthy was the second of his family to enter the navy. His older brother, Béla (1862–1880), died of injuries suffered in a gunnery accident on the eve of his graduation from the academy. See ibid., 12, and Edgar von Schmidt-Pauli, *Nikolaus von Horthy: Admiral, Volksheld und Reichsverweser,* 42–43.

91. Bayer von Bayersburg, *Auf weiter Fahrt,* 70–76. On the voyage of the *Friedrich,* see Alfred von Koudelka, *Denn Österreich lag einst am Meer: Das Leben des Admirals Freiherr von Koudelka,* 13–20.

92. Bayer von Bayersburg, *Auf weiter Fahrt,* 76–80; and Hamann, "Die österreichische Kriegsmarine im Dienste der Wissenschaften," 77. The *Pola,* an unarmed fully rigged propeller steamer displacing 930 tons, was built in the Pola Arsenal during the years 1869–71.

93. See chart in Lo Giudice, *Canale di Suez,* 188.

94. On the construction of the Budapest-Rijeka line, see Miroslava Despot, *Industrija Gradanske Hrvatske, 1860–1873,* 33.

95. Fulvio Babudieri, *Industrie, commerci e navigazione a Trieste e nella regione Giulia,* 193.

96. Heinz Ploček and Franz Juba, "Geschichte der ungarischen Reederei Adria," 17–18.

97. *Fünfundsiebzig Jahre österreichischer Lloyd,* 59–60.

98. Lo Giudice, *Canale di Suez,* 180.

99. See Baratelli, *La marina militare italiana,* 200–202, 204–9. In recognition of the growing volume of Italian immigration to South America, the Italian navy maintained a permanent presence in the waters off Argentina and Uruguay.

100. Andrássy to Count Zalusky (Habsburg chargé in Rome), Vienna, 15 December 1871, HHSA, PA, XI, Carton 79: Kgr. Italien, Weisungen 1871, fol. 167. The italicized words were added by Andrássy in the margin of the original document.

101. Baratelli, *La marina militare italiana,* 170. For a text of the agreements signed by the three emperors, see F. R. Bridge, *The Habsburg Monarchy among the Great Powers, 1815–1918,* 381–82.

102. Ropp, *The Development of a Modern Navy,* 80.

103. Baratelli, *La marina militare italiana,* 170.

104. Cedric J. Lowe and Frank Marzari, *Italian Foreign Policy, 1870–1940,* 3, treat 1876 as a sort of watershed, contending that Visconti Venosta and the conservatives of the founders' generation did not consider Italy to be a bona fide great power. The Right believed that unity had been achieved by fortuitous circumstances and shrewd diplomacy in the years following the Crimean War, and could just as easily be undone by risky policies and bad judgment.

105. Sokol, *Des Kaisers Seemacht,* 123-25; Rauchensteiner, "Austro-Hungarian Warships on the Danube," 158. According to the *Jahresbericht der k.k. Kriegsmarine* (1878), 23, the navy removed the mines from Klek harbor in January 1879.

106. Sterneck to Richard Sterneck (nephew), Pola, 30 August 1878, Sterneck, *Erinnerungen,* 209-10.

107. Rothenberg, *The Army of Francis Joseph,* 105-6; Reiter, "Entwicklung," 57.

108. Sokol, *Des Kaisers Seemacht,* 128-29.

109. Bayer von Bayersburg, *Österreichs Admirale,* 103; Sokol, *Des Kaisers Seemacht,* 129.

110. Pöck to Francis Joseph, Vienna, 19 March 1880, quoted in Reiter, "Entwicklung," 62.

111. Sullivan, "A Fleet in Being," 110.

112. F. R. Bridge, *From Sadowa to Sarajevo: The Foreign Policy of Austria-Hungary, 1866–1914,* 131.

113. Ibid., 131-32.

114. For a text of the Triple Alliance treaty of 20 May 1882 and notes of 28 May 1882, see Bridge, *The Habsburg Monarchy,* 387–88.

115. Bridge, *Sadowa to Sarajevo,* 132.

116. Baratelli, *La marina militare italiana,* 235.

CHAPTER 3 ≋≋≋≋≋

A DECADE OF UNCERTAINTY

In the decade following the conclusion of the Triple Alliance, the doubts that had plagued the navy during the first fifteen years of the Dual Monarchy gave way to even greater uncertainties. The most obvious questions concerned the strategic role that the fleet would have with a friendly Italy on the other side of the Adriatic. As the navy wrestled with the problem of its overall raison d'être, the radical ideas of the French *Jeune Ecole* revolutionized the strategy and tactics of naval warfare, presenting fresh opportunities but also causing chaos that would spill over into the area of matériel. The navy leadership also faced political uncertainties, both within the service and in its relations with the government—or governments—of the Dual Monarchy. It did not help matters that, as time went on, the Austro-Hungarian relationship did not improve but became more contentious, with the navy becoming one of many pawns in the ongoing struggle between Vienna and Budapest.

FROM PÖCK TO STERNECK:
A CHANGING OF THE GUARD (1882–83)

After the conclusion of the Triple Alliance, it became more difficult than ever for Pöck to secure the funding necessary to keep the navy in fighting shape and abreast of the latest technological developments. In his last years at the helm, however, the budget battles tended to be decided in the council of ministers rather than by the Delegations, a reflection of the extent to which the defeat of the German liberals in the Austrian elections of 1879 and the onset of Taaffe's "Iron Ring" changed the tone of politics not just for the Austrian half of the Dual Monarchy but for the empire as a whole. The new minister-president collaborated with the emperor and with his Hungarian counterpart, Count Kálmán Tisza, to assure that thorny issues such as the military and naval budgets would be resolved in the council before the figures were presented to the Delegations.[1]

Pöck's luck did not change dramatically under the new system, thanks mainly to Hungarian opposition. Even though Francis Joseph and the three joint Austro-Hungarian ministers had approved his fleet plan of 1881 with little debate, the appropriations for new warship construction continued to meet with fierce resistance from Tisza's finance minister, Count Szápáry. The Delegations granted the navy 10.3 million gulden for 1883 and 10.2 million for the following year, each time including money for the *Salamander*'s replacement, to be built in the Pola Arsenal. These sums were so small, though, that the keel of the new warship could not be laid until January 1884, two years and two months after the delegates first voted to fund the project. The "rebuilding" of the *Erzherzog Ferdinand Max*, first funded in the budget for 1883, was also delayed.[2]

In the meantime, in the spring of 1883, Pöck had to decommission the obsolete *Salamander*. In addition to being unseaworthy, the old wooden-hulled armored frigate was also uninhabitable thanks to an infestation of Egyptian cockroaches, a legacy of its last call at Alexandria. The navy's other wooden-hulled ironclads were also deteriorating at an alarming pace and could only be saved by extensive overhaul. In 1880–81 the engineers in the Pola Arsenal had pulled off much of the *Lissa*'s armor in order to replace rotted sections of its wooden hull; in 1881–82 the *Habsburg* underwent similar radical surgery.[3] In taking stock of the battleships that would hold up in combat in case of war, Pöck could really only count the *Tegetthoff* and the five other iron- or iron-and-steel-hulled casemate ships.

Pöck's last hurrah came in September 1882, when Francis Joseph visited Pola for the commissioning of the *Tegetthoff*. During his inspection tour, the emperor boarded the new torpedo ship *Zara* to watch an attack by torpedo boats on the hulk of an old wooden schooner. Before returning to Vienna, he promoted Pöck to full admiral, making him only the second man ever to achieve that rank.[4] Within weeks Pöck had secured the advancement of his second in command, Millosicz, to vice admiral and his protégé Pitner, head of the *Marinesektion*'s presidial (formerly central) chancellery, to rear admiral.[5] To the end,

Pöck never failed to reward the loyal members of his clique within the officer corps.

The torpedo exercises of 1882 were more than just a show for the emperor. Such maneuvers, though modest, were important to the evolution of the navy's use of the torpedo, a weapon all the more vital since Archduke Albrecht and the committee of inquiry had called for the development of tactics for a defensive "little war" in the Adriatic. From a tactical viewpoint, the exercises of the following year were the most innovative to date. Whereas earlier torpedo maneuvers had employed only the torpedo ships and flotillas of torpedo boats, in 1883 three battleships were also involved. A torpedo boat steamed out alongside a battleship, out of sight of the "enemy" vessel. The battleship then fired away with its heavy guns, laying down a carpet of smoke through which the boat then dashed to fire its torpedoes, at close range, into its blinded prey.[6] It was a simple exercise, but it addressed vexing tactical questions: heretofore, there were no satisfactory theories of how to use torpedo boats in operations with battleships, and no one had been able to solve the problem of how to get boats close enough to deliver their torpedoes at an enemy warship with superior guns.

Unfortunately, successes in such experiments were of little solace to Pöck. Exasperated by a dozen years of bitter political infighting and beset by problems that only more money could solve, the admiral by the autumn of 1883 was on the brink of exhaustion. A particularly bitter disappointment came in late September when Francis Joseph sided with Tisza against Pöck as the council of ministers trimmed the navy estimates before the *Marinekommandant* presented them to the Delegations.[7] To be truly effective, a Habsburg navy commander had to have the respect of the army hierarchy and the politicians, enjoy consistent support from the crown, and above all have a reasonably united officer corps behind him. Tegetthoff had been successful in all of these areas, Pöck in none. The burden of failure finally took its toll. In early November, during the session of the Delegations in Vienna, the *Marinekommandant* suffered a nervous breakdown and was ordered to resign his commission; death would cut short his retirement only ten months later. On the morning of 13 November 1883, Francis Joseph summoned to the Hofburg Pöck's most bitter enemy, Max von Sterneck, and appointed him *Marinekommandant* and chief of the *Marinesektion,* with a promotion to vice admiral.[8]

At fifty-four, Sterneck was no longer in his prime; indeed, he was older at the time of his appointment than any entering navy commander in the past three decades. He had not commanded a ship at sea since leading the active squadron in 1874 and 1875, and for the past eight years he had languished in the post of arsenal commander at Pola. But within the corps, he was best remembered as Tegetthoff's flag captain at the Battle of Lissa and as the closest friend and collaborator of Austria's late, great naval hero. From the start, he commanded respect both within the service and in the political arena in a way Pöck never had. Within the navy, there was reason to hope for a brighter future.

THE NAVY UNDER STERNECK:
PERSONNEL, POLICIES, AND POLITICS (1883–92)

After taking command, Sterneck placed the highest priority on the improvement of morale within the officer corps. He put an end to the capricious promotion policies of the Pöck era and implemented a rigid system of advancement by seniority, a policy that in the long run produced an aging leadership. In the short term, however, the effects were positive, because without the blatant favoritism of the past, the battle lines of the multigenerational cliques that had divided the officer corps since the 1850s gradually eroded. In theory his policy eliminated all extraordinary merit promotions, but in this regard Sterneck's own hands were not completely tied because in many cases he could grant rapid promotions to deserving officers under the guise of rectifying the earlier neglect of their seniority. In any event, discontent within the corps declined markedly. In the first dozen years of Sterneck's command, fewer than 5 percent of naval academy graduates resigned their commissions before being promoted to ensign. Under Pöck the attrition rate was 7.5 percent, and it had been even higher in earlier years.[9]

Despite his commitment to break with the policies of his predecessor, when it came to making important appointments, Sterneck, too, did not neglect old friends or younger officers who, like himself, had been outsiders during the Pöck era. Rear Admiral Eberan von Eberhorst, his close friend and academy classmate (class of 1847), became second in command (Stellvertreter) in the Marinesektion, replacing Millosicz, who was ordered to retire along with Pöck. Captain Hermann von Spaun, his aide at Lissa in 1866, was relieved of the duties of personal adjutant to the Archduke Charles Stephen, which he had discharged since returning from the naval attaché's post in London in 1879; a grateful Spaun thereafter enjoyed the best seagoing commands. Sterneck likewise rewarded the long-suffering Rudolf Berghofer; after spending fifteen years at the same grade of lieutenant, Berghofer was promoted four times in twelve years, making it to rear admiral in 1896. Sterneck was also reasonably charitable toward his leading potential adversary. Pöck's protégé Pitner, ousted from his desk job at the *Marinesektion,* was placated with squadron commands in 1884 and 1885. He subsequently received the navy's top consolation prize, the post of harbor admiral in Pola, which he held from 1886 until his retirement in 1898.[10]

In the summer of 1884, Sterneck initiated a reform of the administrative structure by proposing the revival of the post of commander's adjutant (*Marinekommandoadjutant*), left vacant since he had held it himself under Tegetthoff. He also suggested the formation of an admiralty staff (*Admiralstab*), but Francis Joseph questioned the wisdom of creating a naval equivalent of the army General Staff. In August 1885, the emperor approved a revised structure for the *Marinesektion* that included a new operations chancellery (*Operationskanzlei*) alongside the existing presidial chancellery; it assumed the tasks that Sterneck had intended for his proposed admiralty staff but would have none of the status. In the new scheme, the commander's adjutant doubled as head of the operations chancellery. Unlike the position Sterneck had held before 1871—when he reported directly to Tegetthoff—the revived post was placed under the second in command (*Stellvertreter*) of the *Marinesektion.* After 1885 the adjutant's position changed hands frequently and proved not to be a stepping stone to higher office. Sterneck's reformed administration also included a new technical committee to be made up of officers at Pola. The *Marinesektion*'s second staff office (*II. Geschäftsgruppe*), in charge of all technical matters since Tegetthoff's time, retained the ultimate responsibility in all questions of shipbuilding, machinery, and armaments.[11]

In the area of enlisted personnel, Sterneck benefited from the fact that Pöck had secured a lengthening of the term of service for seamen from three to four years, effective in 1882. Under the military law of 1868, common sailors, like soldiers, had served three years on active duty followed by a reserve obligation of seven years; the revised conditions included a commitment of only five years in the reserves following the longer term of active duty. In 1883, when the expansion of the army from 80 to 102 regiments necessitated a revision of the territorial recruiting districts (*Ergänzungsbezirke*), the navy received exclusive rights to coastal areas of Istria, Croatia, and Dalmatia. The military law of 1889 subsequently confirmed these changes and also created a *Seewehr* as the naval equivalent of the Austrian *Landwehr* and Hungarian *Honvéd*. Former sailors were to be liable for three years of *Seewehr* duty, bringing their total obligation to twelve years, the same as the army service liability.[12] The navy reserves and *Seewehr* were important only as pools of manpower in case of war; unlike their army counterparts, they were rarely called upon to participate in training exercises.[13]

The additional year of active duty did not make the navy unattractive as an alternative to the army. Figures from 1887, the first year for which official statistics were tabulated, reveal that significant numbers of men from the interior of the Dual Monarchy opted to fulfill their service obligations in the navy. Of the 7,000 seamen on active duty and 10,000 on the reserve rolls, 7.7 percent were German Austrian, 5 percent Magyar, and 3.1 percent Czech or Slovak, joined by a scattering of Poles, Romanians, and Ruthenians. The Adriatic littoral naturally still produced the majority of seamen: 46.5 percent were Croatian, 33.4 percent Italian, and 3.9 percent Slovene. Throughout the Sterneck era, the annual reenlistment rate for common seamen consistently topped 5 percent, while an average of less than 1 percent were held over for disciplinary reasons beyond the required four years of active duty.[14]

Under Sterneck the navy's growing number of officers and seamen spent more time aboard ship, thanks to a new policy that called for several battleships, the newest cruisers, and all of the torpedo boats to be activated for extensive maneuvers in the Adriatic during the summer months. During the remainder of the year, active vessels were limited to a division consisting of a composite frigate (the *Radetzky* or *Laudon*) and a few other smaller unarmored ships. The new timetable represented a dramatic break from the rhythm of past years. From 1870 through 1883, the navy more often than not (in 106 months out of 168) had just one armored warship in service; in 32 months Pöck had two ironclads in active commission, and in 9 months none at all. Only on rare occasions—the Bosnian crisis of 1878, the summer maneuvers of 1883— did the navy have three battleships in service at the same time, just 21 months in all. Pöck usually activated the newest or newly renovated warships, but owing to the tight budget some vessels were laid up in reserve for extended periods of time between their sea trials and first tour of duty. The worst example was the *Erzherzog Albrecht,* commissioned in 1875 but not placed in active service until the spring of 1881.[15]

In 1884 the summer squadron in the Adriatic included six of the fleet's ten armored warships. They were joined by six torpedo boats, which repeated the same exercises that were first tried the previous year off Pola, only this time on the open sea. The fleet separated into two divisions of three battleships, each with a torpedo boat alongside. Steaming in parallel lines two thousand yards apart, the battleships squared off for an artillery duel and, once the requisite smokescreens were laid, the torpedo boats carried out their simulated attacks on the opposing division. The maneuvers made a strong impression on a group of observers from the French navy, confirming the Austrian position in the forefront of the development of torpedo tactics.[16]

The summer exercises of 1884 also impressed Francis Joseph, who spent three days aboard the imperial yacht *Miramar* in his longest visit thus far with the fleet. Afterward the emperor expressed his satisfaction that "the spirit of Tegetthoff lives on undiminished" in the navy.[17] During 1884 Sterneck put more ships in service and more men to sea than the navy had in any year since the war of 1866. In addition to the squadron in the Adriatic, he sent an unprecedented five vessels on overseas missions. The corvette *Helgoland* visited West and South Africa, returning to Pola later in the year. The corvette *Frundsberg* cruised through the Suez Canal to the Red Sea and East Africa, and the corvette *Aurora* visited several South American ports; both ships returned home in 1885. The corvette *Saida* also cruised South American waters before visiting South Africa and Australia on an extended mission that did not end until 1886. The gunboat *Nautilus* likewise spent the years 1884–86 on a lengthy cruise to East Asia.[18]

Four missions left Pola during 1885, all returning the following year: the corvette *Zrinyi* for the West Indies; the corvette *Donau* to the West Indies, New York, and a number of northern European ports; the *Frundsberg* to East Asia; and the gunboat *Albatros* to South America and West Africa. There were only two departures the next year, both for more extended cruises. The *Saida,* just back from the Pacific, visited South American and East African ports in 1886–87; highlights of the mission included a reception by the soon to be deposed Dom Pedro II in Brazil and the conclusion of a commercial treaty in Zanzibar with the local sultan. Meanwhile, the *Aurora* spent the years 1886–89 on a voyage to East Asia, studying the feasibility of extending Austro-Hungarian shipping lines beyond their terminus at Hong Kong. The Austrian Lloyd, which had been serving Singapore and Hong Kong with regularly scheduled steamers since 1880, subsequently extended its lines to Japan in 1891.[19] In 1887–88 the corvette *Fasana* visited the Persian Gulf, the East Indies, and East Asia, while the *Albatros* cruised to South America and South and West Africa. The busy *Saida* then visited the West Indies and North American waters in 1888–89, and in 1889–90 Captain Berghofer commanded the *Fasana* on the fourth circumnavigation of the globe by a Habsburg vessel. The same ship repeated the feat in a subsequent voyage in 1891–93. Meanwhile the *Aurora,* under Captain Count Rudolf Montecuccoli, cruised via the Suez Canal to East Africa and the Indian Ocean during 1889–90, and in 1890–91 the *Zrinyi* visited East Asia, the fifth warship assigned to the Orient in the past six years.

The large number of overseas missions and the larger squadrons in home waters allowed the navy to continue the practice of giving newly mustered out cadets immediate experience at sea. For its cruise of 1887–88, the *Fasana's* cadets included a Habsburg archduke, Leopold Ferdinand of the exiled Tuscan branch of the family, who had opted for a career in the navy. Unlike his cousin Charles Stephen, the maverick archduke at his own request attended the naval academy in Rijeka as a regular student. Francis Joseph, not keen on the idea of a Habsburg prince being treated as any other cadet, gave his permission only reluctantly. Leopold Ferdinand began his studies in 1883 and finished at the top of the class of 1887; he was the only Habsburg ever to graduate from the academy. The school's muster rolls likewise included relatively few names from the high nobility. According to Leopold Ferdinand, the emperor's unwillingness to see him attend the academy in the first place stemmed largely from a concern that his classmates, mostly boys with vastly inferior bloodlines, would be "totally unfit companions." The archduke alleged that Francis Joseph looked down on the navy officer corps as "a disgustingly democratic institution, largely composed of the prosperous sons of . . . the *haute bourgeoisie.*"[20] At the academy, roughly equal numbers of students were sons of navy personnel, army personnel, Habsburg civil servants, and private citizens, but by the mid-1890s the latter group accounted for a clear plurality of over 30 percent.[21]

Under Sterneck the academy graduated an average of twenty-five cadets per year, ultimately too few to serve the needs of an expanding navy. In 1885 the *Marinekommandant* revived the practice of taking on provisional sea cadets or *See-Aspiranten*, which Pöck had ended eleven years earlier. Once again *Gymnasium* and *Oberrealschule* graduates could become provisional cadets en route to commissions as regular cadets, then ensigns. By the turn of the century, the average academy graduate spent five years as a cadet before becoming an ensign; provisional sea cadets typically became cadets following two years of naval training and advanced to ensign after another four years. In the years 1885–95, just over 90 percent of all provisional sea cadets (107 of 118) stayed with the program and became ensigns. Their attrition rate was double that of academy graduates but still remarkably low; during this period they accounted for almost 30 percent of all men reaching ensign's rank.[22]

Even though the fleet of the late 1880s had two archdukes in its officer corps, and Sterneck enjoyed better relations with Francis Joseph than Pöck had, the navy still had no dedicated, highly placed ally within the imperial house willing to lend the sort of support that Ferdinand Max had provided in the 1850s and early 1860s. As a young man, Crown Prince Rudolph had been given an appropriate navy captain's rank to complement his titular status within the army officer corps. He was promoted rapidly to the top in both services, becoming a vice admiral (as well as *Feldmarschalleutnant*) by the time Sterneck took command.[23] After Count Karl Bombelles, a career navy officer, became Rudolph's chamberlain, there was at least some hope that the crown prince would take an interest in the fleet. Bombelles had been a close friend of Ferdinand Max, whom he accompanied to the New World as commander of the imperial Mexican guard; after the debacle in Mexico, he returned to the corps of sea officers and in 1882 was promoted to rear admiral.[24] But Rudolph did not share Bombelles's love of the sea. While he had a certain fascination with the life and career of his late uncle, counting among his most prized possessions the navy sabre of Ferdinand Max, there is little evidence that he ever took much of an interest in the fleet.[25] Voyages to Spain in 1879 and to the Levant in 1881 and 1885, all aboard the imperial yacht *Miramar*, were his only trips overseas. In the summer of 1887, he did not even attend the christening of the new battleship *Kronprinz Erzherzog Rudolf*, the replacement for the old *Salamander*. His death by suicide two years later, though a terrible personal tragedy for Francis Joseph and the imperial family, was not greatly mourned by the navy. Indeed, his passing paved the way for a future heir to the throne who would prove to be a much greater friend of the fleet.[26]

As the navy made its transition in leadership from Pöck to Sterneck, construction began on the pair of battleships ultimately named for the crown prince and his wife, the first armored warships laid down by Austria-Hungary since 1876: the 6,900-ton *Kronprinz Rudolf*, laid down at the Pola Arsenal in January 1884; and the 5,100-ton *Kronprinzessin Stephanie*, begun by the Stabilimento Tecnico Triestino in November 1884. Launched in 1887 and in service by 1889—just in time for Mayerling to make their names somewhat of an embarrassment— the two ships carried the heaviest primary armament ever for Habsburg warships: three 12-inch Krupp guns for *Rudolf* and two for *Stephanie*. Designed by Moriz Soyka, the navy's chief engineer since Romako's retirement in 1882, the ships were Austria-Hungary's first pre-dreadnoughts. The guns were mounted in turrets on deck rather than in a casemate and, reflecting the prevailing style of French battleships, each gun had its own turret.[27]

While Pöck's program of 1881 had provided for the construction of the *Kronprinz Rudolf* ("Ersatz Salamander") as a new replacement battleship, Sterneck built the new *Kronprinzessin Stephanie* with the money appropriated for the "rebuilding" of the old armored frigate *Erzherzog Ferdinand Max*. Pöck already had set the precedent for such sleight of hand in the mid-1870s, constructing the casemate ships *Kaiser Max, Don Juan d'Austria*, and *Prinz Eugen* under the guise of "rebuilding" old armored frigates bearing the same names. But in the earlier cases, the new ships had the same dimensions and tonnage as the old ones; furthermore, the old engines and armor plate had been salvaged and used in building the new vessels. In contrast, the *Kronprinzessin Stephanie* was built entirely from new material and, aside from having the same displacement (5,100 tons), bore no resemblance to the *Erzherzog Ferdinand Max*; indeed, the latter even remained afloat, anchored in Pola, while the *Stephanie* was under construction in Trieste! As a fig leaf, Sterneck had the *Stephanie* listed under the name *Ferdinand Max* in all official naval publications, at least during the first two years of its construction. Thereafter it appeared as the *"Ersatz Ferdinand Max"* and did not receive the name *Stephanie* until just before its launching in 1887.[28] During the previous year, Sterneck ordered the old *Erzherzog Ferdinand Max* converted to a stationary school ship; its sister ship *Habsburg* likewise left the battle fleet in 1886 but served for another dozen years as harbor watch in Pola. The two new battleships, along with the eight casemate ships and the *Habsburg*, left the navy with the eleven armored warships Pöck had called for in his fleet plan of 1881.

Early in his tenure, Sterneck's greatest contribution to the matériel of the fleet came in the dramatic expansion of the number of torpedo boats and other smaller vessels. Austria-Hungary had only ten torpedo boats when Sterneck took command, none of them displacing more than 47 tons; by 1891 he had added fifty-three more, ranging in size from 55 to 78 tons, along with six new *Torpedofahrzeuge* (destroyers) ranging from 350 to 540 tons. A pair of 450-ton river monitors, the *Körös* and *Szamos*, doubled the size of the Danube flotilla, but Sterneck's most significant additions were his cruisers. On the last day of 1885, the navy took possession of two modern light cruisers from the firm of Armstrong, Mitchell & Company of Newcastle. Originally classified as torpedo ships, the *Leopard* and *Panther*—at 1,500 tons apiece—were much larger than the four torpedo ships constructed under Romako's direction in the late 1870s; they also had no masts or yards. Sterneck praised the British design as "a triumph of naval technology" and had the Stabilimento Tecnico Triestino build the *Tiger*, a slightly larger copy, in the years 1886–88.[29] Officially the trio were added within the framework of the fleet plan of 1881, which had called for three new cruisers to be built by 1887. In 1887, four years after introducing the classifications "battleship" and "cruiser" for armored and unarmored warships, respectively, the navy officially redesignated all of its remaining wooden cruisers—primarily the composite ships—as "Schiffe für specielle Zwecke." Their "special purposes" included coastal defense, employment as school ships, and showing the flag overseas.[30]

New ships, of course, cost money, as did the more extensive operations. But in the area of securing funding, Sterneck from the start was successful, dramatically so when compared to Pöck. In November

1884, after meeting with the Delegations in Budapest, Sterneck could boast that the navy had found "much sympathy" with the politicians and would "no longer be treated as a stepchild." While he was critical of his own performance ("As a parliamentarian, I still have to overcome my stage fright"), the navy received eleven million gulden for 1885, the largest allocation in thirteen years.[31] Over the winter of 1884–85, Sterneck, an old bachelor and reluctant socialite, lobbied for the navy in the highest circles of Vienna. "Soirées, balls, and dinners are the order of the day, and I, poor devil, must attend in order to win delegates."[32] He developed a similar routine for the summer, frequenting the spas for friendly informal discussions with political and military figures.[33]

As the Delegations prepared to meet in Vienna in October 1885, the *Marinekommandant* confided to his nephew that he "hope[d] to find no spirited opposition" to his proposals.[34] Political and diplomatic developments worked in his favor, as another German liberal defeat in the Austrian elections of 1885 strengthened Taaffe's "Iron Ring." Although Sterneck personally disliked the minister-president, the conservative successes at the polls reduced the size of the antinavy faction in the *Reichsrat* and Austrian Delegation. Then, in September, a Balkan crisis over Bulgaria left the Austrians and especially the Hungarians in a more bellicose mood, willing to spend more on armaments. Sterneck received just under 11.2 million gulden for 1886, the highest navy appropriation since Ferdinand Max's last budget in 1864.[35]

In September 1886, just before the meeting of the Delegations, Sterneck presided at the dedication of the Tegetthoff monument in Vienna's Praterstern. The occasion, attended by all of the leading political and military figures of the Dual Monarchy, served as a timely reminder of the navy's success in battle twenty years earlier. During the ensuing budget debate, foreign minister Kálnoky actively pressured the Delegations for a higher naval outlay. The continuing Bulgarian crisis and disarray in the Hungarian ranks also worked to Sterneck's favor.[36] The appropriation of 13.2 million gulden for 1887 included a special credit for the construction projects then underway, most of it going to the *Tiger*, the destroyers, and torpedo boats.[37] It was the second highest allocation ever granted to the navy and would be its largest until 1895.

Sterneck could boast that the summer maneuvers of 1887, coinciding with the launching of the *Kronprinz Rudolf*, were attended not just by Francis Joseph but also by "representatives from both halves of the empire."[38] It did no harm to give the politicians direct exposure to the fleet; that autumn the Delegations once again posed no difficulties, voting the navy 13.1 million gulden for the following year, including a continuation of the special construction credit. The budget for 1888 also provided for moving expenses for the navy's administrative offices, which occupied new quarters in Vienna, the Maximilianhof in the Währingerstrasse. The impressive building, adjacent to the newly completed Votivkirche, would house the *Marinesektion* for the next two decades. Concurrent with the move, Sterneck sought to maintain the political momentum of his first years in office by having the *Marinesektion* actively propagandize for the navy's cause. Captain Josef von Lehnert, promoted in 1890 to head of the presidial chancellery, took charge of the effort to enlighten the public and the politicians on a variety of subjects: the navy's past history, its present needs, and the relative weakness of the Austro-Hungarian fleet compared to other navies.[39]

In October 1888, Francis Joseph promoted Sterneck to full admiral and sent him to Athens as his special envoy to the silver jubilee of King George of Greece.[40] Such honors raised Sterneck's spirits and his prestige, but in the years to come he could not sustain the momentum of his early political victories. In 1888 the Delegations were "again very gracious" but slashed his budget all the same; the appropriation for 1889 fell to 12.1 million gulden.[41] In the deliberations for 1890, Sterneck won praise for having accomplished so much as *Marinekommandant* without spending an inordinate amount of money; nevertheless, his reward took the form of another budget cut, to 11.4 million. His luck improved the following year, as a supplementary credit increased the outlay to just under 11.6 million.[42]

The new decade was to be an era of growing political instability for the Dual Monarchy; at the same time, the politicians grew less predictable in their attitude toward military and naval spending. The year 1890 marked the end of Kálmán Tisza's fifteen-year reign as minister-president of Hungary, and the Austrian *Reichsrat* elections of 1891 saw Karl Lueger's Christian Socials, German Nationalist groups, and the Young Czechs all make gains at the expense of Taaffe's "Iron Ring" while the German liberals held their ground. Taaffe survived for another two years, but his conservative coalition no longer held a majority of the seats in the *Reichsrat* and consequently was unable to control the Austrian contingent to the Delegations.[43]

Sterneck's success in the area of finances, while not spectacular, had been remarkable in that it came during a decade in which the Italian threat in the Adriatic was not a factor. It helped still more that the *Marinekommandant* was careful to make the most of every budget.[44] When domestic industry could not meet his needs for a reasonable price, Sterneck used less expensive foreign suppliers for raw materials and even entire ships. It was not a new policy. Tegetthoff had rearmed the entire battle fleet with British Armstrong cannon, and the casemate ships laid down before his death all had imported British armor and Krupp guns, the latter becoming standard equipment for all Austro-Hungarian battleships and cruisers until late in the century. The *Tegetthoff* also had British wrought-iron armor, but by the time the *Kronprinz Rudolf* and *Kronprinzessin Stephanie* were under construction, German firms had secured the navy's biggest contracts. The steel works of Dillingen on the Saar provided the compound (iron and steel) armor for both of the new battleships, while Krupp supplied the 12.5-ton steel ram bow for the *Stephanie* and the stern post, rudder, and other steel components for the *Rudolf.* Nevertheless, British firms still played a significant role: the *Stephanie*'s engines came from Maudsley Sons & Field of London, Langley & Company of London provided the *Rudolf*'s anchors, and Watson & Company of Newcastle supplied the pumps for both battleships. And while their guns came from Krupp, Armstrong of Newcastle built the hydraulic machinery for their turrets. All of these imports entered Austria duty free under a program designed to stimulate domestic shipbuilding; unfortunately the same laws discouraged the growth of related industries to support the shipyards.[45]

Dependence upon foreign industry was even greater with the navy's smaller vessels. The *Panther* and *Leopard,* built by Armstrong, were the only cruisers ordered from abroad, but of Sterneck's six destroyers only one was of domestic construction; four were built by the Schichau firm of Elbing, Germany, and one by Palmers of Newcastle. While the Whitehead factory in Rijeka continued to supply all of the navy's torpedoes, many of the torpedo boats were imported. Of the original ten boats introduced under Pöck, six had been purchased from Thornycroft of London. Ten of the fifty-three torpedo boats added under

Sterneck were built in foreign yards, eight by Schichau and two by Yarrow; of the forty-three built in Pola or Trieste, twenty-five were copies of Schichau boats and ten had Schichau engines.[46]

When the *Tegetthoff* was renovated in the early 1890s, its original Stabilimento Tecnico Triestino engines were replaced by new machinery from Schichau. The pride of the fleet after finally being commissioned in September 1882, the ship made it through only three years in the active squadron (1883, 1887, and 1888) without suffering from some sort of debilitating engine trouble.[47] Almost all of the older Habsburg ironclads had had Stabilimento Tecnico engines, too, but none was as large as the 7,550-ton *Tegetthoff*. The ship's engine woes bore witness to the fact that Austro-Hungarian domestic industry could not yet build machinery capable of providing reliable power for such a large vessel. When the time came, Sterneck decided to order British machinery for the *Kronprinzessin Stephanie* even though the ship was being built by the San Rocco yard of the Stabilimento Tecnico. Nevertheless, financial constraints compelled the navy to contract with the Stabilimento Tecnico for engines for the *Kronprinz Rudolf*, which at 6,900 tons was almost as large as the *Tegetthoff*.

Altogether, during the years 1884–1891, 26 percent of the outlay for the construction, modernization, and maintenance of Austro-Hungarian warships went to foreign firms.[48] Although years had passed since the crash of 1873, the economy still had not fully recovered, and Austrian heavy industry could have used the additional business, but Sterneck hesitated to turn to relatively unproven domestic suppliers, regardless of their future promise. After expanding into steel production in 1886, Emil von Skoda received no major contracts from the Habsburg navy until after he first demonstrated that he could do business with the German navy and foreign merchant fleets.[49] In Sterneck's first eight years, the navy purchased 400,000 gulden worth of machine guns and light artillery from Skoda, a negligible sum compared to the outlay for heavier guns from Krupp. In 1890 Skoda established a partnership with the Krupp works to produce heavy guns, but the navy continued to buy the latter directly from Krupp.[50]

Even firms that had done business with the navy for years could not count on preferential treatment from Sterneck. The foreign construction of the light cruisers *Leopard* and *Panther* prompted Trieste representative Raffaele Luzzatto to make an impassioned plea on behalf of the Stabilimento Tecnico in the Delegations of November 1886. The work force of the San Rocco yard, reduced to less than three hundred men in 1882 following the completion of the *Tegetthoff*, had expanded more than threefold after the firm won the contract for the *Kronprinzessin Stephanie;* nevertheless, the future appeared far from secure. In his remarks, Luzzatto attributed the collapse of the Navale Adriatico in 1875 and the closing of its San Marco yard to the dearth of navy contracts. He feared that the same would happen to the Stabilimento Tecnico, with dire consequences for "the significant number of more than 1,000 workers . . . who otherwise would fall into poverty." He regretted that the merchant marine had done little to help the situation.[51] Indeed, in 1886 the Austrian Lloyd's fleet of eighty-seven steamers included forty-six that were constructed in foreign shipyards. The Lloyd's own arsenal in Trieste built thirty-nine of the remaining vessels but had been operating at such a deficit that the company's directors even closed it for six months in 1884.[52] This depressed situation would not last much longer, at least for navy shipbuilding. The conditions of the past dozen years encouraged the formation, in 1886, of an iron and steel cartel. After the cartel developed ties to the shipyards and the leading banks, and after political leaders embraced the cause of industry, the navy ultimately would have to rely upon domestic sources even when foreign matériel was available at a lower cost.[53]

Sterneck's fleet also relied heavily on foreign sources, mostly British, for the coal that fueled its warships. Because few mines in the Dual Monarchy produced coal that burned clean enough for use in the engines of ships, imported coal had been used ever since the navy purchased its first steamer in the mid-1830s. This practice would continue, out of necessity, until the end of the First World War. In the last nine years of Sterneck's tenure (1889–97), the navy purchased 307,803 tons of coal for warship use, with annual amounts ranging from 15,102 in 1889 to 47,803 in 1893. Ninety-nine percent came from Britain, 0.8 percent from domestic mines, and 0.2 percent from Germany. Most domestic coal went to harbor use and to the Pola Arsenal ("für den Arsenalsbedarf"). The mines of Trbovlje (Trifail) in southern Styria supplied the largest amount, followed by Pécs (Fünfkirchen) in southern Hungary. Other sources ranged from Ostrava in Moravia to Siverić in Dalmatia.[54]

In his quest for higher budgets, Sterneck's good relations with the army were a tremendous asset; indeed, before the early 1890s, the war ministers only rarely caused difficulties for him in the council of ministers. His adoption of the defensive "little war" strategy for the Adriatic endeared him to Archduke Albrecht, while Count Friedrich Beck, chief of the General Staff from 1881 to 1906, included navy officers in General Staff war games, which heretofore had involved only the army.[55] War minister Bylandt-Rheidt (in office from 1876 to 1888) and his successor, Baron Ferdinand von Bauer (1888–93) actually supported the navy's independence from the army and the creation of a separate navy ministry. Sterneck opposed the idea of an independent ministry, however, on the grounds that it would increase the navy's administrative costs and also necessitate separation of the post of *Marinekommandant* from the ministerial position. Besides, under the present system the chief of the *Marinesektion* already enjoyed prerogatives normally reserved for a minister, and as time went on Sterneck attended enough meetings of the council of ministers to warrant recognition as a de facto minister. In 1885 Francis Joseph even gave the *Marinesektion* the right to comment, in an official capacity, on matters pertaining to the merchant marine. Thereafter, Sterneck encouraged Vienna and Budapest to make the annual subsidies to Austrian and Hungarian steamship lines contingent on their introduction of larger, faster vessels that could serve the navy as auxiliary cruisers in wartime.[56]

In the area of questioning the navy's budget, the Hungarian minister-president more than made up for the war ministry's passive stance. Sterneck faced stiff opposition from Tisza especially on the budgets for 1886, 1888, 1889, and 1890,[57] but in general he had fewer problems with the Hungarians than Pöck had. In 1888 the Hungarian ministry for agriculture, industry, and trade even agreed to finally pay a modest sum (less than 30,000 gulden) to the navy toward the cost of the Petz mission to the Far East, which it had been haggling over for the past two decades.[58] The opposition from Hungary typically focused on all joint Austro-Hungarian military expenditure and was not strictly anti-navy. Indeed, army bills usually generated more controversy in Hungary than did naval appropriations, especially when issues arose that concerned their reserve force, the *Honvéd,* which many Hungarians considered the catalyst for a future independent national army. The military law of

1889, which confirmed German as the language of command in the Aus-tro-Hungarian army, sparked stormy debates in the Hungarian parlia-ment and riots in the streets of Budapest and other cities. Passage of the law came only after the armed forces were redesignated "Imperial and Royal" (*kaiserliche und königliche,* or *k.u.k.*) rather than the traditional "Imperial Royal" (*kaiserliche königliche,* or *k.k.*), in order to emphasize the kingdom of Hungary's equal status within the empire.[59] The change applied not just to the army but also the navy, which became the *k.u.k. Kriegsmarine,* officially "Austro-Hungarian" rather than "Austrian," some twenty-two years after the *Ausgleich.*

Under Pöck the navy already had made important concessions to the Hungarians in revising the curriculum of the naval academy, and the results were soon reflected in the national profile of the navy officer corps. The Hungarian share of the corps peaked at 14.7 percent in 1885, second only to the German Austrians at 44.9 percent; in the same year the Magyars accounted for just 5.6 percent of the seamen. In the army, Hungarians provided a similar share of the officer corps, if reserve officers are counted, but provided almost 20 percent of the common manpower.[60]

By the early 1890s, Sterneck could look back at his first years in office with some satisfaction. He had accomplished much in the im-proved training of personnel, the reform of the administrative struc-ture and policies, and in his own personal development as a politician and public advocate for the navy's cause. But in the category of larger warships, the material state of the fleet left much to be desired. Other than the recently launched *Kronprinz Rudolf* and *Kronprinzessin Ste-phanie,* only the *Tegetthoff* could be considered a respectable battleship, and it would have to undergo extensive remodeling in 1892–93 to be brought up to date. In addition to the new Schichau engines, the mod-ernization process included the removal of the ship's full set of masts and yards, and the installation of a lighter battery of six 9.4-inch Krupp guns. After its recommissioning, the *Tegetthoff* at least would be able to keep up with the two newer battleships on squadron maneuvers.[61] The sad state of the armored fleet reflected Sterneck's commitment to tailor the navy for defensive "little war" tactics and his infatuation with the controversial doctrines of the French *Jeune Ecole;* it also left him open to criticism within the officer corps. The early years of the new de-cade thus found the navy divided in philosophy, if not in spirit, as Vice

Admiral Pitner, Pöck's former protégé, led the opponents of the *Jeune Ecole* back toward a commitment to battleship construction, opposing Sterneck and the proponents of torpedo boats and unarmored cruisers.

TORPEDO BOATS AND CRUISERS: AUSTRIA-HUNGARY AND THE *JEUNE ECOLE*

The "young school" of naval strategy that emerged in France during the 1880s ultimately caused a philosophical schism not just within the Austro-Hungarian navy but also in the French fleet and among navy men worldwide. Admiral Hyacinthe-Laurent-Théophile Aube, the founding father of the *Jeune Ecole,* actually belonged to the older generation; indeed, he was three years older than Sterneck. From the onset of his naval service in 1843 until the early 1880s, Aube spent almost all of his time on distant stations, either in the Far East, the West Indies, or African waters. His own career experiences left him with a strategic outlook that focused on the defense of worldwide interests and, in wartime, on a *guerre de course* attacking enemy commerce.[62]

Aube took a disparaging view of ironclads from the time of their introduction,[63] and his "discovery" of the torpedo boat in 1883, upon his return to home waters from a post in Martinique, confirmed his view that ironclads were worthless. That same year he invited Gabriel Charmes, a young journalist and foreign policy expert, on a cruise with the French Mediterranean fleet. During these maneuvers, two 46-ton torpedo boats rode out a heavy storm better than some of the larger vessels of the fleet, prompting Charmes, as Aube's mouthpiece, to write several articles arguing that torpedo boats could be used as autonomous seagoing warships.[64] The marriage of torpedoes and torpedo boats with the overall *guerre de course* outlook was a match made in heaven. According to Aube and Charmes, torpedo boats would join larger unarmored cruisers in a ruthless campaign of commerce raiding that would cripple the economy of an enemy state and ensure victory in war.

This new strategic school of thought quickly gained the support of younger French officers and, naturally, of those who saw Britain as their country's most likely future enemy. Aube and the *Jeune Ecole* felt that France could never match Britain in battleships, and that battleships in any event had been rendered obsolete by the perfection of the torpedo. They were also aware that Britain always had placed its faith in a seagoing deterrent and had done little to develop harbor defenses and coastal fortifications. Surprise torpedo attacks on ports and indiscriminate shelling of the enemy coastline thus found their place in the strategy of the *Jeune Ecole,* alongside commerce raiding.[65]

In the area of coastal defense, Aube copied freely from the strategies of the Imperial German navy. In the 1870s and 1880s, before the era of William II and Tirpitz, the German fleet was, in the words of one historian, "merely the part of the army that happened to watch the sea frontier." Warships dispersed in fortified coastal bases were to conduct sorties to break an enemy blockade and prevent attempts to land troops on the coast, or at least delay a landing until the army could send help. Telegraph and semaphore stations along the coast linked the naval bases together and provided an early-warning network for the army inland. But the *Jeune Ecole* also maintained that such a coastal defense could be a springboard for offensive operations. Fear of torpedo boat attacks probably would deter an enemy blockade in the first place, and if one were attempted, Aube contended, the telegraph would work in favor of the blockaded fleet, facilitating coordinated feints and break-outs from many ports that would confuse the enemy and enable commerce raiding cruisers to slip out to open sea. An optimistic Aube believed that whole squadrons could break out in the same manner, rendezvous at sea, and enjoy temporary superiority over the enemy fleet.[66]

The latter point may have caused the most concern at the British Admiralty, but for a majority of Aube's critics the most controversial aspect of the *Jeune Ecole* strategy was the appeal for ruthless commerce raiding, ultimately for an unrestricted torpedo boat warfare against all enemy shipping. Aube declared that "war is the negation of law. . . . Everything is therefore not only permissible but legitimate against the enemy."[67] Despite the hue and cry over the morality of these aspects of the strategy, the ideas of the *Jeune Ecole* had a profound and immediate effect on all navies. Shipyards came alive with the feverish construction of torpedo boats, and doubts about the efficacy of the battleship could be heard from every corner. In June 1886, in a debate over the funding of the 12,000-ton British pre-dreadnoughts *Nile* and *Trafalgar,* Lord Northbrook, the First Lord of the Admiralty, conceded that these battleships probably would be the last of their size ever to be added to any navy.[68] In France the heyday of the *Jeune Ecole* came in 1886 and 1887, when Aube served briefly as navy minister.

While the French developed strategic theories calling for torpedo attacks in a wide variety of circumstances, they left much work to be done in the applied science of tactics. It was here that the Austro-Hungarian navy excelled, indeed impressing the French. Long before Aube became navy minister, the two fleets were sharing a remarkable amount of information, and the conclusion of the Triple Alliance in 1882 did not stop the exchanges. With the dawning of the *Jeune Ecole,* even more Frenchmen toured the Whitehead torpedo factory in Rijeka and the navy base at Pola; the visitors included interested members of the Chamber of Deputies as well as French navy officers.[69] One mission remained in Rijeka and Pola from 1884 until 1886. It was this group of French observers that had been so impressed by Sterneck's summer exercises in 1884, which included the use of torpedo boats in a simulated action between squadrons of battleships at sea. The same maneuvers marked the abandonment of Tegetthoff's line abreast in favor of a return to the line ahead; just as in the 1860s, the Habsburg navy led the way in a significant shift in squadron tactics. The French adopted the Austrian tactic of "hiding" a torpedo boat beside each battleship in the line until smoke provided safe cover for their attacks, and used it until 1902. As late as 1901—just five years before his *Dreadnought* revolutionized naval warfare—Britain's great innovator Sir John Fisher offered the same idea to his colleague, Sir Arthur Wilson, as if it were his own![70] Sterneck also promoted the development of torpedo tactics for coastal flotillas. Here, the French concluded that the Austrians were ahead of even the Germans.[71]

If the French were impressed by Austrian tactics, Sterneck was equally enamored of French strategy. At the time, the Dual Monarchy maintained only one naval attaché, in its London embassy, but the *Marinekommandant* was fortunate enough to have a personal connection in the French capital. His nephew Richard Sterneck, later a representative of Carinthia in the Austrian *Reichsrat,* held a post in the Austro-Hungarian embassy in Paris during the mid-1880s and served as the admiral's contact with the *Jeune Ecole.* Charmes's *La réforme de la Marine* (1886) was among the books he received from his nephew; the *Marinekommandant* instructed the younger Sterneck to convey to Charmes his "special admiration" of the Frenchman's work. It gave Sterneck great satisfaction that he had already tried at sea many of the maneuvers that Aube's chief publicist was still discussing in the realm of theory. "It appears as if we have had the same ideas simultaneously, with the difference that I can put them into action immediately."[72]

By adding dozens of torpedo boats to the fleet and introducing the first destroyers and light cruisers, Sterneck reflected his commitment to *Jeune Ecole* thinking. Some of the defensive aspects of the new strategy fit his navy perfectly; as the French visitors noted, "the Adriatic was ideal for mine and torpedo warfare."[73] But Sterneck eventually concluded that Aube and Charmes were wrong in their assertion that torpedo boats could act as autonomous warships. In the summer of 1887, he confided to his second in command, Eberan, that torpedo attacks in daylight would be "foolhardy" and likely to fail.[74] Thereafter the navy's maneuvers included simulated night attacks by torpedo boats on battleships. One such exercise targeted the *Erzherzog Albrecht* at a time when the archduke himself was aboard observing navy maneuvers as Sterneck's guest. Albrecht, seventy years old at the time, was more annoyed than pleased by the surprise attack, but the *Marinekommandant* offered no apologies for the loss of sleep.[75] Such defensive strategies, after all, had been mandated by the archduke's own committee of inquiry in 1880.

Like other European navies, the Austro-Hungarian fleet had mixed results in experiments with floodlights to illuminate targets for torpedo attacks at night; it also enjoyed considerable success in equipping battleships with defensive torpedo nets.[76] The latter were hung from swinging booms attached to the hulls of the ships. When fully extended, they gave battleships the unflattering appearance of huge armored fishing trawlers, but the nets sufficed to stop most of the slow-moving torpedoes of the 1880s before they could strike their target and detonate. Concurrent experiments with lighter, stronger all-steel armor likewise demonstrated that the threat of torpedo attack would not make the battleship obsolete.[77] It also became clear to Sterneck that torpedo boats operating alone were worthless, at night as well as in the daytime, even for coastal defense. They had to be supported by larger ships.[78]

This conviction shaped Sterneck's approach to the design and construction of his cruisers, an area in which he broke with the purists of the *Jeune Ecole*. In part the Habsburg navy had to devise its own scheme for cruisers on practical grounds because the commerce raiding and worldwide cruiser warfare of Aube's strategy did not apply to Austria-Hungary. As Pöck had observed in the committee of inquiry in 1880, Italy—at that time the navy's probable enemy—had neither overseas colonies nor a large merchant marine. By the late 1880s, Italy was an ally and, owing to tensions in the Balkans, war with Russia appeared likely, but the Russians also had no colonies and their merchant fleet was even smaller than the Austrian. As a result, Sterneck's first larger cruisers were designed not with an eye toward independent operations as commerce raiders but to lead the navy's torpedo flotillas.

These ships, the so-called "ram cruisers" *Kaiser Franz Joseph I* and *Kaiserin Elisabeth*, proved to be Sterneck's undoing. Built in the late 1880s, their size (4,000 tons) and speed (nineteen knots) reflected the thinking of the *Jeune Ecole*, while their ram bows were reminiscent of Tegetthoff's tactics at Lissa. As Sterneck's "battleship of the future," the ram cruiser would lead a torpedo division consisting of two light cruisers such as the *Leopard* and *Panther*, two destroyers, and a dozen torpedo boats.[79] Because tacticians assumed that a torpedo attack on enemy battleships in any case would come under cover of smoke or darkness, Sterneck envisioned clashes that would be chaotic melees not unlike Lissa. A ram bow could be a considerable asset in such a battle, and he saw no contradiction between ramming tactics and other elements of the *Jeune Ecole*.

Owing to the widespread popularity of the *Jeune Ecole*'s strategies, Austria-Hungary's ram cruisers were not entirely unique. Aside from their pronounced ram bows, what distinguished them most from similar warships in other navies was their heavy armament—two 9.4-inch Krupp guns, mounted in turrets fore and aft—backed by a secondary battery of six 6-inch Krupps. According to an article published by Captain Lehnert, Sterneck's publicist in the *Marinesektion*, the heavy artillery was supposed to enable the ram cruiser to exchange fire at a distance with armored enemy battleships and thus cover the attacking torpedo boats while serving as a flotilla leader.[80] There was also a political reason for mounting such heavy guns aboard the two cruisers. Because Sterneck intended to have his unarmored "battleships of the future" replace obsolete armored warships, they had to have some of the characteristics of genuine battleships. Still operating within the framework of Pöck's fleet plan of 1881—the last such program to receive official approval—the *Marinekommandant* presented his pair of ram cruisers to the Delegations as successors to the casemate ships *Kaiser* and *Lissa*. The former, last activated in 1875, had been slated for replacement by Pöck in the years 1886–89; the latter, in reserve since 1885, was to be retired instead of the older but more seaworthy *Habsburg*. The *Habsburg,* scheduled for "rebuilding" during the years 1886–89, instead became the harbor watch ship in Pola.[81]

The politicians of the Dual Monarchy initially found the ram cruiser very appealing, but mostly because of the price tag. The *Kaiser Franz Joseph I,* first included in the budget for 1887, and the *Kaiserin Elisabeth,* initially funded in 1888, together cost just 5.36 million gulden, compared to 5.44 million for the *Kronprinz Rudolf* alone.[82] Yet even laymen could see that the relatively small unarmored cruisers likely would be blown out of the water by the 10,000-ton battleships of an enemy fleet long before they could use their rams. As early as 1889, skeptics in the council of ministers suggested postponement of the appropriation of funds for a third ram cruiser.[83] After the two ships were launched—the *Kaiser Franz Joseph I* in 1889 by the Stabilimento Tecnico Triestino, the *Kaiserin Elisabeth* in 1890 by the Pola Arsenal—the design also drew criticism from officers and seamen. The latter referred to the cruisers as "Sterneck's sardine-boxes."[84]

As the new decade began, Sterneck stood by the concept of the ram cruiser and also clung to many other aspects of *Jeune Ecole* thinking, even though by then the school of thought was passing out of fashion in other navies. Death stopped the polemics of Charmes in 1886, and in the summer of 1887 ill health forced Aube into early retirement. They left behind a French navy officer corps bitterly divided between their followers and their opponents, and for the remainder of the century, French strategy swung from one extreme to another at the whim of the faction in power.[85] In 1889, just three years after Lord Northbrook had sounded the death knell of the large armored warship, the British Parliament passed the Naval Defence Act, which provided for the construction of a homogeneous class of eight 14,000-ton battleships.[86] The Italians likewise turned away from torpedo boats as abruptly as they had embraced them. Italy had 4 of the boats as of 1881, added 159 during the years 1881–88, then did not build another until 1897.[87] In 1890 the proponents of the battleship found their Aube across the Atlantic when Captain Alfred Thayer Mahan of the United States Navy published *The Influence of Sea Power upon History,* which affirmed the importance of a battle fleet in the quest to gain command of the sea.

But Sterneck refused to yield without a fight. The navy's maneuvers in June 1891 again included torpedo boat exercises, which he called "the most interesting maneuvers that we have yet conducted."[88] Early the following month, the *Marinekommandant* visited Francis Joseph at the emperor's summer retreat in Bad Ischl armed with a new fleet plan, the first since Pöck's a decade earlier. Sterneck called for a fleet of nine battleships, six ram cruisers, twelve light cruisers, twelve destroyers, and seventy-two torpedo boats, with each type divided equally among three squadrons. Except for one light cruiser, the larger vessels of the first squadron were already in place: the battleships *Tegetthoff, Kronprinz Rudolf,* and *Kronprinzessin Stephanie,* the ram cruisers *Kaiser Franz Joseph I* and *Kaiserin Elisabeth,* and the light cruisers *Leopard, Panther,* and *Tiger.* Also in service were most of the smaller ships for the entire program: six destroyers and over sixty torpedo boats, although some of the latter were already obsolete. The construction of the rest of the larger ships would be the most expensive item. Sterneck called for the completion of the second squadron by 1896 and the third by 1901.

True to the precepts of the *Jeune Ecole,* the *Marinekommandant* argued that the primary purpose of the fleet still would be coastal defense. Indeed, he proposed that the three new battleships of his second squadron should be *Küstenverteidiger* (coast defenders), small, heavily armed vessels designed specifically for operations in coastal waters. The navy's secondary goal in wartime would be the destruction of enemy commerce, to be accomplished by the cruisers and smaller vessels. Sterneck made no provision for ships to defend trade or show the flag overseas, even though most of the vessels then employed for these purposes—the composite ships—had been in service for two decades and would not hold up much longer.[89]

Because the fleet plan embodied concepts that other navies clearly were abandoning, it ran into trouble even before Sterneck presented it to the council of ministers. Major General Arthur Bolfras, head of Francis Joseph's military chancellery, commented that it "appears questionable . . . whether the range of possibilities and effectiveness of the torpedo, upon which the plan places the greatest emphasis, are as significant and certain as has been assumed." Bolfras called for a more "objective consideration" of the torpedo issue in particular and the fleet plan in general.[90] When Sterneck turned to senior navy officers for support, they came up with a plan quite different from his own. In the summer of 1891, a commission convened in Pola under the harbor admiral, Maximilian von Pitner, produced an alternative proposal for a fleet of twenty battleships, four light cruisers, twelve destroyers, and seventy-two torpedo boats, with each type divided equally among four squadrons. The number of destroyers and torpedo boats was the same in both plans, but the Pola group's emphasis on battleships over cruisers repudiated the *Jeune Ecole* philosophy. Pitner's commission left out ram cruisers altogether on the grounds that they were too heavy and expensive for the task of leading torpedo flotillas.[91]

As he prepared for the budget process for 1892, Sterneck predicted "hard days of disappointment" for the navy.[92] In September 1891, when he presented his fleet plan and the related budget estimates to the council of ministers, he defended, in vain, the concept of the ram cruiser. The proposal for coastal defense battleships rather than "colossal armored ships" appealed to the ministers, but the Hungarians argued that the construction timetable of the three required for Sterneck's second squadron could be delayed. Echoing Szápáry's words of a decade earlier, Hungarian finance minister Alexander Wekerle argued that no new ships should be laid down until all current projects were finished. Kálnoky supported the need for a stronger navy, but the Triple Alliance had just been renewed for another five years, and the international situation appeared calm. In dismissing the urgency of new warship construction, Austrian finance minister Emil Steinbach employed reasoning similar to that which Metternich had used in 1815 when arguing against an earlier expansion of the fleet: if war broke out and Austria were allied with Britain, the British navy would shoulder the bulk of the burden of the war at sea; if Austria were not allied with Britain, any operation bolder than coastal defense would be out of the question. War minister Bauer, an ally in previous council meetings, alluded to the serious discrepancies between Sterneck's fleet plan and the one produced by Pitner's commission at Pola. Faced with such overwhelming opposition, Francis Joseph could not support Sterneck. The council cut 1.5 million from his estimates for new construction, his fleet plan did not receive imperial or ministerial endorsement, and the budget for 1892 subsequently emerged from the Delegations looking much the same as the 1891 outlay (just under 11.7 million gulden).[93]

While the financial and diplomatic arguments against Sterneck carried considerable weight, he had managed to overcome similar resistance in the past; Hungarian opposition likewise had never caused him to suffer such a complete defeat. His fleet plan of 1891 failed for three reasons: it lacked the support of the army, the emperor, and of Sterneck's own officer corps. The latter, in particular, was a decisive factor. Just as Sterneck's vacillation on the issue of battleship construction had undermined Pöck's position in the committee of inquiry in 1880, the lack of support from Pitner's commission highlighted the fact that Sterneck's tactical philosophy and vision of the future did not reflect a consensus of his highest ranking subordinates.

While neither of the two competing fleet plans of 1891 was ever formally adopted, in the long run the course of Austro-Hungarian naval expansion more closely resembled Pitner's program. The navy built no new ram cruisers and added only one destroyer and two torpedo boats during the remaining six years of Sterneck's command. The new warship *Kaiserin und Königin Maria Theresia* reflected the shift away from the influence of the *Jeune Ecole.* Laid down in Trieste in 1891 as a 4,000-ton ram cruiser, the ship was modified while under construction and launched in 1893 as a 5,200-ton armored cruiser.[94] A stubborn Sterneck continued to refer to the *Maria Theresia* as a "ram cruiser," even though its armored belt made it a far different warship from the *Franz Joseph* and *Elisabeth.* The navy even listed the ram cruisers and *Maria Theresia* as "battleships" until 1895, when they were placed in the same class with the *Leopard, Panther,* and lighter cruisers. As late as 1902, a new armored cruiser under construction was referred to in the Delegations as a "ram cruiser" and listed in the navy almanac as a "torpedo ram ship."[95] But actions spoke louder than words, and in the future the navy's cruiser projects conformed to the established international norms: those larger than the ram cruisers were armored, and those smaller than 4,000 tons were built with an emphasis on speed rather than firepower.

THE NAVY AND
GRAND STRATEGY: THE TRIPLE ALLIANCE
AND THE MEDITERRANEAN AGREEMENTS (1882–92)

The Triple Alliance, though disastrous from the navy's point of view, provided Austria with the greatest degree of security it had ever enjoyed. Kálnoky felt confident that the scenarios requiring the Dual Monarchy to come to the aid of Germany or Italy were farfetched compared to the likelihood of a future Austro-Russian war, in which the guarantee of Italian neutrality would be crucial. He placed little faith in the Three Emperors' League, the loose Austro-German-Russian alignment that his predecessor, Haymerle, had renewed in 1881, a few months before his death. Beck and the army General Staff found neither alliance particularly reassuring; on an almost annual basis, staff officers continued to draft contingency plans for war against Russia, Italy, or a combination of both powers.[96]

It was in this context that the navy prepared plans to defend the Adriatic against a Russian attack. In theory the tsar could send ships to support future hostile activity by Montenegrins or Bosnian rebels, but such assistance was highly unlikely because it would have had to come from the Baltic fleet. As early as 1872, two years after the remilitarization of the Black Sea, the Russian navy deployed twenty-seven steamers there, but none was armored or larger than a corvette.[97] In the early 1880s, Russia still had no Black Sea fleet capable of breaking out into the eastern Mediterranean. As recently as the Russo-Turkish War of 1877–78, the Ottoman navy, at least on paper, had enjoyed a wide superiority over its Russian rival in the war zone.[98]

Meanwhile, should Italy break the Triple Alliance, Sterneck planned to use the *mezzi insidiosi* of mines and torpedoes to wage a defensive "little war" in the Adriatic against the materially superior Italian fleet. But in spite of the tremendous respect that the *Duilio* and the rest of Italy's huge pre-dreadnoughts commanded, in fact they were not ideally suited for action in the closed forum of the Adriatic. They had been built so large in the first place in part to accommodate a greater coal capacity for an extended cruising range, an asset that would mean nothing in the Adriatic. And even if they were deployed against Austria-Hungary, the Italian battleships would have to operate from Taranto because Venice, the only major Italian base in the Adriatic, was treacherous for larger warships owing to its relatively shallow, silted lagoon. In any event, the *Duilio* and the other pre-dreadnoughts were too big to use the Venice Arsenal for repairs. Ironically, while Habsburg navy men bemoaned the inadequacies of their own small casemate ships, the Italians considered them perfectly suited for Adriatic warfare.[99] For

Italy the Triple Alliance had been bought, in part, by conceding the Adriatic to Austria-Hungary. Benedetto Brin's impressive battleships were designed for a Mediterranean war against France.

Thus, when it came to justifying higher navy budgets, Sterneck was in an unenviable position. The two most likely adversaries were allies of the Dual Monarchy, and both possessed either insufficient or ill-suited means to threaten the Adriatic coastline. But the changing international situation of the mid-1880s strengthened Sterneck's hand in Vienna and afforded opportunities for the navy to be more active at sea. In 1884 Russia began building 10,300-ton armored warships for the Black Sea fleet. The *Ekaterina II* class included four battleships, of which three were completed before the end of the decade.[100] The following autumn, when Bulgaria's annexation of Eastern Rumelia led to increased Austro-Russian tensions, the Three Emperors' League became a dead letter. In the winter of 1885–86, with the Bulgarian crisis still unresolved, a war scare between Greece and Turkey added more fuel to the fire. In January 1886, Britain demanded that the Greeks demobilize. When they refused, the British took the lead in organizing an international naval demonstration in Greek waters.

Russia, wary of isolation, supported the British demobilization demand, and of all the great powers only France declined to contribute warships to the demonstration. Because Sterneck's deployment policies customarily kept the navy's armored warships in port except for during summer maneuvers, at the onset of the crisis Austria-Hungary had just the composite frigate *Radetzky* and two old wooden propeller gunboats cruising in the Mediterranean. This "winter squadron," under the command of Captain Spaun, was soon reinforced by the casemate ship *Kaiser Max*, the torpedo ship *Lussin*, six torpedo boats, and an obsolete wooden steamer serving as a torpedo boat tender. It was a motley assortment of warships, but, aside from Britain, no one else made a better showing. Russia sent two ships and Germany just one, while Italy was represented by three older ironclads rather than the *Duilio* or the other pre-dreadnoughts. After a demonstration by one armored ship from each of the five powers off Piraeus failed to cow the Greek government, in May 1886 the British, Italian, and Austrian contingents each blockaded part of the Greek coast; Spaun's squadron sealed the port of Volos north of Athens. In June a new Greek regime capitulated to the demands of the powers and demobilized the army. The last of the Habsburg warships left Greek waters in August. Spaun received his personal reward while the operation was still underway, in the form of a promotion to rear admiral.[101]

Although Sterneck lamented that the operation had upset his budget ("the [expletive deleted] Greeks are costing me more money than they are worth"), causing the cancellation of summer maneuvers, the affair gave the navy a valuable opportunity to support Austro-Hungarian diplomacy outside of the Adriatic.[102] The new diplomatic climate brought a chill to Austro-French naval cooperation, but the successful blockade of Greece demonstrated to Britain the possibilities of Mediterranean cooperation with Italy and Austria-Hungary. After the Liberal ministry of the traditionally anti-Austrian William Gladstone fell in the summer of 1886, the more sympathetic Conservatives under Lord Salisbury returned to power. Salisbury saw international peace and British interests threatened by the growth of Russia's power in the Black Sea and Near East as well as by France, where at the time Aube served as navy minister and the bellicose General Georges Boulanger as war minister. With Bismarck's encouragement, on 12 February 1887 Salisbury concluded an agreement with Italy to maintain the status quo in the Mediterranean. On 24 March, the prime minister exchanged similar notes with Kálnoky, including special references to the Black Sea and the Aegean. Spain entered the picture on 4 May via a separate agreement pledging not to collaborate with France in partitioning unclaimed lands in North Africa. A more specific exchange of notes among Austria-Hungary, Italy, and Britain on 12 December pledged the three powers to defend Turkey against Russian aggression. Should the sultan succumb to Russian pressure to alter the status quo in the Balkans or at the Dardanelles, the powers asserted their right to intervene "either jointly or separately" to preserve Ottoman territorial integrity and uphold existing treaties.[103]

These so-called Mediterranean Agreements, though not including Germany, formed a valuable part of Bismarck's system of alliances at the confusing zenith of his diplomacy. Along with other arrangements made during the first half of 1887—the renewal of the Triple Alliance on 20 February and the conclusion of the secret Russo-German "Reinsurance Treaty" of 18 June—the Mediterranean Agreements joined the often contradictory web of commitments and obligations that had as their one common goal the continued isolation of France. Italy emerged as the big winner, gaining the closest thing to a British alliance that it would have at any time before 1915. In an addendum to the renewed Triple Alliance, the Italians also secured a pledge of German support in the event of a Franco-Italian war, not just if France attacked Italy proper but also if Italy went to war with France as a consequence of a French move to annex Tripoli or Morocco. A separate Austro-Italian corollary, conceded by Kálnoky under pressure from Bismarck, virtually guaranteed Italy an equal voice with Austria-Hungary throughout the Balkans. If either party found it necessary to change the status quo in the region of the Balkans, Adriatic, and Aegean through a temporary occupation or permanent annexation of territory, such action would be taken only after consultation with the other party, which would be guaranteed "reciprocal compensation" for any gains made by the active party.[104] Kálnoky sought warmer relations with Italy in part for the sake of maintaining his new friendship with Salisbury. He knew that if Austro-Italian relations soured, Britain's sympathies would be with Italy.[105]

Franco-Italian tensions increased after August 1887, when Francesco Crispi took over as prime minister in Rome. The following February, the French broke off negotiations for a trade agreement with the Italians, coincidentally at a time when the French navy was testing a new system of mobilization. Though Aube no longer held the navy portfolio in Paris, his belligerent *Jeune Ecole* rhetoric was still ringing in Italian ears. Crispi concluded that the fleet at Toulon was preparing for a preemptive strike against Italy and asked Bismarck for support. Urgent appeals from Rome and Berlin prompted Salisbury to dispatch a British squadron to Genoa as a sign of solidarity with the Italians.[106]

Three months later, in May 1888, the four parties to the Mediterranean Agreements staged a joint display of friendship at the opening ceremonies of the Barcelona World's Fair. The Spanish hosts welcomed British, Italian, and Austro-Hungarian squadrons; the latter, commanded by Rear Admiral Moriz Manfroni von Manfort, consisted of the casemate ships *Tegetthoff, Custoza, Kaiser Max, Don Juan d'Austria,* and *Prinz Eugen,* the new torpedo cruisers *Panther* and *Leopard,* and the destroyer *Meteor.* The five armored vessels were the most the Habsburg navy had ever sent out of the Adriatic in a single squadron. Crispi's Italy, eager to make an impression on French observers (and everyone else), sent the *Duilio,* the *Italia,* and fifteen smaller escorts. Queen Maria Christina of Spain, a Habsburg by birth and sister of the navy's own Archduke Charles Stephen, paid special attention to the Austro-Hungarian squadron, inspecting the *Tegetthoff* and *Custoza.* En route home, the *Custoza, Kaiser Max, Prinz Eugen,* and *Leopard* visited Malta and received a cordial welcome from their British hosts.[107]

During the first half of 1889, Crispi sought to supplement his country's tenuous claim on British support with specific naval commitments from his Triple Alliance partners. Bismarck supported the idea, but Kálnoky did not, fearful that binding commitments for Austro-Italian naval cooperation would draw the Dual Monarchy into a war with France.[108] The Italians tried to sweeten the deal by offering the Habsburg fleet anchorage rights at Taranto. While they had developed the port initially as a springboard for their own ambitions in the Balkans and eastern Mediterranean, for Austria-Hungary it could serve as a base for operations in the western Mediterranean.[109] But Sterneck rejected the Italian overtures, even with the offer of Taranto. Aside from his general suspicion of Italian intentions, which virtually all Austrian navy men shared, he feared that any interaction with the Italian navy would grow to include the sharing of technology. The Italians certainly could benefit from Austrian expertise in the use of mines and torpedoes, while the Habsburg navy would have no use for Brin's innovative but impractical ship designs. Sterneck believed that close cooperation with the Italians ultimately would cause the navy to throw away its edge in the *mezzi insidiosi,* and he wanted no part of it.[110]

There was also the matter, of course, that Austro-Italian naval cooperation would be aimed against the French, and Sterneck—even more so than Kálnoky—had no intention of involving the Dual Monarchy in a war with France. On a practical level, he had no reason to fear a hostile French fleet entering the Adriatic as long as Britain honored the Mediterranean Agreements and remained informally aligned with the Triple Alliance. Furthermore, his faith in Aube and the *Jeune Ecole* strategies and his earlier willingness to welcome French observers at Pola and Rijeka attest to his cordial personal feelings toward the French navy; the Triple Alliance notwithstanding, he would never have similar sentiments for the Italians. For their part, the French never planned for a naval war against Austria-Hungary. Despite their admiration for Sterneck's torpedo tactics and defensive strategy in the Adriatic, they concluded that the Habsburg navy in its present condition played no role at all in their strategic considerations.[111]

Kálnoky all along considered the Triple Alliance and the Mediterranean Agreements valuable to the Dual Monarchy primarily for the security they provided against the perceived threat from Russia. After the Bulgarian crisis of 1885 and the collapse of the Three Emperors' League, the relationship between the Austro-Hungarian and Russian navies reflected the overall tensions between the two empires. Official visits by Russian officers to Pola, Trieste, and Rijeka, which had occurred on a regular basis ever since the remilitarization of the Black Sea (in 1872, 1876, 1880, and 1884), were discontinued,[112] and the navy's contingency plans for war focused on Russia as the most probable enemy. The British commitment to preserve the Mediterranean status quo implied a commitment to stop a Russian naval offensive at the Dardanelles, leaving Sterneck with no further reason to plan for a defensive war against a Russian attack in the Adriatic; consequently, in 1887 he turned his attention to offensive operations in the Aegean and Black Sea. A proposal for a joint Austro-German-Turkish effort against Russia included a Habsburg squadron operating out of Varna, Bulgaria, or from Trebizond on the northern coast of Asia Minor. But the most ideal scenario would involve Britain and Italy as well. A plan from 1892 less optimistically conceded that it would be impossible to establish an offensive base against Russia even in Salonika or Constantinople without British support.[113]

At the same time, Germany had a far different strategic vision of Austria-Hungary's role in a European naval war, reflecting Berlin's focus on France as the primary enemy. In 1887 German plans called for an Austro-Italian fleet to assemble in the western Mediterranean, compelling the French to reinforce their Mediterranean fleet at Toulon with their Atlantic forces from Brest; this redeployment would leave only the French Channel forces at Cherbourg to face an attack from the German fleet. The scheme envisioned only a defensive holding action in the east against the Russian Baltic fleet and did not consider the Russian Black Sea fleet at all. Five years later, the German High Command, like Sterneck, was less optimistic, theorizing that the Austro-Italian Mediterra-

nean combination at best would keep the fleet at Toulon from supporting the French Atlantic and Channel forces against the German fleet
in the north.[114] Their strategic sketches notwithstanding, German navy
leaders harbored no illusions about the prospects for close cooperation
between the Italian and Austro-Hungarian fleets. While they had a low
opinion of the Italians, their evaluation of the Habsburg navy was
kinder: "small but capable."[115] The feelings were mutual, for while Sterneck rejected the notion of cooperating at sea with Italy, he welcomed
the opportunity for joint maneuvers with the Germans. In 1890 Emperor William II invited him to participate in summer exercises in the
Baltic with the German fleet, and Sterneck responded by sending his
three newest vessels: the battleships *Kronprinz Rudolf* and *Kronprinzessin Stephanie,* and the ram cruiser *Kaiser Franz Joseph I.* Rear Admiral
Johann von Hinke commanded the squadron, but Sterneck traveled
overland by rail to meet his ships upon their arrival in the north. Even
though the *Rudolf,* like the *Tegetthoff* in earlier years, had trouble with its
Stabilimento Tecnico engines, the cruise was a great success, especially
from the diplomatic perspective. En route to the Baltic, Hinke stopped
at Gibraltar and in Britain, where Queen Victoria, the Prince of Wales,
and Admiral Prince Louis Battenberg reviewed the squadron at Cowes.
While in northern waters, the ships visited Copenhagen and Karlskrona,
Sweden. Hinke paid his respects to the French and Italians on the return
trip, visiting Cherbourg and Palermo.[116]

The joint maneuvers with the German fleet no doubt stirred feelings of envy among Habsburg sea officers, especially the older ones.
The German navy's Prussian predecessor had had only two ironclads in
1866, but a decade later Germany already had more armored warships
than Austria-Hungary. In 1890, well before William II and Admiral Tirpitz launched their dramatic plans for naval expansion, Germany could
boast of twenty-five armored warships to Austria-Hungary's eleven and
held a similar margin of superiority in total number of ships and in overall tonnage.[117] The Germans also enjoyed an enormous lead over their
ally in naval technology. Just a quarter century earlier, General Albrecht
von Roon, then Prussian minister for war and navy, had visited Trieste
and considered having the Austrian shipyards build ironclads for him.[118]
Now, Austria-Hungary was totally dependent upon Krupp for its heavy
naval guns and ordered smaller vessels, machinery, and building materials from other German firms.

The squadron's visit to Germany came just months after William II's dismissal of Bismarck. The new chancellor, General Leo von Caprivi, soon embarked upon a "new course" in foreign policy that quickly destroyed much of the delicate network of German alliances. Caprivi did not renew the "Reinsurance Treaty" with Russia, considering it incompatible with Germany's obligations to Austria-Hungary. In the Triple Alliance, he proved to be less willing than Bismarck to accommodate the Italians. Caprivi, Germany's navy minister from 1883 to 1888, actually welcomed the construction of a new French naval base at Bizerte in Tunisia, reasoning that as long as the French naval threat in the central Mediterranean caused concern in both Italy and Britain, the Italians would remain loyal to the Triple Alliance and the British faithful to the Mediterranean Agreements. It never occurred to Caprivi that Germany could lose the friendship of both powers.[119]

In February 1891, the marquis of Rudini succeeded Crispi as Italian prime minister, and within weeks Italy took the initiative in pursuing an early renewal of the Triple Alliance. During the summer, after the three powers agreed to extend the pact until 1902, Rudini revived Crispi's earlier appeal for naval cooperation within the alliance. In November Francis Joseph shocked Sterneck by informing the new Italian naval attaché in Vienna, Captain Raffaele Volpe, that he personally favored Austro-Italian naval cooperation in the interest of strengthening the Triple Alliance. Obliged to discuss the matter with Volpe, Sterneck deliberately obstructed their negotiations by demanding an Austrian commander for any joint fleet. He subsequently requested a secret meeting in Venice with the Italian navy minister, Vice Admiral Simone di Saint-Bon, but nothing came of the scheme before Saint-Bon's death in 1892. No doubt it would have been an interesting session, matching two former opposing ship captains from the Battle of Lissa.[120]

In the spring of 1892, Rudini's government gave way to the first ministry of Giovanni Giolitti, in which the navy's own Benedetto Brin held the portfolio of foreign minister. When King Umberto visited Berlin in June 1892, Brin repeated the appeal for a Triple Alliance naval agreement but received no encouragement from Caprivi and the Germans. Later that summer, Tirpitz was a guest at Italian naval exercises, and in the spring of 1893, on a visit to Italy, William II also viewed maneuvers at Venice. Both went home unimpressed, dashing Italian hopes for a naval treaty.[121]

CHAPTER 3

By then, however, the international situation had changed dramatically. After Caprivi cut Russia loose from the German alliance system, France quickly exploited the opportunity. In the summer of 1891, a French squadron visited the base of the Russian Baltic fleet at Kronstadt, near St. Petersburg, sending shock waves through the chancelleries of Europe.[122] But the evolving Franco-Russian friendship, finally formalized in January 1894, initially caused as much, if not more, concern in Britain than it did for the powers of the Triple Alliance. In the summer of 1891, Salisbury, eager to breathe new life into the Mediterranean Agreements, sent a British squadron to Venice. After the ships were reviewed by King Umberto, the flagship *Victoria* cruised to Rijeka for an inspection by Francis Joseph and Sterneck.[123] The following summer, however, Salisbury's fall and Gladstone's return to power cast doubt over the future of the agreements. Gladstone maintained cordial ties with Italy but had no intention of pursuing a policy that might require supporting Austria-Hungary in the Balkans, even against Russia.[124]

The summer of 1892 featured naval reviews to commemorate the four hundredth anniversary of Columbus's discovery of America. An improvement in Franco-Italian relations was manifested in the French navy squadron sent to Genoa for the Italian festivities. Austria-Hungary was represented at Genoa by Rear Admiral Spaun with the battleships *Kronprinz Rudolf* and *Kronprinzessin Stephanie* and the ram cruiser *Kaiser Franz Joseph I.* The latter ship, commanded by Captain Montecuccoli, went on to the Gulf of Cadiz for the Spanish celebration, where it was dwarfed by Italy's pre-dreadnoughts *Lepanto* and *Duilio.* During the visit to Genoa, the *Kronprinz Rudolf* was inspected by King Umberto and the Italian crown prince, the future Victor Emmanuel III.[125]

The deterioration of the German alliance system after 1890 ultimately proved to be fatal for both the Second Reich and the Dual Monarchy, but from the perspective of 1892 Austria-Hungary's situation hardly appeared bleak. Fear of the new Franco-Russian combination had the potential of pushing Britain closer to the Triple Alliance than ever before. The Mediterranean Agreements appeared likely to lapse, but the British, for the sake of their interests in Egypt and the security of the Suez Canal, maintained their own commitment to stop the Russian navy at the Dardanelles, providing a measure of security for Austria-Hungary in the Adriatic even without a formal agreement.

For its part, the navy had exploited the diplomatic climate of the past decade to the fullest extent possible. In the tense years of 1886–87, Sterneck depicted the Russian danger in terms dark enough to secure budgets of over thirteen million gulden for 1887 and 1888, over a million more than in the preceding and following years. Meanwhile, cooperation under the auspices of the Triple Alliance and Mediterranean Agreements had opened possibilities for operations with allies outside of the Adriatic, and the navy no longer appeared doomed to a future of purely defensive preparations in the Adriatic. But while there was talk of an offensive role, if only in league with other powers, it remained to be seen whether the Dual Monarchy would be willing to invest in a fleet strong enough to stand up to other navies. The modest force tailored more or less for the defense of the Adriatic was a far cry from one that would be a factor in the European balance of naval power.

Ten years after the conclusion of the Triple Alliance, the status of Austro-Italian relations—always crucial to the navy—remained uncertain. The French appearance at Genoa for the Columbus commemoration bore witness to an easing of Franco-Italian tensions, and a rapprochement between Paris and Rome certainly would destroy the alliance and once again make the Italian navy a threat to Austro-Hungarian security in the Adriatic. But the same festivities in Genoa had included the tour of Spaun's flagship by the Italian king and crown prince. While on the surface an event of little significance, the visit was the first by an Italian or Habsburg monarch aboard a warship of the other navy. It came a full decade after the conclusion of the Austro-Italian alliance and twenty-six years after the Battle of Lissa.

In the area of naval strategy and tactics, Austria-Hungary had played an important part in the era of the *Jeune Ecole*. Even though it would have no enduring impact on the navy, the *Jeune Ecole* philosophy filled an important strategic void in the decade following the initial signing of the Triple Alliance, a time in which the future role of the fleet was very much in doubt. And just as Aube's strategy was important to Sterneck and his navy, the Austro-Hungarian navy was important to the *Jeune Ecole*. In contrast to so many other times in their history, in the 1880s the Austrians were near the leading edge of naval developments in their pioneering torpedo tactics, an area crucial to the new strategy. From the

113

perspective of the First World War, Aube's predictions seemed prophetic, especially his conviction that battleships ultimately would stay in port while smaller vessels ventured out to fight. Indeed, Germany's deadly campaign of submarine warfare in the First World War seemed to vindicate the *Jeune Ecole*. But the torpedo boat of the 1880s was not the sort of weapon that the submarine ultimately would become. Sterneck and his colleagues in other navies learned through their maneuvers and exercises that the boats were too vulnerable to enemy fire and—notwithstanding the initial arguments of Aube and Charmes— were not viable as autonomous seagoing warships, as submarines later would be.

As for the coastal defense strategies of the *Jeune Ecole* era, the terrain of the Adriatic hinterland and problems with communications made an integrated system such as the one adopted by the German navy in the 1870s and 1880s hardly feasible for Austria-Hungary. A Habsburg army could not rush from Bosnia to Dalmatia, over rugged mountains on poor roads with no railroads, in the same way that a German corps could ride the rails across the flatlands of northern Germany to the Baltic or North Sea coast. Indeed, in 1869 and 1882, when the army had to suppress rebellions in remote areas of southern Dalmatia and Hercegovina, it had relied upon the navy for much of its transport. In the committee of inquiry of 1880, Archduke Albrecht and the army leadership had encouraged the navy to develop itself as a purely defensive force; ironically, the army was in no position to participate in an integrated system of coastal defense in the Adriatic littoral.

The navy's relatively cordial relationship with the army was one of the only political factors that Sterneck could count on, yet after almost a decade of consistent support, key military figures failed to rally behind his fleet plan of 1891. Even though Sterneck enjoyed the emperor's sympathies—in the first twelve years of his command there were five formal imperial visits to the fleet, compared to just two in Pöck's dozen years at the helm—Francis Joseph also did not intervene to save the plan. Sterneck had been more successful than Pöck in promoting the navy's cause (and in promoting his own image as a successful *Marinekommandant*), but as his tenure continued into the 1890s, he would have to restore or renew his ties with the army and the emperor and overcome the schism within the corps caused by the philosophical conflict over the ideas of the *Jeune Ecole*.

On the broader level of Austro-Hungarian politics, Sterneck had endured and at times managed to overcome Budapest's general resistance to joint military and naval expenditure. But in the future, he would have to appease more than just the two governments of the Dual Monarchy. The expansion and modernization of the fleet promised to generate economic benefits, and the competing regions of the empire would demand their fair share, making the equitable distribution of navy contracts a heated political issue. This conflict, like the overall nationality problem of the 1890s, would involve the Czechs as well as the German Austrians and Hungarians.

Faced with an ever more complex political scene, the navy badly needed a powerful patron whose influence could overcome most, if not all, obstacles. Indeed, the reversal of Sterneck's fortunes in the early 1890s demonstrated that progress and growth could not be sustained without one. Archduke Ferdinand Max had been such a man, but thirty years later there was little hope that another Habsburg so close to the throne would take such a strong interest in the fleet. In December 1892, at the end of an eventful year, the navy attached little importance to the departure of Archduke Francis Ferdinand aboard the ram cruiser *Kaiserin Elisabeth* on the first leg of a trip around the world.

NOTES

1. Reiter, "Entwicklung," 75.

2. *StPD*, XVII (10 November 1882), 24–26, 182, 188; ibid., XVIII (10 November 1883), 23–27, 48, 51; *Jahresbericht der k.k. Kriegsmarine* (1884), 42, 44.

3. *Jahresbericht der k.k. Kriegsmarine* (1880), 26; (1881), 29; on the *Salamander*'s cockroach problem, see Koudelka, *Denn Österreich lag einst am Meer,* 14–15.

4. See Bayer von Bayersburg, *Österreichs Admirale,* 139–40; and Harbauer, *Der Kaiser,* 130–37. The navy's first full admiral was Baron Anton Bourguignon von Baumberg. Born in 1808, Bourguignon entered naval service at the age of seventeen and rose as high as second in command under Ferdinand Max. He never commanded the navy and served as harbor admiral in Pola from 1865 until his death in 1879. Francis Joseph promoted Bourguignon to full admiral in 1875, on his fiftieth anniversary in the service. On Bourguignon's activity before 1866, see Sondhaus, *The Habsburg Empire and the Sea,* 151, 187, and 197n. 32.

5. Pitner's promotion took effect in October 1882, Millosicz's in November. See *Rangs- und Eintheilungsliste der k.k. Kriegsmarine* (1883) and Bayer von Bayersburg, *Österreichs Admirale,* 129.

6. See Ropp, *The Development of a Modern Navy,* 136.

7. HHSA, PA, XL, Carton 293: GMR 315 (23 September 1883).

CHAPTER 3

8. On Pöck's mental health, see Höbelt, "Die Marine," 701; Sterneck to Richard Sterneck, Vienna, 13 November 1883, Sterneck, *Erinnerungen,* 217. According to *StPD,* XVIII (10 November 1883), 9, Pöck was present at the morning meeting of the Austrian Delegation just three days before Sterneck replaced him. The record shows that the admiral did not address the Delegations in defense of either of his last two budgets, passed in November 1882 and November 1883, respectively.

9. Among 322 cadets from the graduating classes of 1884–96, only 16 (4.9 percent) resigned their commissions before being promoted. See Salcher, *Marine-Akademie,* 66.

10. Höbelt, "Die Marine," 734, characterizes the position of Pola harbor admiral as the de facto "number two" office in the navy, at least during peacetime. The post acquired its prestige thanks to Bourguignon, who was the highest ranking officer in the navy for the last eleven of his fourteen years as harbor admiral. See note 4 above.

11. Wagner, "Die obersten Behörden," 75–77.

12. Wagner, "Die k.(u.)k. Armee: Gliederung und Aufgabenstellung," 491–92. The army's *Landwehr* or *Honvéd* obligation was for two years, following the initial three years of active duty and seven years in the reserves. In each year, a share of the army's draftees were assigned directly to the *Landwehr* or *Honvéd.*

13. Höbelt, "Die Marine," 741–42.

14. Figures from *Militärstatistisches Jahrbuch* (1887).

15. The change in philosophy is explained at length in the *Jahresbericht der k.k. Kriegsmarine* (1885), 24–25.

16. See Sokol, *Des Kaisers Seemacht,* 143; Ropp, *The Development of a Modern Navy,* 136.

17. Francis Joseph to Sterneck, Pola, 9 July 1884, text in Sterneck, *Erinnerungen,* 220–21. See also Harbauer, *Der Kaiser,* 139–50.

18. For details on these overseas missions and those mentioned below, see Bayer von Bayersburg, *Auf weiter Fahrt,* 80–112, 115–17.

19. See Babudieri, *Industrie, commerci e navigazione,* 141.

20. Leopold Wölfling, *My Life Story: From Archduke to Grocer,* 31–32; see also Salcher, *Marine-Akademie,* 73–74. Leopold Ferdinand, born in 1868, was the eldest son of Ferdinand IV, the last Habsburg grand duke of Tuscany. He was ultimately the black sheep of the family, and his memoirs are perhaps more entertaining than accurate.

21. See Sondhaus, "The Austro-Hungarian Naval Officer Corps," 66–67.

22. Figures from Salcher, *Marine-Akademie,* 66. A total of 256 academy graduates reached the rank of ensign in the years 1885–95.

23. The *Almanach für die k.k. Kriegsmarine* lists Rudolph for the first time in 1879 (185), with the rank of captain first class (*Linienschiffskapitän*), equivalent to a colonel in the army. In the autumn of 1883, he was promoted to vice admiral, the rank he held at the time of his death.

24. Bombelles was born in 1832, the son of a tutor to Francis Joseph and Ferdinand Max. After growing up as a boyhood companion to the imperial princes, he entered the army in 1849 as an officer in the 5th Hussars. When Ferdinand Max entered the navy in 1851, Bombelles transferred to the naval infantry regiment; he became a sea officer in 1854. Bombelles became Rudolph's chamberlain in 1877, eight years after reentering Austrian service. See *Österreichisches Biographisches Lexikon 1815–1950* (Graz: Verlag Hermann Böhlaus Nachfolger, 1957), 1:101.

25. The sword is now on display in the navy exhibit of the Heeresgeschichtliches Museum in Vienna.

26. In the summer of 1887, Rudolph was in England attending the fiftieth jubilee of Queen Victoria. Sokol, *Des Kaisers Seemacht,* 139, is almost alone among Austrian naval historians in his favorable view of Rudolph.

27. See Schöndorfer, "Kriegsschiffbau," 33-34. Höbelt, "Die Marine," 708, comments on the factor of French influence.

28. *Almanach für die k.k. Kriegsmarine* (1885), 156; (1886), 157; (1887), 157; (1888), 155. The project was always presented to the Delegations as a "rebuilding" of the *Ferdinand Max,* appearing under both names after its launching. This practice continued until the summer of 1889, when the Delegations voted the last installment to fund its construction. See *StPD,* XXV (8 July 1889), 12.

29. Sterneck to Richard Sterneck, Vienna, 3 March 1886, Sterneck, *Erinnerungen,* 232.

30. *Jahresbericht der k.u.k. Kriegsmarine* (1897), 119.

31. Sterneck to his sister, Vienna, 27 November 1884, Sterneck, *Erinnerungen,* 228; *StPD,* XIX (14 November 1884), 78-80, 119-20.

32. Sterneck to Richard Sterneck, Vienna, 3 January 1885, Sterneck, *Erinnerungen,* 229. Sterneck clung to his bachelorhood until 1896 when, at the age of sixty-seven, he married the young widow of his nephew Richard.

33. E.g., Sterneck to Richard Sterneck, Corfu, 9 June 1886, Sterneck, *Erinnerungen,* 240, commenting on his itinerary for the summer. Sokol, *Austro-Hungarian Navy,* 64, calls Sterneck "an accomplished courtier," a characterization far from accurate for his early years as commander.

34. Sterneck to Richard Sterneck, Vienna, 21 October 1885, Sterneck, *Erinnerungen,* 231.

35. *StPD,* XX (9 November 1885), 30-34. On the mood of the Hungarians in the fall of 1885, see Sterneck to Richard Sterneck, Vienna, 19 November 1885, Sterneck, *Erinnerungen,* 232. On Sterneck's view of Taaffe, see Sterneck to wife, n.d. [1896], ibid., 283. In the 1885 elections, the German liberal share of the *Reichsrat* fell from 170 seats (48 percent) to just 114 (32 percent). On the 1864 budget, see Sondhaus, *The Habsburg Empire and the Sea,* 225.

36. Reiter, "Entwicklung," 173; Sterneck to Eberan, Pest, 21 November 1886, Sterneck, *Erinnerungen,* 249.

37. *StPD,* XXI (23 November 1886), 55-61; Reiter, "Entwicklung," 86. Most of the special credit mentioned here and below (3.5 million gulden) was granted in March 1887 as part of a 52.5 million gulden supplement to the war ministry budget. See *StPD,* XXII (7 March 1887), 13.

38. Sterneck to Richard Sterneck, Trieste, 11 June 1887, Sterneck, *Erinnerungen,* 258, which also praises Francis Joseph for dutifully attending the tactical and torpedo maneuvers, in lieu of the grand fleet reviews staged for monarchs in other maritime countries.

39. *StPD,* XXIII (17 November 1887), 18-22, 54; Wagner, "Die obersten Behörden," 82. Koudelka, *Denn Österreich lag einst am Meer,* 58, dates Lehnert's campaign from 1888.

40. Sterneck to sister, Vienna, 21 October 1888, Sterneck, *Erinnerungen,* 265.

41. Sterneck to sister, Pola, 10 November 1888, Sterneck, *Erinnerungen,* 265; *StPD,* XXIV (25 June 1888), 42-48.

42. *StPD,* XXV (8 July 1889), 10-14; ibid., XXVI (18 June 1890), 9-12, 16; ibid., XXVII (3 December 1891), 184-85.

CHAPTER 3

43. In the 1891 *Reichsrat* elections, the German liberals retained their 32 percent share, while the Young Czechs won 10 percent, various German Nationalists 6 percent, and Christian Socials 3 percent. For a detailed analysis, see Lothar Höbelt, "Die Linke und die Wahlen von 1891," 270–301.

44. Under Pöck the navy almost always came in under its budget; under Sterneck's command, as in the Tegetthoff era, the navy almost always overstepped its appropriation. The years under budget were 1868, 1873–1885, 1888, and 1889; the navy exceeded its budget in the years 1869–72, 1886–87, and 1890–96. In 1890 the navy spent almost 800,000 more than it had been allotted. Figures from table in *StPD*, XXXV (12 January 1900), 338.

45. Handelsministerium to Seebehörde Triest, Vienna, 7 June 1888, Österreichisches Staatsarchiv, Verwaltungsarchiv (cited hereafter as VA), Handel 4/b, 23306/1888, discusses the duty-free list of shipbuilding materials. The navy rarely did business with French companies but contracted with the Muraille firm of Toulon for the water-distilling equipment for both *Rudolf* and *Stephanie;* see *Jahresbericht der k.k. Kriegsmarine* (1885), 53–54; (1886), 51; (1887), 54. See also Alfred von Zvolensky, *Handbuch über die k.k. Kriegs-Marine,* 15.

46. Construction data for light cruisers, destroyers, and torpedo boats from Bilzer, "Die Schiffe und Fahrzeuge der k.(u.)k. Kriegsmarine," passim, and *Jahresbericht der k.u.k. Kriegsmarine* (1913), 98–111.

47. Bilzer, "Schiffstypenblatt S.M.S. *Tegetthoff,*" 34.

48. Figure from *StPD*, XXVII (3 December 1891), 137.

49. Skoda won a competition to provide stern posts for two German pre-dreadnoughts; merchant marine contracts came in from Germany, Russia, Denmark, Holland, and even Italy. See Josef Mentschl and Gustav Otruba, *Österreichische Industrielle und Bankiers,* 159.

50. See René Greger, *Austro-Hungarian Warships of World War I,* 9–10; *StPD*, XXVIII (19 October 1892), 187; Brousek, *Die Grossindustrie Böhmens,* 131.

51. *StPD*, XXI (23 November 1886), 58. Employment figures for the Stabilimento Tecnico Triestino for 1882 in Sema, *Il Cantiere San Rocco,* 18.

52. Fulvio Babudieri, *L'industria armatoriale di Trieste e della regione Giulia dal 1815 al 1918,* 207–10; Giovanni Gerolimi, *L'Arsenale Triestino, 1853–1953,* 51–53.

53. On the founding of the iron and steel cartel, see Wilhelm Kestranek, *Die Eisenindustrie der österreichisch-ungarischen Monarchie,* 12–13; and David F. Good, *The Economic Rise of the Habsburg Empire, 1750–1914,* 220.

54. Figures from *Jahresbericht der k.u.k. Kriegsmarine* (1913), 92, 94.

55. Glaise-Horstenau, *Franz Josephs Weggefährte,* 411.

56. Wagner, "Die obersten Behörden," 77; *StPD*, XX (9 November 1885), 34. In the years 1862–65, the short-lived Ministry of Marine had had jurisdiction over both the navy and the merchant marine, a configuration of responsibilities criticized by those holding the office of minister. See Sondhaus, *The Habsburg Empire and the Sea,* 244–45.

57. Reiter, "Entwicklung," 84–88.

58. Hungarian Pénzügyministerium to Reichsfinanzministerium, Budapest, 15 October 1888, FA, 4,069-RFM/1888, indicates that the sum would be included in the Hungarian budget for 1889.

59. See Rothenberg, *The Army of Francis Joseph,* 109, 119–120.

60. Figures from *Militärstatistisches Jahrbuch* (1885).

61. Bilzer, "Schiffstypenblatt S.M.S. *Tegetthoff,*" 34–35.

62. Aube's views also reflected the influence of his father-in-law, Louis Faidherbe, one of the foremost proponents of French colonial expansion. See Ropp, *The Development of a Modern Navy*, 155–56. For a detailed analysis of the strategy of the *Jeune Ecole*, see Volkmar Bueb, *Die "Junge Schule" der französischen Marine: Strategie und Politik 1875–1900*. See also Lawrence Sondhaus, "Strategy, Tactics, and the Politics of Penury: The Austro-Hungarian Navy and the *Jeune Ecole*"; and Lothar Höbelt, "Von der Jeune Ecole zur Flottenpolitik: Die Rolle der österreichisch-ungarischen Kriegsmarine im letzten Viertel des neunzehnten Jahrhunderts."

63. Aube was influenced by other French critics of armored warships, most notably Captain Louis Grivel, whose writings in the 1860s emphasized the disruption of enemy commerce as the ultimate goal of any naval war. See Ropp, *The Development of a Modern Navy*, 19, 156.

64. Ibid., 132, 159–60.

65. Marder, *The Anatomy of British Sea Power*, 86–87; Ropp, *The Development of a Modern Navy*, 160–65.

66. Ropp, *The Development of a Modern Navy*, 28–30, 157.

67. Aube quoted in ibid., 165.

68. Marder, *The Anatomy of British Sea Power*, 125.

69. HHSA, AR, F 44 - Marinewesen, Carton 4: Varia ab 1871 (Austausch 1874–96) contains a far greater exchange of information with France than with Britain or Germany, even though Austria-Hungary accredited a naval attaché to the former and was closely allied with the latter. Much of the interaction concerned developments in artillery. In ibid., Carton 6: Generalia ab 1871, Besuche 1/48, Pöck's second in command, Millosicz, gives the navy's permission for a French deputy to visit Pola in late summer 1882.

70. Ropp, *The Development of a Modern Navy*, 234.

71. See ibid., 134, 136.

72. Sterneck to Richard Sterneck, Vienna, 3 March 1886, Sterneck, *Erinnerungen*, 232. Marder, *The Anatomy of British Sea Power*, 86n, calls Charmes's *La réforme de la Marine* "the first written formulation of the complete theory" of the *Jeune Ecole*.

73. Ropp, *The Development of a Modern Navy*, 136.

74. Sterneck to Eberan, Pola, 7 June 1887, Sterneck, *Erinnerungen*, 254.

75. Episode recounted in Koudelka, *Denn Österreich lag einst am Meer*, 35. A young officer aboard one of the attacking torpedo boats, Koudelka places the exercise in the summer of 1888; the *Jahresbericht der k.k. Kriegsmarine* (1888), 32, describes such a simulated attack occurring on 12 July 1888. The record shows, however, that Archduke Albrecht visited the navy in 1887, not in 1888, and that the *Erzherzog Albrecht*, a participant in the summer maneuvers of 1887, was not involved in 1888. See ibid. (1887), 28–29.

76. Floodlights and torpedo nets mentioned in Sterneck to Eberan, Pest, 12 October 1886; and same to same, Pola, 7 June 1887, Sterneck, *Erinnerungen*, 244, 254.

77. Ironically, the French navy led the way in adopting steel armor in 1884, two years before Aube became navy minister. See Ropp, *The Development of a Modern Navy*, 67.

78. Sterneck to Richard Sterneck, Trieste, 11 June 1887, Sterneck, *Erinnerungen*, 256.

79. See Höbelt, "Die Marine," 710.

80. Josef von Lehnert, "Rückblick auf die Entwicklung der k.k. Flotte," 233. Zvolensky, *Handbuch*, 32, refers to the Italian navy's 3,100-ton *Giovanni Bausan* as the first

ram cruiser. Built by Armstrong in the years 1882–85, the *Bausan* had a ram bow, very little armor, and carried two 10-inch and six 6-inch guns. See also Giorgerini, *Almanacco*, 284–85.

81. *StPD*, XXI (23 November 1886), 58, first refers to "Rammkreuzer A" (the future *Kaiser Franz Joseph I*) as *Ersatz Lissa;* ibid., XXIII (17 November 1887), 19, refers to "Rammkreuzer B" (the *Kaiserin Elisabeth*) as *Ersatz Kaiser.*

82. Figures from *Jahresbericht der k.u.k. Kriegsmarine* (1913), 112–13.

83. Reiter, "Entwicklung," 87. The initial funds for "Rammkreuzer C" were appropriated anyway, as part of the budget for 1890.

84. Schöndorfer, "Kriegsschiffbau," 34–35. See also Koudelka, *Denn Österreich lag einst am Meer,* 58.

85. Ropp, *The Development of a Modern Navy,* 178–80.

86. Marder, *The Anatomy of British Sea Power,* 143.

87. See Baratelli, *La marina militare italiana,* 259–60; and Giorgerini, *Almanacco,* 419–27.

88. Sterneck to Richard Sterneck, Vienna, 6 July 1891, Sterneck, *Erinnerungen,* 269.

89. Reiter, "Entwicklung," 89–91. On the question of the defense of overseas commerce, Sterneck ironically also conformed to the strategy of the *Jeune Ecole*. Reflecting the fact that it was, at heart, a French strategy for warfare against Britain, Aube's theory had assumed that the ruthless destruction of commerce in wartime would be mutual but was feasible nonetheless because, owing to Britain's dependence on maritime trade, it would hurt her more than it would hurt France. To embrace the *Jeune Ecole* fully, one had to write off the merchant marine of one's own country. To do so in a country with constitutional government would involve alienating a navy's most important domestic constituencies.

90. Bolfras quoted in Höbelt, "Die Marine," 709.

91. Höbelt, "Die Marine," 709.

92. Sterneck to Richard Basso (personal adjutant), Vienna, 22 August 1891, Sterneck, *Erinnerungen,* 270.

93. On the deliberations of the council, see HHSA, PA, XL, GMR 370 (20 September 1891). The budget approved in December 1891 was for just over 11.5 million gulden; a supplementary credit brought the sum to just under 11.7 million. See *StPD*, XXVII (3 December 1891), 183–84; ibid., XXVIII (19 October 1892), 190. On Metternich and the navy in 1815, see Sondhaus, *The Habsburg Empire and the Sea,* 42–43.

94. Some sources refer to the *Maria Theresia* as a protected cruiser because its waterline belt armor was only four inches thick; Austria-Hungary's subsequent armored cruisers were built with waterline belts of eight inches. By definition, a protected cruiser had an armored deck but not an armored hull, while an armored cruiser had both. On the importance of 1891 as a watershed year in the navy's history, see Höbelt, "Die Marine," 711. On the *Maria Theresia*'s origins as "Rammkreuzer C," see note 83 above.

95. Cf. *Almanach für die k.u.k. Kriegsmarine* (1894), 187; and (1895), 300; see also ibid. (1902), 287; and *StPD*, XXXVIII (9 June 1902), 549–50.

96. See Wagner, "Die k.(u.)k. Armee," 382–83.

97. Stefan von Herzfeld (consul) to Andrássy, Moscow, 10 February 1872, HHSA, AR, F 44 - Marinewesen, Carton 9: Varia 2/7.

98. Ropp, *The Development of a Modern Navy,* 87; Höbelt, "Die Marine," 707–8.

99. On the *Duilio's* various problems, see Ropp, *The Development of a Modern Navy,* 80, 84, 85–86, 102.

100. Ropp, *The Development of a Modern Navy,* 203, 240.

101. Even though Austria-Hungary had more warships involved than any power besides Britain, its largest vessel (the 3,600-ton *Kaiser Max*) was dwarfed by the largest battleships of the other powers: the British *Neptune* (9,300 tons), the German *Friedrich Karl* (6,000 tons), the Russian *Dmitri Donskoi* (5,800 tons), and the Italian *Ancona* (4,500 tons). HHSA, PA, XVI, Cartons 80 and 81, Liasse IV: Griechenland, Flottendemonstration 1886, contains diplomatic and operational instructions to Spaun as well as his reports. For a brief overview of the operation, see Sokol, *Des Kaisers Seemacht,* 144–45; and Koudelka, *Denn Österreich lag einst am Meer,* 26–30.

102. Sterneck to Richard Sterneck, Vienna, 3 March 1886, Sterneck, *Erinnerungen,* 233.

103. See Cedric J. Lowe, *Salisbury and the Mediterranean, 1886–1896,* 8–25. According to Lowe, the nine points included in Salisbury's note "were literally translated word for word" from an earlier version proposed by Kálnoky (24). See note from Salisbury to Károlyi (Austro-Hungarian ambassador) and Catalani (Italian ambassador), London, 12 December 1887, text in Cedric J. Lowe, *The Reluctant Imperialists: British Foreign Policy, 1878–1902,* 2:61–62.

104. On the renewal of the Triple Alliance, see Bridge, *From Sadowa to Sarajevo,* 164–66; for text of Austro-Italian Balkan agreement, 416. On the depth of the British commitment, Lowe, *The Reluctant Imperialists,* refers to the Mediterranean Agreements as "the nearest thing to an alliance that Britain had ever made in peacetime"(1:120).

105. See Bridge, *Sadowa to Sarajevo,* 176.

106. Ropp, *The Development of a Modern Navy,* 191–92; Lowe, *Salisbury,* 35–36. The British visited Genoa in mid-February and again at the end of March, when a French move against Italy again was rumored. On both occasions, the ships were provided by the Channel squadron, which was already on an extended cruise in the Mediterranean.

107. Baratelli, *La marina militare italiana,* 272–73; Ropp, *The Development of a Modern Navy,* 195; Sokol, *Des Kaisers Seemacht,* 147–48; *Jahresbericht der k.k. Kriegsmarine* (1888), 27–33. Ropp incorrectly places the Barcelona demonstration in March 1888; Sokol contends that a French squadron was also present. Manfroni, promoted to rear admiral in 1884 by Sterneck, fell ill on the voyage to Barcelona and had to retire, for health reasons, upon returning home. He died a year later, at the age of fifty-seven. See Bayer von Bayersburg, *Österreichs Admirale,* 124–25.

108. Bridge, *Sadowa to Sarajevo,* 183.

109. Höbelt, "Die Marine," 712.

110. Ibid., 712. Early in 1887, in the cordial atmosphere surrounding the renewal of the Triple Alliance, the Italian military attaché in Vienna had requested detailed information on the Austro-Hungarian system of coastal defense. In a very brief reply, a suspicious Sterneck gave no specifics, merely citing the importance of mines and torpedoes in the navy's defensive strategy. Sterneck to Min. des Äussern, Vienna, 27 January 1887, HHSA, AR, F 44 - Marinewesen, Carton 8: Varia 1/22.

111. Ropp, *The Development of a Modern Navy,* 193.

112. Russian visits to Rijeka, Trieste, and Pola are discussed in several letters from Pöck to the foreign ministry (Min. des Äussern) in HHSA, AR, F 44 - Marinewesen, Carton 6: Besuche 1/2 (23 January 1872), Besuche 1/16 (22 January 1876), Besuche 1/8 (2 March 1876), Besuche 1/36 (25 March 1880), Besuche 1/37 (15 June 1880); also in Eberan to Min. des Äussern, Vienna, 4 April 1884, ibid., Besuche 1/58.

113. Höbelt, "Die Marine," 707-8.

114. Ivo Lambi, *The Navy and German Power Politics, 1862-1914,* 25, 71-72.

115. Ibid., 45.

116. Sokol, *Des Kaisers Seemacht,* 148; Koudelka, *Denn Österreich lag einst am Meer,* 38-43. Sterneck to Min. des Äussern, Vienna, 3 April 1890, PA, XL, Carton 146: Korr. mit inneren und Militärbehörden 1890-91, indicates that plans for the visit to Germany started in March 1889. Kálnoky to Sterneck, Vienna, 17 April 1890, ibid., conveys William II's formal invitation to the navy to participate in joint maneuvers.

117. Figures from *Jahresbericht der k.u.k. Kriegsmarine* (1913), 118-21. Eleven of the twenty-five German armored warships were 1,100-ton coastal defense gunboats, roughly one third the size of the smallest Austro-Hungarian ironclads.

118. Roon's interest in Austrian-built ironclads is referred to in Count B. Chotek (chargé) to Mensdorff, Berlin, 2 November 1864, HHSA, AR, F 44 - Marinewesen, Carton 3: Generalia 1860-70; and Chotek to Mensdorff, Berlin, 6 January 1865, ibid. See also Sondhaus, *The Habsburg Empire and the Sea,* 243.

119. Ropp, *The Development of a Modern Navy,* 194-95.

120. Baratelli, *La marina militare italiana,* 243-44. For a text of the renewed alliance (dated Berlin, 6 May 1891), see Bridge, *The Habsburg Monarchy,* 388-90.

121. Ibid., 244-45.

122. On the Kronstadt visit, see George F. Kennan, *The Fateful Alliance: France, Russia, and the Coming of the First World War,* 97-115; and Ropp, *The Development of a Modern Navy,* 239 and chapter 14 passim.

123. Marder, *The Anatomy of British Sea Power,* 173; Sokol, *Des Kaisers Seemacht,* 149. Bridge, *The Habsburg Monarchy,* 191, indicates that the British visited Rijeka first, then Venice. In any event, it was the first significant British naval visit to a Habsburg port in a decade. In June 1881, shortly after France's annexation of Tunisia, the British Mediterranean squadron had visited Trieste. See *Jahresbericht der k.k. Kriegsmarine* (1881), 19.

124. On the continuation of an informal Anglo-Italian entente, see Marder, *The Anatomy of British Sea Power,* 171.

125. Christopher Seton-Watson, *Italy: From Liberalism to Fascism, 1870-1925,* 177; Baratelli, *La marina militare italiana,* 273. In addition to the royal inspection, Spaun hosted a shipboard reception for Genoese high society. According to Koudelka, then a lieutenant aboard the *Kronprinz Rudolf,* the admiral's charm and diplomatic tact made the visit to Genoa a great success. See Koudelka, *Denn Österreich lag einst am Meer,* 45-46.

C H A P T E R 4 ≋

NAVALISM ASCENDANT

In the early 1890s, the navy's future appeared to be more muddled than ever, as changes in strategy and tactics at sea coincided with a transformation in Austrian domestic politics and a realignment in the European balance of power. The abandonment of the *Jeune Ecole*, the collapse of Taaffe's "Iron Ring," and the Mediterranean repercussions of the new Franco-Russian alliance left Sterneck searching for answers on virtually every front. But the navy's decade of uncertainty gave way to an unexpected era of good fortune. Foreign policy considerations supported the revival of the battle fleet, and the construction of battleships—though far more expensive than the cruisers of the *Jeune Ecole*—ironically enabled the navy to build an unprecedented base of political support. As Sterneck increased his patronage of domestic industry, former political enemies became friends, and the fleet also gained allies among the wide array of new emerging parties. Most important of all, at least in the long run, future heir to the throne Francis Ferdinand became a convert to the cause of navalism.

THE NAVY UNDER STERNECK: DOMESTIC AND FOREIGN POLICY (1892–97)

Francis Ferdinand's cruise of 1892–93 was not his first sea voyage or his first formal contact with the navy. As the eldest son of Emperor Francis Joseph's younger brother, Charles Ludwig, the archduke grew up in relative obscurity, dogged by poor health. In early 1885, at the age of twenty-one, he recuperated from a lung ailment on an extended sea and land trip to the eastern Mediterranean and Near East.[1] Francis Ferdinand's first official visit with the navy came in 1887, when he and his stepmother, Archduchess Maria Theresa, accompanied Francis Joseph to Pola for the launching of the *Kronprinz Rudolf.* During fleet maneuvers, the twenty-three-year-old archduke joined the imperial party aboard the flagship *Prinz Eugen* but did not make much of an impression on Sterneck. In a long letter to his nephew describing the visit, the *Marinekommandant* mentioned the archduchess but not Francis Ferdinand.[2]

In January 1889, the suicide of Crown Prince Rudolph brought the archduke much closer to the throne, although his father technically became the emperor's heir. In the meantime, his army career continued to occupy much of his time. His first active commission, in 1883, had been in the 4th (Austrian) Dragoons, but subsequent transfers took him first to the 102nd (Bohemian) Infantry, which was 90 percent Czech, then to the 9th (Hungarian) Hussars. No friend of restive nationalities, Francis Ferdinand did not enjoy life with the 102nd and had an even worse time with the 9th Hussars, which he commanded from the spring of 1890 until his departure aboard the *Kaiserin Elisabeth* late in 1892. The regiment's official languages were Hungarian and German, but in a stormy meeting with his officers, Francis Ferdinand insisted that they speak only German in his presence. Accounts of the incident soon appeared in the leading Hungarian newspapers, giving the archduke the anti-Hungarian label he would carry for the rest of his life.[3] During his years with the 9th Hussars, the archduke's nebulous Habsburg conservatism started to jell into a more specific philosophy: he became convinced that in political life and especially within the armed forces, the dynasty must overcome the disintegrating influence of nationalism, above all the aspirations of the Hungarians.

By December 1892, when he boarded the *Kaiserin Elisabeth,* Francis Ferdinand was badly in need of the escape and diversion of foreign travel. Sterneck entrusted Captain Alois von Becker with the command of the cruiser and included among its complement of officers Archduke Leopold Ferdinand, by then a veteran of over five years of naval service. Their route went from Trieste via the Suez Canal to Ceylon, then Bombay, where Francis Ferdinand and his personal entourage disembarked for a tour of India. The *Kaiserin Elisabeth* met Francis Ferdinand at Calcutta, and the voyage proceeded by way of the Dutch East Indies to Sydney, where the archduke again left the ship in order to tour the Australian outback. From Sydney the cruise continued through the islands of the southwest Pacific, then to Singapore, Hong Kong, and Japan. The *Kaiserin Elisabeth* left Francis Ferdinand at the end of his Japanese tour and went on to show the flag in East Asian waters before returning home by way of the Suez Canal later in 1893. The archduke continued his circumnavigation of the globe, traveling from Yokohama to Vancouver aboard a Canadian passenger liner, traversing North America by rail, then crossing the Atlantic aboard a French steamer. In October 1893, he arrived in Vienna from Le Havre, to be welcomed home by Francis Joseph.

Of all his experiences on the journey, Francis Ferdinand recalled with the greatest fondness the months aboard the *Kaiserin Elisabeth.* Like all larger Habsburg warships, the cruiser was a floating Austria-Hungary in miniature; its German-speaking officer corps included men from several nationalities, and the crew of almost four hundred sailors was even more diverse. But the professionalism of the officers and discipline of their crew allowed the ship to function with no sign of the divisive problems that the archduke had experienced in the army, problems that plagued the Dual Monarchy as a whole. In sharp contrast to his recent criticism of his subalterns in the 9th Hussars, Francis Ferdinand praised the "agreeable circle of officers" aboard the *Kaiserin Elisabeth* who made him feel like "a member of a great family."[4] He commended the crew for their loyalty and patriotism; indeed, in his account of a farewell ceremony held in his honor in Yokohama harbor, he recalled that the songs and speeches of the seamen "moved me almost to tears."[5] In taking leave of the ship, he lauded the superior brand of *Kameradschaft* "that reigns in our sea officer corps" and the manner in which the crew, especially the Croatians, "persevered in the faithful performance of their duties."[6] In addition to his new respect for the navy as an example of a multinational Habsburg institution that actually worked, Francis Ferdinand also developed a strong conviction that true great power status required sea power. From that time onward, he intended to help Austria-Hungary build a respectable fleet.[7] For the immediate future, however, the archduke returned to the army, taking command of a brigade in Bohemia in the spring of 1894.[8]

While Francis Ferdinand's cruise aboard the *Kaiserin Elisabeth* ultimately led to better times for the navy, his potential usefulness would not be realized for several more years. But if Sterneck could not yet benefit from the help of the archduke, at least he was able to exploit the political situation in Austria following the defeat of Taaffe's "Iron Ring" in the elections of 1891. Even though the 11.7 million gulden appropriation for 1892 had included no money for new battleships or cruisers, the meeting of the Delegations in December 1891 had been a turning point in the political history of the navy. Conveniently forgetting the traditional posture of the German liberals and his own virulent antinavy rhetoric of the years before the "Iron Ring," Victor Wilhelm Russ of Bohemia called the fleet an "important part of our armed forces" and lamented that it had not received sufficient attention from the public or the Delegations, implying that the relative neglect had been Taaffe's fault. In a clear departure from the mentality of earlier years, Russ praised Sterneck for having the cruiser *Maria Theresia* laid down by the Stabilimento Tecnico Triestino even though a foreign shipyard had submitted a lower bid for the contract.[9] For his part, Sterneck used the occasion to announce that for the first time in over twenty years, the navy again was buying domestic armor plate: after the steel works of Witkowitz (Vítkovice) in Moravia won a competition with foreign manufacturers to provide steel armor for the river monitors *Körös* and *Szamos,* the navy also awarded Witkowitz the far more lucrative armor contract for the *Maria Theresia.* Russ welcomed the development as "a great success for Austrian industry."[10]

When the Delegations convened in the autumn of 1892 to approve the budget for the following year, Alois Spinčić of Istria argued that the delegates would approve greater expenditure for warships built in Austria from Austrian materials, in order to "support domestic industry" and "free ourselves entirely" from dependence on foreign imports.[11] Sterneck's allies also included the German Nationalists, a growing factor in Austrian politics, whose pronavy sentiments reflected those of Georg von Schönerer's Linz Program of a decade earlier, which had called for the "extensive expansion" of the navy.[12] The budget for 1893 rose only modestly, to twelve million gulden, but the appropriation included money to start one of the proposed trio of *Küstenverteidiger* (coast defenders), small, heavily armed battleships designed for service in the Adriatic. Not taking for granted the growing political support for battleship construction, Sterneck listed the 5,600-ton coast defense battleship *Monarch,* laid down in Pola in the summer of 1893, not as an additional warship but as a replacement for the harbor watch armored frigate *Habsburg*, which was dropped from the battle fleet in 1886.

International developments also worked in favor of the navy. The new Franco-Russian alliance initially had caused no great alarm in Austria-Hungary, but Italy's reaction to the realignment soon raised fears in Vienna. With France no longer isolated, Italy almost immediately started hedging its bets, and the subsequent mixed signals from Rome spawned fresh doubts over Italian fidelity to the Triple Alliance. For Habsburg military planners, the nightmare scenario of a two-front war against both Russia and Italy no longer seemed so improbable. In January 1893, Count Beck, on behalf of the General Staff, proposed an overall strengthening of the armed forces. While he concluded that "in our next war . . . the fleet will play only a secondary role," Beck believed that the navy should be able to defend the coast and "if possible" secure the Adriatic against enemy fleets. He recommended an increase in the navy budget and called for the construction of vessels designed for coastal defense.[13]

Beck's conclusions naturally lent support to Sterneck's program of coastal defense battleships. In February 1893, the foreign minister, Kálnoky, and the Hungarian minister-president, Wekerle, both spoke out in favor of an accelerated strengthening of the armed forces, and the council of ministers agreed to fixed increases in the army and navy budgets for the years 1894 through 1899. Subject to the approval of the Delegations, appropriations for the fleet would rise by 500,000 gulden per year to the end of the century.[14] Later in the year, the legislators concurred in the increase, at least for 1894, granting the navy 12.5 million gulden. The estimates provided for two sister ships for the coastal defense battleship *Monarch*, with both of the contracts going to the Stabilimento Tecnico Triestino. The *Wien* and *Budapest* were the first battleships since the *Tegetthoff* eighteen years earlier to be laid down as additions to the fleet rather than as replacement vessels.

Even though the status of the Mediterranean Agreements was in doubt, Austria-Hungary could take comfort in the fact that Britain remained committed to preventing a Russian naval sortie from the Black Sea into the eastern Mediterranean. In October 1893, a Russian squadron called at Toulon, returning the courtesy of the French naval visit to Kronstadt two years earlier. The British responded by reaffirming their friendship with the powers of the Triple Alliance, dispatching a squadron to the Italian base at La Spezia.[15] But even though the Foreign Office sought to preserve Britain's friendship with Italy as insurance against the new Franco-Russian threat in the Mediterranean, the British Admiralty by the early 1890s no longer had much confidence in the alliance value of the Italian fleet. In the late 1880s, Italy's program of naval expansion had left it with the third largest fleet in the world, trailing only Britain and France, but in 1893 the rapidly reviving Russian navy surpassed the Italians in battleship tonnage, as did the German navy in 1894. By the middle of the decade, few British naval leaders wanted to rely upon an Italian alliance to deny France control of the Mediterranean.[16] After succeeding Gladstone as prime minister in March 1894, Lord Rosebery informed Kálnoky that the British Mediterranean fleet would not be able to defend Constantinople and the Dardanelles against a Russian attack for fear of having the French fall upon it from the rear.[17]

The Russian visit to Toulon and Rosebery's revelations set the tone for the debate over the budget for 1895. In the council of ministers, Kálnoky and Sterneck painted the Mediterranean strategic picture in dark tones. Kálnoky cited "the importance of pursuing the development of the navy and the securing of our coasts, with the greatest possible speed." Joint finance minister Benjamin Kállay theorized that if war broke out and a Dalmatian port such as Cattaro fell to the enemy, the results would be devastating for the Habsburg position in the Adriatic. Prince Alfred zu Windischgrätz, Taaffe's successor as Austrian minister-president, likewise supported a stronger fleet.[18]

When the Delegations met in October 1894, Sterneck found almost unanimous support in the Austrian contingent. Along with his purchases of steel and small caliber guns from the Skoda works, his commitment to use nickel steel armor from Witkowitz for all three battleships of the *Monarch* class, even though foreign armor was available at a much lower price, endeared him to the representatives of Bohemia and Moravia, Germans as well as Czechs.[19] Indeed, politicians whose disputes on other subjects carried them to the brink of violence agreed on the need for a stronger navy. Young Czech representative Jan Kaftan called for the fleet to show the flag in promotion of overseas trade and even advocated the conquest of colonies to provide markets for domestic industries and settlement possibilities for the empire's growing number of emigrants. Kaftan's colonialism placed him in a distinct minority in the Austrian Delegation; an Austro-Hungarian Colonial Society, founded in 1894, likewise attracted little support.[20] In any event, supplementary credits ultimately brought the 1895 appropriation to just over 13.2 million gulden, the most in thirty-one years. Sterneck had hoped for even more but was pleased to see the promise of fixed annual increases honored once again.

In May 1895, Francis Joseph and Francis Ferdinand attended the launching of the *Monarch*.[21] Designed by navy engineer Siegfried Popper, the vessel had four heavy 9.4-inch Krupp guns paired in two turrets and a secondary armament of six 6-inch Krupps. The 5,600-ton *Monarch* was less than half as large as the newest battleships of the European navies, but its modest size was comparable to that of the coastal defenders *Maine* and *Texas*, also launched in 1895 by another up-and-coming naval power, the United States. In July the *Monarch*'s sister ship *Wien* was launched in Trieste, followed in April 1896 by the *Budapest*.[22]

Francis Ferdinand's visit with the navy in 1895 came on the eve of another crisis with his health. Diagnosed as having tuberculosis, the archduke spent the autumn of 1895 on the island of Lussinpiccolo off the Istrian coast then went to Egypt for the winter aboard the composite corvette *Donau*. After moving on to Monte Carlo for the spring, he was en route back to Vienna in May 1896 when he received word of the death of his father, Charles Ludwig. At thirty-two, Francis Ferdinand became heir to the throne, but his continued poor health cast doubts over his future.

By then Kálnoky had given way to Count Agenor Goluchowsky, a Polish aristocrat with no great love for Russia. The new foreign minister sought to strengthen Anglo-Austrian ties, and the return to power of Lord Salisbury later in 1895 raised hopes of a revival of the Mediterranean Agreements. But Salisbury only confirmed the impossibility of a more active British posture against Russia, and as Anglo-German relations deteriorated over the issue of William II's support for the Boers in South Africa, the Anglo-Austrian relationship became more correct than cordial. In the winter of 1895–96, the Habsburg naval attaché in London, Captain Ladislaus Sztranyavszky, complained of new restrictions on his access to information from the British Admiralty. Salisbury denied that there was a problem, but Austria-Hungary's military attaché subsequently reported a similar change in his relationship with British army leaders.[23] Apparently the British became concerned that the representatives of the Dual Monarchy would pass along sensitive military and naval information to their German allies.[24] Goluchowsky quite correctly concluded that Britain would be of no use to Austria-Hungary should Russia pursue further expansion at the expense of the Turks; with no other alternative, he sought an understanding with Russia over the future of the Balkans. His campaign led to an Austro-Russian rapprochement, ultimately concluded in the spring of 1897, that would last for a decade. Austria-Hungary agreed to consult Russia prior to any change in the status quo of the Balkans, a commitment identical to the Austro-Italian Balkan clause of the Triple Alliance.[25]

Well before the consummation of the rapprochement, the reduction of Austro-Russian tensions affected the budget debates in Vienna and Budapest. Ironically, however, the navy came away from the proceedings in 1895 with a higher appropriation for 1896: the 13.5 million gulden already promised, plus another one million for new cruisers to replace the obsolete composite ships. These fully rigged vessels still shouldered most of the burden of the overseas missions, including those to the Far East, where most of the other great powers now employed modern warships. Before leaving office, Kálnoky had called for the construction of the cruisers on the grounds that Austria-Hungary had to make a better showing in East Asian waters. The Young Czech Kaftan personally supported the appropriation and regretted that party loyalty compelled him and other Czechs to vote with the opposition ("If we vote against the passage of the budget, it is for political reasons"). Wekerle, the Hungarian minister-president, opposed the special credit but fell from power before the autumn meetings of the Delegations. His successor, Deszö Bánffy, acquiesced in the appropriation, paving the way for the first of the new ships, the 6,300-ton armored cruiser *Kaiser Karl VI* and 2,300-ton light cruiser *Zenta*, to be laid down in the summer of 1896.[26]

The *Zenta* and its sister ships *Szigetvár* and *Aspern*, all built in the Pola Arsenal, were the navy's first larger vessels equipped with an all-Skoda armament; each carried eight 4.75-inch guns. The *Zenta* was launched in August 1897, but the limited capacity of the Pola facility caused delays in the completion of the *Szigetvár* and *Aspern,* which were not launched until May 1899 and October 1900. Henceforth the Pola Arsenal was used only to build smaller vessels and for repair projects. The Stabilimento Tecnico Triestino received the contract for the *Kaiser Karl VI,* which was launched in October 1898.[27]

While the navy added more modern warships, Austria-Hungary maintained its close alliance with Germany and in the summer of 1895 sent another squadron to German waters. Under the command of Rear Admiral Archduke Charles Stephen, the armored cruiser *Maria Theresia,* the ram cruisers *Kaiser Franz Joseph I* and *Kaiserin Elisabeth,* and the destroyer *Trabant* represented the Dual Monarchy at the opening of the Kiel Canal. The ships called at Brest en route and at Plymouth on the way home but did not visit an Italian port, evidence of the prevailing uncertainty in Austro-Italian relations.[28] But the Italians left no doubt about their feelings for the Germans. The Francophobe Francesco Crispi, a great friend of the Triple Alliance, had returned as prime minister in December 1893. He sent an impressive squadron to the opening of the Kiel Canal: four pre-dreadnought battleships—the *Andrea Doria,* the *Ruggiero di Lauria,* and two new 13,800-ton vessels, the *Re Umberto* (built 1884–93) and *Sardegna* (built 1885–95)—escorted by four modern cruisers.[29] Unfortunately, the *Sardegna* ran aground on the day of the opening ceremonies at Kiel, partially blocking the canal for several days.[30] For William II and Tirpitz, the ineptitude of the *Sardegna*'s captain only confirmed their earlier appraisals of the Italian navy.

Crispi was destined to endure greater embarrassments than the Italian showing at Kiel. A staunch colonialist, he sought to build an empire in East Africa, where Italy already had a foothold. Frustrated by the French occupation of Tunis, in 1885 the Italians established a colony on the Red Sea coast of Eritrea; four years later, during Crispi's first ministry, Italy seized part of Somalia. But complete dominion over East Africa required the conquest of Ethiopia, which Crispi ordered early in 1896. Italian troops moved southward from Eritrea, only to be repulsed at Aduwa by the Ethiopians. The humiliation was more than the Italian public could bear, and amid a great national loss of confidence, Crispi fell from power.[31] His resignation ushered in a prolonged chill in Italy's relations with its Triple Alliance partners; over the next fifteen years, genuine Italian enthusiasm for the pact would be hard to find. Only after Italy satisfied its colonial appetite in the annexation of Libya—in the process incurring the wrath of France—would Rome again actively value the friendship of Berlin and Vienna.

The domestic stock of the Italian navy rose after Aduwa, if only because the army had been so humbled.[32] Benedetto Brin returned for his last term as navy minister, and the fleet soon had a chance to recover Italy's lost prestige. In May 1896, the Greeks of Crete rebelled against their Turkish masters; nine months later, Greece proclaimed its annexation of Crete, sending ships and "volunteer" troops to secure the conquest. The six great powers agreed to a joint intervention, and after Italy committed a large contingent to the blockading fleet, an Italian admiral, Felice Canevaro, was named commander of the entire force.[33] The Austro-Hungarian contingent, commanded by Rear Admiral Hinke, was the largest after the Italian and the British, consisting of the battleship *Kronprinzessin Stephanie,* the armored cruiser *Maria Theresia,* the torpedo cruisers *Tiger, Leopard,* and *Sebenico,* three destroyers, and eight torpedo boats. A Lloyd steamer also brought a battalion of the predominantly Slovene 87th Infantry Regiment to Crete, where the troops supplemented marine detachments from the various warships. In March 1897, Captain Kneissler, who had distinguished himself as leader of a landing party against Cattaran rebels fifteen years earlier, commanded an Anglo-Austrian detachment that skirmished with Greek rebels. The Habsburg ships also sank one Greek schooner and took several prizes, including one large Greek steamer.[34] A compromise solution ultimately left Crete under Turkish sovereignty but with a Greek prince as governor. The outcome pleased Germany and Austria-Hungary less than the other powers; in a sign of dissatisfaction, they withdrew their ships early, in March 1898. Their Triple Alliance partner did not join them. In part to demonstrate a willingness to cooperate with the French, Canevaro and the Italian squadron stayed on longer with the ships of the remaining powers.[35]

The operations off Crete wreaked havoc with Sterneck's budget for 1897, as the navy spent 800,000 gulden more than its authorized appropriation of 14 million. Nevertheless, the Austro-Hungarian contingent had been outclassed by the other squadrons of the international fleet, and even if the battleships of the *Monarch* class had been fitted out in time for the campaign, they would have been dwarfed by the newest warships of the other powers. It was still more embarrassing that as the crisis unfolded over the winter of 1896–97, the active squadron had consisted of just a composite frigate and an assortment of old unarmored escorts, as it had in virtually every winter since Sterneck assumed command. Aside from years in which special operations changed the agenda—the international actions in Greek waters in 1886 and 1897, the cruise to Barcelona in 1888, and the visits to the German navy in 1890 and 1895—the navy adhered to the annual ritual of mobilizing most of its newer warships every summer for maneuvers in the Adriatic, saving expenses by maintaining only a skeleton force in the winter months. In his next confrontation with the ministers, Sterneck used the embarrassment at Crete to the navy's advantage, arguing that the fleet needed more formidable warships and enough money to maintain a respectable cruising presence in the Mediterranean on a year-round basis. Sterneck's budget estimates for 1898 included money for the first of three new larger battleships with a displacement of 8,300 tons. The design, once again prepared by Siegfried Popper, had one less heavy gun than the *Monarch* class but double the secondary battery: three 9.4-inch guns, backed by a dozen 6-inch guns. They were much smaller than the newest battleships of other fleets but still the largest ever proposed for the Habsburg navy.[36]

Given the recent breadth of political support for the fleet, Sterneck was not overly concerned that in March 1897 *Reichsrat* elections under a new, broader franchise had resulted in significant gains by the Czechs, German Nationalists, Christian Socials, and Social Democrats, the latter gaining seats for the first time.[37] But Austrian minister-president Count Casimir Badeni, striving since 1895 to defuse German-Czech tensions, subsequently failed to secure passage of a new language ordinance for Bohemia and Moravia and resigned in November, just as the Delegations convened. During the height of the language debate in the *Reichsrat*, the Young Czechs, whose obstructionist tactics had been criticized by Sterneck as early as 1893,[38] repeatedly disrupted the speeches of their opponents. When Schönerer's disciples and other German representatives responded with similar behavior, the parliamentary process ground to a halt. After fistfights broke out in the *Reichsrat*, Vienna's new mayor, Karl Lueger, had the police intervene to arrest the brawling politicians. Meanwhile, the army had to be called in to keep order on the Ringstrasse outside. With no other solution in sight, speculation abounded that Francis Joseph would resort to an authoritarian ministry.

Sterneck, like Tegetthoff before him, was a liberal at heart and did not object in principle to the political procedures he faced on an annual basis; indeed, he had been uncomfortable even with the benign authoritarianism of Taaffe's "Iron Ring." But the chaos of 1897 was too much for Sterneck, and he speculated privately that the navy might do better financially under a dictatorship.[39] With good reason, though, he wondered if the loyalty of the multinational army would hold up in the wake of a suspension of the constitution. During a wave of unrest four years earlier that had helped force Taaffe from power, the 28th (Prague) Infantry had wavered when called upon to disperse Czech rioters. In the unrest of 1897, army reserve officers figured prominently in the German Austrian backlash against the Czechs, most notably in Graz, where almost three dozen had to be stripped of their commissions. And most ominous of all, in a protest against the German language of command, Czech nationalist recruits were insisting upon answering roll call with the Czech *Zde* instead of the German *hier.*[40]

But with equally good reason, Sterneck did not doubt the loyalty of the navy, which managed to remain remarkably well insulated from the nationality problems that had paralyzed the political life of the empire and were threatening the army. The reenlistment rate for common seamen reached a peak of 8.5 percent in 1890 and averaged close to 7 percent per year toward the end of the decade; meanwhile, the number held over for disciplinary reasons remained at less than 1 percent per year, and desertions were rare. Thanks in part to Sterneck's propaganda efforts, the interior lands of the Dual Monarchy sent more men to sea, but as late as 1896 the crews of the fleet still were drawn primarily from the littoral. Of the 8,000 active seamen and 14,000 in the reserves or *Seewehr,* 41.7 percent were Croatian, 27.3 percent Italian, and 4.1 percent Slovene. German Austrians accounted for 12.1 percent, while the Magyar contingent remained modest at 6.4 percent. The Czech share was 6.3 percent, but the men of Bohemia and Moravia—German as well as Czech—were heavily represented among petty officers, by the mid-1890s outnumbering those from the Küstenland and Dalmatia. Bohemians and Moravians also accounted for a growing share of machinists.[41]

The empire's dominant nationalities were more heavily represented in the officer corps, which was 55 percent German and 10.9

percent Magyar as of 1896. Czechs accounted for 9.9 percent of sea officers, followed by Italians (8.5 percent), Croatians (7.6 percent), Slovenes (4.7 percent), and Poles (3.3 percent).[42] The nationalities of the littoral complained about underrepresentation in the corps, but there was no systematic discrimination on ethnic grounds. Sterneck even promoted Italians to the rank of admiral, breaking an informal policy that the navy had followed since 1848. Italian-surnamed officers reaching rear admiral included Count Oscare Cassini (1892), Baron Francesco Minutillo (1894), and Count Rudolf Montecuccoli (1897).[43]

Significantly, all three Italians breaking this barrier were of aristocratic birth, a relative rarity in the higher levels of the navy officer corps. Montecuccoli, a Modenese whose ancestors had served the Habsburgs since the 1600s, was the first admiral to come from the circle of prestigious older noble families traditionally well represented in the army, ministerial, and diplomatic corps. The navy's rosters included a smattering of officers with names such as Auersperg, Crenneville, Liechtenstein, and Windischgrätz, and after 1867 the Hungarian nobility was represented as well; before the unification of Germany, even a duke of Württemberg and a Prince Wrede from Bavaria had entered the corps. None, however, rose above the rank of captain and most left after just a few years of service.[44]

In addition to the dearth of high aristocrats, by the late 1890s there were no archdukes on active service with the fleet. Leopold Ferdinand, after setting sail with Francis Ferdinand aboard the *Kaiserin Elisabeth* in 1892–93, shipped out during the cruise and returned home, officially because of illness but, according to his memoirs, after a bloody fight with his imperial cousin, whom he considered a "licentious cad."[45] Transferred to the army against his will—at the bidding of an angry Francis Ferdinand, he contended—Leopold Ferdinand soon left Austria, renounced his rights as an archduke, and lived out his life as Leopold Wölfling. Among the most rebellious Habsburgs ever to disgrace the family name, he later recalled that "my years in the navy were the happiest of my life."[46]

The story was quite different for Archduke Charles Stephen. After entering the service in the late 1870s, he had risen rapidly through the officers' ranks. Hailed by some of his younger peers as a natural leader, he was thoroughly disliked by others and had a chilly relationship with Sterneck, who never assigned him to duties of any great importance.[47]

The climax of his career came in 1895, when he commanded the Austro-Hungarian squadron at the opening of the Kiel Canal. The following year, at the age of thirty-six, he retired from active duty after inheriting the Habsburg family estates in Galicia upon the death of his guardian, Archduke Albrecht. Charles Stephen remained on the *Rangliste* and continued to be promoted, ultimately reaching full admiral in 1911, but he spent most of his time in Galicia and went to sea only as a summer yachtsman in the Mediterranean. In sharp contrast to Leopold Ferdinand, he was a good friend of Francis Ferdinand, sharing not only his cousin's love of the sea but also his conservative political philosophy and pro-Russian views in foreign policy.[48]

Sterneck never benefited directly from the nascent pronavy sympathies of Francis Ferdinand. The aging *Marinekommandant* had learned his political skills on the job and continued to depend on his own talents and connections. He also relied on his instincts in dealing with divisions in the officer corps; fortunately the most recent schism healed as quickly as the *Jeune Ecole* passed out of fashion. Nevertheless, in the twilight of his career, Sterneck took care to grant appropriate rewards to his closest friends. In 1896 his second in command, Eberan, became the first sea officer other than a *Marinekommandant* or harbor admiral to be promoted to full admiral. He retired in October 1897, at sixty-eight, after fifty years with the navy, but Sterneck, at the same age, served on. For Eberan's replacement, he had to choose between his nemesis Pitner and his friend Spaun, both vice admirals, both sixty-four years old. It was an easy choice. Spaun, though slightly inferior in seniority, became second in command, while Pitner remained in Pola as harbor admiral. Two months later, the appointment took on a far greater significance. In early December, during the session of the Delegations, Sterneck died.[49]

The stunned Austrian delegates, preparing to approve a 15.5 million gulden navy budget for 1898, stood in silence as the president of their body, Count Franz Thun, began his eulogy by praising Sterneck's bravery as Tegetthoff's flag captain at the Battle of Lissa. Then, as Thun continued with remarks on the admiral's long tenure as *Marinekommandant*, he was interrupted repeatedly by cheers of approval and agreement from the floor.[50] Francis Joseph joined the political and military leaders of the empire at Sterneck's funeral in the Votivkirche, adjacent to the *Marinesektion*'s offices in the Maximilianhof. The emperor subsequently appointed Spaun chief of the *Marinesektion* and *Marinekommandant*, ultimately with a promotion to full admiral. Rear Admiral Berghofer, another protégé of Sterneck, was called to Vienna in January 1898 to take over as second in command. Pitner subsequently received a promotion to full admiral, just before his retirement later in 1898. With the death of Sterneck and departure of Pitner, the remnants of the navy's two principal cliques from the 1850s finally died out. From the start, Spaun was free to battle external opponents and obstacles, of which there would be no shortage.[51]

Even though his plan of 1891 had never been formally adopted, until his death Sterneck still used it as a yardstick to gauge the material progress of the fleet.[52] Toward his goal of nine battleships the navy could count the *Kronprinz Rudolf*, the *Kronprinzessin Stephanie*, the renovated casemate ship *Tegetthoff*, and the three coast defenders of the *Monarch* class, with funding approved for the first of another class of three battleships. The news was not so good for the smaller categories of warships, where the numbers reflected the sharp turn away from the philosophy of the *Jeune Ecole*. If his ram cruisers are classified as large cruisers, Sterneck's goal had been for six large and twelve small cruisers; counting all programs approved as of 1897, including ships still on the drawing board, the navy could claim only four large and six small cruisers. Even stronger evidence of the abandonment of the *Jeune Ecole* could be found in the destroyer and torpedo boat programs, where construction had come to a standstill. Sterneck had arrested the overall material decline of the fleet, but there was much work to be done before it could claim to be in the same class with the navies of the other European powers. In a time of increasing domestic political tensions, in an era of growing international naval competition, Spaun would be in an unenviable position.

OVERSEAS MISSIONS
UNDER STERNECK AND SPAUN (1892–1904)

In addition to the impression it had made on Francis Ferdinand, the voyage of the *Kaiserin Elisabeth* in 1892–93 was significant for another reason: it was the first cruise outside of European waters by a modern, unrigged, steel-hulled warship of the Habsburg navy. For the remainder of the 1890s, however, most overseas missions were still carried out by the aging composite ships, which used their sails more than their engines when on the high seas.[53]

In recognition of Austria-Hungary's growing trading interests with Brazil, Sterneck continued to schedule cruises to the South Atlantic and South American ports. In 1893–94 the composite corvette *Zrinyi* visited South Africa, West Africa, and South America; the itinerary included an extended stop in Rio de Janeiro, where the ship found two Austrian Lloyd steamers and one of the Hungarian Adria Line stranded by a dockworkers' strike and threatened by civil unrest against the government of the new Brazilian Republic. The two steamship lines, forbidden by a 1891 agreement from operating on the same routes, had arranged to share the lucrative Brazilian coffee trade,[54] and both companies would have incurred losses if their valuable cargoes were destroyed. Shore parties from the *Zrinyi* helped load the steamers and stood watch until their departure. In 1897–98 the ship returned to South American and West African waters on a less eventful voyage; in the meantime, in 1896–97, the corvette *Frundsberg* visited Brazil on a cruise that included stops in East and South Africa and the West Indies.

Other missions concentrated on the North Atlantic. In 1894–95 the *Donau* visited the United States on a cruise that also included stops in South America and South and West Africa. During its stay in New York, the ship's officers were treated to a tour of the Naval War College at Newport, Rhode Island. The same vessel went on another Atlantic cruise in 1897–98, visiting ports in the West Indies and North America. The navy's next visitor to the same waters was given a less friendly reception. In May 1898, one month after the outbreak of the Spanish-American War, Spaun sent Captain Julius von Ripper with the armored cruiser *Maria Theresia* to the West Indies to safeguard Austrian interests and, if necessary, evacuate consular personnel and other Habsburg subjects from the war zone. Unfortunately, the similarity between the Austrian and Spanish flags, and the fact that the Spanish fleet included a cruiser *Maria Teresa*, almost led to a tragic mistake when the Austrian cruiser appeared off Santiago on the morning of 3 July, just in time to see the Spaniards attempt to break the American blockade. As the Spanish cruisers dashed for open sea, the Americans mistook the *Maria Theresia* for an enemy warship and stalked it for several hours.

The 10,300-ton battleship *Indiana* was cleared for action and on the verge of opening fire before its captain realized his error. After the battle, Ripper's cruiser evacuated dozens of European and Latin American refugees from Cuba to Jamaica. The ship remained in the West Indies after the Spanish-American armistice of August 1898 but returned home before the end of the year.

While the crew of the *Maria Theresia* was spared from a possible bloodbath, the officers and men of the composite gunboat *Albatros* were not so lucky. In 1895 the vessel left for the Solomon Islands in the Pacific carrying a civilian scientific expedition led by the geologist Baron Heinrich Foullon von Norbeeck. In May 1896, while on the island of Guadalcanal, Foullon was ambushed and killed by hostile local inhabitants; a detachment from the *Albatros* then engaged in a skirmish with the attackers in which a cadet and two seamen were killed and several others wounded. The gunboat cruised to Australia, and the crew recovered during a stay of several months in Sydney before leaving early in 1897 to return home via Singapore and the Indian Ocean.

Under both Sterneck and Spaun, frequent cruises to the Pacific reflected the expansion of the Dual Monarchy's economic interests in East Asia. In a mission overlapping with that of the *Kaiserin Elisabeth,* in 1892–94 the *Saida* visited Australia, China, and Japan. The *Fasana* followed these ships in 1893–95, calling at Indian and Australian ports. In 1895–97 the *Saida* again showed the flag in East Asian waters while on a circumnavigation of the globe, the sixth by a Habsburg vessel. The composite corvette *Aurora* joined the *Saida* in the Orient in 1895–96, inaugurating a policy under which the navy tried to maintain two warships on the East Asian station, with missions staggered in order to ensure that at least one vessel would be there at all times. In 1896 the light cruiser *Panther* relieved the *Aurora;* the following year, it was reinforced by the ram cruiser *Kaiser Franz Joseph I.* While in Chinese waters, the *Panther* sent a landing party ashore in Shanghai to help marines from the American paddle steamer *Monocacy* defend the local American community during riots.[55] Both cruisers returned home in 1898, after the old corvettes *Frundsberg* and *Saida* arrived in the Far East. They were joined in 1899 by the ram cruiser *Kaiserin Elisabeth,* but all three vessels returned home later that year, leaving the Far Eastern station to the new light cruiser *Zenta.*

In April 1900, amid growing violence against the foreign presence in China, the Austro-Hungarian ambassador in Beijing employed the *Zenta* in a bit of gunboat diplomacy. After a Chinese mob sacked the Catholic mission church in Sikiao (Hsi-chiao), injuring an Austrian priest, the cruiser made a timely appearance to secure a payment of damages.[56] As the Boxer Rebellion reached its peak, the European powers, joined by Japan and the United States, reinforced their presence in Chinese waters. In late June, the Dual Monarchy followed suit; after the Boxers and Chinese regulars laid siege to the embassies in Beijing, the armored cruiser *Maria Theresia* left Pola for the six-week voyage to the Far East. The ram cruiser *Kaiserin Elisabeth* and the new light cruiser *Aspern* followed a month later. By early September, all four ships had joined the international fleet off Taku, roughly one hundred miles southeast of Beijing. Rear Admiral Montecuccoli, arriving with the *Elisabeth,* took command of the Austro-Hungarian squadron.[57]

Most of the fighting was over by the time the reinforcements arrived; in mid-August an international landing party already had broken the siege of the embassies. Detachments of sailors from the *Zenta* were the only Habsburg forces to see action. Some had been sent to the capital in early June, the day before the Boxers blocked the Taku-Beijing railway; they helped defend the Austro-Hungarian embassy during the ten-week siege. Another party from the *Zenta* participated in the rescue mission. In all, four Habsburg casualties were among fifty-one deaths suffered by the international forces. During September the squadron shelled and helped capture several Chinese coastal forts, and by early October the hostilities ended.[58]

After the defeat of the Boxers, the navy maintained its presence in Chinese waters and also continued to provide guards for the embassy in Beijing.[59] The *Kaiserin Elisabeth* and *Zenta* returned home later in 1900, but the *Aspern* and *Maria Theresia* remained in the Far East. The composite corvette *Donau,* circumnavigating the globe with the academy class of 1900, reached China in the spring of 1901; the *Donau's* commander, Captain Anton Haus, took command of the *Maria Theresia,* and there was a partial exchange of crews. Haus continued to show the flag and even ventured where other captains had never gone. In the summer of 1901, he took his ship up the Yangtze as far as Hankow; no foreign vessel as large as the *Maria Theresia* had ever steamed so far upstream.[60]

In 1900–1901 the light cruiser *Leopard* temporarily reinforced Haus's squadron, visiting the Far East while on a voyage to Australia and the East Indies.

After the *Maria Theresia* and *Aspern* returned home in 1902, the new armored cruiser *Kaiser Karl VI* took over the East Asian station for 1902–3 and was present in Shanghai for the inauguration of the Austrian Lloyd's Trieste-Shanghai service. The *Aspern* returned in 1903–4, followed by the *Kaiserin Elisabeth* in 1904–5. Austria-Hungary never considered claiming a Chinese port for itself, but its warships were always welcomed at Kiaochow Bay, which Germany had annexed in 1898. While the Habsburg presence in the Far East was modest compared to the other powers, the Dual Monarchy nevertheless gained recognition as a great power with Chinese interests. Indeed, U.S. Secretary of State John Hay included Austria-Hungary among the recipients of his Open Door note of 1900, articulating the American policy regarding China.[61]

After the turn of the century, cruises to East Asia accounted for all but three of the missions Spaun sent overseas. In 1901–2 the new light cruiser *Szigetvár* visited the West Indies, Mexico, and several ports along the Gulf and Atlantic coasts of the United States. While at Veracruz, the staff of the cruiser celebrated the recent resumption of Austro-Mexican diplomatic relations, which had been broken since 1867. President Porfirio Diaz greeted the officers in Mexico City and allowed them to lay a wreath at the Maximilian Chapel in Queretaro, on the site where the former navy commander and Mexican emperor had been executed. Before returning home, the *Szigetvár* called at several ports in the Baltic and North Sea; heads of state inspecting the cruiser included William II at Kiel, Tsar Nicholas II at Kronstadt, and the kings of Denmark and Sweden. In 1902 the light cruiser *Panther* visited the Atlantic coast of Morocco on a brief voyage outside the Mediterranean, and later the same year the *Zenta* called at ports in Africa and South America before returning home in 1903. While the *Zenta* was docked near Durban in South Africa, its officers were treated to a tour of the major battlefields of the recent Boer War.

By the time of his death in 1897, Sterneck had sent thirty-one missions overseas in a span of fourteen years, a dramatic rise from the average of one per year under Pöck; over half of the cruises included visits to China, Japan, or Singapore. Starting with Francis Ferdinand's voyage aboard the *Kaiserin Elisabeth* in 1892–93, modern steel-hulled cruisers gradually replaced the aging composite ships on overseas duty. The *Donau's* world cruise in 1900–1901, the navy's seventh circumnavigation of the globe, was the last mission undertaken by a fully rigged, wooden-hulled vessel. Spaun's deployment of the squadron of four modern cruisers in Chinese waters during the Boxer Rebellion represented the high-water mark in the navy's history of overseas missions. After 1904 Austria-Hungary would continue to maintain at least one warship on the East Asian station at all times and usually had two cruisers there. At the same time, however, the growing manpower requirements of an expanding fleet in home waters reduced dramatically the number of cruises to destinations other than the Far East.

SPAUN AND THE POLITICS OF
NAVAL EXPANSION (1898–1901)

Vice Admiral Baron Hermann von Spaun came to the office of commander with ample experience as a sailor-diplomat. He had served as naval attaché in London from 1873 to 1879, commanded the navy's contingent in the squadron off Greece in 1886, represented Austria-Hungary at an international naval conference in Washington, D.C., in 1889, and commanded the Habsburg squadron at the Genoa Columbus festivities in 1892. A few months before taking over as *Marinekommandant*, he had captained the *Wien*, one of the new coast defense battleships, to Great Britain for a naval review in commemoration of Queen Victoria's sixtieth anniversary on the throne. But Spaun had no experience whatsoever in domestic politics. Normally the second in command, as *Stellvertreter* in the *Marinesektion* in Vienna, was involved to some extent in helping the *Marinekommandant* prepare the budget and pilot it through the council of ministers and Delegations. Spaun, however, had served in this capacity for just two months before succeeding Sterneck, time enough only to see the former commander present one budget to the Delegations. To make matters worse, Spaun's own second in command, Berghofer, had no administrative experience other than in matters related to technology. He had served from 1891 to 1895 as head of the *II. Geschäftsgruppe* of the *Marinesektion* and was chairman of the technical committee in Pola when called to Vienna in January 1898.[62]

Spaun's weak political background made the support of Francis Ferdinand all the more important. In March 1898, Francis Joseph placed the archduke "at the disposition of the Supreme Command," a vague assignment that would leave him free "to gain insight into all aspects of the armed forces on land and at sea."[63] Francis Ferdinand gained access to all military conferences chaired by the emperor and was to be kept informed of all decisions affecting the joint Austro-Hungarian war ministry as well as the Austrian and Hungarian defense ministries. His personal entourage expanded to include military staff personnel, the nucleus of what eventually would become the Military Chancellery of Francis Ferdinand. After 1898 the archduke's Vienna residence, the Belvedere, was home to an evolving military-political think tank, characterized by some as a "shadow cabinet," a rival center of power to the Hofburg and the official organs of government.[64] When the heir to the throne finally took up the cause of naval expansion, he would do so from a position of considerable influence.

In May 1898, just six weeks after being placed "at the disposition of the Supreme Command," the archduke visited Pola as the guest of Vice Admiral Hinke, Pitner's successor as harbor admiral.[65] In his subsequent report to Francis Joseph, he praised the personnel of the fleet and their level of training and readiness, areas in which "our navy may be counted with the best in the world." The archduke also paid his customary respects to the South Slavs, noting that "it is recognized by all seafaring nations that the Dalmatian is the best sailor." He inspected the new coast defense battleships *Monarch, Wien,* and *Budapest,* but Hinke also took care to show him the trio of 3,600-ton casemate ships that were to join the new battleships in the active squadron for the summer of 1898. A quarter century old, with engines and armor salvaged from frigates built in the early 1860s, the *Kaiser Max, Don Juan d'Austria,* and *Prinz Eugen* were "clumsy and slow, and would be of minimal use before the enemy." After an eight-hour cruise along the Istrian coast aboard the *Kaiser Max,* Francis Ferdinand concluded that it was "absolutely and urgently necessary, that . . . the matériel of our fleet be increased and improved." He called for the navy "to acquire several large battleships of at least 8–10,000 tons" along with "more good and fast cruisers."[66] It was his first appeal to the emperor for a larger and stronger fleet; he would pursue the cause until his death.

Unlike Crown Prince Rudolph in earlier years, Francis Ferdinand had not received nominal promotions in the navy corresponding to his advancements in the army; he held no naval rank at all until 1902, when he added the title of full admiral to his army rank of general (*General der Kavallerie*).[67] Thereafter he wore the navy's uniform proudly, not unlike Emperor William II in Germany. The passage of Admiral Tirpitz's First Navy Bill (April 1898) provided a strong example of what the influence of a pronavy emperor could do for a second-rate naval power; the Austro-Hungarian navy expected similar good fortune in the near future, after Francis Ferdinand took the throne. For all who placed their hopes in him, the archduke's fearlessness in challenging Francis Joseph—manifested dramatically in his morganatic marriage to Countess Sophie Chotek in 1900—was a heartening sign, even though the marriage controversy and his ensuing preoccupation with family responsibilities temporarily left him with little energy to voice strong opinions on political, military, or naval questions.[68] The heir to the throne was self-assured, often mean-spirited and obstinate, and could be ruthless in dealing with opponents. These characteristics earned Francis Ferdinand many enemies but also were the same qualities that would make him so valuable to the navy in future political battles.

By the time Francis Ferdinand conducted his inspection tour of Pola, Spaun already had proposed a new fleet plan of twelve battleships, twelve cruisers, twelve destroyers, seventy-two torpedo boats, and six monitors for the Danube. He called for the goals to be met over the next ten budget years (1899–1908), an ambitious target because, of the ships in the present fleet, Spaun counted only the three *Monarch*-class battleships, the armored cruiser *Maria Theresia,* and other vessels completed since 1890. Battleships as new as the *Kronprinz Rudolf* and *Kronprinzessin Stephanie,* both commissioned in 1889, and the renovated casemate ship *Tegetthoff* (which still had engine trouble even with its new German Schichau machinery) were reckoned as reserve ships, as were the ram cruisers. To fund the nine new battleships and dozens of smaller vessels, Spaun proposed that the navy budget continue to rise by 500,000 gulden per year not just through 1899 but through 1904, to be supplemented by a credit of 5.5 million per year for the years 1899–1908.[69]

It was a bold program, even when compared to the the one approved the same spring by the German *Reichstag:* the goals of Tirpitz's First Navy Bill were nineteen battleships and forty-two cruisers, but only seven battleships and nine cruisers would have to be built in order to reach those levels.[70] At the time, most of Europe perceived Germany's naval expansion not as a challenge to Britain but as a commitment to a more aggressive colonial policy. When the legislators of the two Habsburg parliaments learned of Spaun's program just as word arrived of Tirpitz's success in the *Reichstag,* opponents of the navy in Vienna and especially in Budapest naturally accused the *Marinekommandant* and the joint Austro-Hungarian ministers of harboring colonial ambitions of their own.

Defending Spaun's program in the council of ministers, Goluchowsky cited the traditional goals of coastal defense and the protection of overseas commerce but added that a stronger navy would be essential to the defense of Austria-Hungary's interests in the Balkans. In the wake of the Crete affair, the foreign minister considered the collapse of the Ottoman Empire to be imminent; he did not want to enter the upcoming competition for territory and spheres of influence with a navy incapable of a strong showing in the Ionian and Aegean seas. Kállay, the joint finance minister, also approved of the program.[71] Goluchowsky subsequently chose to emphasize the economic argument in supporting Spaun in May 1898 at the budget hearings of the Delegations in Budapest, contending that the expansion of the fleet was "necessary not only from the standpoint of our defense, but even more from the standpoint of our commercial policy."[72]

No Habsburg foreign minister had ever assumed such a strong pronavy posture. In the ensuing debate over the budget for 1899, his support for Spaun clearly made a strong impression, at least on the Austrian delegates. Baron Max von Kübeck of Moravia echoed Goluchowsky's remarks, arguing that Austria-Hungary's "economic independence would be lost forever" as a result of "an unfavorable outcome of a conflict at sea." He called for a fleet capable of offensive action, citing among other battles the shocking outcome of the Spanish-American clash in the Philippines just three weeks earlier, in which Admiral Dewey's squadron of cruisers and gunboats had destroyed a larger Spanish force that had remained on the defensive in Manila Bay. Kübeck called naval expansion a matter of "national honor," not just for power-political reasons but because "each warship is a complete microcosm," an advertisement of the industrial capability of the power whose flag it flies.[73]

The Young Czech Kaftan reiterated the economic points raised by his German colleague, specifically calling for a stronger Mediterranean naval presence to support Habsburg commerce in the Levant, "our nearest sphere of interest."[74] The *Bund österreichischer Industrieller,* for the first time formally petitioning the Delegations in support of a stronger navy, likewise argued that a better showing at sea could arrest the Dual Monarchy's relative decline as a political and economic power in the Levant.[75] In his own comments before the Austrian Delegation, Spaun affirmed the necessity "that our warships visit the Levant frequently" and also seconded the argument that cruisers were needed to show the flag and promote commerce in distant waters. But he sought above all to focus attention on the need for his battleship program. Because "even smaller states and nations are precisely informed of the sea power of every other state," the flag of a power such as Austria-Hungary "will find no respect . . . if the nation or state in question knows that it only has to deal with a single cruiser, behind which no fleet stands." Of course, the Germans and Czechs of Bohemia and Moravia continued to be so enthusiastic about the navy primarily because of its patronage of the booming industries of their provinces. Spaun cultivated their support by praising the Skoda works of Pilsen, which began providing six-inch guns for the navy in 1895, fashioned from nickel steel produced by the Prager Eisenindustrie-Gesellschaft (P.E.G.) in Kladno. He looked forward to the day when Skoda could produce the heavy guns that still had to be imported from Krupp.[76]

In contrast to the Austrian Delegation, the Hungarians were not impressed by Goluchowsky's economic arguments. In their debate over the budget for 1899, Hungarian delegates charged that the reasoning of the ministers applied only to the Austrian half of the Dual Monarchy; Hungary certainly did not intend to make financial sacrifices to expand a fleet that would promote Austria's overseas trade. The representatives from Budapest also raised a constitutional question in reminding Goluchowsky and his colleagues that Austria and Hungary were separate countries in economic matters. Because the arrangement of 1867 left each half of the empire in control of its own economic policies, they contended that any naval expansion for commercial reasons would have to be negotiated between Vienna and Budapest. Strictly speaking, the joint ministries and the Delegations had no jurisdiction in matters not pertaining to military and foreign policy or their financing.[77]

Hungarian opposition ended Spaun's hopes for a long-term commitment to naval expansion, but the representatives from Budapest were willing, as before, to increase the budget modestly on a year-to-year basis.[78] Funding for new battleships likewise would have to be secured one ship at a time. Sterneck's last budget, for 1898, had included funding to start the first of three 8,300-ton battleships. Construction on the vessel—named Habsburg—did not begin until 1899; nevertheless, the navy overstepped its budget for 1898 by some 500,000 gulden, spending 16 million. For 1899 Spaun had to settle for 16.8 million rather than the 20.5 million he had proposed, but the budget did include money for a second 8,300-ton warship. Just as Sterneck dared not name the battleship Wien without christening one of its sisters Budapest, Spaun made a gesture to the Hungarians by naming the Habsburg's first sister ship Arpád, after a medieval Magyar dynasty. Initial work on the new battleships, along with the construction of the cruisers begun under Sterneck, pushed naval expenditure to 17.8 million gulden for 1899, the highest figure ever.[79]

Unfortunately, Goluchowsky and other supporters of the navy unwittingly played into the hands of Spaun's opponents in the months after the passage of the 1899 budget. In the wake of its disastrous defeat at the hands of the United States and loss of colonies in the Pacific and Caribbean, Spain considered divesting itself of its remaining colonies; later in 1898, the Spanish offered to sell Rio de Oro (the Spanish Sahara or Western Sahara) to the Austro-Hungarian Colonial Society. The society's vice president, Ernst Franz Weisl, negotiated a deal with the complicity of Goluchowsky and lesser foreign ministry officials, only to have Budapest intervene to veto the sale on the eve of its consummation. While it would not have been much of an economic asset, the arid colony on the Atlantic coast of Africa south of Morocco would have opened new strategic horizons for Austria-Hungary, with Rio de Oro's lone port, Villa Cisneros (Dakhla), offering the fleet a base on the Tropic of Cancer some three hundred miles due south of the Canary Islands. If nothing else, an Austro-Hungarian colonial presence in the region might have had some influence on the course of the subsequent Moroccan crises.[80] The affair had a far clearer immediate impact on domestic politics, to the detriment of Spaun and the navy. The attempt by the Colonial Society and the foreign ministry to present them with such a fait accompli in Rio de Oro naturally reinforced the suspicions of Hungarian leaders that the campaign to expand the fleet ultimately would go hand in hand with a quest for colonies.

The commercial arguments of navalism and colonialism were based on the assumption that trade would follow the flag. But more often than not, the flag followed trade, for the Dual Monarchy no less than for other European powers. While this phenomenon caused Britain, France, and Germany to turn African and Asian trading posts into protectorates, and protectorates into possessions, it gave all powers a good reason to maintain squadrons in distant waters, especially the Far East. Indeed, Austria-Hungary would not have sent cruisers to China during the Boxer Rebellion of 1900 if not for the fact that the Austrian Lloyd already had lucrative trading interests in East Asia. By the turn of the century, Trieste had enjoyed regular service with Hong Kong for twenty years and with Japanese ports for a decade, and the Lloyd was soon to add Shanghai to its itinerary. Thanks to the eastern activity of the Lloyd, Austria-Hungary in 1893 surpassed Italy to trail only Britain, Germany, and France in its use of the Suez Canal; thereafter, the Dual Monarchy remained fourth in canal use in every year except 1896, the year of Crispi's Ethiopian venture.[81]

The success of the Lloyd also led to an increase in the prosperity of Trieste, but in the last two decades of the century, this growth was far from spectacular. In 1882 the port handled 310.4 million gulden worth of imports and exports, the first time that the 300-gulden level had been surpassed in any single year, but eighteen years later the figure stood at just 356.3 million. In 1900 the average nominal wage of the Trieste worker still lagged behind that of his counterparts in Vienna, Salzburg, and Graz and had not gained significantly in the past decade.[82] Such conditions naturally affected the shipyards, where navy projects would be interrupted by strikes throughout Spaun's time in office. Trieste did not have an organized workers movement in the modern sense until the founding, in 1894, of the Social Democratic League, a local Italian branch of the Austrian Social Democratic party.[83] The Social Democrats supported a shipyard strike in 1897, the first in fourteen years, which delayed work on the armored cruiser *Kaiser Karl VI*. By then, however, Slovene migration to Trieste already had transformed the local labor market and complicated efforts to organize unions. As late as the 1880 census, there were few Slovenes in Trieste, but toward the end of the century their numbers increased dramatically. The Social Democratic League and its affiliated unions, though antinationalist in ideology, did not welcome the migrants; as a result, in 1896 a Yugoslav Social Democratic party was founded in Trieste, and Slovenes also ultimately formed their own unions. To the outbreak of the First World War, labor organizers would be plagued by the lack of a consistent common front of Italian and Slovene workers.[84]

There were no similar divisions in the ranks of the capitalists. By the time of Sterneck's death, the leading banks, already well connected with the iron and steel cartel, were forging their first ties with the shipyards. In 1897 the Rothschilds—founders and owners of the Witkowitz works—developed a stake in the shipbuilding industry when their bank, the Creditanstalt, became the largest stockholder in the Stabilimento Tecnico Triestino. The infusion of capital enabled the company to buy the San Marco shipyard, closed since the bankruptcy of the old Navale Adriatico in 1875. After renovating the facilities, the Stabilimento Tecnico moved its warship projects to the much larger San Marco yard and used its old San Rocco yard only for civilian and repair contracts. The *Kaiser Karl VI*, launched in October 1898, was the last Austro-Hungarian warship constructed at San Rocco; the *Habsburg* and *Arpád* were laid down at San Marco in March and June of 1899.[85]

Although many Magyar leaders still refused to concede that Hungary had significant maritime interests, the growth of their own port of Rijeka in part caused the stagnation of Trieste. After Budapest terminated its share of the Lloyd's subsidy and placed all of its support behind the Adria Line in 1892, the company quickly tripled the size of its fleet and at the turn of the century owned twenty-five modern, British-built steamers. In the early 1880s, the port of Rijeka annually handled less than half the tonnage of Trieste, but by 1900 volume had improved to 78 percent of Trieste's total, thanks largely to the Adria Line's virtual monopoly of western Mediterranean and Western European trade under the Austro-Hungarian flag.[86] The prosperity of Rijeka and the success of the Adria Line were facts not in harmony with the Hungarian contention that overseas trade was a purely "Austrian" affair.

Without the support of Goluchowsky and Kállay in the council of ministers, Spaun would not have had as much luck with his first budget. But his success came in spite of the tenacious opposition of General Edmund von Krieghammer, since 1893 the joint war minister of the Dual Monarchy. Francis Joseph had appointed Krieghammer on the advice of Beck, but the chief of the General Staff quickly changed his mind about the "power hungry" war minister. Krieghammer directed his efforts primarily against the navy, seeking to assert his authority over the *Marinesektion*.[87] His relationship with Spaun worsened during the Boxer Rebellion, when he protested to Francis Joseph that the navy had arranged to send the cruiser squadron to the Far East after direct consultations with the foreign ministry. The emperor agreed that Spaun should have dealt with Goluchowsky through Krieghammer, and ordered him henceforth to communicate with other ministries only through the war minister.[88]

In the summer of 1900, Spaun brought the conflict to a head, proposing to reorganize the navy administration and redefine its relationship to the army. The *Marinesektion* would be replaced by a new organization, the Admiralty, which still would be under the war ministry. In addition to all of the prerogatives of the chief of the *Marinesektion*—direct access to the monarch, the preparation of the budget, and the right to defend the budget in the council of ministers and before the Delegations—the chief of the Admiralty also would be free to correspond directly with other ministers on matters related to the navy. In October 1900, Francis Joseph rejected the proposal, standing by the existing administrative structure.[89]

After failing to reorganize the administration, Spaun redoubled his efforts to pursue his material goals for the fleet. He benefited from the overall policies of Austria's new minister-president, the career bureaucrat Ernst von Koerber, to whom Francis Joseph had turned in January 1900 in an effort to put an end to the political chaos that had reigned since Badeni's last year in office. Relying initially on emergency powers available under Article 14 of the Austrian constitution—which interim governments had employed during 1898 and 1899—Koerber used an extensive public-works program as the salve to soothe the conflicts among nationalities. He took care to distribute the benefits equitably over all parts of the Austrian half of the Dual Monarchy, providing contracts for heavy industry and employment opportunities in all provinces.[90] The leaders of most parties and nationalities rallied around Koerber's government for fear of being left out, and in two years the *Reichsrat* was able to resume its constitutional functions. Koerber's philosophy shared some characteristics with the recent *Sammlungspolitik* of Imperial Germany or with the revived coalition of special interests and parties pieced together by Chancellor Bernhard von Bülow, both of which had embraced the cause of German naval expansion on economic as well as nationalistic grounds.[91] In Austria, no less than in Germany, the government was more than happy to pump money into the economy via the navy. Indeed, military and naval spending soon rivaled railway construction and other civilian projects as an important stimulus for heavy industry.[92] As Spaun continued to develop his political skills, Koerber joined Goluchowsky and Kállay among the valuable cards in his hand.

But the political-economic coalitions supporting German *Weltpolitik* at the turn of the century shared one important characteristic with the earlier Bismarckian political constellation of the 1880s that Koerber's coalition lacked: an alliance of "iron and rye" linking industrialists and agrarian interests in which the latter supported costly projects such as naval expansion in exchange for the promotion of domestic agriculture against foreign competition. In the month of Koerber's appointment, in a belated debate over the budget for 1900, Austrian delegates supporting a larger fleet raised the possibility of such an alliance as a means of gaining Hungarian support for Spaun's efforts. Unfortunately, it came in the form of a warning rather than an olive branch. With the Hungarian Delegation once again hostile to naval expansion and unreceptive to the related economic arguments, Albert Gessmann of Lower Austria, a colleague of Lueger in the leadership of the Christian Social party, bluntly threatened retaliation: if Hungary did not support the interests of Austrian industry, Austria should not support Hungarian agriculture.[93] The prospect of economic warfare with Hungary drew cheers from some in the Austrian Delegation, most notably the German Nationalists, but such a course would have been destructive for both halves of the Dual Monarchy. Almost two thirds of Hungary's agricultural exports went to Austria, but Austrian industry also dominated the Hungarian market, producing well over 80 percent of Hungary's imported manufactured goods.[94]

In 1900 construction projects raised the naval outlay to 22.4 million gulden, including money to start the *Babenberg,* the last battleship of the 8,300-ton *Habsburg* class, and the 7,400-ton armored cruiser *Sankt Georg.* In the new Austro-Hungarian kronen, which replaced the old imperial currency at a rate of 2:1, the total came to 44.8 million.[95] Threats of "if no iron, then no rye!" failed to move the Hungarians, and gestures such as giving Hungarian names to warships (the battleship *Árpád,* the cruiser *Szigetvár*) also did little good. Ultimately only promises of a share of the industrial contracts would win them over. In 1901 Spaun gave Budapest a written promise to spend in Hungary a share of his budget equivalent to the Hungarian contribution to the joint budget of the Dual Monarchy, which at that stage stood at 34 percent. If Hungary provided nothing at all in one area, it would receive as compensation more than 34 percent of the navy's business in another. This sweeping commitment, though important as a political gesture, bordered on the preposterous. As recently as 1897, the navy had spent only 12.3 percent of its budget in Hungary, mostly on foodstuffs and other supplies.[96]

As of 1900, 90 percent of the navy's expenditure for warship construction and maintenance (not including coal) went to domestic firms, but aside from the steel mills of Diósgyör and Resicza and another plant in Diósgyör producing small caliber shells, no Hungarian industries had significant contracts with the navy.[97] Because shipbuilding consumed such a large share of the annual budget, warships would have to be constructed in the Hungarian half of the empire in order for Spaun to honor the new obligation. Thus far the only ships built in Hungary were the four Danube river monitors. Spaun ordered two more—the *Bodrog* and *Temes,* both completed at Budapest in 1904—but together they cost less than 2.8 million kronen. In contrast, the battleships of the *Habsburg* class, built in Trieste, cost roughly 18 million apiece.[98] Only a similar commitment to stimulate the Hungarian economy would suffice to overcome antinavy sentiments in Budapest.

The navy spent 45.7 million kronen in 1901, a new record high for the third straight year. The Stabilimento Tecnico Triestino finally started work on the *Babenberg* in January, and the Pola Arsenal laid down the

Sankt Georg in March; the budget also included money to start the first of a new class of three 10,600-ton battleships, again designed by Siegfried Popper. The new vessels would have a primary armament of four 9.4-inch guns backed by a secondary battery of a dozen 7.5-inch guns, making them the most heavily armed as well as the largest warships ever built for the navy. Known as the *Erzherzog* class, the three battleships were to be named after archdukes who had supported or commanded the navy in the past. In June 1901, when the Delegations met to debate the budget for 1902, Spaun announced that recent tests of 9.4-inch Skoda guns had been successful.[99] The *Babenberg*, when completed, would be the first battleship with an all-Skoda armament; Skoda would also provide all of the guns for the *Sankt Georg* and the three *Erzherzog*s.

Coming a decade after Austria-Hungary became self-sufficient in armor plate, the breakthrough in heavy artillery made the navy's shipbuilding program virtually independent of foreign industry. The delegates applauded the news and also passed a resolution commending the navy for its performance during the Boxer Rebellion.[100] In spite of Spaun's deteriorating relationship with the army and the lingering problem of opposition from Hungary, the praise of the politicians held the promise of an even brighter future. But the summer of 1901 represented a high-water mark, at least for Spaun. During the remainder of his tenure, things would get no better for the navy.

LABOR UNREST, POLITICAL PROBLEMS, AND THE DETERIORATION OF AUSTRO-ITALIAN RELATIONS (1901–4)

Counting a supplementary credit, the Delegations voted the navy 49.1 million kronen for 1902, including money to start a second 10,600-ton battleship. Spaun's political successes fueled a shipbuilding boom in Trieste, where the Stabilimento Tecnico grew to employ 2,200 workers by 1901, double the number of fifteen years earlier.[101] But unfortunately for the *Marinekommandant*, labor problems in the shipyards delayed his projects. In 1901 the riveters of San Marco went on strike, followed in 1902 by the drillers, but in scope (if not in duration) these actions paled in comparison to the general strike of February 1902.[102]

The trouble began in January 1902 when the Austrian Lloyd stokers' union went on strike, idling all of the company's ships that were not at sea. Their demand for an eight-hour work day was rejected by the Lloyd directors, who hired Italian, Greek, and Arab replacements; the navy also loaned some of its stokers for the duration of the strike. On 12 February, as the strike entered its third week, the other unions of Trieste agreed to a general strike in support of the stokers' demands; by the morning of 14 February, the entire city was shut down. Later that day, strikers clashed with troops from the local garrison; the soldiers opened fire, killing eight and wounding twenty-five. Further violence the following day brought the casualty total to fourteen dead and fifty wounded; two soldiers and five policemen also suffered serious injuries, and one policeman died from his wounds. On the evening of 15 February, a Saturday, the Lloyd agreed to almost all of the strikers' demands. The stokers returned to work the following Monday , along with the workers of the Lloyd Arsenal and the San Marco shipyard. Martial law remained in effect for several more days, enforced by the local police and garrison and thousands of additional troops summoned from as far away as Ljubljana and Marburg (Maribor) at the height of the unrest. Spaun also sent the winter squadron to Trieste, but its battleships—the *Monarch, Wien,* and *Budapest*—did not arrive until after the strike ended. Nevertheless, the navy took no chances. On 17 February, sailors from the *Monarch* were deployed at the San Marco shipyard to guard the *Babenberg,* which was still under construction; on the following day sailors joined troops in patrols of downtown Trieste.[103]

Initial accounts in the Vienna press reassured readers that the strike had "an exclusively Social Democratic character" and no Italian nationalist overtones; Slovene and Croatian workers participated in the walkout, and the group that negotiated with the Lloyd directors to end the strike included equal numbers of Italians and Slovenes. For political reasons, the official police account blamed "anarchists" rather than Social Democrats for inciting the violence that caused the deaths; nevertheless, Valentino Pittoni, head of the local Social Democratic League, was censured for his leading role in the strike.[104] Spaun also faced criticism when he appeared before the Delegations in Budapest in June 1902. No one questioned his decision to send the squadron to Trieste or even the deployment of sailors to guard the *Babenberg,* but the use of navy stokers as strikebreakers troubled some delegates. Spaun argued that he had loaned stokers to the Lloyd in the "public interest," citing the company's government postal contracts, and accepted "full responsibility" for the decision.

In July 1902, two years after the Delegations first voted to fund it, the 10,600-ton battleship *Erzherzog Karl* was finally begun in the San Marco yard in Trieste, on a slip vacated the previous autumn by the *Arpád*. Three months later, on the same day that the launching of the *Babenberg* freed an adjacent slip, the Stabilimento Tecnico laid down the *Erzherzog Friedrich*. These projects pushed the navy outlay for 1902 to 50.6 million kronen, exceeding the budget by only a modest sum but still enough to draw sharp protests from war minister Krieghammer, who complained to Francis Joseph that Spaun was ignoring his right of final approval on all large expenditures of money.[105] In 1903, when no new battleships or cruisers were begun, spending leveled off at 50.3 million, around a million more than the authorized budget. In 1904 the start of construction on the last *Erzherzog*, the *Ferdinand Max*, drove naval spending to an unprecedented 56.1 million kronen, almost 5 million over budget, primarily because the navy's contracts with the Stabilimento Tecnico now required the company to use only domestic materials and to respect the Hungarian quota.[106]

The construction of so many battleships promised to increase the strength of the fleet, if not the number of ships. As Francis Ferdinand observed in his report of 1898, the fleet that Spaun had inherited was largely obsolete; in most cases, the new vessels were merely long-overdue replacements for older warships. The last two wooden-hulled ironclads, the harbor watch frigate *Habsburg* and the ancient *Kaiser*, had already been deleted from the list of battleships in 1897. The *Erzherzog Albrecht* left the fleet in 1901, followed by the *Custoza, Prinz Eugen, Don Juan d'Austria*, and *Kaiser Max* in 1903. The lone remaining casemate ship, the *Tegetthoff*, assumed duties as harbor watch in Pola. With the modern cruisers now handling overseas missions, the last of the composite ships also left active service. Few of the deactivated ships were scrapped; most became training ships or accommodation hulks for sailors awaiting assignment. When a new ship assumed the name of an old vessel, the latter was renamed for its second life in the harbor.[107]

Given the continuing difficulties with the Hungarians, Spaun could be thankful that international developments underscored the need for sea power. It did not escape notice in Vienna or Budapest that naval weakness had played a significant role in Spain's loss of its colonial empire to the United States in 1898. Furthermore, in the summer of 1900, the decision of Spaun and Goluchowsky to dispatch the cruiser squadron to the Far East during the Boxer Rebellion had played much better in the arena of public and political opinion than it had with Krieghammer and the war ministry. It also helped the cause that, after 1900, Spaun and Goluchowsky no longer could be charged with copying German colonial ambitions: in the wake of the Boxer Rebellion, the Dual Monarchy could have laid claim to a Chinese port but did not. At the same time, Tirpitz's Second Navy Bill of June 1900—which doubled the projected fleet strength from nineteen to thirty-eight battleships—showed that Germany intended to compete with Britain in the North Sea rather than strictly in a new scramble for colonies.[108]

Austria-Hungary could not be accused of harboring similar grandiose ambitions, but at the turn of the century, it appeared increasingly likely that the Adriatic would be home to a future naval competition just as heated as the race in the North Sea, albeit on a much smaller scale. After the fall of Crispi in 1896, Italy never again had a prime minister so committed to the Triple Alliance. A further blow fell in 1900 when an anarchist assassinated King Umberto, whose visit to Vienna in 1881 had paved the way for the initial treaty; Victor Emmanuel III did not share his father's enthusiasm for the ties to Germany and Austria-Hungary. As early as 1896, Beck drafted fresh plans for an Austro-Italian war, and after 1900 Koerber's public works included the completion of the Tauern railway. This direct link from Prague to Trieste via Linz would be invaluable in the event of mobilization against Italy.[109]

Meanwhile, at least superficially, the Triple Alliance remained in force. In December 1900, the three powers even concluded a naval convention against the Franco-Russian threat. It assigned the defense of the Baltic, North Sea, and Atlantic to Germany; the western Mediterranean to Italy; the Adriatic to Austria-Hungary; and designated the eastern Mediterranean as a joint Austro-Italian zone. The clauses on joint operations were vague, however, and the ships of the three powers cooperated actively only in the Far East. The navies adopted a joint signal code in 1901 and shared information on the French fleet until 1902; thereafter, Italian interest waned and the convention became a dead letter.[110] The Triple Alliance was renewed in February 1902, but by then Italy was actively playing a double game. In December 1900, while the

Italians were in Berlin signing the naval convention ostensibly against the Franco-Russian threat, the octogenarian Visconti Venosta, in his last term as foreign minister, secured from the French a free hand for Italy in Libya in exchange for similar considerations for France in Morocco.[111] The deal settled the disputes in North Africa that had divided the two powers since the French occupation of Tunisia in 1881, disputes that inspired Italy to join the Triple Alliance in the first place.

As a sign of the change of policy, in 1901 the Italian navy visited Toulon; by 1902 its leaders clearly considered the Austro-Hungarian fleet, not the French navy, to be their most likely future rival.[112] For the immediate future, Italy's admirals could feel confident of their vast superiority over their "ally" across the Adriatic. Counting vessels still under construction, the Italian navy in 1902 had 16 pre-dreadnought battleships, 7 armored and 27 unarmored cruisers, 11 destroyers, and 145 torpedo boats. The *Affondatore* and 7 other older ironclads were still in service, but all would be scrapped by 1910.[113] All of the battleships were larger than Austria-Hungary's new *Habsburg* class, but they were no monuments to Italian industrial prowess. Produced by inefficient shipyards, the building times of the dozen completed by 1902 averaged eight years, nine months; in contrast, the six newest Austro-Hungarian battleships—the *Monarch* class and the *Habsburg* class—were completed in an average of just over four years.[114] Most of the Italian torpedo boats dated from the 1880s; there had been even more, but twenty were either lost at sea or scrapped before 1902. Italy had so many unarmored cruisers because it had continued to build them even after the *Jeune Ecole* went out of fashion. The Italians were slow to introduce destroyers, and in 1902 most of their eleven were still under construction. Whereas foreign observers of the Habsburg navy always praised the personnel and the operational skill of the fleet and gave low marks to the matériel, the Italian navy was admired for the quality of its matériel and rated low in personnel and operations. As recently as 1896 and 1897, British observers of Italian naval maneuvers had filed very unflattering reports.[115]

Naval maneuvers under Spaun more often than not included battleship exercises and in general reflected the new focus on Italy as the most likely enemy. In the summer of 1898, the maneuvers had included the *Wien, Monarch,* and *Budapest,* then the navy's newest battleships, and the old casemate ships *Prinz Eugen, Kaiser Max,* and *Don Juan d'Austria;* it marked the first time since 1887 that the summer exercises had involved two full divisions of battleships. The same six vessels participated in the 1899 maneuvers. In 1900 and 1901, the operations in the Far East strained manpower resources so much that the battleships had to be kept in reserve; summer exercises were conducted with makeshift squadrons consisting mostly of smaller ships.[116] The maneuvers of 1902, the last ever attended by Francis Joseph, simulated an amphibious assault against Pola. The attacking force, led by the three *Monarch*-class battleships, included Lloyd steamers carrying troops from two infantry regiments. Rear Admiral Ripper commanded the ships, while the troops were led by Major General Baron Franz Conrad von Hötzendorf, a rising star who had already attracted the attention of Francis Ferdinand. The defense of Pola was left to Vice Admiral Minutillo, Hinke's successor as harbor admiral, with the ram cruiser *Kaiser Franz Joseph I,* several smaller vessels, and troops from a *Landwehr* regiment. The attackers left Trieste for Pola, fending off simulated torpedo boat attacks en route. Ripper put Conrad's troops ashore, and Pola was on the verge of falling to a land assault when the emperor declared the exercise over.[117] Francis Ferdinand, also in attendance, became more convinced than ever that an Italian landing attempt could be repulsed only by a superior force at sea.[118] Similar maneuvers in 1903 included the new battleships *Habsburg* and *Arpád* along with the *Wien,* a cruiser division, and a torpedo flotilla. The 1904 maneuvers were the first involving two homogeneous divisions of modern battleships, the three ships of the *Habsburg* class against the three *Monarchs.*[119]

Spaun's navy made a stronger showing on a year-round basis thanks to the abandonment of Sterneck's practice of maintaining only a skeleton squadron in the winter months. As late as 1896–97, the most formidable warship in the winter squadron had been the old composite frigate *Laudon,* but under Spaun it became customary for at least one armored warship to be cruising in the Adriatic and Mediterranean at all times. In 1898–99, the winter squadron included the *Budapest* and *Maria Theresia;* in 1899–1900, all three *Monarch*-class battleships; in 1900–1901, the *Kaiser Karl VI;* in 1901–2, the three *Monarchs;* in 1902–3, the *Budapest,* joined in January by its sister ships *Monarch* and *Wien* along with the newly commissioned *Habsburg.* Both the *Habsburg* and the new *Arpád* were in the winter squadron of 1903–4. Significant visits included a cruise by the winter squadron of 1899–1900 to Malta in December 1899; the British Mediterranean squadron reciprocated by calling at

Trieste in July 1900, and another British squadron visited Pola in October 1904. Austro-Hungarian admirals and British Mediterranean commanders remained on relatively cordial terms, though the overall Anglo-Austrian relationship continued to cool.[120]

The more active Italian threat provided further grist for the mill of Spaun's supporters in the Austrian *Reichsrat* and Delegation. Taking nothing for granted, he ensured continued support from Hungary by agreeing to a more rigid revision of the quota arrangement of 1901. The new terms committed the navy to honor the Hungarian quota of 34 percent even in its ordinary day-to-day spending.[121] Spaun's campaign to replace obsolete battleships with larger, more modern designs would have involved higher expenditure in any event, but the concurrent shift to a reliance on domestic industry—purely for political reasons—forced costs even higher. As early as 1898, when delegates blamed the iron and steel cartel for the rise in warship costs, Spaun commented that he had "no influence" over the price increases; four years later, he lamented that the navy was "powerless" vis-à-vis the cartel's price-fixing tactics. The problem would only grow worse in the future. Since its founding in 1886, the cartel had been a relatively loose arrangement, with the firms renegotiating its terms every three to five years; in 1902, however, the cartel was renewed for a period of fifteen years, and for the first time all iron and steel works in Austria were included.[122]

Competition from foreign firms would have driven prices down, but by the turn of the century, it was politically impossible for the navy to consider using foreign sources for matériel. The same did not hold true for fuel purchases, since almost all domestic coal was unsuitable for warship use. During Spaun's seven years in office, the navy purchased 380,202 tons for its fleet coal stocks; 98 percent came from British mines, just over 1 percent from the Pocahontas seam of Virginia, and less than 1 percent from domestic suppliers. Discounting 1898, when barely 20,000 tons were purchased, orders averaged around 60,000 per year, almost double the average of Sterneck's last decade.[123]

Throughout the Spaun era, the machine shops of the Stabilimento Tecnico Triestino continued to supply the engines for Austro-Hungarian warships, with better results thanks to licensing arrangements that gave the firm access to the latest foreign technology. The first such agreement, concluded in 1897 with Yarrow of Britain, resulted in significant improvements in the Stabilimento Tecnico's boiler construction. Of the newer vessels, only two had foreign engine components: the *Budapest* and the *Kaiser Karl VI*, both equipped with Stabilimento Tecnico engines and Maudsley boilers imported from Britain.[124]

Of all the industries supporting the naval buildup, the Skoda works profited the most from developments in the Spaun era. Among the larger warships, the armored cruiser *Kaiser Karl VI* (commissioned in 1900) embodied the transition from Krupp to Skoda armament, carrying two 9.4-inch Krupp guns and a secondary battery of eight 6-inch Skodas. The *Arpád* and *Habsburg* likewise had Krupp heavy guns with a Skoda secondary armament, but all warships from the *Babenberg* onward would be armed exclusively with Skoda guns.[125] The increase in business brought changes at the Skoda firm, which became a joint-stock company in 1899 to raise capital for expansion. Initially Emil von Skoda held a majority of shares, but the Creditanstalt soon acquired a controlling interest. Already in control of the Witkowitz works and the Stabilimento Tecnico Triestino, the Rothschild bank had a greater stake than ever in the naval buildup. Confident of a successful future, in 1902 Skoda ended its decade-long partnership with Krupp in the development of heavy guns.[126]

The navy's last foreign-built surface warships were the destroyer *Huszár* and torpedo boat *Kaiman* (later renamed *Torpedoboot 50-E*), both laid down by Yarrow in 1904 and completed a year later. The 400-ton destroyer was used as a model for eleven sister ships, while the 210-ton torpedo boat became the prototype for another twenty-three vessels. To satisfy the quota for the Hungarian half of the empire, contracts for six destroyers and ten torpedo boats went to the Danubius firm of Rijeka, which opened a shipyard in 1903. The rest were built by the Stabilimento Tecnico.[127]

Funding for Spaun's twelve destroyers and two dozen torpedo boats came from a special credit granted by the Delegations in May 1904 in response to the deterioration of Austro-Italian relations. Over the previous winter, the anti-Austrian rhetoric in the Chamber of Deputies in Rome had reached disturbing levels, and rumors abounded of irredentist plans for assaults against the Trentino (Italian South Tyrol) and Trieste. The Japanese surprise attack on the Russian Pacific Fleet in Port Arthur at the start of the Russo-Japanese War generated fears among the leaders of the Dual Monarchy that Italy would attempt a similar preemptive strike against Pola. Half of the allocation of 121 million kronen was to be used to place the fleet in a state of war readiness, while the remainder would go toward building the destroyers and torpedo boats and completing the three *Erzherzogs* and the armored cruiser *Sankt Georg*.[128]

The new destroyers and torpedo boats would strengthen an area of the fleet that had been neglected in recent years, but Spaun was disappointed that the outlay did not provide for new battleships. He was even more concerned by the rather novel concept—devised by the Austrian finance minister, economist Eugen Böhm von Bawerk—that the navy should repay the money with interest over the next twenty-five years out of its future budgets.[129] Having come to terms with the Hungarians, Spaun had felt reasonably confident about the financial future of the navy. Now, he and his successors would be faced with having a substantial portion of their annual outlay used to service a debt, and to make matters worse it was a debt not incurred for battleship construction. Spaun feared that this burden would place a cap on the navy's budget and bring an end to the recent trend of rising appropriations. In early October 1904, the disheartened *Marinekommandant* handed the emperor his resignation. Francis Joseph, caught off guard, accepted it with the promise that a warship would be named in Spaun's honor.[130] It was an extraordinary tribute to a commander—last accorded posthumously to Tegetthoff—belying the fact that their relationship had not always been so cordial.

Spaun was seventy-one at the time of his retirement, a veteran of fifty-four years of naval service, but age and health were not factors in his decision to resign; he would survive for another fifteen years, until 1919, outliving Austria-Hungary by several months. At any earlier point in the navy's history, it would have been unthinkable for a commander to resign under the circumstances that Spaun enjoyed in 1904: the navy was receiving unprecedented higher budgets in the midst of a period of significant expansion, with broad political support at least in the Austrian half of the empire. Furthermore, the renewed Italian threat and Francis Ferdinand's keen interest in the fleet held the promise of an even brighter future. But Spaun's resignation in spite of such positive conditions underscores the extent to which the political and financial situation had become more challenging than ever. When it came to

spending, the navy was trapped in an upward spiral. Political considerations dictated that domestic industry be used, even in underdeveloped
Hungary; this, in turn, pushed up costs; higher costs required larger
budgets and an even broader base of support in the Delegations; and to
win these supporters, the navy had to patronize even more domestic
firms.

For the moment, political considerations played a greater role in
driving up expenditure than did rapid technological change. Warships
were getting larger and their guns and engines more powerful, but in the
nearly two decades since the heyday of the *Jeune Ecole,* there had been
no fundamental changes in battleship design. The relative calm would
soon give way to a new storm. Improvements in gunnery training and
tactics, especially in the area of long-distance range finding and fire control, promised to increase dramatically the distance at which battleships would fight one another. In May 1905, in the decisive Battle of
Tsushima, Japanese warships applied theory to practice in destroying
their Russian counterparts after opening fire at unprecedented dis-
tances.[131] The leading navies took their designs for an all big-gun
battleship from the drawing board to the shipyard. Thanks to Sir John
Fisher's *Dreadnought,* laid down one year after Spaun's retirement, a
British design would give its name to the largest, fastest, most powerful—and most expensive—battleships the world had ever known.

The deterioration of Austro-Italian relations during the Spaun era was
detrimental to the Dual Monarchy's overall strategic health but certainly played to the advantage of the navy. In the 1880s, Italian foreign
policy had rested on the assumption that France would remain isolated,
with Britain and Germany generally friendly toward each other. The
Franco-Russian alliance of the early 1890s prompted the Italians to
start hedging their bets, and after the turn of the century the growing
hostility between Britain and Germany drove an alarmed Italy even
farther from its allies. In the spring of 1904, when Britain joined France
in the Entente Cordiale, Italy's strategic position as a member of the
Triple Alliance became completely untenable. By the time of Spaun's
resignation, it appeared likely that the Austro-Hungarian navy and the
Italian fleet would be on opposite sides in any future war. It would be

left to his successor to narrow the gap in matériel between the two adversaries.

Spaun's relations with the army and the emperor were cooler than those Sterneck had enjoyed, but the burgeoning political support for naval expansion in the Austrian half of the empire more than balanced the equation. Leaders from the increasingly restive Slavic nationalities gave Spaun high marks for his treatment of their conationals,[132] and his agreements with Hungarian leaders, though bad for the budget, at least bought their support for the near future. While Sterneck's last budget was significantly larger than his first, the navy's share of defense expenditure barely rose at all during his fourteen-year tenure; in contrast, in 1904 the navy spent 11.7 percent of the defense budget, compared to just 7.5 percent in 1898, Spaun's first full year at the helm.[133] Indeed, Spaun would be a hard act to follow. In order to be as effective, his successor would have to master the intimidating array of political, economic, and technological challenges facing the fleet.

NOTES

1.   Rudolf Kiszling's *Erzherzog Franz Ferdinand von Österreich-Este: Leben, Pläne und Wirken am Schicksalsweg der Donaumonarchie* is the most comprehensive chronological biography of the archduke; for a more detailed account of the period covered in this section, see 9–37.

2.   Sterneck to Richard Sterneck, 11 June 1887, Sterneck, *Erinnerungen,* 258.

3.   The incident is recounted in Francis Ferdinand to Friedrich von Beck (chief of General Staff), Territet, 6 May 1896, in Glaise-Horstenau, *Franz Josephs Weggefährte,* 476–78.

4.   Francis Ferdinand, *Tagebuch meiner Reise um die Erde, 1892–1893,* 1:525.

5.   Ibid., entry for 24 August 1893, 2:414.

6.   Ibid., entry for 25 August 1893, 2:419–20. Francis Ferdinand's *Tagebuch meiner Reise um die Erde* contains many complimentary references to the South Slavs of the crew. He did not even object to their singing of old national songs, admiring their "melancholy . . . heroic sagas of Marko Kraljević, Peter Klepec, and others." See entry for 23 December 1892, 1:16.

7.   Kiszling, *Erzherzog Franz Ferdinand,* 28.

8.   Those close to Francis Ferdinand later traced his idea of "trialism"—converting the Dual Monarchy into a Triple Monarchy, including a South Slav kingdom led by the Croatians—to this time. Because his only contact with Croatians, as of 1894, would have come aboard the *Kaiserin Elisabeth,* where they accounted for the largest single group among the crew, his high opinion of their loyal service to the empire and of the need to reward it politically may also be traced to his cruise with the navy. See Kiszling, *Erzherzog Franz Ferdinand,* 28, 120.

9. *StPD*, XXVII (3 December 1891), 137, 139.

10. Ibid., 138–39. The *Maria Theresia* also had a ram bow made from Skoda steel; just a few years earlier, the steel ram of the *Kronprinzessin Stephanie* had to be imported from Krupp. See Gellner and Valentini, *San Rocco,* 38.

11. *StPD*, XXVIII (19 October 1892), 183.

12. In point 33 of the 36-point Linz Program; see text in Kolmer, *Parlament und Verfassung in Österreich,* 3:214. The German Nationalist program included a number of other points that Sterneck and other navy leaders could not support: the cession to Hungary of Dalmatia and Bosnia-Hercegovina, and a union between Austria and Hungary only in the person of the Habsburg monarch. Andrew G. Whiteside, *The Socialism of Fools: Georg Ritter von Schönerer and Austrian Pan-Germanism,* 92, characterizes the German Nationalist maritime position as "curious" in light of the anti-militarist, anti-imperialist tone of other points in the program.

13. Beck *Denkschrift* of 25 January 1893, excerpt in Reiter, "Entwicklung," 94.

14. Reiter, "Entwicklung," 94–95.

15. Kennan, *The Fateful Alliance,* 220–22; Seton-Watson, *Liberalism to Fascism,* 176.

16. Marder, *The Anatomy of British Sea Power,* 171–72; for a comparison of battleship tonnage figures, see *Jahresbericht der k.u.k. Kriegsmarine* (1897), 120–29.

17. Ropp, *The Development of a Modern Navy,* 205. The French and Russians actually did little in the area of joint naval planning before 1900, but the British navy took no chances. The Admiralty prepared new war plans for the Mediterranean that assumed a Russian fleet would pass through the Dardanelles and secure a base on the Aegean coast of Asia Minor. The British would concentrate on holding Gibraltar, Malta, and Alexandria and preventing a union of the French and Russian fleets in the Mediterranean. See text of British naval intelligence office memo of 28 October 1896, reproduced in Marder, *The Anatomy of British Sea Power,* 578–80.

18. HHSA, PA, XL, Carton 296: GMR 384 (28 March 1894).

19. The *Jahresbericht der k.u.k. Kriegsmarine* (1893), 10, notes that the navy made the commitment to buy the higher-priced Witkowitz armor "solely in the interest of domestic industry." Ibid. (1894), 11–12, identifies the Witkowitz armor for the *Monarch* class as nickel-steel plate.

20. *StPD*, XXX (3 October 1894), 63–64; on the founding of the Colonial Society, see "Kolonialpolitik" in *Kolonial-Zeitung* 13 no. 5/6(1915): 17.

21. Francis Joseph to Sterneck, Fasana, 11 May 1895, Sterneck, *Erinnerungen,* 279–80, conveys the emperor's congratulations on the launching of the *Monarch.*

22. The *Maine,* at 6,700 tons, and the *Texas,* at 6,300 tons, were almost identical in armament and speed (seventeen knots) to the Austro-Hungarian coastal defense battleships. The first modern battleships of the United States navy, they were commissioned in the late summer of 1895. See John D. Alden, *The American Steel Navy,* 361. For details on the *Monarch* class, see Schöndorfer, "Kriegsschiffbau," 35.

23. In Salisbury to Count Franz Deym (Austro-Hungarian ambassador), London, 26 December 1895, HHSA, AR, F 44 - Marinewesen, Carton 10: Varia 2/5, the prime minister contends that he has "endeavored to persuade the authorities to relax their rules as far as possible in favor of your embassy." Subsequent correspondence indicates that the problem continued. Edmund Krieghammer (war minister) to Min. des Äussern, Vienna, 30 October 1898, ibid., reports that the army's attaché in London, *Feldmarschalleutnant* Prince Esterhazy, was having similar problems.

24. During the last half of 1895, Salisbury and Goluchowsky both were interested in reviving Anglo-Austrian cooperation in the Near East, but for entirely different reasons: the British prime minister sought to build an international coalition against the sultan on behalf of the Armenian minority, then being subjected to vicious pogroms by the Turks, while the Habsburg foreign minister sought joint action with the British to avert an Anglo-Russian partition of the Ottoman Empire, which would have benefited the Russians in the Balkans. See Lowe, *Salisbury,* 102.

25. On this period of "Austro-Russian entente," see Bridge, *The Habsburg Monarchy,* 224–87; Barbara Jelavich, *The Habsburg Empire in European Affairs, 1814–1918,* 138–40.

26. Reiter, "Entwicklung," 102–3. Kaftan quoted in *StPD,* XXXI (24 June 1895), 63.

27. Schöndorfer, "Kriegsschiffbau," 35–36.

28. Bayer von Bayersburg, *Auf weiter Fahrt,* 135–41.

29. Baratelli, *La marina militare italiana,* 273–74.

30. R. J. B. Bosworth, *Italy, the Least of the Great Powers,* 24.

31. Seton-Watson, *Liberalism to Fascism,* 181–83.

32. Sullivan, "A Fleet in Being," 112.

33. Seton-Watson, *Liberalism to Fascism,* 204; Baratelli, *La marina militare italiana,* 148.

34. Sokol, *Des Kaisers Seemacht,* 156–60.

35. Seton-Watson, *Liberalism to Fascism,* 205.

36. Reiter, "Entwicklung," 104.

37. No party or faction won as much as one fifth of the *Reichsrat,* and the Czechs—dominated by the liberal nationalist Young Czechs—emerged as the largest single group with 18.5 percent of the seats. The German liberal share of seats fell from 32 percent in 1891 to 18 percent in 1897, while the German Nationalists rose from 6 percent to 11 percent, the Christian Socials from 3 percent to 7 percent, and the Social Democrats from zero to 3 percent.

38. Sterneck to Richard Sterneck, Vienna, 30 May 1893, Sterneck, *Erinnerungen,* 272.

39. Sterneck to wife, [Vienna,] June 1897, Sterneck, *Erinnerungen,* 317–18.

40. Rothenberg, *The Army of Francis Joseph,* 121, 129–30.

41. See *Militärstatistisches Jahrbuch,* 1891, 1896, and *Jahresbericht der k.u.k. Kriegsmarine,* 1896. In 1896, 27.2 percent of all active petty officers were from Bohemia and Moravia, compared to just 26.4 percent from Dalmatia and the Küstenland; in 1893 the percentages had been 23.6 percent and 32.4 percent, respectively. By 1896, 38.4 percent of all machinists' petty officers were from Bohemia and Moravia.

42. See *Jahresbericht der k.u.k. Kriegsmarine,* 1896.

43. See Sondhaus, *In the Service of the Emperor,* 103.

44. Höbelt, "Die Marine," 748, comments on the shortage of noblemen in the corps. By 1914, however, the sea officers may have had a higher percentage of nobles than any part of the Austro-Hungarian armed forces, other than the army's cavalry officer corps. See Sondhaus, "The Austro-Hungarian Naval Officer Corps," 69–71.

45. Wölfling, *My Life Story,* 82, 88–91. Horthy corroborates the general outlines of Leopold Ferdinand's version of the story. Horthy, a friend who had graduated from the academy a year before the archduke, "went so far as to advise him against going" on the cruise with Francis Ferdinand. "The two archdukes were temperamentally so different that I could foresee nothing but trouble" (*Memoirs,* 62–63).

46. Wölfling, *My Life Story,* 33.

47. For a positive view of Charles Stephen's leadership qualities, see Theodor Winterhalder, *Die österreichisch-ungarische Kriegsmarine im Weltkriege,* 66. Winterhalder, who rose to the rank of rear admiral during the First World War, entered the officer corps during Sterneck's tenure as commander.

48. Bayer von Bayersburg, *Österreichs Admirale,* 72–73; Kiszling, *Erzherzog Franz Ferdinand,* 54.

49. Sterneck died on 5 December 1897; he had presented his budget to the Hungarian Delegation on 23 November and to the Austrian on 29 November. See Sterneck, *Erinnerungen,* 325. Eberan lived on in retirement until 1915; see Bayer von Bayersburg, *Österreichs Admirale,* 62.

50. *StPD,* XXXIII (7 December 1897), 165.

51. See Bayer von Bayersburg, *Österreichs Admirale,* 25, 144, 170. Francis Joseph promoted Spaun to full admiral in May 1899.

52. Sterneck's timetable of five-year plans for the construction of new squadrons had been revised in 1896 and projected through 1909. See Reiter, "Entwicklung," 104.

53. Unless otherwise noted, my source for this section is Bayer von Bayersburg, *Auf weiter Fahrt,* 122–34, 143–81.

54. Ploček and Juba, "Geschichte der ungarischen Reederei Adria," 18–19.

55. On the landing at Shanghai, see Sokol, *Des Kaisers Seemacht,* 189.

56. See Richard Georg Plaschka, "Von Pola nach Taku: Der Druck der Mächte auf China 1900 und Österreich-Ungarns Beteiligung an der maritimen Intervention," 43–44.

57. Ibid., 46–48.

58. Ibid., 48–53. Plaschka is highly critical of the morality of Austro-Hungarian involvement in China; see ibid., 53–54.

59. On the navy's role in garrisoning the Beijing embassy compound, see Bayer von Bayersburg, *Unter der k.u.k. Kriegsflagge,* 57.

60. See *Jahresbericht der k.u.k. Kriegsmarine* (1901), 36.

61. See David L. Anderson, *Imperialism and Idealism: American Diplomats in China, 1861–1898,* 183. In 1899, Hay's first Open Door note was sent to all of the powers except Austria-Hungary.

62. See Bayer von Bayersburg, *Österreichs Admirale,* 25, 168–70.

63. Imperial resolution of 29 March 1898, quoted in ibid., 37.

64. See Rothenberg, *The Army of Francis Joseph,* 141. According to Carl von Bardolff, chief of staff at the Belvedere from 1911 to 1914, the Military Chancellery of Francis Ferdinand gained official status as a military staff only in November 1908, by decree of Francis Joseph. See Carl von Bardolff, *Soldat im alten Österreich: Erinnerungen aus meinem Leben,* 118.

65. Hinke, passed over for the post of second in command despite enjoying six years of seniority over Berghofer, was appeased with the position in Pola. He served as harbor admiral until 1901, when he retired at the age of sixty-four. See Gilbert von Randich, "Johann Edler von Hinke: Ein k.(u.)k. Admiral," 132–34.

66. Francis Ferdinand, report on inspection of Pola, 9–11 May 1898, reproduced in Randich, "Die Besichtigung Polas im Mai 1898," 90–91.

67. Kiszling, *Erzherzog Franz Ferdinand,* 58.

68. Samuel R. Williamson, Jr. comments on the archduke's distractions between 1898 and 1906, years in which he "made little attempt to use his constitutional position" ("Influence, Power, and the Policy Process: The Case of Franz Ferdinand, 1906–1914," 420).

69. Höbelt, "Die Marine," 715; Reiter, "Entwicklung," 105–6.

70. Holger Herwig, *"Luxury" Fleet: The Imperial German Navy, 1888–1918*, 42; Jonathan Steinberg, *Yesterday's Deterrent: Tirpitz and the Birth of the German Battle Fleet*, 128. Herwig erroneously counts eight coastal defense battleships as armored cruisers in his version of Tirpitz's figures.

71. Reiter, "Entwicklung," 106–8.

72. Goluchowsky quoted in ibid., 116–17.

73. *StPD*, XXXIV (25 May 1898), 218–220.

74. Ibid., 223.

75. Reiter, "Entwicklung," 115–16.

76. *StPD*, XXXIV (25 May 1898), 220, 227, 259; see also *Jahresbericht der k.u.k. Kriegsmarine* (1895), 11.

77. Reiter, "Entwicklung," 118–19.

78. See Paul G. Halpern, *The Mediterranean Naval Situation, 1908–1914*, 154.

79. Figures on total annual expenditure from Wagner, "Die k.(u.)k. Armee," 591.

80. For an account of the Rio de Oro affair, see *Kolonial-Zeitung* 13 no. 5/6 (1915): 17. Spain kept Rio de Oro until 1975, evacuating the colony only after the death of Francisco Franco.

81. Lo Giudice, *Canale di Suez*, 180, 202; Babudieri, *Industrie, commerci e navigazione*, 141.

82. Good, *Economic Rise*, 122; Lo Giudice, *Canale di Suez*, 188, 228.

83. Piemontese, *Il movimento operaio a Trieste*, 73.

84. Marina Cattaruzza, "Sloveni e Italiani a Trieste: La formazione dell'identità nazionale," 28–29; Cattaruzza, "Organisierter Konflikt," 347.

85. The Creditanstalt became the largest stockholder in Stabilimento Tecnico by purchasing all new shares in a new stock issue in 1897. See Cupez, *Cantieri Riuniti dell'Adriatico*, 5; Gellner and Valentini, *San Rocco*, 48; Gerolimi, *Cantiere Riuniti dell'Adriatico*, 29, 33.

86. Ploček and Juba, "Geschichte der ungarischen Reederei Adria," 18–19; Babudieri, *Industrie, commerci e navigazione*, 193.

87. Glaise-Horstenau, *Franz Josephs Weggefährte*, 401.

88. Wagner, "Die obersten Behörden," 86.

89. Ibid., 86–87.

90. See Good, *Economic Rise*, 166.

91. A. J. P. Taylor, *The Habsburg Monarchy, 1809–1918*, 199, compares Koerber to Bülow in less than flattering terms.

92. See Good, *Economic Rise*, 165.

93. *StPD*, XXXV (12 January 1900), 233.

94. Figures from David F. Good, "Economic Union and Uneven Development in the Habsburg Monarchy," 69.

95. Figures on total annual expenditure from Wagner, "Die k.(u.)k. Armee," 591.

96. Höbelt, "Die Marine," 754; Louis A. Gebhard, Jr., "The Development of the Austro-Hungarian Navy, 1897–1914: A Study in the Operation of Dualism," 120.

97. *Jahresbericht der k.u.k. Kriegsmarine* (1899), 11; and (1900), 13; see also Spaun's remarks in *StPD*, XXXV (12 January 1900), 237.

98. See *Jahresbericht der k.u.k. Kriegsmarine* (1913), 98, 118.

99. *StPD*, XXXVII (7 June 1901), 336.

100. Ibid., 345.

CHAPTER 4

101. Figure from Arthur Lengnick, "See-Interessen und See-Politik," 312.

102. Cattaruzza, "Organisierter Konflikt," 348.

103. The story of the Trieste general strike dominated the pages of the *Neue Freie Presse* from 14 to 19 February; on the navy's role, see 18 February, 2 (morning and evening editions). The most detailed account of the strike is a commemorative volume issued on the eightieth anniversary, *La lotta dei fuochisti: 1902–1982.* See also Piemontese, *Il movimento operaio a Trieste,* 109–18; Marina Cattaruzza, *La formazione del proletariato urbano: Immigrati, operai di mestiere, donne a Trieste dalla metà del secolo XIX alla prima guerra mondiale,* 142–43. The anniversary of the strike is still celebrated as a holiday by the parties of the Left in Trieste.

104. *StPD,* XXXVIII (9 June 1902), 539. The *Neue Freie Presse,* 16 February 1902, 3, attributes the strike to the Social Democrats, but ibid., 18 February 1902, 2, cites a police report blaming "anarchists" for the "excesses" of the past few days. On Pittoni's role, see 18 February 1902 (evening edition), 2.

105. Wagner, "Die obersten Behörden," 87.

106. *StPD,* XXXIX (5 February 1904), 401.

107. For political purposes, the *Marinekommandant* presented all of his larger projects to the Delegations with the *"Ersatz"* prefix, although the designations often were ridiculous: the three 10,600-ton *Erzherzog*-class battleships initially were labeled *Ersatz Laudon, Ersatz Drache,* and *Ersatz Novara,* after a 3,400-ton composite ship deactivated in 1897, a 2,800-ton armored frigate scrapped in 1875, and a 2,500-ton wooden propeller frigate decommissioned in 1876.

108. After the defeat of the Boxers, even Italy received a Chinese concession at Tientsin; see Seton-Watson, *Liberalism to Fascism,* 211. On Tirpitz's Second Navy Bill, see Herwig, *"Luxury" Fleet,* 42–43.

109. On the Tauern railway, see Bridge, *Sadowa to Sarajevo,* 236; and Good, *Economic Rise,* 182.

110. See Halpern, *Mediterranean Naval Situation,* 220–22; and Baratelli, *La marina militare italiana,* 337–41.

111. Seton-Watson, *Liberalism to Fascism,* 212.

112. Ropp, *The Development of a Modern Navy,* 338; Seton-Watson, *Liberalism to Fascism,* 359; Sullivan, "A Fleet in Being," 112.

113. Giorgerini, *Almanacco,* 220–26, 284–91, 350–51, 418–27.

114. Cf. Bargoni, *Corazzate italiane (1880–92)* and *Corazzate italiane classi Re Umberto - Ammiraglio di Saint Bon (1893–1901),* passim; and Greger, *Austro-Hungarian Warships,* passim.

115. Marder, *The Anatomy of British Sea Power,* 271.

116. *Jahresbericht der k.u.k. Kriegsmarine* (1898), 40–47; (1899), 37–41; (1900), 35–38; (1901), 33–34.

117. Harbauer, *Der Kaiser,* 224–33.

118. On the archduke's view of joint maneuvers and landings, see Kiszling, *Erzherzog Franz Ferdinand,* 66.

119. *Jahresbericht der k.u.k. Kriegsmarine* (1903), 36–39; (1904), 36–39.

120. *Jahresbericht der k.u.k. Kriegsmarine* (1898), 47; (1899), 37–41; (1900), 35–38; (1901), 33–34; (1902), 36–39; (1903), 36–39; (1904), 36–39.

121. See Höbelt, "Die Marine," 754; and Louis Gebhard, "The Croatians, the Habsburg Monarchy and the Austro-Hungarian Navy," 155. Spaun made the greater commitment, even though the navy still had not been able to honor his promises of 1901. In 1902,

for example, only 20.93 percent of the navy's budget had been spent in Hungary. Figure from Gebhard, "Austro-Hungarian Navy," 133.

122. *StPD*, XXXIV (25 May 1898), 227; ibid., XXXVIII (9 June 1902), 542. On the cartel agreement of 1902, see Kestranek, *Eisenindustrie,* 12–13.

123. Figures from *Jahresbericht der k.u.k. Kriegsmarine* (1913), 92–95. All of the Pocahantas coal (3,917 tons) was purchased in 1900.

124. Data on engines from *Jahresbericht der k.u.k. Kriegsmarine* (1913), 98–111. Greger, *Austro-Hungarian Warships,* 19, 30, identifies the boiler manufacturer as Belleville rather than Maudsley.

125. On the dates of introduction of various types of Austro-Hungarian naval guns, see Greger, *Austro-Hungarian Warships,* 9–10.

126. Brousek, *Die Grossindustrie Böhmens,* 131.

127. Greger, *Austro-Hungarian Warships,* 42, 55; on the founding of the Danubius shipyard, see Babudieri, *Squeri e cantiere,* 27.

128. According to Gebhard, 76 million of the special appropriation was designated for construction ("Austro-Hungarian Navy," 146). See also Höbelt, "Die Marine," 715–16; Reiter, "Entwicklung," 131.

129. The repayment scheme is explained in considerable detail in *StPD*, XL (1 June 1904), 370–71. See also Höbelt, "Die Marine," 715–16; Reiter, "Entwicklung," 132.

130. Francis Joseph to Spaun, Radmer, 5 October 1904, text in Harbauer, *Der Kaiser,* 238–39.

131. On the evolution of fire control around the turn of the century, see Ropp, *The Development of a Modern Navy,* 300–304, and Jon Tetsuro Sumida, "British Capital Ship Design and Fire Control in the *Dreadnought* Era: Sir John Fisher, Arthur Hungerford Pollen, and the Battle Cruiser," 205–17. For Tsushima's impact on future naval artillery, see Höbelt, "Die Marine," 718; Baratelli, *La marina militare italiana,* 356; and Herwig, *"Luxury" Fleet,* 54.

132. See Gebhard, "The Croatians," 153.

133. See tables in Wagner, "Die k.(u.)k. Armee," 590–91. In 1884, Sterneck's first full year as commander, the navy spent 7.4 percent of the defense outlay; in 1897, the share was 7.5 percent.

NAVALISM TRIUMPHANT

Spaun's unexpected retirement led to the appointment of Vice Admiral Count Rudolf Montecuccoli as chief of the *Marinesektion* and *Marinekommandant.* For the navy, it was a fortunate choice; a far better politician than Spaun, Montecuccoli would be able to build on the achievements of his predecessor and in less than a decade increase the navy's share of the overall Austro-Hungarian defense outlay twofold. As the pronavy coalition continued to grow and lucrative navy contracts silenced Hungarian opposition, it became unnecessary to justify the fleet purely in defensive terms. As late as the spring of 1904, Spaun still felt compelled to refer to the new battleship *Erzherzog Friedrich* as a "coast defender." Eight and a half years later, after Austria-Hungary had one dreadnought in service and another three under construction, Montecuccoli proudly declared before the Delegations: "We are a Mediterranean power."[1]

MONTECUCCOLI, FRANCIS FERDINAND, AND THE MODERN BATTLE FLEET (1904–9)

A veteran of forty-five years of naval service, Montecuccoli first saw action at the age of sixteen, after he and his classmates were mustered out of the naval academy early at the start of the war of 1859. He later served at Lissa aboard the wooden frigate *Adria* and would be the last veteran of 1866 ever to lead the navy. The culmination of Montecuccoli's career as a seagoing captain came in 1900, when he commanded the cruiser squadron sent to China during the Boxer Rebellion. In April 1903, the retirement of Vice Admiral Berghofer had opened the way for his appointment as second in command under Spaun.[2]

Montecuccoli thus reached the top via the same route as his predecessor, after a brief time in the second highest post. But when it came to administrative and political experience, there was a great difference between his eighteen months as *Stellvertreter* in the *Marine-sektion* and the few weeks that Spaun had held the same position before Sterneck's death. The new *Marinekommandant* had been a party to the passage of two budgets and the extraordinary credit of May 1904, not to mention Spaun's most recent bargain with the Hungarians. Sixty-year-old Rear Admiral Leodegar Kneissler filled the vacant position of *Stellvertreter*. Like Montecuccoli, the new second in command was a veteran of Lissa, where he earned a decoration for bravery. He distinguished himself in leading landing parties against the Cattaran rebels in 1882 and on Crete fifteen years later. In 1896 he caught the attention of Francis Ferdinand while serving as captain of the *Donau*, which transported the ailing archduke on his convalescent visit to Egypt. Two years later, after the blockade of Crete, he was elevated to the nobility as Kneissler von Maixdorf.[3] In 1905, a few months after their appointments, both men received promotions, Montecuccoli to admiral, Kneissler to vice admiral.

The new leadership assumed command of a force of just under 700 sea officers, 10,000 seamen on active duty, and 16,000 reserves and *Seewehr*. While the precise percentages fluctuated annually, the national composition of the navy had changed little since Sterneck's time. Among the sea officers, Germans (54.6 percent) and Magyars (11.9 percent) still dominated, followed by Italians (9.6 percent), Czechs (8.9 percent), Croatians (7.6 percent), Slovenes (4.2 percent), and Poles (3.2 percent). Among the men, Croatians still claimed the largest contingent at 35.8 percent, followed by Italians (25 percent), Germans (13.9 percent), Czechs (10 percent), Magyars (8.1 percent), and Slovenes (5 percent). Since 1896 the Italians had edged past the Czechs to become the third-largest group in the officer corps; otherwise, the order of nationalities had not changed either for officers or common seamen. In a continuation of earlier trends, Czechs and Germans from Bohemia and Moravia supplied the largest number of petty officers and over 40 percent of machinist petty officers.[4] With a growing number of men from the interior provinces entering the navy, the share of experienced seamen among the recruits continued to decrease. In January 1907, Montecuccoli reported to the Delegations that in recent years, career merchant mariners made up between 11 and 13 percent of new recruits. In 1884, the figure had been 21 percent.[5]

Montecuccoli inherited a fleet significantly more modern than the one Sterneck had left to Spaun seven years earlier.[6] The *Monarch* and *Budapest* had been commissioned in the spring of 1898, a year after the activation of their sister ship *Wien*. Between March 1899 and March 1904, the navy laid down an unprecedented six battleships in five years; the three vessels of the *Habsburg* class all were in service in time for the summer maneuvers of 1904, and the three *Erzherzogs* were on their way to completion by the time Montecuccoli assumed command. After Spaun removed all of the casemate ships from the active fleet, Montecuccoli retired the *Kronprinz Rudolf* and *Kronprinzessin Stephanie*; worthless after barely fifteen years of service, they bore witness to the rapid pace of technological change. Like Spaun, Montecuccoli employed the old vessels as training ships and hulks. The casemate ship *Tegetthoff*, eventually renamed *Mars*, continued to serve as harbor watch in Pola, while the *Kronprinzessin Stephanie* and later the *Kronprinz Rudolf* filled the same role in Cattaro.

In addition to its nine newer battleships, the fleet also included three armored and three unarmored cruisers built within the past decade; of the former, the *Sankt Georg* and *Kaiser Karl VI* were significantly larger than the coast defense battleships of the *Monarch* class. The old ram cruisers were still in service, as were the smaller *Leopard* and *Panther*, but Montecuccoli had the *Tiger* rebuilt as the admiral's yacht *Lacroma*. The twelve *Huszár*-class destroyers and the two dozen torpedo boats authorized in the special outlay of 1904 helped modernize the navy's stock of smaller vessels. Unfortunately, construction delays, especially in the less experienced Danubius yard in "Hungarian" Rijeka, would delay the completion of the last of the destroyers and torpedo boats until 1909 and 1910, respectively.

Montecuccoli maintained Spaun's active posture in the Adriatic and Mediterranean. The winter squadron of 1904–5 was the most formidable ever, consisting of all three *Habsburg*-class battleships. Thereafter the navy always kept its three newest battleships on active duty on a year-round basis. From 1905–6 onward, the winter squadron included an armored cruiser—either the *Sankt Georg* or *Kaiser Karl VI*—in addition to the trio of battleships. Every summer Montecuccoli mobilized the six newest battleships, which were organized into two divisions for

the annual exercises. Starting in 1906, the summer squadron also included a cruiser flotilla consisting of the armored cruisers and any unarmored cruisers not involved in overseas missions. During the same
year, Montecuccoli created the reserve squadron, a ready-reserve force
that remained on alert in Pola except for the summer months, when the
ships and their crews joined the rest of the fleet for maneuvers. Initially
consisting of the three *Monarch*-class battleships, the reserve squadron
usually included the second-oldest trio of battleships and the armored
cruiser (*Sankt Georg* or *Kaiser Karl VI*) not serving with the winter
squadron.[7] Montecuccoli did not ignore the Danube flotilla, activating
all six of its monitors during 1905. Four monitors participated in that
autumn's army maneuvers in Hungary.[8]

The stronger showing was impressive, but only by the standards of
the navy's own past history. For the first time in over a quarter century,
the Italian fleet was the yardstick against which Austria-Hungary had to
measure its own naval power, and the disparity in strength was just as
disheartening to Montecuccoli as it had been for Spaun. After two more
battleships were laid down in 1903, Italy had eighteen pre-dreadnoughts
built or building. Improvements in the shipyards shortened construction times, and the newest vessels were completed just a few months
after the commissioning of the last of the *Erzherzogs*—the *Ferdinand Max*—
in December 1907. By then, however, the *Duilio* and the six other battleships launched in the 1880s were obsolete; four of these ships were
scrapped in the years 1909–11 and a fifth in 1914, while two survived to
serve as harbor watch vessels in the First World War. But the eleven
remaining battleships (commissioned in the years 1893–1908) compared very favorably to the nine most modern battleships of the Austro-
Hungarian fleet. Nine of the eleven were larger and more powerful than
even the *Erzherzog* class and were double the size of the tiny *Monarch*
class.[9] By 1905 the Italians also had six armored cruisers in roughly the
same class as Austria-Hungary's three, with four more (ranging in size
from 9,800 to 10,700 tons) laid down in the years 1905–7.[10] Italy had a
great advantage in light cruisers and torpedo boats and was catching
up in destroyers; for these smaller vessels, the Italians, like the Austrians, relied in part on purchases from Yarrow, Thornycroft, and
Elbing. Meanwhile, domestic construction benefited from a number of
Anglo-Italian corporate partnerships. Among engine manufacturers, the
Italian Ansaldo firm was affiliated with Maudsley and Guppy with

Hawthorn; in armaments, mergers linked Pozzuoli with Armstrong and Terni with Vickers.[11] This heavy dependence upon British technology made it all the more unlikely that Italy would support its Triple Alliance partners in a war in which Britain would be among the opponents.

All things considered, Montecuccoli had no shortage of evidence to support an argument for further naval expansion. Indeed, the Italians were so far ahead that catching them seemed almost a hopeless task, especially in battleships. But developments in Italy gave Montecuccoli some breathing space. After laying down two battleships in 1903 (the last two of four *Regina Elena*-class warships), the Italian navy committed itself to the program of four large armored cruisers begun in the years 1905–7. Also in 1903, a scandal over armor contracts with the Terni steel works led to an investigation that put the navy's construction program in limbo for three years.[12] A total of six years were to pass before Italy, in 1909, finally laid down another battleship.

Unfortunately, the political situation within the Dual Monarchy made it difficult for Montecuccoli to take advantage of the respite. Indeed, throughout his time in office, political instability in Austria and especially in Hungary prevented the Delegations from convening on a regular basis. The budgets would include a bewildering array of multi-year special credits, supplementary credits, and one-time emergency appropriations. At times expenditure raced ahead of allocations, and funding was granted ex post facto; at other times sums appropriated actually were more than the navy could spend, and balances had to be carried over to subsequent years. The confusion continued from 1904 through 1912, when the books were balanced once again.

Montecuccoli took office amid a crisis in Budapest over the issue of the Magyarization of the army's Hungarian line regiments. The imbroglio lasted until the spring of 1906; in the meantime, foreign developments such as the Russian Revolution of 1905 and Norway's unilateral dissolution of its dynastic union with Sweden (June 1905) encouraged the more rebellious Hungarian faction favoring complete independence. The crisis in Hungary also had a profound effect on political life in the Austrian half of the empire. In the council of ministers, Koerber—who had objected even to Spaun's concessions to Hungary—took an uncompromising position vis-à-vis the demands from Budapest, arousing the ire of Francis Joseph, who dismissed him late in

1904.[13] Future Austrian ministers would try to copy his methods but with far less success.

The emperor finally appeased Hungarian leaders by upgrading the status of their *Honvéd* (including the addition of artillery units) in exchange for a larger future contingent of recruits and recognition that German should remain the language of command for the regular army.[14] In April 1906, as soon as the dust settled, Montecuccoli protected the navy's interests by renewing Spaun's earlier Hungarian quota agreement.[15] Owing to the political turmoil, the Hungarian share of the special appropriation of 1904 was not paid until August 1906,[16] but on the bright side, the funding of the same special credit in Austria had caused enough problems to force the resignation of the finance minister, Böhm von Bawerk, late in 1904. Thereafter Böhm's stipulation regarding the repayment of the credit, which had driven Spaun to resign, lost most of its support. A total of 22.1 million kronen was deducted from the 1905 share of the special credit, but when the Delegations finally met again in July 1906 for a belated approval of the budget for 1906, the politicians voted to end the repayment scheme.[17]

Naval spending reached new record heights in 1905 (64 million kronen) and in 1906 (70.5 million), but neither appropriation included money for additional battleships. The launching of the *Erzherzog Friedrich* and *Erzherzog Ferdinand Max,* in April and May 1905, respectively, left both of the large slips at the San Marco yard empty for the first time in more than six years. Speaking before the Austrian Delegation in July 1906, Montecuccoli lamented the lost momentum in battleship construction: "The best defense of a coast lies certainly in a powerful offensive. But . . . we could not go on the offensive against the fleet of any great power."[18] Pronavy delegates placed the blame squarely on Budapest's doorstep. Josef Wolfgang Dobernig, a German Nationalist from Carinthia, stated bluntly that Austria "must shout across the Leitha: 'Hands off our navy!'"[19]

Following the constitutional crisis, an exhausted Francis Joseph conceded an unprecedented amount of influence to Francis Ferdinand, and by the end of 1906 the archduke had registered a series of impressive political victories. To varying degrees, he was instrumental in the appointment of a new Austrian minister-president, Baron Max von Beck;[20] the replacement of Goluchowsky with a new foreign minister,

Count Alois Lexa von Aehrenthal;[21] the retirement of the aging chief of the General Staff, Friedrich von Beck, in favor of his own protégé, *Feldmarschalleutnant* Conrad von Hötzendorf;[22] and the appointment of a new war minister, General Baron Franz von Schönaich.[23]

Early in 1906, before this dramatic purge of military and civilian leaders, Francis Ferdinand had appointed Major Alexander Brosch von Aarenau as head of his personal staff in the Belvedere. The relatively minor move ultimately became more significant than any of the other changes. The tactful and patient Brosch became the archduke's alter ego, restraining his volatile personality and directing his energies into constructive channels. Under Brosch the disorganized and understaffed Military Chancellery of Francis Ferdinand soon became a center of power and influence. A network of friendly journalists and editors coordinated from the Belvedere publicized the archduke's ideas, attacked his opponents, and attempted to shape public opinion. Brosch also identified sympathetic experts from the various nationalities of the empire and introduced them to Francis Ferdinand's circle at the Belvedere. The ultimate goal was to hit the ground running on the day of the archduke's accession to the throne; in the process of building this brain trust for the future reign, Brosch's office eventually received and processed over ten thousand pieces of correspondence per year. Shortly after the First World War, a relatively hostile observer, R. W. Seton-Watson, conceded that Brosch was "a soldier of quite unusual breadth of vision and understanding."[24]

The non-German proponents of Francis Ferdinand's plans to reorganize the Habsburg Empire often doubled as important supporters of the fleet. The Slovene Ivan Šušteršić authored a South Slav program compatible with the archduke's "trialism," which envisioned a Triple Monarchy in which the South Slavs would have equal status with German Austrians and Hungarians; he also led the fight for naval expansion in the *Reichsrat* and the Austrian Delegation, as early as 1905 calling for a fleet of fifteen battleships.[25] Among the German Austrian parties, the Christian Socials so closely reflected Francis Ferdinand's own sympathies—Catholic, prodynastic, German Austrian, and anti-Semitic—that they became known as the "party of the heir to the throne (*Thronfolgerpartei*)." The archduke made no secret of his admiration for the party's leader, Karl Lueger; he could also count on Albert Gessmann to rally

Christian Social support for the navy in the *Reichsrat* and Austrian Delegation.[26] The German Nationalists, who took their cue from Berlin in much the same way that future communist politicians would follow the lead of Moscow, had to be manipulated via the German ambassadors in Vienna. Francis Ferdinand and Brosch used Baron Ludwig Oppenheimer, an ally of the Belvedere with close ties to the German embassy, to engineer German Nationalist support for increased expenditure on the Habsburg army "in the interest of Germany" and the alliance.[27] Fortunately for Montecuccoli and his predecessors, the German Nationalists in the *Reichsrat* had always supported the navy because of the economic interests of their constituents and also out of a belief that a strong Austrian navy dominating the Adriatic would secure an outlet to the Mediterranean for German *Mitteleuropa*. The press connections of the Belvedere included the Christian Social daily *Reichspost*, edited by Friedrich Funder, who often printed pronavy articles and editorials. Other allies of the archduke included former liberal Baron Leopold von Chlumecky of the *Österreichische Rundschau* and Friedrich Danzer of the *Armeezeitung*.[28]

Such ties to the nationalities, political parties, and the press became all the more important after December 1906, when the new Austrian minister-president, Max von Beck, secured passage of a bill expanding the franchise for *Reichsrat* elections to a universal suffrage for males twenty-four and older. The Austrian elections of 1907 left German Austrian parties in control of just over half of the *Reichsrat* but also brought the death of the traditional liberal and conservative factions. The Christian Socials absorbed most of the former German conservative vote and emerged as the largest party, with 19 percent of the seats (up from 7 percent a decade earlier); the Social Democrats became the second-largest party, at 17 percent (1897: 3 percent), while German Nationalists secured 15 percent of the seats (1897: 11 percent). Given the opposition of the Social Democrats to all military and naval spending, Montecuccoli would rely heavily upon Francis Ferdinand's ability to control the Christian Socials, influence the German Nationalists, and muster sufficient non-German support.

From the onset of his tenure, Montecuccoli also enjoyed the support of the Austrian Navy League. Founded in September 1904 on the model of the phenomenally successful German Navy League, the organization grew from a charter membership of 39 to over 4,300 members by 1910. Count Ernst Sylva-Tarouca, a friend of Francis Ferdinand and member of the Belvedere circle, served as first president of the new pronavy lobby. Some of the oldest and wealthiest aristocratic families were represented in the circle of leaders: Count Josef Thun-Hohenstein served as the League's second president, and in 1910 Prince Alfred von und zu Liechtenstein became the third man to hold the office. Prominent politicians among the charter members included South Slav leaders Ivan Šušteršić and Ante Vuković. Industrialists, provincial political figures, and leading clerics also rallied to the cause. Although he did not officially become patron of the Navy League until 1908, Francis Ferdinand naturally took an interest in the organization from the outset.[29]

The archduke's favorite politician, Karl Lueger, served as first vice president of the League. The popular mayor of Vienna was fascinated with modern technology, held neomercantilist economic views, and had nothing but contempt for Italians; to some degree, each of these sentiments drew him to the navy's cause. With the creation in 1906 of the Christian Social *Knabenhorte*, Lueger even extended his navalism to the streets and neighborhoods of the imperial capital. The boys of the *Knabenhorte*, considered by some historians to be models for the Hitler Youth of Nazi Germany, wore sailor suits as their uniform.[30]

In October 1905, the League's publication, *Die Flagge*, began to appear on a monthly basis. In its opening manifesto, "What We Want," the editors proclaimed their intention to "arouse the mind of the people for the navy, to support our maritime interests in the representative bodies, to influence negotiations over the regulation of tariffs and trading relations with overseas lands, and to make the heroic deeds of our navy universally known." The spokesmen of Austrian navalism made no secret of their intention to emulate the Germans, citing their common need for sea power as well as strong armies: "Germany is powerful on land . . . [and] therein lies its strength. But history teaches us that no nation can maintain its great power status in the long run without naval prestige, without sea power!"[31]

Founding members of the League's presidium included two retired navy men, former second in command Alexander Eberan von Eberhorst and former rear admiral Karl von Pöltl. While the navy welcomed the creation of a pronavy lobby, its leaders at least initially were careful not to identify themselves too closely with the League in order to maintain the fiction that the military services remained above politics. Spaun joined in 1905 after his retirement, and later that year both Montecuccoli and future commander Anton Haus purchased memberships in their wives' names, but the officer corps successfully enforced an unofficial ban on membership by active navy men. In the autumn of 1906, Montecuccoli lifted the prohibition, and over one hundred thirty active officers promptly joined the League. In subsequent years, several hundred navy officers purchased memberships.[32]

The League took up the cause of Montecuccoli's first fleet plan upon its promulgation in July 1905. The proposal actually differed little from Spaun's plan of 1898. The *Marinekommandant* called for thirteen battleships (instead of Spaun's twelve), twelve cruisers, eighteen destroyers (instead of twelve), and eighty-two torpedo boats (instead of seventy-two); he also proposed the construction of six submarines.[33] Because Montecuccoli considered only the six battleships of the *Habsburg* and *Erzherzog* classes to be credible as modern warships, battleship construction was his first priority. In November 1906, his budget proposal to the Delegations included starting costs for a new class of three 14,500-ton battleships. Thanks to the recent renewal of the quota agreement, the Hungarians were actually enthusiastic in approving his program. The only grumbling came from the Austrian Delegation, where the promoters of industries that had benefited from naval contracts in the past protested the extent of the concessions Montecuccoli had made in order to win Hungarian support. When questioned about the ability of the Rijeka shipyards to fulfill navy contracts, he could offer only a lame response: "We hope for the best." Young Czech leader Karel Kramář retorted with the observation that "ships are not built with hopes."[34]

Montecuccoli's victory in the budget battle for 1907 coincided with a revolutionary development in naval technology. A few weeks earlier, in October 1906, Britain had launched its *Dreadnought,* the first all big-gun battleship. At 17,900 tons, carrying ten 12-inch guns, and capable of 20.9 knots, the *Dreadnought* was the largest, most powerful, and fastest battleship ever constructed. In the years to come, navy men would argue that the slate had been wiped clean the minute the *Dread-*

nought had been launched; all pre-dreadnoughts were considered obsolete and only battleships of the dreadnought design could be counted in calculating the strength of one's battle fleet.

Even Germany, Britain's most determined naval rival, did not respond immediately to the *Dreadnought* challenge. Tirpitz's first four dreadnoughts were not laid down until the summer of 1907. The French navy, Europe's third-largest, went ahead in 1907 with the construction of a new class of six pre-dreadnought battleships. Fortunately for Austria-Hungary, chief naval architect Siegfried Popper made his new *Radetzky* class as powerful as possible without fully embracing the dreadnought design. Their 14,500 tons made them the navy's largest battleships ever and, even more important, larger than any Italian warships. Each would have a primary armament of four 12-inch guns and a powerful secondary battery of eight 9.4-inch guns, a caliber as heavy as the primary armament of the *Monarch*s, the *Habsburg*s, and the *Erzherzog*s. Their capacity for 20.5 knots and cruising range of 5,600 miles put them in the same league with the *Dreadnought* in terms of speed.

The new design was impressive in other ways as well. An American officer, touring one of the *Radetzky*s at the end of the First World War, observed that "the ship was constructed with an eye to comfort—for the officers." The design featured "large, airy rooms with ports of almost window size for even the junior officers," and the captain's quarters consisted of "a magnificent seven-room suite in the stern of the ship." In contrast, "the crew's quarters were cramped, dark, and stuffy."[35] Similar differences in living conditions could be found on the navy's older, smaller battleships; aboard the *Monarch* and its sister ships, the crew's quarters below were so crowded that sailors had to change clothes on deck.[36] Unfortunately for Austria-Hungary and for other countries that would experience naval mutinies during the First World War, such a lack of consideration for the basic needs of the crew only widened the traditional gulf between officers and their men.

The navy awarded all three of the new battleship contracts to the Stabilimento Tecnico Triestino. The armament came from Skoda and the armor from Witkowitz. The machine shop of the Stabilimento Tecnico built their engines, which featured British-style Yarrow boilers manufactured domestically under a licensing arrangement. The teak backing for their side armor was the only imported material.[37] The

Erzherzog Franz Ferdinand—laid down in September 1907, launched in September 1908—was the first of the new ships to be completed, followed by the *Radetzky* (begun November 1907, launched July 1909). The *Zrinyi* completed the class (January 1909, April 1910). The warships would have been launched even faster if not for strikes by welders in 1908 and riveters in 1909, both supported by the Trieste Social Democratic League.[38] Thanks to these expensive projects, overall naval spending, which had fallen to 63.4 million kronen in 1907, rebounded to a new record high of 73.4 million in 1908, the first year of a new three-year 54 million kronen supplementary special credit.

Montecuccoli also oversaw the completion of the last of the destroyers and torpedo boats authorized in the special outlay of 1904. These included a dozen 110-ton coastal torpedo boats, in service by 1910, which had the distinction of being the navy's first oil-burning vessels.[39] In another breakthrough, in May 1908 the navy laid down the 3,500-ton light cruiser *Admiral Spaun* in the Pola Arsenal, the first Austro-Hungarian warship to be built with turbine engines. The Stabilimento Tecnico Triestino concluded an arrangement with the Parsons firm of Britain, pioneers in turbine construction, which enabled the engines to be constructed in Trieste from domestic resources. Designed for scouting purposes, the *Spaun* would have a top speed of more than twenty-seven knots. It also fulfilled Francis Joseph's promise to name a vessel after the former *Marinekommandant*.[40]

Francis Ferdinand showed a natural interest in the battleship named for him, and his wife Sophie also christened the *Radetzky* at its launching.[41] The *Zrinyi*, named as a gesture to Hungary, received less attention from the archduke. But Montecuccoli could not afford to snub the Hungarians, even less so after the fall of 1907, when the decennial revision of the Austro-Hungarian economic relationship called for Hungary to provide 36.4 percent of the common budget. Hungarian leaders naturally demanded from the navy a new quota conforming to this higher figure, which Montecuccoli quickly conceded. Fully aware of what was at stake, he was never too proud to pander to the sentiments of the politicians in Budapest. Speaking to the Hungarian Delegation in October 1908, he won a rousing response by ending his address with a quote from the patriot Lajos Kossuth, who had proposed a Hungarian maritime policy sixty years earlier: "Tengere a Magyar! (Go to sea, Magyars!)"[42] The Delegations voted the navy an unprecedented 97.2 million kronen for 1909, with the additional funds intended to hasten the completion of the three *Radetzkys*.[43] Montecuccoli's remarks, though very effective, sparked protests in the Austrian Delegation, where many already felt that Montecuccoli had gone too far in courting Hungarian support. The Croatian delegate Juraj Biankini argued that the Hungarians should be told to "go back to the Puszta" because the Adriatic "belongs to the Croatians."[44] Leopold Steiner of Lower Austria quipped that "it is certainly possible that one fine day a ship will be christened *Kossuth*."[45] Fortunately for the navy, the commander had the political talent to prevent such minor storms from assuming more significant proportions. Nevertheless, the tense internal political balance of Austro-Hungarian Dualism challenged him no less than it had his predecessors. In building better relations with the Hungarians, Montecuccoli imperiled his ties with the politicians and industrialists of the Austrian half of the empire; in particular, he risked alienating Francis Ferdinand, whose anti-Magyar sentiments were no secret to anyone. Indeed, the archduke loathed all Austrian military and political figures who were "too soft" toward the Hungarians. He even conspired to end the careers of some deemed to be in this category—most notably Baron Heinrich von Pitreich, Schönaich's predecessor as war minister, and minister-president Max von Beck[46]— but both Spaun and Montecuccoli appeared to enjoy a unique immunity from his wrath. The archduke never openly questioned the necessity of their arrangements with the politicians in Budapest, and when it came to Montecuccoli, he went out of his way to show favor to the admiral, especially in the presence of army leaders.[47] Such signs of approval no doubt were comforting, since the support of the Hungarians had been just as vital as the backing of the archduke and his Austrian connections in securing the funding for the *Radetzky* class of battleships, and the *Marinekommandant* certainly could not risk alienating either camp. With the dawning of the dreadnought era and the likelihood that he would propose bigger, more expensive warships in the future, Montecuccoli continued to walk a political tightrope.

The war scare over Austria-Hungary's annexation of Bosnia-Hercegovina ultimately provided further impetus for the cause of naval expansion, but the navy's actual role during the crisis was minimal. Against landlocked Serbia the navy could employ only its flotilla of river monitors; at the height of the crisis, they cruised down the Danube to Belgrade, where their appearance caused a panic.[48] Even though Russia threatened war in support of Serbia, navy strategists did not take seriously the possibility of a sortie through the Dardanelles by the Black Sea fleet. Austria-Hungary's attentions focused instead on its "ally" Italy, which reacted with unexpected hostility to the change in the Balkans. Citing the danger of war with Italy, in January 1909 Montecuccoli sent a memorandum to Francis Joseph proposing a new fleet plan of sixteen battleships, twelve cruisers, twenty-four destroyers, seventy-two seagoing torpedo boats, and twelve submarines. The plan included six destroyers and six submarines more than his proposal of 1905, and ten fewer torpedo boats, but the additional battleships drew the most attention, especially because Montecuccoli proposed that four of the new total of sixteen should be 20,000-ton dreadnoughts. After the emperor endorsed the plan, the *Marinekommandant* circulated it among the appropriate ministries in Vienna and Budapest.[49]

In Rome and other Italian cities, anti-Austrian street demonstrations continued throughout the winter of 1908–9, while bellicose statements from Conrad von Hötzendorf and the construction of the three *Radetzky*s combined to heighten Italian perceptions of an Austrian threat. Even though the new warships were far from ready for battle, Italy had nothing to match them; upon their completion, Austria-Hungary arguably would enjoy a material naval advantage over Italy for the first time since before the commissioning of the *Duilio* in 1880. The Italian navy, which laid down its last pre-dreadnoughts in 1903, had to get back into the game of battleship building. While the budget for the Italian fiscal year 1907–8 had included a modest sum to start a dreadnought program, little had been done before the onset of the Bosnian crisis. At the end of 1908, panicky Italian admirals had called for a two-to-one ratio of superiority over the Habsburg navy, only to have their government reject this goal on financial grounds. But in April 1909, after reports of Montecuccoli's dreadnought project appeared in the Italian press, public and political concern reached new heights. Taking advantage of the hysteria over the new Austro-Hungarian proposals, the Italian navy finally threw down the gauntlet. In June 1909, the 19,500-ton *Dante Alighieri* was laid down at Castellammare.[50]

As Montecuccoli focused his energies on matching the Italian move with at least one dreadnought of his own, Austria-Hungary received an aggravating reminder that Italy was still formally an ally: in late June, the Italian navy asked permission for four of its officers to visit the Whitehead torpedo factory in Rijeka. In calmer times, such a routine request would be granted without question, but in the tense atmosphere of the summer of 1909, the *Marinekommandant* considered it a provocation. Italy was well aware that Austria-Hungary had a virtual open-door policy for all foreign visitors to the Whitehead factory; to bar the officers of an "allied" country from touring Whitehead would spark a diplomatic incident and perhaps even a formal breach between Rome and Vienna. A frustrated Montecuccoli agreed to allow the visit, but the foreign ministry respected his wishes in treating it as a matter of the greatest delicacy. In a cipher telegram, the Ballhausplatz called for police agents to shadow the four officers with the "greatest possible inconspicuous surveillance" during their stay in Rijeka.[51]

The navy continued to encourage tours of Rijeka, Trieste, and Pola by friendlier visitors, and Montecuccoli did everything possible to facilitate Austro-Hungarian overtures to the states of southeastern Europe. In the years before the First World War, the navy accommodated cadets from Romania at the academy in Rijeka and allowed a number of Romanian officers to serve aboard the ships of the fleet. In addition to Romanians, a Greek and several Bulgarians were admitted to the torpedo course at Pola.[52] The Austro-Hungarian presence in the Far East also prompted requests from Asian countries for visits and training experiences. Japanese officers had been touring Habsburg installations on a regular basis since the 1870s and returned again in 1909; the Chinese navy asked if its officers could serve aboard the cruisers stationed in East Asian waters; and from Bangkok came requests for torpedo instructors and for places at the academy for Siamese cadets. While some of the requests from the Asians had to be denied,[53] Montecuccoli could take pride in the fact that his navy still enjoyed an excellent reputation abroad for the training and education of its personnel.

THE NAVY, THE ECONOMY, AND OVERSEAS INTERESTS (1904–13)

By the time Montecuccoli assumed command of the fleet, its golden age of overseas cruises already had drawn to a close. During Spaun's time in office, the navy had followed the trend common to the other fleets of Europe at the turn of the century, curtailing its worldwide missions to show the flag and concentrating instead on expanded operations in or near home waters. For Austria-Hungary, the change meant extensive cruises throughout the Mediterranean and vastly expanded year-round operations in Mediterranean and Adriatic waters, with the resulting strain on matériel and manpower necessitating a reduction in the number of overseas voyages.

Nevertheless, the navy under Montecuccoli remained an active instrument of diplomacy and economic expansion. In 1905, in part to spite an Italy still smarting from the Aduwa fiasco of 1896, Austria-Hungary concluded a treaty of trade and friendship with Ethiopia. The mission to Addis Ababa was led by Captain Ludwig von Höhnel, who earlier had participated in two scientific expeditions to East Africa. With Italy in control of the Eritrean and Somalian coasts, the cruiser *Panther* docked at the French enclave of Djibouti, and Höhnel's entourage went overland to meet Emperor Menelik at the Ethiopian capital.[54] Höhnel subsequently commanded the armored cruiser *Sankt Georg* on a voyage to Hampton Roads for the United States' Jamestown tricentennial in the summer of 1907. Accompanied by the light cruiser *Aspern*, Höhnel's ship also visited Annapolis and New York.[55] In the last transatlantic cruise ever undertaken by an Austro-Hungarian warship, the armored cruiser *Kaiser Karl VI* visited Brazil and Uruguay in the summer of 1910, then represented the Dual Monarchy at Argentina's centennial celebration.[56]

The navy maintained a continuous overseas presence only on the East Asian station, where the old ram cruisers, too slow and weak for use in the Adriatic in case of war, shouldered most of the burden. The *Kaiser Franz Joseph I* replaced the *Kaiserin Elisabeth* on the station in 1905, staying on until 1908; the *Elisabeth* then returned for another two years, followed by the *Franz Joseph* from 1910 until 1913. The *Elisabeth* returned again in 1913 and was still in the Far East when the First World War began.[57] More often than not, another warship could be found along with a ram cruiser on the East Asian station. The light cruiser *Szigetvár* visited Singapore in 1907, while the *Leopard* spent the years 1907–9 in the Far East, followed in 1909–10 by the *Panther.* In 1912–13 the *Szigetvár* returned for a cruise through the East Indies. These missions overlapped with those of the ram cruisers and provided the latter with at least a partial exchange of crews almost on an annual basis. Owing to the turmoil in China, life on the station was often eventful. In 1911 and 1912, during the Chinese Revolution, detachments from the

Franz Joseph joined with forces of other powers to protect the foreign communities in Shanghai and other ports.[58]

The navy's emphasis on Asian waters reflected the growing importance of the Austrian Lloyd's East and South Asian trade. In 1913 the Lloyd ran fifty-four voyages to India, China, and Japan, with cargoes that amounted to just under 30 percent of the company's total volume. In the same year, the Far East alone accounted for almost 17 percent of Trieste's trade, and the overall value of the city's trade with Asia (including Asiatic Turkey) by far surpassed the figure for the Asian trade of all ports of the kingdom of Italy combined.[59]

Trade with Asia was just one aspect of a spectacular growth in the prosperity of Trieste after the turn of the century. The value of the port's trade mushroomed from 712.6 million kronen (356.3 million gulden) in 1900 to 1,801.6 million kronen in 1913.[60] The relative importance of Trieste, and of all maritime commerce, in Austria-Hungary's overall foreign trade picture likewise grew during the prewar boom. The German Empire by far was Austria-Hungary's largest trading partner, consistently producing between 35 and 40 percent of its imports and taking between 40 and 50 percent of its exports, and of course virtually none of this German trade went by sea; but maritime commerce became a very significant factor in the rest of Austria-Hungary's foreign trade, accounting for at least one fourth and as much as one third of annual traffic with countries other than Germany.[61]

The boom in maritime commerce went hand in hand with an expansion of the merchant marine and the emergence of several new shipping companies. The most successful was the Austro-Americana, formed in 1895 as a joint venture by British and Viennese investors; the line expanded dramatically after 1903, when it absorbed the Cosulich Brothers line, a small family firm that had been operating since 1857.[62] After becoming a public company, the Austro-Americana prospered thanks to an influx of capital from Albert Ballin's Hamburg-Amerika Line and the North German Lloyd, which pooled their resources to buy 5 million kronen worth of stock. The Rothschilds' Creditanstalt also purchased shares.[63] The Austro-Americana filled a void by concentrating on traffic between Trieste and the ports of North America, which were not served by the Lloyd or Hungary's Adria Line. The company also profited from the booming Austro-Hungarian, Russian, and Balkan emigration to North America; in 1913 more than 43,000 emigrants used Trieste as their port of departure to a North American destination, and 56.5 percent sailed aboard vessels of the Austro-Americana.[64] After 1906 the Austro-Americana also carried Italian emigrants to North America, adding stops in Palermo and Naples to its Trieste-New York routes, and in 1907 it started to serve South American ports previously monopolized by the Lloyd and the Adria Line.[65]

By 1913 the Austro-Americana had a fleet of thirty-five steamers, eleven of domestic and twenty-four of British construction, with a total capacity of 150,000 tons, carrying over 1 million tons of cargo annually. In comparison, in the same year the Lloyd's sixty-two steamers, totaling just under 240,000 tons, carried just over 1.5 million tons of cargo. While the Lloyd remained the largest of the Trieste lines, over the years it had become notorious for its inefficiency, a complacency bred by decades of government subsidies. The Austro-Americana had little difficulty establishing a better reputation with both freight customers and passengers.[66]

The emergence of the Austro-Americana pushed the Hungarian Adria Line into third place among Austro-Hungarian steamship companies: in 1913 the Adria's fleet included thirty-five steamers totaling 78,000 tons and carried just under 950,000 tons of cargo.[67] The line never extended its routes across the North Atlantic, mainly because the Hungarian government contracted with the Cunard Line to carry emigrants from Rijeka to North American ports. This arrangement, which initially threatened the prosperity of the Austro-Americana, was maintained until 1911.[68] Rijeka continued to handle more trade with western Mediterranean and Western European ports than Trieste—thanks to the Adria Line's virtual monopoly over Austro-Hungarian routes to those destinations—and the total tonnage of ships docking at the port continued to rise, but the boom in Rijeka paled in comparison to the growth of Trieste. In 1913 the total traffic in Rijeka harbor equaled just 53 percent of the tonnage handled by Trieste, down from 78 percent in 1900.[69]

Budapest certainly could not be blamed for the less impressive boom in Rijeka. The Hungarian government's improving disposition toward the navy's ever larger budget requests went hand in hand with a willingness to pour money into harbor facilities at Rijeka—some fifty million kronen before the outbreak of war in 1914—and into Hungarian merchant shipping. Ironically, the Adria Line did not patronize the shipyards of Rijeka, continuing to the end to purchase all of its steamers from British builders. In the last prewar years, the company received an annual grant of four million kronen, making it the most heavily subsidized Habsburg steamship line. Budapest also provided funding for other smaller shipping firms, most notably the Ungaro-Croata, which handled many of the shorter Dalmatian coastal routes abandoned in earlier years by the Lloyd.[70]

In addition to supporting Montecuccoli's quest for a larger fleet, Francis Ferdinand and the Belvedere's allies also promoted a general expansion of Austro-Hungarian maritime interests. The archduke criticized the Austrian government's policy regarding the support of merchant shipping; unlike its Hungarian counterpart, the Austrian *Reichsrat* traditionally had approved of subsidies only for the Lloyd. As early as 1907, Francis Ferdinand, in a letter to Brosch, theorized that the growth of smaller lines in the Adriatic would not hurt the Lloyd's business and could do wonders for the economy of the more impoverished parts of the littoral.[71] The archduke expressed a special concern for the Dalmatian economy, and with good reason. While the major ports of the Adriatic expanded and prospered, Dalmatia continued to register the lowest per capita income of any province in the Austrian half of the Dual Monarchy.[72]

On the eve of the First World War, the Dual Monarchy had the seventh-largest steam-powered merchant marine in Europe, trailing (in order) Britain, Germany, France, Norway, the Netherlands, and Italy. Of these countries, Norway and the Netherlands had much smaller navies than Austria-Hungary, while Russia had a larger navy than the Dual Monarchy but ranked tenth in merchant sea power, also trailing Sweden and Spain. In 1913, 57.4 percent of the foreign trade of Austrian ports and 36.1 percent of the foreign trade of Hungarian ports was handled by domestic lines. Austria's figure ranked second in the world behind only Britain, which carried 59 percent of its own trade, and even the Hungarian percentage compared very favorably to those of the great powers at the bottom of the list, Russia (9.1 percent) and the United States (13.7 percent).[73] In an important step early in 1914, Austrian investors bought up the German-held shares of the Austro-Americana, the only steamship line in which foreign investment had been a significant factor.[74] In the 1830s, when the Lloyd received its first subsidy from Vienna, early promoters of Austrian maritime commerce had feared that if domestic shipping lines were not promoted and supported, the empire's foreign trade would fall completely into foreign hands. They would have taken pride in the growth of the merchant marine and in the level of self-sufficiency achieved over the next three quarters of a century.

The growth of the merchant marine naturally had an impact on the shipyards of the littoral, where civilian projects supplemented the business generated by warship construction. While the Adria Line relied on foreign builders, the Lloyd and the Austro-Americana provided subsidized contracts for the shipyards of the Austrian littoral.[75] In 1907 the Austro-Americana and the Skoda works, backed by a consortium of Vienna banks, established the Cantiere Navale Triestino at Monfalcone, a few miles west of Trieste. After opening in the spring of 1908, the new firm built a number of ships for the Austro-Americana. These included the 12,600-ton *Kaiser Franz Joseph I*, launched in 1911, the largest commercial vessel ever to fly Austro-Hungarian colors. Skoda controlled a majority of the shares in the Cantiere Navale Triestino until 1913, when the Boden-Creditanstalt of Vienna secured the dominant interest. Thanks to the Skoda connection, the shipyard was able to expand its operations into warship construction.[76] The Austrian Lloyd continued to build most of its own vessels but ultimately outgrew the facilities of the Lloyd Arsenal, which dated from 1861. In 1910 the Lloyd sold its shipyard property to the Stabilimento Tecnico Triestino, which owned the adjacent San Marco yard. The Lloyd and the Stabilimento Tecnico then pooled their resources to revitalize the San Rocco shipyard, which had finished its last battleship in 1898. The joint San Rocco shipbuilding company became the Lloyd's primary construction facility.[77] On the eve of the war, the company operated sixty-two steamers, of which only fourteen were constructed abroad, all in Britain.[78]

By 1913 the average nominal wage of workers in Trieste had surpassed the figures for workers in Prague, Graz, and Salzburg, reaching a level 89 percent of the Lower Austrian average, up from just 74.2 percent in 1900.[79] The great expansion in the shipbuilding industry created thousands of jobs, but shipyard wages did not rise significantly even for skilled workers. In the years before the First World War, even master mechanics and other skilled, experienced workers seldom earned more than six kronen per day, a sum barely higher than the top daily wage of the mid-1880s.[80] Migration from adjacent provinces had a tremendous impact on the prewar labor market in Trieste, keeping the shipyards supplied with cheap labor. Amid the boomtown atmosphere, the population of the city rose from 178,500 in 1900 to 229,500 in 1910, with Slovenes from nearby rural lands accounting for much of the growth; their share of the population rose from 13 percent at the turn of the century to 26 percent a decade later. Indeed, by 1910 there were more Slovenes in Trieste than in any other city of the empire, including Ljubljana. Relations remained strained between the Slovenes and the Italian majority, and ethnic divisions continued to plague the workers' movement. In 1905 the Slovenes formed the Narodna Delavska Organizacija, a union whose members included shipyard workers.[81] The Italian-dominated Social Democratic League remained in control of most other shipyard unions.

While the Slovene factor kept wages down in the navy-related industries of Trieste, in the interior provinces the sheer power and influence of firms such as Skoda and Witkowitz enabled them to control their respective labor markets, keeping labor costs low and profits high. Most of the politicians of Bohemia and Moravia, Czechs as well as Germans, continued to welcome the expansion of their local armaments industry, but a vocal minority ultimately called attention to the negative consequences of having a handful of companies dominate the industrial economy of an entire region. In the Austrian Delegation of 1910, František Tomášek of Moravia leveled harsh criticism against both Skoda and Witkowitz: "These proprietors . . . plunder the state on one side and rob the workers on the other." He alleged that the Skoda works in Pilsen held its six thousand workers "in nothing short of slave conditions." According to Tomášek, the only unions at Skoda were controlled by the company and supported by dues deducted from the workers' paychecks. Things were even worse at Witkowitz, where some workers earned as little as 1.20 kronen for a twelve-hour shift. As many as five thousand accidents had been reported at the Witkowitz works in a single year, and in 1908 alone seventeen workers were killed on the job. To make matters worse, the long arm of the company stretched far beyond the factory gates. "The Witkowitz works dominate not only the worker, but the entire region [and] the local government," Tomášek contended, with "the law courts and the political authorities" controlled by the company. He also charged that Witkowitz was used as an instrument to Germanize Czech workers: "At the beginning of every school year . . . . officials of the company persuade the workers to send their children to German schools." Tomášek acknowledged that the naval armaments industry created jobs, but he argued that too little of the money ended up in the workers' pockets. The naval race with Italy soon would lead to unprecedented expenditure for Austria-Hungary's first dreadnoughts and provide even more industrial jobs, but the lot of the individual worker remained unchanged. While 70 percent of the price of a British dreadnought went to workers' salaries, similar labor costs would account for 32 percent of expenditure on Austro-Hungarian dreadnoughts.[82]

THE DREADNOUGHT PROGRAM AND THE AUSTRO-ITALIAN NAVAL RACE (1909–13)

The onset of construction on the Italian dreadnought *Dante Alighieri* in June 1909 sparked the greatest crisis of Montecuccoli's career as *Marinekommandant*. His own proposal for Austro-Hungarian dreadnoughts had been decisive in prompting the Italian move, yet the project remained just as theoretical as it had been when first drafted in January. To make matters worse, in April 1909, the same month that Montecuccoli's plans found their way into the press, the fall from power of Hungarian minister-president Alexander Wekerle marked the start of an interregnum in Budapest that did not end until a new parliament was seated in May 1910. With no Hungarian government, no Hungarian Delegation could be selected and the budget process of the Dual Monarchy ground to a halt. Montecuccoli, preparing estimates for 1910 that included funding for the start of his dreadnought program, would have no Delegations to address.[83]

In July 1909, the launching of the *Radetzky* by Stabilimento Tecnico Triestino left just its last sister ship, the *Zrinyi*, still under construction. Pending the resolution of the constitutional impasse and the approval of a new budget, the Trieste shipyard, the Witkowitz foundry, and the Skoda works each faced a hiatus in its lucrative relationship with the navy and a curtailment of operations. To avoid long-term losses, the industrialists late in July offered to undertake the construction of three dreadnoughts "at their own risk," with the understanding that the government would buy them as soon as the Delegations authorized a budget. After consulting the joint ministers for foreign affairs, war, and finance, Montecuccoli arranged for the construction of two dreadnoughts under these terms. The scheme also received an energetic endorsement from Conrad von Hötzendorf. Given the likelihood of a future war with Italy, the chief of the General Staff argued that the ships should be completed as soon as possible. If the dreadnoughts failed to gain retroactive approval, Conrad proposed their "sale to a reliable ally," meaning Germany, Austria-Hungary's only remaining "reliable ally."[84]

The arrangement, of course, was unconstitutional in that it committed the Dual Monarchy to spend money without the prior approval of the representatives of the Austrian and Hungarian parliaments. As a result, all parties concerned endeavored to keep it secret for as long as possible. Because Italy already had a dreadnought under construction, Montecuccoli could argue that an emergency situation existed; when the truth came out, he reasoned, only the most bitter antinavalists would argue that Austria-Hungary's security was not threatened. But the colossal sums of money involved in the construction of dreadnoughts made the arrangement a potential political time bomb. The *Habsburg* class of battleships, laid down in the years 1899–1901, had cost an average of eighteen million kronen apiece; for the *Erzherzogs*, begun in 1902–4, it was twenty-six million, while the *Radetzkys* of 1907–9 cost more than forty million kronen each. The dreadnoughts were projected at sixty million apiece, but Montecuccoli had yet to negotiate a specific price with the builders.[85]

Considering the fact that for the years 1907 and 1908—with expenditures inflated by the cost of beginning the first two *Radetzkys*—the entire outlay for the navy had been just 63.4 million and 73.4 million, respectively, Montecuccoli feared that the politicians and the public would find it hard to accept a price tag of 60 million for a single dreadnought. In 1909 the navy spent a whopping 100.4 million, mostly because of the acceleration of work on the three *Radetzkys*; with materials still being assembled for the two dreadnoughts, their cost was not yet a factor. It became apparent that in the future, the navy would have to ask the Delegations for sums far in excess of 100 million kronen per year just to meet basic needs in operations, maintenance, and new construction.

In the meantime, pending the resolution of the constitutional crisis in Budapest, the cooperation of the Vienna Rothschilds would be essential to the success of Montecuccoli's secret arrangements. The family certainly had a vested interest in the success of the dreadnought program: they controlled the Witkowitz works and, through their Creditanstalt, had a considerable stake in both the Skoda works and the Stabilimento Tecnico Triestino. At the same time, in shouldering the short-term burden of the dreadnought project, the Rothschilds and their bank understandably wanted a guarantee from a higher power than Montecuccoli that in two or three years they would not be stuck with 120 million kronen worth of finished battleships. According to legend, this led to a most extraordinary meeting in which Francis Ferdinand, swallowing his anti-Semitism, paid a personal visit to Baron Albert Rothschild in order to promise the eventual purchase of the ships. In return, he received assurances that the Rothschild money would continue to flow until the Delegations convened to legitimize the whole arrangement.[86]

A full year passed between the initial promulgation of the dreadnought project in April 1909 and the first public revelations of Montecuccoli's secret deal. During this time, the rumored construction of dreadnoughts in Austria-Hungary attracted the attention of diplomats and navy men throughout Europe. Underestimating the extent of Austro-Italian animosity and overestimating Vienna's subservience to Berlin, British observers tended to view Montecuccoli's dreadnoughts "as a concealed addition to the German fleet."[87] Officials in the Admiralty, locked in a bitter naval race with Tirpitz, from the outset believed that Germany inspired or even directed Austria-Hungary to build dreadnoughts. In the spring of 1909, when Montecuccoli sent Captain Alfred von Koudelka, a *Marinesektion* official, to consult with Tirpitz on various aspects of dreadnought construction, a British spy shadowed the emissary during his stay in Berlin and on the train trip back to Vienna.[88]

In the dreadnought era, all countries placed a shroud of secrecy over their warship construction projects, in sharp contrast to the openness and technology transfers of the last decades of the 1800s. The Austrians were no exception, and in the atmosphere of 1910 their behavior only helped fan the flames of suspicion. Viscount Faramond de Lafajole, the French naval attaché in Vienna, complained of a pervasive secrecy even when warship construction was not a factor. Naval officials prohibited photography in Pola, where the well-preserved ruins of the Roman coliseum afforded foreign tourists a bird's-eye view of the inner harbor installations. Foreign officials in Austrian ports, especially naval attachés, were watched constantly by the police.[89]

Ultimately, the Austrian Social Democrats broke the dreadnought story in April 1910 in their *Arbeiter Zeitung*. The Christian Social Party's *Reichspost*, with the blessing of the Belvedere, promptly confirmed Montecuccoli's secret deal and argued strongly in favor of it. Francis Ferdinand hastened to use his other press organs to stir up support for the program. The Navy League also rallied support for Montecuccoli, and ultimately the dreadnought issue only won more converts for the cause of navalism in Austria-Hungary. Over the next four years, the League experienced more than a tenfold increase in membership, from 4,389 in 1910 to 44,617 in 1914, becoming the second largest organization of its type in Europe, smaller only than the German Navy League.[90]

By the time the Delegations finally met in October 1910, Austria-Hungary had two dreadnoughts under construction: the *Viribus Unitis*, named after Francis Joseph's personal motto, had been laid down in July 1910, followed by the *Tegetthoff* in September 1910. The 20,000-ton warships, designed by Siegfried Popper, would carry twelve 12-inch Skoda guns, matching the firepower of the Italian *Dante Alighieri*. The navy's first battleships with turbine engines, their projected speed was 21.5 knots. Popper provided for the guns to be mounted in four triple-gunned turrets, a revolutionary design also employed by the Italians in building their *Dante*.[91] As he prepared to face the Delegations, Montecuccoli's hand was strengthened by the fact that the Italians, after laying down their first dreadnought in the summer of 1909, had begun another three in the summer of 1910: the *Giulio Cesare, Leonardo da Vinci,* and *Conte di Cavour*. The trio of 23,000-ton warships would carry thirteen 12-inch guns apiece and were designed to be at least a knot faster than the Austro-Hungarian dreadnoughts.[92] For many who questioned whether the *Dante Alighieri* alone posed a threat to the Dual Monarchy's security in the Adriatic, the prospect that the navy would face four Italian dreadnoughts dispelled all doubts over the need to respond in kind.

The Delegations convened twice in the last months of 1910. The first meeting, in October and November, approved the long-overdue budget for 1910, while the second, which dragged on from December until March 1911, passed the budget for 1911. In the first session, Montecuccoli concentrated on securing retroactive approval and funding for the first pair of dreadnoughts. Notwithstanding the fact that the navy and Francis Ferdinand, with the complicity of the three joint ministries, had committed the government to purchase the two warships, Montecuccoli argued that because no specific price had been negotiated and no government funds had yet gone to the companies involved, the constitutional prerogatives of the Delegations had not been violated.[93]

The vast majority of the representatives accepted his flimsy reasoning. In the Hungarian Delegation, István Tisza and his supporters, once bitter opponents of naval expansion, backed Montecuccoli and ensured the easy passage of his budget. Tisza's ally Gyula Rosenberg, converted to the maritime cause after being appointed to the board of directors of the Adria Line, went so far as to argue that the Dual Monarchy needed a battle fleet capable of engaging navies of other great powers.[94] The Austrian Delegation, dominated by spokesmen of the coalition of pronavy special interests, likewise sanctioned Montecuccoli's actions. While the Czechs were not unanimous in their support of the *Marinekommandant*, their leader, Kramář, explained away his acquiescence by conceding that he had "a certain weakness for the navy." In the entire process, the Social Democrats in the Austrian Delegation were Montecuccoli's most vocal opponents—indeed, his only opponents. In condemning the nascent Austro-Italian naval race, Karl Seitz, future president of the Austrian Republic, called for immediate negotiations with Italy for a mutual cessation of naval construction. Italian Socialists made similar appeals in Rome, but neither initiative attracted support outside of the ranks of the far Left.[95] The navy ended up spending 100.6 million kronen in 1910, slightly more than in 1909.

Emboldened by the support of Francis Ferdinand and the growing pronavy sentiment in both halves of the Dual Monarchy, Montecuccoli in the second session asked the Delegations for a commitment to his entire fleet plan of January 1909. This would involve money to start building two more dreadnoughts and a further commitment for three 3,500-ton scout cruisers (sisters for the *Admiral Spaun*), another six destroyers, twelve torpedo boats, and six submarines. He estimated that the entire package would cost 312.4 million kronen and proposed that the expenditure be divided over the next six budget years. He made 1920 the target year for achieving the goals of his fleet plan: sixteen battleships, twelve cruisers, twenty-four destroyers, seventy-two torpedo boats, and twelve submarines. Introducing a concept embodied in Tirpitz's German navy laws, Montecuccoli called for the automatic replacement of battleships after twenty years, cruisers and destroyers after fifteen, and torpedo boats after twelve.[96]

The long-term nature of the proposals naturally provoked further debate and discussion. In the Austrian Delegation, even the Christian Social Party's contingent pondered the consequences before voicing its approval. Other delegates voiced a wide variety of reasons for voting with the majority. The Slovene leader Šušteršić concluded that the program was in the best interest of the Habsburg state and the Slovene people. Eduard Stransky of Bohemia, a self-styled "German Radical," supported a stronger navy because it enhanced "the alliance value of this state for the German Empire." Among Czech leaders, Tomás Masaryk stood almost alone in rejecting the program. The Social Democrats again posed the only real opposition, submitting a resolution condemning Montecuccoli's "repeated and habitual disregard" for the constitutional prerogatives of the Delegations. Its seven cosponsors included German Austrians, Czechs, and Valentino Pittoni of Trieste.[97]

On the Hungarian side, Montecuccoli spared no effort in ensuring a victory. In January 1911, the influential *Magyar Figyelo,* a journal founded by Tisza, published an interview in which the *Marinekommandant* made a case for the significance of sea power to Hungary's future. Meeting with Hungarian leaders later the same month, Montecuccoli guaranteed that 113 million kronen (the 36.4 percent quota) of the cost of his program would be spent in Hungary. To balance the sum of three dreadnought contracts awarded to the Stabilimento Tecnico Triestino, Hungarian firms would build the remaining dreadnought, two of the light cruisers, six destroyers, and six submarines. To compensate for the fact that all armor plate and guns would be produced in the Austrian half of the monarchy, Hungarian companies would provide most of the electrical equipment for the new vessels, including those built at Trieste, and the navy pledged to purchase 50 percent of its shells in Hungary. The dreadnought constructed in Hungary would be named *Szent István,* after the kingdom's patron saint. With good reason, the Hungarian Delegation greeted Montecuccoli with an ovation and quickly passed his budget.[98]

The approval of the Delegations did not bring an end to the financial difficulties. Alarmed at the scope of the program, Faramond, the French naval attaché, in December 1910 advised his government not to allow Austria-Hungary to list bonds on the Paris money market. "It would be a generous folly on our part," he argued, "to aid the development of the Austro-Hungarian navy with our money."[99] Montecuccoli could take solace in the fact that at least for the moment, the British were not being as vigilant as their Entente partners; in their case, however, the issue was coal rather than capital. The expansion of the Habsburg fleet, involving the commissioning of much larger warships, necessitated a dramatic increase in its annual coal purchases, from 56,967 tons in 1904, the last year of Spaun's command, to 153,248 tons in 1912, Montecuccoli's last full year in office. The international situation notwithstanding, most foreign coal purchased for fleet use continued to come from Britain, but for security reasons the *Marinekommandant* had to end the traditional 98–99 percent dependence on British suppliers. He hedged his bets by buying from other, friendlier sources, even when the costs were higher. German mines supplied an unprecedented 5.6 percent of the fleet's coal in 1909, then 13 percent in 1910 and 9.8 percent in 1911. The following year, the German share dropped to 4.6 percent, but American Pocahontas coal accounted for another 3.6 percent.[100] The navy also had to import oil, the fuel burned by the submarines and newer torpedo boats. In the spring of 1910, the fleet commissioned its own tanker, the *Vesta,* which subsequently plied the route between the Romania's Black Sea oil terminal, Constanza, and Pola, a round-trip voyage of three weeks.[101]

The availability of foreign capital and foreign fuel posed problems for Montecuccoli, but he also faced new internal obstacles. Notwithstanding the approval of the ambitious program, naval spending rose only modestly in 1911, to 120.7 million kronen. War minister Schönaich, fearing trouble with the army's share of the budget, insisted that the navy should get by with an increase of only 1.5 million kronen in areas other than construction. This poisoned his relationship with both Montecuccoli and Francis Ferdinand. It did not help his cause that the chief of the General Staff, Conrad von Hötzendorf, also disliked him; in September 1911, he was fired.[102] His successor, General Moritz von Auffenberg-Komarów, had been a classmate of Conrad at the Wiener Neustadt Military Academy and was Francis Ferdinand's personal choice. It remained to be seen whether he would be a better friend of the navy than Schönaich.

Before promoting Auffenberg's candidacy for the war ministry post, the archduke sounded out his opinions on naval expansion and took care to give him a clear indication of his own sentiments. In June 1911, three months prior to his appointment, Auffenberg was Francis Ferdinand's guest when the *Viribus Unitis* slid down the ways at San Marco amid an unprecedented extravaganza. The fleet, expanded for summer maneuvers, was anchored in Trieste harbor during festivities that brought together the leaders of politics and industry with dozens of archdukes, archduchesses, and other dignitaries. Francis Joseph did not attend but used the occasion as a pretext for awarding Montecuccoli the prestigious Order of the Golden Fleece.[103] The workers of the Stabilimento Tecnico also took advantage of the launching. In May 1911, with the date already set, the metal workers of the new Unione Metallurgica refused to work the overtime hours necessary to complete the project on time unless all San Marco workers received a raise. A desperate Stabilimento Tecnico management quickly caved in and granted a raise of over one kronen per day to all employees. Aside from this "passive" strike, the first Austro-Hungarian dreadnought projects were free from labor problems.[104] The launching of the *Viribus Unitis* occurred as scheduled on 24 June; the only tense moment came when Auffenberg almost fell into the water when walking up the gangway of the yacht *Lacroma* for his meeting with Francis Ferdinand.[105]

Bad weather delayed the launching of the navy's second dreadnought, the *Tegetthoff,* until March 1912. By then work already was underway on the remaining pair of dreadnoughts, the *Prinz Eugen* at the Stabilimento Tecnico Triestino and the *Szent István* at the Danubius yard in Rijeka, both begun in January. The Rijeka shipyard had to be expanded before the *Szent István* could be laid down; the largest warships previously constructed there had been 400-ton destroyers of the *Huszár* class. Even after the expansion, the Danubius establishment was barely half the size of the Stabilimento Tecnico's warship construction operation, employing just 2,000 workers to San Marco's 3,700.[106]

Danubius subsequently built two 3,500-ton light cruisers on the model of the *Admiral Spaun:* the *Helgoland* (laid down in October 1911, commissioned in August 1914) and the *Novara* (February 1912–January

1915). Their sister ship, the *Saida*, was constructed in Monfalcone by the new Cantiere Navale Triestino (September 1911–August 1914). The six destroyers promised to Hungary were built in the Danubius yard at Porto Ré (Kraljevica), down the coast from Rijeka. Designated the *Tátra* class, these 870-ton vessels were laid down between October 1911 and September 1912; all were completed by July 1914.[107] War clouds over the Balkans prompted Montecuccoli to order two more river monitors. Completed early in the First World War, they increased the strength of the Danube flotilla to eight ironclads.[108]

Montecuccoli had included six submarines in the package of contracts promised to the Hungarians early in 1911; ultimately, however, the focus on dreadnought construction left little room in the construction budget for anything else besides the scout cruisers and destroyers. By the summer of 1911, the navy still had only its six original submarines, all of which displaced between 230 and 240 tons. Two had been built in the Pola Arsenal from a design provided by the American firm of Simon Lake, two were purchased from the Germania shipyard of Kiel, and two were built in Rijeka by Whitehead from a design provided by the American Holland firm. The six additional submarines initially promised to Hungarian builders finally were ordered from Germania of Kiel in the winter of 1913–14. Reflecting the conventional wisdom of the prewar years, the undersea boats were considered defensive weapons. The submarine station, established at Pola in January 1909, remained under the command of the local harbor admiral until January 1917, long after the submarine had become a tool of offensive warfare. Lieutenant Erich Heyssler served as head of the station until February 1912, when Lieutenant Franz von Thierry replaced him; Thierry would remain head of the submarine service through the end of the First World War. While both men were promoted to the lowest grade of captain (*Korvettenkapitän*) within months of their appointment, the assignment of the command to such junior officers reflects the relative level of importance of the station in the prewar years.[109] Even though submarines were far from the top of Montecuccoli's list of priorities, he appreciated the necessity of keeping the undersea program a mystery to outsiders. Indeed, the level of secrecy surrounding the construction and testing of Austro-Hungarian submarines approached that of the dreadnought program. In October 1909, Montecuccoli informed the foreign ministry of the need to censor the details of submarine sea trials, and four months later a visiting Uruguayan officer was allowed to see everything but the undersea boats.[110]

In addition to the modest scope and delayed pace of submarine construction, the two dozen new torpedo boats of Montecuccoli's program likewise were postponed; eight were finally constructed in Trieste in the years 1913–14, sixteen by Danubius in 1913–16.[111] In general terms, even before the dreadnought program entered the picture, the Austrians already were losing their edge in the so-called *mezzi insidiosi* of naval warfare, an advantage that had worried the Italians ever since the *Jeune Ecole* era. By 1914 Italy had twenty submarines in service and many more seagoing torpedo boats in its fleet. Austria-Hungary soon would suffer the consequences of Italy's superior ability to wage the unconventional "little war" so fitting to the Adriatic.[112]

On the bright side, Montecuccoli took notice of the new technology of aviation and as early as 1910 budgeted money for experimental seaplane construction. In 1911 the first navy officers were sent to the army's aviation school at Wiener Neustadt for pilot training, and in February 1912 a naval air station opened at Pola. In spite of his age and portly physique, the *Marinekommandant* resolved to experience the new technology firsthand and took to the skies as a passenger aboard the navy's rather flimsy first seaplane. When war broke out in the summer of 1914, the navy had an air arm of twenty-two planes.[113]

Even without the torpedo boats and submarines, the cost of the construction program inflated Montecuccoli's last budgets to levels unthinkable at the beginning of his tenure. It certainly helped that the last prewar Austrian elections, held in June 1911, left the balance of power in the *Reichsrat* practically unchanged, preserving the pronavy majority coalition in the Austrian Delegation.[114] The navy spent 170.2 million kronen in 1912, bringing the total appropriation and expenditure for the years 1904–12 to just over 819 million kronen. The navy had exceeded its allocation in 1904, 1906, and 1908 through 1910; in the remaining years, more money was appropriated than spent, balancing the overruns of the other budgets. In 1913 naval spending would rise again to 210.2 million; in that year, as in 1912, the figure represented roughly one quarter of the total military budget. It was a far cry from the lean years under Pöck and Sterneck, when the navy had taken barely 7 percent of the military outlay.[115] Critics hastened to point out that Montecuccoli's concessions to the Hungarians, though politically necessary, had only made matters worse. The most outrageous example was the award of a dreadnought contract to the Danubius firm at a time when it did not yet have the capacity to build such a vessel.

While the quota system requiring the granting of navy contracts to Hungarian firms generated heated debates, policies encouraging greater Hungarian involvement in the service caused an even greater controversy among other Habsburg nationalities. The Croatians, in particular, bristled at Montecuccoli's appeals for young Magyars to attend the naval academy at Rijeka and enter the officer corps; even though their nationality had provided a plurality of the navy's common seamen in recent decades, Croatians had never received similar encouragement. As a condition to their approval of Montecuccoli's budget of 1907, the Hungarian Delegation in December 1906 secured a promise that all naval academy students from the Hungarian half of the monarchy be required to study the Magyar language in each of their four years at the school. The policy was supposed to go into effect in the 1909–10 school year, but there is no evidence that Croatians from Croatia-Slavonia ever were required to comply with it. Because the political system of Hungary stifled the voice of non-Magyar nationalities, the Croatians of Istria and Dalmatia—represented in the Austrian *Reichsrat*—became the most outspoken opponents of Montecuccoli's alleged pro-Magyar personnel policies. In both the *Reichsrat* and the annual Austrian Delegation, Juraj Biankini of Zara was their leading spokesman. In a spirit of Slavic solidarity, Czech and Slovene deputies supported his resolutions.[116]

Those protesting Magyar influence in the navy could point to the rising star of Captain Miklós Horthy, appointed in 1909 as naval aide-de-camp *(Flügeladjutant)* to Francis Joseph. The navy had provided one of the emperor's aides-de-camp since Sterneck's time, but Horthy was the first Magyar ever to hold the post. The duties gave the captain access to high court circles, where he was already well connected thanks to the fact that his brother, an officer in the Hungarian hussars, served as riding instructor to the young Archduke Charles, next in line to the throne after Francis Ferdinand.[117] In the First World War, Horthy would benefit from having friends in high places; meanwhile, he was an exception to the rule. There were few Magyars in the upper echelons of the corps and no Magyar admirals.

Personnel figures for the navy as a whole likewise hardly bore out the fears of a great expansion of Magyar influence. At the end of 1910, the sea officer corps was just 12.9 percent Magyar, compared to 11.9 percent in 1904, the first year of Montecuccoli's command. A bare majority of the officers were German (51 percent), while Croatians and Italians each accounted for 9.8 percent, followed by Czechs (9.2 percent), Slovenes (4.2 percent), and Poles (2.8 percent). Among the seamen, the share of Magyars rose significantly under Montecuccoli, to 12.6 percent in 1910 (up from 8.1 percent in 1904), but only as a part of an overall increase of recruits from the kingdom of Hungary: the share of Slovaks rose eightfold, to 2.4 percent (1904: 0.3 percent), while Romanians, often completely unrepresented in the past, contributed 0.4 percent. The Croatian plurality continued to erode, but they remained the largest nationality (29.8 percent). Contrary to the assertions of Biankini and his colleagues regarding the Magyars, in fact an influx of German Austrians was responsible for diluting the Croatian domination of the crews: in 1910, 24.5 percent of the seamen were German, compared to just 13.9 percent six years earlier. Among the remaining nationalities, the Italians (18.3 percent) were followed by the Czechs (7.1 percent) and Slovenes (3.6 percent). The Croatians had some grounds for protest only in the ranks of the petty officers, where the men of the Küstenland and Dalmatia now found themselves outnumbered almost two to one by the Czechs and Germans of Bohemia and Moravia, but this continuation of an old trend could hardly be blamed on ethnic discrimination. As the navy modernized, a greater percentage of the noncommissioned positions of responsibility involved the supervision of machinists and machinery; these assignments naturally went to men from the more industrialized parts of the empire, such as Bohemia and Moravia. But this does not explain why the total share of petty officers from Hungary (excluding Croatia-Slavonia) also rose significantly under Montecuccoli, from 6.9 percent in 1905 to 11.7 percent in 1911.[118]

More pronounced than the rise of the Magyars was the decline of the Italian representation within the navy. Overall, the Italians slipped to third place among the seamen, trailing the Germans as well as the Croatians, after having always been either first or second. There was no mystery behind their fall: in a time of increased tensions between Austria-Hungary and the kingdom of Italy, the navy simply stopped taking as many Habsburg Italians into its ranks. As recently as 1899, 36 percent of the annual contingent of recruits had been Italian, and in 1905, Montecuccoli's first full year as *Marinekommandant,* they still accounted for 28 percent, but by 1911 the Italian share of incoming seamen fell to just 14.4 percent.[119] Ironically, Montecuccoli, the first *Marinekommandant* of Italian descent since 1848, led the way in the final "de-Italianization" of the navy.

Notwithstanding the perennial hue and cry in the *Reichsrat* and the Austrian Delegation, there was little evidence to support the argument that Montecuccoli was letting the Magyars take over the navy. It became an annual ritual for the Hungarian Delegation to demand equal status for the Hungarian flag and national crest, and some radical Magyars even called for some ships or squadrons to be designated as "Hungarian,"[120] but after a while such pronouncements took on a pro forma character. What really mattered in Budapest was that Hungary got its share of navy contracts. Hungarian leaders indeed drove a hard bargain, which in turn drove up the cost of everything, but their firms were relative newcomers to the game. Other than the navy itself, the Austrian industries and their stockholders were the biggest winners in the game of naval expansion. In contrast to Spaun's acquiescence, Montecuccoli at times complained vigorously about the price gouging of the iron and steel cartel, but with little effect.[121] The navy in Austria-Hungary—like any military force in any modern state—was wedded to its military-industrial complex for better or worse, and the marriage had its benefits. Indeed, if not for the connections between a banking house and the leading shipyard, armor factory, and armaments producer, Montecuccoli's secret deal to build the first two dreadnoughts would have been far more difficult to arrange. In the end, the navy got its battleships, and the firms involved registered their profits. By February 1911, shares of Stabilimento Tecnico Triestino stock carried a price over two and a half times greater than their value of January 1909. During the same period, Skoda's stock almost doubled in price.[122]

In October 1912, the *Viribus Unitis* received its commission and joined the fleet. Austria-Hungary's first dreadnought held the dubious honor of being the most expensive warship ever built anywhere, but its completion, in just twenty-seven months, confirmed that the shipyards of Trieste were in the same league with those of Britain and Germany when it came to battleship construction. The Dual Monarchy also became the first European power after Britain and Germany to have a dreadnought in active service. The Italian *Dante Alighieri,* begun thirteen months before the *Viribus Unitis,* was not commissioned until January 1913.

Even before the completion of its first dreadnought, the navy was capable of impressing the most critical of observers. In the years before the outbreak of the First World War, Emperor William II made it an annual ritual to cruise the Mediterranean aboard the Imperial German yacht, *Hohenzollern,* in the late winter months. In March 1911, Francis Ferdinand, an occasional visitor to German naval maneuvers, sailed to Corfu to meet him with a fleet of forty-seven ships ranging in size from torpedo boats to the newest battleships of the *Radetzky* class. The ships staged a review for the German emperor on a scale that would have been impossible in earlier years. Three months later, when the archduke visited Britain for the coronation of King George V, the *Radetzky* attracted much attention while representing Austria-Hungary at a naval review off Spithead. Such festive events were a boost to Francis Ferdinand's ego, but he had every reason to be proud. Without his patronage, Montecuccoli's political efforts on behalf of the fleet no doubt would not have met with such success.[123]

THE ITALO-TURKISH WAR, THE BALKAN CRISIS, AND THE TRIPLE ALLIANCE (1911–12)

By the time Austria-Hungary and Italy launched their first dreadnoughts, their relationship was strained to the breaking point. With the Triple Alliance due to expire at the end of 1912, few statesmen in Vienna, Rome, or Berlin held out much hope for a renewal. But the Italo-Turkish war of 1911–12 and the subsequent Balkan Wars led the Austro-Italian relationship through a strange series of twists and turns, many of which involved the navy or had a direct impact on its future strategy. Circumstances were to push Italy closer to Germany and Austria-Hungary than it had been in years, breathing new life into the doomed alliance.

The groundwork for Italy's declaration of war on Turkey in late September 1911 had been laid over a decade earlier. In the Franco-Italian rapprochement of 1900, Italy had conceded the French a free hand in Morocco in exchange for similar considerations in Libya. When the Moroccan crisis of 1911 led to a French protectorate over most of Morocco, Italy exercised its option in Turkish Libya.[124] Austria-Hungary's position on the issue was somewhat ambiguous. Before leaving office in 1906, Goluchowsky also had given Italy a free hand to claim Libya, but only in the event of the complete dismemberment of the Ottoman Empire.[125]

The first days of the conflict brought the two nominal allies to the brink of war, as Italy clearly intended to make Adriatic waters a part of the war zone. On the heels of news that an Italian destroyer had seized an Ottoman merchant ship in the Turkish Albanian port of Valona, word reached Vienna that an Italian squadron had sunk two Ottoman torpedo boats off the Albanian coast. Foreign minister Aehrenthal demanded that the Italian navy cease operations against the Turks in the Adriatic Sea, and Montecuccoli sent reinforcements to the base at Cattaro to back up the threat. Virtually acknowledging Austria-Hungary's hegemony over the Adriatic, Italy promptly complied.[126] Francis Ferdinand did not applaud the tough stand. The Belvedere's Brosch conveyed his disgust that Aehrenthal had done "next to nothing (gar nichts)" to show the Dual Monarchy's displeasure; he contended that Rome should have informed Vienna in advance of any decision to extend the war into the Adriatic.[127]

Francis Ferdinand's old protégé Conrad von Hötzendorf went far beyond the position taken by the archduke, pressing Aehrenthal either to agree to a preventive war against Italy or to secure compensation in Turkish Balkan territory for what the Italians were taking in Libya. Amid bitter clashes with the foreign minister, Conrad even argued for the annexation of Venetia as a legitimate war aim. When Francis Joseph began to contemplate Conrad's dismissal, Francis Ferdinand did not intervene to save him, in part because he had reversed his earlier support for the dreadnought program. Conrad later recalled receiving "many reproaches" for his argument that the sixty million kronen appropriated for the Szent István should be redesignated "as a loan for the most urgent needs of the army." He was fired in November 1911, and three months later Aehrenthal, on his deathbed with leukemia, was also asked to resign. Count Leopold Berchtold, a former ambassador to Russia, replaced Aehrenthal as foreign minister. One year later, Conrad would return as chief of the General Staff.[128]

Early in 1912, Italy's relations with France became seriously compromised when the Italian navy stopped and searched two French merchant steamers suspected of carrying arms to the Turks in Libya. Thereafter, British and Russian commerce was disrupted when Italy extended the war into the Aegean Sea, taking the Dodecanese Islands and blockading the Dardanelles. This campaign culminated in a daring nighttime raid through the straits in July 1912 by a flotilla of Italian torpedo boats. The attack foreshadowed Italian boldness in similar ventures in the Adriatic after 1915; while it failed in its mission to destroy the Turkish fleet at anchor, it raised spirits on the home front in Italy.[129]

Having incurred the wrath of the entire Triple Entente, Italy also faced disapproval from its allies, both of whom expressed concern for their economic ties to the Ottoman Empire. While German fears centered around the fate of the celebrated Baghdad railway project, Austria-Hungary had far broader commercial interests at stake, standing second only to Britain on the list of Turkish trading partners. Over one fourth of Trieste's trade was with the Ottoman Empire, the Balkans, or Greece, and most of the rest also passed through the eastern Mediterranean war zone.[130] Pressured from all sides, the Italians opened peace talks with the Turks and in October 1912 signed the Treaty of Ouchy, which gave Libya to Italy and promised the eventual return of the Dodecanese to Turkey. The Italians ultimately kept the islands as a part of the peace settlement after the First World War.

Just days before the Italo-Turkish war officially came to an end, Montenegro declared war on the Ottoman Empire. Within a week, Serbia, Bulgaria, and Greece joined in the effort to push the Turks out of what remained of their Balkan possessions. Russia gave strong diplomatic support to the coalition, and both the Russian and Austro-Hungarian armies mobilized partially in preparation for a general war. The navy mobilized the Danube flotilla, which soon was active enough to draw complaints from a nervous Serbia.[131]

Montecuccoli also sent the *Maria Theresia* to Salonika to protect Austro-Hungarian business interests and the thousands of Habsburg subjects living there. He could have made a better choice; as the Dual Monarchy's consul in Piraeus had observed the previous winter, the old 5,200-ton armored cruiser "cannot make much of an impression as a representative of our maritime *Macht*."[132] Once coveted by Sterneck as an ideal future Habsburg foothold on the Aegean, Salonika ultimately fell into Greek hands. In November 1912, as Francis Ferdinand met with William II in Berlin to discuss contingency plans for war, Montecuccoli sent the *Radetzky, Zrinyi,* and *Erzherzog Franz Ferdinand* to the eastern Mediterranean along with the light cruiser *Admiral Spaun* and two destroyers. The squadron showed the flag in the Aegean for a month before returning to Pola, where, in December, the entire fleet was placed on a war footing. The mobilization included thirteen battleships, ranging in age from the new *Viribus Unitis* to the three old *Monarch*s. The Delegations approved a special credit of 151 million kronen for the mobilization, including 26 million for the navy.[133]

In early December 1912, everyone but the Greeks agreed to an armistice, and in mid-month representatives of the belligerents and the six great powers convened in London to determine the peace settlement. The conference agreed in principle to create an independent Albania and to strip the Ottoman Empire of all of its remaining European territory except for a modest foothold guarding the straits. A second round of fighting in the Balkans would postpone the definitive drawing of borders until May 1913, when the Treaty of London was finally signed. For Austria-Hungary and Italy, the war presented an ironic opportunity for cooperation, as both Berchtold and his Italian counterpart, Antonio di San Giuliano, energetically opposed Serbian designs on an Albanian outlet to the sea, but for very different reasons. Berchtold simply wanted to keep Serbia off of the Adriatic, while San Giuliano, expecting an eventual Austro-Hungarian annexation of Serbia, worked from the assumption that Serbian control over Albania would lead to Austro-Hungarian control over Albania.[134] The foreign ministers concurred in the selection of William of Wied, a minor German prince, as the new Albanian ruler.

Owing to the fact that the Italo-Turkish war had already poisoned Italy's relations with the Triple Entente, especially France, the cooperation between Berchtold and San Giuliano over Albania came within the framework of a renewed Triple Alliance. In December 1912—in a move that would have been unthinkable just one year earlier—the three powers agreed to extend the thirty-year-old pact for another five years. Thanks to their arms race against each other, Austria-Hungary had one dreadnought in service and three more under construction, while Italy, after laying down another pair early in 1912, had six under construction. The simple arithmetic was not lost on the Germans or on Italian and Austrian proponents of the alliance: while Austria-Hungary and Italy had a combined strength of ten dreadnoughts built or building, France at the end of 1912 had only seven, all still under construction. With Britain concentrating its resources in the North Sea for the contest against Germany and with Russia unable to lend a hand, the possibility arose that a reinvigorated Triple Alliance could make a bid to dominate the Mediterranean.

"We are a Mediterranean power," Montecuccoli informed the Delegations in October 1912, a fact that required "a stronger navy with which we can assume our proper place among the Mediterranean powers."[135] Scarcely a decade earlier, it would have been politically suicidal for a navy commander to characterize Austro-Hungarian sea power in such terms. The explosion in naval spending under Montecuccoli strained the budget and consumed resources that may have been better spent elsewhere—such as on the army, as Conrad von Hötzendorf argued. But the navy was a popular cause, and a profitable one, too, for some of the most important people and institutions in the economy of the Dual Monarchy. Throughout Europe, navalism became a sort of ideology in which patriotism, economics, and self-interest embellished legitimate defense and security concerns; the armies were also arming, and some countries eventually had proarmy lobbying groups that imitated the more successful navy leagues, but the phenomenon was not quite the same. The emergence of navalism in a land power such as Austria-Hungary attests to its significance as a reflection of the overall spirit of the times. In the words of one historian, "a strong vested interest was created . . . that could only be satisfied by being fed another dreadnought. The longer the process continued, the more difficult it was to stop."[136] Generals complained, at the time and in their post-1918 memoirs, that the naval craze "took money away" from their armies, and historians have been too quick to accept their line of reasoning. One must, however, keep in mind that a reduction or cancellation of funding in one branch of a country's armed forces in no way guarantees an increase in the funding of a rival branch, or vice versa; before 1914, no less than at the present, military and naval programs prospered or languished on the strength of their individual political popularity. There is no reason to believe that in Austria-Hungary, a country traditionally disinclined to provide adequate funding for its army, a reduction in naval spending would have brought a corresponding increase in the army budget. The political leaders of the non-German parties, in particular, were converted to the *navy's* cause much more than to the cause of an overall defense buildup; indeed, many of the same politicians who supported the navy continued to view the army as an oppressive institution, a "prison of the nationalities," and would never have agreed to grant comparable sums for the army with the same enthusiasm. Bankers and industrialists likewise favored a navy buildup for the large, lucrative contracts it provided to leading heavy industries; an army buildup, in contrast, typically generated relatively smaller contracts, albeit for a greater number of businesses.

But politicians and capitalists were not the only ones with vital interests linked to the growth of the navy. In November 1912, Count Vinzenz Baillet de Latour of the Austrian House of Lords estimated that an end to naval expansion would cost the workers of Austria-Hungary 12,000 to 13,000 jobs and 21 million kronen per year in wages.[137] His figures were on the conservative side; several thousand more workers in the private sector could have been defined as dependent upon the naval armaments industry for their livelihood. He also did not consider the navy's own Pola Arsenal, where 5,000 men were employed.[138]

Amid the pragmatic considerations, there was also an irrational element, indeed personified in the actions of the *Marinekommandant* himself. Since taking command, Montecuccoli had registered remarkable successes in building up the fleet, but his public references to the "Italian threat" only drove Italian leaders to spend more money on their navy in order to maintain a secure advantage over the Austro-Hungarian fleet. Like Tirpitz in Germany's naval race against Britain, Montecuccoli had posed a challenge to a numerically stronger opponent and in the process aroused in that opponent the resolve to stay ahead. And then, with the changes in the European diplomatic climate, came new hopes for a peaceful future between Austria-Hungary and Italy. Could cooperation replace confrontation? Shortly after the renewal of the Triple Alliance in December 1912, the Italians suggested that the dormant Austro-German-Italian naval convention of 1900 should be revived.

CHAPTER 5

NOTES

1. *StPD*, XL (1 June 1904), 386; ibid., XLVI (15 October 1912), 903.
2. Bayer von Bayersburg, *Österreichs Admirale*, 118–21.
3. Ibid., 102–5. See also Dieter Winkler, "Admiral Leodegar Kneissler von Maixdorf," 1–2.
4. Percentages from *Militärstatistisches Jahrbuch* (1904); overall number of officers and men from *Jahresbericht der k.u.k. Kriegsmarine* (1905).
5. *StPD*, XLI/2 (5 January 1907), 1176–77.
6. The additions and deletions of warships discussed in this section are based upon data in Greger, *Austro-Hungarian Warships*, passim.
7. According to Vego, "Anatomy," 1:96, the new system followed "the Italian example." The reserve squadron was used to train recent recruits, a task formerly handled by the active squadron.
8. On the Danube maneuvers, see *Jahresbericht der k.u.k. Kriegsmarine* (1905), 46.
9. See Bargoni, *Corazzate italiane (1880–1892)*, passim; and Giorgerini, *Almanacco*, 222–25.
10. Giorgerini, *Almanacco*, 290–93.
11. On the corporate partnerships, see Halpern, *Mediterranean Naval Situation*, 188–89.
12. On the Terni scandal, see Seton-Watson, *Liberalism to Fascism*, 242, 265, 358–59; and Baratelli, *La marina militare italiane*, 327.
13. On Koerber and the Hungarian crisis, see Rothenberg, *The Army of Francis Joseph*, 133. Spaun angered Koerber by not informing him of his negotiations with Budapest; see Louis Gebhard, "Austria-Hungary's Dreadnought Squadron: The Naval Outlay of 1911," 248n. According to Gebhard, "Austro-Hungarian Navy," 132, relations between Koerber and Spaun had soured as early as 1902.
14. Rothenberg, *The Army of Francis Joseph*, 136.
15. Höbelt, "Die Marine," 754; Gebhard, "Dreadnought Squadron," 248.
16. Höbelt, "Die Marine," 718–19.
17. *StPD*, XLI/1 (4 July 1906), 474. See also Gebhard, "Austro-Hungarian Navy," 147; and Höbelt, "Die Marine," 719n.
18. *StPD*, XLI/1 (4 July 1906), 468.
19. Ibid., 457.
20. Beck, an expert on constitutional law, had been one of the archduke's tutors in his youth. See Kiszling, *Erzherzog Franz Ferdinand*, 12, 20.
21. Notwithstanding Goluchowsky's success in engineering and maintaining an Austro-Russian rapprochement in the Balkans, Francis Ferdinand believed firmly that a Polish foreign minister would be a liability in future relations with St. Petersburg. Aehrenthal came to Vienna after several years of service as Habsburg ambassador to the tsar. See Kiszling, *Erzherzog Franz Ferdinand*, 33–34, 94.
22. Rothenberg, *The Army of Francis Joseph*, 137.
23. Schönaich replaced Baron Heinrich von Pitreich, Krieghammer's successor after 1902. See Kiszling, *Erzherzog Franz Ferdinand*, 90–91.
24. R. W. Seton-Watson, *Sarajevo: A Study in the Origins of the Great War*, 84n. On Brosch and the Belvedere, see Williamson, "Franz Ferdinand," 421; and Georg Franz, *Erzherzog Franz Ferdinand und die Pläne der Habsburger Monarchie*, 26–28.
25. Kiszling, *Erzherzog Franz Ferdinand*, 234; Reiter, "Entwicklung," 134.

26. On Lueger and the *Thronfolgerpartei,* see Franz, *Erzherzog Franz Ferdinand,* 35–36.

27. Leopold von Chlumecky, *Erzherzog Franz Ferdinands Wirken und Wollen,* 284.

28. Francis Ferdinand lamented the fact that the strong clerical identity of the *Reichspost* made it popular only in Christian Social and conservative circles; the *Armee-zeitung,* published weekly, and the *Österreichische Rundschau,* appearing twice a month, likewise appealed to limited audiences. For years the archduke promoted the idea of a more secular daily newspaper as an additional mouthpiece for the Belvedere. At one time, he negotiated with Arthur Krupp, Viennese cousin of the German arms manufacturer, for financing, but could not persuade him to support the scheme and ultimately had to abandon it. See Theodor von Sosnosky, *Franz Ferdinand: Der Erzherzog-Thronfolger,* 120; and Franz, *Erzherzog Franz Ferdinand,* 36. The Viennese Krupp (1856–1938), a member of the Austrian House of Lords, was the nephew of Alfred Krupp; his branch of the family controlled the Berndorfer Metallwarenfabrik, a manufacturer of consumer goods, since 1843. See Mentschl and Otruba, *Österreichische Industrielle,* 170–73.

29. *Die Flagge,* Probenummer (August 1905), 8.

30. Richard S. Geehr's *Karl Lueger: Mayor of Fin de Siècle Vienna* is the most recent biography of the Christian Social leader. On Lueger and technology, see 279–80; on his protectionist economic views, 146; on his view of Italians, 147; on the *Knabenhorte,* 291–92. Curiously, Geehr does not mention Lueger's connection with the Navy League at all and offers no explanation for the mayor's choice of uniforms for the *Knabenhorte.*

31. Ibid., 2.

32. As early as October 1905, several army officers were League members, including war minister Heinrich von Pitreich. Cf. membership rosters in *Die Flagge* (October 1905), 11–12; (December 1905), 12; (September 1906), 11–12.

33. Gebhard, "Austro-Hungarian Navy," 170–71.

34. *StPD,* XLI/2 (5 January 1907), 1187; Gebhard, "Austro-Hungarian Navy," 179.

35. E. E. Hazlett, Jr., "The Austro-American Navy," 1759, commenting on the *Zrinyi's* appearance in November 1918.

36. Alexander Ranzenhofer, *Mit der Kriegsmarine kreuz und quer im Mittelmeer: Eine Mittelmeerreise mit S.M. Schiffen "Monarch," "Wien," und "Budapest" im Frühjahr 1901,* 10.

37. In 1908 the teak used in the construction of the *Erzherzog Franz Ferdinand* and *Radetzky* was the navy's only foreign purchase other than coal. See *Jahresbericht der k.u.k. Kriegsmarine* (1908), 19.

38. On the strikes of 1908 and 1909, see Cattaruzza, "Organisierter Konflikt," 348.

39. Greger, *Austro-Hungarian Warships,* 56. The *Erzherzog Ferdinand Max* (launched in May 1905) and all subsequent Habsburg battleships were equipped to burn oil as well as coal. See *Jahresbericht der k.u.k. Kriegsmarine* (1908), 14.

40. Greger, *Austro-Hungarian Warships,* 33. On the development of turbine engines, see Herwig, *"Luxury" Fleet,* 46. On the licensing agreement between the Stabilimento Tecnico and the Parsons Marine Steam Turbine Company of Wallsend-on-Tyne, see *Jahresbericht der k.u.k. Kriegsmarine* (1908), 14. Turbine engines were first installed in the British destroyer *Velox* (1901), followed by the cruiser *Amethyst* (1903) and the celebrated battleship *Dreadnought* (1906).

41. Franz, *Erzherzog Franz Ferdinand,* 103–4.

42. Montecuccoli's quote repeated in *StPD,* XLIII (31 October 1908), 613. On Kossuth's initial remark, which was also the title of his article in the weekly journal *Hetilap* dated 27 January 1846, see Paul Jonás, "Lajos Kossuth's Maritime Policies," 209.

43. The sum included 33.8 million from a three-year special credit of 54 million for 1908–10.

44. *StPD,* XLIII (31 October 1908), 613.

45. Ibid., XLI/2 (5 January 1907), 1177.

46. The archduke condemned Pitreich for being too conciliatory toward the Hungarians during the army crisis of 1905–6; he turned against Max von Beck after his old friend in 1907 agreed to the Hungarian quota of 36.4 percent in the decennial revision of the Austro-Hungarian economic relationship. Francis Ferdinand contended that Hungary should have been required to contribute a greater share to the common budget of the Dual Monarchy. On the dismissal of Pitreich, see Kiszling, *Erzherzog Franz Ferdinand,* 90–91; on the fall of Beck, see Franz, *Erzherzog Franz Ferdinand,* 35. The archduke toppled Beck in November 1908 by turning the Christian Social party against him in the *Reichsrat.*

47. While attending joint army-navy maneuvers in Dalmatia in 1906, Francis Ferdinand spoke exclusively with the *Marinekommandant* at all meals, completely ignoring the field marshals in attendance. See Glaise-Horstenau, *Franz Josephs Weggefährte,* 433.

48. Gebhard, "Austro-Hungarian Navy," 186.

49. Ibid., 196–97.

50. See Bridge, *Sadowa to Sarajevo,* 312; Seton-Watson, *Liberalism to Fascism,* 359–60; Halpern, *Mediterranean Naval Situation,* 190. On the Italian dreadnought appropriation for 1907-8, see Vego, "Anatomy," 1:99, 111–12.

51. Min. des Äussern to interior ministry, Vienna, 22 June 1909, HHSA, AR, F 44 - Marinewesen, Carton 7: Generalia ab 1871, Instruktionsreisen (cipher telegram).

52. HHSA, AR, F 44 - Marinewesen, Carton 7: Generalia ab 1871, Kommandierungen 2/1, 2/7, 2/10, 2/11.

53. Ibid., Kommandierungen 1/1, 2/2, 2/6, 2/12. The Siamese requests were turned down because no instructors could be spared and no places were available at the academy; the Chinese requests likewise were rejected on the grounds that conditions for officers aboard the East Asian cruisers already were too crowded.

54. Bayer von Bayersburg, *Auf weiter Fahrt,* 181–86.

55. Ibid., 192–94.

56. Ibid., 195–99.

57. Ibid., 187–92, 195, 200.

58. See ibid., 200; Bayer von Bayersburg, *Unter der k.u.k. Kriegsflagge,* 57; Sokol, *Des Kaisers Seemacht,* 230–31.

59. Lo Giudice, *Canale di Suez,* 235, 238; Babudieri, *Industrie, commerci e navigazione,* 165.

60. Lo Giudice, *Canale di Suez,* 228.

61. German trade figures cited in Richard L. Rudolph, "Quantitative Aspekte der Industrialisierung in Cisleithanien 1848–1914," 247. In 1909 seagoing trade accounted for 16 percent of all Austro-Hungarian exports and 17 percent of imports. Figures cited in *StPD,* XLV (2 March 1911), 530.

62. On the creation of the Austro-Americana, see Horst F. Mayer and Dieter Winkler, *In allen Häfen war Österreich: Die österreichische-ungarische Handelsmarine,* 65–67; Babudieri, *L'industria armatoriale di Trieste,* 144–45.

63. On the Austro-Americana's connections with the Hamburg-Amerika Line and the North German Lloyd, see Karl Bachinger, "Das Verkehrswesen," 314; and Wladimir Aichelburg, *Die Handelsschiffe Österreich-Ungarns im Weltkrieg 1914–1918,* 9. On the com-

pany's ties with the Creditanstalt, see Eduard März, "The Austrian Credit Mobilier in a Time of Transition," 126.

64. Figures from Babudieri, *Industrie, commerci e navigazione*, 159. North America was the destination of 85 percent of emigrants leaving Trieste in 1913; the rest went to South American ports. Of those leaving for North America, 44 percent were Austrian or Hungarian subjects, 38 percent were Russians, and the remaining 18 percent from other countries, mostly in the Balkans. The British Cunard Line, which before the creation of the Austro-Americana had dominated commerce between Trieste and North America, carried 32.7 percent of the emigrants leaving the city in 1913. The Canadian Pacific Line carried the remaining 10.8 percent.

65. Mayer and Winkler, *In allen Häfen war Österreich*, 68.

66. Eduard G. Staudinger and Siegfried Beer, "Die aussenwirtschaftlichen Beziehungen zu Grossbritannien," 736; Bachinger, "Das Verkehrswesen," 314–15. The Lloyd, a giant by Austro-Hungarian standards, was roughly one fourth the size of Ballin's Hamburg-Amerika Line, which in 1913 had 172 steamers totaling just over one million tons. See W. O. Henderson, *The Rise of German Industrial Power, 1834–1914*, 206. On the Lloyd's reputation, see Ronald E. Coons, review of Dieter Winkler and Georg Pawlik, *Die Dampfschiffahrtsgesellschaft Österreichischer Lloyd 1836–1918* (Graz: H. Weishaupt Verlag, 1986), in *Austrian History Yearbook* 22 (1991): 207.

67. Ploček and Juba, "Geschichte der ungarischen Reederei Adria," 19, 21.

68. Mayer and Winkler, *In allen Häfen war Österreich*, 141.

69. See figures in Sokol, *Des Kaisers Seemacht*, 201.

70. Bachinger, "Das Verkehrswesen," 315; Ploček and Juba, "Geschichte der ungarischen Reederei Adria," 19.

71. Francis Ferdinand to Brosch, Sonnwendhütte, 16 July 1907, in Chlumecky, *Erzherzog Franz Ferdinands Wirken und Wollen*, 45.

72. Good, *Economic Rise*, 150.

73. See figures from the summer of 1914 in Babudieri, *Industrie, commerci e navigazione*, 154, 194.

74. Mayer and Winkler, *In allen Häfen war Österreich*, 69. Francis Ferdinand wanted to bring the Austro-Americana completely under Austrian control but almost ruined the deal early in 1914 because it would have benefited the Boden-Creditanstalt, which was led by Rudolf Sieghart, a Jewish opponent of the archduke. Ultimately a consortium of banks bought up the shares of stock being sold by the Germans; it included the Boden-Creditanstalt, but in the long run the Rothschilds' Creditanstalt gained a controlling interest. See Rudolf Sieghart, *Die letzten Jahrzehnte einer Grossmacht*, 166.

75. Ernst Becher (president of the *k.k. Seebehörde*) to Handelsministerium, Trieste, 11 November 1894, Verwaltungsarchiv, Handel 3/a, 63163/1894, compares the Austrian and Hungarian shipbuilding subsidy laws of 1893. For example, an Austrian shipyard building a 1,000-ton iron-hulled steamship for overseas trade would receive a government subsidy of between 64,350 and 73,125 gulden (128,700 to 146,250 kronen) depending upon the source of the raw materials; a Hungarian shipyard building the same ship would receive a subsidy from Budapest of between 77,214 and 94,954 gulden (154,428 to 189,908 kronen). Higher subsidies were offered as an incentive to use domestic raw materials.

76. On the founding of the Cantiere Navale Triestino, see Fulvio Babudieri, "L'industrializzazione nelle costruzioni navali nella regione Giulia," 32; and Babudieri, *L'industria armatoriale di Trieste*, 145.

77. Aichelburg, *Die Handelsschiffe Österreich-Ungarns*, 8.

78. Staudinger and Beer, "Die aussenwirtschaftlichen Beziehungen zu Grossbritannien," 736.

79. Good, *Economic Rise*, 121.

80. Babudieri, *Squeri e cantiere*, 87–88. In 1884 the top shipyard wage was 2.5 gulden (5 kronen) per day.

81. Marina Cattaruzza, "I conflitti nazionali a Trieste nell'ambito della questione nazionale nell'Impero Asburgico, 1850–1914," 137, 147; Cattaruzza, "Sloveni e Italiani a Trieste," 29, 51.

82. Tomášek quoted from *StPD*, XLIV (16 November 1910), 466–67. Number of Skoda workers in 1910 cited in Fritz Weber, "Die wirtschaftliche Entwicklung Cisleithaniens vor dem Ersten Weltkrieg," 115.

83. Gebhard, "Austria-Hungary's Dreadnought Squadron," 252. Gebhard's article gives a comprehensive account of the constitutional and political issues facing Montecuccoli in his quest to build the dreadnought squadron.

84. Ibid., 252; Franz Conrad von Hötzendorf, *Aus meiner Dienstzeit, 1906–1918*, 1:360.

85. Figures from *Jahresbericht der k.u.k. Kriegsmarine* (1913), 112.

86. Of the archduke's biographers, Maurice Muret, *L'archiduc François-Ferdinand*, 132, gives the most attention to this episode. Gebhard, "Austro-Hungarian Navy," 203–4, discusses the Rothschild connection but, doubting their genuine links to the firms involved, draws no conclusions. None of the accounts of the meeting between the archduke and Baron Rothschild provides a specific date or month for the encounter.

87. Bridge, *Sadowa to Sarajevo*, 330. This British interpretation held that the dreadnought squadron was the quid pro quo for Germany's diplomatic support of the Dual Monarchy during the recent Bosnian crisis.

88. Koudelka, *Denn Österreich lag einst am Meer*, 116–18. The Admiralty's convictions never represented the official view of the British government. Winston Churchill, appointed First Lord of the Admiralty in 1911, personally doubted the alleged Austro-German connection. See Halpern, *Mediterranean Naval Situation*, 41; and Vego, "Anatomy," 1:141–43.

89. Halpern, *Mediterranean Naval Situation*, 160; Viscount Faramond de Lafajole, *Souvenirs d'un attaché naval en Allemagne et en Autriche, 1910–1914*, 27.

90. On the *Reichspost* and the growth of the Navy League, see Halpern, *Mediterranean Naval Situation*, 156, 160.

91. For specifics on the dreadnought design, see ibid., 162–63; and Greger, *Austro-Hungarian Warships*, 23–25.

92. Halpern, *Mediterranean Naval Situation*, 190–91.

93. Ibid., 161.

94. Gebhard, "Austro-Hungarian Navy," 211.

95. Kramář quoted in *StPD*, XLIV (17 November 1910), 789; Seitz's resolution in committee report in ibid., 846.

96. Halpern, *Mediterranean Naval Situation*, 161–62.

97. *StPD*, XLV (2 March 1911), 901, 906–9, 925; see also Gebhard, "Austro-Hungarian Navy," 213.

98. Ibid., 213–14.

99. Faramond, *Souvenirs d'un attaché naval*, 30.

100. *Jahresbericht der k.u.k. Kriegsmarine* (1913), 92–95. Figures do not include coal purchased for harbor use or the Pola Arsenal.

101. HHSA, AR, F 44 - Marinewesen, Carton 11: Kriegsschiffe 1/26 includes documentation on the voyages of the *Vesta* between 1911 and 1914. The ship, completed in 1892 by Armstrong of Newcastle, was purchased by the navy in December 1909. See Greger, *Austro-Hungarian Warships*, 112–13.

102. Gebhard, "Austria-Hungary's Dreadnought Squadron," 257; Kiszling, *Erzherzog Franz Ferdinand*, 160, 162.

103. Koudelka, *Denn Österreich lag einst am Meer*, 156–57.

104. Cattaruzza, *La formazione del proletariato urbano*, 121; Cattaruzza, "Organisierter Konflikt," 349. Ironically, the successful action of the Unione Metallurgica did not result in much of an increase in its membership.

105. Moritz von Auffenberg-Komarów, *Aus Österreichs Höhe und Niedergang*, 146, recounts the near-mishap.

106. Halpern, *Mediterranean Naval Situation*, 163. Numbers of workers cited in Weber, "Die wirtschaftliche Entwicklung Cisleithaniens," 115.

107. Greger, *Austro-Hungarian Warships*, 35, 44. Francis Ferdinand was not pleased that the *Saida* contract went to the Cantiere Navale Triestino because of its connection to the Boden-Creditanstalt. See note 74 above.

108. The first of the monitors was laid down in 1912 by the river shipyard of Stabilimento Tecnico Triestino at Linz in Upper Austria, the second in 1913 by the Budapest yard of the Danubius firm. They were completed in October 1914 and April 1915, respectively. See Greger, *Austro-Hungarian Warships*, 141–42.

109. Wladimir Aichelburg, *Die Unterseeboote Österreich-Ungarns*, 1:31–48, 58, 143.

110. Montecuccoli to Min. des Äussern, Vienna, 13 October 1909, HHSA, AR, F 44 - Marinewesen, Carton 4: Generalia ab 1871, Auskünfte 1/1; Montecuccoli to Min. des Äussern, Vienna, 1 Feb. 1910, ibid., Carton 7: Generalia ab 1871, Instruktionsreisen 2/14.

111. Greger, *Austro-Hungarian Warships*, 58–60.

112. On Italy's first submarines, see Giorgerini, *Almanacco*, 492–95.

113. Vego, "Anatomy," 1:286; Peter Schupita, *Die k.u.k. Seeflieger: Chronik und Dokumentation der österreichisch-ungarischen Marineluftwaffe 1911–1918*, 10–11, 85. While some of the early Habsburg seaplanes were imported, the Dual Monarchy quickly developed its own aircraft industry, thanks mostly to the efforts of Camillo Castiglioni of Trieste. In 1909 he founded the Motor-Luftfahrgesellschaft (MLG), followed in 1912 by the Ungarische Flugzeugfabrik (UFAG) in Budapest, and in 1914 the Albatros-Werke (later renamed the Phönix Flugzeugwerke AG) in Vienna. He also owned the Hansa-Brandenburg-Werke, one of the largest aircraft plants in Germany. Because the same firms that built airplane engines also manufactured automobiles, Castiglioni became involved as an investor in automobile companies. During the war, he purchased an interest in the Daimler-Motoren-Gesellschaft of Wiener Neustadt and in 1917 he bought the Rapp-Werke of Munich, which he renamed the Bayerische Motoren-Werke (BMW). See ibid., 12n.

114. The elections left the three principal German groups still in control of roughly half of the seats in the *Reichsrat*. German Nationalists became the largest bloc, with 20.2 percent of the seats, up from 15.3 percent in 1907. The Social Democrats fell slightly, to 15.9 percent (1907: 16.7 percent), and the Christian Social party, rocked by the death in 1910 of Karl Lueger, fell to 14.7 percent (1907: 18.9 percent).

115. See Akos Paulinyi, "Die sogenannte gemeinsame Wirtschaftspolitik Österreich-Ungarns," 574.

116. Gebhard, "The Croatians," 153–56 passim.

117. See Horthy, *Memoirs*, 43–60, 76–77. Horthy and Charles first met in 1901, when the future emperor was fourteen.

118. Percentages for nationalities from *Militärstatistisches Jahrbuch*, 1904 and 1910; other figures from *Jahresbericht der k.u.k. Kriegsmarine*, 1905 and 1911.

119. Figures from *Jahresbericht der k.u.k. Kriegsmarine*, 1899, 1905, 1911. In the last full peacetime year (1913), the Italian share of new recruits again was 14.4 percent; see ibid., 1913.

120. Gebhard, "Austria-Hungary's Dreadnought Squadron," 255.

121. Gebhard, "Austro-Hungarian Navy," 100, 241–43.

122. Ibid., 213n.; Brousek, *Die Grossindustrie Böhmens*, 162.

123. On the review of 28 March 1911 at Corfu, see Sosnosky, *Franz Ferdinand*, 113. On the *Radetzky's* cruise to Britain, see Sokol, *Des Kaisers Seemacht*, 231. Ironically, Francis Ferdinand missed the Spithead review, cutting short his visit in order to be in Trieste to preside over the launching of the *Viribus Unitis* on 24 June 1911. See Wladimir Aichelburg, Lothar Baumgartner, et al., *Die "Tegetthoff"-Klasse: Österreich-Ungarns grösste Schlachtschiffe*, 3.

124. The Moroccan crisis officially ended with the Franco-German agreement of November 1911, in which France ceded parts of the French Congo to Germany in exchange for German recognition of the French protectorate over Morocco. The protectorate was formally established in March 1912.

125. See Kiszling, *Erzherzog Franz Ferdinand*, 163n.

126. Ludwig Rudnay (consul) to Min. des Äussern, Durazzo, 5 October 1911, HHSA, AR, F 44 - Marinewesen, Carton 10: Varia 2/77. See also Baratelli, *La marina militare italiana*, 414; Bosworth, *The Least of the Great Powers*, 175–76. On 8 October 1911, Italy agreed not to pursue the war in the Adriatic, the northern Ionian Sea, or the Red Sea.

127. Brosch to Leopold von Chlumecky, 5 October 1911, in Chlumecky, *Erzherzog Franz Ferdinands Wirken und Wollen*, 103.

128. Sosnosky, *Franz Ferdinand*, 142; Rothenberg, *The Army of Francis Joseph*, 163–64; Kiszling, *Erzherzog Franz Ferdinand*, 163–65. Conrad von Hötzendorf quoted in *Aus meiner Dienstzeit*, 1:358.

129. See Halpern, *Mediterranean Naval Situation*, 194–95; Bosworth, *The Least of the Great Powers*, 181–93 passim.

130. Babudieri, *Industrie, commerci e navigazione*, 163–64. In the Ottoman fiscal year 1911–12, the total value of Britain's trade with Turkey was 1.59 billion piastres, followed by Austria-Hungary (1.03 billion), France (862 million), and Germany (668 million). In 1913, 27.1 percent of Trieste's trade was with the Ottoman Empire, Greece, and other Balkan ports.

131. Serbian concerns on the Danube are addressed in Montecuccoli to Min. des Äussern, Vienna, 10 October 1912, HHSA, AR, F 44 - Marinewesen, Carton 10: Varia 2/83. See also Sokol, *Des Kaisers Seemacht*, 223–24. On the army's preparations during the First Balkan War, see Rothenberg, *The Army of Francis Joseph*, 166–67.

132. Walter Princig von Herwalt (consul) to Aehrenthal, Piraeus, 10 December 1911, HHSA, AR, F 44 - Marinewesen, Carton 11: Kriegsschiffe 1/24. See also Sokol, *Des Kaisers Seemacht*, 222–23.

133. *Jahresbericht der k.u.k. Kriegsmarine* (1912), 56. On Francis Ferdinand's trip to Berlin, see Williamson, "Franz Ferdinand," 428.

134. See Bridge, *Sadowa to Sarajevo,* 347; Seton-Watson, *Liberalism to Fascism,* 396. On Austria-Hungary's willingness to go to war in order to block Serbia's access to the Adriatic, see Samuel R. Williamson, Jr., *Austria-Hungary and the Origins of the First World War,* 127, 173.

135. *StPD,* XLVI (15 October 1912), 903.

136. Gebhard, "Austro-Hungarian Navy," 231.

137. *StPD,* XLVII (19 November 1912), 195.

138. Figure cited by Montecuccoli in ibid., XLV (2 March 1911), 918.

CHAPTER 6 ≋

THE EVE OF WAR

Supported by a broad coalition of political parties, the patronage of Francis Ferdinand, and the interests of a booming military-industrial complex, Montecuccoli by 1912 had transformed the Austro-Hungarian navy from a force capable of defending the Adriatic to a fleet that was a factor even in the Mediterranean calculations of Britain, the greatest naval power. But success unfortunately bred arrogance, which in turn led to scandal. Far from resting on his laurels, the aging admiral remained at the center of controversy right up to his retirement. Financial irregularities cast a shadow over Montecuccoli's last year in office, and in the resulting row with the war ministry only the direct intervention of Francis Ferdinand saved the *Marinekommandant* from suffering a serious disgrace.

MONTECUCCOLI IN TROUBLE: FRANCIS FERDINAND, FINANCES, AND THE REORGANIZATION OF THE NAVY (1912–13)

While Montecuccoli's latest questionable financial arrangements remained secret until the beginning of 1912, the scandal had its roots in decisions made two years earlier. After concluding his own deal with the banks and the industrialists for the construction of the navy's first two dreadnoughts during the budget year of 1910, when the Hungarian constitutional crisis prevented the Delegations from meeting, Montecuccoli had continued the practice of borrowing money in private arrangements between the *Marinesektion* and the banks to supplement the navy's budget allocation. The previously unreported borrowing began in February 1910 and continued through the end of 1911. The navy incurred most of the illegal debt during 1911, after the Delegations approved Montecuccoli's fleet program but, at the insistence of Auffenberg's predecessor, Schönaich, granted the navy a sum that the *Marinekommandant* considered inadequate to support both the construction program and the rest of the fleet's needs. Montecuccoli borrowed 13.7 million kronen from the Creditanstalt and 18.5 million from the Länderbank, in the latter case incurring an interest debt of another 1.3 million. He also authorized the Stabilimento Tecnico Triestino to do 24.8 million worth of work beyond what had been funded by the budget for 1911; by the end of the year, the navy owed the shipyard another 2.2 million in interest on this unpaid debt. Altogether, the *Marinekommandant* ran up a bill of over 60 million kronen without securing the approval of any higher authority.[1]

Because Montecuccoli's arrangement with the Länderbank called for that loan to be repaid beginning in January 1912, his activity could not be concealed beyond that time, and the war ministry had to be asked for the necessary funds. Auffenberg was outraged that such sums had been spent by a branch of the armed forces without his knowledge. In March he protested to Francis Joseph that the war minister was officially responsible for the budget of the entire armed forces, and that all expenditures undertaken in the name of the army or navy had to be reported directly to him. Auffenberg intended to give Montecuccoli a harsh reprimand, but Francis Ferdinand succeeded in having the letter watered down before it was delivered. The *Marinekommandant*, after all, had "only the best of intentions."[2]

Montecuccoli's quest for money went beyond contracting bank loans. The sale of obsolete warships also promised to raise a modest amount of supplemental income for the navy, and in this area, as in his dealings with the banks, the *Marinekommandant* circumvented the war minister. In 1912 he corresponded directly with the foreign ministry on a plan to sell old battleships, presumably the *Monarch* and its sisters, to the Netherlands. The Dutch initiated the request but ultimately rejected the proposed terms of the sale. Four years earlier, a similar scheme to sell the *Kronprinz Rudolf*, *Kronprinzessin Stephanie*, and the casemate ship *Tegetthoff* to Uruguay likewise had fallen through.[3] Though they had long outlived their usefulness as seagoing units, the old battleships would remain on hand to see action in various supporting roles in the First World War.

After the budget controversy between Auffenberg and Montecuccoli, Francis Ferdinand concluded that something had to be done to redefine the relationship between the army and the navy. His personal staff in the Belvedere, since late 1911 under the direction of Brosch's successor, Colonel Carl von Bardolff, was already working on a plan to create a separate navy ministry as soon as Francis Ferdinand succeeded to the throne. A similar proposal had been drafted during 1911 by the presidial chancellery of the *Marinesektion,* most likely a direct result of Montecuccoli's difficulties with Schönaich over the budget for that year. But there were considerable obstacles to the creation of a navy ministry, all of them Hungarian. The three existing joint Austro-Hungarian ministries were all housed in Vienna; it was likely that if a fourth joint ministry were created, the Hungarians would insist that two of the four be housed in Budapest. There was also the possibility that if the armed forces had separate ministries for war and the navy, the Hungarians would insist that one of the two ministers be a Magyar. Since there were no Magyars among the navy's most senior officers, the war ministry would have to be headed by a Magyar, an intolerable situation for an army officer corps that was over three-quarters German Austrian. Furthermore, the parties in Budapest favoring a greater autonomy or even independence for Hungary would reject out of hand any expansion of the common Austro-Hungarian bureaucracy.[4]

Francis Ferdinand and his circle in the Belvedere did not worry about offending Magyar sensibilities when drafting their political and constitutional proposals for the future reign; neither did the archduke abandon the notion of creating a navy ministry simply because the Hungarians would not approve. In any event, as long as Francis Joseph remained alive, all of the archduke's plans would remain on the drawing board. In the spring of 1912, Francis Ferdinand resolved to do what he could to reorganize the navy's administrative structure and pave the way for the creation of a separate ministry later on. He focused his attention on the traditional policy of having the *Marinekommandant*— the chief of naval operations—also head the navy's administration as chief of the *Marinesektion.* The two positions had been linked since the time of Tegetthoff but would have to be separated before the *Marinesektion* could be converted into an independent body under a navy minister. Faced with strong opposition in the upper echelons of the navy, Francis Ferdinand argued that administrative duties had kept Montecuccoli and his predecessors in Vienna most of the time, leaving them less familiar with the ships and personnel of the fleet. The *Marinekommandant* in fact would be ill prepared to command the navy should war break out.[5]

Francis Ferdinand also took into account the aging of the sea officer corps, which had become a serious problem. The average age of all active admirals had risen steadily in the last decades of the nineteenth century (from 49 in 1870 to 53 in 1880, 58 in 1890, and 59 in 1900) as did the average number of years needed to reach rear admiral's rank (26 in 1870, 30 in 1880, 36 in 1890, 39.5 in 1900).[6] Tegetthoff had taken command of the navy at forty, Pöck at 46, Sterneck at 54, and Spaun at 64; Montecuccoli became *Marinekommandant* at 61 but was 69 in 1912. Tegetthoff, the hero of 1866, had excellent credentials as a commander and was intimately acquainted with the personnel and matériel of his fleet; at the same time, his prestige as a victorious admiral made him an effective political figure as head of the *Marinesektion*. Montecuccoli, in comparison, distinguished himself as a political admiral after his career at sea came to an end; he had not commanded a ship at sea since heading the cruiser squadron in the Far East during the Boxer Rebellion. A short, stout man who became even stockier with age, he hardly had the look of a fighting admiral as he neared seventy. In May 1912, Francis Ferdinand formally proposed to Montecuccoli the creation of a new post of fleet inspector (*Flotteninspektor*) based at Pola to assume most of his responsibilities for the fleet and coastal installations. In case of war, the fleet inspector would mobilize the navy, then assume active command of it.[7] Montecuccoli had little choice but to agree to the change, especially given the role the archduke had played in blunting Auffenberg's reprimand over the private arrangements with the Vienna banks. The only question concerned whom to appoint to the new position.

In July 1912, Vice Admiral Anton Haus received the post; he was Francis Ferdinand's personal choice but also the obvious man for the job. The son of an estate overseer, Haus had graduated from the Ljubljana gymnasium and entered the navy as a provisional cadet in 1869, at the age of eighteen. In addition to his native German, he spoke Italian, Slovenian, English, French, Spanish, and Portuguese. He wrote a text on oceanography, and his early career included service as an instructor at the naval academy from 1886 to 1890. Haus mastered the technical aspects of naval artillery and torpedo technology and headed the navy's torpedo school from 1896 to 1899. He received his first significant independent command at the age of forty-nine, taking the old composite corvette *Donau* on its circumnavigation of the globe in 1900–1901. Haus left the ship in the Far East to assume command of the cruiser *Maria Theresia* and was the highest-ranking officer on the East Asian station until his return home in 1902. He headed the presidial chancellery of the *Marinesektion* from 1902 to 1905 and, after a promotion to rear admiral, served as Austro-Hungarian delegate to the Hague Peace Conference of 1907. Haus led the active squadron from 1908 to 1910 and commanded it again during the summer of 1911 after advancing to vice admiral. At the time of his appointment, he chaired the technical committee at Pola.[8]

In a close-knit corps in which the sea officer's closest friends usually were his classmates from the naval academy, Haus, having never attended the academy, was always a sort of outsider among officers at his own rank. As a senior officer, he reinforced these barriers by habitually criticizing his peers in front of junior officers. But through his work as an instructor at the academy and torpedo school, he built an extensive network of protégés, and much to the chagrin of other senior officers, he was the admiral most respected by the younger men of the corps.[9] He first came to the attention of Francis Ferdinand in 1902, when he was commander of the imperial yacht *Miramar* during fleet maneuvers. According to legend, the archduke at that point resolved that some day Haus would command the navy.[10] While his overall credentials no doubt impressed Francis Ferdinand, Haus's recent experience as a seagoing commander was the strongest factor in his favor. The archduke, though concerned about the aging of the navy leadership, chose to overlook the fact that Haus already was sixty-one years old.

With Haus clearly being groomed to succeed Montecuccoli as *Marinekommandant,* his appointment to the new position raised the possibility of friction between the two men. Montecuccoli had not gone out of his way to promote Haus's career in the past; indeed, as recently as June 1911, when Vice Admiral Kneissler retired from his post as second in command, Montecuccoli had passed over Haus and filled the

Stellvertreter position with Vice Admiral Alois von Kunsti, a man with two years' less seniority. According to Alfred von Koudelka, then head of the presidial chancellery in the *Marinesektion,* the old *Marinekommandant* was "absolutely dissatisfied" with Haus's appointment as fleet inspector.[11] Nevertheless, the new arrangement worked because of the clear division of responsibilities: Montecuccoli remained in Vienna, concerned primarily with administrative and political affairs, while the fleet in Pola preoccupied Haus.

Much more so than the relationship between Haus and Montecuccoli, the new fleet inspector's position vis-à-vis the harbor admiral at Pola promised to be awkward. The post of Pola harbor admiral had been an important "consolation prize" ever since the 1860s, often going to a senior officer no longer in line to become *Marinekommandant.* At the time of Haus's appointment, Admiral Julius von Ripper had held the post since 1905. Ripper had eight years' more seniority than Haus, and to complicate matters further, the two men were known not to be the best of friends.[12] In the new arrangement, Ripper remained harbor admiral, directly responsible for Pola, but he was subordinate to Haus because of the fleet inspector's accountability for the readiness of the entire fleet as well as all coastal installations. The informal code of the corps prevented an officer from serving at sea under an officer of inferior seniority, but Ripper could stay on because his post did not involve sea duty.

Francis Ferdinand hoped that after the retirement of Montecuccoli, Haus would stay at Pola as *Marinekommandant* but with the same duties he had already assumed as fleet inspector. To fulfill the goal of separating the command of the fleet from the administrative leadership of the navy, another admiral would succeed Montecuccoli in his capacity as chief of the *Marinesektion.* For this post, the archduke promoted the candidacy of Rear Admiral Richard von Barry, a distinguished officer currently serving as commandant of the naval academy for the 1912–13 school year. With Barry heading the administration in Vienna and Haus still at Pola, the way would be cleared for the future conversion of the *Marinesektion* into an independent navy ministry without further disrupting the operational command of the fleet.[13]

Montecuccoli finally stepped down on 22 February 1913, six days before his seventieth birthday. The last active veteran of the Battle of

Lissa, he retired as the most decorated admiral in the navy's history; his more recent honors included the Grand Cross of the Order of Leopold as well as the Order of the Golden Fleece.[14] A week later, Ripper left the post of harbor admiral, and within a month Kunsti was ousted as second in command, retiring before his fifty-ninth birthday. The clean sweep eased the transition to a younger leadership. Haus, eight years younger than Montecuccoli, became *Marinekommandant* and chief of the *Marinesektion,* with a promotion to full admiral; Karl Kailer von Kaltenfels, the new *Stellvertreter* in the *Marinesektion,* had just been promoted to rear admiral at the beginning of 1913 and was eight years younger than the outgoing Kunsti; and the new harbor admiral at Pola, fifty-seven-year-old Eugen von Chmelarž, was nine years younger than Ripper.

The changes reversed the long trend toward a graying leadership. Becoming second in command at fifty-one, Kailer, an 1880 graduate of the naval academy, was the youngest officer since Pöck in the 1870s to hold such a high position. By the summer of 1914, other retirements and promotions brought the average age of admirals down to fifty-three; for this group, an average of thirty-two years of service had been required to reach rear admiral.[15] By putting the navy's future in the hands of younger admirals, Francis Joseph and the new war minister, Baron Alexander Krobatin, heeded Francis Ferdinand's wishes. In the specific appointments, however, the Hofburg and the war ministry either ignored or overruled the Belvedere. Barry did not receive a major office, and even more important, the archduke saw his overall plans foiled by the selection of Haus for the position of chief of the *Marinesektion* as well as *Marinekommandant.* The abolition of the admiral's superfluous title of fleet inspector in March 1913 confirmed the return to the status quo ante: the unification of the operational and administrative commands of the navy, with the commander residing in Vienna. Francis Ferdinand was disappointed but not prepared to abandon his goal. Just as Montecuccoli's last months in office had been dominated by the reorganization plans of the archduke, the same would be true of the first months of the Haus era.

THE HAUS ERA:
PREWAR POLICIES AND POLITICS (1913–14)

Haus assumed command of a navy far larger than the one Montecuccoli had inherited from Spaun just over eight years earlier. The material expansion of the fleet, crowned by the dreadnought program, naturally had attracted most of the attention, but under Montecuccoli there had been an equally dramatic growth in the area of personnel. In 1905 there were 698 sea officers, 10,000 seamen on active duty, and 16,000 reserves and *Seewehr;* at the onset of Haus's tenure in 1913, there were 871 sea officers, almost 18,000 seamen on active duty, and more than 22,000 in the reserves and *Seewehr.* In the early months of 1913, the special fleet mobilization resulting from the Balkan War brought 25,000 men onto active duty, of whom 21,000 were serving aboard ships. Never before had so many sailors worn the navy's uniform, and never before had so many been at sea at one time.[16]

The navy was able to place so many men on active duty thanks to recent legislation increasing the supply of recruits for both the army and navy. In June 1912, the Austrian and Hungarian parliaments passed a military law guaranteeing the armed forces a total annual contingent of 181,000 men, up from the previous ceiling of 139,000. The law envisioned a continuing growth in the annual contingent over the next five years to 243,000.[17] The navy's share represented only a tiny fraction of the whole, but it sufficed to raise the number of incoming seamen from fewer than 3,700 in 1911 to more than 5,500 in 1913; it was projected that 7,000 per year would be added after 1916.[18] With the parliaments committed to increasing manpower levels as the fleet continued to grow in size, the future appeared secure.

With the appointment of Haus to the offices of *Marinekommandant* and chief of the *Marinesektion,* Francis Ferdinand was back at square one in his plans to reorganize the navy's command structure. To achieve his original goal, he would have to persuade Haus to give up either his administrative authority or fleet command. In late March 1913, when Francis Ferdinand visited Haus to plead his case, the admiral rejected the archduke's scheme.[19] After months of haggling, however, Haus agreed to a compromise solution. He would move from Vienna to Pola but retain his titles of *Marinekommandant* and chief of the *Marinesektion.* The second in command would remain behind in Vienna as the de facto head of the administration. The fact that Haus and Kailer were good friends enabled the commander to make the move with few misgivings. In other significant administrative changes, the position of commander's adjutant (*Marinekommandoadjutant*), revived by Sterneck in 1885 and linked to the post of head of the operations chancellery of the

Marinesektion, was moved to Pola. Future adjutants chaired a naval command chancellery (*Marinekommandokanzlei*) in Pola, which served as a naval equivalent of the army General Staff, only without the designation of *Admiralstab* or the corresponding status. Meanwhile, in Vienna the operations chancellery remained in existence but had less extensive responsibilities than before. The *Stellvertreter* in the *Marinesektion* also received a *zugeteilter Flaggenoffizier* to function as a third in command.[20]

The reforms took effect in August 1913, the same month that Francis Joseph named Francis Ferdinand inspector general of the armed forces (*Generalinspektor der gesamten bewaffneten Macht*). The new appointment, coming fifteen years after the emperor had placed the archduke "at the disposition of the Supreme Command," finally gave him an official military position, one even more powerful than that held by Archduke Albrecht in the last decades of the nineteenth century. As had been the case with Albrecht, it was assumed that Francis Ferdinand would serve as supreme commander of the armed forces in case of war; Francis Joseph, now eighty-three, certainly was in no condition to fulfill this constitutional obligation.[21] One would assume that the archduke's new official powers would have made Haus less willing to challenge him, but this was not the case. According to one account, the *Marinekommandant* "had a sharp eye for human folly and an even sharper tongue."[22] Known for his frankness in all matters, he was to have his share of disagreements with the Belvedere in the months to come.

During the negotiation and implementation of the latest administrative changes, Haus had to contend with the last flare-up of the First Balkan War and, in the summer of 1913, the eruption of a second Balkan conflict. In April 1913, one month before the Treaty of London ended the war between the Balkan states and Turkey, Austria-Hungary provided most of the ships for an international naval demonstration off the coast of Albania. This show of force, involving vessels from all of the great powers except Russia, succeeded in pressuring Montenegro and Serbia to evacuate the city of Scutari and other territory promised to the new Albanian state. The navy's contingent included the three battleships of the *Radetzky* class, the old light cruiser *Aspern,* and torpedo boats, under the command of Rear Admiral Maximilian Njegovan. After the Montenegrin and Serbian withdrawal, landing parties from the Austro-Hungarian ships policed the disputed territory for several months until the Albanians established control.[23] The dreadnought *Viribus Unitis,* though ready for action, was kept in Pola throughout the operation; the navy's second dreadnought, *Tegetthoff,* commissioned in July 1913, likewise did not take part.

The great powers were still well represented in Albanian waters in late June 1913, when Bulgaria, disappointed at its spoils from the Treaty of London, attacked its former allies Serbia and Greece. Montenegro and Turkey then declared war on Bulgaria, and even Romania joined the fray. Austria-Hungary ultimately threatened Serbia in support of the beleaguered Bulgarians, a course Italy strongly opposed.[24] Because the Second Balkan War quickly turned into a defensive struggle for the Bulgarians along all of their borders, it had no naval dimension. In August 1913, the Treaty of Bucharest restored the peace, with the other combatants all making minor gains at the expense of Bulgaria. The cessation of hostilities in the Balkans enabled the new state of Albania to finally establish some measure of control over its assigned territory, and in March 1914 an international naval escort accompanied the new Albanian monarch, Prince William of Wied, on his journey from Trieste to Durazzo (Durrës). Austro-Hungarian cruisers and other smaller naval vessels, active in Albanian waters throughout the previous winter, remained offshore to support William's shaky throne. With Vienna and Rome still in agreement over the need for an independent Albania, over the next six months the captains of their warships cooperated to support the prince and his entourage against his own hostile Muslim subjects. In September 1914, William abdicated, leaving Albania in chaos. By that time, Haus and his navy were too preoccupied with a greater conflict to take much notice.[25]

In addition to directing these prewar operations from his headquarters in Pola, Haus also traveled to Vienna for important meetings with government ministers and presented the navy budget to the Delegations. It was of some comfort that Montecuccoli's goal of sixteen battleships would be reached as soon as the four dreadnoughts were completed; however, this figure included the three tiny vessels of the *Monarch* class, twenty years old and barely a quarter the size of dreadnoughts. As early as October 1912, Montecuccoli had proposed the construction of two additional dreadnoughts as replacements for two of the *Monarchs,* and in March 1913 Bardolff, on behalf of Francis Ferdinand, urged Haus to pursue the construction of a "second dreadnought division" to replace the obsolete warships, if necessary by the same extralegal means that Montecuccoli had used in 1909–10.[26] The Creditanstalt, Stabilimento

Tecnico Triestino, Skoda, and Witkowitz offered to play the same roles as before, building dreadnoughts "at their own risk" pending the Delegations' authorization of the expenditure. Bardolff even negotiated the necessary bank loans on the navy's behalf. But despite the pressure from the Belvedere, Haus refused to go behind the backs of the politicians, in May 1913 revealing the offer in the council of ministers. He found Hungarian opposition to further increases in naval spending to be particularly strong; minister-president László Lukács even threatened to resign if the navy placed an order with the shipyard before the next meeting of the Delegations.[27]

In the fall of 1913, Haus decided not to include new dreadnoughts in his 1914 budget proposals for the Delegations. He did take the scheme back to the ministers, however, and in October secured their approval for a program of four dreadnoughts (to replace the three *Monarchs* and the *Habsburg*, the next-oldest battleship), three 4,800-ton cruisers (to replace the *Zenta, Aspern*, and *Szigetvár*, built in 1896–1900), six more *Tátra*-class destroyers, another two Danube monitors, and a supply ship, at a cost of 426.8 million kronen.[28] The support of the council, contrasting with the cool reception of the previous May, came largely because Lukács had fallen from power and Tisza, a convert to the cause, had returned as Hungarian minister-president.

Owing to a decision to change the Austro-Hungarian fiscal year from January–December to July–June, the Delegations convened in Vienna late in 1913 to approve a budget for the first six months of 1914; they met again in Budapest in the spring of 1914 to allocate funds for 1914–15, the first full fiscal year on the new calendar. In part to absorb the tremendous overrun of 1913 (the navy had been allocated 142.7 million kronen and spent 210.2 million), Haus asked the Delegations for 133.5 million for January through June 1914. Most of the sum was to come from supplementary credits: another installment of the six-year, 312.4 million credit for 1911–16, plus more than 40 million to defray the cost of the Balkan crisis. Even though Haus decided not to formally propose the 426.8 million kronen program until the session in Budapest, his supporters in the Austrian Delegation used the Vienna session as a forum to rally support for the new quartet of dreadnoughts. Albert von Mühlwerth, a German Nationalist from Bohemia, offered a simple analogy: "If my coat is old and threadbare, I buy myself a new one. . . . It is the same with warships."[29]

When the Delegations met in Budapest to approve the budget for 1914-15, Haus presented his program and asked for the special credit to cover the cost. The 426.8 million kronen were to be allocated over the next five fiscal years, through 1918-19, in installments of 45.3, 100, 100, 100, and 81.5 million. In the Hungarian Delegation, Tisza's party supported the navy, but Haus, like Montecuccoli, had to pay dearly for their votes. The emergence of the Cantiere Navale Triestino at Monfalcone, which was awarded the contract for the light cruiser *Saida* in 1911, had raised fears in Budapest that future dreadnought contracts might be divided between the shipyards of Trieste and Monfalcone, but early in 1914 Haus reassured Tisza that Rijeka would continue to get its share. In fact, two of the four dreadnoughts, all six destroyers, and both Danube monitors were promised to Hungary.[30] In the Austrian Delegation, the Social Democrats, as before, voiced the only real opposition. Karl Leuthner of Lower Austria, editor of the *Arbeiter Zeitung*, lamented that still more big, expensive battleships would be launched "into the ocean of the Austrian state debt."[31]

German Nationalists continued to support naval expansion because it enhanced the Dual Monarchy's alliance value to the Second Reich. Austrian House of Lords delegate Count Heinrich Lützow, a former Habsburg ambassador to Italy, contended that "every supporter of the Triple Alliance . . . must vote for the strengthening of our navy."[32] The pro-Russian Young Czechs naturally rejected such pro-German reasoning. Speaking for his colleagues, Karel Kramář reaffirmed that "we have a certain partiality for the navy" but argued that the Russian Black Sea fleet was not a potential rival for the Austro-Hungarian navy, and that the fate of the Dardanelles should be of no concern to the Dual Monarchy.[33] But once again, the strange bedfellows of the pronavy majority maintained their coalition. The cause even gained support from traditionally antinavy agrarian politicians, who feared competition from cheap Balkan grain and blamed a weak Habsburg foreign policy for the recent strengthening of the Balkan states.[34]

With almost everyone but the Social Democrats converted to navalism, the only real friction came when the parties bickered over the spoils. In the Budapest session, Kramář conceded that the Young Czechs were "happy when Skoda has business"—indeed, by 1913 the firm provided 9,600 jobs—but expressed regret that Skoda and Witkowitz so dominated the economy of their region. Unlike his countryman Tomášek four years earlier, he did not address the plight of the workers, instead focusing on the problems these powerful firms caused for other businesses: "We in Bohemia and Moravia have the fortune, or misfortune, that the most expensive [components], namely the Witkowitz steel plates and Skoda guns, are manufactured by us." The two giants consumed almost all of Bohemia and Moravia's share of the overall naval armaments pie, leaving little for the local machine-building and electrical industries.[35] Delegates from other provinces, already jealous of the relative prosperity of Bohemia and Moravia, gave him no sympathy. Indeed, in the future Kramář's constituents were likely to receive a somewhat smaller share of the navy's money. In the spring of 1913, the Hungarian government concluded agreements with both Skoda and Krupp to produce naval guns in partnership with a government-owned factory to be located at Győr. The new plant, scheduled to open in the spring of 1915, would produce guns of all calibers and supply the weaponry for all warships constructed by Danubius.[36]

The division of gun contracts promised to create more jobs for the Hungarian half of the Dual Monarchy, and the diffusion of navy contracts to areas other than the Adriatic littoral and the Bohemian-Moravian industrial heartland only attracted more support to the navy's cause. In this atmosphere, the opponents of navalism could do little other than lay their deepest concerns at Haus's feet and hope to strike a responsive chord. With the budget for 1914–15 certain to pass, Leuthner and other Social Democrats implored the *Marinekommandant* to consider the plight of the many thousands of workers whose livelihood depended upon naval armaments and appealed to the navy to do what it could to improve their working conditions.[37]

Final approval of the navy budget for 1914–15—the largest in history—came with less fanfare than any in recent years. The Hungarian Delegation, once a forum for the most bitter antinavy diatribes, passed it without debate in just fifteen minutes; the Magyar politicians also endorsed a program of incentives designed to encourage the Adria Line and other Hungarian steamship companies to order their steamers from Danubius rather than British shipyards. Austrian delegate Otto Lecher commented sarcastically that the two Delegations appeared to be engaged in a contest to see which could approve the navy budget the faster. In a front-page story, the *Neue Freie Presse* noted that the massive outlay had passed "with little resistance." Once a mouthpiece for liberal opponents of the fleet, the prominent Vienna daily concurred in the need for naval expansion, referring to the Adriatic Sea as "one of the main arteries through which the monarchy draws its blood."[38] The annual meeting of the general assembly of the Austrian Navy League in late May 1914 coincided with the passage of the budget. Prince Alfred von und zu Liechtenstein urged the members in attendance to continue to work for a stronger fleet "with which to defend our interests and preserve the peace, and if necessary, to fight and win for *Kaiser* and *Vaterland!*"[39]

The unprecedented breadth and depth of pronavy sentiment in the Dual Monarchy made even the cynical Haus optimistic about the future. Having secured the necessary funding for his program, he planned to lay down the first two new dreadnoughts in September and October, respectively. Designed by Franz Pitzinger, *Generalschiffbauingenieur* and successor to the retired Siegfried Popper, they were to be larger and more powerful than the first class of Austro-Hungarian dreadnoughts, displacing 24,500 tons and carrying ten 14-inch guns. The Stabilimento Tecnico Triestino, which had laid off a thousand workers after the completion of the *Prinz Eugen* in the spring of 1914, was eager to begin work on the vessels and received both contracts.[40] Danubius of Rijeka would start the remaining pair of dreadnoughts at a later date. Political considerations had forced Haus to promise two dreadnoughts to Rijeka, even though Danubius had been far less efficient than its Trieste counterpart in fulfilling its first dreadnought contract. The *Prinz Eugen* and *Szent István* both were laid down in January 1912, but the Trieste yard launched the former in November 1912, while Danubius did not launch the latter until January 1914. The navy ultimately commissioned the *Prinz Eugen* in July 1914; the *Szent István* entered service in November 1915. The feat of the Trieste yard was even more impressive given the fact that two strikes by machinists, in August 1912 and March 1913, had delayed work on the *Prinz Eugen*'s engines.[41]

After attending the launching of each of the navy's first three dreadnoughts, Francis Ferdinand expressed his displeasure over the delays at Danubius (and his general sentiments toward the Hungarians) by boycotting the launching of the *Szent István*. His absence caused Haus considerable embarrassment, especially since members of the Delegation and other dignitaries from Budapest had been invited to attend the ceremonies. An angry Haus aired his displeasure over the archduke's conduct in a private letter to a member of Francis Joseph's inner circle, ensuring that his account of the near-fiasco would reach the emperor.[42]

While Haus had few of Montecuccoli's political skills and certainly a less diplomatic personality, he succeeded in continuing the program of fleet expansion. Of course, the public and political coalition supporting navalism was already firmly established by the time he took the helm; nevertheless, securing a special credit of 426.8 million kronen from the Delegations was no small feat. The latest appropriation appeared to guarantee that the Austro-Hungarian navy in the near future would progress from a position of mere respectability as an Adriatic force to a new stature as a potent offensive factor in the Mediterranean. If not for the First World War, the Dual Monarchy by the end of the decade would have had a fleet of sixteen battleships launched since 1900, including eight dreadnoughts and the three battleships of the *Radetzky* class, considered "semi-dreadnoughts" by foreign observers. Even taking into account financial restrictions and construction delays, especially in Rijeka, the last of the new class of dreadnoughts should have been in service by the end of 1918.[43] In contrast to the relative certainty concerning the completion of the program, the purpose of such a fleet remained a cloudy matter. During the prewar period of Haus's tenure as commander, the revival of the Triple Alliance and the prospect of alliance naval cooperation shifted the focus from competition with Italy, the traditional nemesis, to cooperation with the Italians against the Triple Entente in the Mediterranean.

THE TRIPLE ALLIANCE
NAVAL CONVENTION AND PREWAR PLANS
FOR MEDITERRANEAN COOPERATION (1913–14)

Following the renewal of the Triple Alliance in December 1912, Montecuccoli's last weeks in office witnessed the reactivation and strengthening of the Austro-German-Italian naval convention of 1900. The recent Italo-Turkish war had strained Italy's relations with the powers of the Triple Entente, especially France, while at the same time, the bitter Anglo-German naval race in the North Sea caused the British to redistribute their naval power toward home waters, leaving the French to shoulder more of the Triple Entente's responsibilities in the Mediterranean.[44] Given the poor state of Franco-Italian relations, the resulting French buildup in the western Mediterranean caused alarm in Italy. At the same time, the weaker British naval presence in the region caused some Italian policymakers to reconsider the traditional belief that they could never pursue a foreign policy in conflict with British vital interests.[45] With France as the primary rival and Britain less of a consideration than ever before, Italy took the initiative in suggesting a revival of Triple Alliance naval cooperation.

The initial Italian overture came to Vienna indirectly, by way of Berlin. In correspondence with his German counterpart, General Helmut von Moltke, the chief of the Italian army General Staff, Lieutenant General Alberto Pollio, outlined Italy's position in the event of war with France; Pollio included observations on the changing balance of power in the Mediterranean and appealed for naval talks within the alliance. Moltke was spurred on by visions of a Franco-German war in which an Austro-Italian fleet would surprise French troop convoys en route from Algeria to Toulon, depriving France of valuable reinforcements as the German army drove toward Paris. He quickly seized the initiative, sending a memorandum on the Mediterranean to Conrad von Hötzendorf, recently reinstated as chief of the Habsburg army General Staff. Meanwhile, the chief of the German *Admiralstab,* Vice Admiral August von Heeringen, raised the issue with Montecuccoli. In mid-January 1913, Francis Joseph authorized the *Marinekommandant* to open negotiations for a Triple Alliance naval convention.[46]

Even though Austria-Hungary did not take the initiative in opening the discussions, the growth of the navy had transformed the strategic balance in the Mediterranean and helped create the conditions that inspired the British redeployment decision. In 1912 British naval strategists theorized that once Austria-Hungary had two dreadnoughts in service, these plus the three *Radetzky*s would pose a danger to the British fleet at Malta, which could be cut off or defeated should war break out. Under the circumstances, the most sensible course was to scale down the force at Malta, rely on the French in the Mediterranean, and focus on the defense of home waters against the German threat.[47]

The Austro-Hungarian naval leadership also anticipated the revival of Triple Alliance naval cooperation as early as October 1912, when the

Balkan states went to war against Turkey. The operations chancellery of the *Marinesektion*, then under the leadership of the future second in command, Kailer, prepared a memorandum for Montecuccoli outlining the prospects for the Mediterranean theater of a war between the Triple Entente and Triple Alliance. The pragmatic analysis called for joint Austro-Italian naval operations if such cooperation would enable Habsburg forces to better protect the Austro-Hungarian coastline and seagoing commerce. The French fleet alone would be superior to an Austro-Italian combined fleet, but offensive operations would be feasible provided that the British Mediterranean fleet grew no stronger and the Russian Black Sea fleet remained behind the Dardanelles. Under these ideal conditions, the memorandum recommended an aggressive campaign against the enemy's naval forces, North African colonies, and Suez Canal trade. Montecuccoli agreed with Kailer's conclusions and added that upon the outbreak of such a war, an Austro-Italian fleet should assemble in the Ionian Sea in order to threaten Malta and cut off the western Mediterranean from the eastern.[48]

Thus, by the time Francis Joseph sanctioned the negotiations, the navy already was well armed with its own plans for cooperation. Conrad von Hötzendorf, who had called for a preventive war against the Italians barely a year earlier, supported the talks but remained skeptical of Italy's fidelity to the alliance; Francis Ferdinand, owing to the rigidity of his own Italophobe convictions, chose not to get involved at all. On the Italian side, it helped matters that both General Pollio and foreign minister San Giuliano were friends of the Triple Alliance; indeed, Conrad professed to have "complete trust" in Pollio, if not in Italy's political leaders. For their part, the Germans from the start were well aware that they would have to act as the go-between to open and sustain an Austro-Italian naval dialogue; they did not, however, foresee much of a future role for German warships in the Mediterranean.[49]

At the end of March 1913, a French squadron visited the British Mediterranean fleet at Malta. Amid reports of the "extraordinary enthusiasm" of the reception, Anglo-French ties appeared stronger than ever.[50] Notwithstanding the ensuing new sense of urgency, changes in the naval leadership of both Austria-Hungary and Italy delayed the start of formal talks. Shortly after Haus replaced Montecuccoli as *Marinekommandant*, the Italians announced that Vice Admiral Paolo Thaon di

Revel would replace Admiral Rocca Rey as chief of the Italian navy General Staff. After his appointment became official in April 1913, Thaon di Revel dispatched his trusted aide, Captain Angelo Ugo Conz, to Berlin and Vienna to lay the groundwork for a naval conference. A former head of Italian naval intelligence and fluent speaker of German, Conz was well suited to the task at hand, which hinged on securing Austria-Hungary's agreement to war plans that would call for its fleet to deploy in the western Mediterranean against the French. In a triangular exchange of obligations on land and sea, Italy would pay for the Austro-Hungarian naval help by committing one or more army corps to a front in southern France; this would enable the German army to divert one or more corps from the western front to the east, helping the Dual Monarchy against Russia. Conz went first to Berlin to secure German agreement to the scheme. At the same time, underscoring Italy's value to Germany on the issue dearest to Moltke's heart, Thaon di Revel ordered the first Italian naval maneuvers in years that were clearly anti-French in tone: held in the Tyrrhenian Sea, their goal was to intercept a simulated French troop convoy en route from North Africa to Toulon. Conz had little trouble winning over the Germans; he then proceeded to Vienna for an appointment with Haus.[51]

After hearing the details of the Italian grand strategy, Haus pointed out to Conz that while he personally welcomed the overture, only the chief of the General Staff, Conrad von Hötzendorf, had the authority to agree to such sweeping war plans, and he could do so only with the approval of the emperor and, informally, Francis Ferdinand. Conz promptly secured an appointment with Conrad. Despite his reluctance to trust the Italians, the chief of staff was swayed by the prospect of having more Germans standing alongside his own troops on the eastern front against Russia. On 9 May, four days after the Italian envoy arrived in Vienna, Francis Joseph endorsed the negotiation of a naval convention based on the strategic scheme that Conz had outlined. Fearing trouble from the Belvedere, Haus and Conrad appear to have made no great effort to inform Francis Ferdinand of Conz's presence in Vienna; in any event, the archduke was conveniently away on a hunting trip in Styria and did not learn of the latest turn of events until 10 May. Bardolff subsequently requested that Francis Ferdinand receive advance copies of Haus's instructions to the Austrian delegate to the forthcoming naval conference, and the archduke himself ordered all officers involved in the negotiations to be careful what they revealed to the Italians. Irritated at the *Marinesektion*'s failure to keep him informed, Francis Ferdinand admonished Haus not to withhold information from the Belvedere in the future.[52]

The conference was scheduled to open on the first of June in Vienna, in the Marxergasse building that had been home to the *Marinesektion* since 1908. In the intervening month, the operations chancellery formulated the navy's negotiating position. Haus wanted to retain the scheme of zones outlined in the dormant naval convention of December 1900, which had assigned the defense of the Baltic, North Sea, and Atlantic to Germany, the western Mediterranean to Italy, and the Adriatic to Austria-Hungary, giving Italy and Austria-Hungary joint responsibility for the eastern Mediterranean. The question of command in case of joint operations had been a thorny issue in 1900; the original convention ultimately left it to the senior officer of the country in whose zone the operations were taking place. Haus was willing to see this formula preserved, even though in the event of an Austrian deployment in the western Mediterranean, it would mean an Italian command over the Austro-Italian force. On the question of formulating a new wireless signal code for the three navies to share, the Austrians were determined to let the Germans or Italians take the initiative and keep their own techniques secret. In general, Haus would let the Italians take the lead in the discussions. Aside from the actual purpose of drafting a new naval convention, he viewed the conference as an opportunity to learn more about the strategic and tactical ideas of a traditional rival. To avoid a further clash with Francis Ferdinand, Haus forwarded his ideas to the Belvedere well before the first of June.[53]

For their part, the Italians went into the conference hoping to designate a supreme commander for all Mediterranean operations. Even though Italy would provide the majority of the ships for the proposed combined operations against France, not to mention its bases and coaling facilities, Thaon di Revel was willing to have Haus be the supreme commander. Since the Italian strategy ultimately called for compensating the Austro-Hungarian deployment outside of the Adriatic with only an additional German army corps or two against Russia in the east, he considered the appointment of Haus vital to guaranteeing Vienna's agreement to send ships to the western Mediterranean. In return, Thaon di Revel also hoped to secure concessions on other points. Considerations of rank and protocol also influenced his decision: after becoming *Marinekommandant,* Haus had been promoted to full admiral, and the Italian navy at present had no candidate for active command at such a high grade.[54]

Haus entrusted the duties of chief Austrian negotiator to Kailer's successor as head of the operations chancellery, Captain Alfred Cicoli. Born in Venice in 1866 just months before the city was ceded to Italy, Cicoli was fluent in Italian and a good match for Italy's Conz.[55] When the conference opened as scheduled in the Marxergasse, they were joined by Captain Erich Köhler of the German *Admiralstab* and Captain Alfred Saalwachter, a German navy expert on wireless signals. The hosts took great care to provide a cordial atmosphere, even changing the decor of the *Marinesektion* building. Conz noted later that "innocuous travel scenes" were hanging in place of the traditional paintings of Austria's victory over Italy in the Battle of Lissa.[56]

As soon as the talks opened, Conz shocked Cicoli with his proposal to give the joint command to Haus, but by the second day of the conference, the Austrians had accepted the offer and, in return, conceded that Haus's eventual successor in the position should be an Italian admiral. Cicoli also agreed to abandon completely the scheme of zones from the 1900 convention. The Italians also got their way on most of the details of the operational plan. While the preliminary Austrian plans called for an Austro-Italian rendezvous in the Ionian Sea, with the Italian port of Taranto as the principal base, the Italians preferred Messina, on the strait between Sicily and the tip of the Italian boot, a center of gravity two hundred miles farther away from the Adriatic and much closer to the French navy. Cicoli ultimately agreed to a rendezvous at Messina.[57]

Other Austrian concessions included the assignment of the navy's best torpedo boats to the force designated for the joint operation, the granting of a free hand to the Italians to use their pre-dreadnoughts in the Tyrrhenian Sea in whatever way they wished, and agreement that the Austrians would not have a similar freedom of action with their pre-dreadnoughts that remained behind in the Adriatic. Conz sent glowing reports of these successes to Thaon di Revel, boasting of the ease with which he had dominated the conference, not knowing that Cicoli was under orders to play his cards close to the vest and wait for Conz to tip his hand. The meetings concluded on 23 June, just over three weeks after they had begun. As the sessions were winding down, Cicoli raised the issue of the new joint code, suggesting that the Germans devise it. Conz, unaware of the importance that the Austrians attached to keeping their own wireless techniques secret, considered the issue of signals a trivial point and agreed to Cicoli's request. The representatives of all three navies left the conference satisfied with the results. Conz felt he had won a great victory for Italy, Köhler was amazed and heartened by the level of Austro-Italian cooperation, and Cicoli had played the game exactly as Haus had wanted him to. In the months that followed, the naval and political leaders of the three countries refined the agreements prior to their final ratification. The convention went into effect on 1 November 1913.[58]

An annex to the convention specified the ships that each of the allies would contribute should hostilities with the Triple Entente break out during 1914. The Austrians and Italians each were to provide three dreadnoughts, eleven pre-dreadnoughts or armored cruisers, and four scout cruisers; the Austrians would contribute eighteen destroyers and twelve torpedo boats, while the Italians would provide twenty-six destroyers and fifty-four torpedo boats. For the larger vessels, the Italians fulfilled their obligations by listing the dreadnoughts *Dante Alighieri, Giulio Cesare,* and *Leonardo da Vinci,* of which the latter two finally entered service only in May 1914; the four pre-dreadnoughts of the *Regina Elena* class (completed in 1907–8); and seven armored cruisers. Austria-Hungary, meanwhile, committed the dreadnoughts *Viribus Unitis, Tegetthoff,* and *Prinz Eugen,* although the latter would not be in commission until July 1914; nine pre-dreadnoughts (the ships of the *Radetzky* class, the *Erzherzog* class, and the old *Habsburg* class); and the armored cruisers *Sankt Georg* and *Kaiser Karl VI.* Any German ships in the Mediterranean at the outbreak of war were also to be placed under the joint command. At the end of 1913, these included the battle cruiser *Goeben,* sent to protect German interests during the Balkan Wars, and three scout cruisers.[59] The combined force would be more than strong enough to overwhelm the French. An annex to the convention stipulated that the objective of the fleet commander was "the securing of naval control in the Mediterranean through the swiftest possible defeat of the enemy fleets."[60]

In October 1913, after all of the allies had ratified the convention, Thaon di Revel sought a meeting with Haus to discuss the prospective combined operations. The *Marinekommandant,* who had been forced to miss the Vienna naval conference because of hospitalization for abdominal surgery, promptly accepted the offer, but the meeting was delayed for several weeks while plans for a secret rendezvous were worked out. Both admirals realized that the tense international atmosphere made secrecy essential; a public conference would only alarm the Triple Entente and cause diplomatic complications for their respective governments. Thaon di Revel and Haus finally agreed to meet at a hotel in Zurich, in neutral Switzerland.[61]

Prior to his departure from Vienna a week before Christmas, Haus informed Francis Joseph and Francis Ferdinand of his plans. Both agreed that the visit was necessary, the archduke only reluctantly. He cautioned Haus to reveal no secrets to the Italians, advice that offended the admiral.[62] Conz accompanied Thaon di Revel to Zurich; Haus brought with him Captain Josef Rodler, since October 1913 his personal adjutant and head of the new naval command chancellery in Pola. Strategic issues on the agenda included the Austrian fear that a quick move by the combined fleet from Messina northward into the Tyrrhenian Sea would automatically leave the rest of the Mediterranean in Anglo-French hands and expose the Adriatic to an enemy incursion. Specifically, Haus theorized that the French would move southward from Toulon, west of Corsica and Sardinia, and execute a rendezvous south of Sicily with their own North African squadron and British units from Malta. In response, Thaon di Revel could only offer to put his strategy to the test in a naval war game during the autumn 1914 maneuvers. The two admirals also agreed to give the *Goeben* and the German Mediterranean division considerable leeway in its wartime sphere of operations; they could hardly do otherwise, having not invited a German to their meeting.[63]

Other matters discussed in Zurich included details of the supply and reinforcement of Austro-Hungarian units operating in the western Mediterranean. For example, in a protracted war Haus envisioned sending relief crews to Venice and then by rail to La Spezia or some other location on the western coast of Italy, where they could replenish the manpower of his warships as they came into port. The talks ranged widely and were not limited to the projected campaign against France or an Anglo-French combination. The admirals even discussed mining the harbor of Mahón in the Balearic Islands in the event that Spain joined the Triple Entente. And because both Austria-Hungary and Italy at the time were at odds with Greece over the delineation of the Greco-Albanian border, they also addressed the issue of a blockade of the Greek coast. At the close of their secret conference, Haus and Thaon di Revel sent a joint letter to Admiral Hugo von Pohl, Heeringen's successor as chief of the German *Admiralstab*, informing him of their deliberations.[64]

Notwithstanding the Austro-Italian cooperation at the Vienna naval conference and the unprecedented Zurich meeting of the two admirals, the Germans continued to be the glue that held the Triple Alliance together, both in general terms and in the Mediterranean. Rear Admiral Wilhelm Souchon, appointed commander of the German Mediterranean division in October 1913, met with Haus and Thaon di Revel before the end of the year and in January 1914 had an audience with Victor Emmanuel in Rome. Souchon brought the *Goeben* to the upper Adriatic in March 1914, escorting the imperial yacht *Hohenzollern* and William II, who took time off from his annual cruise to Corfu for a side trip north.[65] In Trieste the German emperor disembarked for a journey by rail to Vienna and a meeting with Francis Joseph, their last, as it turned out. Returning to Trieste, William held talks with Francis Ferdinand at Miramar, Ferdinand Max's old palace, then joined the archduke for a review of the Austro-Hungarian fleet and tour of the *Viribus Unitis.* While in the upper Adriatic, the *Goeben* and *Hohenzollern* also called at Venice, where William met with Victor Emmanuel. In an effort to do his part to improve Austro-Italian relations, he invited both Francis Ferdinand and the king of Italy to German army maneuvers in the fall of 1914.[66]

In the year between the negotiation of the naval convention and the outbreak of war, the Italians sent clear signals that their affection for the Triple Alliance was in fact for a German alliance. In the late summer of 1913, Victor Emmanuel attended the Kiel Regatta, and in September Vice Admiral Luigi of Savoy, the duke of the Abruzzi, accompanied Conz to German naval maneuvers in the North Sea. The same month, Pollio attended German army maneuvers in Silesia and had cordial discussions with Moltke and Conrad von Hötzendorf; the three chiefs of staff discussed war plans, and Pollio promised to lobby Rome for a greater military commitment in a war against France, to enable him to send Italian divisions to Germany via the Austrian Tyrol as reinforcements for the German army on the Rhine.[67]

At the same time, Italy offered no similar gestures of friendship to Austria-Hungary. In April 1914, in a conversation with the German military attaché in Rome, Pollio made the rather remarkable offer of Italian aid to a Habsburg army campaign against Serbia, but the attaché suspected that such assistance would come only at a high price, probably Austria's cession of either Trieste or Italian-speaking southern Tyrol.[68] The foreign ministers Berchtold and San Giuliano held an inconclusive meeting at the Istrian resort of Abbazia (Opatija) in mid-April 1914, but there were no direct high-level discussions between naval or military officials of the two countries after the December 1913 Zurich meeting of Haus and Thaon di Revel.

Contrary to the spirit of the naval convention, the Italian navy continued to shroud its activities in secrecy and viewed Austro-Hungarian visitors with great suspicion. In the autumn of 1913, after being denied an invitation to Italian naval gunnery exercises, the Habsburg naval attaché in Rome, Prince Johannes von und zu Liechtenstein, attempted to view them from aboard a passing civilian steamer. His ingenuity led to an unpleasant brush with Italian officials, briefly stirring up speculation that he might be expelled from the country. The Austrians likewise tended to be wary of Italian visitors, but as late as March 1914, Haus's second in command, Kailer, gave permission for five Italian navy officers to tour the Whitehead torpedo factory in Rijeka.[69]

In a further manifestation of the tension between the two allies, in March 1914 it was agreed that the warship representing Italy in the international escort of Prince William of Wied from Trieste to his new Albanian throne would not enter Trieste harbor. City officials feared that the appearance of an Italian vessel would only provoke local irredentist demonstrations, and Rome recognized that the ensuing Austrian police crackdown would only stir up anti-Austrian sentiments in Italy. Ultimately the Italian ship joined the escort at sea.[70] Riots broke out anyway two months later, when Italian and Slovene workers clashed in the Trieste May Day celebration. After the press in Italy depicted the Italian workers as victims of the Slovenes and the Austrian police, anti-Austrian sentiment erupted in several Italian cities. In Naples a mob stormed the Austrian consulate, while in Rome violent student protests forced the university to close for several days.[71] Watching the demonstrations in Rome, naval attaché Liechtenstein had good reason to doubt that Italy's government could ever lead the country to war on the side of the Dual Monarchy.[72]

The Germans, despite their cordial relations with both alliance partners, likewise wondered how well things would work in the event of war. The *Admiralstab* in Berlin suspected that Austria-Hungary would be reluctant to use its fleet in operations far from the Adriatic. Regarding the Italians, Moltke placed little faith in Pollio's promised help on land against France. In internal memoranda, the Italians themselves conceded that their army would distract few French troops from the Rhine frontier opposite Germany. Indeed, an amphibious assault on the Riviera would take so long to organize that the Germans were likely to be in Paris before the troops ever landed.[73]

As for the primary target of the projected naval cooperation, the French learned of the Triple Alliance naval convention in October 1913, before it even went into effect, thanks to an intercepted Italian diplomatic dispatch. When questioned by the French ambassador in Rome, San Giuliano acknowledged that the leaders of the Italian armed forces, like their counterparts across Europe, were preparing for various scenarios, but gave assurances that the Triple Alliance was still purely a defensive pact.[74] He was, of course, correct in stating that the alliance was defensive and that Italy's relationship with its allies had remained unchanged: in the event of an unprovoked French attack on Germany, Italy was pledged to come to the aid of Germany; in the event of an unprovoked French attack on Italy, Germany and Austria-Hungary were to come to the aid of Italy. Supplementary accords such as the naval convention would be relevant only after the casus foederis had been satisfied.

German and Austro-Hungarian military and naval leaders, oblivious to the limited nature of the authority of their Italian counterparts, doubtless would have been shocked at San Giuliano's remarks to the

French ambassador. Unlike its two alliance partners, Italy was a true constitutional monarchy in which a responsible ministry reflecting a majority in the lower house of parliament actually ran the government. Career soldiers or sailors such as Pollio and Thaon di Revel could generate plans to their hearts' content but could not determine policy. Pollio's statements and actions indicate that he had no idea of how narrowly defined the casus foederis of the alliance actually was, and in this regard he had much company among army and navy leaders. Indeed, Italian foreign ministers always considered the exact text of the Triple Alliance to be the dearest of state secrets, and San Giuliano was no exception.[75]

In the same way, Pollio and Thaon di Revel did not keep their political bosses, the war and navy ministers, informed of their war plans; ministerial offices, after all, changed hands frequently with the rise and fall of cabinets, and it would be imprudent for so many people to have knowledge of the most sensitive military and naval plans.[76] As in any constitutional system, too often the right hand was unaware of what the left hand was doing. The Italians responsible for initiating the negotiations for a naval convention and eventually hammering out the terms—Pollio, Thaon di Revel, and, specifically, Conz—operated strictly in a world of strategy and tactics, out of the loop of Italian diplomacy, not fully aware of just how conditional their "commitments" to Germany and Austria-Hungary actually were.

While it remained to be seen what would happen to the naval convention in a major European war, the plans began to generate a reality of their own. The special credit of May 1914, providing 426.8 million kronen to fund Haus's building program, included money for the dramatic expansion of facilities at Sebenico that would be necessary to extend the range of the fleet into the Mediterranean.[77] The navy also repainted many of its warships from the dark green suitable for camouflage in the Adriatic to the light gray used by the other powers for vessels operating in the open waters of the Mediterranean. Meanwhile, the Germans completed the new Triple Alliance signal code, all three navies exchanged intelligence on the British and French fleets, and on Sicily the Italians even stockpiled coal for the Austro-Hungarian navy at Augusta, south of Messina, as prescribed in the convention's operational plan.[78]

The naval convention naturally poisoned Italian and Austro-Hungarian relations with France, but it did not appear to affect their ties with Britain, which remained on remarkably cordial terms with Austria-Hungary to the eleventh hour. Between 4 and 18 May, the British battle cruisers *Indomitable* and *Inflexible* visited Trieste, accompanied by five smaller escorts. Later that month, the dreadnoughts *Viribus Unitis* and *Tegetthoff* returned the visit at Malta, leaving on 28 May, exactly one month before Sarajevo and two months before the first shots of the war.[79]

THE NAVY, THE JULY CRISIS
OF 1914, AND THE ONSET OF WAR

In late June 1914, Francis Ferdinand and his personal entourage left Vienna to attend army maneuvers in Bosnia-Hercegovina. The archduke's itinerary called for him to visit Sarajevo, the Bosnian capital, with his wife, Sophie, after the maneuvers ended. On 24 June, he boarded the *Viribus Unitis* at Trieste for a brief cruise down the Dalmatian coast to the mouth of the Narenta River; there, he transferred to the yacht *Dalmat*, which steamed upstream into the interior of Hercegovina. After disembarking and observing the three days of maneuvers, Francis Ferdinand proceeded to Sarajevo and a reunion with Sophie, who had come from Vienna by rail. On 28 June, while riding through the Bosnian capital in an open car, they were shot and killed by the young Serbian radical, Gavrilo Princip.[80]

The bodies of Francis Ferdinand and his consort were transported from Sarajevo to the Neretva, where the *Dalmat* had been waiting for the archduke to return. Downriver, the two caskets were transferred to the *Viribus Unitis*. Upon receiving word of the assassination, Haus raced from Pola to the mouth of the Narenta aboard the yacht *Lacroma*, escorted by the dreadnought *Tegetthoff*, the scout cruiser *Admiral Spaun*, and every torpedo boat that was ready to put to sea. The hastily assembled escort fleet was on hand in time to witness the transfer of the bodies to the *Viribus Unitis;* thereafter, the entire force moved slowly up the coast to Trieste, remaining within sight of land much of the way. As the sad convoy passed coastal villages and towns, church bells intoned somber salutes and local inhabitants lined the shore to pay their respects.[81]

The assassination of Francis Ferdinand touched off a month of intense diplomatic activity during the so-called July Crisis, the particulars of which will forever provide material for lively debate among historians. After Serbia rejected the Austro-Hungarian ultimatum of 23 July, the Dual Monarchy declared war on 28 July. The ensuing chain reaction of declarations of war brought most of Europe into the conflict by mid-August. The turn of events certainly would have chagrined the late heir to the throne. He had been a war hawk as recently as the fall of 1912, during the First Balkan War, but by the time of the second Balkan flare-up in the summer of 1913 he stood firmly against a belligerent policy, concluding that at least in the short run, war would bring the Dual Monarchy nothing but grief. Ironically, in a meeting with Haus in January 1914, Francis Ferdinand had predicted that a general European war would not break out until the end of 1918 or early 1919.[82]

Not surprisingly, the July Crisis strained the relationship between Vienna and Budapest, as the Hungarian government seized the opportunity to assert a degree of national sovereignty. As the crisis unfolded and a general war appeared increasingly likely, the countries of Europe began to exchange diplomatic notes precisely defining their territorial waters. When Berchtold proposed to the council of ministers that the Dual Monarchy issue a declaration regarding the Adriatic coast, the Hungarian ministers rejected the wording "Austro-Hungarian monarchy," insisting instead upon a definition of separate Austrian and Hungarian territorial waters. While the Hungarian Delegation had discussed the issue of separate Austrian and Hungarian squadrons within the navy almost on an annual basis, such resolutions had taken on a pro forma character; the question of actually dividing the territorial waters had never been raised. A compromise solution ultimately dodged the issue. Maintaining a common front before the rest of the world, the notes from Vienna to the other capitals referred to the waters of "both states of the Austro-Hungarian monarchy."[83]

Throughout the July Crisis, Haus remained in Pola, while Kailer represented the navy in Vienna. When called upon to do so, the second in command joined Conrad von Hötzendorf in presenting the views of the armed forces in the council of ministers. On 18 July, Haus received orders to mobilize the navy for a Balkan war, and on 22 July he sent the *Radetzky* and its two sister ships to Cattaro, which had been guarded only by the old harbor watch *Kronprinz Rudolf* and lighter craft. The

battleships were withdrawn to Pola less than two weeks later, after Cattaro was reinforced by a torpedo flotilla (destroyers and torpedo boats)
and a seaplane detachment. On 23 July, the day of the fateful ultimatum
to Serbia, Haus mobilized the river monitors of the Danube flotilla. On
the night of 28–29 July, just hours after the Austro-Hungarian declaration of war, the monitors *Temes*, *Bodrog*, and *Szamos* bombarded Belgrade. Their shots were the first fired by naval vessels in the First World
War.[84]

As Haus implemented the prescribed Balkan mobilization, he was
preoccupied with the position of Italy and the prospects for an activation of the Triple Alliance naval convention. Unfortunately for the
alliance, in recent months Austro-Italian relations again had taken a
turn for the worse. The Delegations' approval of Haus's program in the
spring of 1914 and their grant of the special credit of 426.8 million kronen caused considerable anxiety in Italy.[85] It did not help matters that
this news came on the heels of the well-publicized May Day riots in
Trieste. On the diplomatic front, Austro-Italian cooperation in Albania
had held up through two Balkan wars but was breaking down by the
summer of 1914. Berchtold suspected that Italy secretly was inciting the
Muslim rebel movement that sought to overthrow the shaky regime of
William of Wied, on the grounds that he was too pro-Austrian.[86]

The navy's buildup at Cattaro at the end of the third week of July
caused further concern in Italy. Over the winter of 1913–14, the Italians had feared that Austria-Hungary would try to buy or annex the
Mount Lovčen area of Montenegro; the region bordered the Bocche di
Cattaro, and Montenegrin batteries on the mountain overshadowed the
navy base below, seriously compromising its security. The elimination
of Mount Lovčen as a potential hostile factor would make the bay a safe
anchorage and open the way for Austria-Hungary to station more, and
larger, warships there.[87] Italian fears of an Austrian preventive strike
against Montenegro escalated after the murder of Francis Ferdinand.
On 10 July, San Giuliano told the German ambassador in Rome that to
compensate for an Austrian annexation of Mount Lovčen, Italy would
have to receive the entire Italian-speaking South Tyrol. Any lesser compensation, or no compensation at all, would be unacceptable. In the words
of the foreign minister, the issue was explosive enough to lead "not only
[to] the end of the Triple Alliance but war between Italy and Austria."[88]

Such a statement, coming from a man considered to be a friend of the Triple Alliance, certainly did not bode well for its future. To make matters worse, General Pollio died of a heart attack just three days after the assassination of Francis Ferdinand; pro-German if not pro-Austrian, the chief of the General Staff had been the leading friend of the alliance within the Italian army hierarchy.[89] Meanwhile, on the naval side, Italian admirals continued to act as if the plans for Austro-Italian naval cooperation would indeed go into effect. In the waters off Albania, the local Italian commander kept his Austrian counterpart "confidentially" informed of Italian warship movements until mid-July,[90] and as late as 29 July, Thaon di Revel gave a warm reception to the Austrian naval attaché, Prince Liechtenstein, passing along information on the war readiness of Italy's dreadnoughts and the status of coal stocks designated for use by the Habsburg fleet. Such reports naturally raised Haus's spirits, but his hopes were dashed on 31 July when he received word via Vienna that San Giuliano had characterized Austria-Hungary's declaration of war on Serbia as an act of aggression, the consequences of which would not activate the casus foederis of the Triple Alliance. The same day, Austria-Hungary declared a general mobilization, responding to the Russian mobilization of the previous day; on 1 August, both France and Germany mobilized their forces, and Germany declared war on Russia. Liechtenstein cabled home reports of Italy's rapid drift toward neutrality, which became official on 2 August. It was of little consolation that Turkey on the same day concluded an alliance with Germany and Austria-Hungary. The German invasion of Belgium and declaration of war on France came on 3 August, leading to Britain's entry into the war on the following day. On the morning of the fourth, the German battle cruiser *Goeben* fired the first shots of the war in the Mediterranean, shelling the French Algerian port of Philippeville.[91]

Of all the Triple Alliance naval forces in the theater, the German Mediterranean division, which in the summer of 1914 consisted of the 24,500-ton *Goeben* and light cruiser *Breslau,* had attracted the most prewar attention from the French and British. Supposedly capable of a remarkable twenty-eight knots, the *Goeben* had held the honor of being both the largest and fastest warship in the Mediterranean since its deployment there in 1912, fresh from the shipyard, after the outbreak of the Balkan Wars. But the *Goeben's* assignment to active duty immediately after its initial sea trials turned out to be premature; it suffered from defective boiler tubes and failed to reach its advertised top speed while in the Mediterranean. Rear Admiral Souchon kept the difficulties with his flagship's engines a closely guarded secret, however, and the British and French never suspected that the *Goeben*'s capabilities were impaired.[92]

In the spring of 1914, Souchon made arrangements to have the *Goeben* relieved in early October by the battle cruiser *Moltke,* but the assassination of Francis Ferdinand changed his plans. Fearing that a general war would prevent the scheduled exchange from taking place, he received permission from Haus to put in at the Pola Arsenal. During July, representatives of the original German engine manufacturer supervised the repair of the defective boiler tubes. The *Goeben* left Pola as the war began and on 2 August entered Messina, the designated rendezvous point for Triple Alliance forces. Souchon was greeted with the news of Italy's neutrality and promptly left for his raid on the Algerian coast, anticipating the onset of hostilities with France.[93]

The saga of the *Goeben* and its escort *Breslau,* and their dash to the sanctuary of the Dardanelles, no doubt was the most dramatic story of the early war in the Mediterranean. But during the days when the fate of the *Goeben* was still in doubt, the issue of the deployment of Austro-Hungarian warships either to save the German battle cruiser or join it in a bold run for the Black Sea caused the first serious clash between the strategists of the two allies.[94] The controversy began when Souchon, after learning of the British declaration of war on Germany, abandoned the Algerian coast and returned to Messina. Blockaded there by British units from Malta, on 5 August he sent a cable to Pola pleading for Austrian help. The appeal placed Haus in a dilemma, since Germany was at war with both Britain and France but thus far neither power had declared war on Austria-Hungary; indeed, Austro-Russian hostilities did not even become official until the following day. In any event, Haus was not inclined to risk the fleet for the sake of saving the German battle cruiser and its small escort. While his own forces, supplemented by the *Goeben* and *Breslau,* would have been more than a match for the British Mediterranean fleet, the untimely appearance of French warships would have spelled disaster, and by the time Souchon's telegram arrived, Haus already knew that French units had left Toulon and Corsica on 4 August, heading southward. But the *Marinekommandant* could not simply ignore Souchon's call for help, especially after it was repeated, via Berlin, directly to Vienna. Haus then justified staying in port by pointing to simple problems of geography and speed. The bulk of his fleet was at Pola, five hundred eighty miles from Messina, much farther away from the *Goeben* than either the French or British fleets. Furthermore, even with lingering engine problems, the German battle cruiser still was a few knots faster than the Austrian dreadnoughts and *Radetzkys*; if the *Goeben*'s goal was merely to flee from the enemy threat, a battleship escort would only slow it down.[95]

Souchon slipped out of Messina on 6 August and headed for the mouth of the Adriatic with his former blockaders in hot pursuit. Berlin issued a modified appeal for Austrian help, calling for Haus to come as far south as Brindisi, on the boot heel of the Italian peninsula, for a rendezvous with the *Goeben* and *Breslau*. Assuming that Souchon would seek sanctuary in the Adriatic, on 7 August Haus hastened southward with a formidable force: the dreadnoughts *Viribus Unitis, Tegetthoff,* and *Prinz Eugen,* the *Radetzky* and its sister ships *Erzherzog Franz Ferdinand* and *Zrinyi,* the armored cruiser *Sankt Georg,* the scout cruiser *Admiral Spaun,* six destroyers, and thirteen torpedo boats. It was a risky venture for the same reason that Haus, two days earlier, had not wanted to go to Messina. The Austro-Hungarian fleet and the two German warships were capable of defeating the British, but a joint Anglo-French force would have overwhelmed them. As it turned out, the sortie came to an abrupt end before the ships were halfway down the Adriatic. On the afternoon of the seventh, the German *Admiralstab* sent word that Souchon's move toward the mouth of the Adriatic on the previous day had been a diversion and that the *Goeben* and *Breslau* already had rounded Cape Matapan in southern Greece en route to the Dardanelles, the Black Sea, and future action against the Russian navy. The Germans also offered the advice that by following Souchon's lead and running for the Black Sea, the Austro-Hungarian fleet would perform its greatest service to the common cause. Haus ordered his ships back to Pola.[96]

Ironically, the harebrained notion that the battle fleet should abandon the Adriatic in favor of the Black Sea actually originated in Vienna. Rear Admiral Erwin Raisp von Caliga, the navy's representative to the army high command (*Armeeoberkommando*) from the start of the war until his death in October 1915, raised the idea on 4 August on his own initiative. A furious Haus dismissed it the next day as soon as he learned of it. Even Conrad von Hötzendorf, who ultimately would criticize the navy's reluctance to take risks, hesitated before presenting Raisp's bold plan to Berchtold. Much to Haus's dismay, the foreign minister, eager to pressure Bulgaria and Romania into joining the Central Powers against Russia, concluded that an Austrian naval deployment in the Black Sea would serve his diplomatic efforts perfectly, all the more so since the Germans loved the idea.[97]

On 8 August, after returning with the fleet to Pola, Haus moved quickly to quash the whole scheme. He pointed out that there was no guarantee that the fleet could make it to the Black Sea from the Adriatic without being intercepted by a superior Anglo-French force, and even if it deployed there, it would be able to return to home waters only after the end of the war. Furthermore, of the Turkish ports on the Black Sea, Constantinople alone had the basic facilities to support a fleet, and it was too far from the Russian coastline to serve as a base for offensive operations. Haus also argued that if Austria-Hungary's Adriatic coast were left virtually defenseless, the prospect of easy conquests in the littoral inevitably would tempt Italy to join the Entente, with disastrous consequences for the Dual Monarchy. The German naval attaché subsequently came to Pola to plead the case for a Black Sea deployment. The Germans reduced their request first to include only the three pre-dreadnoughts of the *Radetzky* class, then to just two warships, but Haus refused to budge. A frustrated Berchtold confided in Conrad that he was "very disturbed" over the *Marinekommandant*'s intransigence.[98]

The Germans hoped that Haus's attitude would change after Britain and France finally declared war on Austria-Hungary on 12 August, but the certainty of a hostile encounter with Anglo-French forces en route to the Dardanelles only made the *Marinekommandant* all the more certain of the foolishness of the idea. Haus's responses to the plight of the *Goeben* and to the suggestion of a Black Sea deployment confirmed prewar German doubts about the navy's willingness to send significant forces outside of the Adriatic. At one point, their frustrated attaché in Vienna complained arrogantly to Conrad that no German warship would remain in port when there was an enemy to be defeated at sea. In time, owing to the wartime inactivity of their own High Seas

Fleet, the hypocrisy of German appeals for Austro-Hungarian naval action would become increasingly apparent.[99]

On 13 August 1914, the senior Entente commander in the Mediterranean, Vice Admiral Augustin Boué de Lapeyrère, received word of the declarations of war on Austria-Hungary along with orders to proceed immediately into the Adriatic with as many French and British warships as possible. He was instructed to take care to pass within sight of the Italian coast, in case Italy needed any further persuasion to remain neutral, and to proceed against the Austrian target of his choice. He selected the ships blockading the small Adriatic foothold of Montenegro, which had declared war on the Dual Monarchy a week earlier. When the first shots were exchanged on the sixteenth, the war at sea finally began for the Austro-Hungarian navy, almost three weeks after the Danube monitors had fired their initial salvoes at Belgrade.[100]

On the eve of the conflict in 1914, the admirals, like the generals, did not believe war would last long. The cult of the offensive and the quest for "one big battle" to decide an entire campaign had colored the strategic thinking of navies as well as armies. Just as the German Schlieffen plan envisioned knocking out the French in another Sedan, Haus dreamed of a Trafalgar in the western Mediterranean in which a Triple Alliance fleet would defeat a French or Anglo-French force; at the least, in an Austro-Italian war, he could expect another Lissa. But by mid-August 1914, the navy found itself in almost the worst possible scenario, standing alone against the combination of Britain and France. The only greater nightmare would be an enemy coalition of Britain, France, and Italy.

NOTES

1. Gebhard, "Austro-Hungarian Navy," 225–226.
2. Quoted in ibid, 226. See also Wagner, "Die obersten Behörden," 87.
3. Montecuccoli to Min. des Äussern, Vienna, 26 December 1912, HHSA, AR, F 44 - Marinewesen, Carton 4: Auskünfte 1/4, refers to the Dutch inquiry; the commander's reference to ammunition being included as part of the deal indicates that the battleships under discussion must have been the *Monarchs*. In the Uruguayan scheme, Kneissler to Min. des Äussern, Vienna, 22 October 1908, ibid., Carton 10: Varia 2/41, offers the *Rudolf* for 5 million kronen, *Stephanie* for 4 million, and *Tegetthoff* for 4.5 million.

4.	Gebhard, "Austro-Hungarian Navy," 235–36; Wagner, "Die obersten Behörden," 89. Unlike the navy officer corps, the army corps had always been overwhelmingly German. According to the official statistics, in 1911 Germans accounted for 76.1 percent of all active career officers, compared to 10.7 percent for the Magyars; if reserve officers are also counted, the figures were 68.6 percent and 16.1 percent, respectively. See *Militärstatistisches Jahrbuch*, 1911. On the validity of the official statistics, see Deák, *Beyond Nationalism*, 178–85; and Sondhaus, "Austro-Hungarian Naval Officer Corps," 57–58.

5.	Wagner, "Die obersten Behörden," 89.

6.	Cf. rosters of naval officers in the *Militär-Schematismus* (1871) and the *Almanach für die k.u.k. Kriegsmarine* (1881, 1891, 1901).

7.	Wagner, "Die obersten Behörden," 90–91.

8.	For a biographical sketch of Haus, see Heinrich Bayer von Bayersburg, *Unter der k.u.k. Kriegsflagge*, 7–12.

9.	On Haus's criticism of his peers, see Koudelka, *Denn Österreich lag einst am Meer*, 161; according to Koudelka, Haus's detractors considered him an egomaniac. Gottfried von Banfield, *Der Adler von Triest*, 26, confirms that Haus was well-liked by junior officers. Banfield, a flying ace in the First World War, was a lieutenant at the time of Haus's promotion to commander.

10.	Gebhard, "Austro-Hungarian Navy," 249.

11.	Koudelka, *Denn Österreich lag einst am Meer*, 161. Kunsti, born in 1854 at Ferrara in the Papal State, was the son of a Habsburg army colonel killed in the war of 1866. He graduated from the naval academy in Rijeka in 1871. See Bayer von Bayersburg, *Österreichs Admirale*, 27–28.

12.	On Ripper's view of Haus, see Koudelka, *Denn Österreich lag einst am Meer*, 161.

13.	Wagner, "Die obersten Behörden," 92–93.

14.	Sokol, *Des Kaisers Seemacht*, 237.

15.	Data from *Almanach für die k.u.k. Kriegsmarine* (1915).

16.	Figures from *Jahresbericht der k.u.k. Kriegsmarine* (1905), 96–97; (1913), 124–25. Under normal circumstances, as many as 75–80 percent of seamen on active duty would be aboard ship during the summer months; the share would fall to around two thirds in the winter. During the mobilization of early 1913, over 80 percent of those on active duty were aboard ship.

17.	See Rothenberg, *The Army of Francis Joseph*, 165.

18.	Figures from *Jahresbericht der k.u.k. Kriegsmarine* (1911), 142; (1913), 127. See also Höbelt, "Die Marine," 742.

19.	Wagner, "Die obersten Behörden," 93–94.

20.	Ibid., 96–98; Höbelt, "Die Marine," 738. On the close friendship of Haus and Kailer, see Gebhard, "Austro-Hungarian Navy," 250.

21.	See Rothenberg, *The Army of Francis Joseph*, 170.

22.	Paul G. Halpern, *The Naval War in the Mediterranean, 1914–1918*, 15.

23.	Vego, "Anatomy," 307–17, gives the most detailed account of the Scutari affair. See also Williamson, *Origins*, 135–40; and Sokol, *Des Kaisers Seemacht*, 254–56. The international squadron included two Italian pre-dreadnoughts, a British pre-dreadnought and light cruiser, a French armored cruiser, and a German light cruiser. Even though Austria-Hungary provided the bulk of the warships, the Italians insisted that a British admiral be named overall commander of the force.

24.	Seton-Watson, *Liberalism to Fascism*, 399.

25. On the navy's Albanian operations in 1914, see Sokol, *Des Kaisers Seemacht*, 258–66.

26. Halpern, *Mediterranean Naval Situation*, 170; Gebhard, "Austro-Hungarian Navy," 252–53.

27. Williamson, "Franz Ferdinand," 426; Halpern, *Mediterranean Naval Situation*, 176–77; Gebhard, "Austro-Hungarian Navy," 253.

28. Halpern, *Mediterranean Naval Situation*, 177–78.

29. *StPD*, XLVIII (16 December 1913), 288–89.

30. Horst F. Mayer, "Die k.u.k. Kriegsmarine 1912–1914 unter dem Kommando von Admiral Anton Haus," 71; Gebhard, "Austro-Hungarian Navy," 266n.

31. Leuthner's remarks are in *StPD*, XLIX (28 May 1914), 532–39.

32. Ibid., 540.

33. Ibid., 545.

34. Reiter, "Entwicklung," 162–63.

35. *StPD*, XLIX (28 May 1914), 546, 548. Number of Skoda workers cited in Weber, "Die wirtschaftliche Entwicklung Cisleithaniens," 115.

36. Vego, "Anatomy," 322n.

37. *StPD*, XLIX (28 May 1914), 550–51.

38. Lecher quoted in *Neue Freie Presse*, 27 May 1914 (evening edition), 5; see also ibid., 29 May 1914, 1; Mayer, "Die k.u.k. Kriegsmarine 1912–1914," 73, 84.

39. Quoted in ibid., 26 May 1914, 13.

40. Halpern, *Mediterranean Naval Situation*, 178; Vego, "Anatomy," 2:399. For a biography of Pitzinger, see Bayer von Bayersburg, *Österreichs Admirale*, 136–38.

41. Greger, *Austro-Hungarian Warships*, 25. On the strikes at the Stabilimento Tecnico, see Cattaruzza, "Organisierter Konflikt," 350.

42. Gebhard, "Austro-Hungarian Navy," 251.

43. Halpern, *Mediterranean Naval Situation*, 179.

44. In March 1912, First Lord of the Admiralty Winston Churchill informed the House of Commons that the British dreadnoughts at Malta would be moved to Gibraltar to be closer to the British Isles in case of emergency; the old Gibraltar squadron was to return to home waters. See Samuel R. Williamson, Jr., *The Politics of Grand Strategy: Britain and France Prepare for War, 1904–1914*, 265–66. The redistribution of the burden in the Mediterranean was finally confirmed in a secret Anglo-French naval agreement of March 1913; see ibid., 320–25. Halpern, *Mediterranean Naval Situation*, 148–49, criticizes this "somewhat hazy plan" and the absence of greater Anglo-French prewar cooperation in the Mediterranean.

45. Bosworth, *The Least of the Great Powers*, 268.

46. Halpern, *Mediterranean Naval Situation*, 226–27, 229–31.

47. Ibid., 31, 45–46. Britain ultimately chose to cover the Mediterranean station with four battle cruisers and an assortment of pre-dreadnought battleships and smaller vessels.

48. Ibid., 228–29.

49. On Conrad's view of Pollio, see *Aus meiner Dienstzeit*, 3:153. Pollio had served as Italian military attaché in Vienna during the 1880s and had a Viennese wife. San Giuliano was the founding vice president of the Italian Navy League before the turn of the century; an old Francophobe, he had always considered France to be Italy's primary rival at sea. See also Halpern, *Mediterranean Naval Situation*, 226, 231–34; and Bosworth, *The Least of the Great Powers*, 74.

50. HHSA, AR, F 44 - Marinewesen, Carton 13: Kriegsschiffe Frankreich 65, includes detailed reports and press clippings from the Austro-Hungarian consul in Malta regarding the visit of the French squadron, which lasted from 30 March to 3 April.

51. Halpern, *Mediterranean Naval Situation*, 202, 242–44.

52. Ibid., 244–47.

53. Ibid., 247–48.

54. Ibid., 248.

55. For a biographical sketch of Cicoli, see Bayer von Bayersburg, *Österreichs Admirale*, 45–47. Cicoli had just returned from commanding the cruiser *Kaiser Franz Joseph I* on the East Asian station from 1910 until early 1913. See Sokol, *Des Kaisers Seemacht*, 230–31.

56. Halpern, *Mediterranean Naval Situation*, 249–50.

57. Ibid., 249–51.

58. Ibid., 251–53. For a complete text of the convention, see Alfred Francis Pribram, ed., *The Secret Treaties of Austria-Hungary*, 1:282–305.

59. Halpern, *Mediterranean Naval Situation*, 255–56.

60. Quoted in ibid., 254.

61. Ibid., 256. On 9 June 1913, Haus had surgery to remove part of his large intestine and a benign stomach tumor. Ibid., 251.

62. Ibid., and Höbelt, "Die Marine," 720.

63. Halpern, *Mediterranean Naval Situation*, 256–58.

64. Ibid., 257–58.

65. Ibid., 265–66; Sokol, *Des Kaisers Seemacht*, 247.

66. Kiszling, *Erzherzog Franz Ferdinand*, 272–74; Sokol, *Des Kaisers Seemacht*, 247.

67. Halpern, *Mediterranean Naval Situation*, 262–63, 269.

68. Ibid., 270.

69. Ibid., 277; Kailer to Min. des Äussern, Vienna, 1 March 1914, HHSA, AR, F 44 - Marinewesen, Carton 6: Besuche Italien 2/1.

70. Halpern, *Mediterranean Naval Situation*, 278. Koudelka, promoted to rear admiral and district commander (*Seebezirkskommandant*) of Trieste in the summer of 1913, disagreed with the governor, Prince Conrad Hohenlohe, over the seriousness of the irredentist threat in the city. See Koudelka, *Denn Österreich lag einst am Meer*, 181–83.

71. Kiszling, *Erzherzog Franz Ferdinand*, 278–79; Seton-Watson, *Liberalism to Fascism*, 409.

72. Halpern, *Mediterranean Naval Situation*, 277.

73. Ibid., 267–73 passim.

74. Ibid., 273–74.

75. Ibid., 223–24.

76. Ibid., 239.

77. Gebhard, "Austro-Hungarian Navy," 265.

78. Halpern, *Mediterranean Naval Situation*, 260–61, 275, 278–79. The German edition of the Triple Alliance naval code (the *Triplecodex*) was completed by the summer of 1914, but its translation into Italian was still in progress at the outbreak of war.

79. Koudelka, *Denn Österreich lag einst am Meer*, 195–200, provides a detailed account of the British visit; as *Seebezirkskommandant* in Trieste, he was the host. In addition to visiting Malta, the *Viribus Unitis* and *Tegetthoff* cruised the eastern Mediterranean, putting in at Smyrna, Beirut, Alexandria, and other ports. See Aichelburg, et al., *Die "Tegetthoff"- Klasse*, 4.

80. On Francis Ferdinand's last cruise aboard an Austro-Hungarian warship, see Sokol, *Des Kaisers Seemacht,* 281; and Bardolff, *Soldat im alten Österreich,* 181.

81. Sokol, *Des Kaisers Seemacht,* 281–82.

82. Ibid., 282. On Francis Ferdinand and the Balkan Wars, and on his subsequent role as an advocate of a less belligerent foreign policy, see Williamson, "Franz Ferdinand," 429–33.

83. HHSA, AR, F 44 - Marinewesen, Carton 14: Kriegsschiffe 2/1, contains documentation of this thorny debate.

84. Wulff, *Donauflottille,* 31–32.

85. Seton-Watson, *Liberalism to Fascism,* 408–9.

86. Ibid., 405.

87. Bridge, *Sadowa to Sarajevo,* 365.

88. Seton-Watson, *Liberalism to Fascism,* 409.

89. On the death of Pollio, see Halpern, *Mediterranean Naval Situation,* 270.

90. HHSA, AR, F 44 - Marinewesen, Carton 13: Kriegsschiffe Italien 37, includes documentation of the sharing of such information from as late as 4 July 1914, covering Italian movements for the subsequent two weeks.

91. Halpern, *Naval War in the Mediterranean,* 13, 16.

92. Ibid., 12–13.

93. Ibid.

94. On the stormy relationship between the two allies, see Gerard E. Silberstein, *The Troubled Alliance: German-Austrian Relations, 1914 to 1917;* Gary W. Shanafelt, *The Secret Enemy: Austria-Hungary and the German Alliance, 1914–1918;* and Holger Herwig, "Disjointed Allies: Coalition Warfare in Berlin and Vienna, 1914," 265–80.

95. Egon Pflügl (consul) to Min. des Äussern, Naples, 4 August 1914 (cipher telegram), HHSA, AR, F 44 - Marinewesen, Carton 13: Kriegsschiffe Frankreich, Kriegs-Operationen 2, reports a French squadron leaving Corsica on the morning of the fourth "with orders to intercept Austro-Hungarian and German ships." On the same morning, the bulk of the French fleet left Toulon. See also Halpern, *Naval War in the Mediterranean,* 17–18.

96. Hans Hugo Sokol, *Österreich-Ungarns Seekrieg, 1914–18,* 1:68–69.

97. Conrad von Hötzendorf, *Aus meiner Dienstzeit,* 4:174. Raisp, born in 1862, graduated from the naval academy at Rijeka in 1881 in the bottom third of his class. He was promoted to rear admiral in November 1913 in the prewar "youth movement" instigated by Francis Ferdinand.

98. Ibid., 4:179; Halpern, *Naval War in the Mediterranean,* 19–21. The text of Haus to *Armeeoberkommando,* Pola, [8 August 1914], is quoted at length in Sokol, *Österreich-Ungarns Seekrieg,* 1:73–74.

99. Halpern, *Naval War in the Mediterranean,* 18, 20. By 12 August, Conrad had accepted Haus's objections to the Black Sea scheme, specifically the logistical arguments and the threat of an Italian attack in the Adriatic. See Conrad von Hötzendorf, *Aus meiner Dienstzeit,* 4:205–6.

100. Halpern, *Naval War in the Mediterranean,* 27–28.

CHAPTER 7 ≋

THE NAVY AT WAR
IN THE HAUS ERA

Within days of the assassination at Sarajevo, Francis Joseph dissolved the Military Chancellery of Francis Ferdinand. With remarkable speed, imperial officials invaded the Belvedere, boxing up and sealing all files for storage in the imperial archives. Bardolff and other officers from the archduke's staff were in the field with their former regiments by the time the fighting began in August. The navy would be dogged by controversy in wartime even more so than in peacetime and would sorely miss its powerful patron and the services of the Belvedere. In the first days, Haus was already at loggerheads with Berchtold and the foreign ministry; Conrad von Hötzendorf and other army leaders soon would join the critics of the fleet's relative inactivity.

Meanwhile, within the alliance of the Central Powers, the friction between Haus and the German naval hierarchy continued at disturbing levels, while the *Marinekommandant* tried to pursue a war against the Anglo-French alliance, a war the navy had not been prepared to fight and could not win. It was a bleak scenario, but not completely hopeless. Owing to the British focus on the North Sea, the French navy would provide most of the opposition for the fleet, and thanks to the prewar naval buildup, Austria-Hungary at least could deny France control of the Adriatic. The Dual Monarchy still could not compete on even terms with a naval power of the first rank, but the gap was far smaller than it had been the last time Austria and France went to war, fifty-five years earlier, before the construction of the first Habsburg ironclad fleet. In the war of 1859, the army had to devote precious manpower to guard against an enemy landing in the littoral of the upper Adriatic.[1] At least that would never be the case during the First World War.

"I CONSIDER IT MY FIRST DUTY
TO KEEP OUR FLEET INTACT":
HAUS AND THE FRENCH WAR (1914–15)

The mobilization for war brought unprecedented numbers of men into active naval service. By the end of August, some 28,000 sailors manned the battle fleet and warships designated for coastal defense. Supplementing the cohort of officers and cadets were the young men of the naval academy's class of 1915, mustered out a year early.[2] The battle fleet included twelve battleships, three armored and five unarmored cruisers, eighteen destroyers, twenty-eight torpedo boats, and six submarines, supported by seven auxiliary vessels and a dozen merchant steamers, most of them requisitioned from the Lloyd for use as colliers.[3] On the navy's initial order of battle, the First Battle Squadron, under the command of Vice Admiral Njegovan, consisted of Haus's flagship, *Viribus Unitis*, and the other completed dreadnoughts *Tegetthoff* and *Prinz Eugen* (designated the First Battle Division), along with the *Radetzky* and its sister ships *Zrinyi* and *Erzherzog Franz Ferdinand* (the Second Battle Division). The Second Battle Squadron, under Rear Admiral Franz Löfler, consisted of six older battleships: the *Erzherzog Karl*, *Erzherzog Friedrich*, and *Erzherzog Ferdinand Max* (Third Battle Division), along with the *Habsburg* and its sister ships *Árpád* and *Babenberg* (Fourth Battle Division). The armored cruisers *Sankt Georg*, *Kaiser Karl VI*, and *Maria Theresia* and light cruisers *Aspern*, *Zenta*, and *Szigetvár* were grouped together in the Cruiser Flotilla under the command of Vice Admiral Paul Fiedler. The First Torpedo Flotilla, led by the new scout cruiser *Saida*, consisted of the six *Tátra*-class destroyers and six older *Huszár*-class destroyers, plus ten torpedo boats and a depot ship. The Second Torpedo Flotilla, led by the scout cruiser *Admiral Spaun*, consisted of the remaining six *Huszár*-class destroyers, eighteen torpedo boats, and a depot ship.[4] Haus's choice of subordinate commanders for the squadrons and cruiser group reflected the emergence of Kailer's generation within the naval leadership: Njegovan, an 1877 graduate of the academy, was fifty-six; Fiedler (class of 1878) and Löfler (class of 1879) were both fifty-three.

Ships designated for coastal defense included the Fifth Battle Division—the *Monarch* and its sister ships *Wien* and *Budapest*—and the old cruisers *Kaiser Franz Joseph I* and *Panther*.[5] Rear Admiral Barry, Francis Ferdinand's candidate for chief of the *Marinesektion* less than two years earlier, left his position as head of the naval academy to assume command of this group.[6] Local defense forces at Pola included three obsolete destroyers and fifteen old torpedo boats, all dating from Sterneck's time, plus all six of the navy's submarines. Trieste and Lussin (Lošinj) were covered by four old torpedo boats apiece, Sebenico by ten, and Cattaro by six. An obsolete destroyer joined the forces at each of the latter three ports. Several old torpedo boats and ten small (47-ton) tugboats were outfitted as minesweepers and dispersed along the coast.[7] The harbor watch ships *Kronprinz Rudolf* and *Mars* (the former casemate ship *Tegetthoff*) contributed to the defense of Cattaro and Pola, respectively. Considered secure because of the proximity of Pola, Rijeka was left virtually undefended. After the naval academy moved inland to a site near Marchegg on the Morava River, the city had no naval installation of any kind.[8]

The British and French declarations of war found Haus busily redeploying his forces. The *Radetzkys*, which were sent to Cattaro in late July, were back in Pola in time to sail with the rest of the battle fleet on the abortive mission to rescue the *Goeben* and *Breslau*. The First Torpedo Flotilla went to Sebenico, and in late July the Second Torpedo Flotilla and the Cruiser Flotilla started to relocate to Cattaro; these vessels were helping to defend the Bocche when Montenegro's declaration of war finally came on 8 August. Thereafter Haus reinforced their exposed position with Barry's Fifth Battle Division—the trio of old *Monarchs*—keeping the twelve newest battleships at Pola.[9] As luck would have it, only two of the navy's ships were caught outside of the Adriatic: the yacht *Taurus*, station ship at Constantinople, which quickly ran for home, and the old ram cruiser *Kaiserin Elisabeth,* on station in the Far East.

Immediately after the Montenegrin declaration of war, the light cruisers *Zenta* and *Szigetvár* bombarded the port of Antivari (Bar). In the days that followed, elements of the Cruiser Flotilla and Second Torpedo Flotilla maintained a blockade of Montenegro's narrow coastal foothold.[10] They remained offshore until 16 August, when word arrived of Lapeyrère's vastly superior fleet approaching from Malta. The French force included fourteen battleships: the 23,400-ton dreadnoughts *Courbet* and *Jean Bart,* the six 18,000-ton pre-dreadnoughts of the *Danton* class (all completed in 1911), and the six 14,900-ton pre-dreadnoughts of the older *Patrie* class (completed 1907–8). Lighter vessels accompanying the impressive armada included a token British contribution of the cruiser *Defence* and one destroyer. Lapeyrère found the coast of Montenegro covered by only the light cruiser *Zenta* and destroyer *Ulan;* the latter managed to escape northward to Cattaro, but the *Zenta* was not so fortunate. Caught by the vanguard of the pursuing force, Captain Paul Pachner and the crew of the 2,300-ton cruiser fought on in an impossible situation. In their enthusiasm, the French expended five hundred heavy shells in subduing the tiny vessel, which finally went down with flags still flying. Their heroism made the men of the *Zenta* the navy's first martyrs of the First World War. Setting the tone for things to come, the French left the scene without attempting to rescue the survivors.[11]

Following up the success off Antivari, on 1 September the French sent two dreadnoughts, ten pre-dreadnoughts, four armored cruisers, and lighter craft on a sortie to Cattaro, where they bombarded the forts at the entrance to the Bocche before withdrawing. Lapeyrère subsequently kept submarines stationed offshore to prey upon any Austro-Hungarian warships attempting to enter or leave the base. On 19 September, in one of four sorties during that month, he sent four armored cruisers as far north as Cape Planka near Sebenico. The French attempted three full-scale sorties in October, and as late as 1 November Lapeyrère's forces made a half-hearted attempt to take the island of Lissa, but circumstances ultimately prevented the French admiral from maintaining an aggressive posture.[12] While he possessed the forces to overwhelm the Austro-Hungarian navy, he was plagued at every turn by problems. He toyed with the idea of a feint toward Trieste to goad Haus into coming out of Pola but quickly dropped it because the losses would be prohibitive. His hands were also tied by the fact that the French army—which in early September barely stopped the Germans at the Marne—was in no position to contribute manpower to amphibious operations in the Adriatic.[13]

With actual assaults on the coast out of the question, Lapeyrère also found it difficult to exploit his advantages at sea. His main base at Malta was almost five hundred miles from the Straits of Otranto at the mouth of the Adriatic. Antivari, though in Franco-Montenegrin hands, was worthless to him; it had no harbor defenses or port facilities adequate for warships of any great size and, being less than forty miles from the Austrian stronghold at Cattaro, would be dangerously exposed to enemy attack. In August and September, Lapeyrère could refuel his fleet at sea, but the coaling and oiling operations, which involved thousands of tons of fuel per day, would be impossible with the onset of rougher weather. By October he had devised a scheme for rotating ships back and forth to Malta for supply and repair, a solution that naturally weakened the force available in the lower Adriatic at any given time. Nevertheless, Pola and Trieste continued to receive false intelligence of an impending all-out French offensive almost on a weekly basis. As late as 20 October, the Austro-Hungarian consul in Corfu telegraphed news that the "French fleet with almost all ships, around 45, has left for northern Adriatic." Haus naturally could not afford to dismiss such reports out of hand.[14]

Lapeyrère's problems, combined with the perilous situation on the western front in France, limited the extent to which the French could support their Montenegrin allies. In mid-September, a French detachment of one hundred forty men with eight heavy cannon went ashore at Antivari, and a month later the battery was in place on Mount Lovćen, above the navy's base at Cattaro, supplementing the weaker Montenegrin artillery already there. The three *Monarch*s in the Bocche, each mounting four 9.4-inch guns, answered the French bombardment. They were soon joined by the *Radetzky,* which was sent from Pola on temporary assignment to the Fifth Battle Division. The semi-dreadnought's four 12-inch and eight 9.4-inch guns dramatically increased the firepower available on the Austro-Hungarian side. Two of the French cannon were disabled, and the rest pulled back beyond the effective range of the battleship guns below. In late November, the French mission withdrew altogether and handed over the remaining cannon to the Montenegrins. The navy could claim a victory, in more ways than one. The display of firepower against Mount Lovćen bred a new French respect for the Austro-Hungarian squadron at Cattaro, persuading Lapeyrère that future convoys with supplies for Montenegro would have to be escorted by battleships in order to ensure their safety.[15]

Notwithstanding Lapeyrère's difficulties, Haus remained in a defensive posture and refused to risk his larger units in a clash with the enemy. Defeat, of course, would be disastrous, and even a miraculous victory over the superior enemy fleet would weaken the navy enough to leave Italy free to dominate the Adriatic in the future. In early September, he explained his position to Kailer in a letter to the *Marinesektion:* "So long as the possibility exists that Italy will declare war against us, I consider it my first duty to keep our fleet intact . . . for the decisive struggle against this, our most dangerous foe."[16] Francis Joseph supported this conservative strategy, as did William II and the head of the German emperor's naval cabinet, Admiral Georg von Müller, but Haus still had his share of detractors. Kailer, as the chief naval official in Vienna, had to fend off criticism from the Habsburg army General Staff, the German naval and military attachés, and especially Berchtold and the foreign ministry.[17] Against charges of inaction at sea, the second in command could point to regular sorties from Cattaro by Barry's three *Monarchs* as well as the lighter craft of the Bocche, which harassed the Montenegrin coast in spite of the tremendous risk of being caught and annihilated by the French fleet.[18]

Concern for coal supplies also played a role in Haus's decision to keep the battle fleet in port. Cut off from Britain, its traditional source of imported coal, the navy would have to get through the war on its prewar stocks, supplemented by German and suitable domestic coal sent to the Adriatic bases overland by rail. Fortunately, the Balkan crisis and fleet mobilization of 1913 had prompted Haus to stockpile coal in unprecedented amounts; by the end of the year, the navy had purchased 405,302 tons for fleet use, more than double the previous high, in 1912, of 153,248 tons. Reflecting the changing international situation, 12.1 percent came from German mines and 11.6 percent (47,001 tons) from the Pocahontas seam in Virginia. Austro-Hungarian sources, most notably the mines of Ostrava in Moravia, accounted for another 1.6 percent, a minuscule proportion, yet the largest domestic share of any year since 1889. The remaining 75 percent of purchases (over 300,000 tons) still came from British suppliers.[19] The stockpiling continued through the first half of 1914. As soon as war was declared and British sources no longer were available, Haus began to conserve his resources. A sortie by the entire fleet consumed 1,000 tons of coal per hour, and in the event of a long war, the stocks would be depleted rapidly. Common sense dictated that coal-hungry battleships remain idle unless there were some compelling reason to send them out.

While he fended off the allegations of inactivity in fleet operations, Haus certainly could not be accused of complacency in the area of command personnel. The acerbic *Marinekommandant* reacted to the loss of the *Zenta* by criticizing the commander of the Fifth Battle Division at Cattaro, Barry, for failing to react to the approach of the superior French force. Their relationship deteriorated thereafter, and in October, Barry lost his command to the younger Rear Admiral Alexander Hansa.[20] Junior officers also did not escape Haus's wrath. In particular, Captain Bogumil Nowotny, a native of Galicia and one of the highest-ranking Poles in the officer corps, was singled out for the allegedly shoddy conduct of destroyer operations off the Montenegrin coast.[21] But Haus's relationship with the head of the submarine service, Captain Thierry, was the stormiest of all. Submarines fascinated Haus, yet from the onset of his tenure, he rarely saw eye-to-eye with Thierry on any point regarding their role or stationing. At times he annoyed the captain by soliciting the opinion of Heyssler, Thierry's predecessor, on submarine affairs. Fortunately, Thierry was on better terms with Kailer and could count on the second in command to mediate his disputes with the *Marinekommandant*, thus saving his own position notwithstanding their serious disagreements. Haus only slowly recognized the offensive potential of the undersea boat and initially insisted on keeping all of the navy's submarines in Pola. On 27 July, the day before the declaration of war on Serbia, Thierry suggested that the four newest boats be transferred to the Bocche di Cattaro, an ideal base for offensive operations at the mouth of the Adriatic. He repeated his proposal in mid-August, after Britain and France declared war on Austria-Hungary, but again Haus refused to let any submarines leave Pola.[22]

Shortly after the shake-up in the command at Cattaro, the fate of an Austro-Hungarian warship half a world away finally was decided as the *Kaiserin Elisabeth* became the navy's second casualty of the war. The navy's largest vessel lost before the end of 1917, the old 4,000-ton ram cruiser had relieved the *Kaiser Franz Joseph I* late in 1913 and was trapped in East Asian waters by the outbreak of the war. Too old and slow to operate as a commerce raider, it entered Kiaochow Bay and put in at Tsingtao, Germany's Chinese port, shortly after the onset of hostilities. The position of the cruiser and Germany's small East Asian squadron became far more precarious after Japan's decision to enter the war. Allies of the British since 1902, the Japanese declared war on 23 August with the transparent goal of gobbling up Germany's Pacific possessions. Indeed, the British themselves did nothing to encourage Japanese intervention, realizing that it would benefit no one but Japan. In any event, a small number of British vessels ultimately joined the Japanese fleet in a blockade of Kiaochow Bay. Japan initially did not declare war on Austria-Hungary, and the navy held out some hope of saving the cruiser by arranging to have it disarmed and interned at Shanghai under Chinese supervision, but when William II personally insisted that the *Kaiserin Elisabeth* be placed at the disposal of the German commander in Kiaochow Bay, Francis Joseph could hardly refuse. The forces at Tsingtao held out for several weeks, but the struggle was hopeless. On 3 November the *Kaiserin Elisabeth* was scuttled with flags flying, and four days later the garrison surrendered. Captain Richard Makoviz and four hundred of his men became prisoners of war; another ten were killed in the brief campaign. With the sinking of the old cruiser, the navy lost its last surface vessel outside of the Adriatic.[23]

While the *Kaiserin Elisabeth* was the only warship trapped overseas in 1914, for the merchant marine the losses were far greater. The wide variety of ports in which Austro-Hungarian merchantmen were seized or interned attests to their worldwide scope of activity on the eve of the war. The Austrian Lloyd had eight steamers seized or interned in foreign ports: four by the British, three in China, and one in Portugal.[24] The Hungarian Adria Line also lost eight vessels: two in Spain, two in Brazil, and one apiece in the Netherlands, Portugal, France, and Russia.[25] The Austro-Americana suffered the greatest losses of all, with eighteen ships seized or interned overseas: eight in the United States, five in Spain, two in Brazil, two in Argentina, and one in Cuba.[26] In a war that would soon feature the sinking of passenger vessels by submarines, the first great disaster involving civilian loss of life ironically occurred entirely by accident. Two weeks after the outbreak of war, the Lloyd steamer *Baron Gautsch* strayed into an Austrian navy mine field off Pola while en route from Cattaro to Trieste. Booked full of returning vacationers who had been stranded in various eastern Mediterranean ports by the outbreak of war, the *Gautsch* went to the bottom with 147 lives lost; there were 159 survivors. Out of concern for public morale, censors kept word of the disaster out of the newspapers.[27]

With little good news coming from the Adriatic or the high seas, the navy could take solace in the fact that its Danube flotilla remained active in the campaign against Serbia. After firing the first shots against Belgrade in late July, the monitors in mid-September once again shelled the Serbian capital. Along with their tiny patrol boat escorts, the monitors expanded their campaign to the Sava River, but with less favorable results. In late October, while on duty on the Sava, the monitor *Temes* struck a Serbian mine and sank. Fortunately for the flotilla, in a relatively shallow river such a loss was not permanent; the *Temes* eventually was raised, repaired, and recommissioned. On 2 December, the remaining monitors supported the army's occupation of Belgrade.[28] The campaign on land, though bungled, appeared to have succeeded, but on the very day of the Austro-Hungarian entry into the capital, the Serbs launched a counteroffensive that forced Habsburg troops to abandon the country altogether just two weeks later. The demoralized army assumed a defensive posture north of the Danube-Sava line and, in the west, along the Bosnian frontier. The war against Serbia did not resume until October 1915, after Bulgaria joined the Central Powers. In the meantime, the Danube flotilla added two new monitors in the summer of 1915, bringing its total strength to ten.[29]

As the men of the Danube flotilla went onto a less active footing, their counterparts aboard the seagoing warships in the Adriatic continued to see little action. While the larger units of the navy remained safely in Pola and Cattaro, in much the same way that the German High Seas fleet confined itself to port in Wilhelmshaven, the possibility arose that Austria-Hungary also could imitate Germany's success in using the submarine as an offensive weapon against enemy warships and shipping. Unfortunately, the navy had started the war with very few undersea boats in its inventory. The six original submarines were joined by a seventh in late August 1914. A Holland-type boat like the *U5* and *U6* already in service was purchased from the Whitehead firm of Rijeka, which had built it on speculation; the navy designated it *U12* in anticipation of the delivery of submarines ordered in Germany back in 1913, under Montecuccoli's last program. During the autumn of 1914, Thierry finally prevailed on the question of the move to Cattaro, but Haus approved the redeployment only reluctantly and in a piecemeal fashion. *U3* and *U4* were transferred in late September, *U5* in late October, *U6* and *U12* in December. The older *U1* and *U2*, too unseaworthy for offensive operations, remained in the upper Adriatic throughout the war. Thierry's frustrations were compounded in late November, when the submarines under construction for the navy in Germany were taken over by the German fleet. Help would finally arrive in the summer of 1915, but until then Austria-Hungary had to make ends meet with seven boats.[30]

Thierry could take heart in the knowledge that his boats, when finally turned loose, registered the navy's first great success against the enemy. On 21 December 1914, the *U12*, commanded by Lieutenant Egon Lerch, torpedoed the 23,400-ton dreadnought *Jean Bart*, Lapeyrère's flagship, during a French attempt to convoy supplies to the Montenegrins at Antivari. The battleship took on water but made it back to Malta, where it remained out of action for several months. Even though the *Jean Bart* was saved, the near-catastrophe had a considerable impact on Entente strategy. The strength of the Austro-Hungarian navy at Cattaro meant that convoys to Montenegro had to be escorted by battleships, and the new danger of submarine attack, Lapeyrère concluded, made the deployment of battleships as convoy escorts too risky. The French went to the extreme of never again sending a battleship into the Adriatic.[31] Montenegro had to be left to its own devices and remained temporarily secure only because the Serbian counteroffensive had so weakened the Austro-Hungarian army's Balkan position.

Over the winter of 1914–15, the navy registered another pair of far less dramatic successes against the French. The day before the torpedoing of the *Jean Bart*, the French submarine *Curie* was sunk by fire from shore batteries and torpedo boats while on a daring raid of Pola harbor. At the end of January 1915, the boat was raised and taken to the Pola Arsenal for repairs; in June 1915, it was commissioned as the Austro-Hungarian *U14*.[32] Meanwhile, on 24 February, the French destroyer *Dague* sank after striking an Austrian mine off Antivari.[33] Regular raids by warships operating out of Cattaro made the Montenegrin port a dangerous place, and not just for French vessels. On the night of 1–2 March, the destroyer *Csikós* attacked Antivari and torpedoed the *Rumija*, the 140-ton royal yacht of the king of Montenegro.[34]

In the first months of 1915, the French and British blockade line was moved out of the lower Adriatic to the southern extreme of the Straits of Otranto, almost two hundred miles south of Cattaro. The cautious Lapeyrère kept his battleships and cruisers even farther out of reach, employing destroyers as his advance force. The admiral intended to harass traffic in and out of Cattaro with submarines, but three quarters of the time, rough winter seas prevented his undersea boats from even entering the Adriatic. The French, with British approval, in effect gave the Austro-Hungarian navy free run of the Adriatic and were satisfied merely to prevent it from breaking out into the Mediterranean, a move that Haus clearly had no intention of attempting. The standoff left the Dual Monarchy's merchant ships free to ply their routes unmolested, if only within the confines of the Adriatic.[35] But the subsequent lack of action once again left Haus open to criticism from the usual quarters, especially after mid-February, when the British, with nominal French support, attacked the Dardanelles.

The Dardanelles project originated with Winston Churchill, then First Lord of the Admiralty. Frustrated by the stalemate on the western front, he advocated an attack on some area vital to the enemy yet peripheral enough to be relatively weakly defended. In the search for a "soft underbelly," foreshadowing his strategic thinking during the Second World War, he considered Schleswig and the Adriatic before settling on the Turkish straits. The attack began on 19 February and had as its climax the unsuccessful attempt, on 18 March, to force the Dardanelles. Thereafter the Turks had the upper hand, although troops landed by the British—primarily Australians and New Zealanders—were left to languish on the Gallipoli peninsula until the end of 1915.

Through mid-March 1915, while the issue was still very much in doubt, the Germans pressured Haus to do something to help save the Turks. At one time, he considered sending a shipment of munitions aboard the new scout cruiser *Novara*, a sister ship of the *Admiral Spaun* that had just entered service in January 1915. The commander of the *Novara*, the daring Captain Horthy, was well suited for the task, but Haus ultimately considered the risk too great for the modest cargo that the cruiser would have been able to carry. The Germans also asked for two submarines to slip out of the Adriatic and operate against the Entente fleet at the Dardanelles, but at the time Austria-Hungary had only five undersea boats capable of offensive action, and Haus was disinclined to commit two outside of the Adriatic, where their impact on the campaign, in any event, would have been minimal. To distract the French from their support of the British at the Dardanelles, the Germans suggested a strike at the French forces at the mouth of the Adriatic. Haus retorted that his situation remained unchanged; the token French support for the British at the straits consisted of a handful of old battleships, none of which had been detached from the force deployed against him. Indeed, Lapeyrère had contributed nothing to the Dardanelles campaign.[36]

The criticism did not subside even after the Turkish position stabilized. When the Entente fleet failed in its attempt to storm the Dardanelles, Count István Burián, Berchtold's successor as Austro-Hungarian foreign minister, argued that a naval victory over the French would compound the enemy's woes in the Mediterranean and deter Italy from entering the war. The German embassy in Vienna likewise persisted in pressuring Haus, even employing Baron Max von Beck, the retired Austrian minister-president, as a go-between. In his response to Beck, Haus did not diverge from his earlier reasoning. An Austrian attack on the French fleet made *"absolutely not the least strategic sense."*[37] Ironically, the episode involving Beck rallied at least some army support behind the *Marinekommandant*. After Haus sent army headquarters a copy of his reply to Beck, Francis Joseph's cousin Archduke Frederick, titular head of the *Armeeoberkommando,* instructed him not to respond to future German overtures made outside of proper channels.[38]

Notwithstanding the storm of criticism, the navy in the spring of 1915 was far from inactive. The submariners, emboldened by the crippling of the *Jean Bart,* expanded their radius of action to adjust to the more distant positioning of the enemy blockade. On the night of 26–27 April 1915, the *U5*, under the command of Lieutenant Georg von Trapp, ventured into the northern Ionian Sea and torpedoed the 12,500-ton armored cruiser *Léon Gambetta* off Cape Santa Maria di Leuca, the tip of the Italian boot heel. Aware that most of the French seamen would have no way of saving themselves, Trapp nevertheless considered the action to be morally defensible in light of the French navy's failure to pick up survivors after sinking the *Zenta* in the first days of the war. Almost seven hundred men went down with the ship, and barely a hundred survived the disaster. After the sinking of the *Léon Gambetta,* the French became even more timid about maintaining a vigilant blockade of the mouth of the Adriatic. Lapeyrère resolved that, except in special circumstances, only vessels smaller than cruisers would venture north of the parallel of the Ionian island of Cephalonia (Kefallinia), some three hundred miles south of Cattaro. Ultimately, because Malta was tied up supporting the effort at the Dardanelles, French cruisers had to go all the way to Bizerte to take on coal. Operating from Tunisia, they could hardly claim to be blockading the mouth of the Adriatic.[39]

The weakness of the blockade became all the more apparent in the first half of May 1915, when the navy assisted in the breakout from the Adriatic of two German submarines assembled at Pola. The partially finished boats were sent by rail from Germany in March 1915, after the Germans, frustrated by Haus's refusal to commit his submarines to the Dardanelles, resolved to deploy their own. Plans called for Austro-Hungarian warships to tow the boats to Greek waters, from which point their own cruising range easily could take them to the coast of Asia Minor without refueling. The German *UB8* left Pola on 2 May, towed by Horthy's cruiser *Novara.* They passed through the Straits of Otranto and were not sighted by the French until the sixth, off Cephalonia. Horthy cut loose the submarine, then raced northward to the safety of the Adriatic. His sortie, to a point three hundred miles south of Cattaro, by far was the longest of the war to date. On the night of 15–16 May, the destroyer *Triglav* repeated the feat by towing the *UB7* out of the Adriatic and into the Ionian Sea. By then, the first German submarine to reach the Mediterranean by sea already had put in at Cattaro. For the remainder of the war, German undersea boats would operate out of Austrian bases.[40]

Pleased with Haus's cooperation in the submarine deployment, Admiral Gustav Bachmann, the new chief of the German *Admiralstab,* pledged to head off future criticism from Berlin. For their part, the Austrians felt confident enough to raise the issue of replacement submarines for the boats expropriated in November 1914 in the shipyard at Kiel. In May the German navy sent the recently completed *UB1* and *UB15* by rail to Pola, where they were recommissioned as the Austro-Hungarian *U10* and *U11.* By the time they entered service in June and July, respectively, the captured and repaired French submarine *Curie* had received its Habsburg commission as *U14.* At just over 400 tons, *U14* became the navy's largest submarine, an honor it retained for the remainder of the war. Lieutenant Trapp received command of the new prize later in 1915, but from the start he lamented its engineering flaws, speculating that his grandmother could have designed a better submarine. Nevertheless, the desperate shortage of undersea boats made any additions welcome. The flotilla of ten submarines soon would to be joined by another three—the future *U15, U16,* and *U17*—under construction in Bremen.[41]

The replacement submarines from Germany filled the only remaining hole in the last program approved under Montecuccoli; the other warships were either already in service or nearing completion. Haus's program of May 1914, for which the Delegations had voted 426.8 million kronen, did not fare as well. The outbreak of war found the Stabilimento Tecnico Triestino assembling materials for the first of the new 24,500-ton dreadnoughts, but in August the government suspended contracts for all four dreadnoughts, the three 4,800-ton cruisers, and the six *Tátra*-class destroyers. Improvements on the harbor at Sebenico, included in the budget package, were never begun. Except for the two Danube monitors, which entered service in the summer of 1915, Haus's entire program ultimately died on the drawing board, but he and his aides did not give in without a fight. As early as October 1914, the Hungarian finance ministry suggested that the program be cancelled. The matter finally came to a head in a meeting of the council of ministers in February 1915, when Kailer finally agreed to postpone the special credit until the end of the war. In doing so, he made clear the navy's view that the credit was being suspended, not cancelled. The savings were reflected in the overall naval expenditure for fiscal year 1914–15 (July 1914 through June 1915), which coincided with the first twelve months of the war. Even with the added expenses of wartime operations, the navy spent only 190 million kronen, some twenty million less than in 1913.[42]

The navy could do little to make up for the lost warships. At the start of the war, Austria-Hungary expropriated the *Lung Tuan,* a 400-ton destroyer built by Stabilimento Tecnico Triestino for the Republic of China. Almost identical to the older *Huszár*-class destroyers, it was rechristened the *Warasdiner* and entered service in September 1914. The navy also planned to take over a 4,900-ton cruiser and three 1,860-ton cruisers initially ordered by China from the Cantiere Navale Triestino in Monfalcone, but the shipyard made little progress on the vessels before the Italian declaration of war on 23 May 1915, and days later the Italian army overran Monfalcone.[43]

The suspended contracts and limited possibilities for acquiring warships from other sources only reinforced Haus's resolve to take no unnecessary risks with the existing fleet. His belief that Italy ultimately

CHAPTER 7

would enter the war proved to be correct, and when the time came, he had at his disposal almost all of the vessels that had been in service or under construction as of the summer of 1914. Other than the *Zenta* and *Kaiserin Elisabeth,* the only Austro-Hungarian warship lost by the spring of 1915 was the old *Torpedoboot 26,* sunk in late August 1914 after accidentally striking one of the navy's own mines at the entrance to Pola harbor.[44] From the beginning of the war, Haus had argued that he was saving his fleet for the inevitable future conflict with Italy; it remained to be seen how he would use it once this campaign was underway.

For the navy, May 1915 marked the end of the initial phase of the war, and with some justification Haus could claim victory in the first round of the action. Even though France, the primary adversary, deployed a much larger fleet, Austria-Hungary's coastline had not been seriously threatened, and its seaports had not been shelled. By the end of 1914, at least between its own ports in the Adriatic, merchantmen could move freely without fear of enemy attack. In material losses, the balance tipped heavily in favor of the Austrians. In addition to the *Léon Gambetta* disaster, the French had lost a destroyer, a submarine, and, temporarily, one of their newest dreadnought battleships. On the negative side, the navy had been able to do nothing to disrupt the Entente's activities in the Mediterranean. French troop transports moved between Algeria and Toulon—and British transports, from the Suez Canal to Gibraltar—all with little concern for the Austro-Hungarian fleet. Italian neutrality and the likelihood of Italy's eventual intervention on the side of the Entente almost completely neutralized the navy as an offensive factor in the Mediterranean. Less than one year into the conflict, the prewar British fears of Habsburg dreadnoughts swooping down on Malta seemed ludicrous indeed.

THE ITALIAN NAVY, THE ENTENTE,
AND INTERVENTION (1915)

In September 1914, just over a month after Italy's declaration of neutrality, navy chief of staff Thaon di Revel drafted his first detailed plan for operations against Austria-Hungary. He envisioned a blockade of the Straits of Otranto, the occupation of some Dalmatian islands, and the mining of channels along the Dalmatian coast. The primary seaports, Rijeka and Trieste, could be shelled, although operations against the latter would be a sensitive matter owing to its large Italian population. The plan was not particularly original; indeed, similar schemes dominated Italian strategic thinking before the brief, superficial warming of Austro-Italian relations in the years 1912–13.[45]

By January 1915, the course of the Anglo-German campaign in the North Sea had caused Thaon di Revel to revise his thinking; instead of heavier units, the admiral now foresaw a campaign in which torpedo boats and submarines would dominate a "naval guerrilla war" along the coast, especially in the northern Adriatic between Venice and Pola. Rather than risk Italian battleships to mines and torpedoes, the admiral foresaw holding them back for a decisive encounter against the Austro-Hungarian battle fleet should it venture out. The Italian navy would adhere to the basic principles of this amended strategy throughout the war, ultimately exposing its leaders to criticism from their allies that they were "afraid to risk their battle fleet."[46]

In the early months of 1915, as Italy's intervention on the side of the Triple Entente grew increasingly likely, Italian naval war planning focused on the question of securing a base of operations in the Dalmatian islands. The remarkable Captain Conz, instrumental earlier in the negotiation of the Triple Alliance naval convention, more recently was purported to have engaged in espionage along the Austrian coast "disguised as a mendicant friar or fisherman." Conz recommended an operation to seize the channel between the island of Curzola (Korčula) and the mainland, a location between Cattaro and Pola that would be close enough to threaten the former but far enough away from the latter to be reasonably secure.[47] Such a plan, of course, hinged on the army's willingness to participate in an amphibious operation to secure the base. Unfortunately for Thaon di Revel, his army counterpart, Pollio's successor General Luigi Cadorna, was lukewarm toward the idea. Cadorna's plans called for a heavy commitment of Italian resources to an advance out of Venetia, across the Isonzo River to Trieste. He was willing to commit only one reserve infantry regiment to the scheme of seizing a Dalmatian base for the navy and let it be known that in the event of war against the Austrians he would expect the navy to concentrate on supporting the army's effort, not vice versa. Thaon di Revel's final prewar plan, in April, deemphasized the goal of permanently occupying Curzola or some other strong point along the Dalmatian coast.[48]

CHAPTER 7

Over the winter of 1914–15, Sidney Sonnino, San Giuliano's successor as Italian foreign minister, negotiated with both alliance systems
in an effort to secure the best deal for Italy in exchange for its intervention in the war. Sonnino not surprisingly found that Germany and
Austria-Hungary could make few territorial concessions to Italy. Berlin
pressured Vienna to appease the Italians, but ultimately the price was
too high. Italy demanded the Trentino and Trieste in exchange merely
for its continued neutrality. Austria-Hungary initially offered only to
recognize Italian possession of the Albanian port of Valona (Vlore),
which Italy had already seized in December 1914 to protect its interests in the wake of the abdication of William of Wied.[49] In March 1915,
the Habsburg foreign minister, Burián, offered to give up the Italian-
speaking Tyrol, but it was too little, too late. In any event, Italy's insistence that cessions of Austrian territory had to be immediate, rather than
promised as part of an overall postwar settlement, was unacceptable in
Vienna.

The diplomats of the Entente were able to offer Italy a much better
deal, embodied on 26 April 1915 in the Treaty of London. From Switzerland in the west to the Julian Alps in the east, Sonnino demanded and
received promises of a border that would include not only the ethnic
Italian population of the Habsburg Empire but hundreds of thousands
of German Austrians and Slavs. Trieste, Pola, and the entire Istrian peninsula would go to Italy in a postwar settlement. Regarding Dalmatia,
Russian support for Serbia's claims to a substantial outlet to the sea
complicated the negotiations; nevertheless, much of the Dalmatian coast
was designated for cession to Italy. The Entente confirmed Italy's possession of Valona and a sphere of influence in Albania, which would
enable the Italians to control the mouth of the Adriatic. The Italians also
expected a share of Germany's African colonies as well as Turkish land
in the Middle East.[50]

The third article of the Treaty of London committed the British and
French navies to support Italy "until the destruction of the Austro-Hungarian fleet or until the conclusion of peace."[51] Anglo-French-Italian naval discussions began in Paris on 2 May and culminated eight days later
in a formal naval convention. The accord called for the establishment
of a First Allied Fleet, predominantly Italian and based at Brindisi, and
a Second Allied Fleet, predominantly French and based at Taranto,
Malta, and Bizerte. The First Fleet was to include the newest units of the

Italian navy, a French contingent of a dozen destroyers and six submarines, and a British detachment of four pre-dreadnought battleships and four light cruisers. The Second Fleet essentially would be the force that Lapeyrère already commanded in the Ionian Sea, joined by whatever units the Italians chose to send him. Should the First Fleet move north to Venice, plans called for the Second Fleet to deploy in the lower Adriatic, using Brindisi and Taranto as bases. For operations in the Adriatic, all British and French commanders would be subordinated to the Italian commander in chief, who was initially the Duke of the Abruzzi. This posed a dilemma, since the British already had agreed to a French commander in chief, Lapeyrère, for the entire Mediterranean. Technically, Abruzzi was subordinate to Lapeyrère, but Lapeyrère would take orders from Abruzzi when operating in the Adriatic![52]

For the moment, the new partners left this thorny question of command unresolved. The Second Fleet would not enter the lower Adriatic until the First Fleet redeployed to the upper Adriatic, and Thaon di Revel did not foresee that happening very soon after Italy's intervention. Incredibly, the three navies did not formulate any specific operational plans in advance of the Italian declaration of war. The disposition of the First Fleet was left to the discretion of Abruzzi, whose initial goal was to secure the Adriatic south of the line of Spalato (Split). The duke planned to keep his battleships and most of his cruisers outside the Adriatic at Taranto while lighter units swept the lower Adriatic of all Austro-Hungarian torpedo boats and submarines. Only after this phase of the operation ended would the bulk of the First Fleet round the Italian boot heel to deploy north of the Straits of Otranto. Then, Abruzzi hoped, the enemy could be lured out of Pola to do battle in the lower Adriatic, where the Italians would have the advantage.[53]

At the time of Italy's declaration of war, the Italian navy had an active fleet of seventeen battleships, ten armored and seven unarmored cruisers, four auxiliary cruisers, thirty-three destroyers, forty-eight torpedo boats, and eighteen submarines. The order of battle found the Italian contribution to the First Fleet still divided between Taranto and Brindisi, with all of the dreadnoughts at Taranto: the *Dante Alighieri, Giulio Cesare, Leonardo da Vinci,* the recently completed *Conte di Cavour* (April), and the *Duilio* (May), the latter not yet ready for action. They were joined by four armored cruisers, five unarmored cruisers, four auxiliary cruisers, eleven destroyers, eighteen torpedo boats, and four submarines. The squadron at Brindisi included the six newest pre-dreadnoughts: the *Regina Elena* and its three sister ships, *Vittorio Emanuele, Roma,* and *Napoli* (completed 1907–8), along with the slightly older *Regina Margherita* (1904) and *Benedetto Brin* (1905). The four newest and largest armored cruisers, *Pisa, Amalfi, San Giorgio,* and *San Marco* (1909–11), the unarmored cruiser *Piemonte,* and ten destroyers rounded out the contingent. Defensive forces at Venice included the three oldest active pre-dreadnoughts—the *Sardegna* (1895), *Emanuele Filiberto* (1901), and *Ammiraglio di Saint Bon* (1901)—along with one armored and one unarmored cruiser, a dozen destroyers, thirty torpedo boats, and fourteen submarines. Harbor watch and auxiliary vessels included the pre-dreadnoughts *Sicilia* (1895), *Re Umberto* (1893), and *Dandolo* (1882), along with several obsolete cruisers and torpedo boats.[54]

Officials in Austria-Hungary were not oblivious to the preparations in Italy. The day after the signing of the Treaty of London, the *Armeeoberkommando* warned Haus that Italy might launch an attack even without first declaring war. On 4 May, the Italians went through the formality of declaring their departure from the Triple Alliance, leaving little doubt that hostilities were imminent. Nevertheless, the navy's hands were tied until Francis Joseph authorized action. On 20 May, the emperor gave permission to attack the Italian navy if it made a move to convoy troops across the Adriatic to Antivari to reinforce Montenegro. By then, Haus already had a screen of light cruisers, destroyers, and submarines scattered from Trieste to Antivari on the lookout for Italian warships, while at Pola the battle fleet stood ready for a sortie as soon as word arrived of an Italian declaration of war. When the news came to Pola late on the afternoon of 23 May, it was greeted with enthusiasm by officers and seamen alike. Haus and his fleet put to sea just after sunset, steaming for the Italian coast.

The assault on the Italian coast was the navy's first general sortie in nine and a half months, since the fleet steamed half-way down the Adriatic in the abortive mission to save the *Goeben* and *Breslau*. With most of the Italian battle fleet far away at Taranto, Haus's goal was to bombard cities and towns and to destroy sections of the Italian coastal railway, which in many places was well within range of naval guns. The armored cruiser *Sankt Georg,* with an escort of two torpedo boats, shelled Rimini; the scout cruiser *Novara,* one destroyer, and two torpedo boats attacked Porto Corsini near Ravenna; the *Radetzky* and two torpedo boats went to the mouth of the Potenza; and its sister ship *Zrínyi*, also escorted by two torpedo boats, bombarded Senigallia. The bulk of the fleet steamed for Ancona: the dreadnoughts *Tegetthoff, Viribus Unitis,* and *Prinz Eugen,* the six pre-dreadnoughts of the *Erzherzog* and *Habsburg* classes, the *Radetzky*'s sister ship *Erzherzog Franz Ferdinand,* four destroyers, and twenty torpedo boats. Haus led the attack himself aboard the *Habsburg,* the oldest of the ten battleships in the group; keenly aware of the danger from enemy mines, he did not want to lead the force into coastal waters with one of his dreadnoughts. Other vessels were deployed on reconnaissance patrols to the south of Ancona to provide ample warning should the Italian battle fleet venture northward up the Adriatic: these included the scout cruisers *Admiral Spaun, Saida,* and *Helgoland,* the old light cruiser *Szigetvár,* and nine destroyers. Meanwhile, detachments of seaplanes bombed Venice and Ancona.[55]

At Rimini the *Sankt Georg* damaged a freight train and railway bridge, while at Senigallia the *Zrinyi* destroyed a train and damaged the railway station and a bridge. The *Radetzky* damaged a bridge over the Potenza, and at Porto Corsini the group led by Horthy's *Novara* destroyed coastal installations and dueled with shore batteries. After the latter action, Horthy reserved special praise for Captain Nowotny, commander of the destroyer *Scharfschütze.* Most of the attacks brought no response from the lightly defended coastline; the only casualties were six killed aboard the *Novara,* which was also the only ship in the entire fleet to absorb significant damage. Ancona naturally bore the brunt of the assault. The bombardment temporarily disrupted electricity, gas, and telephone service, all but destroyed the railway station, and left the city's coal and oil stockpiles ablaze. In the port, shells damaged three merchant steamers and sank a fourth. Buildings damaged in the city included the police and army barracks, the military hospital, a sugar refinery, and the offices of the Bank of Italy. Thirty military personnel and 38 civilians were killed, another 150 wounded or injured.[56]

The cruisers and destroyers on reconnaissance patrol far to the south also got into the act of shelling points along the coastal railway. At Barletta the *Helgoland* bombarded the fortress and hit a freight train. At Termoli the *Admiral Spaun* damaged a railway bridge and freight train, then destroyed station buildings and a freight yard at Campomarino. At Manfredonia two destroyers shelled the railway station and yard and damaged a viaduct, machine shop, and factory. Unlike their more numerous counterparts to the north, the reconnaissance screen did encounter Italian naval units, but only two cruisers and two destroyers. Near the island of Pelagosa (Palagruža), the *Helgoland* and the destroyers *Lika, Csepel,* and *Tátra* hunted down and sank the destroyer *Turbine.* Before going down, the *Turbine* scored hits on the *Csepel,* causing light damage and wounding some of the crew. After the battle, the destroyer's captain, Janko Vuković de Podkapelski, commented favorably on "the performance of the [*Csepel's*] sailors of Italian nationality," which "exceeded all expectations."[57]

The attacks did not put the Italian coastal railway out of commission for any great length of time, but in the first days of the campaign, troop trains bound for the front from central and southern Italy had to be diverted to other routes. Perhaps far more important, the raid had a "depressing impact" on the Italian public. Inhabitants of the shelled cities and towns—and their representatives in Rome—had to wonder how the Austro-Hungarian navy could bombard so many targets along three hundred miles of coastline with impunity, then return to its ports without losing a ship.[58]

"COMMAND OF THE SEA IN THE ADRIATIC": HAUS AND THE ITALIAN WAR (1915–17)

While the navy did not cause a significant disruption in the Italian mobilization, at the opening of the Austro-Italian war, the Habsburg army needed all the help it could get. Decimated by the initial Russian offensive of the previous summer and fall, by the spring of 1915 Austro-Hungarian forces on the eastern front depended heavily upon their German allies, placing Conrad von Hötzendorf and the *Armeeoberkommando* in an uncomfortable position of subservience to the German army command. In April 1915, General Erich von Falkenhayn, chief of the German army General Staff, rejected a request from Conrad for permission to transfer several Habsburg army divisions from the Russian front to the Italian border. Falkenhayn, as insensitive as his counterparts in the German navy to Austro-Hungarian interests and concerns, went so far as to suggest that Trieste should be sacrificed for the sake of maintaining the focus on defeating Russia in the east. The Italophobe Conrad, confident of his ability to defeat Italy if given the necessary manpower, had to assume a defensive posture and guard the border with makeshift forces. On 23 May 1915, only one division was fully deployed along the Isonzo River. In the Alps, reserve formations such as the Tyrol Home Guard (*Standschützen*) held most of the line.[59]

In addition to its contribution at sea, the navy did its part on land. The Trieste marine battalion (*Seebataillon Triest*), which had been formed the previous September, was grouped with army units in the 187th Infantry Brigade and sent to the front. Rear Admiral Alfred von Koudelka, the Trieste district commandant (*Seebezirkskommandant*), was appointed commander of the brigade's 10,800 men, becoming the only admiral to lead significant land forces during the war.[60] In June, with the Austro-Hungarian front as strong as it would be for the immediate future, 228,000 troops stood opposite an Italian force more than twice as large—460,000 men—that also enjoyed a three-to-one superiority in heavy guns. Not without justification, General Cadorna in April 1915 had boasted that it would take him just one month to get to Trieste. Fortunately for Austria-Hungary, Italy's mobilization had been both slow and inefficient, and the first of a dozen bloody battles of the Isonzo did not even begin until 23 June, exactly one month after the Italian declaration of war.[61]

By then, the navy's activities against Italy reached far inland. In the prewar years, the Naval Intelligence Service (*Nachrichtendienst*) had operated from headquarters at Trieste, with branches at Constantinople and Corfu, but after Italy entered the war, the head of the service, Captain Rudolf Mayer, transferred his seat to Zurich in neutral Switzerland. There he held consular status, and the Intelligence Service operated out of its own building, labeled "Austro-Hungarian General Consulate, Second Section." Over the next two years, Mayer would assemble and coordinate the activities of a network of spies and saboteurs operating throughout Italy, ultimately providing an invaluable service not just to the navy but to the overall war effort.[62]

The start of the Italian offensive on land found the navy busy trying to foil Abruzzi's plans at sea. On 5 June, enemy warships shelled the lower Dalmatian coast and succeeded in breaking the rail line between Ragusa (Dubrovnik) and Cattaro, but four days later the *U4* torpedoed the British light cruiser *Dublin* off the coast of Albania. The best of the four British cruisers attached to the First Fleet, the *Dublin* limped to Brindisi, where it would be laid up for extensive repairs. The submarines were also active off Venice, where *U11* sank the Italian submarine *Medusa* on 10 June and *U10* sank the Italian torpedo boat *PN-5* on 26 June. Such successes kept morale high among Austro-Hungarian submariners and throughout the fleet. Their spirits were buoyed still more when the heir to the throne, Archduke Charles, visited Pola and went for a brief cruise aboard the newly commissioned *U14*.[63]

In the first weeks of the campaign, the boldest Italian moves in the upper Adriatic came in the air. Reflecting the prewar Italian emphasis on airships rather than planes, dirigibles were used to bomb Sebenico on 26 May and Pola four days later; neither raid caused significant damage. The Austro-Hungarian naval air arm—forty-three seaplanes at the time of the Italian declaration of war, compared to twenty-seven for the Italian navy—was more than strong enough to command the skies, but local authorities took no chances, imposing nightly blackouts to protect Pola and other coastal targets. All civilians were evacuated from Pola, and those remaining in homes on the fringe of town were advised to paint their roofs in camouflage colors. The navy scored its first success in the air war on 8 June over the island of Lussin, when a seaplane shot down the airship *Città di Ferrara,* which had been en route to bomb Rijeka. The loss had a demoralizing effect on the home front in Italy, all the more so since the dirigible had been paid for entirely through public donations. While Italian air raids ended at least temporarily, Austro-Hungarian planes continued to bomb Venice on a regular basis throughout the rest of the year. Nevertheless, their raids were small—the largest involved five planes dropping twenty-six bombs—and reconnaissance remained the primary duty of the air arm.[64]

Meanwhile, at the mouth of the Adriatic, Abruzzi still had not moved his dreadnoughts from Taranto to Brindisi. In early June, the duke had his twelve battleships—the four completed Italian dreadnoughts, the four newest Italian pre-dreadnoughts (the *Regina Elena* class), and four old British pre-dreadnoughts—practice joint maneuvers in the Gulf of Taranto. While one British officer characterized his own navy's pre-dreadnoughts as an "antediluvian quartette" that did not maneuver well as a squadron, the same observer characterized the Italian maneuvering as "abominable" and added the remark: "God help us if we have to tackle the Austrian battle fleet."[65] But the fleet sortie of 23–24 May had no sequel. Owing to the makeshift nature of the Isonzo front, Haus from the start feared that

Trieste would fall to the Italian army, making Pola too vulnerable for use as main base. Contingency plans called for a transfer of the base from Pola to Cattaro, the only alternative site and unfortunately an exposed one, where the fleet would be more vulnerable to an Entente attack. In the event of a move to Cattaro, Haus would need every available battleship; as before, he clung to his conviction that they should not be risked in actions of marginal importance.[66]

In mid-June, the navy resumed its raids against various targets on the Italian coast, albeit not on the same scale as the sortie of 23–24 May. Thaon di Revel responded by sending the four *Pisa*-class armored cruisers, Italy's newest and largest, from Brindisi to Venice. While the Italian dreadnoughts, the old British battleships, and most of the rest of the First Fleet remained at Taranto, the defense of Brindisi fell to the *Regina Elena* and its three sister ships. Capable of twenty-three knots, the armored cruisers should have been a powerful deterrent against raids in the upper Adriatic by Austro-Hungarian light cruisers, destroyers, and torpedo boats. Instead, they just provided bigger targets for the submarines operating out of Pola. On 7 July, shortly after the warships arrived in the north, the 9,800-ton *Amalfi* was torpedoed and sunk by the *U26* while on patrol twenty miles off Venice.[67]

It is not entirely accurate to refer to the *U26* as an "Austrian" submarine because it was, in fact, the German *UB14*. After 23 May 1915, the Adriatic and Mediterranean operations of the Central Powers were complicated by Italy's decision to declare war on Austria-Hungary but not on Germany; the Italians would not declare war on the Germans until fifteen months later. In the meantime, German submarines active in the theater flew the flag of the Dual Monarchy when attacking Italian naval and merchant shipping. This practice and the close Austro-German submarine cooperation make it difficult, after the fact, to distinguish between the undersea boats of the two navies. Some German submarines were turned over to Austria-Hungary but kept their German crews until Habsburg navy seamen were trained to replace them; these included the *U10* (former German *UB1*) and *U11* (former *UB15*), which were so successful off Venice in June 1915. Many more were double-numbered and went through the war with dual identities in the two navies; between June 1915 and October 1918, fifty-six German submarines (including the *UB14* or *U26*) received Austrian numbers. Of these, only two were ever actually turned over to the Austro-Hungarian navy, while three were lost en route to the Mediterranean, and two others were double-numbered but never left German waters. These boats had German commanders and crews and usually an Austrian officer aboard as second in command. Others never received an Austrian number but still flew the Habsburg flag while surfaced, either to attack Italian vessels or simply to keep the enemy fleets confused about the actual number of German undersea boats deployed in the Mediterranean. Ultimately the two navies formulated a policy under which many German submarines already active in the theater were double-numbered retroactively, becoming "Austrian" as of the dates they had first passed Gibraltar and entered the Mediterranean. The growing German presence warranted the creation in July 1915 of a "Half-Flotilla" and special command (*Marine-Spezial-Kommando*) at Pola, which coordinated activities with the Austro-Hungarian navy, supervised the repair of submarines in the Pola Arsenal, and oversaw the assembly of the boats brought overland from Germany by rail. In the fall of 1915, the Germans established a separate submarine flotilla command at Cattaro.[68]

Within the Italian navy leadership, the sinking of the *Amalfi* touched off a bitter debate between Thaon di Revel and the Duke of the Abruzzi. The duke had opposed the redeployment of the armored cruisers to Venice and held the chief of staff responsible for the loss, but Thaon di Revel, under pressure from Cadorna to provide naval support for the army's thrust across the Isonzo to Trieste, defended his decision. Within days the Entente powers tried to regain the momentum by seizing an Austrian island in the lower Adriatic and making their presence felt on the Dalmatian coast itself. On 11 July, the Italians occupied Pelagosa, some fifty miles south of Lissa, and a week later Abruzzi ordered his remaining division of armored cruisers—the 7,350-ton *Garibaldi, Varese,* and *Ferruccio*—to shell the coastline between Ragusa and Cattaro, where the Austrians had repaired the rail line damaged six weeks earlier. On 18 July, the cruiser sortie met with disaster when the *U4*, commanded by Lieutenant Rudolf Singule, torpedoed and sank the *Garibaldi* fifteen miles offshore. Admiral Haus, always hard on his submariners, subsequently criticized Singule for not sinking all three cruisers while he had the chance. Nevertheless, Singule was rewarded with the Order of Maria Theresa, which Trapp received for torpedoing the *Léon Gambetta*. Meanwhile, on the Italian side, the sinking of the *Garibaldi* caused the cancellation of plans to take the island of Lagosta (Lastovo), just a few miles south of Curzola.[69]

Thereafter the ebb and flow of the war in the Adriatic swung back in Austria-Hungary's favor. In late July, a force of light warships shelled the coast around Termoli while seaplanes bombed between Ancona and Fano. At the same time, the navy turned its attentions to the Italians on Pelagosa. The garrison withstood an attack on 28 July, but a week later, while hunting in the waters surrounding the island, the *U5*—then still under Trapp's command—torpedoed and sank the Italian submarine *Nereide*. Pelagosa was evacuated on 18 August, one day after a heavy shelling from the scout cruisers *Saida* and *Helgoland* and several destroyers. Abruzzi's goal of securing the lower Adriatic was no closer to fruition than it had been three months earlier, at the start of the campaign. Captain Herbert Richmond, the British liaison officer to the duke, complained in his diary that "in spite of inferior naval force . . . the Austrians have command of the sea in the Adriatic." He speculated that his Italian allies would make better organ-grinders than seamen.[70]

The months of July and August also went well enough for Austria-Hungary in the upper Adriatic. In a span of thirty-nine days, the Italian torpedo boats *OS-17* and *PN-6* and submarines *Nautilus* and *Jalea* all were sunk by mines in the Gulf of Trieste, while the dirigible *Città di Iesi* was shot down during a bombing raid over Pola.[71] But both navies had sown mines in the upper Adriatic, as the *U12* discovered off Venice on 11 August when it struck an Italian mine and was lost with all hands. The dead included Lieutenant Lerch, hailed as a war hero in the Dual Monarchy by virtue of his torpedoing of the *Jean Bart* eight months earlier. Just one day later, far to the south, the French destroyer *Bisson* sank the *U3* off Brindisi.[72]

Thierry's tiny undersea force could ill afford to lose two boats, not to mention their experienced crews. Fortunately, within a month the *U15*, *U16*, and *U17* were completed in Bremen and sent by rail to Pola. The Germans also contributed to the cause by training Austro-Hungarian submarine machinists in Germany. The trio of new vessels were in service by the end of October, bringing the strength of the submarine service (not including the double-numbered German units) to eleven boats. While the undersea effort depended heavily on German assistance, Whitehead of Rijeka continued to supply all of the torpedoes for the submarines. Indeed, Austrian torpedoes remained a hot commodity in the international arms market of the war years, and the navy, which took control of production at the start of the war, did not hesitate to demand a high price. In October 1915, answering an inquiry from neutral Holland, Kailer offered to provide torpedoes for the Dutch navy in exchange for one ton of East Indian rubber and ten tons of ammonium nitrate *per torpedo*. At that price, the Dutch decided not to do business.[73]

The submarines *U3* and *U12* were the first Austro-Hungarian vessels lost in the Adriatic since the sinking of the *Zenta* and *Torpedoboot 26* twelve months earlier. In comparison, Italy had suffered staggering losses in the first three months of its war at sea: two armored cruisers, one destroyer, three torpedo boats, four submarines, and two airships. To make matters worse, the shelling of the Italian coast, while only sporadic after the first night of the war, prompted representatives from coastal cities and towns to raise protests in the Chamber of Deputies in Rome. While things were going no better for the army, either in the Alps or on the Isonzo, at least Cadorna was keeping the Habsburg troops on the defensive. The navy became the focal point of Italian frustrations, and within the navy, Thaon di Revel became the principal target. During the course of an investigation, the navy minister, Vice Admiral Leone Viale, suggested that his own position and the post of naval chief of staff be combined under one man; on 24 September he submitted his resignation to help facilitate the change. Thaon di Revel, under fire from the deputies and still feuding with Abruzzi, stood on very shaky ground. While the prime minister, Antonio Salandra, pondered the alternatives, the Italian fleet suffered its biggest loss to date: on 27 September, the 13,400-ton pre-dreadnought *Benedetto Brin* blew up in Brindisi harbor, apparently the victim of sabotage. The disaster claimed the lives of 23 officers and 433 seamen. Two weeks later, Thaon di Revel was banished to the post of commander of the navy's contingent at Venice. Vice Admiral Camillo Corsi, Viale's replacement as navy minister, assumed the duties of chief of staff while Abruzzi remained fleet commander.[74]

The reorganization of the Italian naval hierarchy coincided with a temporary lull in the action in the Adriatic as attentions shifted back to the Balkans. Over the summer of 1915, the Central Powers registered dramatic successes against the Russians, and by September the front stretched from Latvia in the north to the eastern edge of Galicia in the south. Swayed by the Russian defeats, Bulgaria signed treaties of alliance with Germany and Austria-Hungary on 6 September. This turn of events increased the vulnerability of Serbia, which had been relatively secure since the failure of the initial Habsburg army invasion nine months earlier. Alarmed by the prospect of a collapse of the Balkan front, Britain and France arranged with neutral Greece to land troops at Salonika. A force of two divisions disembarked on 3 October, just three days before the Central Powers renewed their campaign against the Serbs. While one German and one Austro-Hungarian army attacked Serbia from the north and west, two Bulgarian armies attacked from the east. The monitors of the Danube flotilla bombarded Belgrade in support of the army, which occupied the Serbian capital at the end of the first week of the fighting.[75]

While the Bulgarians held off the small Anglo-French force, the advancing German and Austro-Hungarian armies pushed the Serbs farther southward. Unable to fall back to the Greek border, they retreated southwestward toward Albania. In mid-November, the Entente powers worked out a scheme under which supplies for the Serbian army, which Britain, France, and Russia paid for, would be collected at Brindisi and convoyed by the Italian navy across the Adriatic to Albania for transshipment to the interior. The Italians also reinforced their garrisons in Albania. Haus responded by ordering the light forces at Cattaro to maintain a vigorous surveillance of the Albanian coast. The scout cruisers *Helgoland, Saida,* and *Novara,* joined by destroyers and torpedo boats, sank at least a dozen supply vessels in a three-week period. The sorties were not aimed at enemy warships, and only one was sunk: on 5 December, en route home to Cattaro as an escort of the *Novara,* the destroyer *Warasdiner* sank the French submarine *Fresnel* off the coast of Montenegro. The greatest enemy setbacks came as a result of Austrian mines. The Italian navy lost the 3,000-ton auxiliary cruiser *Re Umberto* and the destroyer *Intrepido,* both off Valona on 4 December.[76]

For the admirals of the Entente, the problems with the supply operation brought the eruption of tensions that had been growing for two months. In October 1915, the French navy withdrew its twelve destroyers from the First Fleet in the Adriatic for duty in the Aegean in support of the Anglo-French landing at Salonika. Abruzzi subsequently complained that he did not have enough vessels suitable for convoy duty, but Corsi could provide no replacements. When the Austro-Hungarian raids against the convoys proved to be so successful, the Italians naturally blamed the French. In early December, just as the beaten and hungry Serbian army started to cross the border into Albania, Italy abruptly cut off its supply operation and vowed not to resume the convoys until the French returned at least six of their destroyers to the Adriatic. Vice Admiral Louis Dartige du Fournet, Lapeyrère's successor as French—and overall Entente—commander in the Mediterranean, met with Abruzzi at Taranto in mid-December and quickly agreed to the Italian demand. By then all of Serbia was in the hands of the Central Powers, and the situation in Albania was deteriorating by the day. With the advancing Habsburg army bearing down on the routed Serbs, the question of supply gave way to one of evacuation. Over the next two months, in almost 250 individual steamer passages, the Entente navies successfully ferried 260,000 Serbian troops and civilian refugees to Corfu. While the island became a long-term haven for the refugees and sick or wounded soldiers, 130,000 Serbian troops were shipped on from Corfu to Salonika in the spring of 1916 to bolster the Anglo-French force along the Greco-Bulgarian border.[77]

The evacuation of the Serbian army to Corfu and the subsequent transport of so many Serbs to Salonika were remarkable operations, made all the more extraordinary by the fact that not a single transport steamer was torpedoed in either case. German submariners had enjoyed good luck in the Aegean in the fall of 1915,[78] but in a dramatic reversal of fortune they had no luck at all during the ensuing winter and spring months. The Austro-Hungarian effort at sea suffered a similar turn of fate. After disrupting the supply line between Brindisi and the Albanian coast in November and early December, the same light cruisers, destroyers, and torpedo boats continued their sorties throughout the time of the Serbian army evacuation, but to no avail. The Italians ultimately lost only the auxiliary cruiser *Città di Palermo* and two transports, and the French, two transports, all of which struck mines.[79]

An Austro-Hungarian sortie on 29 December 1915 escalated into the greatest sea battle in the Adriatic thus far. Captain Heinrich Seitz and the *Helgoland*, escorted by five *Tátra*-class destroyers, raided the Italian-held Albanian port of Durazzo early in the morning and destroyed a handful of merchant ships; on the way out of the harbor, however, the destroyers *Lika* and *Triglav* ran into a minefield. Attempts to save the crew of the *Lika* and tow the *Triglav* to safety kept Seitz off Durazzo for hours, and by the time he turned north to head back to Cattaro, a superior enemy force from Brindisi blocked his way. The afternoon of the twenty-ninth featured a dramatic high-speed chase as the cruiser and three surviving destroyers sought to elude an Anglo-French-Italian force that grew to include four cruisers and nine destroyers. In a bold gamble, Seitz ran due west for the Italian coast, banking on the fact that he would eventually gain enough of a lead on his pursuers to turn north and head for home. After the captain radioed Cattaro for help, the commander of the Cruiser Flotilla, Vice Admiral Fiedler, sent out the armored cruiser *Kaiser Karl VI*, which found Seitz's pursuers but was too slow to keep up with the chase. Even though a late-afternoon sun on the port side of the Austro-Hungarian vessels gave the enemy a good silhouette to fire upon, they steamed on unscathed and reached the Italian coast off Bari around sunset. Seitz was able to turn north well in front of the enemy and run for Sebenico, which he reached before dawn on 30 December. Seitz's peers hailed his successful escape, but Haus was not so charitable. He held the captain responsible for bungling the attack on Durazzo and losing the two destroyers and criticized him for his failure to turn on his pursuers after nightfall. It was of no consolation to Haus that one enemy vessel had been destroyed in the action: the French submarine *Monge*, which was struck by the *Helgoland* before dawn on the twenty-ninth, when Seitz was still en route to Durazzo, and subsequently sunk by fire from the destroyer *Balaton*. In January 1916, Seitz lost his command; he would remain inactive as long as Haus commanded the fleet. Meanwhile, across the Adriatic, Entente commanders were furious that their superior force had failed to trap Seitz's flotilla and finish it off.[80]

The navy's subsequent role in the collapse of Montenegro, though far less dramatic than the battle of 29 December 1915, was far more significant for the course of the war. On 8 January, the warships of the Fifth Division and the Cruiser Flotilla in the Bocche di Cattaro began a three-day bombardment of the Montenegrin positions on Mount Lovčen; particularly effective were the 9.4-inch guns of the *Kaiser Karl VI*, the old coast defender *Budapest*, and the still older ram cruiser *Kaiser Franz Joseph I*. After storming the mountain on 11 January, the army's

XIX Corps moved on to take Montenegro's capital, Cetinje, on the thirteenth. Four days later, the Montenegrins surrendered, and the Austro-Hungarian corps moved on into northern Albania. Once there, they disrupted the last stages of the Serbian evacuation effort; at the end of February, they took Durazzo from the Italians. The Entente then stabilized the Balkan front along a line stretching eastward from Valona. Italian troops held the southern half of Albania, and an Anglo-French-Serbian force occupied the Greek territory around Salonika; in between lay the rest of Greece, still neutral.[81] The advances on land left Cattaro more secure than ever before. After February 1916, the Cruiser Flotilla, which had been divided between Pola and the Bocche for the first year and a half of the war, made Cattaro its permanent home. Hansa and the Fifth Battle Division were subordinated to Vice Admiral Fiedler, the cruiser commander.[82]

In the last months of 1915, as the war in the Balkans heated up, the submarines of the Central Powers remained active in the Adriatic and Mediterranean. Because Germany still was not at war with Italy, German submarines stalking Italian vessels continued to do so under their ally's flag. Remarkably enough, this practice caused no great diplomatic complications until November 1915, when the German *U38* (a.k.a. Austro-Hungarian *U38*) torpedoed the 8,200-ton passenger liner *Ancona* while hunting off the Tunisian coast. The ship, en route from Messina to New York, was fully booked and more than two hundred lives were lost, some of them American. Coming six months after the torpedoing of the *Lusitania* off the Irish coast, the *Ancona* sinking only added to the growing American outrage over unrestricted submarine warfare. Robert Lansing, Woodrow Wilson's secretary of state, sent a sharply worded protest to Vienna.[83]

Lansing's note prompted Count Burián and the Austro-Hungarian foreign ministry to ask the *Marinesektion* for details of the existing arrangements for German use of the Austrian flag. Burián, no doubt shocked to learn of the extent of the practice, subsequently took most of the fire over the *Ancona* incident. In December the United States demanded that Austria-Hungary denounce the sinking and punish the captain of the submarine responsible for it. The Germans, eager to keep the United States neutral, advised Burián to give in to the American demands. Ultimately Vienna agreed to pay an indemnity and also assured Washington that the captain would be punished, although because the captain was, in fact, a German navy officer, this promise was meaningless. Once the affair was settled, Austria-Hungary formally requested that German submariners refrain from torpedoing passenger vessels when flying the Austrian flag. Burián's diplomatic retreat angered Haus, who had advocated a harder line after the *Ancona* sinking. He justified the targeting of the ship on the grounds that on its return voyage from the United States, it could have been used to transport arms or Italian emigrants returning home for military service.[84] The controversial undersea campaign also divided Germany's leaders. In March 1916, a bitter debate in Berlin led to the resignation of the leading proponent of unrestricted submarine warfare, the once-powerful state secretary in the Imperial Navy Office, Admiral Tirpitz. The Germans themselves then yielded to American pressure for an end to unrestricted submarine warfare in the Atlantic. In late April 1916, Chancellor Theobald von Bethmann Hollweg called off the campaign.[85]

Even at times when the Central Powers were not torpedoing civilian vessels, the submarine threat to enemy warships led the Entente navies to devise ingenious counterstrategies. Late in 1915, after it became clear that German submarines were using the Austrian bases in the Adriatic, the British resolved to close the Straits of Otranto with antisubmarine nets. They assembled a force of dozens of armed trawlers and auxiliary steamers to drag the nets, but operational and maintenance problems were to plague the effort throughout the war. The "drifters," as the vessels were known, were of course quite vulnerable to attack. In May 1916, the scout cruiser *Helgoland* led a small flotilla in a raid on the barrage line and sank one of the drifters; in early July, Captain Horthy's *Novara* sank or damaged several trawlers, and in late August, another was sunk by an Austro-Hungarian seaplane.[86] But the British strategy could claim some successes. In May 1916, the *U6*, the first submarine snagged in the nets, had to be scuttled by its own crew.[87]

The loss of the *U6* reduced the Austro-Hungarian submarine fleet to ten boats, but by the summer of 1916, eleven more were under construction in various Habsburg shipyards. Four boats (the future *U20* through *U23*) were laid down before the end of 1915 by the Ungarische Unterseebootsbau AG, more commonly known by the acronym UBAG, a new subsidiary of the Whitehead firm of Rijeka. Between March and August 1916, four submarines (the future *U29* through *U32*) were begun in Rijeka by the Danubius firm, while the Cantiere Navale Triestino, displaced by the land war from its own shipyard in Monfalcone, built another three (*U27, U28,* and *U40*) in the Pola Arsenal. With normal political life suspended and the annual Delegations not meeting, funding for new construction came through the joint consent of the heads of the two cabinets of the Dual Monarchy, Count Karl Stürgkh in Austria and Count Tisza in Hungary; it was at the latter's insistence that most of the contracts went to Hungarian firms. The appropriation was supplemented by 2.2 million kronen raised by the Austrian Navy League, enough to pay for one of the undersea boats, the *U40.* The submarine program did little to strain the budget, but operational expenses and wartime inflation combined to drive naval spending for 1915–16 to 276 million, a dramatic increase from 190 million in 1914–15. Inflation was largely responsible for another rapid escalation, to 379 million, in 1916–17. Owing to construction delays, most notably on the four UBAG boats, none of the eleven submarines entered service before the beginning of 1917.[88]

In the meantime, the navy's older submarines continued to account for most of the successes against the enemy. Before being caught in the Otranto nets, *U6* torpedoed and sank the French destroyer *Renaudin* off Durazzo in March 1916. On 8 June, *U5* sank the 7,900-ton transport *Principe Umberto* off Valona, drowning two thousand Italian soldiers. Two weeks later in the Straits of Otranto, *U15* sank the French destroyer *Fourche* and the 3,500-ton Italian auxiliary cruiser *Città di Messina,* both of which had been deployed to guard the drifters on the antisubmarine barrage. At the end of June, the Italians lost the torpedo boat *Serpente* to shipwreck, and in early July, *U17* torpedoed the Italian destroyer *Impetuoso* while hunting in the Straits of Otranto. During the same month, the Entente lost another three submarines in the Adriatic: the Italian *Ballila,* sunk north of Lissa by the torpedo boats *65-F* and *66-F;* the British *H3,* which struck a mine off Cattaro; and the Italian *Pullino,* stranded on a reef while attempting a raid on Rijeka. The crew of the latter included the Istrian émigré Nazario Sauro, who was considered a martyr in Italy after his subsequent execution by the Austrians on charges of high treason.[89]

The navy's luck continued into the late summer and fall of 1916. After Romania joined the Entente in August, the Danube flotilla once again became an active player in the war. In the first days of the campaign, the monitors ventured far down the river to bombard Giurgiu.

Later they covered river crossings into Romania by the armies of the Central Powers attacking from Bulgaria, most notably on 23 November at Svishtov, paving the way for the fall of Bucharest two weeks later.[90] Meanwhile, back in the Adriatic, the Italians lost an airship and the destroyer *Audace* to accidents during August, and in September another dirigible was destroyed in a bombing raid on the airfield of Iesi, near Ancona. The same month, an Austro-Hungarian seaplane bombed and sank the French submarine *Foucault* off Cattaro, and in October *U16* torpedoed the Italian destroyer *Nembo* off the Albanian coast. The string of good fortune came to an end, however, when the Italian auxiliary cruiser *Bermida* rammed and sank the *U16* shortly after the sinking of the *Nembo*.[91] Three days before Christmas, in the last action of the year, Captain Nowotny's *Scharfschütze* led three other destroyers in a night-time raid against the Otranto barrage line. After sinking two British drifters, they encountered a flotilla of six French destroyers, reinforced by five Italian destroyers and a British cruiser; fighting a rearguard action en route home to Cattaro, the Habsburg vessels damaged two French destroyers.[92] For the year 1916, the Entente's losses of naval vessels in the Adriatic (two auxiliary cruisers, five destroyers, four submarines, one torpedo boat, and one large transport) far outweighed those of the Austro-Hungarian navy (two submarines). Nevertheless, for the small undersea force, the loss of two boats was a significant blow.

Though relatively heavy, the enemy losses included no regular warship larger than a destroyer. From the start of the war, the Entente commanders were careful with their battleships, but after the campaigns of 1914 and 1915, they were equally cautious in deploying their cruisers. In April 1916, Abruzzi secured the recall from Venice of the three surviving *Pisa*-class armored cruisers, which had remained in port almost continuously since the sinking of the *Amalfi* in July 1915. The three cruisers went first to Valona, then to Brindisi in May 1916, when the four pre-dreadnoughts of the *Regina Elena* class were sent from Brindisi to Valona.[93] The redeployment bolstered the Italian position in southern Albania, which had been threatened earlier in the year by the defeats of Serbia and Montenegro and the Austro-Hungarian occupation of northern Albania. It also confirmed the Italian and overall Entente strategy of drawing the line at the mouth of the Adriatic and conceding the sea itself to Austria-Hungary, especially in light of the submarine threat. The great Anglo-German Battle of Jutland (31 May), the only fleet-scale action of the war in the North Sea, did not inspire either Abruzzi or Haus to seek a similar encounter in the Adriatic. Even though their battle fleets were stronger than ever—the fourth Austro-Hungarian dreadnought, *Szent István*, had been commissioned in November 1915, and the sixth Italian dreadnought, *Andrea Doria*, had entered service in March 1916— both commanders continued to strike at one another with submarines and light surface vessels, while the dreadnoughts remained safely at anchor in Pola and Taranto.

At least on the Italian side, however, home ports were not always such safe places. On 2 August 1916, just over ten months after losing the pre-dreadnought *Benedetto Brin*, the Italian navy suffered its greatest disaster of the entire war when a mysterious explosion wracked the 23,000-ton dreadnought *Leonardo da Vinci* in Taranto harbor. The ship went down with 21 officers and 227 seamen still aboard, apparently another victim of sabotage. In material terms, the new dreadnought represented a much more serious loss than the ten-year-old *Benedetto Brin;* the Italian government launched an investigation but censored all news of the disaster, fearing the negative impact on public morale. A similar shroud of secrecy surrounded the accidental sinking of the 13,400-ton pre-dreadnought *Regina Margherita*, sister ship of the *Benedetto Brin*, which struck a mine while leaving Valona harbor on the evening of 11 December; 15 officers and 659 seamen drowned. The loss was finally made public in January 1917, with no details of where or when the accident had occurred.[94]

Amid all of the bad news, the Italian navy could take some solace in the development of a new weapon, the *motobarche anti-sommergibili* or *MAS*, a twelve-ton motor torpedo boat designed initially as a submarine chaser but ultimately much more successful against enemy surface vessels. Between the ordering of the first prototypes in March 1915 and November 1918, 244 of the boats entered service; at the end of the war, another 175 were under construction, including models ranging up to 44 tons displacement. The Italians used the motorboats to take advantage of the bravery and audacity of their junior officers, and the results at times were spectacular. They first demonstrated their offensive potential in a nighttime raid on Durazzo in June 1916 in which *MAS-5* and *MAS-7* torpedoed and sank the Austro-Hungarian merchant steamer *Lokrum*. Those in charge of local security in the harbors of the Dual Monarchy, heretofore concerned mostly with enemy submarine infiltration, would have to devise new measures against surface attacks by the small high-speed torpedo boats.[95]

Seaports and naval bases also had to be defended against an increasing threat from the air, for by the autumn of 1916, Italy had wrested control of the skies over the Adriatic away from Austria-Hungary. Thanks in part to licensing arrangements that enabled French-designed aircraft to be built in Italy, the Italian naval air service grew from 39 planes at the end of 1915 to 172 a year later. Mounting Austro-Hungarian losses reflected the changing balance in the air. In 1914 no planes or pilots were lost through enemy action, and in 1915 only three planes were shot down, with three pilots killed. For 1916 the figures were twelve planes and twenty pilots. For the entire war through 1916, the navy's pilots shot down only five enemy planes. Lieutenant Gottfried Banfield registered four of the kills and was rewarded with the Order of Maria Theresa in August 1917.[96]

In the future, air superiority and the new *MAS* would give the Italians the decisive edge in the *mezzi insidiosi* of the "little war" in the Adriatic. In the meantime, the loss of the battleships—especially the *Leonardo da Vinci*—exacerbated frustrations in Italy over the general poor performance of the navy. The Duke of the Abruzzi, whose record as commander of the First Fleet had not lived up to expectations, was forced to retire in early February 1917 "for reasons of health." Though immensely popular with his own officer corps, he would never again hold a naval command. The shake-up revived the career of Thaon di Revel, since October 1915 in exile as commander of Venice. He returned to his old post as navy chief of staff and also inherited Abruzzi's powers as commander in chief of the Italian fleet. Admiral Corsi, who had served as both navy minister and chief of staff for the past sixteen months, soon lost his portfolio in the cabinet as well.[97]

Thaon di Revel would be in no better position than his predecessor to launch an aggressive campaign in the Adriatic. In January 1917, just before his dismissal, Corsi attended an allied naval conference in London, hoping that the recent Italian battleship losses would prompt the British Admiralty to agree to replace the four aging British pre-dreadnoughts of the First Fleet with four dreadnoughts. Much to his shock, the British instead announced the withdrawal of three of the pre-dreadnoughts and offered no replacements at all; the lone battleship *Queen* would remain at Taranto, but only as a depot ship for the drifters of the Otranto barrage line. The French offered Corsi the support of their fleet from the Ionian Sea—which now included seven dreadnoughts—but only in an emergency and on the condition that the Italian fleet commander would be subordinated to the new French commander in chief, Vice Admiral Dominique-Marie Gauchet, even in the Adriatic.[98]

The winter of 1916–17 also brought a revision of the strategy of the Central Powers, coinciding with a great transformation in the political and military leadership in Austria-Hungary. On 21 November, Francis Joseph died, and the crown passed to his great-nephew, Charles. In early December, the new emperor took personal command of the armed forces and moved the *Armeeoberkommando* from Teschen (Těšin) to Baden, south of Vienna, where he could take an active part in its proceedings. The changes undercut the positions of Archduke Frederick, titular commander since the beginning of the war, and Conrad von Hötzendorf, who as chief of the General Staff had been the de facto operational commander of the army. Frederick stayed on for two months as Charles's "assistant," then was retired; Conrad lasted another month before being demoted to a field command in the Tyrol in March 1917. The purge also claimed war minister Krobatin, an old friend of Conrad. Generals Arthur Arz von Straussenburg and Rudolf Stöger-Steiner became chief of the General Staff and war minister, respectively. The change of monarchs also affected operations against the enemy. Allegedly under pressure from his strong-willed wife, the Empress Zita, Charles reserved the right to authorize the use of gas on the battlefield and ordered an end to all aerial bombardment that might endanger civilians.[99] After being hit by twenty-seven air raids over the past eighteen months, Venice—the favorite urban target of Austro-Hungarian seaplanes—enjoyed a respite of five months before the unrealistic humanitarian measures were rescinded.[100]

The new empress was known to oppose the German philosophy of submarine warfare,[101] but at least in this area, she had little influence on her husband. On 15 December 1916, William II made his first wartime visit to Pola, accompanied by Charles. In inspecting the fleet and harbor installations, the two monarchs paid special attention to the submarines and the facilities supporting them.[102] Following William's return to Berlin, the German *Admiralstab* resolved to resume unrestricted submarine warfare, after a hiatus of eight months. After the German government formally endorsed the policy, foreign secretary Arthur Zimmermann and *Admiralstab* chief Admiral Henning von Holtzendorff traveled to Vienna to secure their allies' agreement. From Pola, Haus wholeheartedly supported the German proposal, but in the imperial capital, the reaction was far less enthusiastic. Count Ottokar Czernin, Burián's successor as foreign minister, had grave misgivings about unrestricted submarine warfare, as did the emperor himself; Count Tisza, the Hungarian minister-president, shared their doubts. Haus and the Germans ultimately swayed them, in part by citing Entente sinkings of unarmed Austro-Hungarian vessels in the Adriatic.[103] There were nine such cases, among them the torpedoing of the 3,200-ton Habsburg army hospital ship *Elektra* in March 1916 by a French submarine.[104]

On 20 January, Zimmermann and Holtzendorff met in Vienna with Haus, Czernin, Tisza, and Austrian minister-president Count Heinrich Clam-Martinic, successor to Stürgkh, who had been assassinated the previous autumn. Czernin's postwar account of the session, emphasizing his own opposition to the resumption of the campaign, observes that "Admiral Haus agreed *unreservedly* with the arguments of the German navy." On the danger of provoking the United States into joining the Entente against the Central Powers, Haus "declared that *no great anxiety need be felt*." The ministers reluctantly gave their consent.[105] An aide of Emperor Charles, Arthur Polzer-Hoditz, later offered his own version of the meeting in which a noncommittal Czernin "sagte nicht ja und nicht nein" on the question of resuming the campaign. Polzer-Hoditz's account asserts that Charles did not sanction the policy until Holtzendorff informed him that the orders already had been issued to German submarine commanders; unrestricted warfare would resume on 1 February 1917. The emperor then gave his approval "under angry protest."[106]

Shortly after the Vienna conference, Charles arranged to meet with William II at German supreme headquarters at Schloss Pless. Haus and his adjutant, Rear Admiral Rodler, head of the naval command chancellery in Pola, accompanied the emperor on his trip to Germany. The negotiations over the terms of the campaign in the Mediterranean, which were held on 26 January, were greatly simplified by the fact that Italy finally had declared war on Germany on 28 August 1916, making it unnecessary for German submarines to pretend to be Austrian when attacking Italian targets. Under an Austro-German agreement of October 1916, three German submarines—*U35, U38,* and *U39*—still identified themselves as Austrian vessels to avoid raising suspicions among the Entente and neutral powers over what would have been a very sudden end to "Austrian" submarine activity outside of the Adriatic. At Schloss Pless, it was agreed that the same boats would retain their dual designation. Haus promised to deploy submarines against Entente convoys between Malta and Salonika and to disarm the aging cruisers *Maria Theresia* and *Panther* in order to provide the manpower to service the increasing German submarine traffic at Cattaro.[107]

For Haus, the meeting at Schloss Pless was the high-water mark of an often stormy wartime relationship with his counterparts in the Imperial German navy. The future cooperation would be unprecedented, but it would also come under a new navy leadership. The sixty-five-year-old Haus, already in ill health, succumbed to pneumonia on the trip to Germany and died on 8 February aboard his flagship, the *Viribus Unitis.* The emperor, who felt personally responsible for hastening the admiral's demise, came to Pola for the funeral, accompanied by the former admiral Archduke Charles Stephen as well as Krobatin and Conrad, then in their last days in office.[108] Having been awarded the new designation of grand admiral (*Grossadmiral*) just a few months earlier, Haus went to his grave as the highest-ranking officer in the history of the navy.

Haus's tenure of almost exactly four years was the shortest of any *Marinekommandant* since Tegetthoff, but the war made the last two and a half years the most active time in the navy's history. If judged on the balance of naval losses alone, the campaign thus far merited the highest marks. Under Haus's command, the fleet had lost only the old cruisers *Zenta* and *Kaiserin Elisabeth,* the destroyers *Lika* and *Triglav,* one old torpedo boat, and four submarines. During the same time, the Entente forces in the Adriatic theater lost one dreadnought, two pre-dreadnought battleships, three armored cruisers, one light cruiser, three auxiliary cruisers, eight destroyers, four torpedo boats, eleven submarines, and four airships. The navy still was able to do little to disturb the Entente's Mediterranean activities, but the German submarines had become a serious concern to the enemy, and without access to Adriatic bases their operations would have been impossible.

The Austro-Hungarian dreadnoughts and the rest of the battle fleet at Pola remained in port, but as a "fleet in being," they served several purposes. The deployment protected the largest and most populous port cities, Trieste and Rijeka, which were threatened only by isolated attacks from Italian torpedo boats, submarines, and airships, all of which failed miserably. The Italian squadron at Venice had to remain in port for fear of being caught at sea by a superior force from Pola. Any move by the Entente navies to reinforce Venice with dreadnoughts or additional older battleships would have provoked a fleet-scale action in the northern or central Adriatic on terms very favorable to the Austrians, something that Abruzzi, in particular, had no intention of doing. At the same time, the raids and patrols by the light cruisers, destroyers, torpedo boats, and submarines based at Cattaro foiled Italian plans to dominate the southern Adriatic and created an atmosphere in which the fear of torpedo attacks kept larger Entente warships south of the Straits of Otranto. While the Habsburg army continued to hold the line on the Isonzo and in the Alps against a numerically superior enemy, the navy likewise managed to protect the Adriatic border in spite of being vastly outnumbered by its foes.

NOTES

1. See Sondhaus, *The Habsburg Empire and the Sea*, 190–93.

2. Sokol, *Des Kaisers Seemacht*, 284; Edgar Tomicich, "Die k.(u.)k. Marineakademie," 40.

3. The twelve steamers requisitioned by the navy in July 1914 ranged in size from the *Austria* (7,588 tons) to the *Urano* (2,627 tons), both of the Lloyd. See Greger, *Austro-Hungarian Warships*, 113–14, 118–20.

4. See order of battle in ibid., 11–12.

5. Ibid., 12.

6. Bayer von Bayersburg, *Österreichs Admirale*, 15–16.

7. Greger, *Austro-Hungarian Warships*, 14–15.

8. Tomicich, "Die k.(u.)k. Marineakademie," 40. The academy, minus the senior class already with the fleet, remained at Schlosshof for the 1914–15 school year. Sailing instruction was limited to two small cutters brought from Rijeka for use on the Morava, today the border between Austria and Slovakia.

9. Sokol, *Österreich-Ungarns Seekrieg*, 1:76, 88–89.

10. Ibid., 1:77–80.

11. Adrien Thomazi, *La guerre navale dans l'Adriatique*, 39–40; Sokol, *Österreich-Ungarns Seekrieg*, 1:80–87. Of the 312 officers and men aboard the *Zenta*, 139 survivors—including Pachner—made it ashore and were taken prisoner by the Montenegrins. They were freed early in 1916 after the defeat of Montenegro.

12. Thomazi, *La guerre navale*, 45, 50; Sokol, *Österreich-Ungarns Seekrieg*, 1:113–14, 115–16, 122–31. Haus, "Promemoria über die Kriegslage in der Adria," Pola, 24 October

1914, text in Conrad von Hötzendorf, *Aus meiner Dienstzeit,* 5:303, places the first eight sorties on 16 August; 1, 6, 18, and 19 September; and 4, 5, and 17 October.

13. Halpern, *Naval War in the Mediterranean,* 28–30, 33.

14. Ibid., 29; Gottlieb von Pára (consul) to Seebezirkskommando Triest, Corfu, 20 October 1914 (cipher telegram), HHSA, AR, F 44 - Marinewesen, Carton 13: Kriegsschiffe Frankreich, Kriegs-Operationen 7.

15. Thomazi, *La guerre navale,* 52–57; Sokol, *Österreich-Ungarns Seekrieg,* 1:88–96. The use of battleships as convoy escorts caused French fuel costs to escalate dramatically. Haus, "Promemoria," 5:304, estimates that the French burned the equivalent of 200,000 to 300,000 kronen worth of coal on each operation to resupply the Montenegrins.

16. Haus to Kailer, Pola, 6 September 1914, quoted in Halpern, *Naval War in the Mediterranean,* 30.

17. Ibid., 38–39.

18. Sokol, *Österreich-Ungarns Seekrieg,* 1:97–100.

19. *Jahresbericht der k.u.k. Kriegsmarine* (1913), 92–95. Figures do not include coal purchased for harbor use or for the Pola Arsenal.

20. Halpern, *Naval War in the Mediterranean,* 30. An 1882 graduate of the academy, Hansa, at fifty-one, was two years younger than Barry.

21. Ibid., 39.

22. Aichelburg, *Die Unterseeboote,* 1:63–66; Halpern, *Naval War in the Mediterranean,* 40.

23. Sokol, *Österreich-Ungarns Seekrieg,* 2:753–69; Bayer von Bayersburg, *Auf weiter Fahrt,* 200–203. Nine officers were sent home from the ship on the first of August, before the Japanese blockaded Kiaochow Bay.

24. Dieter Winkler and Georg Pawlik, *Die Dampfschiffahrtsgesellschaft Österreichischer Lloyd, 1836–1918,* 83.

25. Plocek and Juba, "Geschichte der ungarischen Reederei Adria," 20.

26. Lothar Baumgartner et al., "Die Austro-Americana: Geschichte einer österreichischen Reederei," 45.

27. Winkler and Mayer, *In allen Häfen war Österreich,* 182–84.

28. Wulff, *Donauflottille,* 35–45 passim; Greger, *Austro-Hungarian Warships,* 141. The *Temes* was raised in the summer of 1916 and recommissioned a year later. In September 1914, the navy also lost two small patrol boats on the Sava, and in May 1915, a third boat ran aground and burned on the Danube at Belgrade after being shelled by Serbian batteries.

29. On the failed Balkan campaign of 1914, see Gunther E. Rothenberg, "The Austro-Hungarian Campaign against Serbia in 1914," 127–46. On the new monitors, see Greger, *Austro-Hungarian Warships,* 142.

30. Aichelburg, *Die Unterseeboote,* 1:49–50, 67–68.

31. Thomazi, *La guerre navale,* 68–70, 74; Aichelburg, *Die Unterseeboote,* 1:75–76.

32. Thomazi, *La guerre navale,* 67–68; Aichelburg, *Die Unterseeboote,* 1:70–74, 77–83.

33. *Jahresbericht der k.u.k. Kriegsmarine* (1914–17), 18.

34. Sokol, *Österreich-Ungarns Seekrieg,* 1:101–5.

35. Halpern, *Naval War in the Mediterranean,* 73, 94, 102–3.

36. Ibid., 69–70, 72–73, 102–3.

37. Haus to Beck, Pola, 31 March 1915, text in Erwin Sieche, "Die diplomatischen Aktivitäten rund um das Haus-Memorandum vom März 1915," 95. Emphasis in Haus's original.

38. Archduke Frederick to Haus, [Teschen,] 8 April 1915, text in ibid., 97.

39. Halpern, *Naval War in the Mediterranean*, 95; Thomazi, *Le guerre navale*, 77–79; Aichelburg, *Die Unterseeboote*, 1:87–88. For evidence of the extent to which the *Zenta* affair set the moral tone for Austro-Hungarian submariners, see Georg von Trapp, *Bis zum letzten Flaggenschuss: Erinnerungen eines österreichischen U-Boots-Kommandanten*, 37.

40. Halpern, *Naval War in the Mediterranean*, 109. A third German submarine, *UB3*, followed the example of the *UB7* and *UB8*, arriving at Pola in April 1915. An Austro-Hungarian warship towed the boat to the Straits of Otranto on 23 May, the day Italy declared war. Thereafter, *UB3* disappeared, never to be heard from again. See ibid., 116.

41. Ibid., 111–12; Greger, *Austro-Hungarian Warships*, 73–74. On the quality of construction of the *U14*, see Trapp, *Bis zum letzten Flaggenschuss*, 101.

42. Halpern, *Mediterranean Naval Situation*, 178; Greger, *Austro-Hungarian Warships*, 26, 36, 47; Aichelburg, *Die Unterseeboote*, 1:114; Sokol, *Österreich-Ungarns Seekrieg*, 1:319. On the Hungarian campaign to cancel the program, see Mayer, "Die k.u.k. Kriegsmarine 1912-1914," 85.

43. Greger, *Austro-Hungarian Warships*, 35, 44.

44. *Jahresbericht der k.u.k. Kriegsmarine* (1914–17), 15.

45. Halpern, *Naval War in the Mediterranean*, 85.

46. Ibid., 85–86. According to Halpern, "Allied charges that the Italians were afraid to risk their battle fleet are unfair and not true." Sullivan claims that the Italian admirals "had no intention of risking their ships by trying to seize the initiative: the army could win this war, while they husbanded their battleships for the next war against the French" ("A Fleet in Being," 114).

47. Halpern, *Naval War in the Mediterranean*, 87.

48. Ibid., 88–91.

49. Jelavich, *The Habsburg Empire in European Affairs*, 166.

50. Ibid.

51. For a complete text of the Treaty of London, see Ufficio Storico della R. Marina, *La marina italiana nella grande guerra*, 1:416–22. Source cited hereafter as *La marina italiana* with volume and page number(s).

52. For the most complete account of the negotiations, see Paul G. Halpern, "The Anglo-French-Italian Naval Convention of 1915," 106–29. For a text of the convention, see *La marina italiana*, 1:435–37; or Thomazi, *Le guerre navale*, 82–85.

53. Halpern, *Naval War in the Mediterranean*, 100–101.

54. See Thomazi, *La guerre navale*, 218–19; Giorgerini, *Almanacco*, passim; Bargoni, *Corazzate italiane (1893–1901)*, passim; Bargoni, *Corazzate italiane (1880–1892)*, 5.

55. Sokol, *Österreich-Ungarns Seekrieg*, 1:197.

56. Ibid., 1:198–209; *La marina italiana*, 2:22–32. For a detailed report of the damage in Ancona, see ibid., 2:573–79.

57. Sokol, *Österreich-Ungarns Seekrieg*, 1:210–14; *La marina italiana*, 2:33–65. Vuković quoted in Sokol, 1:214.

58. Ibid., 1:218. The "depressing impact [deprimierenden Eindruck]" was noted by an Austro-Hungarian consular official en route out of Italy via the coastal railway following the breach of diplomatic relations.

59. Rothenberg, *The Army of Francis Joseph*, 189-90.

60. Koudelka, *Denn Österreich lag einst am Meer*, 205, 212-13.

61. Rothenberg, *The Army of Francis Joseph*, 190; John Whittam, *The Politics of the Italian Army, 1861-1918*, 192-93.

62. Sokol, *Österreich-Ungarns Seekrieg*, 1:465-67.

63. *Jahresbericht der k.u.k. Kriegsmarine* (1914-17), 16-17; *La marina italiana*, 2:89-90, 108-11; Aichelburg, *Die Unterseeboote*, 1:121.

64. Thomazi, *La guerre navale*, 89; Schupita, *Die k.u.k. Seeflieger*, 85-86, 96, 171, 246, 251, 253. On the measures taken in Pola, see Trapp, *Bis zum letzten Flaggenschuss*, 125.

65. Midshipman Charles Drage, quoted in Halpern, *Naval War in the Mediterranean*, 126, 128. The four British warships, with years of launching, were the *London* (1899), *Implacable* (1899), *Queen* (1902), and *Prince of Wales* (1902), all displacing 15,000 tons. See Marder, *The Anatomy of British Sea Power*, 548.

66. Koudelka, *Denn Österreich lag einst am Meer*, 219, contends that as late as August 1916, Haus was still using the potential move to Cattaro as an excuse for keeping the battle fleet in port.

67. Halpern, *Naval War in the Mediterranean*, 129-32 passim; *La marina italiana*, 2:119-25. Of the cruiser's complement of 754 men, 682 survived the sinking.

68. Greger, *Austro-Hungarian Warships*, 82-83; Halpern, *Naval War in the Mediterranean*, 133, 152, 191, 252. German submarines sometimes flew the Turkish flag when surfaced in the eastern Mediterranean. See Halpern, 153.

69. Ibid., 133-35; *Jahresbericht der k.u.k. Kriegsmarine* (1914-17), 16; *La marina italiana*, 2:178-88. Of the 578 men aboard the *Garibaldi*, 525 were saved.

70. Halpern, *Naval War in the Mediterranean*, 136-38. Richmond quoted, 138. See also *La marina italiana*, 2:189-214.

71. *Jahresbericht der k.u.k. Kriegsmarine* (1914-17), 15-16.

72. Halpern, *Naval War in the Mediterranean*, 139; Thomazi, *La guerre navale*, 97.

73. Kailer to Min. des Äussern, Vienna, 26 October 1915, HHSA, AR, F 44 - Marinewesen, Carton 8: Torpedoausfuhr 1/40. Baron Karl von Giskra (ambassador) to Min. des Äussern, The Hague, 13 January 1916, ibid., 1/45, reports Dutch displeasure at the notion of bartering raw materials for torpedoes; the war had disrupted imports from the East Indies, and there was "hardly any rubber in the country." Kailer to Min. des Äussern, Vienna, 30 January 1916, ibid., 1/46, reiterates the original terms. On the new submarines, see Aichelburg, *Die Unterseeboote*, 1:102-5.

74. Halpern, *Naval War in the Mediterranean*, 141-47; *La marina italiana*, 2:308-16. Just over half of the men aboard the *Benedetto Brin* (482 of 938) survived the disaster. Halpern contends that the post of chief of staff was left vacant after the reassignment of Thaon di Revel; Ceva, *Le forze armate*, 462, lists Corsi as Thaon di Revel's successor.

75. See Wulff, *Donauflottille*, 61-71.

76. Halpern, *Naval War in the Mediterranean*, 208-9; Thomazi, *La guerre navale*, 109; *Jahresbericht der k.u.k. Kriegsmarine* (1914-17), 16.

77. Halpern, *Naval War in the Mediterranean*, 206-7, 209-12, 215-16, 242; Thomazi, *La guerre navale*, 114-19. *La marina italiana*, 2:467-532, provides the most detailed account of the Serbian evacuation. On Lapeyrère's resignation, see Halpern, 174.

78. Halpern, *Naval War in the Mediterranean*, 191.

79. Ibid., 216-17; Thomazi, *La guerre navale*, 117, 227, 228. The *Città di Palermo* was sunk in January 1916, the other four ships in February. In commenting on the navy's inability to sink any of the transports involved in the Serbian army evacuation, Sokol,

Österreich-Ungarns Seekrieg, 1:286–87, cites "great difficulties of a geographical, meteorological, and navigational nature" but also admits that the failure is hard to explain.

80. Karl von Lukas, "Der Durchbruch der *Helgoland* am 29.12.1915," 63–78; Thomazi, *La guerre navale,* 110–14; *La marina italiana,* 2:433–66.

81. Rothenberg, *The Army of Francis Joseph,* 191; Sokol, *Österreich-Ungarns Seekrieg,* 1:264–70. According to Rothenberg, Conrad von Hötzendorf's decision to detach a corps for the conquest of Montenegro angered the Germans, who wanted all Habsburg army resources on the Balkan front to remain focused on the pursuit of the retreating Serbs.

82. Lukas, "Der Durchbruch der *Helgoland,*" 69 and passim, places the commander of the Cruiser Flotilla, Vice Admiral Fiedler, in Cattaro at the time of Seitz's battle of 29 December 1915. Sokol, *Österreich-Ungarns Seekrieg,* 1:329–30, contends that Fiedler arrived in early February 1916 with the armored cruiser *Sankt Georg.*

83. Aichelburg, *Die Unterseeboote,* 1:129–30; Halpern, *Naval War in the Mediterranean,* 194.

84. Aichelburg, *Die Unterseeboote,* 1:130–32; Halpern, *Naval War in the Mediterranean,* 195–98, 203.

85. According to Herwig, *"Luxury" Fleet,* 164–65, German unrestricted submarine warfare started on 28 February 1915 and proceeded until a "virtual cancellation" on 18 September, some seven weeks before the torpedoing of the *Ancona;* the campaign resumed on 23 February 1916 and ended after the American protest of 20 April.

86. *Jahresbericht der k.u.k. Kriegsmarine* (1914–17), 17, claims that Horthy sank five trawlers on 9 July 1916; Halpern, *Naval War in the Mediterranean,* 280, contends that two were sunk and two damaged. The *Helgoland's* sortie is recorded in Halpern (ibid., 279) but not mentioned in the official Austrian record.

87. *Jahresbericht der k.u.k. Kriegsmarine* (1914–17), 15. The crew of the *U6* was rescued by British trawlers.

88. Greger, *Austro-Hungarian Warships,* 76; Aichelburg, *Die Unterseeboote,* 1:114–16. Budget figures from Sokol, *Österreich-Ungarns Seekrieg,* 1:319, 465.

89. Thomazi, *La guerre navale,* 126–28, 228; Halpern, *Naval War in the Mediterranean,* 255, 277, 280. On the capture and execution of Sauro, see Sondhaus, *In the Service of the Emperor,* 107–8; *La marina italiana,* 3:180–81.

90. Rothenberg, *The Army of Francis Joseph,* 197–98; Wulff, *Donauflottille,* 82–105.

91. *Jahresbericht der k.u.k. Kriegsmarine* (1914–17), 15, 17–18; Halpern, *Naval War in the Mediterranean,* 255, 277; Thomazi, *La guerre navale,* 227. The official *Jahresbericht* does not acknowledge the loss of the *U16* or its earlier torpedoing of the *Nembo;* it does, however, claim as "Austrian" the loss of the *U24* (actually the German *UC12*), which was never heard from again after a mine-laying mission off Taranto in March 1916. Aichelburg, *Die Unterseeboote,* 1:142, reports that the *Nembo* sank the *U16.*

92. Sokol, *Österreich-Ungarns Seekrieg,* 1:367–75; Thomazi, *La guerre navale,* 138–39. In the confusion of the pursuit, another French destroyer and an Italian destroyer were damaged in collisions.

93. Halpern, *Naval War in the Mediterranean,* 265.

94. *Jahresbericht der k.u.k. Kriegsmarine* (1914–17), 17; *La marina italiana,* 3:215–24, 516–18; Thomazi, *La guerre navale,* 128, 137–38. A total of 942 men survived the *Leonardo da Vinci* disaster, while 275 survived the sinking of the *Regina Margherita.*

95. *La marina italiana,* 3:50–55; Giorgerini, *Almanacco,* 531–33, 552–65 passim.

96. Schupita, *Die k.u.k. Seeflieger,* 178–79, 245, 251; Banfield, *Der Adler von Triest,* 89.

CHAPTER 7

97. Halpern, *Naval War in the Mediterranean,* 333–36. Corsi left the navy ministry in June 1917. His replacement, Rear Admiral Arturo Triangi, held office for only a month before giving way to Vice Admiral Alberto Del Bono, who remained in office until 1919. See Ceva, *Le forze armate,* 459.

98. Thomazi, *La guerre navale,* 140–43; Halpern, *Naval War in the Mediterranean,* 331–33. Dartige du Fournet was fired in January 1917, just before the allied naval conference, for his alleged mismanagement of operations involving neutral Greece. See ibid., 300.

99. Rothenberg, *The Army of Francis Joseph,* 203.

100. According to Shanafelt, *The Secret Enemy,* 111, Zita specifically had opposed the bombardment of Venice. For details on the number and frequency of raids, see Schupita, *Die k.u.k. Seeflieger,* 246.

101. Shanafelt, *The Secret Enemy,* 111.

102. Aichelburg, *Die Unterseeboote,* 1:142.

103. Halpern, *The Naval War in the Mediterranean,* 307–9.

104. The *Elektra* was one of six requisitioned steamers to serve as Habsburg army hospital ships; the navy had one hospital ship of its own. See Greger, *Austro-Hungarian Warships,* 123. Thomazi, *La guerre navale,* 130, repeats the French contention that the *Elektra* was not well marked.

105. Ottokar Czernin, *In the World War,* 124. The italics are in Czernin's original account.

106. Arthur Polzer-Hoditz, *Kaiser Karl: Aus der Geheimmappe seines Kabinettchefs,* 273–74.

107. Halpern, *Naval War in the Mediterranean,* 251–52, 310.

108. The most detailed account of Haus's death and funeral is in the memoir of *Admiralstabsarzt* Anton von Eiselsberg, *Lebensweg eines Chirurgen,* 310–13. Eiselsberg performed the abdominal surgery on Haus in 1913 and remained close friends with the *Marinekommandant* until his death.

THE NAVY AT WAR: FROM NJEGOVAN TO HORTHY

While the passing of Haus initiated a reordering of the navy command structure, the frustrations generated by the late *Marinekommandant's* strategy for the war in the Adriatic had been largely responsible for the concurrent shake-up on the Italian side. Returning to power in Italy the day after Haus's death, Thaon di Revel would face the problem of fighting a war in league with allies whose patience with Italy had reached a low ebb. Both on land and at sea, Italy's entry into the war had not had the decisive effect that Britain and France had hoped for back in the spring of 1915. Indeed, the Italian navy's lack of confidence in its ability to contain the Austro-Hungarian fleet on its own had necessitated the detachment of a significant number of British and French warships to the Adriatic theater. But as Corsi learned at the recent Entente naval conference in London, Italy's allies were no longer in a mood to indulge every plea that came from Rome.

In sharp contrast, Haus's successors inherited a navy bound, for better or worse, closer than ever to its German ally. As the campaign of unrestricted submarine warfare resumed, the tensions of the past thirty months seemed to be laid to rest, replaced instead by a *Nibelungentreue* reminiscent of the prewar years and the perennial mutual assurances that when the chips were down, the two empires would stand together to the end.[1] But the common expressions of solidarity obscured the fact that Austria-Hungary essentially would be fighting for German war aims in the future. Ironically, with Habsburg territory completely free of enemy troops and secure on all fronts, and with the Balkans almost entirely under the domination of the Central Powers, the very success of the German alliance had left Austria-Hungary with no compelling reasons of its own to continue fighting. From the perspective of Vienna and

Budapest, the rationale for the German alliance all along had been to safeguard the Dual Monarchy against threats from other great powers, and by the start of 1917, the partnership already had served its purpose.[2]

THE NAVY UNDER NJEGOVAN
(FEBRUARY 1917–FEBRUARY 1918)

At the beginning of 1917, with the reorganization of the army command already underway, the military chancellery of Emperor Charles had produced a contingency plan to replace the ailing Haus and reshuffle the navy leadership. It embodied elements of Francis Ferdinand's schemes of 1912 and 1913, including the separation of the administrative command from the operational command of the fleet. A week after Haus's death, the plan went into effect. In the *Marinesektion,* Vice Admiral Kailer was promoted from *Stellvertreter* to chief; Rodler was brought from Pola to Vienna to serve as his second in command. The position of third in command (*zugeteilter Flaggenoffizier*), held since its creation in 1913 by Rear Admiral Franz von Keil, was abolished. The operational command of the fleet passed to Vice Admiral Njegovan, commander of the First Battle Squadron and the flag officer next in seniority after Haus. The Croatian received a promotion to full admiral but not the office of *Marinekommandant,* which remained vacant. Rear Admiral Franz von Holub took over for Rodler as fleet commander's adjutant and head of the naval command chancellery in Pola. But Charles's plan to finally divide the operational command of the fleet from the administrative command was foiled ten weeks after Haus's death when Kailer died just one month short of his fifty-fifth birthday. The emperor decided to keep Rodler in Vienna as *Stellvertreter,* in charge of the navy administration in the same way that Kailer had been under Haus. On the last day of April 1917, Admiral Njegovan, fleet commander in Pola, received the posts of *Marinekommandant* and chief of the *Marinesektion.*[3]

The changes in leadership affected the squadron and flotilla commands as well. In Pola, Vice Admiral Anton Willenik succeeded Njegovan as head of the First Battle Squadron, and Rear Admiral Karl Seidensacher became commander of the Second Battle Squadron. In Cattaro, Rear Admiral Hansa replaced Fiedler as head of the Cruiser Flotilla. Later in the year, Fiedler succeeded the retiring Admiral Chmelarž as harbor admiral in Pola. Captain Thierry remained head of the submarine command and, after January 1917, enjoyed a higher status directly under the fleet commander; in the past, his chain of command in Pola went through the harbor admiral, and since October 1915 the submarines at Cattaro had been subordinated to the head of the Fifth Battle Division. Overall, the changes resulted in a slightly younger leadership. After Chmelarž's retirement, the seven most prominent admirals all were under sixty.[4]

Owing to the light losses suffered in the war thus far, the new commanders had at their disposal virtually the same warships that Haus had inherited from Montecuccoli, built or building, four years earlier. The fleet at Pola included the four 20,000-ton dreadnoughts *Viribus Unitis, Tegetthoff, Prinz Eugen,* and *Szent István,* along with the 14,500-ton *Radetzky* and its sister ships *Erzherzog Franz Ferdinand* and *Zrinyi.* The nine older battleships—three each of the 10,600-ton *Erzherzog* class, the 8,300-ton *Habsburg* class, and the 5,600-ton *Monarch* class—remained armed and manned but were of dubious value; the latter trio had spent most of the war at Cattaro, used strictly for local defense. Of the armored cruisers, the obsolete *Maria Theresia* had been disarmed in one of Haus's last actions as commander. The *Kaiser Karl VI* and *Sankt Georg* remained with the Cruiser Flotilla at Cattaro, even though their limited speed kept them from operating with the newer scout cruisers—*Admiral Spaun, Saida, Novara,* and *Helgoland*—which shouldered the burden of the surface warfare in the lower Adriatic. Older unarmored cruisers likewise were of limited value; Haus had decommissioned the *Panther* but kept the *Aspern, Szigetvár,* and *Kaiser Franz Joseph I* in service. Not counting obsolete coastal defense vessels, there were seventeen destroyers (thirteen 400-ton *Huszárs* and four 870-ton *Tátras*) and fifty-one torpedo boats displacing between 210 and 270 tons.

After being down to nine submarines at the end of 1916, the navy added another fourteen between January 1917 and February 1918. The three boats built in the Pola Arsenal by Cantiere Navale Triestino (*U27, U28,* and *U40*) and the four laid down by Danubius of Rijeka (*U29* through *U32*) were all commissioned between January and August of 1917. The four UBAG submarines (*U20* through *U23*) entered service between August and November 1917. In July 1917, the navy gained two more boats when the Germans turned over *UB43* and *UB47* to the Austro-Hungarian fleet as *U43* and *U47*, respectively. Another three were begun in Pola over the winter of 1916–17 by Cantiere Navale Triestino; one, the *U41*, was completed in February 1918, the last new submarine to enter service.[5] Between July 1917 and January 1918, the navy also added four new *Tátra*-class destroyers built by Danubius's Kraljevica shipyard. Authorized in part to make up for the loss of the *Triglav* and *Lika* in December 1915, they were the navy's only surface vessels built entirely during the war.[6]

Fifty-eight at the time of his appointment, Njegovan hardly could be characterized as young, yet he was the youngest man to be named *Marinekommandant* since Sterneck thirty-four years earlier. He had a temperament akin to that of Haus, and the similarities did not end there. He spoke several languages fluently—his native Croatian, German, Italian, French, and English—and his rise to the top followed the same pattern. As a young officer, Njegovan served as an instructor at the naval academy and torpedo school. He went on to head a *Marinesektion* department, in his case the operations chancellery, from 1909 to 1911, and on the eve of the war, he chaired the technical committee in Pola. Like Haus, he held a number of significant ship and squadron commands, punctuating these assignments on land.[7] Even though Njegovan's recent experience as head of the idle squadron of dreadnoughts and *Radetzkys* at Pola had left him frustrated with Haus's cautious use of larger warships, he had little alternative to continuing the same course. Haus's conservative policies left the navy with reasonably healthy coal stocks of 400,000 tons,[8] but the strategic realities remained unchanged, and large-scale operations by the surface fleet would be no more feasible than before.

Less than a month after Haus's death, the navy suffered a serious setback far from the Adriatic, in Zurich, home to the operational headquarters of the Naval Intelligence Service ever since May 1915. The head of the service, Captain Mayer, had made good use of his own consular status and the cloak of diplomatic immunity that protected the "Austro-Hungarian General Consulate, Second Section." His spies in Italy provided a constant stream of valuable information, and the successes of his saboteurs—assuming that the most costly of "accidents" indeed were acts of sabotage—were nothing short of spectacular, including the sinkings of the pre-dreadnought *Benedetto Brin* and dreadnought *Leonardo da Vinci*. But the Italians ultimately traced such activities to Mayer's "consulate," and on the night of 25 February 1917 their own agents ransacked the place, dynamiting the door to the captain's safe and stealing his files. Italian authorities identified and arrested countless Austrian agents, the sabotage campaign ground to a halt, and the quality of the navy's information on Entente operations out of Italian ports deteriorated markedly. Mayer was so discouraged that he did not attempt to rebuild his network and retired from the navy in early May.[9]

The collapse of the intelligence network within Italy coincided with Austria-Hungary's commitment to join in and to support German unrestricted submarine warfare. By the time Njegovan became *Marinekommandant* and chief of the *Marinesektion,* the enemy already was feeling the effects of the undersea campaign. In April 1917, their most effective month of the entire war, German submarines sank 860,000 tons of enemy shipping, of which just over a quarter of a million tons were in the Mediterranean. For the same month, Austro-Hungarian submarines sank only one tenth the German Mediterranean total (23,000 tons), but the Habsburg navy's undersea force was only a fraction the size of Germany's, and most of it still was deployed in the Adriatic. The sinkings in the Atlantic prompted the United States to declare war on Germany on 6 April, but the weight of American power would not be felt on the western front in France until the summer of 1918. Aside from the depressing psychological impact, the American intervention did not have a direct effect on the Austro-Hungarian navy until December 1917, when Congress finally got around to declaring war on the Dual Monarchy.[10]

Not all of the action in the spring of 1917 was undersea, but the navy's main sortie had as its goal the destruction of the antisubmarine Otranto barrage. The nets dragged by the line of drifters at the mouth of the Adriatic had claimed the *U6* in May 1916, and either the nets or the mines sown by the Entente navies probably were responsible for the loss of the new *U30* on the last day of March 1917, just six weeks after it entered service. In mid-May, Rear Admiral Hansa, new commander of the Cruiser Flotilla at Cattaro, authorized a raid on the barrage line by Captain Horthy's *Novara,* escorted by the *Saida* and *Helgoland,* the latter under former submariner Erich Heyssler. At the same time, Captain Prince Johannes von und zu Liechtenstein would attack the Albanian coast with the destroyers *Balaton* and *Csepel,* mostly to create confusion, while the *U4* would lie in ambush off Valona and the *U27* off Brindisi along with the German *UC25* to attack enemy ships venturing out to repel the raiders.[11]

Just before 3:30 on the morning of 15 May, Liechtenstein's destroyers fired the first shots of the operation after intercepting a small Italian convoy headed for Valona. They sank the Italian destroyer *Borea* and 1,650-ton freighter *Carroccio,* which was carrying a cargo of munitions, and damaged two other vessels so badly that they had to be abandoned. Just minutes later, around fifty miles to the southwest, Horthy started to attack the line of drifters. Of forty-seven vessels on the barrage line, the cruisers sank fourteen and damaged four others. British officers subsequently praised the Austrians for permitting the crews of the trawlers to abandon ship before their vessels were destroyed and for taking time to rescue the survivors of vessels that resisted the attack. Such humanitarian gestures in darkness and amid the confusion of battle delayed the progress of the operation and limited the number of drifters the three cruisers destroyed.[12]

The attacks left Liechtenstein's destroyers 150 miles due south of Cattaro and Horthy's cruisers 180 miles south-southwest of the same port, making their run home the greatest challenge. By dawn an Anglo-French-Italian force of three cruisers and thirteen small destroyers was combing the seas between Brindisi and Durazzo, hoping to catch the raiders on their way northward. Two cruisers and five destroyers intercepted Liechtenstein off the Albanian coast. His destroyers exchanged fire with the enemy vessels after 7:30 and by 8:30 succeeded in outrunning them, putting in safely at Austrian-held Durazzo. During the skirmish, fire from the 870-ton *Csepel* disabled the 1,750-ton Italian destroyer *Aquila.* For Horthy and the cruisers, the battle did not begin until 9:00 but lasted until noon, with most of the Entente ships being involved in some way in the effort to block or chase Horthy's smaller force. Around 10:00, at the peak of the action, his *Novara* (3,500 tons, 3.9-inch guns) closed under cover of smoke to engage the British *Dartmouth* (5,300 tons, 6-inch guns). It was the sort of boldness that Haus had found lacking in Seitz's action of December 1915, and Horthy paid dearly for it: he was seriously wounded and his ship so heavily damaged that it had to be taken in tow by the *Saida.* Receiving the flotilla's distress signals back in Cattaro, Hansa sent out the armored cruiser *Sankt Georg* along with two destroyers and four torpedo boats. When the Entente captains sighted *Sankt Georg*'s smoke on the northern horizon, they broke off the action and returned to Brindisi. Liechtenstein's destroyers then came out of Durazzo for the general rendezvous, and the entire force returned home safely.[13]

Seaplanes from both sides dropped bombs and engaged each other throughout the battle, but no ships were damaged by air attack, and only one Italian plane was shot down. In pursuing Horthy and Liechtenstein, the Entente captains were mindful of the fact that Austro-Hungarian submarines were present, although neither *U4* nor *U27* ultimately played a role in the battle. The German *UC25* had much better luck, torpedoing the *Dartmouth*—the largest warship actively involved in the engagement—before it could make it back to Brindisi. Initially given up for lost, the ship was towed back to port, repaired, and reactivated three months later. The French destroyer *Boutefeu* also went down on the afternoon of 15 May, the victim of a mine laid by *UC25* off Brindisi.[14]

When the Austro-Hungarian force steamed into Cattaro, the crews of the warships anchored in the port greeted them with rousing cheers. With good reason the navy claimed victory. In addition to disabling one third of the barrage line, Horthy's raid prompted the Entente navies to deploy the vulnerable drifters only during the daylight hours for the next six weeks, making the Straits of Otranto much safer for the passage of submarines. The action also stirred bitter debate between the British and Italians over the responsibility for protecting the drifters. The Italians continued to insist that they needed more help at the mouth of the Adriatic. The British, adhering to their recent hard line against Italian demands, sent only one light cruiser, forcing the Italians to pull destroyers out of Venice for duty at Brindisi. They also opened a British seaplane station at Otranto, reinforcing the Entente's superiority in the skies over the straits.[15]

These tensions were eased somewhat by the arrival of other allied forces: during the spring and summer of 1917, Japan sent a cruiser and fourteen destroyers to the Mediterranean, while Australia contributed six destroyers to the Otranto barrage, and the United States sent three light cruisers and seven old gunboats to Gibraltar. After Greece declared war on the Central Powers in July 1917, the modest Greek navy could be thrown into the balance as well, at least in the Aegean Sea. By then, however, Anglo-French friction over the protection of convoys led the British to appoint their own Mediterranean commander in chief, Admiral Somerset Gough-Calthorpe, who would not be subordinate to the French commander, Gauchet. If nothing else, the German and Austro-Hungarian navies could count on continuing confusion and division in the enemy camp.[16]

The battle in the Otranto Straits was the most important clash of the spring and summer of 1917—indeed, in numbers of ships involved, it was the biggest engagement of the entire war in the Adriatic—but the navy was involved in other actions as well. In late May and early June, the war in the northern Adriatic heated up, at least temporarily. On 24 May, two British monitors deployed in Venice since the end of 1916 shelled the coast a few miles west of Trieste and retired only after being bombed by Austro-Hungarian seaplanes.[17] Then, on the night of 3–4 June, the Habsburg navy destroyer *Wildfang* was sunk by a mine during a raid on Goro at the mouth of the Po River by an expedition of destroyers, torpedo boats, and seaplanes.[18] A most unlikely confrontation occurred a week later off Crete, where the *U27* was hunting as part of the navy's commitment to unrestricted submarine warfare in the Mediterranean: on 11 June, the submarine torpedoed and heavily damaged the Japanese destroyer *Sakaki*. Most of the crew was killed, but the ship did not sink and was later repaired. The navy was not yet aware that Japan had sent vessels to the Mediterranean; the official *Jahresbericht*, published late in 1917, listed the destroyer as British![19]

It was not a comforting sign that the array of enemies facing the Central Powers in the Mediterranean had grown to include even the Japanese. Emperor Charles likewise could take no solace in the domestic situation within the Dual Monarchy. After taking the throne in November 1916, he came under great pressure to summon the Austrian *Reichsrat*, which had not met since the spring of 1914. In May 1917, Charles finally relented, at the same time ordering minister-president Clam-Martinic to form a multinational cabinet. Charles issued a vague appeal for constitutional reform that would alleviate the nationality problem by promoting "the free national and cultural development of equally privileged peoples," but it was already too late for such promises.[20] The leaders of several of the nationalities had already burned their bridges with Vienna and cast their lot with the enemy; Clam-Martinic's task proved to be hopeless, and he resigned in mid-June. The situation in Hungary was equally chaotic after Charles fired Count István Tisza from his post as minister-president in late May. The dismissal of the count, who had opposed a broadening of the Hungarian franchise, perhaps enhanced the prospects for reform, but on the nationality question, Magyars of all parties were of one mind: the kingdom of Hungary must remain whole and united, whether independent or within the Dual Monarchy. Some Magyar leaders refused even to acknowledge the existence of Croatian, Serbian, Romanian, and Slovakian nationalities.

The revival of political life in the Dual Monarchy brought a renewal of political activity on the part of the navy. In the summer of 1917, Njegovan established a press office (*Pressestelle*) attached to the press office of the *Armeeoberkommando*. Under the leadership of Captain Arthur von Khuepach, the office disseminated news about the navy's contribution to the war effort and coordinated pronavy propaganda throughout the Dual Monarchy. Efforts ranged from the printing of postcards with naval scenes to staging elaborate exhibitions in Vienna and Budapest. Traditional concerns for Hungarian support led Khuepach to concentrate his efforts in Hungary.[21]

In early June, just after the reopening of the *Reichsrat*, Charles escaped the stormy political atmosphere of Vienna long enough to visit Pola. For Njegovan and his officers and seamen, it was quite an occasion, the first formal imperial review of the fleet since 1902, when Francis Joseph last came to the base. A cloudless Sunday afternoon provided an idyllic backdrop for the inspection; crews dressed in their summer whites lined the decks of the ships, flags rippled in the breeze, salutes and cheers for the emperor filled the air.[22] The great spectacle provided a badly needed break from the stifling boredom of life at anchor. Indeed, the festive atmosphere and the spit-and-polish appearances camouflaged the fact that the battle fleet as a whole had not ventured out of Pola in two years, since the initial bombardment of the enemy coastline the day after Italy declared war. From the cheers of the seamen, one would not have guessed that they had been on reduced rations since the first of January.[23]

Just one month after Charles's visit, discontent over the shortages of food and monotony of diet sparked demonstrations in the fleet at Pola, the first signs of a breakdown of discipline after three years of war. Order was restored with little difficulty, and Njegovan chose not to enforce harsh punishments. The seamen were reassured that the navy's rationing was part of a broader program for the entire empire, and that their diet and living conditions were still far better than those of the soldiers at the front.[24] Njegovan and his subordinates failed to consider that the seamen naturally would compare their conditions not to those of the far-away front soldier or civilian but to the officers aboard their own ships, who still ate well.

At least one admiral anticipated the problem and in vain had suggested a remedy. As early as 1916, Koudelka, *Seebezirkskommandant* at Trieste and brigade commander on the left flank of the front against Italy, proposed rotating sailors from the idle ships at Pola through three-month tours of duty along the Isonzo. He reasoned that such service would alleviate boredom and also make the sailors appreciate the sacrifices of their peers at the front. On one occasion, Haus sent Koudelka the occupants of the navy prison in Pola; these unruly seamen made good front soldiers but were sent back to the fleet after their sentences expired. The experiment was never repeated.[25]

Their relative isolation did not completely insulate the men of the fleet from the political climate of the empire as a whole. War weariness made them receptive to the message of socialist and nationalist agitators, and the overall wartime situation in Pola did not help matters. With the outbreak of the war against Italy, the navy had evacuated all civilians from the town—some 64,400 people in all—in part for their own safety from air raids but also because many of them were ethnically Italian. Such evacuations of Habsburg Italians were common in the Tyrol but were not attempted anywhere else in the Adriatic littoral.[26] Since so many of those moved were dependents of the Italian and Croatian workers in the Pola Arsenal, the morale of these men naturally declined as time went on and the "emergency" measure took on a more permanent character. When a serious uprising finally occurred in Pola, the workers rather than the sailors would provide the catalyst.

The demonstrations of July 1917 had ended peacefully, but rationing continued for the seamen, if not the officers. The navy took steps to offset the decreases in bread and meat provisions, calling Vice Admiral Barry out of retirement to organize a fishing operation that grew to include 650 boats and 4,500 seamen, most of whom had been fishermen in civilian life.[27] But in August 1917, again citing shortages throughout the

Dual Monarchy, the navy started to ration clothing and shoes. For the crews, worn and patched uniforms became common, and by the last months of the war, few attempted to keep up appearances, especially outside of the main base at Pola.[28] By late October, when Charles again visited Pola, these measures had combined with the continued rationing of food to bring morale to a new low. When ordered to the decks to cheer the emperor, the sailors aboard some ships replaced the standard *Hurra!* with sarcastic shouts of *Hunger!* Charles, zipping through the harbor in a motorboat, did not hear the protesters, and afterward their officers let the matter drop.[29]

The extent to which the demonstrations and demoralizing shortages affected planning for fleet operations is difficult to gauge, but the navy did not capitalize on the momentum of Horthy's victory at the Otranto Straits. Similar raids, never involving more than one of the scout cruisers, were attempted roughly on a monthly basis, with negligible results.[30] In the meantime, submarines and aircraft were responsible for most of the action in the Adriatic, while in the Mediterranean the German undersea boats still carried the bulk of the burden. After torpedoing just over 250,000 tons of enemy shipping in the record month of April 1917, German submarines in the Mediterranean averaged 120,000 tons per month for the remainder of the year. For Austro-Hungarian submariners, the best month was August 1917, when 38,800 tons were sunk. Trapp's *U14*, hunting in the central Mediterranean, alone claimed 24,800 tons, including the Italian steamer *Milazzo*, which, at 11,480 tons, was the largest enemy merchant ship sunk by the navy during the entire war.[31] The same month, the Italians lost the submarine *W4* to a mine off Brindisi, while in September Austro-Hungarian seaplanes launched two raids on Italian airfields, destroying dirigibles in their hangars at Iesi on the twenty-seventh and at Ferrara on the twenty-ninth.[32]

A week later, the navy suffered its first and only desertion of a vessel at sea when the old *Torpedoboot 11*, part of the coastal defense force at Sebenico since the beginning of the war, defected to Italy. While on a routine patrol on 5 October, the 115-ton boat was seized by a Czech machinist and a Slovene boatswain's mate, who led the crew in subduing the two officers aboard. The mutineers then steered for Recanati, just down the coast from Ancona, and surrendered to the Italians. The peculiar behavior of the crew indicates that they defected out of war weariness and had no treasonous motives; they even destroyed code books and other sensitive materials before reaching Italy.[33]

Such details, of course, were not known to the Central Powers at the time. Njegovan and Austro-Hungarian leaders considered the desertion an isolated incident, but coming in the wake of the demonstrations at Pola three months earlier, it did raise fears, especially in Germany, that the fleet would soon succumb to the same malady that was paralyzing the multinational empire as a whole. The future no longer looked as bright for the Austro-Hungarian navy, but things were going far worse for the Italians, thanks to the temporary collapse of their army late in the month. On 24 October, after two years and five months of stalemate, the twelfth battle of the Isonzo resulted in a breakthrough for a Habsburg army now bolstered by German reinforcements. The Italian line first gave way near the village of Caporetto, signaling the start of three weeks of headlong retreat that only ended when General Cadorna stabilized the front along the Piave River. Meanwhile, to the west, Austro-Hungarian troops under Conrad von Hötzendorf also made modest gains along the Alpine front.[34]

For Austria-Hungary, Caporetto was less than a complete success. Charles, confident of success in a one-on-one Austro-Italian campaign, had asked William II to direct the German High Command to release enough Habsburg troops from the eastern front to enable him to pursue the offensive against Italy with his own manpower, supported only by German artillery. But the German chief of staff, General Erich von Ludendorff, had insisted on a significant German command role and infantry contribution, fearing that a purely Austrian victory against the Italians would give the Dual Monarchy the ideal opportunity to sue for a separate peace. The German role at Caporetto and in the march to the Piave ensured that the Habsburg army would remain in a subordinate position within the alliance. While operational cooperation continued, the tone of the relationship between the two armies actually worsened after the victory.[35]

On the Italian side, the fiasco at the front brought the dismissal of Cadorna in favor of General Armando Diaz. The change of commanders and the stabilization of the Piave line represented an important turning point, but at least in the short term Italy's allies remained skeptical of its ability and willingness to continue the fight. The front now stood just thirty miles from Venice, prompting British and French admirals to fear an amphibious assault on the city, supported by the Austro-Hungarian battle fleet from Pola, which the weak Venetian squadron would be unable to repulse. Thaon di Revel's first moves in the wake of the breakthrough at Caporetto hardly inspired confidence among the British and French. The Italian navy withdrew the old pre-dreadnought *Sardegna* from Venice to Brindisi and made preparations at Ancona to accommodate the Venice squadron should the city have to be abandoned. In his headquarters at Malta, Admiral Calthorpe made contingency plans for the evacuation of British naval forces from all Italian ports in the event that Rome suddenly declared neutrality. The British commander also planned to seize at least part of the Italian fleet should Italy abandon the Entente.[36] It would be no small task for the new prime minister, Vittorio Orlando, to restore the allies' confidence in Italy.

During the Caporetto offensive, there was remarkably little interaction between Njegovan and the army. A company of navy sappers (*Marine-Pionierkompagnie*) and a makeshift flotilla operating in the shallow coastal waters provided logistical support for the advancing left flank of the army. The battle fleet did not launch the dreaded attack on Venice, and the only significant redeployment of warships sent two of the old coast defenders to Trieste, which did not have a harbor watch battleship already on station. The *Wien* and *Budapest* were not welcomed by the local commander, Koudelka, who considered them more of a liability than an asset. On 16 November, the battleships ventured westward along the Venetian coast and shelled Italian positions near the mouth of the Piave; otherwise they remained on guard in Trieste. Serving in this capacity, the 5,600-ton *Wien* fell victim to a torpedo attack on the night of 10 December by *MAS-9* and *MAS-15*, both of which had managed to penetrate the harbor defenses. Obsolete after two decades in service, the *Wien* nevertheless was the navy's greatest loss thus far.[37]

Njegovan promptly sent Captain Vuković to Trieste with the scout cruiser *Admiral Spaun*, the old battleship *Arpád*, and a half dozen destroyers. On 19 December, Vuković led these warships and the *Budapest*, escorted by sixteen torpedo boats, five minesweepers, and seaplanes, on another sortie against the enemy batteries near the mouth of the Piave. Designed to cover a river crossing by a division of Hungarian *Honvéd*, the operation failed largely because of bad weather. Before the end of the year, the entire force withdrew to Pola, and the old cruisers *Szigetvár* and *Aspern* assumed harbor watch duties in Trieste. The spectacular nature of the sinking of the *Wien*—in the first *MAS* raid against an Austro-Hungarian warship—and the fact that the motorboats had returned to Venice unscathed gave Italian morale a badly needed boost. Subsequent *MAS* operations were even bolder, although not always successful. Exactly two months after the sinking of the *Wien,* three *MAS* boats attacked Buccari (Bakar) east of Rijeka, deep inside Austro-Hungarian waters, but failed to hit any of the four steamers they targeted.[38]

The Italian army's defeat at Caporetto and retreat to the Piave coincided with other significant land victories by the Central Powers. In July 1917, Russia, already rocked by one revolution, launched the so-called Kerensky Offensive, which the German and Austro-Hungarian armies soon turned back. In the weeks that followed, the Central Powers advanced eastward with unprecedented speed, and the Russian army gradually disintegrated. In early November, two weeks after the initial breakthrough on the Italian front, the Bolshevik Revolution finally brought an end to the war in the east. In mid-December, Lenin's new regime agreed to an armistice, as did Romania, which for the past year had been clinging to a strip of Moldavia at the southern flank of the Russian army.

While the defeat of Russia left the field marshals planning for the transfer of divisions to the western and Italian fronts, the Austro-Hungarian navy's role in the east was due to expand dramatically. With the enemy blockade in the North Sea and Adriatic affecting the quality and quantity of food available on the home front, the occupation of most of Romania before the end of 1916 had the added significance of opening the way for much of the Romanian harvest of 1917 to be transported up the Danube to Germany and Austria-Hungary. The monitors of the flotilla had played an important role in keeping this lifeline open, and the Central Powers hoped to repeat the success on a grander scale with the Ukrainian harvest of 1918. As 1917 came to a close, it appeared increasingly likely that the Danube flotilla would be called upon to deploy in the Black Sea and even on the rivers of the Ukraine to secure the way for the grain ships.[39]

For the moment, however, the commander of the flotilla, Rear Admiral Viktor Wickerhauser, lacked the manpower and matériel for such extensive operations. As of December 1917, his order of battle included the Monitor Division of seven vessels, under the command of Captain Olaf Wulff, plus three requisitioned paddle steamers, six small patrol boats, and three minesweepers. The original monitors *Maros* and *Leitha,* now forty-six years old, remained with the flotilla as reserves. A tenth monitor, the *Inn,* struck a Romanian mine near Braila in September 1917 and sank. It was raised and sent to Budapest, where it was still under repair a year later. In 1917, two 1,240-ton twin-turreted monitors were laid down in the Linz shipyard of Stabilimento Tecnico Triestino, but they, too, were not ready before the end of the war. It remained to be seen where Wickerhauser and Wulff would find the means to wage a more ambitious campaign.[40]

In November 1917, as the armies of the Central Powers advanced both in Italy and in the east, William II left German headquarters for a brief trip to Pola, his first since December 1916. During the one-day inspection of the Austro-Hungarian fleet and his own German submarine force, the emperor repeated earlier suggestions that Njegovan disarm the more obsolete warships of his battle fleet to free the manpower for other duties, namely, servicing the German submarine traffic at Pola and Cattaro. In January at Schloss Pless, Haus had set the precedent for such a concession by agreeing to decommission the *Panther* and *Maria Theresia.* Njegovan, however, resisted subsequent German appeals to take more aging ships out of service and stood his ground even when faced with direct pressure from William II. Nevertheless, at the end of the year, after the loss of the *Wien,* Njegovan relented and agreed to convert the *Budapest* to an accommodation ship for German submarine crews at Pola. The last of the old coast defenders, the *Monarch,* faced the same fate in Cattaro, where the ram cruiser *Kaiser Franz Joseph I* was disarmed and converted to a headquarters ship. Njegovan also agreed to decommission the next-oldest trio of battleships, the *Habsburg, Babenberg,* and *Árpád.*[41]

These concessions reflected the increasing pessimism that all but paralyzed the *Marinekommandant* by the winter of 1917–18. Whereas Haus had succeeded in deflecting criticism from himself in part by being so hard on his subordinates, Njegovan became a lightning rod for all discontent and frustration within the corps. Unhappy officers complained to the German naval attaché that their commander "seemed to have given up."[42] Njegovan certainly had little reason to be optimistic. In December 1917, the United States finally declared war on the Dual Monarchy, making inevitable the appearance of American warships at the mouth of the Adriatic. As Germany continued to shoulder more of the burden both on land and at sea, the *Marinekommandant* would not be able to refuse German demands in the manner that Haus had earlier in the war. And perhaps most important of all, Njegovan the *kaisertreu* Croatian was in a position to appreciate both the recent erosion of his conationals' traditional loyalty to the crown and the potential of South Slav nationalism as a disintegrating factor within the navy. His mood left him out of step with the military and naval leaders of the Central Powers. The German High Command still hoped to take Paris before the bulk of the American army arrived in France, German navy leaders remained very optimistic that unrestricted submarine warfare would succeed, and the Habsburg *Armeeoberkommando* took comfort in the fact that its troops on the Italian front still stood on the Piave, their deepest penetration of the war.

The conditions that so depressed Njegovan were apparent to Horthy when he returned to active service as captain of the dreadnought *Prinz Eugen* late in 1917, after finally recovering from the wounds suffered in the battle of the Otranto Straits. He recalled later that "the battle fleet was not in good form" owing to the fact that "for three years . . . the crews had been largely inactive." The boredom of years at anchor, combined with the deprivations of the past several months, had created fertile ground for "the underground activities of the socialists" and "the political agitation of Yugoslav, Czech, and Italian nationalists."[43] On Horthy's first day aboard the *Prinz Eugen,* the crew "refused to eat the evening meal" and engaged in a noisy protest that was silenced only with great difficulty. Horthy observed that "a craze for irrational cheering had spread throughout the fleet."[44] Most common at mealtime and at night, the *Hurra-Rufe,* once started, would be answered from other ships; in the case of the battleships, the exchanges ultimately would escalate to involve thousands of seamen. This defiance of discipline worsened after the first of January 1918, when the daily bread and meat rations again were reduced for all military and naval personnel as well as for civilians.[45] Njegovan finally prohibited the cheering, noting in his order that "in the past the cheer *Hurra* was a happy cheer, an enthusiastic greeting," but "the crews of several ships have made it a cheer of protest."[46]

By the end of the month, Njegovan had more to worry about than mere shouting, as a wave of strikes and unrest that started in the interior of the monarchy quickly spread to the littoral. On the morning of 14 January, workers struck the Daimler plant in Wiener Neustadt, which built aircraft for both the army and navy as part of its war production. Later that day, strikes closed the Stabilimento Tecnico Triestino, which by this time had lost its Italian name in favor of the patriotic designation "Austria-Werft." Trieste employees of the Austrian Lloyd joined the walkout, and demonstrators spurred on by local Italian Social Democratic leaders clashed with police in the streets of the city. The wave of unrest, reflecting a general war weariness and more specific discontent over the recent reduction in rations, soon paralyzed all major industrial centers of the empire. At the Skoda works in Pilsen, which had more than tripled in size since 1914, the number of striking workers topped thirty thousand. On 22 January, a general strike brought Prague and all of Bohemia to a standstill. On the same day, the movement spread to the Pola Arsenal.[47]

On the eve of their strike, the Croatian contingent among the arsenal workers formulated a program with strong socialist as well as nationalist overtones, calling for "a South Slav state of workers and peasants." On the twenty-second, 10,000 men of all nationalities stopped work, with Italians accounting for the second largest group. Even the submarine technicians sent to Pola from Germany went out on strike in sympathy with the arsenal workers. On 23 January, sailors from the fleet and soldiers from the local garrison joined the demonstrations and participated in clashes with military police. Social Democratic *Reichsrat* representative Franz Domes hastened to Pola from Vienna to help Fiedler, the harbor admiral, negotiate with the strikers. The navy raised the wages of the arsenal workers, promised them better clothing and shoes, and allowed their families to return to Pola. Army *Landsturm* reservists pressed into service as laborers likewise were promised better conditions. Order was restored on the navy base and aboard the ships of the fleet, and on 28 January work resumed in the arsenal. By then most of the 700,000 workers who had struck throughout the empire were back at work, coerced by demonstrations of force from troops called in from the front lines and by assurances of better future conditions.[48]

For Njegovan and the navy leadership, the Pola strikes of January 1918 posed a threat that made the earlier demonstrations of July 1917 appear mild in comparison. Thankful at having averted disaster, they were confronted just days later with an even greater crisis when word arrived of a general mutiny of the sailors at the base in the Bocche di Cattaro. Though confined to the navy's second-largest anchorage, the rebellion was by far the greatest internal threat the navy had faced since the Venetian Revolution of 1848–49. Unfortunately for Njegovan and many of his subordinates, in the aftermath of the Cattaro mutiny, as in the wake of the Venetian upheaval seventy years earlier, sweeping changes dictated from Vienna would leave the naval hierarchy in the hands of new men.[49]

THE CATTARO MUTINY AND
ITS CONSEQUENCES (FEBRUARY 1918)

Compared to Pola, where the boredom of life at anchor was a significant factor, Cattaro had been a beehive of activity. Home base for the Cruiser Flotilla, the Fifth Battle Division, and the First Torpedo Flotilla, Cattaro's scout cruisers, destroyers, torpedo boats, and submarines made regular sorties and were responsible for most of the navy's overall offensive activities. At the end of January 1918, the vessels shouldering this burden included the *Novara* and *Helgoland,* four *Tátra*-class destroyers, four older *Huszár*-class destroyers, fourteen torpedo boats, and a fluctuating number of German and Austro-Hungarian submarines. Nevertheless, while these units and their crews were worked to the point of mechanical and physical exhaustion, the majority of the men remained relatively inactive aboard the largest ships stationed in Cattaro. The armored cruisers *Kaiser Karl VI* and *Sankt Georg,* the old ram cruiser *Kaiser Franz Joseph I,* and the battleship *Monarch* alone accounted for over two thousand seamen; technically still in active service, these obsolete warships rarely ventured beyond the mouth of the bay. Hundreds more rode at anchor aboard stationary vessels not even reckoned as warships: the harbor watch *Kronprinz Rudolf,* the torpedo depot ship *Gäa,* the hulk of the casemate ship *Kaiser Max,* the auxiliary ship *Cyclop,* the old yacht *Dalmat,* the tug *Büffel,* three obsolete torpedo boats, and two requisitioned merchant steamers.[50]

While the officer corps at Cattaro included some of the navy's best ship captains—among them Prince Liechtenstein of the *Novara* and Erich Heyssler of the *Helgoland*—the quality of leadership of the senior officer, Rear Admiral Hansa, left much to be desired. Under his loose rein, the gulf between officers and seamen, no less a traditional factor in Austro-Hungarian service than in any other navy, had grown unnecessarily wide. Head of the Cruiser Flotilla for the past year, Hansa previously led the Fifth Battle Division from the autumn of 1914 until early 1917. Having spent almost the entire war in the isolated outpost of Cattaro, the admiral had taken great care to provide for his own comfort. His wife and children lived aboard his flagship, the *Sankt Georg;* along with a select circle of senior officers, they shared the sumptuous fare of the admiral's mess. Seamen employed in Hansa's kitchen reported to their mates below deck that the quality of the admiral's food and drink remained impressive, while the quality and quantity of food given to the common sailor continued to deteriorate.[51]

As in the January strikes in Pola and elsewhere, food was a central source of discontent at Cattaro. Seamen complained of rancid meat and coarse bread, the latter often in loaves even lighter than the stipulated ration weight. Officers, meanwhile, had white bread, fruits, and vegetables to supplement a variety of beef, pork, and poultry in their diet. The shortage of clothing likewise caused tension. While officers remained reasonably well attired, seamen received no replacement for threadbare uniforms and worn shoes. Some sailors alleged that officers hoarded articles of clothing intended for their men, especially shoes, in order to sell them on the local black market.

The daily routine of cleaning and scrubbing the decks of idle warships—work for the sake of work—helped to maintain discipline, but at the expense of adding to the monotony of life for the crews. Even worse, Hansa had allowed the customary affronts to the dignity of the common seaman to get out of hand, generating still more discontent. Seamen complained of being ordered to care for the pets of their officers; one reported having to bathe his captain's dog with his own ration of soap. Sailors were detailed to ferry the wives and children of officers from the larger ships to the shore. When it came to walking pets ashore and transporting mistresses back and forth, the duty often required men to be standing by at all hours of the night.

In contrast to the restricted life of the seamen, officers enjoyed free access to shore leave. While Hansa and some senior officers kept their wives and children with them in the commander's quarters of the larger vessels, others had moved their families to lodgings in Cattaro. Officers also had far more frequent access to the taverns and brothels of the town than did their men, to the point of becoming bored with such attractions. Navy pilots were alleged to have used seaplanes to fly to Ragusa to visit a renowned house of prostitution; other fliers reportedly took Red Cross sisters and other girlfriends joyriding aboard navy aircraft. Some of the stories circulating among the seamen were too bizarre to be true, and indeed were not true; nevertheless, most rumors of officers' abuse of rank and privilege contained at least a grain of truth, and such stories only served to stoke the fires of discontent.

The mutiny began at noon on 1 February aboard Hansa's flagship, as the crew assembled for the midday meal. Jerko Šižgorić, a seaman from Sebenico, shot Captain Egon Zipperer von Arbach in the head, seriously wounding but not killing him. A machinist petty officer and a sailor also sustained wounds before the mutineers secured control of the ship. The forbidden *Hurra-Rufe* became the call to action for the mutiny of the other crews. Signals were raised and small boats dispatched to spread the word around the harbor. After securing the *Sankt Georg*, mutineers seized the *Kaiser Karl VI* and the rest of the larger ships, confining officers to their quarters; meanwhile, aboard the smaller ships and boats, many officers raised the red flag of revolt voluntarily to placate rebellious elements in their crews and to avoid being fired upon by the big guns of the mutinous armored cruisers. In his first report to Pola, telegraphed at 2:30 in the afternoon, Hansa reported that the red flag flew above all vessels within sight of his flagship, except the submarines.

On the evening of 1 February, a committee of sailors representing several ships presented Hansa with a list of demands. Half of the points concerned the conditions of service: an end to all "unnecessary work and exercises"; more shore leave, for longer periods of time; three weeks of home leave every six months, with the same provision to apply to both officers and seamen; a more efficient system for transporting men to and from Cattaro on home leave, allowing for more days of the leave to be spent at home; a common mess for officers and seamen; a better supply of tobacco products; an end to the censorship of letters from home; and no future punishment for sailors involved in the mutiny. The remaining points reflected the war weariness of the mutineers and some of their hopes for the future: an appeal for negotiations for an immediate peace; full political independence from other powers [i.e., from Germany]; support for the "Russian democratic proposal" for a peace without annexations or indemnities; a full demobilization and the creation of a voluntary militia in place of the armed forces; national self-determination for all peoples; an answer, in good faith, to Woodrow Wilson's Fourteen Points; better food and clothing for dependents of men in service; and a democratization of the government.[52]

The political demands of the sailors reflected their sympathy with the Bolsheviks, hostility toward the German alliance, and to a remarkable degree, the popularity of the concepts embodied in the Fourteen Points, which were initially proclaimed in Wilson's speech to the U.S. Congress on 8 January. In addition to the ideals of self-determination and arms reduction, the American agenda included several goals especially relevant to the Dual Monarchy. Point Ten stipulated that "the peoples of Austria-Hungary, whose place among the nations we wish to see safeguarded and assured, should be accorded the freest opportunity of autonomous development." Other points called for a "readjustment of the frontiers of Italy . . . along clearly recognizable lines of nationality" and for Serbia to be "accorded free and secure access to the sea." News of the speech reached Austria-Hungary before the strikes of mid-January, but there is little evidence of the workers or their leaders being inspired by it.[53] In contrast, the rhetoric of the Cattaro mutineers, three and a half weeks after the speech, clearly bears witness to the impact of Wilson's peace proposal.

Hansa, of course, could do nothing about the political half of the mutineers' agenda, but he did promise to forward their concerns to the proper authorities. On the remaining demands, the admiral's responses were mixed. He defended the need for work and exercise and characterized as adequate the current policies for home leave, which provided seamen with eighteen days every eight or nine months and officers with fourteen days twice a year. Hansa promised to do what he could to improve conditions for the trips home and to consider more frequent shore leave. He dismissed the points concerning the availability of tobacco and the censorship of letters, since both were beyond his control. Only the demand for a common mess for officers and seamen elicited an unequivocal *"Nein"* from the admiral. Regarding the fate of the mutineers, Hansa pledged not to punish those merely demonstrating or the men presenting the petition of demands, but he promised no quarter to other ringleaders or mutineers who actually fired the weapons they had seized.[54]

The committee of sailors left the meeting with Hansa generally satisfied with his responses. After returning to their ships, some advocated an immediate end to the mutiny, but they found themselves in a distinct minority among their peers. Amid considerable confusion, the radicals vowed to retain control over the fleet. By the morning of 2 February, boatswain Franz Rasch, a Moravian German by birth and recipient of two decorations earlier in the war, had emerged as the de facto leader of the radical mutineers. Rasch, however, resolved to command the revolt through a junior officer with socialist sympathies. His search for such an accomplice remained fruitless until he approached a Dalmatian Croat pilot at the seaplane station, twenty-five-year-old reserve ensign Antun Sešan. The ensign's South Slav nationalist sympathies drove him to agree to lead the mutiny; he was also known to have considerable gambling debts, from which he desperately wanted to escape. On the afternoon of the second, Sešan boarded the *Sankt Georg*, having become a central figure in the rebellion for the strangest mixture of political and personal reasons.[55] He was the only officer to identify himself openly with the mutineers.

By then the local army commander in Cattaro, *Feldzeugmeister* Oskar von Guseck, already had shown his determination to contain the mutiny. In the early afternoon of the second, the harbor watch ship *Kronprinz Rudolf* defied a warning and moved from its position at the entrance of the Bocche to a new anchorage in the central bay. On Guseck's orders, shore batteries opened fire on the rebel vessel, killing one sailor and wounding several others. Sešan subsequently ordered the mutinous ships to maintain their current positions but to remain cleared for action and prepared to move. The solidarity of the rebels started to crumble, however, and on the afternoon of the second, Liechtenstein pulled down the red flags from his *Novara* and moved the cruiser from the central bay of the Bocche into the inner harbor of Cattaro, where the mutiny had not taken hold. Heyssler followed with the *Helgoland*. Thereafter, most of the destroyers and torpedo boats struck their rebel colors and steamed for the inner harbor. The example of the *Kronprinz Rudolf* just hours earlier made a decisive impression. When given the option of facing the hostile fire of the mutinous armored cruisers or the far more numerous guns of the shore batteries, the latter appeared to be the greater of two evils even to the diehard rebels among the crews of the smaller vessels.

The shore batteries made a similar impression on the crew of the *Kaiser Karl VI*, which pulled down its red flags after dark on the evening of 2 February. At the same time, however, the *Sankt Georg* mutineers remained steadfast. Telegrams went out to Viktor Adler and the Austrian Social Democrats in Vienna as well as to Count Mihály Károlyi and the Hungarian opposition party in Budapest, appealing for immediate help.[56] Because Sešan refused to speak with the captive Hansa face-to-face, Rasch continued to serve as chief spokesman of the rebellion. The boatswain informed the admiral that he would remain a prisoner "until peace is concluded." Questioned further by Hansa, Rasch gave full vent to his fearless radicalism: "Blood must flow in every revolution, and it is all the same to me if I am hanged today or tomorrow. The entire navy stands on our side."[57]

But the "entire navy" certainly did not support the Cattaro mutiny. By the predawn hours of 3 February, Heyssler felt confident enough to start issuing ultimata of his own. Having confirmed the loyalty of the other vessels that had taken refuge in the inner harbor, the captain of the *Helgoland,* in his capacity as head of the First Torpedo Flotilla, warned the remaining mutinous ships that they had until 10:00 A.M. to surrender or be sunk. Within hours the loyal forces far outnumbered and outgunned the rebels, thanks to the arrival of Vice Admiral Seidensacher and the Third Battle Division. The *Erzherzog Friedrich, Erzherzog Karl,* and *Erzherzog Ferdinand Max* had left Pola for Cattaro the previous morning; Seidensacher's orders from Njegovan gave him considerable latitude to suppress the mutiny using whatever means he deemed necessary. Each of the 10,600-ton *Erzherzogs* carried four 9.4-inch guns, double the firepower of the 7,400-ton *Sankt Georg,* the largest of the mutineers. For good measure, Njegovan had dispatched an escort of fifteen smaller craft to accompany Seidensacher's battleships. Owing to the recent unrest in Pola, the crews were not informed of their mission until the ships had passed the harbor breakwater and were underway at sea.

Even after they learned of the approach of the Third Battle Division, the mutineers did not lose heart. Aware of the January troubles in Pola, many expected to see the *Erzherzogs* enter the Bocche flying red flags. When the ships appeared flying their battle flags, clearly intending to restore order, the last rebellious vessels surrendered. On the *Sankt Georg,* the red flags came down around 9:00 A.M., but only after a vote by the entire crew. Boatswain Rasch then went below, freed Hansa, and turned himself over to the admiral as his prisoner. At the decisive moment, Antun Sešan was nowhere to be found. Aware of the fate that awaited him, he boarded a seaplane half an hour before the final surrender and flew across the Adriatic to safety in Italy.

The army, fearing a general rebellion in the Cattaro area, had shown little confidence in the navy's ability to suppress its own mutiny. By the time of the capitulation, Guseck had ringed the Bocche with two dozen companies of infantry, many of them armed with machine guns, and the military commander in Sarajevo, *Generaloberst* Baron Stefan Sarkotić, had ordered several thousand more troops from all over occupied Montenegro and Bosnia-Hercegovina to descend on the area. Sarkotić visited Cattaro on 7 February and inspected the ships and shore installations. That same morning, the trial of the chief mutineers began.

Immediately after restoring order, the navy put ashore around 800 unreliable seamen and subjected roughly 600 to a formal inquiry; of this group, charges were brought against 392. While the indicted included men from every nationality of the monarchy, Croatians and Slovenes accounted for the largest number (42.6 percent), followed by Italians (20.6 percent), Czechs and Slovaks (12.7 percent), Germans (11.4 percent), and Magyars (8.1 percent). Most of this group remained in custody for another eight months, since the investigations dragged on almost to the end of the war. Justice was swifter, however, for those identified as leaders of the mutiny. On 10 February, just three days after their trial began, the military court sentenced four of them to death. Jerko Šižgorić, found guilty of shooting Captain Zipperer of the *Sankt Georg* in the chaotic first minutes of the mutiny, faced a firing squad along with Rasch, the Istrian Croat Antun Grabar, and Mate Brničević, a Dalmatian from Split. The death sentences were carried out on the morning of the eleventh. For the sake of preserving calm in the rest of the fleet, the emperor formally suppressed news of the executions.[58]

Meanwhile, on 10 February, Archduke Charles Stephen arrived in Cattaro as special emissary of the emperor with orders to investigate the general causes of the mutiny and to recommend changes for the future.

On the first of these two charges, the judicial proceedings already had unearthed the stories of abuses of rank and privilege responsible for much of the tension. The archduke did not duplicate this process with hearings of his own, relying instead upon inspection tours of the vessels and conversations with officers to form his impressions.[59] Senior officers complained privately that Charles Stephen placed too much stock in interviews with junior officers, and with good reason, for some of their subordinates were brutally frank in holding them responsible for the fiasco. Captain Alphons Wünschek, commander of the destroyer *Lika*, provided the most graphic analogy: "Der Fisch stinkt beim Kopf," and the only solution would be to remove the rotten head of the fish.[60] The archduke was more charitable than that—after all, he had served alongside many of the admirals during his active years with the fleet— but pointed out their "weakness, lethargy, and advanced age" in his report to the emperor. "After seeing the admirals who had been my classmates at the academy, I had to look at myself in the mirror to see whether I, too, had grown so old."[61]

The archduke's recommendations regarding the future command structure of the navy surprised no one. Charles Stephen, like Emperor Charles, was known to have always opposed the concentration of the operational and administrative commands in the hands of a single admiral.[62] Indeed, his own retirement from active service in 1895, at the age of thirty-six, in part came because of frustration over Sterneck's virtual absolute power within the service. Charles Stephen's proposal to divide the commander's powers supported the views of the emperor, who had contemplated sweeping changes in the navy leadership and already resolved to use the Cattaro mutiny as the pretext for a shake-up. On 27 February, after receiving the archduke's report, Charles fired Njegovan from his positions of *Marinekommandant*, chief of the *Marinesektion*, and fleet commander at Pola. He granted the admiral's request that the dismissal be announced as a voluntary retirement. Rodler likewise was fired from his post as *Stellvertreter* in Vienna and placated with a promotion to vice admiral. He spent the remainder of the war as the last commandant of the naval academy, which since 1915 had been at Braunau on the Inn.[63]

Charles subsequently left the office of *Marinekommandant* vacant, as he had a year earlier for the ten weeks between the deaths of Haus and Kailer. Holub was called to Vienna from his post as adjutant and head of the naval command chancellery, promoted to vice admiral, and named to succeed Njegovan as chief of the *Marinesektion*. Rear Admiral Franz von Teichgräber, head of the technical office (*II. Geschäftsgruppe*) of the *Marinesektion*, remained in Vienna as Holub's second in command. Vice Admiral Keil, third in command at the *Marinesektion* (as *zugeteilter Flaggenoffizier*) for four years under Haus, returned to prominence as "admiral at the disposition of the High Command (*Admiral zur Disposition des allerhöchsten Oberbefehls*)," serving as the navy's chief liaison officer to Charles at the *Armeeoberkommando* headquarters in Baden. By far the most controversial aspect of the reshuffling was the emperor's decision to promote his friend Horthy, captain of the dreadnought *Prinz Eugen* in Pola, to rear admiral and fleet commander.[64] The choice of Horthy met with the general approval of junior officers, who respected him as a man of action. In his investigation after the mutiny at Cattaro and during a subsequent stopover in Pola en route back to Vienna, Charles Stephen asked officers for their choice of a commander and heard Horthy's name most often.[65]

The emperor's decision, of course, would most offend those superseded by the extraordinary advancement of Horthy, who was just forty-nine years old, twenty-ninth in overall seniority and eleventh on the captains' list as of the beginning of February 1918. Because the promotion technically only violated the seniority of the ten captains he passed on the *Rangliste*—of whom seven were his own classmates from the academy class of 1886—the admirals ahead of him posed the most serious problem. The traditions of the corps dictated that no one could serve at sea under another officer of inferior seniority; thus all of the admirals had to retire or accept posts on land. Holub, Keil, and Rodler were safe, but the heads of the three principal seagoing units of the fleet—Willenik of the First Battle Squadron, Seidensacher of the Second Battle Squadron, and Hansa of the Cruiser Flotilla—never again held active commands, and all three were to take early retirement before the end of the war. Fiedler, the harbor admiral at Pola, and Koudelka, the local commander at Trieste, should not have been affected, but both came under pressure to retire in order to free their posts for the transfers to land of men standing below themselves and above Horthy on the *Rangliste*. Rear Admiral Alfred Cicoli, who had been instrumental earlier in negotiating the Triple Alliance naval convention of 1913, re-placed Fiedler as Pola harbor admiral in March 1918; a member of the class of 1884, he had two years' seniority over Horthy and thus could not continue as commander of the Second Battle Division (the three *Radetzkys*), a post he had held since the previous August. Koudelka was asked to give way to his own adjutant, Rear Admiral Dragutin Prica (class of 1885), who, like Cicoli, no longer was eligible for service at sea, but the army intervened to save him, citing Koudelka's proven value as a division commander on the left flank of the Italian front. The shake-up even affected the Danube flotilla, where Rear Admiral Wickerhauser (class of 1885) turned over his command to Captain Marjan Ratković.[66]

Charles announced Horthy's promotion in a statement reassuring the "number of senior distinguished, capable admirals and captains" that his decision did not stem from a lack of confidence in their abilities but a "special trust" in Horthy. Charles appealed to their "sense of duty and patriotism" in calling for all sea officers to support the new fleet commander.[67] The emperor subsequently was "very pleased" at the extent to which those affected supported his decision, either by requesting retirement or rallying behind Horthy. He called it "a splendid testimony of the spirit of our sea officers."[68] Fiedler's retirement left Keil, at fifty-six, as the oldest officer still on active duty. Since all seagoing commanders had to be junior to Horthy, for the rest of the war no officer over fifty went to sea.

As for Horthy, the new fleet commander later recalled that he was "taken aback" by the extraordinary promotion and "begged His Majesty to change his mind," on the grounds that the move "would cause much controversy" within the corps. But Charles "adhered to his decision on the grounds that young blood was needed in the higher ranks of the navy."[69] The emperor's desire to give Horthy the greatest possible free hand led to the construction of a complex chain of command with enough loopholes to allow the new fleet commander direct access to the emperor whenever he wanted it. From his post at supreme headquarters in Baden, Keil was responsible for conveying Charles's orders to Holub at the *Marinesektion* in Vienna and to Horthy in Pola, but both Holub and Horthy were authorized to communicate with the emperor either through Keil or directly. In matters relating to operations, Horthy was bound only to consult Charles. On questions of personnel, the fleet commander had to consult Holub and the *Marinesektion*. The new chain of command was a source of confusion for the remainder of the war. Of the three admirals, Keil appears to have been the one most dissatisfied with the arrangement, and understandably so: he could not issue orders on his own authority and was reduced to functioning as reporter to the emperor, albeit only when Horthy and Holub chose to employ his services.[70]

Horthy received carte blanche to reorganize the forces under his command, and the ensuing weeks brought dramatic changes in the deployment of the matériel and personnel of the fleet. Meanwhile, in response to the Cattaro mutiny, Captain Carl Rössler became "leader of the defense against enemy propaganda (*Leiter der Feindespropagandaabwehr*)," and plans were laid to establish a network of "education officers (*Unterrichtsoffiziere*)," one for every larger ship in the fleet; for the smaller vessels, such as destroyers and torpedo boats, there would be one officer per flotilla group. Rössler planned to use films and lectures in all of the Habsburg languages to counter threats of subversion and mutiny. Owing to a shortage of officers and resources, such schemes went nowhere.[71] Horthy ultimately relied on more traditional methods to restore and maintain discipline and could do little more than hope that divisive nationalist and socialist sentiments would not flare up again.

The Germans applauded Horthy's appointment. William II himself reflected the opinion of his own naval hierarchy by observing that such a move was long overdue.[72] As usual, German leaders were less than sympathetic to the political and strategic woes of their ally. To the end, they focused on the stability of Austria-Hungary's home front and the reliability of the Habsburg armed forces, even as the German armed forces and home front began to show many of the same strains. As early as April 1917, serious strikes had slowed war production, and in July the famous Peace Resolution passed the *Reichstag*. Strikes and mutinies plagued the High Seas Fleet throughout the summer of 1917, with poor food, boredom, and political agitation combining to cause the trouble.[73] Finally, in late January 1918, just as the wave of strikes in Austria-Hungary came to an end, workers struck throughout the Reich, paralyzing German industry. As the Dual Monarchy staggered into the war's final year, its domineering ally in many respects was in no better shape to pursue the struggle to a successful end.

THE NAVY UNDER HORTHY
(MARCH 1918–OCTOBER 1918)

As late as March 1918, an American navy memorandum characterized the Adriatic as "practically an Austrian lake in which no Allied Naval operations of importance are undertaken."[74] During 1917 the navy had convoyed 960,000 tons of supplies over the route Rijeka-Split-Cattaro-Durazzo and another 128,500 tons of local traffic between Cattaro and Durazzo. After ferrying 12,388 sick and wounded from northern Albania during 1916, losing six requisitioned steamers in the process, the navy evacuated 60,287 during 1917 and would transport another 55,345 in 1918, losing only three steamers in 1917–18.[75] After the United States finally declared war on Austria-Hungary, the American Mediterranean commander, Vice Admiral William Sims, proposed offensive action in the Adriatic to disrupt this traffic and to bottle up the submarines of the Central Powers.

The plan that Sims promoted mirrored the thinking of the Italians in their optimistic mode of 1915, calling for allied troops to seize Lissa, Lagosta, Curzola, Pelagosa, and other islands in the central Adriatic in order to cut off Cattaro from Pola and the upper Adriatic. He also hinted that the American navy would contribute as many as five pre-dreadnoughts and twenty thousand Marines to an assault on Cattaro itself. All of these operations would require not just American soldiers but contingents of troops from the Entente armies as well. Unfortunately, the Italian army, holding the Piave line only with British and French support, was in no position to provide the necessary manpower, and after the German army launched its final offensive on the western front on 21 March, no one else had troops to spare, either. In early April, Sims conceded that his plans for an Adriatic offensive would have to be put on hold.[76]

The respite gave Horthy an opportunity to take the initiative, but the first months of his tenure were consumed by a reorganization program involving the transfer of dozens of officers and hundreds of men and the decommissioning or reassignment of several warships. As a consequence of decisions made by Njegovan in his last weeks in office, the *Budapest* went from Trieste to Pola as an accommodation ship, while the *Monarch* remained in Cattaro in the same capacity. In Pola the *Habsburg* and *Arpád* were converted to training vessels and their sister *Babenberg* to an accommodation ship. The light cruisers *Aspern* and *Szigetvár*, recently assigned to Trieste, also became accommodation ships. Horthy kept the three 10,600-ton *Erzherzogs* on duty in Cattaro in place of the armored cruisers *Sankt Georg* and *Kaiser Karl VI*, which were disarmed and converted to headquarters ships, the former at Cattaro, the latter at Sebenico.

The changes left the active fleet at Pola with just the seven newest battleships: the four dreadnoughts (First Battle Division), now under the command of Captain Heinrich Seitz, and the three *Radetzkys* (Second Battle Division), under Captain Franz Lauffer. At Cattaro the three *Erzherzogs* assumed the reserve function of the old armored cruisers, standing ready to rescue the scout cruisers and smaller craft should they run into trouble returning from raids at the mouth of the Adriatic. The *Erzherzog Karl* became the flagship of Captain Heyssler, who replaced Hansa as commander of the Cruiser Flotilla. The decommissioning of the *Monarch,* the last remaining coast defender in Cattaro, brought the abolition of the Fifth Battle Division. Responsibility for local defense passed to a new Cattaro harbor admiralty, headed as of June by Rear Admiral Vitus Vončina. Commander of the battleship *Radetzky* for most of the war, Vončina's seniority—one year more than Horthy—made him ineligible for a seagoing position.[77]

The decommissioning of obsolete warships helped address the navy's fuel shortage, especially acute in the case of coal, which all of the larger vessels burned. At the time of Njegovan's dismissal, stocks stood at just 95,000 tons, alarmingly low considering that the battle fleet would consume an average of 1,000 tons per hour on a sortie. Because so few domestic mines produced coal of the quality necessary for warship use, the navy's prewar dependence on British coal gave way after the summer of 1914 to reliance on coal imports from Germany, mostly from Westphalian mines. The shipping of so many tons of coal overland by rail posed a logistical nightmare for the railway systems of both of the Central Powers. When it came to rail transport, the needs of the armies on the various fronts had to be met first; when it came to Westphalian coal, the needs of the German navy naturally took precedence.[78]

In addition to providing manpower to support the submarine and air services, the decommissioning of so many ships in the Adriatic freed seamen for the Danube and for a new Black Sea flotilla, established in

March 1918. The Central Powers had only a dubious claim on ships belonging to the late Imperial Russia; the Treaty of Brest-Litovsk, signed on 3 March, provided for Russian warships to be either disarmed or interned until the end of the European war. To muddy the waters still more, on 9 February, with German approval, Austria-Hungary had already concluded a separate peace with the Ukraine—the so-called *Brotfrieden,* or Bread Peace—staking a stronger claim to the Ukrainian harvest of 1918. Concurrently, the two armies continued to advance until they occupied almost all of the Ukraine. Some vessels of the Russian Black Sea Fleet ran for Novorossiysk, which was under Bolshevik control, but many more fell into German and Austro-Hungarian hands in Odessa and other ports.[79]

Losing no sleep over Soviet Russian or Ukrainian claims to the confiscated warships, the Germans dreamed of using them, along with the *Goeben* and the Turkish navy, to form a powerful new fleet that could break out into the eastern Mediterranean. The Entente powers, suspicious of possible Soviet cooperation with such a scheme, took this threat far more seriously than they should have.[80] In any event, Austria-Hungary's main concern in the east in 1918 was for the security of the Ukrainian harvest and the Black Sea-Danube River supply line to ship the grain home. The 1,600-ton former Russian minelayer *Dunaj,* which had been captured at Odessa, was the largest vessel of the Habsburg Black Sea flotilla; the others were two small steamers, four tugboats, five motorized minesweepers, and one 33-ton midget submarine. The pair of steamers and one tug were armed for escort or transport duties, while the remaining tugs became auxiliary minesweepers. Four monitors and several patrol boats from the Danube joined the Black Sea flotilla to help escort grain ships, and a small naval air station was established at Odessa.[81] The navy planned to move the midget submarine overland to the Adriatic and even sent Lieutenant Trapp to the Black Sea in late March to inspect it. He advised his superiors to drop the plan on the grounds that the submarine would be of little use. It never saw action.[82]

In early April, Charles asked Horthy whether a conventional submarine could be spared to strengthen the Austro-Hungarian representation in the Black Sea. The fleet commander considered sending the *U28,* but ultimately the emperor agreed that the submarine could be put to better use in the Adriatic and Mediterranean, and that the Danube flotilla and the other requisitioned vessels were adequate for showing the flag in the east.[83] A subsequent redeployment sent Captain Wulff from the lower Danube to Odessa with four monitors and two patrol boats. In the months that followed, his vessels could be found not just in coastal waters but also on the Dnieper, Dniester, and Bug rivers. By mid-summer 1918, the Black Sea operation employed more than six hundred Austro-Hungarian navy personnel under the overall command of an old academy classmate of Horthy, Rear Admiral Egon Klein, designated "naval inspector of the eastern army."[84]

The extension of naval operations into the east paradoxically came at a time when the Dual Monarchy's overall health and stability appeared shakier than ever. Trapp's mission to the Black Sea, passing overland across the South Slav provinces, exposed him to the widespread despair and discontent that had overtaken the interior of the empire; he later recalled his shock and dismay at hearing people speak openly of the dismemberment of Austria-Hungary and refer to the emperor as "Charles the Last."[85] The wave of defeatism grew with the failure of Charles's various peace proposals and crested with the sensational news of the so-called "Sixtus Affair."[86] In April 1918, French premier Georges Clemenceau revealed that one year earlier Prince Sixtus of Bourbon-Parma, brother-in-law of Emperor Charles, had visited President Raymond Poincaré on a secret peace initiative. Charles denied the report—he could do little else—and hastened to reassure William II of his fidelity to their alliance. The German emperor publicly accepted his assurances—he, too, could hardly have done otherwise—but their relationship remained strained for the duration of the war. Public opinion in both Germany and Austria-Hungary doubted Charles's denials, and he never recovered from the loss of credibility.

Charles had indeed launched his own peace effort in early February 1917, less than a month after the Schloss Pless conference and his commitment to support the renewal of unrestricted submarine warfare. Sixtus, an officer in the Belgian army, had been a go-between with Poincaré for around two months after the initial contact. The talks collapsed mostly because the emperor was prepared to offer little that would satisfy Italy's war aims. Charles went far beyond keeping the initiative secret from the Germans; he had not even informed his own foreign minister, Count Czernin, the strongest advocate of strict fidelity to the German alliance, who resigned after the scandal broke. István Burián returned to the Ballhausplatz to replace him and remained in office until the last days of the war.[87]

Coinciding with the Sixtus revelations, Italian prime minister Orlando convened a "Congress of Oppressed Nationalities" in Rome in an attempt to fully mobilize the émigré national movements agitating for the dismemberment of Austria-Hungary. Habsburg South Slav exiles were well represented, and for the moment differences between Italian war aims and South Slav national goals appeared to be reconciled.[88] Given the fact that Croatians were still the largest single nationality among Habsburg seamen, the developments in Rome did not bode well for the navy.

Even though the future looked far from promising, Horthy struggled to whip his streamlined battle fleet into shape. Throughout the spring, maneuvers were conducted and gunnery practice held on a scale not seen since before the war.[89] Meanwhile, in the interest of improving morale, Horthy approved a plan to land a band of saboteurs at Ancona. Junior officers had been clamoring for a raid on the port to retake *Torpedoboot 11* ever since the vessel's defection in October 1917, but Njegovan had ignored their appeals, and Horthy likewise rejected a mission purely for the symbolic purpose of restoring the navy's honor. He did, however, authorize a mission designed to destroy Italian submarines docked at Ancona and to commandeer *MAS* boats for the return trip home. Led by a reserve lieutenant, Josef Veith, the operation penetrated the Ancona arsenal but failed to blow up any of the undersea boats and found only one *MAS*, unfortunately immobilized by engine trouble. After two of his men—both Italian—deserted and alerted local authorities, Veith and the other raiders were captured.[90]

Thus a mission intended to boost the spirits of the navy failed miserably, largely because of faulty intelligence (the *Nachrichtendienst* had never recovered from the Zurich disaster of February 1917) but at least in part because of treason. Horthy chose not to dwell on the latter point and instead simply declared that "the entire fleet is proud of our brave comrades, who with such commendable courage volunteered for this dangerous expedition."[91] Nevertheless, paranoia over the loyalty and reliability of the navy naturally increased. A month after the Ancona mission, when a group of *Huszár*-class destroyers were en route

home from an unsuccessful raid on the Italian coast, two of the vessels
suffered engine trouble that left them straggling behind the others and
vulnerable to sinking or capture. Even though all of the destroyers made
it safely to port, Admiral Keil suspected sabotage and requested information on the nationality of the machinists aboard the two ships in
question. An investigation rejected the sabotage theory and concluded
that the mechanical trouble had been legitimate, but Keil's inquiries
were indicative of the prevailing mood of the navy leadership.[92]

When confronted with genuine disloyalty, Horthy responded in a
most decisive fashion. In May, after rumblings of mutiny aboard torpedo boat *80-T* in Pola led to the trial and conviction of two ringleaders,
a Dalmatian Croat and a Czech, the commander promptly authorized
their execution. In sharp contrast to the shroud of secrecy surrounding the executions at Cattaro in February, Horthy ordered contingents
of twenty men from each of the vessels on hand to watch the firing
squad do its work.[93] Such exhibitions *pour encourager les autres,* to use
the French army term, were controversial, and the effects were hard to
measure.[94] Nevertheless, Horthy to some degree succeeded in restoring the navy's traditional iron discipline, which had eroded during
Njegovan's year at the helm.

Horthy and his cohorts felt that a major fleet action ultimately
would be the only cure for low morale, but they did not intend to launch
one until after the fleet was back in fighting trim; from the start, they
assumed that a general sortie before May or June would be impossible.
In the meantime, Horthy continued his drills and maneuvers at Pola,
the lighter craft and submarines carried on their patrols and raids, and
those in charge of harbor defenses along the Austro-Hungarian coastline
remained on guard against raids by *MAS* boats. In the spring of 1918,
the Italians once again demonstrated their ingenuity and prowess in
the "little war" in the Adriatic by unveiling a maritime version of the
tank that could use its caterpillar treads to climb over the defensive
booms strung across the entrances of enemy harbors. None of the odd-
looking vessels ever succeeded in a raid, but the navy guarded the harbor entrances with a renewed vigilance and also tried to use the *Grillo*, a
sea tank captured off Pola in May 1918, as a prototype for a pair of similar boats of its own.[95]

In early June, Horthy concluded that the fleet finally was ready for
its sortie. The operation, set to take place on the morning of 11 June,

would be an attack on the Otranto barrage similar to his successful raid of May 1917, only with the support of the four dreadnoughts from Pola and the three *Erzherzog*-class battleships recently reassigned to Cattaro. The light cruisers once again were to play a pivotal role. Plans called for the *Novara* and *Helgoland* to attack the line of drifters with support from four *Tátra*-class destroyers, while the *Admiral Spaun* and *Saida*, escorted by four torpedo boats, would bombard the seaplane station at Otranto. As in the previous year's battle, German and Austro-Hungarian submarines would be deployed off Valona and Brindisi to try to torpedo enemy vessels that ventured out, and seaplanes from Cattaro were to provide air cover and reconnaissance. The big difference, of course, would be the trailing force of seven battleships, each escorted by destroyers and torpedo boats. In addition to damaging the barrage line, Horthy hoped that the light cruisers, running toward home after their attack on the drifters, would serve as bait to lure unsuspecting British, French, and Italian cruisers northward far enough to be trapped by the overwhelming firepower of the dreadnoughts, supported by the *Erzherzogs*.[96]

Late on 8 June, Horthy left Pola with his flagship, the *Viribus Unitis*, and the *Prinz Eugen;* the following evening, the *Tegetthoff* and *Szent István* departed as well, accompanied by their small escort craft. The plan provided for the dreadnoughts to snake southward through the deep waters of the fractured coastline, using the Dalmatian islands as a screen against observation by the enemy. The first two battleships were almost halfway down the Adriatic when the trailing pair, early on the tenth, were surprised by an *MAS* attack off the island of Premuda. Two of the boats buzzed out of the predawn darkness, the *MAS-15* firing its pair of torpedoes into the *Szent István*, the *MAS-21* missing with both of its shots against the *Tegetthoff*. The *Szent István*, struck at around 3:30 A.M., listed heavily to starboard but remained afloat for more than two hours, its crew feverishly pumping to right the ship while the *Tegetthoff* attempted to take it in tow. Just after six o'clock, the warship capsized, sinking within five minutes. Miraculously, of a crew of over one thousand men, only eighty-five drowned, along with four officers.[97]

Coincidentally, the same person figured prominently in the *MAS-15*'s torpedoing of the *Szent István* and the *MAS-9*'s attack on the *Wien* six months earlier: Captain Luigi Rizzo commanded both missions, and his sinking of the second battleship—the newest dreadnought in the Austro-Hungarian fleet—elevated him to the status of national hero in

Italy.[98] On the Austrian side, the luckless Heinrich Seitz was in command of the *Szent István* at the time of its sinking; prepared to go down with the ship, he was saved after being thrown clear of the bridge when the vessel capsized.[99] Ironically, Seitz also had a personal connection with the *Wien,* having commanded it early in 1917 after Haus's death brought his return to active service, but he was no longer captain of that ship by the time of its demise.

The loss of the *Szent István* forced Horthy to cancel his plans for the operation at the Straits of Otranto. Though he still would have been able to bring overwhelming force to bear against the barrage line itself and whatever forces Brindisi or Valona could send out, the element of surprise was lost, and by the time his dreadnoughts made it to the lower Adriatic, they could expect to meet Italian dreadnoughts from Taranto and French dreadnoughts from Corfu, with British warships from Malta probably not far behind. Even worse, the sinking of the *Szent István*—coming at the end of a crash course of preparedness, with morale in the fleet higher than it had been in quite some time—had a devastating psychological effect on the entire navy. A sortie to the mouth of the Adriatic by the battle fleet, even with all four dreadnoughts, was a risky venture against overwhelming odds; it would be pointless to try it again with just three of the battleships remaining and with the enemy navies in a heightened state of alert.

As late as the beginning of August, Horthy answered an inquiry of the *Armeeoberkommando* by vouching for the battle readiness of the fleet. Indeed, at that stage he expressed greater concern for the manpower shortage than for morale, noting that the navy had received only 1,900 of its quota of 8,000 recruits for 1918. In the face of new commitments in the Black Sea, along with the expansion of the submarine and aviation services, his human resources were stretched to the limit.[100] Notwithstanding the fleet commander's positive appraisal of morale, a pervasive pessimism infected the officer corps while rumors of a South Slav plot at the navy's Sebenico base persisted throughout the summer.[101] Cattaro remained quiet even after a command change at the head of the Cruiser Flotilla, necessitated early in August when the popular Heyssler went on sick leave for eye surgery. Horthy sent Seitz to the Bocche as Heyssler's replacement and turned over the First Battle Division to Captain Adolf Schmidt. Amid the general tension, at least one annual ritual took place in an atmosphere of business as usual: on 15 September 1918, after passing the same rigorous battery of entrance examinations as their predecessors, sixty-five boys—the future class of 1922—were mustered in as the first-year class at the naval academy in Braunau. The 1918–19 school year would be the shortest on record.[102]

In the summer and fall of 1918, the navy continued to work on construction projects likely to have an impact on the war: submarines, aircraft, and surface vessels along the model of the Italian *MAS* and *Grillo*. At the end of the war, fourteen submarines were at various stages of completion, and materials had been assembled for another six that were never laid down.[103] Nine 24.6-ton motor torpedo boats were also begun, three (designated *Mb.107-109*) in the Pola Arsenal in July 1917 and six (*Mb.110-115*) in Trieste in March 1918. *Mb.107* was finished in October 1918; the rest were still under construction when the war ended. The pair of *Grillo*-type "naval tanks," built by the Eppel firm of Vienna, were launched in October but never entered service.[104] In September 1918, a plan for the reorganization of the navy's air service envisioned a fleet of 232 first-line planes by the summer of 1919, including 60 bombers. In October 1918, the navy had 268 planes, many of them obsolete, with another 171 under construction. The active force had grown more than tenfold during the war years but still was dwarfed by the Italian naval air arm, which had 552 planes at the end of the war, supplemented by scores of British, French, and American aircraft.[105]

Austro-Hungarian naval aviators paid dearly for this inferiority in the skies: in 1917, 25 of their planes were lost in action and 43 pilots killed, while only 7 enemy planes were shot down. The figures for the last year of the war were not quite so lopsided: 16 planes and 33 pilots lost, with 12 enemy planes shot down. Navy seaplanes continued to bomb Venice until the last days of the war. Between May 1915 and October 1918, 42 raids involving more than 250 planes dropped more than 1,000 bombs on the city. Pola bore the brunt of the Entente's air assaults, during the same period enduring 41 attacks involving almost 400 planes and 700 bombs. By far the largest attack on Pola came on 17 July 1918, when 66 planes dropped some 200 bombs. Fortunately for the navy, the only vessel hit was the disarmed *Babenberg*, which was then serving as an accommodation ship for submarine crews. During the course of the war, 510 officers and men served in the Austro-Hungarian naval air arm;

of these, 101 lost their lives, and 65 were captured. The aviators suffered the highest casualty rate in the entire service, greater even than the submariners.[106]

Aside from the ill-starred fleet sortie that had ended with the sinking of the *Szent István,* most of the action in the Adriatic during the last year of the war involved the failures or successes of Austro-Hungarian submarines. After an Italian torpedo boat attack claimed the *U23* off Valona in February, the navy lost two more undersea boats in the Gulf of Trieste in July when an Italian submarine sank the *U20* and an enemy mine claimed the *U10.* Entente losses in action were limited to the British destroyer *Phoenix,* sunk in May by the *U27* in the Straits of Otranto, and the French submarine *Circé,* sunk in September by the *U47* off the coast of Albania. Indeed, mishaps claimed far more enemy vessels. In February 1918, the French submarine *Bernouilli* disappeared in the Adriatic, probably after striking a mine. In April a British submarine accidentally torpedoed the Italian submarine *H5,* and two destroyers—the French *Faulx* and the Italian *Cairoli*—were sunk in separate collisions while escorting three of the *Regina Elena*-class pre-dreadnoughts from Brindisi to Taranto. Meanwhile, Austro-Hungarian submarines proved to be even less effective than before against enemy shipping. Throughout the war, the navy had focused its undersea campaign against the Entente's warships operating in the Adriatic, while the German U-boats used the Austrian Adriatic bases to prey upon shipping in the Mediterranean. In any event, Austria-Hungary could have only a limited role in the last phase of the campaign of unrestricted submarine warfare. At the start of 1918, only the nine newest submarines were considered fit for Mediterranean duties; in the first nine months of the year, they claimed just 59,200 tons of enemy shipping. During the same period, German submarines in the Mediterranean *averaged* 80,000 tons per month, a total that would have been higher if not for the success of the allied convoy system.[107]

Less than a week after the sinking of the *Szent István,* with the German army still bearing down on Paris in its most successful western offensive since 1914, the Austro-Hungarian forces along the Piave launched a full-scale attack of their own. The operation commenced on 15 June, supported on its eastern flank by fire from the old coast defender *Budapest,* which had been recommissioned after just a few months as an accommodation ship and fitted out with a single 15-inch howitzer in its forward turret in place of the original pair of 9.4-inch guns.[108] Vice Admiral Koudelka, since December 1915 head of the 94th Infantry Division, commanded forces along the coast and on the left flank; these included the navy's Trieste battalion and sappers, marine field artillery batteries, plus telephone, telegraph, and bicycle detachments charged with maintaining communications behind the lines. Plans called for Koudelka to become harbor admiral of Venice should the offensive succeed in taking the city, but the forces on his flank, weakened by an outbreak of malaria, failed even to establish a bridgehead across the Piave.[109] In the Tyrol, Conrad von Hötzendorf's troops registered modest initial gains, but the entire offensive fizzled out within a week and a half, leaving the front in its original position. After the advance stalled in early July, the navy's land detachments were withdrawn to Trieste. Within days Koudelka announced his retirement; at fifty-four, he had been the oldest admiral other than Keil still on active duty. Conrad became the scapegoat for the overall failure of the offensive and was sacked in mid-July.[110]

Meanwhile, the German drive on Paris sputtered, and the Anglo-French counterattack, backed by fresh American troops, started to push eastward. The war effort of the Central Powers faced its most serious crisis to date on 8 August when the British breakthrough at Amiens marked the definite turning point on the western front. By then the Italians were pressuring Austro-Hungarian forces in Albania while the Anglo-French-Serbian-Greek army around Salonika prepared for an invasion of Bulgaria. On 14 August, Charles, foreign minister Burián, and chief of staff Arz von Straussenburg went to Spa for an emergency meeting with William II and the German High Command. The Austro-Hungarian leaders advocated immediate armistice talks, but the Germans insisted that the western front had to be stabilized first; otherwise, the Central Powers would be bargaining from a position of weakness.[111] The front never did stabilize, and when the German High Command agreed to seek an armistice seven weeks later, the enemy was in no mood to talk.

A counterattack in Albania by the XIX Corps that was launched on 24 August was the last offensive action ever undertaken by the Habsburg army; it recovered all ground recently lost to the Italians and came close enough to Valona to worry the Entente admirals.[112] To the east, the Bulgarians were not so lucky. On 15 September, their lines broke under the weight of an Entente offensive, and within a week and a half their army lay in ruins. As enemy troops poured northward into Serbia and Bulgaria, the position of the navy's eastern forces suddenly became untenable. Bolshevik military successes in the Ukraine had rendered the Austro-Ukrainian treaty of February 1918 meaningless almost as soon as it was signed; only 70,000 tons of Ukrainian foodstuffs ever made it to Austria-Hungary, and in early September Wulff's vessels had been withdrawn from Odessa and the Black Sea to Braila on the lower Danube. After Bulgaria concluded an armistice on 3 October, the Danube flotilla covered the retreat of Central Powers troops northward across the river into Romania. Thereafter, the monitors and their patrol boat escorts executed a slow withdrawal up the Danube.[113]

The collapse of the front in the eastern Balkans caused an immediate crisis for Austria-Hungary on the western end of the Balkan front. The *Armeeoberkommando* concluded that northern Albania could not be held, and on 28 September the navy received instructions to evacuate as many troops as possible via Durazzo. The operation continued for two weeks, during which the port endured one heavy enemy assault. The attack, on 2 October, was spearheaded by Italy's three *Pisa*-class armored cruisers and five British light cruisers. Smaller craft included fourteen British and two Italian destroyers, Italian torpedo boats and *MAS* boats, American submarine chasers (larger, slower versions of the *MAS*), and submarines from the British, French, and Italian navies. British and Italian planes bombed the city to supplement the fire from the fleet. Thaon di Revel supervised the allied operation from aboard the dreadnought *Dante Alighieri,* which did not take part in the attack.[114]

As luck would have it, the harbor was practically empty at the time of the onslaught. The Austro-Hungarian destroyers *Dinara* and *Scharfschütze,* the submarines *U29* and *U31,* and the torpedo boat *87-F* were the only warships on hand, and all survived the action, as did a hospital ship and two of three transports. During the bombardment, the *U31* torpedoed the British cruiser *Weymouth,* which managed to escape without sinking. For his efforts, the commander of the *U31,* Lieutenant Hermann Rigele, received the Order of Maria Theresa. He was the last seaman ever to win the coveted decoration, and the defense of Durazzo would be the last battle ever fought by the Austro-Hungarian navy. Two days later, on 4 October, the Central Powers formally requested an armistice based on the terms of Wilson's Fourteen Points.

After Germany and Austria-Hungary issued their appeal for an armistice, the navy ended all operations except for routine patrols by lighter craft. Thierry's submarines, which had not sunk an enemy vessel since 20 September, remained active for another two weeks, registering no further successes.[115] Upon receiving word of the initiative for a truce, Horthy appointed two officers to serve as the navy's representatives on an armistice commission: his successor aboard the *Novara*, Prince Liechtenstein, and Captain Georg Zwierkowski of the Danube flotilla. But with the Central Powers falling back on the western front and in the Balkans, the time for negotiation had passed. The relatively favorable strategic position that the Dual Monarchy enjoyed on all fronts by early 1917 would not have been achieved without German aid. In return for such support, however, Austria-Hungary had to continue to pursue the war on Germany's terms until such time as the Germans were willing to quit fighting. By the time the German High Command reached this point in the autumn of 1918, all hope of saving the Habsburg Empire even in some radically reformed, restructured condition had been lost.

As the navy's last action, the skirmish at Durazzo typified the overall war effort of the fleet: a defensive action against overwhelming odds pursued successfully with remarkably light losses. The mission of the navy under Njegovan and Horthy was no different than it had been under Haus: to defend the Adriatic front of the Dual Monarchy until the Central Powers achieved victory by breaking through on other fronts. Pursued lethargically under Njegovan, somewhat more energetically—at least initially—under Horthy, the campaign continued in spite of the increasing strength within the navy of the centrifugal forces of nationalism, social discontent, and war weariness. The same forces, of course, were tearing apart the Dual Monarchy as a whole, and for the fleet as well as for the entire empire, the month of October 1918 would see the strains finally reach fatal proportions.

NOTES

1.   On the rhetoric of the *Nibelungentreue,* see Herwig, "Disjointed Allies," 265, 271, 279, and passim.

2. See Shanafelt, *The Secret Enemy*, 150.

3. Wagner, "Die obersten Behörden," 111–13; on Kailer's death, see Bayer von Bayersburg, *Österreichs Admirale*, 95.

4. See order of battle for 20 March 1917 in Sokol, *Österreich-Ungarns Seekrieg*, 2, appendix 9; and Aichelburg, *Die Unterseeboote*, 1:68, 143. The seven leading admirals, ranging in age from fifty-eight (Njegovan) to fifty-two (Holub), graduated from the naval academy between 1877 and 1883.

5. Aichelburg, *Die Unterseeboote*, 1:100, 117.

6. Greger, *Austro-Hungarian Warships*, 47. The four destroyers were laid down in August and September 1916.

7. Bayer von Bayersburg, *Unter der k.u.k. Kriegsflagge*, 21–25.

8. Figure for the end of 1916. By comparison, Italy entered the war in May 1915 with coal stocks of only 493,000 tons. See Sokol, *Österreich-Ungarns Seekrieg*, 1:187n, 416.

9. Ibid., 1:465–67; Bayer von Bayersburg, *Österreichs Admirale*, 126.

10. Halpern, *Naval War in the Mediterranean*, 310–12, 315.

11. Sokol, *Österreich-Ungarns Seekrieg*, 1:376; Halpern, *Naval War in the Mediterranean*, 358.

12. Sokol, *Österreich-Ungarns Seekrieg*, 1:377–81; *La marina italiana*, 4:498–511; Thomazi, *La guerre navale*, 148–49; Halpern, *Naval War in the Mediterranean*, 359. The official *Jahresbericht der k.u.k. Kriegsmarine* (1914–17), 18, claims that twenty drifters were sunk, ten by the *Novara*, eight by the *Helgoland*, and two by the *Saida;* Horthy, *Memoirs*, 81, gives a total of twenty-one.

13. Sokol, *Österreich-Ungarns Seekrieg*, 1:381–91; *La marina italiana*, 4:512–54; Thomazi, *La guerre navale*, 149–51; Halpern, *Naval War in the Mediterranean*, 359–62. An exploding shell left Horthy wounded in the leg by five shell fragments, unconscious, and temporarily deaf in one ear. He had two operations on his leg, one in Vienna and one in Budapest, and did not return to active service until late in 1917. See Horthy, *Memoirs*, 83–86.

14. Sokol, *Österreich-Ungarns Seekrieg*, 1:391–93; Halpern, *Naval War in the Mediterranean*, 362–63; Thomazi, *La guerre navale*, 151–52; *La marina italiana*, 4:554–61. Entente casualties included forty-two killed and forty-five wounded; Austro-Hungarian casualties were sixteen killed and fifty-four wounded. The attack on the drifters resulted in nine killed and an undetermined number of wounded; seventy-two survivors were taken prisoner by Horthy's cruisers. Figures from ibid., 4:568.

15. Halpern, *Naval War in the Mediterranean*, 363–64; Thomazi, *La guerre navale*, 153–54, 158.

16. Halpern, *Naval War in the Mediterranean*, 344, 365, 367–73, 377.

17. Ibid., 366.

18. See Erwin Sieche, "Der Untergang des Torpedofahrzeuges *Wildfang* am 4.6.1917," 52–63.

19. Halpern, *Naval War in the Mediterranean*, 344; *Jahresbericht der k.u.k. Kriegsmarine* (1914–17), 18. Other Entente losses in the first months of 1917 included the Italian torpedo boats *Perseo* and *Scorpione*, both to shipwreck. See Thomazi, *La guerre navale*, 228.

20. See Arthur J. May, *The Passing of the Hapsburg Monarchy, 1914–1918*, 2:640–42.

21. Sokol, *Österreich-Ungarns Seekrieg*, 2:709–10.

22. Eyewitness account by navy physician Rudolf Mosaner, quoted in Sieche, "Der Untergang des Torpedofahrzeuges *Wildfang*," 52.

23. Sokol, *Österreich-Ungarns Seekrieg*, 1:464; rationing also mentioned by Mosaner in Sieche, "Der Untergang des Torpedofahrzeuges *Wildfang*," 52.

24. Winterhalder, *Die österreichisch-ungarische Kriegsmarine,* 39.

25. Koudelka, *Denn Österreich lag einst am Meer,* 274–75.

26. Aichelburg, *Die Unterseeboote,* 1:88; Sondhaus, *In the Service of the Emperor,* 106.

27. Sokol, *Österreich-Ungarns Seekrieg,* 1:464. Some professional fishermen from among the seamen had been assigned to fishing duties earlier in the war. During 1916, the navy's fishermen caught six thousand kilograms of fish, five thousand of which were turned over to the civilian market. See ibid., 1:401.

28. Ibid., 2:705–6.

29. Incident of 27 October 1917 related in a letter by Robert Dietinger (a seventeen-year-old seaman at the time) in *Marine—Gestern, Heute* 12 (1985): 40.

30. Halpern, *Naval War in the Mediterranean,* 410.

31. Ibid., 312, 396; Aichelburg, *Die Unterseeboote,* 2:490–94.

32. *Jahresbericht der k.u.k Kriegsmarine* (1914–17), 17; Thomazi, *La guerre navale,* 157.

33. Sokol, *Austro-Hungarian Navy,* 132; Sondhaus, *In the Service of the Emperor,* 112–13. Two weeks after the desertion, the Italian navy recommissioned the boat under the name *Francesco Rismondo. La marina italiana,* 6:187.

34. Rothenberg, *The Army of Francis Joseph,* 207.

35. Ibid., 206, 208; Shanafelt, *The Secret Enemy,* 150. The request for Austro-Hungarian troops from the eastern front was made by Charles to William II, Reichenau, 26 August 1917, text in Arthur Arz von Straussenberg, *Zur Geschichte des grossen Krieges,* 171.

36. Halpern, *Naval War in the Mediterranean,* 400–405 passim; Thomazi, *La guerre navale,* 167–68.

37. Sokol, *Österreich-Ungarns Seekrieg,* 2:478–86; Koudelka, *Denn Österreich lag einst am Meer,* 262, 272–73. The account in *La marina italiana,* 6:431–35, identifies the boats as *MAS-9* and *MAS-13.* Forty-six men died on the *Wien.*

38. Sokol, *Österreich-Ungarns Seekrieg,* 2:486–88; Koudelka, *Denn Österreich lag einst am Meer,* 274.

39. See Wulff, *Donauflottille,* 127–32.

40. See order of battle for the Danube flotilla, December 1917, in Greger, *Austro-Hungarian Warships,* 15; see also ibid., 138–52.

41. Halpern, *Naval War in the Mediterranean,* 399, 411, 492n; Greger, *Austro-Hungarian Warships,* 19, 29.

42. Halpern, *Naval War in the Mediterranean,* 447.

43. Horthy, *Memoirs,* 87–88.

44. Ibid., 88.

45. Sokol, *Österreich-Ungarns Seekrieg,* 2:706. The bread ration was reduced from 600 grams to 500, the meat ration from 400 grams to 300.

46. "Bis vor wenigen Tagen war der Ruf Hurra ein Freudenruf, eine erhabene Begrüssung. Die Mannschaft einiger Schiffe hat ihn zu einem Demonstrationsruf umgewandelt." Quoted in Richard Georg Plaschka, Horst Haselsteiner, and Arnold Suppan, *Innere Front: Militärassistenz, Widerstand und Umsturz in der Donaumonarchie 1918,* 1:107.

47. Plaschka et al., *Innere Front,* 1:61–75. In 1916 and 1917, Skoda purchased coal and ore mines and secured a controlling interest in steel and iron works, becoming practically self-sufficient. See Brousek, *Die Grossindustrie Böhmens,* 162. Owing to the suspension of battleship and cruiser contracts, almost all of Skoda's wartime business was with the army.

CHAPTER 8

48. Plaschka, et al., *Innere Front*, 1:75–76; Halpern, *Naval War in the Mediterranean*, 453; Sokol, *Österreich-Ungarns Seekrieg*, 2:654.

49. On the reorganization of the Habsburg navy after 1848, see Sondhaus, *The Habsburg Empire and the Sea*, 150–67.

50. Unless otherwise noted, information here and following is based upon Plaschka, et al., *Innere Front*, 1:107–48; and Plaschka's more extensive accounts of the Cattaro mutiny in his *Cattaro - Prag: Revolte und Revolution*, 13–192; and *Matrosen, Offiziere, Rebellen: Krisenkonfrontationen zur See 1900–1918*, 2:155–278. For a concise account of the mutiny highlighting the role of the navy's Italian minority, see Sondhaus, *In the Service of the Emperor*, 113–14.

51. On this point, see Plaschka, *Cattaro - Prag*, 22.

52. For a complete text of the demands, see ibid., 59.

53. When Social Democratic *Reichsrat* representatives agreed to work with government leaders to help end the strike, they limited their comments on the diplomatic situation to the issue of the peace negotiations then underway at Brest-Litovsk between the Central Powers and Soviet Russia. See Plaschka, et al., *Innere Front*, 1:70–71. Even though it would have been difficult for Austria-Hungary to survive under the terms of Wilson's Fourteen Points, the president's use of the word "autonomous" rather than "independent" in Point Ten sparked a storm of criticism from émigré groups and their supporters in Congress and the American press. See May, *The Passing of the Hapsburg Monarchy*, 2:576–80.

54. For the full text of Hansa's response, see Plaschka, *Cattaro - Prag*, 60–61.

55. On Sešan's background and conversion to the mutineers' cause, see ibid., 122–24.

56. For texts of these appeals, see ibid., 155–56.

57. Quoted in ibid., 155.

58. Ibid., 181–89.

59. Sokol, *Österreich-Ungarns Seekrieg*, 2:692–93.

60. For the opinion of a senior officer, see Koudelka, *Denn Österreich lag einst am Meer*, 277. Wünschek quoted in Dora Lauffer, *Die Wellen: Altösterreichische Familiensaga zwischen Adria und Schlesien*, 402.

61. Charles Stephen quoted by Emperor Charles in a postwar memoir dated 8 September 1920, text in Erich Feigl, ed., *Kaiser Karl: Persönliche Aufzeichnungen, Zeugnisse und Dokumente*, 225.

62. Winterhalder, *Die österreichisch-ungarische Kriegsmarine*, 67.

63. Wagner, "Die obersten Behörden," 113; Tomicich, "Die k.(u.)k. Marineakademie," 40, 42. The move to Braunau came after the academy had spent the 1914–15 school year at Schlosshof on the Morava. Because the Inn was too shallow even for small boats to navigate, students had to be taken to the Wolfgangsee for sailing exercises.

64. Wagner, "Die obersten Behörden," 113.

65. Schmidt-Pauli, *Nikolaus von Horthy*, 113, claims that Charles Stephen found "unanimous" support for Horthy. Lauffer, *Die Wellen*, 363, 402, confirms that Horthy was highly regarded in the officer corps. Koudelka, *Denn Österreich lag einst am Meer*, 277, attributes the archduke's verdict to the fact that he only consulted younger officers.

66. For a roster of the corps immediately after Horthy's promotion, see *Almanach für die k.u.k. Kriegsmarine* (1918), 515–17. On the individual personnel changes, see Bayer von Bayersburg, *Österreichs Admirale*, 47, 67, 75, 164; Koudelka, *Denn Österreich lag einst am Meer*, 278–80; Wulff, *Donauflottille*, 140.

344

67. Text of Charles's order of 27 February 1918 in Schmidt-Pauli, *Nikolaus von Horthy*, 114.

68. Charles, memoir of 8 September 1920, in Feigl, *Kaiser Karl*, 225.

69. Horthy, *Memoirs*, 88–89.

70. Wagner, "Die obersten Behörden," 113–15.

71. Sokol, *Österreich-Ungarns Seekrieg*, 2:708. The navy also lacked the resources to participate in a propaganda offensive. Later in 1918, a request by the *Armeeoberkommando* to have navy seaplanes scatter leaflets behind Italian lines had to be denied on the grounds that the fleet did not have enough pilots or aviation fuel to undertake such missions. See ibid., 2:707–8.

72. Halpern, *Naval War in the Mediterranean*, 449.

73. See Herwig, *"Luxury" Fleet*, 230–35.

74. Quoted in Halpern, *Naval War in the Mediterranean*, 439.

75. Sokol, *Österreich-Ungarns Seekrieg*, 1:419–20, 2:631–32.

76. Halpern, *Naval War in the Mediterranean*, 434–41.

77. Ibid., 449–50; Greger, *Austro-Hungarian Warships*, 19–33 passim; Bayer von Bayersburg, *Österreichs Admirale*, 178–79.

78. On the coal shortage, see Winterhalder, *Die österreichisch-ungarische Kriegsmarine*, 77–78; Halpern, *Naval War in the Mediterranean*, 449.

79. Halpern, *Naval War in the Mediterranean*, 542–43.

80. Ibid., 457–59, 543–55.

81. Greger, *Austro-Hungarian Warships*, 81, 152–55; Schupita, *Die k.u.k. Seeflieger*, 223–24.

82. Aichelburg, *Die Unterseeboote*, 1:140; Trapp, *Bis zum letzten Flaggenschuss*, 223.

83. Aichelburg, *Die Unterseeboote*, 1:171. The Habsburg naval attaché at Constantinople, Captain Richard Schönthaler, wanted to pursue the acquisition of one or two Russian destroyers, theorizing that their operation in the Black Sea under the Austro-Hungarian flag would increase the navy's influence with the Turks and open the way for the navy to provide advisors to the Ottoman fleet after the war. For their part, Arz von Straussenburg and the *Armeeoberkommando* proposed confiscating six Russian submarines at Sebastopol for use in the Mediterranean. The Germans vetoed both schemes. See Halpern, *Naval War in the Mediterranean*, 551.

84. Wulff, *Donauflottille*, 153–68; Sokol, *Österreich-Ungarns Seekrieg*, 2:743, 750–51.

85. Trapp, *Bis zum letzten Flaggenschuss*, 223.

86. For a comprehensive treatment of the Sixtus Affair and its consequences, see May, *The Passing of the Hapsburg Monarchy*, 1:439, 483, 486–92, 2:526, 555–56, 596, 631–36, 722.

87. The overture of Sixtus to the French government was followed in December 1917 by a meeting in Geneva between Count Albert Mensdorff, former Austro-Hungarian ambassador to Britain, and Premier Jan Smuts of South Africa, representing the British. See ibid., 2:525–27. On Czernin's defense of the "German course" in Habsburg foreign policy, see Shanafelt, *The Secret Enemy*, 149–91 passim.

88. May, *The Passing of the Hapsburg Monarchy*, 2:596–604.

89. Halpern, *Naval War in the Mediterranean*, 449.

90. Friedrich Jahn and Erwin Sieche, "Der Handstreich auf Ancona am 4. und 5. April 1918," 95–109, 141–47. Ironically, the mission would not have made it as far as the Ancona arsenal if not for the invaluable service of Cadet Icarus Mandolfo (academy class of 1916), who made up for the fact that Veith did not speak Italian.

CHAPTER 8

91. Horthy to Alois von Schinko, Pola, 8 May 1918, reproduced in ibid., 105. Schinko, the father of one of the captured saboteurs, had been a classmate of Horthy at the naval academy (class of 1886).

92. Halpern, *Naval War in the Mediterranean*, 452-53.

93. Plaschka, et al., *Innere Front*, 1:418-20; Horthy, *Memoirs*, 89. In his recollections, written almost forty years later, Horthy identifies the vessel as a "destroyer" rather than a torpedo boat.

94. For a recent discussion of disciplinary strategies during the First World War and their relative success or failure, see Leonard V. Smith, "The Disciplinary Dilemma of French Military Justice, September 1914-April 1917: The Case of the 5e Division d'Infanterie," especially 53-66.

95. Sokol, *Österreich-Ungarns Seekrieg*, 2:628-30; Halpern, *Naval War in the Mediterranean*, 451; Greger, *Austro-Hungarian Warships*, 67.

96. Sokol, *Österreich-Ungarns Seekrieg*, 2:554; Halpern, *Naval War in the Mediterranean*, 501.

97. Sokol, *Österreich-Ungarns Seekrieg*, 2:555-63; Karl Mohl, "Der Untergang der *Szent István* am 10. Juni 1918," 148-53; Halpern, *Naval War in the Mediterranean*, 501-2; *La marina italiana*, 7:570-73.

98. The attack on the *Szent István* had the added effect of salvaging Rizzo's recently tarnished reputation: he had been one of the officers in charge at Ancona on the night of Veith's unsuccessful raid in April 1918 and afterward had spent a week in the local guardhouse on charges of negligence. On this often ignored stain on Rizzo's career, see Jahn and Sieche, "Der Handstreich auf Ancona," 104-5.

99. Mohl, "Der Untergang der *Szent István*," 151.

100. Horthy telegram quoted in Sokol, *Österreich-Ungarns Seekrieg*, 2:704-5.

101. On the Sebenico plot, see Plaschka, et al., *Innere Front*, 1:415-18; Sokol, *Österreich-Ungarns Seekrieg*, 2:710-12.

102. Tomicich, "Die k.(u.)k. Marineakademie," 162.

103. Greger, *Austro-Hungarian Warships*, 78-81.

104. Ibid., 66-67.

105. Schupita, *Die k.u.k. Seeflieger*, 98, 224, 245.

106. Ibid., 155, 237, 245-46.

107. Halpern, *Naval War in the Mediterranean*, 456-57, 462, 511, 538; Aichelburg, *Die Unterseeboote*, 1:169. The three *Regina Elena*-class battleships were pulled back to Taranto after most of their manpower was reassigned to new destroyers and torpedo boats; the *Napoli* remained in Brindisi as a floating battery. See Thomazi, *La guerre navale*, 176. The Habsburg navy also suffered a loss through accident in April 1918 when the destroyer *Streiter* sank after colliding with a supply ship off Rijeka.

108. Greger, *Austro-Hungarian Warships*, 19.

109. Koudelka, *Denn Österreich lag einst am Meer*, 281-83. The Armeeoberkommando did not respond to Koudelka's urgent requests for quinine and mosquito nets.

110. Ibid., 281-84; Rothenberg, *The Army of Francis Joseph*, 214; Sokol, *Österreich-Ungarns Seekrieg*, 2:491. Koudelka and other division commanders blamed the failure of the offensive on the high command's decision to launch simultaneous attacks all along the front, leaving no troops in reserve.

111. Shanafelt, *The Secret Enemy*, 202-3. Arz von Straussenberg, *Zur Geschichte des grossen Krieges*, 281-84, gives an account of the "serious" meeting of 14 August. Arz was struck by the demeanor of William II, who was no longer so animated and bombastic.

346

112. Halpern, *Naval War in the Mediterranean,* 516–18.

113. Wulff, *Donauflottille,* 168–74. On the Austro-Ukrainian treaty, see Shanafelt, *The Secret Enemy,* 172; figure on tonnage of food from Rothenberg, *The Army of Francis Joseph,* 215. On a modest level, the food shipments were supplemented by the personal efforts of soldiers and sailors stationed in the east. Robert Dietinger, a sailor serving in the Black Sea in the summer of 1918, later recalled sending food packages home to his relatives. See Dietinger letter in *Marine—Gestern, Heute* 8 (1981): 75.

114. The account here and below is based on Sokol, *Österreich-Ungarns Seekrieg,* 2:636–46; Halpern, *Naval War in the Mediterranean,* 557–58.

115. On 20 September, *U47* torpedoed the French submarine *Circé,* and *U27* sank seven small Greek sailing ships. See Aichelburg, *Die Unterseeboote,* 2:492–93.

CHAPTER 9 ≋

DAS ENDE

THE OCTOBER REVOLUTION (1918)

As the internal authority of the Dual Monarchy started to collapse, the immediate fate of the navy and the long-term future of Habsburg rule in the Adriatic littoral came to depend largely on the posture of the South Slavs and the actions of their leaders. By the time the Central Powers made their formal overture for an armistice, the signs on the South Slav front already were not good. On 6 October, a national council convened in Zagreb and sent envoys abroad to negotiate with Yugoslav émigré groups. Meanwhile, Croatians still politically active in Vienna spoke out boldly on behalf of their conationals. On the eighth, the *Reichsrat* debated the fate of the hundreds of seamen still in custody as a consequence of their involvement in the Cattaro mutiny eight months earlier. Slovene leader Antun Korošec, who had warned the *Reichsrat* of the tense situation in Cattaro just days before the mutiny, took the lead in calling for all outstanding charges to be dropped. In part to appease South Slav leaders, eleven days later the navy released 348 of the 379 men in question, sustaining charges against only those accused of the most serious offenses.[1]

On 15 October, the Delegations met for the last time. Rather than debate the next year's budget, the two bodies listened to Burián give a dismal report of the outlook in foreign policy and a forlorn appeal for the nationalities to work together to save the Dual Monarchy. After Count Mihály Károlyi delivered a sharp rejoinder criticizing Burián's diplomacy, many of the Hungarian delegates stormed out.[2] The following day, Charles issued his famous manifesto promising to convert Austria into a federal state with German, Czech, South Slav, and

Ukrainian components; the Poles of Galicia would be freed to join a united Poland, and Trieste would be granted some sort of special status. In a last-ditch effort to placate the Hungarians, the statement specifically guaranteed the unity of the lands of the Crown of St. Stephen, but a proviso regarding the preservation of the common armed forces was unacceptable to most Magyar leaders. In any event, it mattered little, for none of the restive nationalities accepted the offer. The proclamation also had no impact in the international arena, even though it was followed on the seventeenth by another goodwill gesture, the end of the navy's participation in unrestricted submarine warfare. On 20 October, Woodrow Wilson confirmed the degree to which he now supported the dismemberment of the Dual Monarchy, informing Austria-Hungary that the United States had made irrevocable commitments to the South Slavs and to the Czechoslovak national committee, even recognizing the latter as a belligerent government. On the twenty-first, the revolution spread to Vienna itself when the Germans of the *Reichsrat* proclaimed themselves to be the "provisional National Assembly for German Austria."[3]

Even though Charles's manifesto of 16 October had met with immediate rejection from all quarters, on the twenty-second Admiral Keil informed Horthy that as far as the emperor was concerned, the plan was still alive; to preserve order and prevent the spread of dangerous rumors, the men of the fleet should be informed of its terms and of the intention to preserve the common armed forces. Over the next two days, the navy conducted meetings, aboard all ships and at all land installations, in which officers and NCOs explained to the men in their own languages the general outlines of the proposal to convert the Dual Monarchy into a federation of autonomous nations.[4] While this useless exercise was still underway, revolution came to the Habsburg littoral. On 23 October, a company from the Croatian 79th Infantry Regiment, professing loyalty to the national council in Zagreb, seized control of Rijeka and disarmed the Hungarian garrison and local police force. The following day, loyal troops restored order in the city, but much to Horthy's chagrin the *Armeeoberkommando* decided to ship the disarmed company of mutineers to Pola for safekeeping.[5]

With the internal collapse of Austria-Hungary well underway, the Italian front finally came alive. On 24 October, the Italian army launched a major offensive all along the Piave and in the Alps. Moving rapidly against little resistance, within days the Italian advance threatened Trieste. Meanwhile, on the Balkan front, the last Austro-Hungarian troops had already retreated across the border from northern Albania, leaving their Italian pursuers just sixty miles from Cattaro. In the face of certain, imminent defeat, Charles resolved to sever the German alliance and throw his empire at the mercy of the Entente. Foreign Minister Burián, like Czernin before him, refused to be a party to an initiative for a separate peace and had to be replaced. Ironically, Count Gyula Andrássy the younger, son of the Habsburg foreign minister who had forged the Austro-German alliance in the 1870s, became the last man to hold the office. On 26 October, Charles informed William II that their partnership had come to an end, but it was far too late for a separate peace to save the Dual Monarchy.[6]

Horthy, desperately trying to maintain order within the fleet, finally appealed to the *Armeeoberkommando* for help on the afternoon of 27 October. Observing that a full-scale mutiny was imminent and that the troops on hand in Pola were likely to join the sailors in revolt, he asked for a "reliable infantry brigade with two mobile batteries" and also requested the removal of the Rijeka mutineers, a destabilizing factor in the days since their arrival.[7] That night the rebellious *Hurra-Rufe* were heard aboard the big battleships at Pola for the first time since the unrest of January 1918. On the morning of the twenty-eighth, the officers of the larger warships informed Horthy that their vessels could not be counted upon; some suggested that disaster could be averted only if the men were sent ashore and permitted to go home without delay. Shortly after 9:00 A.M., the admiral received authorization from the *Armeeoberkommando* to inform the fleet "that we stand on the verge of an armistice and peace negotiations." Horthy was to ask their patience for the next few days with the promise that "extensive furloughing" would occur "as soon as hostilities are ended, even before the demobilization."[8] In the meantime, he would receive no troops to help keep order. Shortly after noon, the commander on the collapsing Italian front, Field Marshal Svetozar Boroević von Bojna, informed the emperor's headquarters that the army could spare no men for Pola.[9]

By the time this bad news had arrived, Horthy and his subordinate commanders were already making the rounds in Pola and speaking aboard the ships and at the land installations with appeals for calm and patience and assurances that the end of the war was imminent. They found many of the vessels already in the hands of their crews, whose elected leaders presented lists of demands reminiscent of those formulated by the Cattaro mutineers, including peace on the basis of the Fourteen Points as well as a common mess and common conditions of service for both officers and seamen. Most vowed to go home, one way or another, on 1 November. The recent Croatian uprising at Rijeka made the navy's Hungarians especially edgy and eager to return home. They realized that if Croatia succeeded in quitting the kingdom of Hungary, the Magyar heartland would be cut off from the sea, and Hungary would no longer have any stake in the future of the navy. While no crews had risen against their commanders, some officers found the increasing tension almost unbearable; aboard the *Prinz Eugen,* the distraught Captain Alexander Milosević committed suicide in his cabin.[10] In recognition of the fact that Thierry's crews were practically the only men in Pola not organizing sailors' councils, Horthy visited the submariners personally aboard their accommodation ship *Babenberg* and implored them to continue to stand fast and do their duty.[11] On this eventful day, the German submariners at Pola, idled a week earlier by the formal suspension of Germany's campaign of unrestricted submarine warfare, finally left Pola, abandoning their quarters hastily and blowing up all submarines not ready to put to sea.[12]

The commotion surrounding the departure of the Germans notwithstanding, by the evening of 28 October Horthy could report that, at least on the surface, order reigned in Pola. Elsewhere, the disintegration of the empire continued. On the twenty-eighth, Czech nationalists seized control of Prague, thanks in part to rebellious naval personnel. Josef Kubát, a Skoda employee and former navy engineering cadet, organized a small armed band of seamen on leave in the city and took over the railway station, in the process disarming a troop of Hungarian soldiers.[13] Meanwhile, to avoid a similar capitulation in the face of violence, the Habsburg army command in Zagreb formally handed over its authority to the South Slav national council.[14] Thus the precedent was set for the surrender of the Austro-Hungarian navy to the same body.

On 29 October, the situation in Pola deteriorated markedly. With sailors' councils controlling virtually all warships and unruly seamen plundering the vacated quarters of the Germans, Thierry spoke with Lieutenant Franz Rzemenowsky, commander of the *U28*, about the possibility of using their undersea boats against mutinous ships. To do so, however, would have violated a direct order from the emperor, since Charles, in the interest of averting senseless bloodshed, had proscribed the use of deadly force against insubordinate or mutinous sailors.[15] Horthy and his officers recognized that only a quick armistice and demobilization could prevent Pola from lapsing into chaos. They could be thankful that most sailors opted for passive resistance; workers in the Pola Arsenal likewise laid down their tools but did not riot. Only the civilians of Pola resorted to violence. On the evening of 28–29 October, a mob gathered under Italian flags, armed itself with stones, and marched on the officers' club (Marinekasino), breaking all of the windows before finally being driven off.[16]

In Zagreb the morning of 29 October saw the national council formally proclaim an end to the dynastic tie between Croatia and Hungary. Its declaration also called for a new union of Croatia with Dalmatia and the unity of all Croatian lands with Serbia. Slovene and Bosnian groups also pledged their allegiance to the Yugoslav concept.[17] Hours later the Hungarian governor of Rijeka boarded a train for Budapest, leaving the city in the hands of Croatians loyal to the national council. The imperial government in Vienna asked Zagreb for assistance in the effort to maintain calm in the fleet, but the South Slav leaders, gaining confidence by the hour, refused to send emissaries to Pola and the other Adriatic bases unless the fleet were first placed under their authority. From imperial headquarters at Baden, Admiral Keil, as late as the twenty-ninth, continued to insist that "the fleet will still be considered a common institution." Owing to the political confusion in both Vienna and Budapest, just what "common" meant was no longer clear. Károlyi and radical Magyars had formed a Hungarian national council four days earlier, challenging the authority of the government in Budapest, while in Vienna the "provisional government of German Austria" on 30 October proclaimed its jurisdiction over all ethnic Germans in the Austrian half of the empire, including those serving in the military.[18]

The domestic and military collapse left Charles with two options regarding the navy: to do nothing, or to turn over the fleet to the Yugoslav national council. An opening presented itself shortly after midnight on the thirtieth when the harbor admiral in Pola, Rear Admiral Cicoli, cabled Vice Admiral Holub at the Marinesektion for instructions regarding the position of Captain Method Koch. The Slovene captain had been elected to a South Slav national committee in Pola on the evening of the twenty-eighth; the following evening, after the Zagreb council had informed Vienna of its desire to take control of the fleet, South Slav leaders in Rijeka informed Horthy that Koch was their choice for navy commander. Cicoli argued that "the position of Koch as a member of the committee is not compatible with his charge as an officer," but Charles, spotting an avenue for a peaceful transition, instructed Holub to convey his permission for Koch to remain an active officer. His telegram to Pola, sent at 1:00 P.M. on the thirtieth, ended with the ominous words: "Dispatch concerning the release of crews and transfer of navy to Yugoslav national council will follow shortly."[19]

Charles made the decision to turn over the fleet after a conference at Schönbrunn with Admiral Keil, Vice Admiral Holub, and the chief of the General Staff, General Arz von Straussenburg. The emperor also spoke by telephone with Count Andrássy, the foreign minister, who endorsed the plan. The ships of the fleet were to be turned over to representatives of the Zagreb authorities with the provision that the other "nations" of the Dual Monarchy would have the right to claim compensation for their share of the total value at a later date. All seamen not belonging to the South Slav nationalities were to be furloughed, and all officers were granted permission to enter the new Yugoslav naval service. Charles, Arz, and the admirals agreed to these terms rather quickly, but because the plan marked his first formal recognition of the fact that the empire was breaking up, the emperor agonized over the decision for three hours before signing the document. Horthy finally received the orders at eight o'clock on the evening of the thirtieth, seven hours after the previous message from Vienna.[20]

Horthy met with the South Slav representatives at nine o'clock on the morning of 31 October in the admiral's cabin of the *Viribus Unitis* to work out the details of the transfer. He later recalled that "the discussion was short and cool"; he had difficulty accepting the presence of one of his own officers, Koch, on the opposite side of the table.[21] The ceremonies in Pola took place at 4:45 that afternoon. For Horthy it was "one of the saddest moments" of his life:

> As I appeared on the deck of the *Viribus Unitis,* the crew stood as
> one man to attention. I was so moved that for a few moments I stood

speechless, unable to begin my short farewell address to the men. As my flag was struck, all the flags on all the ships followed suit. . . . The portrait presented by His Majesty Emperor Francis Joseph to the flagship which bore his personal motto *Viribus Unitis* as her name, the silk ceremonial ensign, and my own Admiral's flag I took with me.[22]

A twenty-one gun salute greeted the raising of the new red-white-blue Yugoslav flag, and Horthy's own flag captain aboard the *Viribus Unitis,* Captain Janko Vuković, took over his duties as commander of the fleet. Captain Franc Vučer succeeded Cicoli as Pola harbor commander, while Koch, the key figure in the local transfer of power, assumed the administrative command in Pola. The Yugoslav national council appointed Rear Admiral Dragutin Prica, formerly Koudelka's adjutant in Trieste, as overall navy commander. His office, initially in Zagreb, would be transferred to Belgrade before the end of the year.[23]

The transition outside of Pola occurred quickly, if not uniformly. In Sebenico, a hotbed of South Slav nationalist activity for many months, the city and torpedo flotilla both passed under the control of the national council on 29 October, coinciding with the takeover in Rijeka. In Trieste, which, like Rijeka, hosted no significant naval forces, the Habsburg governor turned over the reins to local Italians on the thirty-first.[24] Meanwhile, in Cattaro, the first *Hurra-Rufe* broke out on the battleship *Erzherzog Friedrich* on the twenty-sixth, two days before similar demonstrations began in Pola. Late on the afternoon of 29 October, just hours after returning from sick leave to resume command of the Cruiser Flotilla, Heyssler received instructions from Horthy to furlough all German Austrian and Hungarian seamen in Cattaro, starting with those aboard the battleships and those with the most seniority. The orders came on Horthy's own authority, since at that time he still had not received authorization from the emperor to let anyone go.[25]

Otherwise, the turning points in Cattaro occurred a day or two later than in Pola. The German submariners left on 30 October, and the formal transfer of power to the Yugoslavs came at 8:00 A.M. on 1 November. That morning the last two Austro-Hungarian vessels on active sea duty, the *U14* and *U29*, returned to Cattaro. Captain Trapp, head of the Cattaro submarine station for the last three months of the war, later recalled that during the first week of November seamen who had been on leave as of 30 October continued to return to the Bocche, having not heard the news either at home or en route back to Cattaro that the Austro-Hungarian navy no longer existed.[26] Ironically, a *kaisertreu* Croatian from Rijeka, Rear Admiral Vončina, presided at the ceremony turning over the base to the Yugoslavs. Appointed harbor admiral of Cattaro just four months earlier, he retired rather than serve under the new flag.[27]

In late July 1914, the navy had fired its first salvoes of the war not in the Adriatic but on the Danube; it was perhaps fitting that the monitors of the Danube flotilla also fired the last shots of the conflict. Throughout October 1918, Serbian troops advanced northward, reoccupying their country, and by the end of the month those standing on the Danube were in a position to harass the retreat of the flotilla as it passed by on its way home. On the thirtieth, the monitor *Bodrog* fought a duel with Serbian artillery near Visnica, ultimately running aground. The vessel had to be abandoned, but by 2 November the remaining units of the flotilla managed to join forces at Ujvidek for the final withdrawal upriver. Charles's order of 30 October turning over the battle fleet and all Adriatic installations to the Yugoslavs stipulated that the Danube flotilla would belong to the kingdom of Hungary. Upon receiving this news, the flotilla commander, Captain Ratković, surrendered his authority to the head of the Monitor Division, Olaf Wulff. The Hungarian son of Norwegian immigrants, Wulff took command of the flotilla in the name of the Hungarian government. All South Slavs shipped out at Vukovar, the northernmost Croatian port on the Danube. The monitors and patrol boats steamed into Budapest on 6 November, flying the Hungarian flag alongside the Austro-Hungarian ensign.[28]

Years later, Austria-Hungary's motive for turning over the battle fleet to Yugoslavia remained a controversial point for historians as well as the principal parties involved. A half century after the fact, Arthur J. May still cited the often repeated theory that the transfer had occurred "on the advice of Admiral Horthy," and that the "gesture was intended either to exacerbate ill-will between the Italians and South Slavs, or less probably, to win back the Croats to their historic Hapsburg mooring."[29] In a memoir written in 1920, Charles argued that his decision prevented a violent South Slav takeover of the navy, which would have caused deaths among the sailors of the other nationalities and also would have jeopardized the claims of other national groups to a share of the matériel. He also acknowledged a desire to prevent Italy from seizing the mutinous fleet and claiming a final *"granda vittoria"* over Austria-Hungary. The emperor recalled that Horthy, Keil, and the *Marinesektion* all had agreed with his decision.[30] Horthy's first biographer highlights Charles's desire to keep "an autonomous Yugoslavia" in a federation under the Habsburg crown but credits Keil with the scheme of using the fleet as some sort of bait; the same account also implies that the last Austro-Hungarian foreign minister, Count Andrássy, ultimately decided the issue by lending his support to the idea of turning over the navy to the South Slavs.[31] In his memoirs, Horthy alleged that the responsibility for Charles's decision ultimately could be traced to the advice of Croatian generals: "As I heard it, His Majesty was persuaded by generals of Croat nationality to hand over the fleet to the Yugoslavs to prevent it from falling into the hands of the Italians."[32]

While it is indisputable that the Austro-Hungarian government and naval leadership wanted to avoid at all costs a transfer of the fleet to Italy, it is not likely that the leading South Slav generals were involved in any of the eleventh-hour decisions to turn over Habsburg military and naval authority to the Yugoslav national council. Indeed, Field Marshal Boroević, the highest-ranking Croatian in the army, was known to have criticized the *Armeeoberkommando*'s decision to have the military command in Zagreb surrender its powers to the South Slav leadership.[33] In any event, the new Yugoslav kingdom was not destined to become a naval power even on the regional level. The victors recognized the creation of the South Slav state but not the transfer of the fleet, and the postwar settlement would leave Yugoslavia with only a tiny fraction of the Habsburg naval inheritance.

THE SPOILS OF WAR

For the seamen of South Slav origin and the officers choosing to remain aboard ship and serve under the new flag, the transfer of power just before sunset on 31 October touched off a long night of celebration. For the first time since August 1914, blackout rules were ignored, and ships remained fully illuminated. Amid the jubilation, hardly anyone bothered to stand watch. Taking advantage of the opportunity, the Italians sent a torpedo boat and an *MAS* boat to the boom at the entrance of Pola harbor, where they launched their latest innovative weapon. Called a *mignatta* (leech), it was a large self-propelled dummy torpedo equipped with fixtures for two divers to ride on its back. Just before dawn on 1 November, officers Raffaele Rossetti and Raffaele Paolucci, in full diving gear, rode their "leech" underwater to the *Viribus Unitis* and attached explosive devices to its hull. The Yugoslavs then spotted the divers, captured them, and learned of the timed charges that were fixed below the water line of the dreadnought. Vuković ordered his crew to abandon ship but many were not awakened until 6:20 A.M., when the explosion rocked the vessel. The 20,000-ton dreadnought capsized fourteen minutes later, sinking to the bottom of the harbor with around four hundred men still on board. Vuković remained on the bridge and went down with his ship.[34]

There remains some question as to whether those involved in the attack knew that they were targeting a Yugoslav warship. Before the day was over, however, the Italian navy was fully aware of the transfer and was actively working to undo what its leaders considered to be an enemy ploy designed to deny Italy the fruits of victory at sea. Thaon di Revel informed Foreign Minister Sonnino of intercepted radio transmissions indicating that "the entire Austrian fleet or at least a great part of it has pulled down the Austrian flag and raised the Yugoslav. The fleet or a good part of it is already in the hands of the Yugoslav National Committee."[35]

In the meantime, Italian and Austro-Hungarian negotiators engaged in armistice talks at Villa Giusti outside of Padua carried on as if the Habsburg fleet had never been transferred to Yugoslav control. Those signing the Armistice of Villa Giusti on 3 November included Prince Liechtenstein and Captain Zwierkowski on behalf of the navy. The protocols called for an end to hostilities between the Dual Monarchy and the Entente as of 3:00 P.M. on 4 November. Annexes provided for the immediate transfer to Venice of three battleships, three light cruisers, nine destroyers, twelve large torpedo boats, and the fifteen newest submarines. The Italians had intended to ask for the three surviving Austro-Hungarian dreadnoughts, but the sinking of the *Viribus Unitis* caused a change in plans, and the terms called instead for the surrender of the *Prinz Eugen, Tegetthoff,* and the pre-dreadnought *Erzherzog Franz Ferdinand.* The cruisers were to be the *Novara, Saida,* and *Helgoland,* whose yeoman service on raids and patrols in the lower Adriatic had impressed the Entente navies. For destroyers, the Italians wanted only the larger *Tátra*-class vessels.[36]

Amid the general confusion, the Italians occupied the island of Lissa on the morning of 4 November, just hours before the armistice went into effect. It was a symbolic move intended to exorcise the old demons of 1866 and restore the honor of the Italian navy while the war at least technically was still underway. Before the day was over, Italian units entered the harbors of Trieste, Pola, and Rijeka; on the fifth, the Italians took control of all installations in Pola and also occupied Sebenico. Yugoslav officers and seamen retained control of some warships but abandoned to the Italians those that could not be manned adequately. The Italian booty at Pola included considerable fuel stocks. When the Yugoslavs took over the fleet, the navy's stockpile of coal consisted of 167,900 tons, an increase of more than 75 percent from the beginning of 1918, mostly because efforts to procure more coal from Germany had been remarkably successful under Horthy. Ironically, much of the coal that fell into Italian hands was of British origin, indicating that the navy had tried to conserve its high-quality prewar stocks while burning German and domestic coal purchased during the war.[37]

While the Yugoslavs did not resist the Italian occupation of Pola and other coastal bases, their national council did not recognize the legitimacy of these actions. The tension and uncertainty continued through the days that followed. On the seventh, the *Radetzky* raised steam and left Pola under Yugoslav command, putting in hours later at Buccari, a port not yet occupied by the Italians. On 9 November, the Italians raised their flag aboard all former Austro-Hungarian warships remaining in Pola.[38] That same day, cruisers from the British, French, and Italian navies steamed into Cattaro, the last of the former Habsburg ports to be occupied. To prevent Austro-Hungarian colors from being claimed by the Italians as war trophies, the sailors of the Bocche cut their old flags into small pieces, which they distributed as souvenirs. But the Italian navy had far bigger trophies in mind. Later on the ninth at Corfu, Ugo Conz, Italy's negotiator of the Triple Alliance Naval Convention back in 1913, placed before the allies Italy's arguments concerning the fate of the fleet. "There can be no fleet where there is no state. There can be no Yugoslav fleet as long as such a state has not yet been founded or as long as peace has not been definitively concluded." He asked what the British would do if the High Seas Fleet in Kiel or Wilhelmshaven raised the Danish flag on the grounds that Scheswig-Holstein would be given back to Denmark!

Conz concluded that the former Habsburg navy in Yugoslav hands would represent an unacceptable future threat to Italian security. "The Austro-Hungarian fleet must either be given to Italy or destroyed."[39]

A Yugoslav delegation also appeared at Corfu, where it received a sympathetic hearing, especially from the British. According to Captain William Kelly, his delegation was disgusted by the Italian navy's contention that it had achieved "an Italian victory in an Italian war."[40] Nevertheless, there could be no question of any of the victors actually accepting the legality of Austria-Hungary's transfer of the fleet to the South Slavs. On 10 November, Yugoslav officials finally relented and began to give up their warships. The surrender did not follow the terms of the Villa Giusti armistice, instead occurring piecemeal in a process that dragged on for two years. At the end of March 1919, the naval version of the Italian victory parade finally occurred in the lagoon at Venice when the *Tegetthoff* and the *Erzherzog Franz Ferdinand* steamed in, escorted by eight smaller surface vessels and four submarines, all flying the Italian flag.[41]

Because the cash-starved Entente powers viewed the German and Austro-Hungarian battle fleets as unique capital assets, their fate naturally generated considerable debate and disagreement. The German High Seas Fleet, far larger than the Austro-Hungarian navy, attracted most of the attention until June 1919, when the crews of the German ships, after several months of internment at Scapa Flow in Scotland, scuttled their vessels in one last great act of defiance. Denied these spoils of war, the Entente powers bickered all the more over the fate of the Austro-Hungarian warships, postponing their final distribution until 1920.

By the end of 1920, the Italians had received title to the *Radetzky* and *Zrinyi* in addition to the *Tegetthoff* and *Erzherzog Franz Ferdinand;* all four battleships were sold for scrap. The cruisers *Saida* and *Helgoland* and seven *Tátra*-class destroyers were renamed and incorporated into the Italian navy. The French received the remaining dreadnought, *Prinz Eugen,* which they eventually used for target practice, finally sinking it in the summer of 1922. Their spoils included the *Erzherzog Karl* and *Erzherzog Friedrich,* which were scrapped, as well as the light cruiser *Novara* and one *Tátra*-class destroyer, which received commissions in the French fleet. Two older *Huszár*-class destroyers went to France for scrapping, along with several torpedo boats. Of the nineteen submarines, France received five; all went to the scrap yard except the *U14*, the former French *Curie* captured in 1915, which returned to French service under its old name. The remaining undersea boats went to Italy, where all were broken up. Britain received the old coast defenders *Monarch* and *Budapest*, the *Habsburg* and its sister ships *Arpád* and *Babenberg*, the *Erzherzog Ferdinand Max*, the armored cruisers *Kaiser Karl VI*, *Sankt Georg*, and *Maria Theresia*, the light cruisers *Admiral Spaun*, *Aspern*, and *Szigetvár*, the older unarmored cruisers, and a handful of torpedo boats. All were sold to Italian firms for scrap. Greece acquired one *Huszár*-class destroyer and six torpedo boats; most of the latter survived until the German Luftwaffe sank them in its Blitzkrieg victory over the Greeks in 1941. Seven torpedo boats went to Romania, one of which remained in service long after the Second World War and was not scrapped until 1960. Portugal received six torpedo boats, all of which were broken up before 1940.[42]

By the spring of 1921, the victors had left the Yugoslav navy with just twelve torpedo boats, along with an assortment of hulks and auxiliary ships that had been anchored in Cattaro during the war. Most of the Yugoslav vessels that survived the 1920s were sunk during the Second World War, but one of the torpedo boats remained in service until 1963.[43] Cattaro, as Kotor, became the principal base for the Yugoslavs almost by default: the postwar peace treaty allocated Trieste and all of Istria, including Pola, to Italy, and the Italians later seized Rijeka (Fiume).

The Yugoslavs fared better in the division of the spoils on the Danube. Of the ten monitors, four went to Yugoslavia, three to Romania, two were converted to river pontoons, and one was scrapped. The navy's eight small river patrol boats—two of 140 tons, four of 133 tons, and two of 60 tons—were divided evenly between Austria and Hungary, but the Austrian Republic showed little interest in maintaining a river flotilla. In 1927 the Austrians sold three of their boats to the Hungarians, keeping just one 133-ton vessel; two years later, this boat was traded to Hungary for one of the 60-ton vessels. Six of the seven Hungarian patrol boats saw action in the Second World War. The lone Austrian boat was still on active duty at the time of the *Anschluss* in March 1938 and was incorporated into Nazi Germany's Danube flotilla.[44] In the autumn of 1918, the retreating Austro-Hungarian Danube flotilla towed the midget submarine it had captured from the Russians in the Black Sea all the way to Budapest, where the Entente overlooked it in the subsequent division of the monitors and patrol boats. As late as 1933, the Hungarians still had the submarine docked at Budapest, a relic of the Magyar connection to the open seas severed fifteen years before.[45]

Like the fleet itself, the financial and industrial network that had supported the navy and Austria-Hungary's overall maritime interests was broken up after the war. The dismemberment of the empire forced the Creditanstalt to divest itself of its most prized assets: the Skoda works, the shipyards of the Stabilimento Tecnico Triestino, and the Austro-Americana steamship company. The Czech government arranged for the French Schneider-Creusot conglomerate to buy Skoda, while in Trieste the Banca Commerciale Triestina secured a controlling interest in the Stabilimento Tecnico. The Cosulich family, always in control of a minority of Austro-Americana shares, acquired a majority in 1919. The company resumed business in the postwar era under the Cosulich Brothers name; in the early 1930s, after the onset of the worldwide depression, Benito Mussolini's government combined it and other leading shipping companies under the name Italia Line. The Austrian Lloyd likewise fell into Italian hands when the Union Bank of Vienna sold its controlling interest to the Banca Commerciale Italiana. The line resumed service as the Lloyd Triestino, but its directors had little interest in reviving the San Rocco shipbuilding company, which had been established in 1910 in partnership with the Stabilimento Tecnico; after the war, the Stabilimento Tecnico assumed responsibility for operating San Rocco and in 1923 bought it outright. The steamship lines of Trieste recovered quickly after the First World War, only to meet with a greater disaster in the Second World War, thanks to the ambitions of Mussolini. Under the flag of fascist Italy, many former Austro-Hungarian merchant ships convoyed troops to Ethiopia, Spain, and Albania, facilitating the Italian conquests of the 1930s. During the Second World War, vessels of the Lloyd Triestino and Italia Line transported troops to North Africa and also served as hospital ships.[46]

Controlling the former Austro-Americana share of the Cantiere Navale Triestino, the Cosulich family reopened the Monfalcone shipyard in 1919, helped by a fresh infusion of capital from the Banca Commerciale Triestina. In the late 1920s, the Cantiere Navale Triestino and the Stabilimento Tecnico opened merger talks, and in 1930 the two firms combined to form the Cantiere Riuniti dell'Adriatico, bringing all shipbuilding facilities in Trieste and Monfalcone under the control of a single corporation. In the late 1930s, Mussolini's naval buildup gave new life to languishing Trieste shipyards. In addition to smaller vessels, the Cantiere Riuniti built the battleships *Vittorio Veneto* in 1934–40 and *Roma* in 1938–42. At over 40,000 tons apiece, they were more than twice the size of the Austro-Hungarian dreadnoughts of the First World War.[47]

After Italy's annexation of Rijeka, the former Hungarian Adria Line was purchased by the Cosulich family of Trieste, completing the Italian takeover of the major Austro-Hungarian merchant shipping companies. It continued to operate under the Adria name until 1936, when it went out of business. In 1920 the Banca Italiana di Sconto and the Terni steelworks joined forces to buy Rijeka's Danubius shipyard, which was renamed the Cantieri Navali del Quarnero. In 1924 the Banca Nazionale di Credito and the Cantieri Navali del Quarnero bought a majority of shares in the Whitehead torpedo factory, bringing the last of the city's strategic industries under Italian ownership. Meanwhile, in Pola, the Stabilimento Tecnico Triestino reopened the old navy arsenal as a private shipyard, the Cantiere Scoglio Olivi. This venture failed miserably within a few years.[48]

After receiving little of the spoils in the division of the navy, Yugoslavia likewise came away with only a small portion of the Austro-Hungarian merchant marine. Thanks largely to the acquisition of the Lloyd, the Adria, and the Austro-Americana, Italy inherited 210 steamers displacing just over 580,000 tons; in contrast, the new South Slav state received around 100,000 tons. In 1923 a new Yugoslav company, the Jadranska Plovidba, bought up the old Ungaro-Croata and other small Dalmatian coastal lines, assembling some sixty steamers to become the largest Yugoslav line of the interwar years. The Jadranska Plovidba was based at Sušak, the eastern suburb of Rijeka, which did not fall into Italian hands when the rest of the city was annexed. Just as Cattaro became the primary anchorage of the modest Yugoslav navy, Sušak— heir to Rijeka's rail connections with Zagreb and the interior—became the country's principal seaport.[49]

While dozens of former Austro-Hungarian merchant steamers served on into the interwar years and beyond, by the end of 1920 most of the battle fleet either had been broken up or was on the way to the scrap yard. None of the largest and most expensive vessels, the battleships and armored cruisers, ever actually served under another flag; indeed, the 3,500-ton light cruisers *Helgoland, Saida,* and *Novara* by far were the largest units of the fleet incorporated into the navies of the victors after the war.

More so than in Germany and the other European naval powers, in the Dual Monarchy the construction of a respectable fleet had depended upon a remarkable web of political compromises and political-industrial alliances, often involving persons and parties at loggerheads on virtually every other issue. The Austro-Hungarian navy of the First World War was a product of the heyday of popular navalism, and perhaps appropriately the warships left behind after its collapse were victims of the new postwar trend of naval disarmament. As a consequence of the Washington Naval Conference of 1921–22, the three greatest postwar naval powers alone—Britain, the United States, and Japan—scrapped some seventy warships totaling almost 1.7 million tons. In this atmosphere, the leading navies sacrificed all pre-dreadnought battleships and most other vessels predating 1914; some even scrapped their early dreadnought models, which were small and obsolete compared with the so-called super-dreadnoughts launched during the war. Within just a few years of the end of the war, the largest Austro-Hungarian warships, built at such a dear price, were worth far more as scrap metal than they were as naval vessels.

THE LEGACY

While none of the navy's larger ships survived to see action in the Second World War, and the handful of smaller warships that did all served under other names and a variety of flags, the traditions of the service lived on in the next war, thanks to a ploy by Adolf Hitler to use naval symbols to appeal to Austrian opinion after the *Anschluss* of March 1938. In the spring of 1938, Hitler, whose years in Vienna coincided with the peak of pre-1914 navalism, resolved to give an "Austrian" name to a German heavy cruiser then under construction in Kiel. *Tegetthoff* was considered but dropped on the grounds that to name a ship after the victor of Lissa might offend Mussolini and the Italians. Hitler finally settled on *Prinz Eugen,* honoring Prince Eugene of Savoy, an old Habsburg hero claimed by both the Austrians and the Italians; *Prinz Eugen* had also been the name of four Habsburg warships between 1848 and 1918. The cruiser was launched in August 1938 with Hitler and Admiral Horthy, then Regent of Hungary, in attendance. Horthy's wife performed the christening duties. Under pressure from their Führer, the admirals of the Third Reich developed an appreciation for Austro-Hungarian sea power that had been lacking earlier among the admirals of the Second Reich. At a luncheon following the launching of the *Prinz Eugen,* Grand Admiral Erich Raeder assured Horthy that "the German navy would at all times safeguard and follow the great traditions of the Austro-Hungarian navy."[50]

After being commissioned two years later, the *Prinz Eugen* was designated the *"Traditionsschiff"* of the defunct Habsburg fleet. It carried Austro-Hungarian naval memorabilia on board throughout the war, including the ship's bell from the dreadnought *Tegetthoff,* which had been in Italian possession since 1919. German pressure induced the Italians to return other symbolic spoils of war, such as ships' bells, clocks, flags, and other souvenirs taken from the Austro-Hungarian warships that Italy seized after the First World War. Many of these mementoes later found their way to the naval gallery of the Army History Museum in Vienna.[51]

The postwar years saw the personnel of the Austro-Hungarian navy scattered not just among the successor states of the Dual Monarchy but to almost every corner of the earth. More than 98 percent of the roughly 56,000 men in naval service during the war survived, most unscathed. The total casualties from 28 July 1914 through 31 October 1918 included 344 killed (of whom 91 were officers), 639 missing (69 officers), and 313 wounded (24 officers). Another 690 became prisoners of war. The air arm and submarine service, employing relatively small numbers of men, accounted for more than half of the losses. Aviators constituted 30 percent of the dead (101), while 23 percent (80) were submariners; another 21 submariners missing at sea most certainly also died.[52]

In the tumultuous days at the end of the war, while the South Slavs celebrated their acquisition of the navy and the seamen of other nationalities welcomed the opportunity to go home at last, only the career officers appreciated the historic tragedy of the moment. Those not passing on into Yugoslav service received just one month's salary and two weeks of rations to ease their transition into civilian life.[53] The Austrian Republic's citizenship law of 5 December 1918 granted citizenship to all former Habsburg officers whose "ordinary residence" as of 1 August 1914 had been in the Austrian half of the Dual Monarchy, with the exception of Galicia, Istria, and Dalmatia.[54] Ultimately, the navy officers whose residences had been in Trieste, Rijeka, or elsewhere in Istria (including Pola) had the option of accepting Austrian citizenship or becoming subjects of the king of Italy; for those who had made their homes in Cattaro, Sebenico, or elsewhere in Dalmatia, the choice was Austria or Yugoslavia. Because the successor states granting citizenship to former Habsburg officers also assumed responsibility for their pensions, the governments were cautious in crafting their policies. Largely for financial reasons, for hundreds of navy officers the winter of 1918–19 was the most anxious time of their lives.

The winter following the end of the war found most of the officers and men of the *Kaiserin Elisabeth* still far from home. Taken prisoner by the Japanese after their ship was scuttled in Kiaochow Bay in November 1914, they were dispersed among five prisoner of war camps in Japan and practically forgotten by their government. Like their Austro-Hungarian army counterparts who fell into enemy hands, ultimately they were segregated by nationality. After the armistice, the ethnic Italians were the first to be repatriated, followed by those whose homes were in the new successor states of the Dual Monarchy. The German Austrians, accompanied by the ship's captain, Richard Makoviz, finally left Kobe in December 1919 with a group of German navy prisoners of war and reached Wilhelmshaven in February 1920. By far the last Austrian navy personnel to return home, Makoviz and his men arrived by rail at Salzburg in early March.[55]

Of all the veterans of the navy, Miklós Horthy clearly holds the honor of being the most significant historical figure after 1918. His native Hungary lapsed into chaos after the collapse of the Dual Monarchy and in March 1919 fell into the hands of the communist Béla Kun. After only seven months in retirement on his family estate in Kenderes, in June 1919 Horthy reentered public life as commander of the counterrevolutionary Hungarian National Army, which occupied Budapest in November. Thereafter the admiral's political star rose dramatically. In March 1920, after the new regime resolved to proclaim Hungary a kingdom with a vacant throne, the assembly chose Horthy as regent. In the words of one historian, he "was not a particularly talented military commander or politician" but impressed the Entente representatives assigned to Budapest, in part because of "his ability in several languages."[56] Conveniently enough, these included English, French, and Italian, a legacy of his Austro-Hungarian naval education. The Entente governments came to view Horthy as the principal hope for a stable Hungary. Out of concern for their continued support and the certain hostile intervention of Hungary's neighbors, on two occasions—in March and October 1921—Horthy blocked attempts by his old friend and former sovereign, Charles, to return from exile and take the throne as Hungarian king.

Under Horthy's mildly authoritarian regency, Hungary's prewar social, economic, and political elites were restored to power amid the pomp and ceremony of earlier times. Even though Hungary was landlocked, Horthy continued to use his admiral's title and always wore naval uniforms in his formal public appearances. After 1938 his diplomatic alignment with Nazi Germany helped Hungary regain much of the territory it had lost to Czechoslovakia, Romania, and Yugoslavia at the Paris Peace Conference, ultimately at the price of heavy losses on the Russian front in the Second World War, where Hungarians fought alongside the German army. The Germans overthrew Horthy in October 1944 after he sought an armistice with the advancing Soviet army. He remained in custody in Germany for the duration of the war, then went into exile in Portugal, where he died in 1957 at age eighty-nine.[57]

Georg von Trapp ultimately became the most famous alumnus of the navy, at least in the English-speaking world, because of the 1965 film *The Sound of Music*. Thanks to the fortune of his first wife, Agathe von Whitehead, granddaughter of the Rijeka torpedo magnate, the Trapps lived in relative luxury after purchasing the Palais Lamberg near Salzburg.[58] According to the largely fictionalized film account of the captain's second marriage and family life, the musically talented Trapp family fled across the Alps to Switzerland in the wake of the German-Austrian *Anschluss* of 1938 after the former submariner received orders to report for service in Hitler's navy. In fact, Trapp would have had to volunteer for naval duty in Nazi Germany; even though he resided in Austria, he had opted for Italian citizenship after 1918, and this protected him from the service liability. In any event, Habsburg navy veterans with Austrian citizenship were not called to serve in the German navy until 1939 and 1940, well after the *Anschluss*. In the spring of 1938, the Trapp family indeed "escaped" from Salzburg, not by hiking over the Alps to Switzerland but by boarding a train for Italy. In September 1938, they went to the United States for their first concert tour, then returned to Europe early in 1939 for another tour, in Scandinavia. Thereafter Trapp and his family actually went home to Salzburg for several months before departing for a second concert tour of Scandinavia in the summer of 1939. The outbreak of the Second World War found them in Sweden; they emigrated to the United States via Norway in late September 1939 and settled in Stowe, Vermont, where Trapp died in 1947.[59]

While many former officers were repelled by the Nazi movement, at least one—Rear Admiral Heinrich Seitz—was attracted to it at an early stage. Almost fifty when the war ended, Seitz pursued graduate studies at the University of Graz and eventually earned a doctorate in political science; in 1927 he became a convert to National Socialism. After rising to prominence within the party, he served as *Gauleiter* of his native Styria from 1933 until 1934. Following the abortive Nazi putsch that claimed the life of Chancellor Engelbert Dollfuss, Kurt von Schuschnigg's "Austro-Fascist" regime intensified the crackdown against Austrian National Socialists. Seitz's political career came to an end, but he lived on until 1940, long enough to see the *Anschluss*. His tombstone noted that "his life was a struggle for *Grossdeutschland.*"[60]

For at least some of the navy veterans remaining in the Austrian Republic, the *Anschluss* provided a welcome opportunity to serve in the navy of the Third Reich. Renowned submarine commander Hermann Rigele, whose postwar search for employment had taken him to New York, Warsaw, and finally back to Austria, accepted a commission in the German navy. After serving as commander of the training submarine *UD3*, Rigele spent much of the Second World War as harbor commandant in Danzig and Königsberg; when the fall of Mussolini in 1943 brought the German occupation of the former Austrian littoral, he returned to the Adriatic and served until the end of the war as harbor commandant of Trieste.[61] Former submariner Paul Meixner (academy class of 1910), a prisoner of the Italians from 1916 to 1918 after surviving the sinking of the *U16*, coordinated the Mediterranean supply effort of Erwin Rommel's North African campaign during the Second World War and received an extraordinary promotion to admiral.[62] Leo Wolfbauer (academy class of 1913) reached captain's rank and commanded the German supply submarine *U463;* he perished along with his crew when British planes sank the *U463* off the Scilly Islands in 1943.[63] Erich Brauneis, who had entered Austro-Hungarian service in 1913 as a provisional sea cadet, also became a German navy captain and won the highest honor—the knight's cross (*Ritterkreuz*)—for his service as a flotilla commander in the Baltic Sea late in 1944.[64]

Of course, most Habsburg navy veterans were far too old for sea duty in the Second World War, but several took administrative posts and other assignments on land, freeing younger German officers for sea duty. One group of former Austro-Hungarian officers served early in the war at a German coastal observation post in Algeciras, Morocco, across from Gibraltar.[65] Others put their fluent Italian to good use as liaison officers in North Africa and other places where the German and Italian armies operated together. Such services were also needed, oddly enough, in the Baltic, where Italian navy personnel served late in the war in antiaircraft batteries and in other supporting roles at German navy installations.[66] In addition to symbolic gestures, such as the naming of the *Prinz Eugen,* Hitler's regime appealed to retired Austro-Hungarian navy veterans through a National Socialist *Marine-Bund* and through its generous treatment of former officers. They received ranks corresponding to those of German officers who had begun their careers in the same years, thus approximating the levels that they would have achieved if their own careers had not been cut short in 1918. More important, they were granted pensions commensurate with these ranks.[67]

In the postwar years, the new Yugoslav navy, despite its modest size, became the biggest single employer of former Austro-Hungarian officers. Dragutin Prica, appointed overall navy commander by the Yugoslav national council at Zagreb, moved to Belgrade in December 1918 after the formal proclamation of the union of the Serbs, Croats, and Slovenes under the rule of the Serbian Karadjordjević dynasty. But the royal government never recognized the title that Prica had received from Zagreb, and before the end of 1918 the navy was subordinated to the former Serbian army ministry in Belgrade. In the early 1920s, Serbian army cadets were transferred to the navy, and thereafter the officer corps always included enough Serbs and Slovenes to prevent the Croatians from achieving a majority.[68] Nevertheless, Croatians were well represented in the higher ranks. Prica held several temporary positions before finally being reappointed commander of the Yugoslav navy in 1923. He retired in 1929 but survived until 1960, dying in Opatija (Abbazia) at the age of ninety-three.[69] The other prominent South Slav players in the drama of late October 1918 remained in Yugoslav service at least into the early 1920s. Captain Franc Vučer, Cicoli's successor as harbor admiral in Pola, was displaced by the Italian annexation of the port and went on to serve as arsenal commander in Cattaro. Rear Admiral Method Koch, initially the administrative commander in Pola, moved on to become district commander in Sušak.[70] Some non-Yugoslav officers accepted the offer of a Yugoslav commission after 1918. These included Rear Admiral Viktor Wickerhauser, former commander of the Danube flotilla, whose name appears in the Yugoslav records in the Slavicized form "Vikerhauzer." After serving as an administrator in charge of technical, budget, and personnel matters, in 1929 he succeeded Prica as commander of the navy, a position he held until 1932.[71] Nikolaus Sztankovich de Sztapár, a Magyarized Croat who rose to captain's rank in the Austro-Hungarian navy, rediscovered his Slavic roots after 1918 and, as Nikola Stanković, commanded the Yugoslav fleet from 1932 until 1934.[72]

Veterans of Habsburg naval service continued to hold high positions in the Yugoslav navy right up to the Second World War. Some who had witnessed the demise of the Austro-Hungarian navy as junior officers presided over the collapse of the Yugoslav navy after Nazi Germany invaded and dismembered the kingdom of Yugoslavia in April 1941. Rear Admiral Julian Luteroti, a member of the naval academy's class of 1902, was the last man to hold the post of navy commander in the war ministry in Belgrade, while Rear Admiral Milan Domainko (class of 1909) was the last fleet commander in Cattaro. Both had been lieutenants in the Austro-Hungarian navy of 1918. The Slovene Ivan Kern, a twenty-year-old Habsburg navy cadet at the end of the First World War, led the only contingent of Yugoslav vessels to resist the surrender in April 1941. As captain and division commander of Sebenico, he directed a submarine and two torpedo boats on their flight to Malta.[73]

In addition to Horthy, dozens of former officers of Hungarian birth returned to their newly landlocked homeland after 1918. Franz von Thierry, the wartime head of the submarine branch, died in Budapest in 1942.[74] Other, younger officers pursued careers on the water in the Hungarian river watch. Olaf Wulff led the forces on the Danube until 1933, although his small flotilla—seven patrol boats after 1927—hardly justified the rank of vice admiral that Horthy ultimately gave him. Instrumental in organizing the International Danube Commission, Wulff lived in retirement in Hungary until after the communist takeover, finally dying in exile in Costa Rica in 1955.[75] After finishing the war as a submarine lieutenant, Kálmán Hardy joined the Hungarian National Army during the counterrevolution and remained in uniform throughout the 1920s as an adjutant to Horthy. He served in the river watch from 1929 to 1931, then represented Hungary at the Geneva Disarmament Conference in 1932. Thereafter he returned to the army, rising to major general's rank early in the Second World War. In 1942 Hardy transferred back to the river watch as a rear admiral and became its commander; he held the rank of vice admiral when the Germans overthrew Horthy in October 1944.[76] Other Austro-Hungarian veterans who went on to become "admirals" on the Danube after 1918 included Emil Konek Edler von Norwall, Horthy's close friend and former chief of staff.[77]

In postwar Poland, President Josef Pilsudski appointed former destroyer captain Bogumil Nowotny to command the new Polish navy, with the rank of rear admiral. After the cold and hungry winter of 1918–19 drove his men to mutiny, Nowotny fell from favor with Pilsudski and was fired. He went on to form the Sarmacia Line, the first Polish merchant shipping company, which employed a number of former Austro-Hungarian officers. He retired in 1933 and eventually died in exile in Italy in 1960.[78] Other former Habsburg officers entering the Polish navy included Georg Zwierkowski, who had served in the Danube flotilla during the First World War and with Prince Liechtenstein on the armistice commission in the fall of 1918. He held the rank of rear admiral when he died in 1932.[79]

A number of officers accepted Italian citizenship after the First World War and lived under Italian rule in Trieste, Rijeka, or Istria, but few went on to serve in the fleet of the former archenemy. At least one veteran, Konrad Schinko, ultimately lost his life in Mussolini's navy. Commissioned as a sea cadet in 1916, Schinko was captured in the ill-fated raid on Ancona in April 1918 and spent the last months of the war as a prisoner in Italy. Eventually he returned to Pola and became an Italian citizen after Italy annexed the Istrian peninsula. He worked as a merchant captain throughout the 1920s and 1930s while also holding a commission as reserve lieutenant in the Italian navy. Activated after Italy's entry into the Second World War, he received command of the auxiliary ship *Lago Tana* and was killed in November 1942 when his vessel was sunk off Sicily in an allied air attack.[80]

A significant share of Austro-Hungarian sea officers were Germans or Czechs from Bohemia and Moravia, but relatively few of them settled in the new Czechoslovakia after 1918. Exceptions to the rule included Captain Rudolf Mayer, former head of naval intelligence, who returned to his birthplace of Brünn (Brno), where he died in 1927; and Lieutenant Zdenko Hudeček, former commander of *U17* and *U28*, who died in desperate poverty at Frydek Místek in 1974, at the age of eighty-seven. Most of those choosing not to live in Czechoslovakia were ethnic Germans, but some were *kaisertreu* Czechs who identified more with Austria than with the new Czechoslovak state; these included Admiral Chmelarž, the highest-ranking Czech in the history of the navy, who retired to Vienna, where he died in 1945 at age eighty-eight.[81] *General-schiffbauingenieur* Siegfried Popper, the most prominent Jewish figure in the history of the navy, retired to his native Prague after the First World War. Popper had worked as a private engineer for the Stabilimento Tecnico Triestino after leaving active navy service in 1907 and gained international respect for his warship designs, which included all sixteen of the Austro-Hungarian battleships (the 5,600-ton *Monarch*s through the 20,000-ton dreadnoughts) that saw action in the war. Troubled by the intolerant atmosphere of interwar Austria, in 1931 he returned an honorary doctorate he had received years earlier from the Technische Hochschule (today the Technische Universität) in Vienna to protest the open anti-Semitism of members of the school's faculty. In 1933, at the age of eighty-five, Popper was struck by a streetcar and killed while attempting to cross a street in Prague.[82]

Dissatisfied with the options available to them in the successor states of the Dual Monarchy, some officers sought new opportunities in distant lands. Forty-six junior officers, many of them cadets or lieutenants, enlisted at the end of 1920 for five-year terms as officers in the merchant marine of the Netherlands East Indies. The worldwide postwar economic depression in the shipping industry brought most of them back to Austria before their contracts were due to expire, but twelve former Austro-Hungarian sea officers remained in East Indian service, became Dutch citizens, and eventually retired at captain's rank.[83] Few officers had more colorful postwar sea careers than Paul Pachner. Captain of the ill-fated *Zenta* in 1914, he first served in the Spanish merchant marine, then aboard the yacht of the khedive of Egypt, and finally in the Yugoslav merchant marine aboard a humble collier.[84] In their search for opportunities abroad, veterans of the service had help from the remnants of the groups that in better times had lobbied for the cause of Austro-Hungarian naval and overseas interests. In 1919 the Austro-Hungarian Colonial Society still had 180 members; the Austrian Navy League, under the name German-Austrian Navigation League (*Deutsch-österreichische Schiffahrtsverein*), had 1,200 members, including many former sea officers. The two organizations merged to form the Austrian Economic League (*Österreichische Wirtschaftsverein*), which helped facilitate the emigration of former officers.[85]

While some eventually returned to sea, most navy veterans too young to retire after 1918 went on to various careers in civil service or business. Several returned to school, received higher degrees, and went on to take positions in medicine, law, or academia. Rear Admiral Vitus Vončina, the *kaisertreu* Croat, earned a medical degree at the University of Graz and, in his late fifties, became a practicing physician. His second career continued until his death in 1935.[86] From the younger generation, Lieutenant Karl Prett (academy class of 1913) also earned a medical degree.[87] Lieutenant Richard Riebel, who entered the navy in 1914 as a provisional sea cadet, earned a doctorate in chemistry and became manager of the chemical division of a rubber company in Java.[88] About two dozen former officers earned engineering diplomas, but these went on to a wide variety of careers. For example, Lieutenant Friedrich Fikerment, who entered the navy in 1910 as a provisional sea cadet, became manager of the Cathay Hotel in Shanghai; Lieutenant Vinzenz Singer (provisional sea cadet, 1912) became sales representative of a German firm in Hong Kong; and Lieutenant Julius Wassitsch (provisional sea cadet, 1912) became director of Aços Roechling-Buderos do Brazil in São Paulo. A pair of chemical engineers who had entered the navy as provisional sea cadets in 1913 also established themselves in careers far from Austria: Lieutenant Guido Aslan, brother of the famous Burgtheater actor Raoul Aslan, emigrated to Argentina, while Lieutenant Baron Johann Koblitz von Willmburg became a sugar planter in the Dutch East Indies.[89]

Among veterans emigrating to the United States, Anton Sokol ultimately enjoyed the most distinguished academic career. A sea cadet from 1915 to 1918, Sokol served briefly in the merchant marine of the Netherlands East Indies before moving to the United States. He received a doctorate in international relations from Stanford University in 1932 and served on the Stanford faculty from 1934 until his retirement in 1962.[90] Josef Solterer, also a sea cadet from 1915 to 1918, emigrated to the United States after the war and by the 1930s held a position on the economics faculty at Georgetown University.[91] Other former officers pursuing academic careers in the United States included the Hungarian river admiral, Kálmán Hardy. Freed from German captivity in 1945 by American troops, he emigrated to the United States in 1951 and went on to teach German and Hungarian at Georgetown.[92]

Former Austro-Hungarian officers whose postwar lives did not include pursuit of a higher degree or employment in higher education went on to an equally wide variety of civilian careers. Lieutenant Friedrich Zitta (provisional sea cadet, 1909) became owner of a travel agency in Luxembourg. Lieutenant Friedrich Wittek von Salzberg (provisional sea cadet, 1912) worked as a geologist in Mexico. Lieutenant Ludwig Johann Uher (provisional sea cadet, 1912) became a farmer in Brazil. Lieutenant Rudolf Schwenk (provisional sea cadet, 1912) became director of the Zurich branch of Electrolux. Lieutenant Emmanuel Lerch (academy class of 1913), a navy pilot who ended his days in the service as a prisoner of war, went on to become head of the aviation department of a firm in Colombia. Lieutenant Johann Thomas (academy class of 1913) operated a sugar plantation in the Dutch East Indies. Lieutenant Friedrich Schwab (provisional sea cadet, 1914) settled in San Francisco and became a certified public accountant. Sea Cadet Wilhelm von Winterhalder (academy class of 1916) managed a farm in Argentina. And Sea Cadet Alois Lehner (provisional sea cadet, 1917) became owner of a hairdressing salon in Clifton, New Jersey.[93]

CHAPTER 9

A remarkable number of navy veterans survived into the 1960s; thereafter their numbers naturally dwindled, but some enjoyed remarkable longevity. Returning to Austria after his German navy career, former submariner Hermann Rigele served as director general of the Austrian subsidiary of Unilever from 1946 until 1956.[94] He finally died in 1982 at the age of ninety-one, leaving flying ace Gottfried von Banfield as the last surviving recipient, naval or military, of the prestigious Order of Maria Theresa. Just twenty-eight at the end of the First World War, Banfield never piloted another plane during the remainder of his long life. In 1920 he married a daughter of Count Diodato Tripcovich, owner of a small Trieste shipping company; he settled in Trieste, became an Italian citizen, and eventually headed the Tripcovich firm's salvage division. It was in this capacity, over three decades later, that he helped lead the United Nations effort to clear the blocked Suez Canal following the Arab-Israeli War of 1956. President Charles de Gaulle of France subsequently awarded him the Legion of Honor. In his later years, as nostalgia for the old empire grew in his adopted home city, the "eagle of Trieste" became a local celebrity, a last link to the Habsburg past. His memoirs, published in 1984, appeared in Italian as well as German. Banfield died in Trieste in September 1986 at the age of ninety-six. The entourage at his funeral included a delegation of high-ranking officers of the Austrian *Bundesheer;* an Austrian army trumpeter blew taps and retreat. His obituary observed that "an epoch has come to an end."[95]

NOTES

1.   Plaschka, *Cattaro - Prag,* 17–18, 191. The processes continued at Cattaro, and as late as 20 October, thanks to the revelations of those still under custody and to the testimony of other witnesses, the conduct of Captain Milan von Millinković, commander of the destroyer *Orjen* at the time of the mutiny, was called into question. It was of considerable embarrassment to the navy that Millinković in the meantime had been appointed to the sensitive position of navy liaison officer at the headquarters of Field Marshal Svetozar Boroević von Bojna, commander of Habsburg forces on the Piave front. Upon hearing of the allegations of the Cattaro tribunal, the *kaisertreu* Boroević immediately requested that the *Armeeoberkommando* recall Millinković from his headquarters. See ibid., 191–92n.

2.   May, *The Passing of the Hapsburg Monarchy,* 2:766, 779.

3.   Ibid., 2:766–67, 771, 795. On the end of Austro-Hungarian submarine activity, see Halpern, *Naval War in the Mediterranean,* 566.

4.   Sokol, *Österreich-Ungarns Seekrieg,* 2:716.

5.   May, *The Passing of the Hapsburg Monarchy,* 2:779; Plaschka et al., *Innere Front,* 2:187–89.

6. Shanafelt, *The Secret Enemy*, 206-7.

7. Sokol, *Österreich-Ungarns Seekrieg*, 2:718-19.

8. *Armeeoberkommando* to *Flottenkommando*, Baden, 28 October 1918, text in ibid., 2:719.

9. Boroević to *Armeeoberkommando*, 28 October 1918, text in ibid., 2:719.

10. Sokol, *Österreich-Ungarns Seekrieg*, 2:720-21.

11. Plaschka et al., *Innere Front*, 2:225; Aichelburg, *Die Unterseeboote*, 1:189.

12. Halpern, *Naval War in the Mediterranean*, 567.

13. Plaschka, *Cattaro - Prag*, 238.

14. May, *The Passing of the Hapsburg Monarchy*, 2:779; Plaschka et al., *Innere Front*, 2:204.

15. Aichelburg, *Die Unterseeboote*, 1:189. On Charles's orders, see Trapp, *Bis zum letzten Flaggenschuss*, 242.

16. Sokol, *Österreich-Ungarns Seekrieg*, 2:724.

17. May, *The Passing of the Hapsburg Monarchy*, 2:779-80; Plaschka et al., *Innere Front*, 2:205-9.

18. Sokol, *Österreich-Ungarns Seekrieg*, 2:726-27; Plaschka et al., *Innere Front*, 2:229-30.

19. Sokol, *Österreich-Ungarns Seekrieg*, 2:728-29; Plaschka et al., *Innere Front*, 2:233-34.

20. Sokol, *Österreich-Ungarns Seekrieg*, 2:732-33; Plaschka et al., *Innere Front*, 2:235-36.

21. Horthy, *Memoirs*, 91.

22. Ibid., 92.

23. Sokol, *Österreich-Ungarns Seekrieg*, 2:734-35. Koudelka, *Denn Österreich lag einst am Meer*, 278-79, reveals that as early as March 1918 Admiral Keil suspected Prica of having South Slav nationalist sympathies.

24. Plaschka et al., *Innere Front*, 2:234-35.

25. Sokol, *Österreich-Ungarns Seekrieg*, 2:723, 729.

26. Erwin Sieche, "Zeittafel der Vorgänge rund um die Auflösung und Übergabe der k.u.k Kriegsmarine 1918-1923," 133; Trapp, *Bis zum letzten Flaggenschuss*, 244, 246.

27. Bayer von Bayersburg, *Österreichs Admirale*, 179.

28. Wulff, *Donauflottille*, 175-89. German Austrians and Czechs remained aboard until the flotilla reached Budapest; according to Wulff, the flag of the defunct Dual Monarchy was flown alongside the Hungarian out of respect for these non-Hungarian officers and seamen.

29. May, *The Passing of the Hapsburg Monarchy*, 2:780. A recent pictorial history by Horst F. Mayer and Dieter Winkler, *Als die Adria österreichisch war: Österreich-Ungarns Seemacht*, repeats the latter explanation (175).

30. Charles, memoir of 8 September 1920, in Feigl, *Kaiser Karl*, 257.

31. Schmidt-Pauli, *Nikolaus von Horthy*, 125.

32. Horthy, *Memoirs*, 90-91.

33. Plaschka et al., *Innere Front*, 2:215.

34. Sieche, "Zeittafel," 133; Halpern, *Naval War in the Mediterranean*, 567. The saboteurs also sank the requisitioned Austrian Lloyd liner *Wien*, which had housed German submariners in Pola.

35. Thaon di Revel to Sonnino, 1 November 1918, quoted in Sieche, "Zeittafel," 133.

36. Excerpts from Armistice of Villa Giusti, including full text of all naval provisions, in ibid., 134–35. The text lists the older and smaller *Erzherzog Ferdinand Max* rather than *Erzherzog Franz Ferdinand,* certainly an error.

37. Ibid., 136; Sokol, *Österreich-Ungarns Seekrieg,* 2:781.

38. Sieche, "Zeittafel," 137. Hazlett, "Austro-American Navy," 1763, contends that the *Radetzky* was not fired upon by the Italians because its captain "brazenly hoisted the American flag and held its course." His story may stem from the fact that the *Radetzky* was flying the Stars and Stripes when his detachment found the ship docked near Spalato on 17 November. See ibid., 1759.

39. Conz paper, Corfu, 9 November 1918, quoted in Sieche, "Zeittafel," 137–38.

40. Paul J. Kemp, "Grossbritannien und die Aufteilung der k.u.k. Flotte 1918–1923," 44.

41. Sieche, "Zeittafel," 138–40.

42. Greger, *Austro-Hungarian Warships,* 19–23, 27–33, 35, 42–44, 58–60, 63, 68–78.

43. Ibid., 63; Sieche, "Zeittafel," 15.

44. Greger, *Austro-Hungarian Warships,* 138–46; Erwin Steinböck, "Die Nachkriegsschicksale der österreichisch-ungarischen Patrouillenboote."

45. Aichelburg, *Die Unterseeboote,* 1:140.

46. März, "Austrian Crédit Mobilier," 125–26; Cupez, *Cantieri Riuniti dell'Adriatico,* 7–8, 10; Babudieri, *Squeri e cantiere,* 112; Gerolimi, *Cantiere Riuniti dell'Adriatico,* 48; Gellner and Valentini, *San Rocco,* 75, 79; Winkler and Mayer, *In allen Häfen war Österreich,* 204–6, 208.

47. Cupez, *Cantieri Riuniti dell'Adriatico,* 12; Babudieri, *Squeri e cantiere,* 114; Gerolimi, *Cantiere Riuniti dell'Adriatico,* 58–59; Giorgerini, *Almanacco,* 228–29.

48. Ploček and Juba, "Geschichte der ungarischen Reederei Adria," 20; Winkler and Mayer, *In allen Häfen war Österreich,* 202; Babudieri, *Squeri e cantiere,* 113; Cupez, *Cantieri Riuniti dell'Adriatico,* 8; Casali and Cattaruzza, *Sotto i mari del mondo,* 133, 175.

49. Babudieri, *L'industria armatoriale di Trieste,* 176; Winkler and Mayer, *In allen Häfen war Österreich,* 202–204.

50. Horthy, *Memoirs,* 160–61; Raeder quoted by Horthy, 161. See also "Kriegsschiffe mit dem Namen des Prinzen Eugen von Savoyen," *Marine—Gestern, Heute* 13 (1986): 170.

51. "Kriegsschiffe mit dem Namen des Prinzen Eugen von Savoyen," 170.

52. Overall casualty figures from Sokol, *Österreich-Ungarns Seekrieg,* 2:775–76. Figures for aviators from Schupita, *Die k.u.k. Seeflieger,* 245; casualty lists of submariners in Aichelburg, *Die Unterseeboote,* 2:480–82.

53. Trapp, *Bis zum letzten Flaggenschuss,* 243.

54. Wolfgang Doppelbauer, *Zum Elend noch die Schande: Das altösterreichische Offizierskorps am Beginn der Republik,* 22.

55. Erwin Sieche, letter to author, 6 February 1993.

56. Jörg K. Hoensch, *A History of Modern Hungary, 1867–1986,* 101.

57. Bayer von Bayersburg, *Unter der k.u.k. Kriegsflagge,* 27–35, provides the best concise overview of Horthy's life. See also Horthy, *Memoirs;* and Schmidt-Pauli, *Nikolaus von Horthy,* passim.

58. Sieche to author, 6 February 1993.

59. Ruppert von Trapp (son of Georg von Trapp), interview with David Hermges, Radio Austria International, October 1984.

60. Sieche to author, 6 February 1993.

61. Siehe to author, 6 February 1993; Helwig Adolph-Auffenberg, "Dem letzten Theresienritter in Österreich," *Neue Ordnung,* 11 November 1982.

62. Sokol, *Austro-Hungarian Navy,* 139; Aichelburg, *Die Unterseeboote,* 2:481.

63. *Almanach für die k.u.k. Kriegsmarine* (1914), 619; Siehe to author, 6 February 1993.

64. Nikolaus von Preradovich, "Österreicher als Ritterkreuzträger," 61.

65. Lothar Baumgartner, "In memoriam Carl Redl," *Marine—Gestern, Heute* 13 (1986): 186. Redl, one of the Austrians who served at Algeciras, died in August 1986 at the age of ninety.

66. Siehe to author, 6 February 1993.

67. Ibid.

68. Georg Pregel, "Die ersten schwierigen Aufbaujahre der SHS-Marine," 42–44. In 1922-23, 40 Serbian army cadets were transferred to the navy, which at that time had only 145 sea officers.

69. Koudelka, *Denn Österreich lag einst am Meer,* 278n, provides a brief sketch of Prica's Yugoslav career.

70. Pregel, "Die ersten schwierigen Aufbaujahre," 43, 45.

71. Ibid., 44; Siehe to author, 6 February 1993.

72. *Almanach für die k.u.k. Kriegsmarine* (1918), 519; Siehe to author, 6 February 1993.

73. Jerko Kačić-Dimitri, "Das Ende der königlich jugoslawischen Flotte," 9–11. Data on the Austro-Hungarian backgrounds of Yugoslav officers from *Almanach für die k.u.k. Kriegsmarine* (1918).

74. Siehe to author, 6 February 1993.

75. Bayer von Bayersburg, *Unter der k.u.k. Kriegsflagge,* 56–61.

76. "Kálmán Hardy: In Memoriam," *Die Flagge* 3/1980. I am grateful to Mr. Erwin Siehe for this reference.

77. Siehe to author, 6 February 1993.

78. Christian Sandauer, "Konteradmiral Bogumil Nowotny, der Begründer der polnischen Kriegsmarine," 16–19.

79. Bayer von Bayersburg, *Unter der k.u.k. Kriegsflagge,* 62–68.

80. Jahn and Siehe, "Der Handstreich auf Ancona," 145.

81. Bayer von Bayersburg, *Österreichs Admirale,* 42–44, 124–25. Information on Hudeček from Aichelburg, *Die Unterseeboote,* 2:476; and Siehe to author, 6 February 1993.

82. Bayer von Bayersburg, *Österreichs Admirale,* 141–43; Siehe to author, 6 February 1993.

83. Tomicich, "Die k.(u.)k. Marineakademie," 162.

84. Siehe to author, 6 February 1993.

85. Doppelbauer, *Zum Elend noch die Schande,* 90.

86. Bayer von Bayersburg, *Österreichs Admirale,* 179–80.

87. *Almanach für die k.u.k. Kriegsmarine* (1914), 619; Siehe to author, 6 February 1993.

88. *Almanach für die k.u.k. Kriegsmarine* (1918); Siehe to author, 6 February 1993, data from *Marine Almanach,* 1933 (published by the Austrian *Marineverband*).

89. *Almanach für die k.u.k. Kriegsmarine* (1918); Siehe to author, 6 February 1993, data from *Marine Almanach,* 1933.

90. Sokol, *Austro-Hungarian Navy,* 172. Sokol died in 1982 at the age of eighty-five.

91. Sieche to author, 6 February 1993, data from *Marine Almanach,* 1933.

92. "Kálmán Hardy: In Memoriam." Hardy died in 1980 at the age of eighty-eight.

93. *Almanach für die k.u.k. Kriegsmarine* (1918); Sieche to author, 6 February 1993, data from *Marine Almanach,* 1933.

94. Sieche to author, 6 February 1993.

95. Banfield, *Der Adler von Triest,* 122–54 passim; Lothar Baumgartner, "Gottfried von Banfield," *Marine—Gestern, Heute* 13 (1986): 184–85.

EPILOGUE

In December 1946, at Bikini Atoll in the Pacific, an atomic bomb destroyed the *Traditionsschiff* of the Austro-Hungarian navy, the former German heavy cruiser *Prinz Eugen*. The American bomb test targeted several obsolete battleships and cruisers, relics of a bygone age that were overwhelmed by the technology of the future. In naval armaments, the aircraft carrier eclipsed the battleship during the Second World War to become the capital ship of the world's largest navies, but the dreadnought design proved to be more durable than anyone would have predicted. The United States Navy refurbished the super-dreadnoughts of the *Iowa* class during the 1980s, and these warships played an active role as late as the Persian Gulf War of 1991. Of course, in the modern arsenal of a nuclear superpower, battleships more than four decades old—though still potent weapons systems—are little more than a curiosity. It is a far cry from the years before the First World War when dreadnoughts were the yardstick by which great powers were measured. Indeed, in the prewar era the ability to build one's own dreadnoughts became the hallmark of great power status, in much the same way that having one's own nuclear capability became the litmus test of a similar status in the nuclear age.

To be sure, in the prewar years the Austrian Navy League actively copied its German counterpart and parroted many of the same arguments to justify a battle fleet for a traditional land power. The navy's leading prewar patron, Francis Ferdinand, embraced the cause of sea power in a manner similar to that of William II. And the Austro-Hungarian battle fleet—like the German High Seas Fleet—spent much of the First World War bottled up at anchor. Thus, it is easy for the casual observer to dismiss naval developments in Austria-Hungary as a mere imitation of the same phenomenon in Germany. But against the derisive label "Luxury Fleet," used by Winston Churchill (and more recently, Holger Herwig) to describe the navy of William II, the Austro-Hungarian fleet can be defended at least as well as, if not better than, its German counterpart. As we have seen, the navy's fortunes always waxed and waned according to the state of Austro-Italian relations, and with good reason. Italy had long-standing claims to much of the Dual Monarchy's outlet to the sea on historic grounds dating from Venetian times and on ethnic grounds based on the fact that Trieste was an Italian city and Istria and Dalmatia had significant Italian populations. The irredentist movement was both strong and vocal, and even during the years of the Triple Alliance a significant sector of Italian public and political opinion still did not accept Austrian possession of these lands. Consequently, the Triple Alliance notwithstanding, Austria-Hungary could not afford to take Italy's friendship for granted or to lower its guard in the Adriatic. To conceive of a British threat to Germany in the North Sea required some imagination even for the true believers who supported the Tirpitz plan after 1898; in comparison, the deep, historical Austro-Italian animosity and the Italian threat to the Dual Monarchy's coastline were far more genuine. In short, the German case for a battle fleet against Britain rested on far flimsier grounds than the Austro-Hungarian case for naval deterrence against Italy.

Through the expansion of the navy and the construction of its dreadnought squadron, Austria-Hungary maintained the full trappings of great-power status, thus guaranteeing that it would retain its membership in the circle of leading powers until its ultimate demise as a consequence of the First World War. In hindsight, the defensive needs of Austria-Hungary at sea would have been better served if the navy had maintained its early prowess in the defensive "little war" tactics and the *mezzi insidiosi* of mines and torpedoes instead of attempting to build a modern battleship navy. But the force that provides the best *deterrence* against an enemy attack is not always the same as the force that would provide the best *defense* against an attack. Deterrence has always been more psychological than material, subject to the spirit of the times, and aside from the 1880s and the heyday of the *Jeune Ecole,* between the 1860s and 1918 deterrence at sea required battleships. Without its dreadnoughts, Austria-Hungary would not have been a strategic factor in the Mediterranean on the eve of the First World War. And even after the lethal power of the submarine was demonstrated in action during the war, the fear of an Austrian dreadnought sortie *out* of the Adriatic was just as decisive a factor as the fear of a torpedoing by Austrian undersea boats *in* the Adriatic in keeping the Entente navies in their cautious deployment below the Straits of Otranto.

An imperfect institution serving an imperfect regime, the Austro-Hungarian navy nonetheless warrants recognition for the fact that it functioned far better than most organs of the multinational Habsburg state and ultimately also enjoyed a remarkable degree of popular support. After enduring years of neglect and penury, in the age of navalism the fleet provided a unique common cause and rallying point for a wide variety of nationalities and political parties. The navy's broad base of political support made possible the dramatic funding increases that fueled the expansion of the fleet, and the lucrative naval contracts, judiciously distributed, reinforced and further broadened this base of support. To be sure, for many navalists the enthusiasm for the battleship navy had strong overtones of economic self-interest—an enthusiasm that could not have been generated by a less expensive, less ambitious program for a coastal defense navy—but it certainly helped that by the turn of the century the navy enjoyed a much better reputation than the Habsburg army. In the navy, problems between men of different nationalities and tensions between officers and men were far less significant than in the army, despite the fact that shipboard service brought men of a greater variety of nationalities into far closer contact with one another than service in the army's territorially based regiments. Even under the stresses of war, the navy did not experience serious ethnic or class-related problems until 1917, the same year that the first great mutinies wracked the Imperial German navy.

While critics pointed to the general inactivity of the wartime "fleet in being" at Pola, the futility of the cruiser sorties conducted from Cattaro, and the modest size and scope of operations of the Austro-Hungarian submarine force, the navy succeeded in defending the empire's long Adriatic frontier until the end of the war. In the process, the navy made the Adriatic a virtual "Austrian lake," to quote an American observer from the spring of 1918. Throughout the war, Austria-Hungary tied down a significant share of the naval power of the Entente, warships that could have been used elsewhere, most notably in the eastern

Mediterranean at the Dardanelles. Needless to say, an Entente victory at the straits in 1915, opening a supply route from the western allies to Imperial Russia, could have altered the course of the war and perhaps changed the broader course of history.

Evidence of landlocked Austria's naval past remains to this day, aside from the memorabilia in museums. From atop a majestic column, the statue of Tegetthoff still looks down on the Praterstern, now one of the major intersections in Vienna, while in the concert halls, the *Sängerknaben* of the Vienna Boys' Choir still dress in sailor suits. But the accomplishments of the navy that had served Austria-Hungary well against such tremendous odds ultimately lived on only in the memories of the veterans of the service, nurtured eventually by a modest circle of Austrian navy enthusiasts. Their focus naturally was on the exploits of the navy at sea in the various campaigns and expeditions of the nineteenth century but especially in the First World War. The navy's position as the cornerstone of Austro-Hungarian overseas interests, the unlikely phenomenon of navalism in a traditional land power, and especially the role of naval expansion in developing the military-industrial complex within the Dual Monarchy were all but forgotten, even among historians specializing in Austrian and Habsburg history.

The infrastructure that supported Austro-Hungarian navalism survived long after the death of the navy and the dismemberment of the empire. During the prewar arms race, when money flowed freely into the navy's construction budget, naval contracts provided a valuable stimulus to the steel and armaments industries of the Dual Monarchy, in particular in the Bohemian and Moravian lands; later, the same establishments provided the industrial base that set Czechoslovakia apart from its more backward East Central European neighbors. In the years before 1914, while benefiting from the same increases in funding, the shipyards of the Austro-Hungarian littoral outperformed those of France, Italy, and Russia, completing battleships and cruisers at a pace that trailed only the shipyards of Britain and Germany. Unfortunately, the larger former Habsburg shipyards, all in Italian hands after 1918, for the most part languished during the interwar years, cut off from their traditional support industries and forced to compete with Genoa, Castellammare, and Livorno.

Ultimately, in the years after the Second World War, the overall decline of the commercial shipbuilding industry in the Western world affected the Adriatic Italian shipyards as well. The former San Marco and San Rocco wharves were practically idle after the 1960s, and the last Trieste shipyard closed in 1982. By the early 1990s, the successor to the Cantiere Riuniti—the surviving descendant of the Stabilimento Tecnico Triestino of the Habsburg era—operated only the Monfalcone yard that originally belonged to the Cantiere Navale Triestino. Meanwhile, to the east, the Yugoslav annexation of Istria after the Second World War made Pola a Yugoslav naval base and breathed new life into the shipbuilding industry of Rijeka. The former Danubius establishment, christened the Third of May shipyard in memory of the day in 1945 when the city was liberated by Marshal Tito's partisans, remained active through the 1980s, building freighters and oil tankers. The disintegration of Yugoslavia in the early 1990s naturally cast doubt over the future of the Rijeka shipbuilding industry.

In the last decade of the twentieth century, as Yugoslavia and, on a grander scale, the former Soviet Union, disintegrate under the pressure of revived nationalisms and divisive ethnic tensions, the much-maligned Dual Monarchy and its armed forces seem destined to appear in a far better light. True, the Compromise of 1867 and the transformation of the Austrian Empire into Austria-Hungary did not "solve" the Habsburg nationality problem, and the armed forces of the Dual Monarchy, plagued by their share of internal weaknesses, never ranked among the most powerful in Europe, but the political structure did provide a stable framework within which the nationality problem was managed more or less successfully for almost half a century, while the multinational armed forces provided a credible defense, filling what otherwise would have been a power vacuum in East Central Europe and the Adriatic. In a Europe again reminded of the durable and insoluble nature of most ethnic antagonisms, the emergence of similar political and defense structures in the former Soviet Union and Yugoslavia, even if they held the promise only of managing the ongoing crisis and filling a power vacuum, certainly would be welcomed as an alternative to disintegration and chaos.

APPENDIXES

COMMANDERS AND LEADING PERSONNEL OF THE AUSTRO-HUNGARIAN NAVY (1867–1918)

NOTE: ranks reflect the highest reached by the individual while serving in the position listed. Titles of nobility (baron, count, etc.) are not shown. GA = Grand Admiral; Adm. = Admiral; VA = Vice Admiral; RA = Rear Admiral; Capt. = Captain.

NAVY COMMANDER
(Marinekommandant)

VA Wilhelm von Tegetthoff	March 1868–April 1871
Adm. Friedrich von Pöck	April 1871–November 1883
Adm. Maximilian Daublebsky von Sterneck	November 1883–December 1897
Adm. Hermann von Spaun	December 1897–October 1904
Adm. Rudolf Montecuccoli	October 1904–February 1913
GA Anton Haus	February 1913–February 1917
(vacant)	February 1917–April 1917
Adm. Maximilian Njegovan	April 1917–February 1918
(vacant)	February 1918–November 1918

CHIEF OF THE *MARINESEKTION*
(Chef der Marinesektion)

VA Ludwig von Fautz	July 1865–March 1868
VA Wilhelm von Tegetthoff	March 1868–April 1871
(vacant)	April 1871–October 1872

Adm. Friedrich von Pöck	October 1872–November 1883
Adm. Maximilian Daublebsky von Sterneck	November 1883–December 1897
Adm. Hermann von Spaun	December 1897–October 1904
Adm. Rudolf Montecuccoli	October 1904–February 1913
GA Anton Haus	February 1913–February 1917
VA Karl Kailer von Kaltenfels	February 1917–April 1917
Adm. Maximilian Njegovan	April 1917–February 1918
VA Franz von Holub	February 1918–November 1918

ADMINISTRATIVE SECOND IN COMMAND
(Stellvertreter des Chefs)

Capt. Julius von Wissiak	March 1868–January 1870
VA Friedrich von Pöck	February 1870–December 1871
VA Georg von Millosicz	December 1871–November 1883
Adm. Alexander Eberan von Eberhorst	November 1883–October 1897
VA Hermann von Spaun	October 1897–December 1897
VA Rudolf Berghofer	January 1898–April 1903
VA Rudolf Montecuccoli	April 1903–October 1904
Adm. Leodegar Kneissler von Maixdorf	October 1904–June 1911
VA Alois von Kunsti	June 1911–March 1913
VA Karl Kailer von Kaltenfels	March 1913–February 1917
RA Josef Rodler	February 1917–February 1918
VA Franz von Teichgräber	March 1918–November 1918

ADMINISTRATIVE THIRD IN COMMAND
(Zugeteilter Flaggenoffizier)

RA Franz von Keil	November 1913–February 1917

ADMIRAL AT THE DISPOSITION OF THE SUPREME COMMAND
(zur Disposition des allerhöchsten Oberbefehls)

VA Franz von Keil	February 1918–November 1918

FLEET INSPECTOR
(Marine Truppen- und Flotteninspektor 1865-68, Flotteninspektor 1912–13)

Archduke Leopold	July 1865–March 1868

(vacant)   March 1868–July 1912

Adm. Anton Haus   July 1912–March 1913

COMMANDER OF ACTIVE SQUADRON
(in Adriatic and Mediterranean; squadron usually
referred to as "division" during winter months, 1885–95)

Capt. Alois von Pokorny   January 1867–December 1867

RA Friedrich von Pöck   January 1868–December 1869

RA Georg von Millosicz   January 1870–December 1871

RA Alois von Pokorny   January 1872–December 1873

RA Maximilian Daublebsky von Sterneck   January 1874–December 1875

RA Alfred von Barry   January 1876–June 1878

RA Alois von Pokorny   June 1878–June 1879

RA Alexander Eberan von Eberhorst   June 1879–June 1881

RA Alfred von Wiplinger   June 1881–June 1883

RA Johann Pauer   June 1883–December 1883

RA Maximilian von Pitner   December 1883–July 1885

RA Hermann von Spaun   August 1885–September 1886

RA Heinrich von Buchta   September 1886–January 1888

Capt. Josef Wostry (provisional)   January 1888–April 1888

RA Moriz Manfroni von Manfort   April 1888–July 1888

RA Hermann von Spaun   July 1888–July 1889

RA Johann von Hinke   July 1889–June 1891

RA Arno von Rohrscheidt   September 1891–April 1892

RA Hermann von Spaun   May 1892–September 1892

RA Oscare Cassini   October 1892–March 1893

VA Hermann von Spaun   April 1893–August 1893

RA Archduke Charles Stephen   September 1893–March 1894

RA Johann von Hinke   May 1894–August 1894

RA Francesco Minutillo   October 1894–February 1895

VA Hermann von Spaun   April 1895–September 1895

RA Karl Seemann von Treuenwart   October 1895–March 1896

VA Hermann von Spaun	April 1896–August 1896
RA Karl Seemann von Treuenwart	October 1896–December 1896
RA Johann von Hinke	January 1897–April 1898
RA Francesco Minutillo	May 1898–August 1899
RA Rudolf Montecuccoli	September 1899–June 1900
(and cruiser squadron in East Asia, June 1900–September 1901)	
RA Gustav von Brosch	July 1900–July 1901
RA Julius von Ripper	September 1901–September 1902
RA Leodegar Kneissler von Maixdorf	December 1902–June 1904
RA Julius von Ripper	June 1904–September 1904
RA Miecislaus von Siemuszowa-Pietruski	October 1904–June 1905
RA Leopold von Jedina-Palombini	June 1905–December 1906
RA Luzian von Ziegler	January 1907–November 1908
RA Anton Haus	November 1908–September 1910
RA Alois von Kunsti	September 1910–May 1911
VA Anton Haus	June 1911–August 1911
RA August Lanjus von Wellenburg	September 1911–July 1912
VA Anton Haus	July 1912–August 1912
RA Eugen von Chmelarž	September 1912–February 1913
RA Maximilian Njegovan	March 1913–October 1913
RA Franz Löfler	October 1913–July 1914

WARTIME "FLEET COMMANDER" *(Flottenkommandant)*

GA Anton Haus	July 1914–February 1917
Adm. Maximilian Njegovan	February 1917–February 1918
RA Miklós Horthy	February 1918–November 1918

HARBOR ADMIRAL (Pola)

Adm. Anton Bourguignon von Baumberg	1865–79
VA Alois von Pokorny	1879–86
VA Maximilian von Pitner	1886–98
VA Johann von Hinke	1898–1901

VA Francesco Minutillo	1901-5
Adm. Julius von Ripper	1905-13
VA Eugen von Chmelarž	1913-17
Adm. Paul Fiedler	1917-18
RA Alfred Cicoli	1918 (March-November)

SOURCES: Walter Wagner, "Die obersten Behörden der k.u.k. Kriegsmarine 1856-1918"; Heinrich Bayer von Bayersburg, *Österreichs Admirale 1867-1918;* idem, *Unter der k.u.k. Kriegsflagge; Jahresbericht der k.(u.)k. Kriegsmarine.*

ARMORED SHIPS OF THE AUSTRO-HUNGARIAN NAVY (1867–1918)

KEY: builders: N.A. Trieste = Navale Adriatico; S.T.T. Trieste = Stabilimento Tecnico Triestino; Danubius = Danubius of Rijeka

"built": years in which ship was laid down and launched; ships were not ready for service upon launching (e.g., guns, armor, engines were installed later)

"in commission": years of initial commissioning and final removal from the active list of warships

ARMORED FRIGATES	BUILDER	TONS	BUILT	IN COMMISSION
Drache	N.A. Trieste	2,800	1860-61	1862-75
Salamander	N.A. Trieste	2,800	1860-61	1862-83
Kaiser Max (I)	N.A. Trieste	3,600	1861-62	1863-73
Juan d'Austria	N.A. Trieste	3,600	1861-62	1863-74
Prinz Eugen (I)	N.A. Trieste	3,600	1861-62	1863-73
Erzherzog Ferdinand Max (I)	N.A. Trieste	5,100	1863-65	1866-86
Habsburg (I)	N.A. Trieste	5,100	1863-65	1866-86*

* armed as harbor watch vessels: *Habsburg* in Pola (1886-97); *Tegetthoff* in Pola (1905-18; under the name *Mars* after 1911); *Erzherzog Albrecht* in Cattaro (1904-7); *Kronprinzessin Stephanie* in Cattaro (1908-9); *Kronprinz Rudolf* in Cattaro (1910-18)

CASEMATE SHIPS	BUILDER	TONS	BUILT	IN COMMISSION
Kaiser (II)	Pola Arsenal	5,800	1869-71	1874-97
Lissa	N.A. Trieste	6,100	1867-69	1871-92
Custoza	S.T.T. Trieste	7,100	1869-72	1875-1903
Erzherzog Albrecht	N.A. Trieste	5,900	1869-72	1875-1901*
Kaiser Max (II)	S.T.T. Trieste	3,600	1873-75	1877-1903
Don Juan d'Austria	S.T.T. Trieste	3,600	1874-75	1876-1903
Prinz Eugen (II)	Pola Arsenal	3,600	1874-77	1879-1903
Tegetthoff (I)	S.T.T. Trieste	7,550	1876-78	1882-1905*

PRE-DREADNOUGHTS	BUILDER	TONS	BUILT	IN COMMISSION
Kronprinz Rudolf	Pola Arsenal	6,900	1884-87	1889-1905*
Kronprinzessin Stephanie	S.T.T. Trieste	5,100	1884-87	1889-1905*
Monarch	Pola Arsenal	5,600	1893-95	1897-1918†
Wien	S.T.T. Trieste	5,600	1893-95	1897-1917§
Budapest	S.T.T. Trieste	5,600	1894-96	1898-1918†
Habsburg (II)	S.T.T. Trieste	8,300	1899-1900	1902-18†
Arpád	S.T.T. Trieste	8,300	1899-1901	1903-18†
Babenberg	S.T.T. Trieste	8,300	1901-2	1904-18†
Erzherzog Karl	S.T.T. Trieste	10,600	1902-3	1906‡
Erzherzog Friedrich (II)	S.T.T. Trieste	10,600	1902-5	1907‡
Erzherzog Ferdinand Max (II)	S.T.T. Trieste	10,600	1904-5	1907‡
Radetzky (III)	S.T.T. Trieste	14,500	1907-9	1911‡
Erzherzog Franz Ferdinand	S.T.T. Trieste	14,500	1907-8	1910‡
Zrinyi (II)	S.T.T. Trieste	14,500	1909-10	1911‡

DREADNOUGHTS	BUILDER	TONS	BUILT	IN COMMISSION
Viribus Unitis	S.T.T. Trieste	20,000	1910-11	1912‡
Tegetthoff (II)	S.T.T. Trieste	20,000	1910-12	1913‡
Prinz Eugen (III)	S.T.T. Trieste	20,000	1912	1914‡
Szent István	Danubius	20,000	1912-14	1915-18§

ARMORED CRUISERS	BUILDER	TONS	BUILT	IN COMMISSION
Maria Theresia	S.T.T. Trieste	5,200	1891–93	1895–1917†
Kaiser Karl VI	S.T.T. Trieste	6,300	1896–98	1900–1918†
Sankt Georg	Pola Arsenal	7,400	1901–3	1905–18†

* armed as harbor watch vessels: *Habsburg* in Pola (1886–97); *Tegetthoff* in Pola (1905–18; under the name *Mars* after 1911); *Erzherzog Albrecht* in Cattaro (1904–7); *Kronprinzessin Stephanie* in Cattaro (1908–9); *Kronprinz Rudolf* in Cattaro (1910–18)
† ships removed from the active list before the end of the war
§ *Wien* was sunk in December 1917, *Szent István* in June 1918
‡ still on active list of warships as of 31 October 1918

SOURCES: Franz F. Bilzer, "Die Schiffe und Fahrzeuge der k.(u.)k. Kriegsmarine," *Marine— Gestern, Heute* 12 (1985), no. 2–15 (1988), no. 3 (continuing series in fourteen parts); René Greger, *Austro-Hungarian Warships of World War I; Jahresbericht der k.(u.)k. Kriegsmarine.*

UNARMORED SHIPS OF THE AUSTRO-HUNGARIAN NAVY (1867–1918)

Sailing ships still in use after 1866 are not included. For wooden and composite ships, paddle steamers and smaller propeller steamers (i.e., schooners and gunboats) are not included. For steel-hulled vessels, ships smaller than those classified as cruisers (i.e., destroyers, torpedo boats) are not included. All navy vessels not armed as warships are not included.

KEY: builders: N.A. Trieste = Navale Adriatico; S.T.T. Trieste = Stabilimento Tecnico Triestino; Danubius = Danubius of Rijeka; Monfalcone = Cantiere Navale Triestino of Monfalcone; Money, Wigram = Money, Wigram & Sons (England); Armstrong = Armstrong, Mitchell & Company (England)

"built": years in which ship was laid down and launched; ships were not ready for service upon launching (e.g., guns, engines were installed later)

"in commission": years of initial commissioning and final removal from the active list of warships

NOTE: most unarmored warships were converted for other purposes (as training ships, auxiliary vessels, etc.) after leaving active service

SHIP OF THE LINE	BUILDER	TONS	BUILT	IN COMMISSION
Kaiser (I)	Pola Arsenal	5,200	1855-58	1861-69

WOODEN FRIGATES	BUILDER	TONS	BUILT	IN COMMISSION
Radetzky (I)	Money, Wigram	2,200	1852-54	1854-69§
Donau (I)	N.A. Trieste	2,200	1855-56	1857-72
Adria	N.A. Trieste	2,200	1855-56	1857-68
Novara (I)	S.T.T. Trieste	2,500	1861-62	1862-76
Schwarzenberg	Pola Arsenal	2,500	1861-62	1862-69

WOODEN CORVETTES	BUILDER	TONS	BUILT	IN COMMISSION
Erzherzog Friedrich (I)	Venice Arsenal	1,500	1854-57	1857-97
Dandolo	Venice Arsenal	1,500	1854-58	1859-79
Helgoland (I)	Pola Arsenal	1,800	1866-67	1869-90

COMPOSITE FRIGATES	BUILDER	TONS	BUILT	IN COMMISSION
Radetzky (II)	S.T.T. Trieste	3,400	1870-72	1873-97
Laudon	S.T.T. Trieste	3,400	1871-73	1874-99

COMPOSITE CORVETTES	BUILDER	TONS	BUILT	IN COMMISSION
Fasana	N.A. Trieste	2,000	1869-70	1871-96
Zrinyi (I)	S.T.T. Trieste	1,300	1870	1871-1902
Frundsberg	N.A. Trieste	1,300	1871-73	1873-1902
Aurora	N.A. Trieste	1,300	1871-73	1874-1902
Donau (II)	N.A. Trieste	2,400	1873-74	1875-1902
Saida (I)	Pola Arsenal	2,400	1876-78	1879-1902

LIGHT CRUISERS (TORPEDO SHIPS)	BUILDER	TONS	BUILT	IN COMMISSION
Zara	Pola Arsenal	850	1878-79	1881-1902
Spalato	S.T.T. Trieste	850	1878-79	1881-1902
Sebenico	Pola Arsenal	900	1880-82	1882-1902
Lussin	S.T.T. Trieste	1,000	1882-83	1884-1902

Leopard	Armstrong	1,500	1885	1886–1914
Panther	Armstrong	1,500	1884–85	1885–1917†
Tiger	S.T.T. Trieste	1,700	1886–87	1888–1905

PROTECTED CRUISERS (RAM CRUISERS)	BUILDER	TONS	BUILT	IN COMMISSION
Kaiser Franz Joseph I	S.T.T. Trieste	4,000	1888–89	1890–1917†
Kaiserin Elisabeth	Pola Arsenal	4,000	1888–90	1892–1914§

LIGHT CRUISERS	BUILDER	TONS	BUILT	IN COMMISSION
Zenta	Pola Arsenal	2,300	1896–97	1899–1914§
Aspern	Pola Arsenal	2,300	1897–99	1900–1918†
Szigetvár	Pola Arsenal	2,300	1899–1900	1901–18†
Admiral Spaun	Pola Arsenal	3,500	1908–9	1910‡
Saida (II)	Monfalcone	3,500	1911–12	1914‡
Helgoland (II)	Danubius	3,500	1911–12	1914‡
Novara (II)	Danubius	3,500	1912–13	1915‡

§ *Radetzky* (I) sank in a powder explosion in February 1869; *Zenta* was sunk in August 1914; *Kaiserin Elisabeth* was scuttled in November 1914

† ships removed from the active list before the end of the war

‡ still on active list of warships as of 31 October 1918

SOURCES: Franz F. Bilzer, "Die Schiffe und Fahrzeuge der k.(u.)k. Kriegsmarine," *Marine— Gestern, Heute* 12 (1985), no. 2–15 (1988), no. 3 (continuing series in fourteen parts); René Greger, *Austro-Hungarian Warships of World War I; Jahresbericht der k.(u.)k. Kriegsmarine.*

AUSTRO-HUNGARIAN BATTLESHIPS

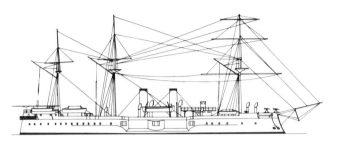

Tegetthoff
(original appearance)

7,550 tons displ.
commissioned 1882

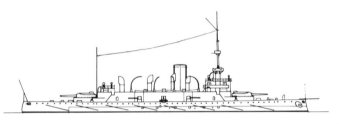

Monarch Wien Budapest

5,600 tons displ.
commissioned 1897–98

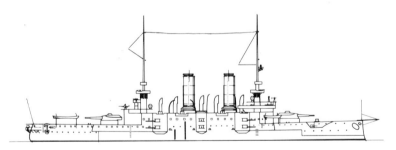

Habsburg Arpád Babenberg

8,300 tons displ.
commissioned 1902–4

Tegetthoff (1882) by Georg Pawlik; all other drawings by Erwin Sieche
Scale: 1:1450

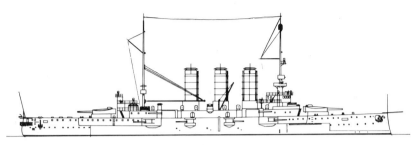

Erzherzog KARL
Erzherzog Friedrich
Erzherzog Ferdinand Max

10,600 tons displ.
commissioned 1906-7

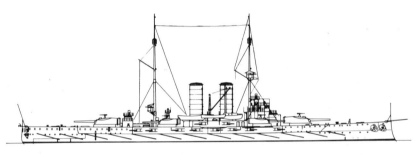

Radetzky
Erzherzog Franz Ferdinand
Zrinyi

14,500 tons displ.
commissioned 1910-11

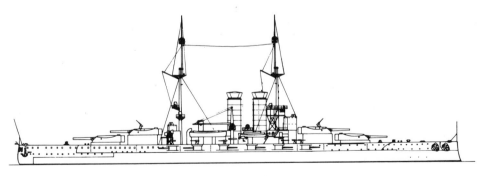

Viribus Unitis
Tegetthoff
Prinz Eugen
Szent István

20,000 tons displ.
commissioned 1912-15

THE AUSTRIAN NAVAL-INDUSTRIAL COMPLEX

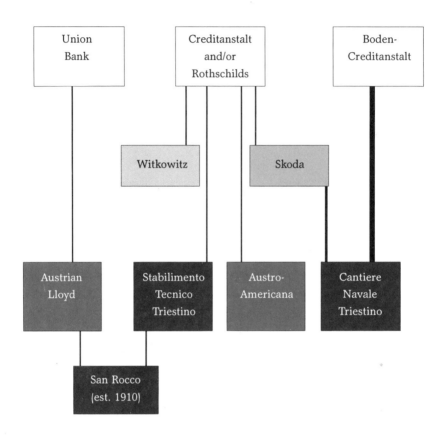

KEY

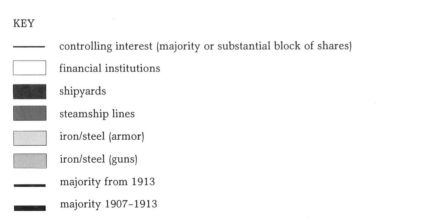

——— controlling interest (majority or substantial block of shares)

☐ financial institutions

■ shipyards

■ steamship lines

▨ iron/steel (armor)

▨ iron/steel (guns)

━ majority from 1913

▰ majority 1907–1913

BIBLIOGRAPHY

PUBLISHED DOCUMENTS

Österreichisches Staatsarchiv, Vienna

Finanzarchiv

Reichsfinanzministerium

Haus- Hof- und Staatsarchiv

Administrative Registratur

F 44 - Marinewesen

Politisches Archiv

I. Kaiserhaus

IX. Frankreich

XI. Italienische Staaten

XL. Interna

Kriegsarchiv

Kriegsministerium

Präsidialreihe

Marineakten

Technisches Archiv

Verwaltungsarchiv

Handel

PUBLISHED DOCUMENTS, LETTERS, AND MEMOIRS

Arz von Straussenberg, Arthur. *Zur Geschichte des grossen Krieges*. Vienna: Amalthea Verlag, 1924.

Auffenberg-Komarów, Moritz von. *Aus Österreichs Höhe und Niedergang*. Munich: Drei Masken Verlag, 1921.

Banfield, Gottfried von. *Der Adler von Triest*. Graz: Verlag Styria, 1984.

Bardolff, Carl von. *Soldat im alten Österreich: Erinnerungen aus meinem Leben*. Jena: Eugen Diederichs Verlag, 1939.

Beust, Friedrich Ferdinand von. *Memoirs of Friedrich Ferdinand Count von Beust*. Edited by Henry de Worms. 2 vols. London: Remington & Co., 1887.

Charles, Emperor of Austria, King of Hungary. *Kaiser Karl: Persönliche Aufzeichnungen, Zeugnisse und Dokumente*. Edited by Erich Feigl. Vienna: Amalthea Verlag, 1984.

Conrad von Hötzendorf, Franz. *Aus meiner Dienstzeit, 1906–1918*. 5 vols. Vienna: Rikola Verlag, 1921–25.

Czernin, Ottokar. *In the World War*. London: Cassell & Company, Ltd., 1919.

Eiselsberg, Anton von. *Lebensweg eines Chirurgen*. Innsbruck: Tyrolia-Verlag, 1949.

Faramond de Lafajole. *Souvenirs d'un attaché naval en Allemagne et en Autriche, 1910–1914*. Paris: Librairie Plon, 1932.

Francis Ferdinand, Archduke. *Tagebuch meiner Reise um die Erde, 1892–1893*. 2 vols. Vienna: Alfred Hölder, 1895–96.

Francis Joseph, Emperor of Austria, King of Hungary. *Briefe Kaiser Franz Josephs I. an seine Mutter, 1838–1872*. Edited by Franz Schnurer. Munich: Verlag Kosel & Pustet, 1930.

Horthy de Nagybánya, Miklós. *Memoirs*. London: Hutchinson, 1956.

Koudelka, Alfred von. *Denn Österreich lag einst am Meer: Das Leben des Admirals Alfred von Koudelka*. Edited by Lothar Baumgartner. Graz: H. Weishaupt Verlag, 1987.

Lauffer, Dora. *Die Wellen: Altösterreichische Familiensaga zwischen Adria und Schlesien*. Graz: Verlag Sterz, 1989.

Paschen, Karl. *Aus der Werdezeit zweier Marinen: Erinnerungen aus meiner Dienstzeit in der k.k. österreichischen und kaiserlich deutschen Marine*. Berlin: Ernst Siegfried Mittler & Sohn, 1908.

Payer, Julius. *Die österreichisch-ungarische Nordpol-Expedition in den Jahren 1872–1874*. Vienna: Alfred Hölder, 1876.

Pribram, Alfred Francis, ed. *The Secret Treaties of Austria-Hungary*. 2 vols. Cambridge, Mass.: Harvard University Press, 1920–21.

Sieghart, Rudolf. *Die letzten Jahrzehnte einer Grossmacht*. Berlin: Verlag Ullstein, 1932.

Stenographische Protokolle der Delegation des Reichsrathes. 50 vols. Vienna: k.k. Hof- und Staatsdruckerei, 1868–1918.

Sterneck zu Ehrenstein, Maximilian Daublebsky von. *Admiral Max Freiherr von Sterneck: Erinnerungen aus den Jahren 1847 bis 1897.* Edited by Jerolim Benko von Boinik. Vienna: A. Hartleben, 1901.

Tegetthoff, Wilhelm von. *Aus Wilhelm von Tegetthoff's Nachlass.* Edited by Adolf Beer. Vienna: Druck und Verlag von Carl Gerold's Sohn, 1882.

——. *Tegetthoffs Briefe an seine Freundin.* Edited by Heinz Steinrück. Vienna: Österreichischer Bundesverlag, 1926.

Trapp, Georg von. *Bis zum letzten Flaggenschuss: Erinnerungen eines österreichischen U-Boots-Kommandanten.* Salzburg: Verlag Anton Pustet, 1935.

Wölfling, Leopold [Archduke Leopold]. *My Life Story: From Archduke to Grocer.* New York: E. P. Dutton & Co., 1931.

Wulff, Olaf Richard. *Die österreichisch-ungarische Donauflottille im Weltkrieg 1914–1918.* Vienna: Wilhelm Braumüller Universitäts-Verlagsbuchhandlung, 1934.

CONTEMPORARY PERIODICALS, TRACTS, AND REFERENCE WORKS

Almanach für die k.u.k. Kriegsmarine. (Annual. Title varies.)

Chiari, Pietro. *L'Albania.* Palermo: Tipografia de Giornale di Sicilia, 1869.

Dorn, Alexander. *Kriegsmarine und Volkswirthschaft in Oesterreich-Ungarn.* Vienna: Alfred Hölder, 1885.

Die Flagge (Austrian Navy League).

Haymerle, Alois von. "Italicae Res." *Streffleurs Österreichische Militärische Zeitschrift* 20 (1879), parts 3/4: 1–144.

Jahrbuch der k.k. Kriegsmarine.

Jahresbericht der k.(u.)k. Kriegsmarine.

Kolonial-Zeitung (Austro-Hungarian Colonial Society).

Lehnert, Josef von. "Rückblick auf die Entwicklung der k.k. Flotte." *Organ der Militärwissenschaftlichen Vereine* 35 (1887): 223–36.

Lengnick, Arthur. "See-Interessen und See-Politik." *Organ der Militärwissenschaftlichen Vereine* 62 (1901): 301–37.

Libert de Paradis, Leonhard. *Das Seewesen in Oesterreich-Ungarn: Seine Wichtigkeit, Entwicklungsfähigkeit und Literatur.* Vienna: Verlag von L. Rosner, 1879.

Militär-Schematismus des österreichischen Kaiserthums. (Annual. Title varies.)

Militärstatistisches Jahrbuch.

Neue Freie Presse (Vienna).

Österreichisches Biographisches Lexikon.

Rangs- und Eintheilungsliste der k.(u.)k. Kriegsmarine. (Irregular. Title varies.)

Zvolensky, Alfred von. *Handbuch über die k.k. Kriegs-Marine.* Vienna: A. Hartleben, 1887.

MONOGRAPHS, ARTICLES, AND GENERAL WORKS

Aichelburg, Wladimir. *Die Handelsschiffe Österreich-Ungarns im Weltkrieg 1914– 1918.* Graz: H. Weishaupt, 1988.

———. *Die Unterseeboote Österreich-Ungarns.* 2 vols. Graz: Akademische Druck- und Verlagsanstalt, 1981.

Aichelburg, Wladimir; Lothar Baumgartner; et al. *Die "Tegetthoff"- Klasse: Österreich-Ungarns grösste Schlachtschiffe.* Munich: Bernard & Graefe Verlag, 1981.

Alden, John D. *The American Steel Navy.* Rev. ed. Annapolis, Md.: Naval Institute Press, 1989.

Anderson, David L. *Imperialism and Idealism: American Diplomats in China, 1861– 1898.* Bloomington: Indiana University Press, 1985.

Babudieri, Fulvio. *L'industria armatoriale di Trieste e della regione Giulia dal 1815 al 1918.* Rome: Archivio economico dell'Unificazione Italiana, 1964.

———. "L'industrializzazione nelle costruzioni navali nella regione Giulia." In *Cantiere: Tecnica, arte, lavoro ottant'anni di attività dello Stabilimento di Monfalcone,* edited by Valerio Staccioli, 24–33. Monfalcone: Edizioni della Laguna, 1988.

———. *Industrie, commerci e navigazione a Trieste e nella regione Giulia.* Milan: Dott. A. Giuffré editore, 1982.

———. *Squeri e cantiere a Trieste e nella regione Giulia dal settecento agli inizi del novecento.* Trieste: Edizioni Lint, 1986.

Bachinger, Karl. "Das Verkehrswesen." *Die Habsburgermonarchie 1848–1918,* vol. 1: *Die wirtschaftliche Entwicklung,* edited by Alois Brusatti, 278–322. Vienna: Verlag der Österreichischen Akademie der Wissenschaften, 1973.

Ballard, G. A. *The Black Battlefleet.* Edited by G. A. Osborn and N. A. M. Rodger. Annapolis, Md.: Naval Institute Press, 1980.

Baratelli, Franco Micali. *La marina militare italiana nella vita nazionale (1860–1914).* Mursia: U. Mursia editore, 1983.

Bargoni, Franco. *Corazzate italiane classi Duilio - Italia - Ruggiero di Lauria (1880– 1892).* Rome: Edizioni dell'Ateneo & Bizzarri, 1977.

———. *Corazzate italiane classi Re Umberto - Ammiraglio di Saint Bon (1893–1901).* Rome: Edizioni dell'Ateneo & Bizzarri, 1978.

———. *Le prime navi di linea della marina italiana (1861–1880).* Rome: Edizioni Bizzarri, 1976.

Baumgartner, Lothar; Franz F. Bilzer; et al. "Die Austro-Americana: Geschichte einer österreichischen Reederei." *Marine—Gestern, Heute* 8 (1981): 45–55.

Bayer von Bayersburg, Heinrich. *Die k.u.k. Kriegsmarine auf weiter Fahrt.* Vienna: Bergland Verlag, 1958.

———. *Österreichs Admirale 1867–1918.* Vienna: Bergland Verlag, 1962.

———. *Unter der k.u.k. Kriegsflagge.* Vienna: Bergland Verlag, 1959.

Beer, Adolf. *Die Finanzen Oesterreichs.* 1877. Reprint. Vienna: H. Geyer, 1973.

Benko von Boinik, Jerolim. *Geschichte der k.(u.)k. Kriegsmarine,* part 3, vol. 1: *Geschichte der k.k. Kriegsmarine während der Jahre 1848 und 1849.* Vienna: Verlag des k.u.k. Reichskriegsministeriums, Marinesektion, 1884.

Bilzer, Franz F. "Die Schiffe und Fahrzeuge der k.(u.)k. Kriegsmarine." Continuing series in fourteen parts. *Marine—Gestern, Heute* 12, no. 2 (1985)–15, no. 3 (1988).

Blumberg, Arnold. *The Diplomacy of the Mexican Empire, 1863–1867.* 1971. Reprint. Malabar, Fla.: Robert E. Krieger Publishing Co., 1987.

Bosworth, R. J. B. *Italy, the Least of the Great Powers.* Cambridge: Cambridge University Press, 1979.

Bridge, F. R. *From Sadowa to Sarajevo: The Foreign Policy of Austria-Hungary, 1866–1914.* London: Allen & Unwin, 1972.

———. *The Habsburg Monarchy among the Great Powers, 1815–1918.* New York: Berg Publishers, 1990.

Brousek, Karl M. *Die Grossindustrie Böhmens 1848–1918.* Munich: R. Oldenbourg Verlag, 1987.

Bueb, Volkmar. *Die "Junge Schule" der französischen Marine: Strategie und Politik 1875–1900.* Boppard am Rhein: Harald Boldt Verlag, 1971.

Casali, Antonio, and Marina Cattaruzza. *Sotto i mari del mondo: La Whitehead, 1875–1990.* Rome: Editori Laterza, 1990.

Cattaruzza, Marina. "I conflitti nazionali a Trieste nell'ambito della questione nazionale nell'Impero Asburgico, 1850–1914." *Quaderni giuliani di storia* 1 (1989): 131–48.

———. *La formazione del proletariato urbano: Immigrati, operai di mestiere, donne a Trieste dalla metà del secolo XIX alla prima guerra mondiale.* Turin: Tommaso Musolini editore, 1979.

———. "'Organizierter Konflikt' und 'Direkte Aktion': Zwei Formen des Arbeiterkampfes am Beispiel der Werftarbeiterstreiks in Hamburg und Triest (1880–1914)." *Archiv für Sozialgeschichte* 20 (1980): 325–55.

———. "Sloveni e Italiani a Trieste: La formazione dell'identità nazionale." *Clio* 25 (1989): 27–58.

Ceva, Lucio. *Le forze armate.* Turin: U.T.E.T., 1981.

Chlumecky, Leopold von. *Erzherzog Franz Ferdinands Wirken und Wollen.* Berlin: Verlag für Kulturpolitik, 1929.

Cooling, B. Franklin. *Gray Steel and Blue Water Navy: The Formative Years of America's Military-Industrial Complex, 1881–1917.* Hamden, Conn.: Archon Books, 1979.

Cupez, Leopoldo. *Cenni sullo sviluppo dei Cantieri Riuniti dell'Adriatico, 1825–1952.* Trieste: Cantieri Riuniti dell'Adriatico, 1953.

Deák, István. *Beyond Nationalism: A Social and Political History of the Habsburg Officer Corps, 1848–1918.* New York: Oxford University Press, 1990.

Despot, Miroslava. *Industrija Gradanske Hrvatske, 1860–1873.* Zagreb: Institut za historiju, 1970.

Doppelbauer, Wolfgang. *Zum Elend noch die Schande: Das altösterreichische Offizierskorps am Beginn der Republik.* Vienna: Österreichischer Bundesverlag, 1988.

Fleischer, Josef. *Geschichte der k.u.k. Kriegsmarine,* part III, vol. 3: *Geschichte der k.k. Kriegsmarine während des Krieges im Jahre 1866.* Vienna: Verlag des k.u.k. Reichskriegsministeriums, Marinesektion, 1906.

Franz, Georg. *Erzherzog Franz Ferdinand und die Pläne der Habsburger Monarchie.* Brünn: Rudolf M. Rohrer, 1943.

Fünfundsiebzig Jahre österreichischer Lloyd. Trieste: Verlag des österreichischen Lloyd, 1911.

Gabriele, Mariano. *La politica navale italiana dall'unita alla viglia di Lissa.* Milan: A. Giuffré editore, 1958.

Gebhard, Louis A., Jr. "Austria-Hungary's Dreadnought Squadron: The Naval Outlay of 1911." *Austrian History Yearbook* 4–5 (1968-69): 245–58.

———. "The Croatians, the Habsburg Monarchy and the Austro-Hungarian Navy." *Journal of Croatian Studies* 11–12 (1970–71): 152–59.

———. "The Development of the Austro-Hungarian Navy, 1897–1914: A Study in the Operation of Dualism." Ph.D. diss., Rutgers University, 1965.

Geehr, Richard S. *Karl Lueger: Mayor of Fin de Siècle Vienna.* Detroit, Mich.: Wayne State University Press, 1990.

Gellner, Ernesto, and Paolo Valentini. *San Rocco: Storia di un cantiere navale.* Trieste: Associazione Marinara Aldebaran, 1990.

Gerolimi, Giovanni. *L'Arsenale Triestino, 1853–1953.* Trieste: La editoriale libraria S.p.A., 1953.

———. *Cantiere Riuniti dell'Adriatico: Origini e sviluppo 1857–1907–1957.* Trieste: Cantiere Riuniti dell'Adriatico, 1957.

Giorgerini, Giorgio. *Almanacco storico delle navi militare italiane: La Marina e le sue navi dal 1861 al 1975.* Rome: Ufficio Storico Marina Militare, 1978.

Glaise-Horstenau, Edmund von. *Franz Josephs Weggefährte: Das Leben des Generalstabschefs Grafen Beck.* Vienna: Amalthea Verlag, 1930.

Good, David F. *The Economic Rise of the Habsburg Empire, 1750–1914.* Berkeley and Los Angeles: University of California Press, 1984.

———. "Economic Union and Uneven Development in the Habsburg Monarchy." *Economic Development in the Habsburg Monarchy in the Nineteenth Century,* edited by John Komlos, 65–80. Boulder, Colo.: East European Monographs, 1983.

Greger, René. *Austro-Hungarian Warships of World War I*. London: Ian Allan, Ltd., 1976.

Gröner, Erich. *Die deutschen Kriegsschiffe 1815–1945*. 8 vols. Coblenz: Bernard & Graefe Verlag, 1989.

Halperin, S. William. *Italy and the Vatican at War: A Study of Their Relations from the Outbreak of the Franco-Prussian War to the Death of Pius IX*. 1939. Reprint. New York: Greenwood Press, 1968.

Halpern, Paul G. "The Anglo-French-Italian Naval Convention of 1915." *The Historical Journal* 13 (1970): 106–29.

———. *The Mediterranean Naval Situation, 1908–1914*. Cambridge, Mass.: Harvard University Press, 1971.

———. *The Naval War in the Mediterranean, 1914–1918*. Annapolis, Md.: Naval Institute Press, 1987.

Hamann, Günther. "Die österreichische Kriegsmarine im Dienste der Wissenschaften." *Schriften des Heeresgeschichtlichen Museums (Militärwissenschaftliches Institut) in Wien*, vol. 8: *Österreich zur See*, 59–90. Vienna: Österreichischer Bundesverlag, 1980.

Handel-Mazzetti, Peter, and Hans Hugo Sokol. *Wilhelm von Tegetthoff: Ein grosser Österreicher*. Linz: Oberösterreichischer Landesverlag, 1952.

Harbauer, Karl. *Der Kaiser und die Kriegsmarine*. Vienna: Verlag des Österreichischen Flottenvereines, 1910.

Hazlett, E. E., Jr. "The Austro-American Navy." *U.S. Naval Institute Proceedings* 66 (1940): 1757–68.

Henderson, W. O. *The Rise of German Industrial Power, 1834–1914*. Berkeley and Los Angeles: University of California Press, 1975.

Herwig, Holger. "Disjointed Allies: Coalition Warfare in Berlin and Vienna, 1914." *The Journal of Military History* 54 (1990): 265–80.

———. *"Luxury" Fleet: The Imperial German Navy, 1888–1918*. Rev. ed. Atlantic Highlands, N.J.: The Ashfield Press, 1987.

Höbelt, Lothar. "Die Linke und die Wahlen von 1891." *Mitteilungen des österreichischen Staatsarchivs* 40 (1987): 270–301.

———. "Die Marine." *Die Habsburgermonarchie 1848–1918*, vol. 5: *Die bewaffnete Macht*, edited by Adam Wandruszka and Peter Urbanitsch, 687–763. Vienna: Verlag der Österreichischen Akademie der Wissenschaften, 1987.

———. "Von der Jeune Ecole zur Flottenpolitik: Die Rolle der österreichisch-ungarischen Kriegsmarine im letzten Viertel des neunzehnten Jahrhunderts." *Etudes danubiennes* 4 (1988): 147–56.

Hoensch, Jörg K. *A History of Modern Hungary, 1867–1986*. London: Longman, 1988.

Iachino, Angelo. *La campagna navale di Lissa 1866*. Milan: Casa editrice Il Saggiatore, 1966.

Jahn, Friedrich, and Erwin Sieche. "Der Handstreich auf Ancona am 4. und 5. April 1918." *Marine—Gestern, Heute* 15 (1988): 95–109, 141–47.

Jelavich, Barbara. *The Habsburg Empire in European Affairs, 1814–1918.* Chicago: Rand McNally, 1969.

Jonás, Paul. "Lajos Kossuth's Maritime Policies." *Southeast European Maritime Commerce and Naval Policies from the Mid-Eighteenth Century to 1914,* edited by Apostolos E. Vacalopoulos, Constantinos D. Svolopoulos, and Béla K. Király, 197–211. Boulder, Colo.: Social Science Monographs, 1988.

Kačić-Dimitri, Jerko. "Das Ende der königlich jugoslawischen Flotte." *Marine—Gestern, Heute* 15 (1988): 4–11.

Karaman, Igor. "Die Industrialisierung des bürgerlichen Kroatiens und ihre wirtschaftliche Infrastruktur bis zum Ersten Weltkrieg." *Festschrift Othmar Pickl zum 60. Geburtstag,* edited by Herwig Ebner et al., 249–55. Graz: Leykam Verlag, 1985.

Kemp, Paul J. "Grossbritannien und die Aufteilung der k.u.k. Flotte 1918–1923." *Marine—Gestern, Heute* 12 (1985): 41–54, 81–99.

Kennan, George F. *The Fateful Alliance: France, Russia, and the Coming of the First World War.* New York: Pantheon Books, 1984.

Kestranek, Wilhelm. *Die Eisenindustrie der österreichisch-ungarische Monarchie.* Vienna: by the author, 1911.

Kiszling, Rudolf. *Erzherzog Franz Ferdinand von Österreich-Este: Leben, Pläne und Wirken am Schicksalweg der Donaumonarchie.* Graz: Hermann Böhlaus Nachfolger, 1953.

Kolmer, Gustav. *Parlament und Verfassung in Österreich.* 8 vols. Vienna: Carl Fromme, 1902–14.

Krenslehner, Erich. "Die k.u.k. Kriegsmarine als wirtschaftlicher Faktor, 1874–1914." Ph.D. diss., University of Vienna, 1962.

La lotta dei fuochisti: 1902–1982. Friuli: C.G.I.L., 1982.

Lambi, Ivo. *The Navy and German Power Politics, 1862–1914.* Boston: Allen & Unwin, 1984.

Lo Giudice, Giuseppe. *Trieste, L'Austria ed il Canale di Suez.* Catania: Università degli studi, 1979.

Lowe, Cedric J. *The Reluctant Imperialists: British Foreign Policy, 1878–1902.* 2 vols. London: Routledge & Kegan Paul, 1967.

———. *Salisbury and the Mediterranean, 1886–1896.* Toronto: University of Toronto Press, 1965.

Lowe, Cedric J., and Frank Marzari. *Italian Foreign Policy, 1870–1940.* London: Routledge & Kegan Paul, 1975.

Lukas, Karl von. "Der Durchbruch der *Helgoland* am 29.12.1915." *Marine—Gestern, Heute* 13 (1986): 63–78.

Marder, Arthur J. *The Anatomy of British Sea Power: A History of British Naval Policy in the Pre-Dreadnought Era, 1880–1905.* New York: Alfred A. Knopf, 1940.

Marraro, Howard R. "Unpublished American Documents on the Naval Battle of Lissa." *Journal of Modern History* 14 (1942): 342–56.

März, Eduard. "The Austrian Credit Mobilier in a Time of Transition." *Economic Development in the Habsburg Monarchy in the Nineteenth Century,* edited by John Komlos, 117–35. Boulder, Colo.: East European Monographs, 1983.

May, Arthur J. *The Passing of the Hapsburg Monarchy, 1914–1918.* 2 vols. Philadelphia: University of Pennsylvania Press, 1966.

Mayer, Horst F. "Die k.u.k. Kriegsmarine 1912–1914 unter dem Kommando von Admiral Anton Haus." Ph.D. diss., University of Vienna, 1962.

Mayer, Horst F., and Dieter Winkler. *Als die Adria österreichisch war: Österreich-Ungarns Seemacht.* Vienna: Edition S, 1987.

———. *In allen Häfen war Österreich: Die österreichisch-ungarische Handelsmarine.* Vienna: Edition S, 1987.

Mentschl, Josef, and Gustav Otruba. *Österreichische Industrielle und Bankiers.* Vienna: Bergland Verlag, 1965.

Mohl, Karl. "Der Untergang der *Szent István* am 10. Juni 1918." *Marine—Gestern, Heute* 15 (1988): 148–53.

Muret, Maurice. *L'archiduc François-Ferdinand.* Paris: Editions Bernard Grasset, 1932.

Novak, Grga. "Narodni preporod u Dalmaciji." *Hrvatski narodni preporod u Dalmaciji i Istri,* edited by Jakša Ravlić, 77–85. Zagreb: Matica Hrvatska, 1969.

Paulinyi, Akos. "Die sogenannte gemeinsame Wirtschaftspolitik Österreich-Ungarns." *Die Habsburgermonarchie 1848–1918,* vol. 1: *Die wirtschaftliche Entwicklung,* edited by Alois Brusatti, 567–604. Vienna: Verlag der Österreichischen Akademie der Wissenschaften, 1973.

Piedmontese, Giuseppe. *Il movimento operaio a Trieste: Dalle origini alla fine della prima guerra mondiale.* Udine: Del Bianco editore, 1961.

Plaschka, Richard Georg. *Cattaro - Prag: Revolte und Revolution.* Graz: Verlag Hermann Böhlaus Nachfolger, 1963.

———. *Matrosen, Offiziere, Rebellen: Krisenkonfrontationen zur See 1900–1918.* 2 vols. Vienna: Verlag Hermann Bohlaus Nachfolger, 1984.

———. "Von Pola nach Taku: Der Druck der Mächte auf China 1900 und Österreich-Ungarns Beteiligung an der maritimen Intervention." *Schriften des Heeresgeschichtlichen Museums (Militärwissenschaftliches Institut) in Wien,* vol. 8: *Österreich zur See,* 43–57. Vienna: Österreichischer Bundesverlag, 1980.

Plaschka, Richard Georg; Horst Haselsteiner; and Arnold Suppan. *Innere Front: Militärassistenz, Widerstand und Umsturz in der Donaumonarchie 1918.* 2 vols. Munich: R. Oldenbourg, 1974.

Ploček, Heinz, and Franz Juba. "Geschichte der ungarischen Reederei Adria." *Marine—Gestern, Heute* 13 (1986): 17–27.

Polzer-Hoditz, Arthur. *Kaiser Karl: Aus der Geheimmappe seines Kabinettchefs.* Vienna: Amalthea Verlag, 1929.

Pregel, Georg. "Die ersten schwierigen Aufbaujahre der SHS-Marine." *Marine—Gestern, Heute* 14 (1987): 41–50.

Preradovich, Nikolaus von. "Österreicher als Ritterkreuzträger." *Feldgrau* 9 (1961): 61.

Randich, Gilbert von. "Die Besichtigung Polas im Mai 1898 durch Erzherzog Franz Ferdinand von Österreich-Este." *Marine—Gestern, Heute* 15 (1988): 89–94.

———. "Johann Edler von Hinke: Ein k.(u.)k. Admiral." *Marine—Gestern, Heute* 13 (1986): 132–34.

Ranzenhofer, Alexander. *Mit der Kriegsmarine kreuz und quer im Mittelmeer: Eine Mittelmeerreise mit S.M. Schiffen "Monarch," "Wien," und "Budapest" im Frühjahr 1901.* Reichenberg: Verlag Paul Sollors Nachfolger, 1913.

Rauchensteiner, Manfred. "Austro-Hungarian Warships on the Danube: From the Beginning of the Nineteenth Century to World War I." *Southeast European Maritime Commerce and Naval Policies from the Mid-Eighteenth Century to 1914,* edited by Apostolos E. Vacalopoulos, Constantinos D. Svolopoulos, and Béla K. Király, 153–73. Boulder, Colo.: Social Science Monographs, 1988.

Reiter, Leo. "Die Entwicklung der k.u.k. Flotte und die Delegationen des Reichsrates." Ph.D. diss., University of Vienna, 1949.

Ropp, Theodore. *The Development of a Modern Navy: French Naval Policy, 1871–1904.* Edited by Stephen Roberts. Annapolis, Md.: Naval Institute Press, 1987.

Rothenberg, Gunther E. *The Army of Francis Joseph.* West Lafayette, Ind.: Purdue University Press, 1976.

———. "The Austro-Hungarian Campaign Against Serbia in 1914." *The Journal of Military History* 53 (1989): 127–46.

Rudolph, Richard L. "Quantitative Aspekte der Industrialisierung in Cisleithanien 1848-1914." *Die Habsburgermonarchie 1848–1918,* vol. 1: *Die wirtschaftliche Entwicklung,* edited by Alois Brusatti, 233–49. Vienna: Verlag der Österreichischen Akademie der Wissenschaften, 1973.

Salcher, Peter. *Geschichte der k.u.k. Marine-Akademie.* Pola: Carl Gerold's Sohn, 1902.

Sandauer, Christian. "Konteradmiral Bogumil Nowotny, der Begründer der polnischen Kriegsmarine." *Marine—Gestern, Heute* 11 (1984): 16–19.

Schmidl, Erwin A. *Jews in the Habsburg Armed Forces, 1788–1918.* Eisenstadt: Österreichisches Jüdisches Museum, 1989.

Schmidt-Pauli, Edgar von. *Nikolaus von Horthy: Admiral, Volksheld und Reichsverweser.* Hamburg: I. P. Toth-Verlag, 1942.

Schöndorfer, Ulrich. "Der österreichische Kriegsschiffbau von 1848 bis 1914." *Schriften des Heeresgeschichtlichen Museums (Militärwissenschaftliches Institut) in Wien,* vol. 8: *Österreich zur See,* 23–42. Vienna: Österreichischer Bundesverlag, 1980.

Schupita, Peter. *Die k.u.k. Seeflieger: Chronik und Dokumentation der österreichisch-ungarischen Marineluftwaffe 1911–1918.* Coblenz: Bernard & Graefe Verlag, 1983.

Sema, Paolo. *Il Cantiere San Rocco: Lavoro e lotta operaia, 1858–1982.* Trieste: Istituto regionale di studi e documentazione sul movimento sindacale e sui problemi economici e sociali di Trieste e del Friuli-Venezia Giulia, 1989.

Seton-Watson, Christopher. *Italy: From Liberalism to Fascism, 1870–1925.* London: Methuen, 1967.

Seton-Watson, R. W. *Sarajevo: A Study in the Origins of the Great War.* London: Hutchinson & Co., Ltd., 1925.

Shanafelt, Gary W. *The Secret Enemy: Austria-Hungary and the German Alliance, 1914–1918.* Boulder, Colo.: East European Monographs, 1985.

Sieche, Erwin. "Die diplomatischen Aktivitäten rund um das Haus-Memorandum vom März 1915." *Marine—Gestern, Heute* 9 (1982): 93–103.

———. "Der Untergang des Torpedofahrzeuges *Wildfang* am 4.6.1917." *Marine—Gestern, Heute* 11 (1984): 52–63.

———. "Zeittafel der Vorgänge rund um die Auflösung und Übergabe der k.u.k. Kriegsmarine 1918-1923." *Marine—Gestern, Heute* 12 (1985): 129–41.

Silberstein, Gerard E. *The Troubled Alliance: German-Austrian Relations, 1914 to 1917.* Lexington: University Press of Kentucky, 1970.

Smith, Leonard V. "The Disciplinary Dilemma of French Military Justice, September 1914–April 1917: The Case of the 5e Division d'Infanterie." *The Journal of Military History* 55 (1991): 47–68.

Sokol, Anthony. *The Imperial and Royal Austro-Hungarian Navy.* Annapolis, Md.: Naval Institute Press, 1968.

Sokol, Hans Hugo. *Des Kaisers Seemacht: Die k.k. österreichische Kriegsmarine 1848 bis 1914.* Vienna: Amalthea Verlag, 1980.

———. *Österreich-Ungarns Seekrieg, 1914–1918.* 2 vols. 1933. Reprint. Graz: Akademische Druck- und Verlagsanstalt, 1967.

Sondhaus, Lawrence. "The Austro-Hungarian Naval Officer Corps, 1867–1918." *Austrian History Yearbook* 24 (1993): 51–78.

———. "Austria-Hungary's Italian Policy under Count Beust, 1866–1871." *The Historian* 56 (1993–94): 41–54.

——. "Croatians in the Habsburg Navy, 1797–1918." *East European Quarterly* 26 (1992): 149–61.

——. *The Habsburg Empire and the Sea: Austrian Naval Policy, 1797–1866.* West Lafayette, Ind.: Purdue University Press, 1989.

——. *In the Service of the Emperor: Italians in the Austrian Armed Forces, 1814–1918.* Boulder, Colo.: East European Monographs, 1990.

——. "Die österreichische Kriegsmarine und der amerikanische Sezessionskrieg 1861–1865." *Marine—Gestern, Heute* 14 (1987): 81–84.

——. "Strategy, Tactics, and the Politics of Penury: The Austro-Hungarian Navy and the *Jeune Ecole.*" *The Journal of Military History* 56 (1992): 587–602.

Sosnosky, Theodor von. *Die Balkanpolitik Österreich-Ungarns seit 1866.* 2 vols. Stuttgart: Deutsche Verlags-Anstalt, 1913.

——. *Franz Ferdinand: Der Erzherzog-Thronfolger.* Munich: Verlag von R. Oldenbourg, 1929.

Staudinger, Eduard G., and Siegfried Beer. "Die Aussenwirtschaftlichen Beziehungen zu Grossbritannien." *Die Habsburgermonarchie 1848–1918,* vol. 6/1: *Die Habsburgermonarchie im System der internationalen Beziehungen,* edited by Adam Wandruszka and Peter Urbanitsch, 711–39. Vienna: Verlag der Österreichischen Akademie der Wissenschaften, 1989.

Steinberg, Jonathan. *Yesterday's Deterrent: Tirpitz and the Birth of the German Battle Fleet.* New York: Macmillan, 1965.

Steinböck, Erwin. "Die Nachkriegsschicksale der österreichisch-ungarischen Patrouillenboote." *Marine—Gestern, Heute* 8 (1981): 60–65.

Sullivan, Brian R. "A Fleet in Being: The Rise and Fall of Italian Sea Power, 1861–1943." *The International History Review* 10 (1988): 106–24.

Sumida, Jon Tetsuro. "British Capital Ship Design and Fire Control in the *Dreadnought* Era: Sir John Fisher, Arthur Hungerford Pollen, and the Battle Cruiser." *Journal of Modern History* 51 (1979): 205–30.

Taylor, A. J. P. *The Habsburg Monarchy, 1809–1918.* Chicago: University of Chicago Press, 1948.

Thomazi, Adrien. *La guerre navale dans l'Adriatique.* Paris: Payot, 1925.

Tomicich, Edgar. "Die k.(u.)k. Marineakademie." *Marine—Gestern, Heute* 11 (1984): 37–43.

Ufficio Storico della R. Marina. *La marina italiana nella grande guerra.* 8 vols. Florence: Vallecchi editore, 1935–42.

Vego, Milan N. "The Anatomy of Austrian Sea Power, 1904–1914." Ph.D. diss., George Washington University, 1981.

Wagner, Walter. "Die k.(u.)k. Armee: Gliederung und Aufgabenstellung." *Die Habsburgermonarchie 1848–1918,* vol. 5: *Die bewaffnete Macht,* edited by Adam Wandruszka and Peter Urbanitsch, 142–633. Vienna: Verlag der Österreichischen Akademie der Wissenschaften, 1987.

————. "Die obersten Behörden der k.u.k. Kriegsmarine 1856–1918." *Mitteilungen des österreichischen Staatsarchivs*, Ergänzungsband 6 (1961).

Wallisch, Friedrich. *Sein Schiff Hiess Novara: Bernhard von Wüllerstorf, Admiral und Minister.* Vienna: Verlag Herold, 1966.

Weber, Fritz. "Die wirtschaftliche Entwicklung Cisleithaniens vor dem Ersten Weltkrieg." *Arbeiterbewegung in Österreich und Ungarn bis 1914*, edited by Wolfgang Maderthaner, 91–123. Vienna: Europaverlag, 1986.

Whiteside, Andrew G. *The Socialism of Fools: Georg Ritter von Schönerer and Austrian Pan-Germanism.* Berkeley and Los Angeles: University of California Press, 1975.

Whittam, John. *The Politics of the Italian Army, 1861–1918.* London: Croom Helm, 1977.

Williamson, Samuel R., Jr. *Austria-Hungary and the Origins of the First World War.* London: Macmillan, 1991.

————. "Influence, Power, and the Policy Process: The Case of Franz Ferdinand, 1906–1914." *The Historical Journal* 17 (1974): 417–34.

————. *The Politics of Grand Strategy: Britain and France Prepare for War, 1904–1914.* Cambridge, Mass.: Harvard University Press, 1969.

Winkler, Dieter. "Admiral Leodegar Kneissler von Maixdorf." *Marine—Gestern, Heute* 9 (1982): 1–2.

Winkler, Dieter, and Georg Pawlik. *Die Dampfschiffahrtsgesellschaft Österreichischer Lloyd 1836–1918.* Graz: H. Weishaupt Verlag, 1986.

Winterhalder, Theodor. *Die österreichisch-ungarische Kriegsmarine im Weltkriege.* Munich: J. F. Lehmanns Verlag, 1921.

INDEX

Unless otherwise indicated, all institutions, titles, and ranks are Austro-Hungarian. Individual ranks reflect the highest levels reached by 1918.

demonstration by, at Naples (1870), 15, 31n. 38, 31n. 39; and occupation of Bosnia (1878), 64–65; demonstration by, at Dulcigno (1880), 65; and Cattaro rebellion (1881–82), 65–66; in demonstration off Greece (1886), 105–6; at Barcelona review (1888), 107–8; in demonstration off Crete (1897–98), 132; during Boxer Rebellion (1900), 140; and annexation of Bosnia (1908), 182–83; during Italo-Turkish War (1911–12), 205; during Balkan Wars (1912–13), 206–7, 226–27, 252n. 23; visits by, to Germany, 110, 131; visits by, to Britain, 110, 142, 204; visits by, to Malta, 108, 158, 244; summer maneuvers of, 82–83, 157–58, 172–73, 198; winter cruises of, 82, 158–59, 172–73; overseas missions of, 23–24, 40–41, 61, 83–84, 137–42, 184–86; importance of, to domestic industry, 8, 91–92, 126, 128, 145–46; importance of, to overseas commerce, 8, 58, 128, 145–46, 148; Italian view of, 14, 15–16, 108, 157, 183; German appraisals of, 110; ethnicity of sailors in, 82, 134; reenlistment rate of seamen in, 82, 134; desertions in, 134; war plans of, against Russia, 68, 109; war plans of, against France, 109–10; respects Austro-Hungarian quota in budgets, 152, 155, 159, 168n. 121, 175, 181, 196–97; dreadnought program of, 191–204, 227–29. See also Fleet plans; Officer corps; warships; names of individual officers, etc.

Austro-Hungarian navy (1914–18): strength of, in 1914, 257–58; during period of Italian neutrality, 249, 258–70; fleet sortie of 23–24 May

1915, 274–76; subsequent operations of, 277–84; battle of 29–30 December 1915, 284–85; strength of, in 1917, 303–4; Battle of Otranto Straits (15 May 1917), 305–7; mutiny of, in Cattaro (February 1918), 318–25; under Horthy, 329–41; Danube flotilla of, 246, 263–64, 283, 288–89, 314–15, 327, 340, 355; Black Sea flotilla of, 331–32, 336, 340; land-based units of, with army, 277, 313, 339; press office of, 309; intelligence service of, 277, 304–5; Adriatic convoys of, 329; submarines and submarine operations, 264–69, 277–82, 287–89, 303–8, 311, 332, 338, 340; collapse of, 349–56; total wartime casualties of, 364. See also Warships; names of individual officers, etc.

Bachmann, Gustav, German admiral, 268
Badeni, Casimir, Austrian minister-president, 133, 150
Baillet de Latour, Count Vinzenz, 209
Balearic Islands, 240
Balkans. See Albania; Bulgaria; Greece; Montenegro; Ottoman Empire; Serbia
Balkan Wars (1912–13), 206–7, 226–27, 234, 239
Ballin, Albert, 186
Baltic Sea, 109–10, 114, 141, 156
Bánffy, Deszö, Hungarian minister-president, 130
Banfield, Gottfried, Lieutenant, 291, 374
Bardolff, Carl von, Colonel, 166n. 64, 220, 227–28, 235, 256
Bari, 285
Barletta, 275

relations of, with Austria-Hungary,
102, 106-9, 112-13, 129-30, 159,
193, 197, 244; and Mediterranean
Agreements (1887), 106-13, 127-28;
relations of, with France, 106, 162,
235; relations of, with Russia, 106,
129; relations of, with Italy, 107,
127-28, 206; relations of, with Germany, 129; alliance of, with Japan,
262-63; in First World War, 247,
248, 250, 272-73, 283, 339; and
liquidation of Austro-Hungarian fleet,
360. *See also* British navy
British navy: peacetime operations of,
in Mediterranean, 105-7, 112, 121n.
106, 127, 132, 158-59, 235; Mediterranean strategies of, 164n. 17, 234,
253n. 44, 270; in First World War,
248-51, 259, 277-78, 288-92, 306-8,
311-13, 338, 340
Brničević, Mate, Cattaro mutineer, 324
Brosch, Gustav von, Rear Admiral, 388
Brosch von Aarenau, Alexander,
Colonel, 176-77, 188, 205, 220
Brown, John, British armor manufacturer, 45, 47
Brown & Lenox, British firm, 47
Buccari (Bakar), 314, 358
Bucharest, Treaty of (1913), 227
Buchta, Heinrich von, Rear Admiral,
387
Budapest: monitors constructed in, 43,
152, 215n. 108, 315; rail connection
of, to Rijeka, 61
Budget. *See* Delegations
Bülow, Bernhard von, German
chancellor, 151
Bug River, 332
Bulgaria, 64, 88, 105, 109, 184, 206,
227; in First World War, 250, 264,
283-84, 339-40

Bund österreichischer Industrieller,
146
Burián, Count István, foreign minister,
267, 272, 286-87, 293, 333, 339, 350
Bylandt-Rheidt, Count Artur, *Feldzeugmeister,* war minister, 55, 57-58, 93

Cadorna, Luigi, Italian general, 271,
277, 280, 282, 312
Cammell, Charles, armor manufac-
turer, 45, 47
Campomarino, 275
Canevaro, Felice, Italian admiral, 132
Cantiere Navale Adriatico, 3, 22, 25,
48, 72n. 46, 92. *See also* Tonello,
Giuseppe
Cantiere Navale Triestino: founded,
189, 396; builds warships in Monfal-
cone, 199, 229; shipyard overrun in
war, 269; builds submarines in Pola
Arsenal, 287-88, 303-4; postwar fate
of, 361-62, 383
Caporetto, Battle of (1917), 312-14
Caprivi, Leo von, German general and
chancellor, 111, 112
Cartel, iron and steel, 92, 159, 203
Cassini, Count Oscare, Rear Admiral,
135, 387
Castellammare, 183, 382
Cattaro (Kotor): rebellion of 1869-70,
13; rebellion of 1881-82, 65-66;
strategic value of, 128; prewar reinforcement of, 205, 246; during First
World War, 258-60, 262-65, 267,
268, 271, 277, 279-80, 283, 285-86,
288-89, 294-95, 298n. 66, 302-3,
305-7, 315, 329-30, 335-36, 350;
mutiny in, 318-25, 348; transfer of
power in (1918), 354-55; as Yugoslav
navy base, 360

203, 219, 228, 231-32, 269, 315, 361-62, 396; during First World War, 258, 263, 270-71, 274, 277, 279-81, 295, 308, 313, 330, 339, 349; wartime unrest in, 317; transfer of power in (1918), 354, 358
Triple Alliance: conclusion of (1882), 66-67; renewed (1887), 106-7; — (1891), 111; — (1902), 156; — (1912), 210; impact of, on navy budget, 77, 102, 105; impact of, on naval operations and strategy, 103-13; naval convention (1900), 156, 210, 236; naval convention (1913), 233-44, 246-47; collapse of, 247, 274
Triple Entente, 207, 234, 239-40
Tripoli, 107. See also Libya
Tsushima, Battle of (1905), 162, 169n. 131
Tunis and Tunisia, 14, 66-67, 111, 131, 157, 268, 286
Turkey. See Ottoman Empire
Tyrol, 15, 241, 339; Home Guard (Standschützen), 277. See also South Tyrol
Tyrrhenian Sea, 235, 237-39

Ukraine, 314, 331, 340
Umberto, King of Italy, 66, 112, 156
Ungarische Unterseebootsbau A.G. (UBAG), 287-88, 303
Ungaro-Croata, steamship company, 188, 362
Union Bank, 361, 396
Unione Metallurgica, labor union, 198, 215n. 104
United States: Tegetthoff's visit to, 9, 10; cruises to, 41, 61, 83, 138, 141, 185; and China, 140-41; merchant

marine of, 188; coal imported from, 159, 197, 261; interns Austro-Hungarian merchant ships, 263; protests submarine warfare, 286-87; enters First World War, 305, 315-16
United States navy: and monitor construction, 43; expansion of, 127; in First World War, 307, 329, 340
Uruguay, 33n. 69, 75n. 99, 185, 200, 219, 251n. 3

Valona (Vlore): during Italo-Turkish War (1911-12), 205; during First World War, 272, 283, 286, 289-90, 306, 335-36, 338, 340
Veith, Josef, Lieutenant, 333, 345n. 90
Venice: as main base of Austrian navy, 3; revolution in (1848-49), 3-4; as Italian navy base, 64, 104-5, 112; in Triple Alliance naval convention, 239; during First World War, 271, 273-74, 278-82, 289, 291, 295, 307-8, 312-14, 337
Venice Arsenal, 3, 73n. 55, 104
Viale, Leone, Italian admiral, 282
Vickers, British armaments manufacturer, 174
Victor Emmanuel II, King of Italy, 14, 50-51
Victor Emmanuel III, King of Italy, 112, 156, 240-41
Vienna: defense of (1866), 1; navy offices in, 26, 40, 89, 137, 236, 237; revolution in (1918), 349
Villa Cisneros (Dakhla), 147
Villa Giusti, Armistice of (1918), 357-58, 359
Vimercati, Count Ottaviano, Italian envoy, 14